ADDITIONAL COOKBOOKS AND DVD SETS AVAILABLE FROM THE PUBLISHERS OF *COOK'S COUNTRY* INCLUDE:

The *Cook's Country* Series

The *Cook's Country* Cookbook

Cook's Country Blue Ribbon Desserts

From Our Grandmothers' Kitchens

Cook's Country Best Lost Suppers

America's Best Lost Recipes

Cook's Country Best Potluck Recipes

Cook's Country Best Grilling Recipes

Cook's Country Annual Editions
from each year of publication (2005–2011)

From the Editors of *Cook's Illustrated*

Cook's Illustrated Cookbook

The Best One-Dish Suppers

The *America's Test Kitchen* Menu Cookbook

Soups, Stews & Chilis

Slow Cooker Revolution

The Best Simple Recipes

More Best Recipes

The New Best Recipe

The Best Skillet Recipes

The Best Slow and Easy Recipes

The Best Chicken Recipes

The Best International Recipe

The Best Make-Ahead Recipe

The Best 30-Minute Recipe

The Best Light Recipe

The *Cook's Illustrated* Guide to
Grilling and Barbecue

Best American Side Dishes

Cover & Bake

Steaks, Chops, Roasts, and Ribs

Baking Illustrated

Perfect Vegetables

Italian Classics

The Best American Classics

1993–2011 *Cook's Illustrated* Master Index

Cook's Illustrated Annual Editions
from each year of publication (1993–2011)

America's Test Kitchen

The Best of *America's Test Kitchen* (2007–2012 Editions)

Light & Healthy (2010–2012 Editions)

Cooking for Two (2009–2011 Editions)

The *America's Test Kitchen* Family Baking Book

The *America's Test Kitchen* Family Cookbook

The *America's Test Kitchen* Healthy Family Cookbook

The *America's Test Kitchen* Series Companion Cookbooks

America's Test Kitchen: The TV Companion Cookbook (2012)

America's Test Kitchen: The TV Companion Cookbook (2011)

The Complete *America's Test Kitchen* TV Show Cookbook (2010)

America's Test Kitchen: The TV Companion Cookbook (2009)

Behind the Scenes with *America's Test Kitchen* (2008)

Test Kitchen Favorites (2007)

Cooking at Home with *America's Test Kitchen* (2006)

America's Test Kitchen Live! (2005)

Inside *America's Test Kitchen* (2004)

Here in *America's Test Kitchen* (2003)

The *America's Test Kitchen* Cookbook (2002)

The *America's Test Kitchen* Series DVD Sets
(featuring each season's episodes from our hit
public television series)

The *America's Test Kitchen* 4-DVD Set (2002–2011 Seasons)

The *America's Test Kitchen* 2-DVD Set (2001 Season)

The *Cook's Country* TV Series DVD Sets
(featuring each season's episodes from our hit
public television series)

The *Cook's Country* 2-DVD Set (Seasons 1–4)

Visit our online bookstore at www.cookscountry.com to order any of our cookbooks and DVDs listed above. You can also order subscriptions, gift subscriptions, and any of our cookbooks and DVDs by calling 800-611-0759 inside the U.S., or 515-246-6911 if calling from outside the U.S.

$35.00

To get home delivery of *Cook's Country*, call 800-526-8447 inside the U.S., or 515-247-7571 if calling from outside the U.S.,
or subscribe online at www.cookscountry.com.

2011 Recipe Index

RC = Recipe card
IBC = Inside back cover

Cook's Country

FEBRUARY/MARCH 2011

Fairy Gingerbread
Lost Recipe, Perfected

Best Weeknight Chicken
Quick Stovetop-to-Oven Method

Lazy Cook's Pot Roast
Easy and Extra-Tender

Slow-Cooker Turkey Chili
Better Than Beef?

Low-Fat Mashed Potatoes
Still Rich and Creamy

From-the-Freezer Meatloaf
No Need to Thaw

Chicken and Slicks
Best Dumplings
You've Never Had

Best Apple Fritters
Awesome Apple Flavor

Silky Chocolate Pudding
Fast as the Box

Popcorn Shrimp
Ultra-Crisp Crust

Breakfast Buttercups
Ham, Eggs, and Toast,
All in One

Rating Milk Chocolate
Face-Off: Hershey's vs. Dove

*Deep in a 19th-century cookbook, we stumbled across a recipe for something called **Fairy Gingerbread**. Intrigued by the name, we had to try it. Good idea: After some re-engineering in the kitchen, we ended up with the best, most delicate ginger cookie we've ever tasted.* PAGE 18

$4.95 U.S./$6.95 CANADA

Dear Country Cook,

The kitchen used to be a frugal place. In the 19th century, a family might spend 30 percent of its household income on food; today, that number is 10 percent. Given the cost back then, nothing was discarded, including the water used to boil vegetables (good for the stockpot) and the brains found in a calf's head, which people bought to make mock turtle soup (fried brain balls were considered a delicacy). Before the Civil War, cooking was mostly about preservation. Every cut of pork was either consumed immediately or brined, smoked, salted, or otherwise put up for later use.

A frugal kitchen meant a creative kitchen. The cook had to make the most of what was available, no matter how pedestrian. Some of America's greatest recipes—Smithfield ham, succotash, corned beef, hoppin' John, Boston baked beans—arose from a need to preserve foodstuffs or from an urge to transform something cheap and plentiful.

The frugal cook has no choice but to explore the tastes and textures of simple ingredients; it takes an intimate acquaintance with black-eyed peas or brisket to know how to dress them up for dinner. One might say that intimacy is at the heart of good cooking, as only then does the sweet potential of a carrot become developed or the true nature of a navy bean get revealed.

I once worked for a dairy farmer, Charlie Bentley. It was grueling work, haying and milking, and Vermonters take a lifetime to offer familiarity. But today, with 50 years behind us, that work has paid off. Like a thrifty cook, hard-ship is a stew that develops over time—a recipe for success in life as well as in the kitchen.

Christopher Kimball
Founder and Editor, Cook's Country

Cook's Country

Founder and Editor Christopher Kimball
Editorial Director Jack Bishop
Executive Editor, Magazines John Willoughby
Executive Editor Peggy Grodinsky
Managing Editor Scott Kathan
Senior Editors Lisa McManus, Cali Rich, Diane Unger
Test Kitchen Director Erin McMurrer
Associate Editor Lynn Clark
Test Cooks Sarah Gabriel, Kelly Price
Assistant Editor Taizeth Sierra
Assistant Test Cook Carolynn Purpura
Copy Editors Nell Beram, Amy Graves
Editorial Assistant Shannon Hatch
Executive Assistant Christine Gordon
Test Kitchen Manager Gina Nistico
Senior Kitchen Assistant Leah Rovner
Kitchen Assistants Maria Elena Delgado,
Ena Gudiel, Ed Tundidor
TV Producer Melissa Baldino
Contributing Editors Erika Bruce, Eva Katz, Jeremy Sauer
Consulting Editor Meg Ragland
Science Editor Guy Crosby, Ph.D.
Executive Food Editor, TV, Radio & Media Bridget Lancaster

Online Managing Editor David Tytell
Online Editor Kate Mason
Online Assistant Editor Mari Levine
Online Editorial Assistant Eric Grzymkowski

Design Director Amy Klee
Art Director Julie Bozzo
Deputy Art Director Susan Levin
Deputy Art Director, Marketing & Web Christine Vo
Staff Photographer Daniel J. van Ackere

Director, Information Technology Rocco Lombardo
Lead Developer Scott Thompson
Web Developers Christopher Candelora,
Jim Madden, Robert Martinez
Web Production Coordinator Evan Davis
Web Production Assistant Jennifer Millet
Systems Administrator Marcus Walser

VP, New Media Product Development Barry Kelly
Lead Developer, New Media Bharat Ruparel
Senior Information Architect Melissa MacQuarrie
Social Media Manager Steph Yiu
Web Programmer, New Media Anand Kumar
Graphic Designer Eggert Ragnarsson

Production Director Guy Rochford
Senior Projects Manager Alice Carpenter
Traffic & Production Coordinator Kate Hux
Asset & Workflow Manager Andrew Mannone
Production & Imaging Specialists
Judy Blomquist, Heather Dube, Lauren Pettapiece

Vice President, Marketing David Mack
Circulation Director Doug Wicinski
Fulfillment & Circulation Manager Carrie Horan
Partnership Marketing Manager Pamela Putprush
Marketing Assistant Lauren Perkins
Database & Direct Mail Director Adam Perry
Senior Database Analyst Marina Sakharova
Products Director Steven Browall
Product Promotions Director Tom Conway
E-Commerce Marketing Director Hugh Buchan
E-Commerce Marketing Manager Laurel Zeidman
Marketing Copywriter David Goldberg
Customer Service Manager Jacqueline Valerio
Customer Service Representatives
Jillian Nannicelli, Kate Sokol

Chief Financial Officer Sharyn Chabot
Human Resources Director Adele Shapiro
Controller Mandy Shito
Finance Director Wayne Saville
Senior Accountant Aaron Goranson
Staff Accountant Connie Forbes
Accounts Payable Specialist Steven Kasha
Office Manager Michael Pickett
Receptionist Henrietta Murray

Sponsorship Sales Director Marcy McCreary
Retail Sales & Marketing Manager Emily Logan
Sponsorship & Marketing Coordinator Bailey Vatalaro
Publicity Deborah Broide

COLOR FOOD PHOTOGRAPHY: Keller + Keller
STYLING: Mary Jane Sawyer
ON THE COVER: Fairy Gingerbread, Keller + Keller

ILLUSTRATION: Ross MacDonald
Greg Stevenson (cover illustration)

Cook's Country magazine (ISSN 1552-1990), number 37, is published bimonthly by Boston Common Press Limited Partnership, 17 Station Street, Brookline, MA 02445. Copyright 2011 Boston Common Press Limited Partnership. Periodicals Postage paid at Boston, Mass., and additional mailing offices. Publications Mail Agreement No. 40020778. Return undeliverable Canadian addresses to P.O. Box 875, Station A, Windsor, Ontario N9A 6P2. POSTMASTER: Send address changes to Cook's Country, P.O. Box 8382, Red Oak, IA 51591-1382. Customer Service: It's easy to subscribe, give a gift subscription, change your address, and manage your subscription online. Visit www.americastestkitchen.com/customerservice for all of your customer service needs or write to us at Cook's Country, P.O. Box 8382, Red Oak, IA 51591-1382. PRINTED IN THE USA

FEBRUARY/MARCH 2011

Contents

BREAKFAST BUTTERCUPS, 15

EASY CHOCOLATE PUDDING, 17

PAPRIKA POTATOES, 10

Features

In Every Issue

You Say You Want a Revolution

Like the slow-cooker recipes we feature in every issue of Cook's Country? Then you'll love this book. A team of ten test cooks at America's Test Kitchen spent a year developing 200 family-friendly recipes that will change how you use your slow cooker. With Slow Cooker Revolution ($26.95), in stores in mid-February, you won't have to choose between convenience and flavor.

America's Test Kitchen is a 2,500-square-foot kitchen located just outside of Boston. It is the home of Cook's Country and Cook's Illustrated magazines and is the workday destination of more than 50 test cooks, editors, and cookware specialists. Our mission is to test recipes until we understand how and why they work and arrive at the best version. We also test kitchen equipment and supermarket ingredients in search of brands that offer the best value and performance. You can watch us work by tuning in to Cook's Country from America's Test Kitchen (CooksCountryTV.com) on public television.

Kitchen Shortcuts

HANDY TIP
Hot Dogs for a Crowd
Sue Jette, St. Paul, Minn.

When I'm cooking hot dogs for a crowd on my grill pan, I've found that I can flip six at a time if I run two skewers through them. This eliminates the rolling and cuts down on the uneven cooking.

DOUBLE DUTY
Easy Cookie Decorating
Maggie Gehman, Los Gatos, Calif.
I use my meat pounder to put a decorative pattern on the top of shortbread cookies. After I've rolled and scored or cut the shortbread dough, I gently press the clean tenderizer into the dough to make a grid pattern on the cookie.

HANDY TIP
Reviving Stale Bread
Molly Perkins, Somerville, Mass.

I love fresh bread from my local bakery, but it often goes a little stale before I can finish the loaf. I've found a way to quickly revive it: I wrap the loaf in a (food-safe) paper bag, brush water on the outside of the bag, and put it in the oven to bake at 350 degrees for 5 to 10 minutes. It's soft again and tastes as good as new.

EASY CLEANUP
Baking Spray Contained
Jill Halpin, Manchester, N.H.

When I used to spray my cake pans with nonstick spray, I would end up with spray all over my counters and floor. Now I just open my dishwasher, place the pan inside, and spray to my heart's content. The mess is gone with the next wash cycle.

DOUBLE DUTY
Mini Strainer
Buck Hamilton, Meridian, Idaho
I use my grid potato masher when draining canned goods like beans. To rinse off the goop, I fill the can with water and drain again. This saves me from having to pull out (and wash) my big colander.

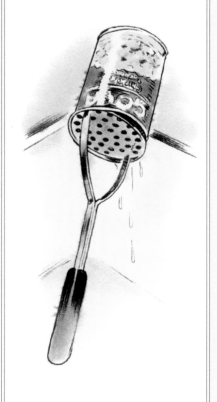

HANDY TIP
Easy Guacamole
Alex Smart, Jacksonville, Fla.

I like making guacamole for parties, but mashing a dozen avocados by hand can be a pain. One day I tried mashing the avocados in a stand mixer with the paddle attachment—it worked great. You can add the lime juice and chopped garlic right to the bowl.

DOUBLE DUTY
Neater Mozzarella Slices
John Jefferson, New York, N.Y.
Because fresh mozzarella is so soft and squishy, I have a tough time slicing it with a knife. It turns out that the perfect tool for the task had been sitting in my utensil drawer all along: An egg slicer makes neat, even slices of mozzarella every time.

If you'd like to submit a tip, please e-mail us by visiting CooksCountry.com/kitchenshortcuts or send a letter to Kitchen Shortcuts, Cook's Country, P.O. Box 470739, Brookline, MA 02447. Include your name, address, and phone number. If we publish your tip, you will receive a free one-year subscription to *Cook's Country*. Letters may be edited for clarity or length.

Ask Cook's Country

Can I make and refrigerate cookie dough and then bake the cookies a few at a time over several days?
Billie Giannone, Ridgefield, Conn.

The amount of time you can refrigerate cookie dough before baking depends on the presence and type of leavener in the dough. To sort through holding times for doughs with different (or no) leaveners, we made four batches of sugar cookies: one with baking powder, one with baking soda, one with both, and the last (an icebox cookie) with neither. We baked six cookies from each batch every day for a week. We found that the dough with baking soda held well for two days, but was a little flatter on the third. Cookies with both baking powder and soda began to lose lift after four days. Baking powder–leavened cookie dough maintained good lift all week. The unleavened cookies held well all week.

The cookies with baking soda were the losers in the holding test because soda is a single-acting leavener, meaning that it begins to make lift-giving air bubbles as soon as it gets wet and comes in contact with an acid. Once started, this action continues until all the leavening power is spent—so there's a time limit. Baking powder is double acting, so it releases gas twice: once when it gets wet, and again when it heats up. So even if the first batch of air bubbles is spent, the second action will allow cookies to rise in the oven.

THE BOTTOM LINE: Cookie dough made with baking soda is best used within two days. Recipes with both powder and soda can be made four days ahead. Recipes with baking powder or no leavener can be made up to seven days ahead.

Why do we eat rare beef but not rare chicken?
Jason Roush, Columbus, Ohio

Whether or not it's safe to eat rare meat has to do with the bacteria associated with the meat. A temperature of 165 degrees is considered a safety point for killing all harmful bacteria. We don't eat raw or rare chicken or turkey because it has an unpleasant texture, but also because it can be infected by the bacteria *Salmonella*, which can live inside the muscle tissue. For beef, the problem isn't the inside of muscle (which is sterile) but the outside, as *Escherichia coli* (or *E. coli*) can reside there. So steaks can safely be cooked rare (burgers are most safely cooked to well-done, as *E. coli* can be mixed into the meat during grinding).

THE BOTTOM LINE: Poultry is safe to eat when it reaches 165 degrees. You can stop cooking it at 160 degrees, as residual heat will take it the final 5 degrees. (Dark meat is best cooked to 175.)

A lot of blueberry muffin recipes call for frozen berries. Is it better to use them straight from the freezer, or do I need to thaw them?
Susan Taigue, Lynbrook, N.Y.

To find out, we baked three batches of the test kitchen's favorite blueberry muffins. For the first, we tossed the berries straight from the freezer into the batter. The muffins baked up moist and delicious, and the blueberries didn't bleed. We made the next two batches with thawed blueberries; for one, we strained out the juice that the berries had exuded during thawing, and for the other, we simply thawed the berries in a bowl and dumped the entire contents, juice and all, into the batter. The batch made with the strained berries produced slightly dry muffins, and the batch made with the thawed berries and their juice was uniformly blue.

We ran the same tests with pancakes, with similar results: Frozen berries straight from the freezer are best.

THE BOTTOM LINE: When making muffins and pancakes with frozen berries, use them frozen—don't defrost them.

THAWED BERRIES
The juice from thawed berries turned our muffins purplish blue.

FROZEN BERRIES
We folded frozen berries straight from the freezer into the batter. Ta-da! No streaking or sogginess.

I don't like the smell that fresh garlic leaves on my hands. Soap and water doesn't do the job. Help!
Ann Arthur, Glens Falls, N.Y.

We know firsthand that garlic odor is hard to remove from your hands. There are plenty of folk remedies for doing this: washing with baking soda, vinegar, lemon juice, salt, or toothpaste, or even rubbing your hands on stainless steel. Do any of these tricks work? To find out, we had five testers mince garlic and rub it on their hands, then try each of the methods listed above (plus washing with soap and water).

Washing with all of these substances lessened the odor at least a little, with baking soda and lemon juice outperforming the others, and rubbing one's hands on stainless steel succeeding just as well. Why? Some of the aromatic compounds in garlic are weak acids that can be neutralized by alkaline baking soda. Because not all aroma compounds are acidic, baking soda can't neutralize the odor 100 percent. Stainless steel removes some of the odor when iron atoms in the stainless steel exchange some of their electrons with sulfur atoms from the volatile aroma compounds, rendering them nonvolatile (i.e., nonstinky). Lemon juice contains lemon oils that dissolve the oil-soluble aroma compounds in garlic, plus its own fragrance masks the remaining odor.

THE BOTTOM LINE: Lemon juice, baking soda, and stainless steel all help a little, but there is no magic cure for removing garlic smell from your hands.

Why does eggplant Parmesan sometimes make my mouth tingle?
Leah Johnstone-Mosher, Somerville, Mass.

Eggplants are members of the botanical genus *Solanum*, a group commonly referred to as nightshades. (Tomatoes and peppers are also in this genus.) Plants in this group often have chemical defenses such as bitter-tasting alkaloids or even, in some cases, poisons. A common example of such a chemical defense is capsaicin, which gives hot peppers their burn. Selective breeding has reduced or eliminated most of these chemicals in many cultivated members of the genus, but bitter alkaloids, which can cause a tingling sensation, are often found in mature eggplants. The bitter alkaloids in eggplant are concentrated in the seeds.

THE BOTTOM LINE: To avoid tingling, select eggplants that are medium-size or smaller. If you're stuck with a large eggplant, slice or cube it, place the pieces in a colander, toss them with salt, and let them sit for 30 minutes to drain. Quickly rinse and thoroughly dry the eggplant before cooking. The salt masks some of the bitterness.

TAMING BITTER EGGPLANT
Salt, drain, then rinse.

Recently, I saw something at the grocery store called "olive pomace oil" and was intrigued by its modest price tag. Bargain or scam?
David Spezzaferro, Tewksbury, Mass.

The International Olive Council defines olive oil as "the oil obtained solely from the fruit of the olive tree (*Olea europaea L.*), to the exclusion of oils obtained using solvents or re-esterification processes and of any mixture with oils of other kinds." Olive pomace oil is made by using solvents (generally hexane, a petroleum product) and extreme heat to extract the last bit of oil from the olive pulp (or pomace) that is left after extracting the higher grades of oil. We tested olive pomace oils side by side with regular and extra-virgin oil in salad dressing and as a frying medium for breaded pork chops. Tasters picked the pomace oil out of the lineup in the dressings, calling it "plasticky," "dusty and stale," and "rancid-tasting." The pomace olive oil wasn't as bad with the breaded pork chops; a few tasters detected a trace of "fishy" flavor, but most couldn't tell a difference.

THE BOTTOM LINE: Don't use olive pomace oil raw (in dressings or marinades). Its nasty flavors are less detectable when it is used to cook with.

What's the proper way to dispose of used frying oil?
Dan Schomburg, Portland, Ore.

When it's warm, peanut (and vegetable, canola, etc.) oil flows easily, and pouring it down the drain seems like the simplest way to dispose of it… until you get the plumber's bill. As it cools, the oil gets thicker (especially used frying oil, which contains food particles), and if it comes in contact with cold water in your plumbing or if the pipes are cold, it may get cold enough to solidify. Solid oil can build up on the inside of pipes, narrowing them, which results in slow drains (think cholesterol in your veins and arteries). In the worst cases, the pipes can clog completely. Happily, the problem is easily avoided: If it's relatively clear, oil can be strained and reused once. When the oil is spent, let it cool completely before throwing it out (or contact your local government for oil recycling guidelines).

THE BOTTOM LINE: To safely and neatly dispose of used oil, wait for it to cool completely, then pour it into a container with a screw cap, seal the container, and put it in the trash.

To ask us a cooking question:
Visit **CooksCountry.com/emailus**. You can also write to Ask Cook's Country, P.O. Box 470739, Brookline, MA 02447. Just try to stump us!

Recipe Makeover Reduced-Fat Mashed Potatoes

Butter and cream supply luxe flavor and texture to traditional mashed potatoes. How do you keep the character of the dish yet slash calories and fat? BY KRIS WIDICAN

VELVETY MASHED POTATOES are as common in country kitchens as they are in white-tablecloth restaurants. But no matter where they come from, they pack a caloric, fatty punch. A single portion of a typical recipe (potatoes, cream, butter, and salt) can deliver 350 calories and 25 grams of fat. Could a much leaner version retain the same silky texture and full flavor?

I found that diet recipes that rely on low-fat milk made wan and watery mashed potatoes, while those that cut out butter altogether were dry and flavorless. Obviously, I'd have to lose at least some of the cream and butter, but how? I began with the potatoes.

Potato types vary only slightly in nutritional value, but their flavor and texture differences are another story. I started with 2 pounds (to feed four people) each of boiled russet, Yukon Gold, and red potatoes and mashed them with equal amounts of cream. The russets were mealy; the red potatoes were dense and bland. The Yukon Golds were buttery, silky, and light.

For 2 pounds of Yukons, I needed about ¾ cup of cream to make a smooth, supple mash. To cut calories I replaced the cream with chicken broth, but it made the potatoes taste like a wet bouillon cube. Potatoes made with fat-free evaporated milk had the right texture but tasted tinny and sweet. Buttermilk tasted too lean, and fat-free half-and-half was just a shade too caloric. Then a fellow test cook reminded me that in leaner times, folks often mashed potatoes with the starchy cooking water. Using the cooking water as the only liquid made bland potatoes, but when I mixed ¼ cup of it with ½ cup of fat-free half-and-half, I'd found my solution. Now I could tackle the butter.

I started with a batch of mashed potatoes made with a full stick as a benchmark for flavor, and gradually cut back the butter in subsequent batches until only 1 tablespoon remained. My tasters and I were amazed that so little could still make its presence felt. I had saved a ton of calories, but unfortunately, the potatoes now lacked the supple, yielding texture of full-fat mashed potatoes. I tried mashing the potatoes with low-fat and fat-free cream cheese,

cottage cheese, and sour cream. None of them gave the potatoes the right texture. Then I noticed a fellow test cook making potato salad. It struck me that the texture of mayonnaise is similar to that of softened butter. On a hunch, I added in a few tablespoons to the next batch of my potatoes. The mayonnaise disappeared into the mash, leaving it silky and smooth. Even better: Low-fat mayonnaise worked just as well.

Although there was no telltale mayonnaise flavor, tasters did complain that the potatoes tasted oddly sweet—the result of both the fat-free half-and-half and the low-fat mayonnaise. To counteract them without adding calories, I steeped two cloves of garlic, a bay leaf, and ¼ teaspoon of black pepper with the butter in the fat-free half-and-half. This brought the flavors into balance. I had saved almost 200 calories and over 20 grams of fat, and finally had a recipe for mashed potatoes I could feel good about eating.

Yukon Golds taste naturally buttery, allowing us to cut back on most of the butter.

The Numbers
All nutritional information is for a single 1-cup serving of mashed potatoes.

Traditional Mashed Potatoes
CALORIES **352**
FAT **25g**
SATURATED FAT **16g**

Cook's Country Reduced-Fat Mashed Potatoes
CALORIES **174**
FAT **3g**
SATURATED FAT **1g**

REDUCED-FAT MASHED POTATOES Serves 4

We prefer Hellmann's low-fat mayonnaise. Use the flat edge of a chef's knife to smash the peeled garlic cloves. A ricer or a food mill makes for an exceptionally creamy mash, but if you don't own either one, use a potato masher.

- 2 pounds Yukon Gold potatoes, peeled and cut into 1-inch pieces
- ½ cup fat-free half-and-half
- 1 tablespoon unsalted butter
- 2 garlic cloves, peeled and smashed
- 1 bay leaf
  Salt and pepper
- 3 tablespoons low-fat mayonnaise

1. Bring potatoes and enough water to cover by 1 inch to boil in large pot over high heat. Reduce heat to medium and simmer until potatoes are tender, 20 to 25 minutes.

2. Meanwhile, bring half-and-half, butter, garlic, bay leaf, 1 teaspoon salt, and ¼ teaspoon pepper to boil in small saucepan over high heat. Remove from heat, cover, and let stand for 15 minutes. Discard garlic and bay leaf.

3. Reserve ½ cup potato cooking water. Drain potatoes thoroughly. Set ricer or food mill over now-empty pot and press or mill potatoes into pot. Stir in warm half-and-half mixture, mayonnaise, and ¼ cup reserved potato water, adding additional potato water as needed. Season with salt and pepper to taste. Serve.

TEST KITCHEN TECHNIQUE
Boosting Savory Flavor

Fat-free half-and-half and low-fat mayonnaise kept our mashed potatoes creamy but made them taste strangely sweet. To counter that sweetness, we steeped smashed garlic and a bay leaf in the half-and-half for 15 minutes and then removed them.

Slow Cooker Turkey Chili

The slow cooker is a perfect place to prepare a long-simmered chili—but if you're using turkey instead of beef, problems loom. BY LYNN CLARK

WITH A WELL-MEANING nod toward healthfulness, many chili recipes swap the usual ground beef for ground turkey. Well, we regret to report that most of the time the results aren't pretty. While ground beef cooks up pleasantly tender with real meaty flavor, ground turkey often dries out or, worse, dissolves into flavorless, wormlike pieces. The slow cooker exacerbates these problems, as the turkey has many hours of opportunity to overcook. We insisted on getting from slow-cooker turkey chili exactly what we expect from ground beef chili: hearty bites of moist, well-seasoned meat in a thick, mellow, gently spicy sauce with plenty of beans.

I used a test kitchen slow-cooker ground beef chili recipe as my base: I sautéed onions, bell pepper, and garlic and added them to the slow cooker along with diced tomatoes, tomato sauce, red kidney beans, spices (chili powder, cumin, and dried oregano), and raw ground turkey. But minus the ground beef, the chili lacked depth. To add meatiness, I stirred in some chicken broth and soy sauce, which has deep,

savory flavors that can actually taste meaty. The broth made the chili too thin, but that was easily fixed: I simply drained the diced tomatoes and stirred in ¼ cup of thick tomato paste (which helped the flavor too). Tasters liked the more complex, smoky heat of chipotles over cayenne, and a tablespoon of brown sugar rounded everything out. Despite these changes, though, the chili base still seemed washed out, so I toasted the spices in a dry skillet to bring out their flavor before cooking the onions and pepper.

My chili was humming along nicely, but the turkey challenge loomed. Its mild flavor added exactly nothing to the chili. Even worse: Right on schedule, the soft raw turkey meat disintegrated into mushy pellets. Until now, I'd avoided precooking the turkey for fear that it would be overcooked before it ever hit the slow cooker. To my great surprise, browning turned out to be essential: Chunks of browned turkey actually held their shape in the slow cooker. On the other account, my fears were realized: The turkey was overcooked.

Puzzling over what to do to fix this, I got a crazy idea. In the test kitchen, we sometimes use a panade—a paste of bread and milk—to tenderize meatballs. Could that do anything for chili? I mashed milk and a couple of slices of white bread into a paste, and mixed it into the ground turkey. I browned the meat (panade and all) and then added it to the slow cooker. After four hours, I gave the chili a taste. It now had chunky bites of moist turkey—score!

But tasters forced me to concede that the overall flavor of the turkey was still nothing to get excited about. Wondering how I could ramp it up, I evaluated the panade: instead of milk, I tried the soy sauce I'd been adding to the chili as a way to season the turkey itself, and I mashed in some of the toasted chili spices and garlic. I made a new batch of chili with my highly seasoned panade and waited for a verdict from tasters. No one could figure out exactly what had changed, but everyone gave the thumbs-up to the transformation. One taster even said that she thought she was eating ground beef chili—which, for me, was the ultimate compliment.

KEY STEP **Pumped-Up Panade**

In the test kitchen, we often use a panade (a paste of bread and milk) to ensure moist meatballs, meatloaf, and even hamburgers. But chili? Yes—lean ground turkey needs all the help it can get to stay tender in the slow cooker. The panade also helped us fix ground turkey's notorious blandness. We made the panade with soy sauce instead of the usual milk, plus we seasoned it with spices and garlic.

Let's talk turkey—ground turkey. Just because the meat spends hours in the slow cooker doesn't mean it has to be bland and mushy.

SLOW-COOKER TURKEY CHILI
Serves 8 to 10
You can use any ground turkey except 99 percent lean (also labeled "fat-free") in this recipe. Serve with shredded cheese, sour cream, and lime wedges. Hunt's are our favorite diced tomatoes.

- ¼ cup chili powder
- 1 tablespoon ground cumin
- 1 teaspoon dried oregano
- 2 slices hearty white sandwich bread, torn into pieces
- ¼ cup soy sauce
- 6 garlic cloves, minced
  Salt and pepper
- 2 pounds ground turkey
- 3 tablespoons vegetable oil
- 3 onions, chopped fine
- 1 bell pepper, seeded and chopped
- ¼ cup tomato paste
- 2 (16-ounce) cans kidney beans, drained and rinsed
- 1 (28-ounce) can diced tomatoes, drained
- 1 (15-ounce) can tomato sauce
- 1¼ cups low-sodium chicken broth
- 1 tablespoon brown sugar
- 2 teaspoons minced canned chipotle chiles in adobo

1. Heat chili powder, cumin, and oregano in large nonstick skillet over medium heat, stirring frequently, until fragrant, about 1 minute. Set aside.

2. Using potato masher, mash bread, soy sauce, 1 tablespoon toasted spices, half of garlic, and ½ teaspoon pepper in large bowl until smooth. Add ground turkey and gently knead until well combined.

3. Heat 2 tablespoons oil in now-empty skillet over medium heat until shimmering. Cook turkey mixture, breaking up meat into 1-inch pieces with wooden spoon, until no longer pink, about 5 minutes. Transfer to slow-cooker insert. Add onion, bell pepper, and remaining oil to now-empty skillet and cook until softened, 6 to 8 minutes. Stir in remaining toasted spices, tomato paste, and remaining garlic and cook until paste begins to darken, 1 to 2 minutes. Transfer to slow cooker.

4. Stir beans, tomatoes, tomato sauce, broth, brown sugar, and chipotle into slow cooker. Cover and cook on low until turkey is tender, 4 to 6 hours. Season with salt and pepper. Serve. (Chili can be refrigerated in airtight container for 3 days.)

Make Ahead Meatloaf

We know the freezer robs moisture and flavor from meatloaf, so we spent weeks engineering a recipe to combat those problems. BY SARAH GABRIEL

Bratwurst helps keep our meatloaf moist and juicy in the freezer.

STASHING A MEATLOAF in the freezer sounds like a great idea… until you factor in the hours of defrosting before baking and the washed-out flavor and dry-as-sawdust consistency you can expect from it. The problem is that the freezer robs food of moisture and flavor. In hopes of making a frozen meatloaf that rivaled a freshly made one, I consulted freezer cookbooks. Alas, none offered strategic advice to prevent the degradation of flavor and texture. And most recipes called for 12 to 24 hours of defrosting in the refrigerator (didn't that miss the point?). More promising were no-defrost, straight-from-the-freezer recipes that simply called for increasing the cooking time by 50 percent. I figured I'd give this method a try with the test kitchen's core meatloaf recipe.

Our meatloaf is baked free-form on a rack to promote browning. It uses half ground beef and half ground pork, eggs, panade (a paste made from crushed crackers and milk), browned onion and garlic, and seasonings. I assembled a loaf, wrapped it well, and stowed it in the freezer. A few days later, I unwrapped the frozen loaf, put it in the oven, and set the timer for an hour and a half. (Our recipe bakes for an hour, but this one needed an extra 30 minutes to get to 160 degrees.) It came out of the oven shrunken, twisted, dry, and bland; it hardly resembled meatloaf. Obviously, I'd need a recipe for a loaf engineered to survive freezing—not to mention a quicker cooking method.

Our science editor gave me three key pieces of information. First, meat gets dry after freezing and cooking because the water in it crystallizes when frozen, punching holes in the cell walls of the meat. When the ice melts during defrosting and cooking, the meat weeps liquid. So in this case, counterintuitively, a drier raw mix should yield a juicier cooked meatloaf because less water should mean less ice damage. Second, fat is less susceptible than meat to ice damage, so I'd have to add extra fat to my raw mixture. And third, salt makes it harder for water to freeze, thereby reducing damage by ice crystals (and helping offset the freezer flavor loss). Armed with science, I set out to make my raw mix drier, fattier, and saltier.

Using less milk in the panade improved the texture of the meatloaf a little by reducing moisture. But trading the milk for heavy cream made a significantly juicier loaf because it contributed both less water and more fat. Unfortunately, with less liquid, the panade was too stiff to easily incorporate into the meat. So I mixed the meat and crushed crackers first, and then added the cream, onion, and seasonings.

To add even more fat, I tried mixing in grated butter and cheese, but they just didn't taste right. Adding an extra egg yolk improved the texture a bit; any more and the loaf tasted, well, eggy. I had better luck trading ground pork for fatty, salty sausage. I tested several types of sausage: breakfast, sweet and hot Italian, and bratwurst. They all vastly improved the texture, but the relatively neutral-tasting bratwurst did the best job at blending into the meatloaf, adding its fat and salt almost undetected. Now I needed to devise a fast, gentle cooking method for the frozen loaf.

We sometimes use a water bath for finicky baking: The bath promotes gentle, even, and efficient cooking. Would it work here? I couldn't plunk my frozen, free-form loaf into the water—I'd need a loaf pan. I found that using two 8-inch pans made for quicker cooking (and more serving options) than a single 9-inch pan. I could still get a flavorful crust on these loaves if I took them out of the pans and glazed and broiled them at the end of cooking. Finally, my meatloaf was moist and tasty enough to actually look forward to.

STEP BY STEP **How to Cook Freezer Meatloaf**

1. A hot water bath ensures that the meatloaf cooks evenly.

2. At 150 degrees, move the loaf to a foil-covered baking sheet.

3. For a classic meatloaf crust, brush the meatloaf with glaze and broil.

MAKE-AHEAD MEATLOAF

Makes two 8-inch loaves, each serving 4 to 6
You'll need two 8-inch disposable loaf pans. If you're baking both loaves at once, increase the cooking time in step 4 by 20 minutes and double the glaze.

MEATLOAF
- 2 teaspoons vegetable oil
- 1 onion, chopped fine
- 3 garlic cloves, minced
- 28 saltine crackers
- 1¾ pounds 85 percent lean ground beef
- ½ pound bratwurst, uncooked, casings removed
- ½ cup heavy cream
- 3 large eggs plus 1 egg yolk, lightly beaten
- 1 tablespoon Dijon mustard
- 1 tablespoon Worcestershire sauce
- ½ teaspoon dried thyme
- ⅓ cup finely chopped fresh parsley
- 1 teaspoon salt
- 1 teaspoon pepper

GLAZE
- ½ cup ketchup
- 2 tablespoons brown sugar
- 1 tablespoon cider vinegar
- ¼ teaspoon hot sauce

1. Heat oil in nonstick skillet over medium heat until shimmering. Add onion and cook until browned, 6 to 8 minutes. Add garlic and cook until fragrant, about 30 seconds. Transfer to large bowl.

2. Process saltines in food processor until finely ground; transfer to bowl with onion mixture. Pulse beef and bratwurst in food processor until just combined. Add meat mixture, cream, eggs and yolk, mustard, Worcestershire, thyme, parsley, salt, and pepper to bowl and knead gently until combined.

3. Press meatloaf mixture into 2 disposable 8-inch loaf pans. Freeze,

uncovered, until firm, at least 1 hour. Tightly wrap pans with plastic wrap, placing plastic directly on surface of meat, then with aluminum foil. Freeze for up to 1 month.

4. Adjust oven rack to middle position and heat oven to 350 degrees. Unwrap 1 meatloaf and set in roasting pan. Place roasting pan on rack and pour boiling water into pan until water reaches 1 inch from top of loaf. Bake until center of meatloaf registers 150 degrees, 40 to 50 minutes.

5. Meanwhile, whisk all glaze ingredients in saucepan until sugar dissolves. Simmer glaze over medium heat until slightly thickened, about 2 minutes. Cover and keep warm.

6. When meatloaf registers 150 degrees, remove pan from oven. Turn meatloaf out onto foil-covered rimmed baking sheet and brush 2 tablespoons glaze over top and sides of loaf. Adjust oven rack to upper-middle position and heat broiler. Broil until glaze begins to brown and center of loaf registers 160 degrees, 5 to 10 minutes. Transfer to serving platter, tent with foil, and let rest 20 minutes. Slice and serve, passing remaining glaze at table.

Wimpy add-ins need not apply. A rich, creamy dip needs assertive playmates for balance. BY KELLY PRICE

AS KIDS, MANY of us in the test kitchen were thrilled when our moms emptied a container of sour cream into a bowl, stirred in an envelope of powdered onion soup mix (or even—gasp!—a can of clams), and announced, "Dip's ready." The carrot and pretzel sticks were a blur of orange and brown, and the dip disappeared in no time. Now that I'm older and wiser, I understand that dip's appeal: The onion soup mix might not have tasted very good, but it was potent (and salty) enough to cut through the richness of the sour cream. We wanted to follow the same formula (rich dairy plus assertive seasonings) for a collection of dips that had the same appeal but fresher ingredients.

The first step to new and improved creamy dips was settling on the base. Many of us grew up eating sour cream dips, but mayonnaise is also standard, and I wondered about a newcomer to American kitchens: rich, creamy, tangy Greek yogurt. We tried the trio every which way before tasters settled on ¾ cup each mayonnaise and Greek yogurt for the best meeting point of flavor and texture.

Now I looked for bold partners for the creamy base: I used lots of chopped chives and basil to give the Creamy Herb Dip the necessary punch. Roasted red peppers, capers, garlic, and basil gave creamy Mediterranean Dip a flavor boost, while pungent Romano cheese and plenty of black pepper did the same for Buttermilk-Peppercorn Dip. Sun-Dried Tomato and Oregano was a bright variation. Finally, Curry-Chutney Dip played up the sweet-and-savory angle by employing mango chutney. A squeeze of fresh lemon juice in each offset the richness and added zing.

The dips were tasty but not well integrated. A colleague suggested whirling them in the food processor to break down the ingredients, which would help incorporate their flavors. Yes, the flavors melded. Unfortunately, the processing also broke down the yogurt, which made the dips runny. For the next test I processed all of the ingredients except for the yogurt, which I stirred in at the end. After an

We start the dip in the food processor to release the flavors of the seasonings. To finish, we stir in the yogurt by hand so that it won't break down and make the dip watery.

hour in the refrigerator, the dips were thick and creamy.

As for the dip-devouring partygoers? They were more enthusiastic than ever. Break out the carrot and pretzel sticks: Dip's ready.

CREAMY HERB DIP
Makes about 1½ cups
You can use either whole or low-fat Greek yogurt and mayonnaise (but don't use nonfat). Let the dips chill for at least one hour or they will be too loose.

- ¾ cup mayonnaise
- 2 tablespoons chopped fresh chives
- 2 tablespoons chopped fresh basil
- 2 teaspoons lemon juice
- ¾ cup Greek yogurt
  Salt and pepper

1. Process mayonnaise, chives, basil, and lemon juice in food processor until smooth. Transfer mixture to medium bowl and stir in yogurt. Season with salt and pepper.

2. Cover dip and refrigerate until thickened, at least 1 hour. (Dip can be refrigerated in airtight container for 2 days.)

BUTTERMILK-PEPPERCORN DIP
Prepare Creamy Herb Dip, omitting chives and basil. Add 6 tablespoons grated Romano cheese, 3 tablespoons buttermilk, and 1½ teaspoons pepper to food processor in step 1.

CURRY-CHUTNEY DIP
Prepare Creamy Herb Dip, omitting chives and basil. Add ½ cup mango chutney, 1 teaspoon curry powder, and ⅛ teaspoon cayenne pepper to food processor in step 1.

MEDITERRANEAN DIP
Prepare Creamy Herb Dip, omitting chives. Add ¼ cup chopped, drained jarred roasted red peppers; 3 tablespoons chopped, drained jarred capers; and 1 clove minced garlic to food processor in step 1.

SUN-DRIED TOMATO AND OREGANO DIP
Prepare Creamy Herb Dip, omitting chives and basil. Add 3 tablespoons rinsed, dried, and chopped oil-packed sun-dried tomatoes; 2 tablespoons grated Parmesan cheese; 1 tablespoon chopped fresh oregano; and 1 clove minced garlic to food processor in step 1.

Lazy Cook's Pot Roast

Onion soup mix? No thank you. Easy, all-in-one dinner from a foil pouch delivering maximum comfort with minimal work? Sign us up. BY SARAH GABRIEL

*T*his recipe swept the country in the 1950s. Whether called "Chuck Roast Winner Dinner," "Beef in Foil," "Foil-Baked Pot Roast," or "Sweep Steak," it always followed the same formula: Rub a chuck roast with dehydrated onion soup mix, seal it in aluminum foil, and cook until tender. Its attractions were obvious. It's quick, it's easy, it makes its own jus, and there's no pan to scrub. Given those virtues, it's no surprise that Peg Bracken featured the recipe (as Sweep Steak) in her 1960 "The I Hate to Cook Book," intended for frustrated housewives seeking merely to survive cooking, not revel in it. But that's not the whole story: At about the same time, a new current was entering the American culinary mainstream. In 1961, Julia Child published "Mastering the Art of French Cooking," then she went on to create her hit PBS series encouraging cooks to try their hand at complex dishes. Our idea was to marry these two seemingly contradictory trends. We wanted to make the super-easy chuck roast in foil recipe so good that even Julia would have wanted to make it.

Wrap the highly seasoned roast and vegetables tightly in foil, cook low and slow, unwrap, and slice. Dinner is served.

There's no question that rubbing a chuck roast with onion soup mix and wrapping it in foil is easy, but what does it taste like? The recipes I tried produced dry, stringy meat and greasy, oversalted, artificial-tasting drippings. But there were two pleasant surprises. First, after steaming in their own juices for almost six hours, the roasts were (somehow) well browned. And second, although none of the recipes called for any liquid, there was over a cup of jus in the foil pouch at the end of cooking. I liked the idea of a pot roast that required no stovetop browning or added liquid, and if I could just get the meat to cook properly and develop a tasty homemade

seasoning mix, I'd have a great lazy cook's pot roast.

I looked at the ingredients on the packet of onion soup mix—as I suspected, onion powder and salt were high on the list, closely followed by sugar and monosodium glutamate (MSG). My homemade mix, then, would start with onion powder, salt, and sugar like the original, as well as black pepper, thyme, and celery seed for seasoning. As for the MSG, I hoped that ground, dried porcini mushrooms would impart the meaty savoriness that MSG gave the Lipton

packet. I rubbed a chuck roast with this mix, sealed it up in foil, and roasted it.

Tasters found the mushroom flavor sour, and as for the roast, it was suspiciously pale—not nicely browned like the ones made with the packaged mix. Working on the flavor first, I tried replacing the dried mushrooms with a paste of sautéed fresh mushrooms, but it didn't bring much flavor. Shifting gears, I turned to soy sauce: Like MSG and mushrooms, it's rich in glutamates, the compounds responsible for savory, meaty flavor (called *umami*). With

a huge boost from soy sauce, my jus was definitely improving. Exchanging the white sugar for light brown added more depth, and an offbeat ingredient, espresso powder, added the last bit of toasty complexity.

To fix the browning, I revisited the ingredient list on the packaged soup mix. Amid vaguely menacing-sounding ingredients, like "disodium inosinate," I spied cornstarch. I assumed it was there as a thickener, but our science editor explained that the cornstarch reacted with the meat juices to form sugars (like glucose and maltose) that brown—even at a low temperature in a moist environment. Surprisingly, 3 tablespoons of cornstarch in my soup mix helped the roast brown perfectly.

Although the roast was now well browned, it was still dry and stringy. I had been following the conventional recipe "wisdom" of roasting at 350 degrees, but I wondered if cooking for longer at a lower temperature would improve the texture. Three hundred degrees was indeed an improvement, but the meat still wasn't meltingly tender and the cooking time was now more than six long hours. I found that I could keep the oven at 300 degrees with one simple trick: cutting the roast in half. The two smaller roasts (wrapped in the same foil packet) needed only 4½ hours or so to achieve tenderness, and the increased surface area allowed me to apply more of my flavorful "soup mix."

Some recipes call for adding carrots and potatoes to the foil packet. I liked this idea, but I expected the vegetables to be overcooked and mushy after four-plus hours of roasting. I was happily surprised that, with just a few tests of different size cuts, the vegetables cooked perfectly—and added flavor and volume to the meat drippings, too. (I threw in a couple of onions to flavor the sauce.) Finally, my pot roast was easy enough for those who hate cooking—and tasty enough for those who love it.

CHUCK ROAST IN FOIL Serves 4 to 6

You will need an 18-inch-wide roll of heavy-duty aluminum foil for this recipe.

RUB
- 3 tablespoons cornstarch
- 4 teaspoons onion powder
- 2 teaspoons light brown sugar
- 2 teaspoons salt
- 1 teaspoon pepper
- 1 teaspoon garlic powder
- 1 teaspoon instant espresso powder
- 1 teaspoon dried thyme
- ½ teaspoon celery seed

CHUCK ROAST
- 1 (4-pound) boneless beef chuck-eye roast
- 2 onions, peeled and quartered
- 6 small red potatoes, scrubbed and quartered
- 4 carrots, peeled and cut into 1½-inch pieces
- 2 bay leaves
- 2 tablespoons soy sauce

1. Adjust oven rack to lower-middle position and heat oven to 300 degrees. Combine rub ingredients in small bowl.

2. Pat roast dry with paper towels. Separate roast into 2 pieces along natural seam and trim fat to ¼-inch thickness. Tie kitchen twine around each roast at 1-inch intervals.

3. Crisscross two 30 by 18-inch sheets of heavy-duty foil inside large roasting pan. Place onions, potatoes, carrots, and bay leaves in center of foil and drizzle with soy. Set roasts on top of vegetables. Rub roasts all over with rub. Fold opposite corners of foil toward each other and crimp edges tightly to seal. Transfer pan to oven and cook until meat is completely tender, about 4½ hours.

4. Remove roasts from foil pouch and place on carving board. Tent meat with foil and let rest 20 minutes. Discard onions and bay leaves. Using slotted spoon, place carrots and potatoes on serving platter. Strain contents of roasting pan through fine-mesh strainer into fat separator. Let liquid settle, then pour defatted pan juices into serving bowl.

5. Remove kitchen twine from roasts. Slice roasts thinly against grain and transfer to platter with vegetables. Pour ½ cup pan juices over meat. Serve with remaining pan juices.

MAKE AHEAD Rub can be made and stored in airtight container at room temperature for 1 month.

WHAT TO DO WITH LEFTOVERS
Quick Sunday Gravy

With a little leftover chuck roast, you can shave hours off the cooking time for this rich, meaty tomato sauce. BY SARAH GABRIEL

SUNDAY GRAVY, THAT cornerstone of Italian-American cooking, is a simmered-for-hours tomato and meat sauce that's an embarrassment of riches. Sausages, meatballs, and pork ribs are a given, and many recipes throw in braciole (stuffed and rolled flank steak), veal chops, and/or neck bones for good measure. Clearly, the time, effort, and ingredient list required for this recipe are significant. I wanted a Sunday gravy that worked for busy cooks on any night of the week. Luckily, I had an ace up my sleeve: some leftover chuck roast.

The tender leftover chuck was a good start, but to approximate the real thing, I'd need more meat. Looking for big flavor in a small, quick-cooking package, I turned to hot Italian sausages. I browned the sausages, pulled them from the pan, and sautéed chopped onion in the seasoned fat. Without the benefit of long cooking to build a slow, deep backbone of flavor, I'd need additional potent ingredients. Into the skillet went lots of garlic, concentrated tomato paste, and a generous pinch of oregano. I deglazed the pan with wine and added a big can of crushed tomatoes with the chuck and the sausages I'd set aside. After just 20 minutes, I finished the sauce with a handful of bright, sweet basil. Served with a pound of my favorite pasta, I now had a hearty supper—even on a Tuesday.

Leftover meat from Chuck Roast in Foil shortcuts time-consuming Sunday gravy.

EASY SUNDAY GRAVY
Serves 4 to 6
This recipe will dress 1 pound of pasta; we prefer tubular shapes here.

- 1 tablespoon vegetable oil
- 1 pound hot Italian sausage
- 2 onions, chopped medium
- 2 tablespoons tomato paste
- 6 garlic cloves, minced
- 2 teaspoons sugar
- ½ teaspoon dried oregano
- ¼ cup red wine
- 1 (28-ounce) can crushed tomatoes
- 2 cups shredded leftover chuck roast meat
  Salt and pepper
- 3 tablespoons chopped fresh basil

1. Heat oil in Dutch oven over medium-high heat until just smoking. Add sausage and cook until well browned, 6 to 8 minutes. Transfer sausage to paper towel–lined plate. Slice in half crosswise; reserve.

2. Cook onions in sausage fat over medium heat until browned, 6 to 8 minutes. Add tomato paste, garlic, sugar, and oregano and cook until tomato paste begins to darken, 1 to 2 minutes. Add wine, scraping up any browned bits, and simmer until reduced to 2 tablespoons, about 1 minute. Add tomatoes, chuck roast, reserved sausage, ¾ teaspoon salt, and ¼ teaspoon pepper.

3. Reduce heat to low and simmer, covered, until slightly thickened, about 20 minutes. Stir in basil. Season with salt and pepper. Serve over pasta. (Sunday gravy can be refrigerated in airtight container for 2 days.)

Paprika Potatoes

It takes more than a sprinkle of spice to make paprika potatoes. We put the pop back into this promising side.

BY JEREMY SAUER

RECIPES FOR PAPRIKA potatoes—one of those old-fashioned Sunday supper side dishes—require boiling new potatoes until tender and flavoring them with sweet, earthy paprika. At first glance, it's a looker: The creamy potatoes are speckled with the pretty brick-red spice. But alas: At first bite, you realize that it's little more than a bland pile of boiled potatoes, with the paprika adding nothing but a flash of color.

The reason for this flavor fake out is that almost every recipe adds the paprika after the potatoes are cooked. Let's be frank: Boiled potatoes don't have much flavor. But boil them with other ingredients and they'll absorb the flavors around them. To get the paprika to soak into the potatoes, I figured I'd just add some to the pot of boiling water. Unfortunately, it took a full handful of the stuff to add any flavor to my pot of water—a flat-out waste of the spice. Then I thought, instead of trying to season a whole pot's worth of water, why not cook the potatoes in a skillet with just a few cups of water? Ultimately, I found that if I cooked the potatoes in a covered skillet, I could reduce the amount of water necessary to just 1 cup. With so little water, 1 tablespoon of paprika was plenty to season it. After the potatoes were tender, I uncovered the pan and let the water boil away.

Paprika, perhaps more than any other spice, needs a bit of TLC to bring out its best. To this end, we usually "bloom" it in a skillet with a bit of oil for a minute or less. Since I was now cooking the potatoes in a skillet, I decided to do just that. For my next test, I cooked the paprika in oil before adding the water. Sure enough, the flavor improved. But I wasn't about to stop there. Adding an onion and four cloves of minced garlic to the pan along with the paprika worked wonders. Next, I replaced the water with an equal amount of chicken broth. This combo gave the potatoes a robust, savory seasoning. Finally, I halved the potatoes before they went into the pan so that they would be sure to soak up all the flavorful pan juices.

The technique and taste were now much improved, but two hitches remained. First, because I was halving the potatoes, their starch leached out into the pan. With nowhere for the starch to go, it soaked back into the potatoes along with the cooking liquid, making the spuds gluey. Up to this point, I had been using all-purpose potatoes (the kind that most recipes call for). Russets were not an option—they contain loads more starch—but waxy red potatoes certainly were a possibility. To get rid of even more starch, I rinsed the cut potatoes before they went into the pan. Gluey quality gone.

Now to address the second hitch. As good as the potatoes tasted, a full tablespoon of paprika created a paste that left their exteriors slightly gummy. Since the potatoes were already cooking in a skillet, I figured that frying them might help. Once the chicken broth evaporated, I added a few more tablespoons of oil to the skillet. The potatoes browned nicely, lending another layer of flavor to the dish. But I'd "solved" the

pastiness problem by creating a grittiness problem. Something had to give.

Removing a teaspoon of paprika improved the texture but dulled the flavor. Would a stronger paprika make up for the smaller amount I was now using? I tried Hungarian (no difference), hot (*reeeally* hot), and gourmet (note: expensive does not equal better). But what about smoked? A newcomer to the supermarket spice aisle, smoked paprika combines the earthiness of sweet paprika with an intense, savory smokiness. Happily, it seemed tailor-made for this dish, especially when I added half of the spice at the end of cooking to refresh the bold, smoky taste. Now all that was needed was a sprinkling of parsley.

Paprika potatoes have always looked the part; now mine tasted it, too.

Paprika is not just the color red. Our potatoes actually taste smoky, earthy, and sweet.

PAPRIKA POTATOES Serves 4 to 6

If you can't find baby red potatoes, substitute larger red potatoes cut into 1-inch pieces.

- 2 pounds baby red potatoes, scrubbed and halved
- ¼ cup olive oil
- 1 onion, chopped
- 4 garlic cloves, minced
- 2 teaspoons smoked paprika
- 1 cup low-sodium chicken broth
  Salt and pepper
- 2 tablespoons finely chopped fresh parsley

1. Place cut potatoes in colander. Rinse under cold water until water runs clear, about 1 minute. Drain potatoes.

2. Heat 1 tablespoon oil in large nonstick skillet over medium heat until shimmering. Add onion and cook until softened, about 5 minutes. Stir in garlic and 1 teaspoon paprika and cook until fragrant, about 30 seconds. Add potatoes, broth, and ½ teaspoon salt and bring to boil.

3. Reduce heat to medium-low and cook, covered, until potatoes are just tender, 12 to 15 minutes. Remove lid and increase heat to medium. Cook, stirring occasionally, until liquid evaporates, about 5 to 8 minutes.

4. Whisk remaining oil and remaining paprika in small bowl. Add paprika oil to pan and cook, stirring occasionally, until potatoes are deep golden brown, about 5 minutes. Off heat, stir in parsley. Season with salt and pepper. Serve.

KEY INGREDIENT
Smoked Paprika

A traditional Spanish ingredient, smoked paprika is made by smoking pimento peppers over oak logs, then drying and grinding the peppers into a potent powder. Spanish cooks so revere this spice that a few varieties have been given Protected Designation of Origin status.

SMOKING PERMITTED
Smoldering sweetness

Broccoli with Cheese Sauce

The secret to making great broccoli with cheese sauce? Get to know your cheeses—and use your oven.

BY KELLY PRICE

BROCCOLI WITH CHEESE sauce is an American classic, one of the handful of vegetable side dishes that almost everybody likes. And why not? Tender, flavorful broccoli topped with a robust, creamy sauce is hard to beat. So I was excited about making my own version—until I cooked five promising-sounding recipes and wound up with multiple variations on watery, mushy broccoli paired with bland, vaguely cheese-flavored sauce. To add insult to injury, most sauces slid right off the broccoli and pooled on the plate. It was time to let this popular dish realize its potential.

I started with the traditional sauce, made by thickening milk with a cooked paste of flour and butter (a roux) and then stirring in cheese. As I should have predicted, the sauce separated. I knew that a higher fat content would help keep the sauce from breaking. (The fat coats the casein proteins in the cheese and prevents them from coagulating.) So I switched from milk to half-and-half. Now the sauce was too thick and rich for everyday eating. I cut the half-and-half with, respectively, chicken broth, milk, and water. The chicken broth added too much chicken flavor (surprise), and though the sauce with milk tasted good, tasters preferred the sauce thinned with water, commenting that it let the cheese flavor come forward yet wasn't in the least watery. (Even thinned by half with water, half-and-half has almost twice the fat content of whole milk.)

I loved the hearty flavor of cheddar cheese, but using it alone was making the sauce gritty—those pesky casein proteins again. As cheddar ages, the caseins tend to clump together and break down; this creates the strong flavor compounds we enjoy in cheddar but also makes the cheese gritty. Using equal parts Monterey Jack and sharp cheddar worked much better. The Monterey Jack kept the sauce nice and creamy (its high moisture content promotes easy blending); the sharp cheddar provided the flavor. But now that I'd cut back on the cheddar... not enough flavor. Fortunately, just a quarter cup of nutty Parmesan added the punch that tasters were after.

Now, how to cook the broccoli? Boiling it left the broccoli wet and limp—only slightly better than something from the frozen foods section. Steaming gave me well-cooked broccoli, but with little flavor. Then I tried roasting. To my delight, the roasted broccoli had a distinct nutty taste that perfectly complemented the cheese flavor. To speed up the roasting, I preheated the baking sheet. Besides yielding tastier broccoli, roasting had another advantage: It produced drier broccoli than steaming or boiling, which meant that the cheese sauce stayed put instead of sliding right off.

Smooth, deeply cheesy sauce over firm, pleasantly nutty, well-cooked broccoli—now that's a dish everyone has reason to like.

BROCCOLI WITH CHEESE SAUCE
Serves 4 to 6

For a silky smooth sauce, wait until the Monterey Jack and cheddar are thoroughly integrated before you add the Parmesan. If the sauce gets too thick, whisk in 1 to 2 tablespoons of hot water.

- 2 pounds broccoli, florets cut into 1-inch pieces, stems peeled and cut into ½-inch pieces
- 2 tablespoons vegetable oil
- Salt and pepper
- 1 tablespoon unsalted butter
- 4 teaspoons all-purpose flour
- ¼ teaspoon dry mustard
- ⅛ teaspoon cayenne pepper
- 1 cup half-and-half
- ½ cup water
- ½ cup shredded Monterey Jack cheese
- ½ cup shredded sharp cheddar cheese
- ¼ cup grated Parmesan cheese

1. Adjust oven rack to lower-middle position, place rimmed baking sheet on rack, and heat oven to 450 degrees.

2. After 15 minutes, toss broccoli, oil, ¾ teaspoon salt, and ¼ teaspoon pepper in large bowl. Arrange broccoli in single layer on hot baking sheet. Bake until spotty brown, 15 to 18 minutes, stirring halfway through cooking.

3. Meanwhile, melt butter in medium saucepan over medium heat. Add flour, mustard, and cayenne and cook, stirring constantly, until golden and fragrant, about 1 minute. Slowly whisk in half-and-half and water and bring to boil. Reduce heat to medium-low and simmer until slightly thickened, 8 to 10 minutes. Off heat, whisk in Monterey Jack and cheddar until smooth. Stir in Parmesan until smooth. Season with salt and pepper. Serve sauce over broccoli.

Three cheeses and the oven collaborate to help a classic American side dish be all it can be.

STEP BY STEP Updating Broccoli with Cheese Sauce
Limp, waterlogged broccoli draped with Velveeta? No thank you. We take this classic American vegetable dish seriously.

1. Instead of steaming or boiling the broccoli, as is customary, we roast it for deep, nutty flavor. A preheated baking sheet cuts down on the roasting time.

2. Processed cheese is definitely out. To get a cheesy, satiny sauce, we combine Monterey Jack, cheddar, and Parmesan.

Chicken and Slicks

If we could figure out how to add flavor to both the broth and the tender noodles, we'd be fast converts to this Appalachian stew. BY LYNN CLARK

Many regions put their own stamp on chicken and dumplings. The Appalachian version is chicken and slicks. The slicks are made from flour, lard (or oil), and water; leavener rarely sneaks in. The dough is rolled out, cut into fat noodles, and dropped into simmering chicken stew. The late Cissy Gregg, food columnist for the "Louisville Courier-Journal" in the 1940s and '50s, distinguished fluffy, leavened "pillows" from slicks, or "sad flats," as she termed them. "Those who call fat bits of fluff-duff with stewed chicken by the name of dumplings are one kind of people, while those who make slick dumplings to go with their chicken are another kind."

We're not sure which kind of folks we are, but one thing we are sure of: We love chicken and slicks. (The name, by the way, refers to the fact that the cooked dumplings are slippery, says Mark Sohn in *Appalachian Home Cooking: History, Culture, & Recipes*.) To make the dish, pieces of chicken, or sometimes the whole bird, are poached in water. The cook then removes and shreds the cooked chicken and returns it to the pot with noodles that she's made as the chicken was simmering. The slicks should be tender with just the slightest bit of chew, while the broth lies partway between a soup and a stew—more body than the former, less than the latter—and has intense chicken-y flavor and a nice peppery kick. This simple dish, by the way, gives the cold shoulder to vegetables (mostly): It's made up of chicken, slicks, a bit of onion, and homey goodness, period.

Because this dish relies on chicken for just about all its flavor, the recipes I tested using modern (read: mild to the point of bland) supermarket birds were disappointing. Without free-range, older, tastier chickens at my disposal, I would have to figure out another way to deepen flavors. A second challenge lay in getting the texture of both broth and noodles right. I headed into the test

Chicken and *what?* Slicks are noodle-like dumplings with a pleasantly slippery texture (which gives them their name).

kitchen and began assembling ingredients and pots and pans.

Using chicken broth as the basis for the stew in place of water was a no-brainer. In Appalachia back in the day, I doubt canned chicken broth was in the pantry, but I had it, and I'd use it. Instantly, both stew and chicken had more depth. Rather than simply

throwing the chicken parts into the simmering broth, I browned them first, to boost the flavor further. (I used both white and dark meat to please fanciers of each, and bone-in for best flavor.) The savory bits (fond) that stuck to the pot went into my broth, fortifying its flavor—but not until I'd taken the opportunity to sauté a chopped onion

in the fat, for (you guessed it) yet more savory flavor, and add flour, for thickening. I discarded the chicken skin—its work was done—and only now tossed the chicken pieces into the broth. I also opted to add thyme and a couple of bay leaves; neither violated the simple spirit of chicken and slicks, and both supplied needed seasoning.

For the sake of simplicity, I was making the dough for the slicks in the food processor, combining water, oil (instead of lard, which most of us don't keep around), flour, and salt, and then kneading the dough briefly before forming the slicks. Obviously, the water added no flavor, so in its place I tried chicken broth. This improvement led me to an even better idea: I set aside some of the rendered chicken fat (from browning the meat) and added that to the dough, too.

Now the dumplings had loads of flavor, and I should have let well enough alone. But I'd seen a couple of recipes that called for baking powder and a few that abhorred its use; one even branded it "scandalous." I was curious (as I'm paid to be). I don't know if baking powder rises to the level of a scandal, but it did make the slicks spongy. After one test, I abandoned it.

I rolled and cut the slicks and then dropped them into the simmering, thickening chicken broth–flour base for about 15 minutes. When the noodles failed to cook through in the thick, soupy base, I turned up the heat. They broke apart. What if, instead of adding the flour to the stew at the start, I made a slurry of flour and chicken broth, set it aside so I could cook the slicks in thin, simmering broth, and added the slurry back in at the end? This time, the slicks cooked perfectly, but the base tasted like raw flour. I brought the liquid to a boil to cook out the floury taste and—whoops—the slicks blew out again. A colleague suggested that I make the slurry with toasted flour (heat it in a pot until its color changes). That did it: The dish had no floury taste, and the slicks were mostly intact.

Mostly—there was the rub. To nudge "mostly" to "entirely," I chilled the slicks before cooking them and noticed a slight improvement. To better my odds, I froze them. This time, the slicks were savory, tender, and shapely. Even just 10 minutes in the freezer had firmed and dehydrated the dough (some of the liquid evaporating, some soaked up by the starch) so that the slicks held up in the simmering broth. To finish, I added the chunks of moist chicken back into the golden broth, stirred in a handful of parsley, and watched as cooks battled to snag bowls of the homey, cheering, and wholly delicious stew.

While I was researching, I'd come across a description of chicken and slicks in a 1938 column from the Middlesboro, Kentucky *Daily News*. After instructing people how to eat it ("Get a spoon and fork and wade in… make as many noises as you please"), the author of the piece added, "What a thrill awaits one who has never tried slickers!"

Indeed.

STEP BY STEP A Slick Production
Sure, making slicks requires a little time (although we minimize it by making the dough in the food processor). But the delicious result is definitely worth a bit of effort.

 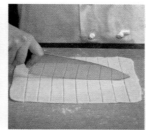 

1. After kneading the dough briefly, roll each dough half into a 10-inch square of ⅛ inch thickness.

2. Using a sharp knife or pizza wheel, cut the dough into 5 by 1-inch rectangles.

3. Stack the slicks between layers of parchment and freeze briefly before simmering.

CHICKEN AND SLICKS Serves 4 to 6
If you're short on chicken fat at the end of step 1, supplement it with vegetable oil.

- 3 **bone-in, skin-on chicken thighs (about 1½ pounds), excess fat trimmed**
- 2 **bone-in, skin-on chicken breasts (about 1½ pounds), halved crosswise**
  Salt and pepper
- 2 **cups plus 6 tablespoons all-purpose flour**
- 3 **tablespoons vegetable oil**
- 1 **onion, chopped**
- 2 **teaspoons minced fresh thyme**
- 7½ **cups low-sodium chicken broth**
- 2 **bay leaves**
- ¼ **cup chopped fresh parsley**

1. Pat chicken dry with paper towels and season with salt and pepper. Toast 6 tablespoons flour in Dutch oven over medium heat, stirring constantly, until just beginning to brown, about 5 minutes. Transfer flour to medium bowl and wipe out pot. Heat 1 tablespoon oil in now-empty Dutch oven over medium-high heat until just smoking. Cook chicken until well browned all over, about 10 minutes; transfer to plate. When chicken is cool enough to handle, remove and discard skin. Pour fat (you should have about 2 tablespoons) into another small bowl; reserve.

2. Add onion and 1 tablespoon oil to now-empty pot and cook over medium heat until softened, about 5 minutes. Stir in thyme and cook until fragrant, about 30 seconds. Add 7 cups broth, chicken, and bay leaves and bring to boil. Reduce heat to low and simmer, covered, until white meat registers 160 degrees and dark meat registers 175 degrees, 20 to 25 minutes. Remove from heat. Transfer chicken to clean plate. When chicken is cool enough to handle, shred into bite-size pieces, discarding bones.

3. Meanwhile, combine remaining chicken broth, reserved fat, and remaining oil in liquid measuring cup. Process remaining flour and ½ teaspoon salt in food processor until combined. With machine running, slowly pour in broth mixture and process until mixture resembles coarse meal. Turn dough onto lightly floured surface and knead until smooth. Divide in half.

4. Following photos 1 to 3, roll each dough half into 10-inch square. Cut each square into twenty 5 by 1-inch rectangles. Place handful of noodles in single layer on parchment-lined plate, cover with another sheet of parchment, and repeat stacking with remaining noodles and additional parchment, ending with parchment. Freeze until firm, at least 10 minutes or up to 30 minutes.

5. Return broth to simmer and add noodles. Cook until noodles are nearly tender, 12 to 15 minutes, stirring occasionally to separate. Remove 1 cup broth from pot and whisk into reserved toasted flour. Stir broth-flour mixture into pot, being careful not to break up noodles, and simmer until slightly thickened, 3 to 5 minutes. Add shredded chicken and parsley and cook until heated through, about 1 minute. Season with salt and pepper. Serve.

MAKE AHEAD Broth and chicken can be made through step 2 and refrigerated in separate airtight containers for 2 days. Dough can be made through step 3, wrapped in plastic wrap, and refrigerated for 1 day. To finish, proceed with step 4.

Fat Is Where the Flavor Is
We bumped up the flavor of the slicks by using chicken broth and rendered chicken fat in the dough.

RENDERED CHICKEN FAT

TEST KITCHEN DISCOVERY
Toasted-Flour Slurry
Flour-thickened stews usually start with a roux of flour cooked in fat to cook off the floury taste. But when we tried starting this recipe with a roux, the slicks failed to cook through in the viscous simmering broth. If we turned up the heat, they broke apart. If we added the flour at the end, our dinner tasted like raw flour. Finally, we got the idea to dry-toast the flour on the stovetop to cook off its raw flavor. We combined the toasted flour with broth to make a slurry, which we stirred into the pot once the slicks were tender at the end of cooking.

Heavenly Hots

Before we could appreciate just how delicious these tiny, fragile sour cream pancakes really were, we needed to get them from pan to plate in one piece. BY ERIKA BRUCE

Don't look for big, hearty pancakes. Delicate, tender Heavenly Hots are pancakes of another (equally delicious) order.

THE APTLY NAMED Heavenly Hots first gained recognition at the Bridge Creek Restaurant in Berkeley, California, but they were immortalized (in the eyes of pancake lovers everywhere, anyhow) in Marion Cunningham's *The Breakfast Book*. These tiny, delicate pancakes are loaded with sour cream—2 cups to four eggs, with a mere ¼ cup of cake flour to (barely) hold the batter together. There's also baking soda and sugar. Together, the unlikely proportions account for the pancakes' incredibly tender texture, which is as much tangy, golden brown soufflé as flapjack. Heavenly Hots live up to their name.

That is, if you work the griddle station in a restaurant and are adept at flipping them in the pan without turning their insides out. This, incidentally, is what happened to me the first time I made them. Dejectedly, I ate what I could of the pancake carnage and was amazed at how delicious it nevertheless tasted. I wanted a foolproof method for these pancakes—one that would work the first time I tried it.

It was not hard to see that the proportion of eggs to flour was off the charts. But as I gradually added more flour to give the pancakes more structure, they lost their ethereal texture and increasingly resembled traditional flapjacks. I switched the tender cake flour that the recipe called for to all-purpose flour plus just a teaspoon of cornstarch. This made the pancakes sturdier but not dense. The batter was slightly easier to flip, but not much.

Next, I tried separating the eggs and whipping the whites, and then folding them in after I'd combined all the other ingredients. This batter showed promise: It was much thicker, and I could spoon it into the skillet instead of pouring it. But once it came time to flip, I realized that the pancakes were more beauty than brawn, and I was yet again scraping pancake guts out of the pan.

To save these pancakes from my apparently lethal spatula, I tried to eliminate flipping altogether. I slid the buttered, pancake-laden skillet under a hot broiler and held my breath. By the time the pancakes had browned on top, they were tragically overcooked inside. What if I covered the pancakes in the skillet, creating, in effect, a gentle mini oven? After about two minutes, the bottoms were golden brown and the centers had partially cooked. They still needed a turn to brown their second side, but flipping the firmer pancakes was a breeze.

Unfortunately, covering the skillet trapped the moisture from the wet batter, causing the pancakes to come out soggy. I already knew that adding more flour would harm their tender texture, so I removed an egg instead. Sigh. While significantly less wet, the pancakes now lacked the lift that fourth egg had provided. So I replaced some of the baking soda (which reacted quickly when it came in contact with the acidic sour cream) with baking powder (which provides a rise activated by heat). Not only did I get an airier pancake, but I fortuitously underlined the tanginess of sour cream (the soda had been neutralizing it). I added a dash of vanilla to round out this pleasant sourness. With a dusting of confectioners' sugar, these pancakes were—I'll say it—heavenly.

HEAVENLY HOTS

Makes 32 pancakes, serving 4
To serve, dust with confectioners' sugar.

- ¼ cup all-purpose flour
- 3 tablespoons sugar
- 1 teaspoon cornstarch
- 1 teaspoon baking powder
- ½ teaspoon salt
- ¼ teaspoon baking soda
- 2 cups sour cream
- 3 large eggs, lightly beaten
- ½ teaspoon vanilla extract
- 3 tablespoons unsalted butter

1. Adjust oven rack to middle position and heat oven to 200 degrees. Combine flour, sugar, cornstarch, baking powder, salt, and baking soda in medium bowl. Whisk sour cream, eggs, and vanilla in large bowl until smooth. Gently fold flour mixture into sour cream mixture until incorporated.

2. Heat 2 teaspoons butter in large nonstick skillet over medium-low heat until butter begins to sizzle. Place five 1 tablespoon scoops of batter in pan, cover, and cook until tops appear dry and bottoms are golden brown, 1½ to 2 minutes.

3. Gently flip pancakes and cook, uncovered, until golden brown, about 30 seconds. Transfer to rimmed baking sheet and place in oven. Repeat with remaining batter, using remaining butter as needed. Serve.

BATTER BREAKDOWN A Fraction of the Flour

The silver dollar–size Heavenly Hots get their soft, custardy texture from the ratio of wet, creamy sour cream (a lot) to flour (very little). Our traditional pancake recipe uses 2 cups of flour in the batter; our recipe for Heavenly Hots requires only ¼ cup.

PANCAKES ON EARTH
2 cups of flour

PANCAKES IN HEAVEN
Just ¼ cup of flour

Breakfast Buttercups

By the time the whites of these baked eggs were properly cooked, the yolks were rubbery. Build me up, buttercup. Don't break my heart. BY SARAH GABRIEL

BREAKFAST BUTTERCUPS LET you get eggs, meat, and toast for the whole family in one fell swoop. The dish is made by pressing bread into muffin tins or ramekins; cracking eggs into them; sprinkling on fixings like bacon, ham, or cheese; and baking until the eggs are soft set and the toast cups are golden.

For the sake of convenience, I decided from the outset to go with a muffin tin rather than ramekins. I prepared several recipes, but the results were disappointing. The toast cups were soggy. The whites breached the bread banks and crusted onto the pan. And by the time the whites set, the yolks were chalky and overcooked.

I couldn't do anything until I fixed the fit. Obviously, the size of the muffin cup was set, and I couldn't make the eggs smaller. Or could I? I reached for a carton of medium eggs instead of the usual large size. As for the toast cups, my testing taught me two valuable lessons: Pretoasting the bread in the tin and separating the egg from the bread were both necessary to prevent soggy cups. Here's the method I ended up with: Trim the crusts, flatten the slices with a rolling pin, press them into the muffin cups, and brush them with butter. After five minutes in the oven, the cups are indeed crisp and golden. Then I made a cone from stacked slices of cheese and ham (cooked bacon proved too crumbly), placed a cone in each cup, and cracked in the eggs. No leaking, no soggy bread.

As for cooking the eggs, testing revealed that room-temperature eggs and a 375-degree oven were best. But the yolks were still overcooked by the time the whites had set. Building on my room-temperature egg discovery, I warmed the eggs (in their shells) in hot tap water for 10 minutes. The white, at the egg's exterior, got a head start but the yolk remained cool, so even oven baking was finally possible. For further insurance, I took the eggs out of the oven about 5 minutes before they were done, covered the pan with foil, and let the eggs finish cooking by residual heat.

Now I had perfectly cooked eggs—except for the center two. Those eggs, insulated on every side, were underdone in every test. The answer was obvious: Leave the center cups empty. Finally, I had both a consistently reliable method and a delicious, all-in-one breakfast.

BREAKFAST BUTTERCUPS
Makes 10 buttercups

Note that while 99 percent of our recipes call for large eggs, medium eggs are called for here.

- 10 medium eggs
- 10 slices hearty white sandwich bread, crusts removed
- 4 tablespoons unsalted butter, melted
- 10 thin slices deli Swiss or cheddar cheese (about 5 ounces)
- 5 thin slices deli Black Forest ham (about 5 ounces), halved crosswise
- Salt and pepper

1. Adjust oven rack to upper-middle position and heat oven to 375 degrees. Place eggs in large bowl and cover with hot tap water. Let sit 10 minutes.

2. Meanwhile, following photos 1 and 2, roll bread as thin as possible with rolling pin and press into 10 perimeter cups of 12-cup muffin tin, leaving 2 center cups empty. Brush bread cups with melted butter and bake until light golden brown, 5 to 7 minutes.

3. Following photos 3 and 4, top each cheese slice with ham slice. Make cut from center to 1 side of each stack. Fold each ham and cheese stack into cone and press into toasted cup. Crack 1 egg into each cup and season with salt and pepper.

4. Return muffin tin to oven and bake until egg whites are barely set and still appear slightly moist, 14 to 18 minutes. Transfer pan to wire rack and cover tightly with aluminum foil. Let sit 5 minutes. Serve immediately.

Use oversize sandwich bread for the toast cups for the best muffin-cup coverage.

STEP BY STEP **Engineering the Cup**

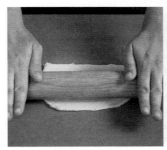  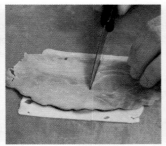 

1. Roll the bread thin before pressing it into the muffin cups; this makes it easy to shape the bread without tearing it.

2. Pinch in the opposite long sides of the bread and press each slice into a muffin cup. Brush with butter and bake until light brown.

3. Cut a slit from the center to one side of each ham and cheese stack.

4. Fold each ham and cheese stack into a cone and place each cone in a toasted cup. Now you're ready to drop in an egg.

Getting to Know Beef Roasts

The best way to sort through the array of beef roasts in the meat case is to understand where on the cow they come from. More active muscles (like the shoulder) have a lot of tough connective tissue that needs slow, moist cooking to become tender. Less active muscles (the rib and loin) are tender to begin with and are usually best cooked quickly. In the U.S., beef is butchered into eight primal cuts for the wholesale market. Six of the eight primal cuts are sources of roasts.

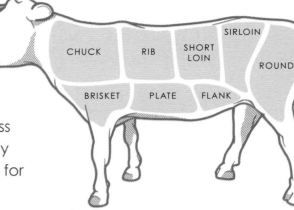

Chuck Shoulder Roast
PRIMAL CUT: CHUCK

The chuck is the primal cut that runs from the steer's neck to the fifth rib. These muscles get a lot of exercise, making for tough but flavorful cuts that are great for long braising. Chuck is often used for pot roast or beef stew. The shoulder roast is affordable, but its comparatively mild flavor means that it's not our favorite cut from the chuck.

Chuck-Eye Roast
PRIMAL CUT: CHUCK

This is a fatty, relatively inexpensive cut with great flavor. Chuck-eye (the term "eye" refers to any center-cut piece of meat) is suited for cutting into stew meat because you can trim out large fat pockets and gristle. It makes a juicy roast, too, but you'll have to maneuver around some fat. Chuck-eye, AKA boneless chuck roll, is our top choice for pot roast.

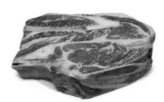

7-Bone Roast
PRIMAL CUT: CHUCK

A shoulder bone shaped like the number seven gives this roast its name; it's also referred to as center-cut pot roast and center-cut chuck roast. Like most cuts from the chuck, it has a rich, beefy flavor and is best slowly braised to tenderness. Because it's thinner than most other chuck roasts, it cooks relatively quickly.

Top Blade Roast
PRIMAL CUT: CHUCK

Top blade is our favorite cut from the chuck for roast beef: It's moist and tender, with big beefy flavor. A line of gristle runs through the center, but it's easy to cut around, either on the platter or on the plate. Top blade has many aliases: chuck roast first cut, top chuck roast, flat iron roast, or simply blade roast.

Rib Roast
PRIMAL CUT: RIB

Rib roasts are tender and extremely flavorful. Enjoy prime rib and rib-eye steaks? This is the same cut. First-cut rib roasts usually contain ribs nine through 12. Second-cut roasts—typically ribs six through nine (from nearer the head)— are slightly fattier and more irregularly shaped, making them harder to cook perfectly. We like to oven-roast rib roasts or grill-roast them for a little smoke flavor.

Top Round
PRIMAL CUT: ROUND

There's no way around saying it: The round is the cow's rump. This round roast is a bargain. It has very good flavor, is relatively juicy, and, when sliced thin, isn't too chewy. Most deli roast beef is cut from top round. Beware, though: Its odd shape can make even cooking (and carving) a challenge. We cook all round roasts the same way: Salt, sear, and then roast in a very low oven.

Eye Round
PRIMAL CUT: ROUND

Falling between top round (which we enthusiastically seek out) and bottom round (which we usually avoid), this roast has a pleasant, mild flavor. We also like its cylindrical shape, which encourages even cooking and neat carving. Like all cuts from the lean round, it's best sliced very thin and benefits from assertive seasoning and/or saucing.

Bottom Round
PRIMAL CUT: ROUND

This roast is attractively priced, but for a reason: It can be exceptionally tough and gamy. To be palatable, it needs a lot of help from the cook. Be sure to season and sear the exterior well (to add flavor) and slice it very thin on the diagonal (to minimize chew). A bottom round roast is our top choice for London broil, which simply means a cheap cut that's cooked quickly and sliced thin.

Top Sirloin
PRIMAL CUT: SIRLOIN

With rich, intense beef flavor and tender texture, top sirloin is our top inexpensive roast. Trim its hefty fat cap to about ¼-inch thickness, and cut around the vein of gristle that runs through this cut. We like to salt top sirloin (about 1 teaspoon of kosher salt per pound) and let it sit, refrigerated, for 6 to 24 hours before searing it on the stove and then finishing it in a gentle 275-degree oven.

Tri-Tip
PRIMAL CUT: SIRLOIN

The sirloin is the hip (between the short loin and the round). This roast is popular in the West (in California, in particular), but it is most commonly cut into steak tips on the East Coast. Tri-tip is also known as triangle roast, thanks to its shape. It has decent beefy flavor and is best not cooked past medium-rare.

Beef Tenderloin
PRIMAL CUT: SHORT LOIN

This incredibly tender roast is known as filet mignon when cut into steaks. Its mild flavor is enhanced by sauces and seasoned crusts. Always buy this costly cut "peeled" or "trimmed," which means that the gristly chain has been removed. For a uniform roast that will cook evenly, tuck the narrow tail under itself and secure it with kitchen twine. Roast at a high temperature to retain juiciness.

Brisket
PRIMAL CUT: BRISKET

Brisket is a tough cut from above the front leg that needs long, low, moist cooking to become tender. A whole brisket is huge— about 12 pounds—so it's usually butchered into the thinner, leaner flat cut and the thicker point cut. In the barbecue belt, brisket is slow-smoked to tenderness. Always slice brisket thin across the grain.

TUSCAN CHICKEN

SHRIMP WITH ARTICHOKES AND MUSHROOMS

OPEN-FACED BEEF WELLINGTON

ITALIAN-STYLE CHICKEN SOUP

SHRIMP WITH ARTICHOKES AND MUSHROOMS Serves 4

WHY THIS RECIPE WORKS: Marinating shrimp with potent garlic and pepper flakes before pan searing yields a light, flavor-packed sauté.

- 2 pounds extra-large (21 to 25 per pound) shrimp, peeled, deveined, and tails discarded
- Salt and pepper
- ¼ cup olive oil
- 3 garlic cloves, minced
- ½ teaspoon red pepper flakes
- 10 ounces white mushrooms, quartered
- 1 (9-ounce) box frozen artichoke hearts, thawed
- ½ cup white wine
- 3 tablespoons unsalted butter, cut into 3 pieces
- 2 tablespoons finely chopped fresh parsley

1. Pat shrimp dry with paper towels and season with salt and pepper. Combine shrimp, 1 tablespoon oil, garlic, and pepper flakes in medium bowl. Cover with plastic wrap and refrigerate for 15 minutes.

2. Meanwhile, heat 1 tablespoon oil in large nonstick skillet over medium-high heat until shimmering. Cook mushrooms until browned, 6 to 8 minutes. Add artichokes and cook until lightly browned, about 3 minutes. Transfer vegetables to medium bowl and tent with foil.

3. Heat 1 tablespoon oil in now-empty skillet over medium-high heat until just smoking. Add half of shrimp and cook without moving until spotty brown on first side, about 1 minute; transfer to bowl with vegetables. Repeat with remaining oil and remaining shrimp. Add wine to now-empty skillet and simmer until reduced to ⅓ cup, 1 to 2 minutes. Whisk in butter until smooth. Stir in vegetable-shrimp mixture and parsley and simmer until shrimp are cooked through, 1 to 2 minutes. Serve.

TEST KITCHEN NOTE: Serve over rice.

TUSCAN CHICKEN Serves 4

WHY THIS RECIPE WORKS: Cooking the chicken skin side down on the stovetop ensures well-rendered skin and juicy meat.

- 2 teaspoons finely chopped fresh rosemary
- 2 teaspoons grated zest and 2 teaspoons juice from 1 lemon
- Salt and pepper
- 8 bone-in, skin-on chicken thighs (about 4 pounds), excess fat trimmed
- 2 tablespoons olive oil
- 2 (16-ounce) cans cannellini beans, drained and rinsed
- 2 tablespoons finely chopped fresh parsley
- 3 garlic cloves, minced
- 4 cups low-sodium chicken broth
- 1½ cups instant polenta

1. Combine rosemary, lemon zest, ¾ teaspoon salt, and ½ teaspoon pepper in small bowl. Pat chicken dry with paper towels and rub all over with rosemary mixture.

2. Heat 1 tablespoon oil in large skillet over medium-high heat until just smoking. Cook chicken skin side down until well browned, about 5 minutes. Add beans and lemon juice. Reduce heat to medium and cook, covered, until meat registers 175 degrees, 12 to 15 minutes. Transfer chicken and beans to platter and sprinkle with parsley. Tent with foil.

3. Heat remaining oil in now-empty skillet over medium heat until shimmering. Cook garlic until fragrant, about 30 seconds. Add broth and bring to boil. Whisk in polenta and cook until thickened, about 3 minutes. Season with salt and pepper. Serve chicken and beans over polenta.

TEST KITCHEN NOTE: Polenta sets up quickly—prepare it just before serving.

ITALIAN-STYLE CHICKEN SOUP Serves 4

WHY THIS RECIPE WORKS: This chicken-fortified version of stracciatella, or Italian egg drop soup, is ready in about 15 minutes.

- 4 boneless, skinless chicken breasts (about 1½ pounds), cut into ¾-inch pieces
- Salt and pepper
- 3 tablespoons extra-virgin olive oil
- 1 onion, chopped fine
- 3 garlic cloves, minced
- 8 cups low-sodium chicken broth
- 2 teaspoons grated lemon zest
- 4 large eggs
- 2 tablespoons finely chopped fresh basil
- ½ cup grated Parmesan cheese

1. Pat chicken dry with paper towels and season with salt and pepper. Heat 1 tablespoon oil in Dutch oven over medium-high heat until shimmering. Cook onion until softened, about 5 minutes. Add garlic and cook until fragrant, about 30 seconds. Stir in broth and bring to boil. Add chicken and zest, reduce heat to medium-low, and simmer until chicken is no longer pink, 3 to 5 minutes.

2. Whisk eggs, ½ teaspoon salt, and ¼ teaspoon pepper in small bowl. While stirring soup in circular motion, slowly pour eggs into pot. Cook until eggs are set, about 1 minute. Break egg into bite-size pieces. Stir in basil and season with salt and pepper. Drizzle with remaining oil and sprinkle with Parmesan. Serve.

TEST KITCHEN NOTE: Serve with crusty Italian bread.

OPEN-FACED BEEF WELLINGTON Serves 4

WHY THIS RECIPE WORKS: This decadent dish usually takes hours to prepare. Our streamlined version delivers similar luxury in a fraction of the time.

- 1 (9½ by 9-inch) sheet puff pastry, thawed
- 4 center-cut tenderloin steaks, about 1½ inches thick
- Salt and pepper
- 1 tablespoon vegetable oil
- 4 tablespoons unsalted butter, cut into 4 pieces
- 10 ounces cremini mushrooms, sliced thin
- 1 shallot, minced
- ½ cup red wine
- ¼ cup low-sodium chicken broth
- 1 tablespoon finely chopped fresh parsley

1. Adjust oven rack to middle position and heat oven to 425 degrees. Cut puff pastry into quarters. Bake puff pastry on parchment-lined baking sheet until golden brown and crisp, about 15 minutes.

2. Meanwhile, pat steaks dry with paper towels and season with salt and pepper. Heat oil in large skillet over medium-high heat until just smoking. Cook steaks until well browned and meat registers 125 degrees for medium-rare, 3 to 5 minutes per side. Transfer to plate and tent with foil.

3. Melt 2 tablespoons butter in now-empty skillet over medium-high heat. Cook mushrooms and shallot until browned, 6 to 8 minutes. Add wine, broth, and any accumulated beef juices and cook until reduced to ¼ cup, about 6 minutes. Off heat, whisk in remaining butter and parsley. Season with salt and pepper. Top each puff pastry with 1 steak and one-quarter of mushroom mixture. Serve.

TEST KITCHEN NOTE: Puff pastry sheets are often sold frozen in packages of 2. For this recipe, thaw 1 sheet in the refrigerator overnight.

TENNESSEE PORK WITH GREENS

STEAK AND BLUE CHEESE PANINI

PASTA AL FORNO

MU SHU PORK

STEAK AND BLUE CHEESE PANINI Serves 4

WHY THIS RECIPE WORKS: Beefy strip steak, blue cheese, and horse-radish elevate this simple pressed sandwich.

- 2 strip steaks, about 1½ inches thick, sliced thin crosswise
  Salt and pepper
- 3 tablespoons olive oil
- 1 small red onion, halved and sliced thin
- 1 tablespoon red wine vinegar
- ⅓ cup mayonnaise
- ¼ cup crumbed blue cheese
- 2 tablespoons prepared horseradish, drained
- 8 slices thick-cut crusty bread

1. Pat steak dry with paper towels and season with salt and pepper. Heat 2 teaspoons oil in large skillet over medium-high heat until just smoking. Cook half of steak until browned all over, about 3 minutes. Transfer to plate. Repeat with additional 2 teaspoons oil and remaining steak. Add onion and 1 teaspoon oil to now-empty skillet and cook until browned, about 6 to 8 minutes. Off heat, add vinegar and transfer onion to plate with meat.

2. Combine mayonnaise, blue cheese, and horseradish in small bowl. Brush remaining oil over 1 side of bread. Place bread, oiled side down, on cutting board. Spread each slice with flavored mayonnaise. Top 4 slices of bread with steak-onion mixture. Top with remaining bread, oiled side up.

3. Heat grill pan or large nonstick skillet over medium heat for 1 minute. Place 2 sandwiches in pan and weight with Dutch oven. Cook sandwiches until golden brown, about 5 minutes per side. Repeat with remaining sandwiches. Serve.

TEST KITCHEN NOTE: For easy cleanup, cover the bottom of the Dutch oven with aluminum foil.

TENNESSEE PORK WITH GREENS Serves 4

WHY THIS RECIPE WORKS: To speed up the classic Southern braise, we use pork medallions and tender greens instead of ham hocks and collards.

- 4 slices bacon, chopped fine
- 2 pork tenderloins (1½ to 2 pounds total), cut crosswise into 1½-inch pieces
  Salt and pepper
- 2 garlic cloves, minced
- 2 pounds Swiss chard, curly-leaf spinach, or beet greens, stemmed and chopped
- 4 teaspoons cider vinegar
- ⅓ cup bourbon
- 2 tablespoons brown sugar
- 2 tablespoons unsalted butter, cut into 2 pieces
- 1 tablespoon Dijon mustard

1. Cook bacon in large skillet over medium heat until crisp, about 6 minutes. Transfer bacon to paper towel–lined plate. Pour off fat, reserving 3 tablespoons.

2. Pat pork dry with paper towels and season with salt and pepper. Cook pork in 2 tablespoons bacon fat over medium-high heat until well browned all over and meat registers 145 degrees, about 10 minutes. Transfer to platter and tent with foil.

3. Add remaining fat and garlic to now-empty skillet and cook over medium heat until fragrant, about 30 seconds. Stir in half of greens and cook, covered, until greens are beginning to wilt, about 1 minute. Add remaining greens and cook until tender, about 5 minutes. Stir in bacon and 2 teaspoons vinegar. Season with salt and pepper and transfer to plate.

4. Add bourbon, brown sugar, and accumulated pork juices to now-empty skillet and cook until thickened, 2 to 3 minutes. Off heat, whisk in butter, mustard, and remaining vinegar. Pour sauce over pork. Serve with greens.

MU SHU PORK Serves 4

WHY THIS RECIPE WORKS: Thin strips of pork tenderloin cook quickly in this single-skillet dish.

- 1 large pork tenderloin (about 1 pound), cut into ½-inch strips
- 1 tablespoon Asian chili-garlic sauce
- 2 tablespoons vegetable oil
- 8 ounces shiitake mushrooms, stemmed and sliced thin
- 1 tablespoon grated fresh ginger
- 1 (14-ounce) bag coleslaw mix
- 1 cup hoisin sauce
- 2 tablespoons dry sherry
- 3 scallions, sliced thin
- 8 (8-inch) flour tortillas, warmed

1. Pat pork dry with paper towels and toss with chili-garlic sauce in medium bowl. Heat 1 tablespoon oil in large nonstick skillet over medium-high heat until just smoking. Cook pork until no longer pink, 3 to 5 minutes. Transfer to plate and tent with foil.

2. Add mushrooms and remaining oil to now-empty skillet and cook over medium-high heat until lightly browned, about 5 minutes. Stir in ginger and cook until fragrant, about 30 seconds. Add coleslaw mix and cook until wilted, about 3 minutes. Stir in pork, along with any accumulated juices, ½ cup hoisin, and sherry, and cook until sauce is slightly thickened, about 1 minute. Sprinkle with scallions. Serve with tortillas, passing remaining hoisin at table.

TEST KITCHEN NOTE: Cut the pork crosswise into ½-inch-thick slices, then cut each slice into ½-inch-thick strips. Wrap tortillas in aluminum foil and place in a preheated 350-degree oven for about 15 minutes to warm.

PASTA AL FORNO Serves 4

WHY THIS RECIPE WORKS: Browned, chopped eggplant adds "meaty" heft to this quick vegetarian baked pasta.

- 2 slices hearty white sandwich bread, torn into pieces
- 2 cups shredded Italian cheese blend
- 3 tablespoons olive oil
- 4 garlic cloves, minced
- 1 medium eggplant (about 1 pound), cut into ½-inch pieces
  Salt and pepper
- 1 onion, chopped fine
- 1 (28-ounce) can diced tomatoes
- ½ cup finely chopped fresh basil
- 12 ounces rotini pasta

1. Adjust oven rack to upper-middle position and heat oven to 475 degrees. Bring 4 quarts water to boil in large pot. Pulse bread, 1 cup cheese, 1 tablespoon oil, and 1 clove minced garlic in food processor until coarsely ground; set aside.

2. Meanwhile, heat remaining oil in large ovensafe nonstick skillet over medium-high heat until shimmering. Add eggplant and ½ teaspoon salt and cook, stirring occasionally, until lightly browned, about 3 minutes. Stir in onion and cook until softened, about 5 minutes. Add remaining garlic and cook until fragrant, about 30 seconds. Stir in tomatoes and simmer until sauce is slightly thickened, about 5 minutes. Off heat, stir in remaining cheese and basil. Cover and keep warm.

3. Add 1 tablespoon salt and pasta to boiling water and cook until al dente. Reserve ½ cup pasta cooking water. Drain pasta and stir into eggplant mixture, adding reserved pasta water as needed. Season with salt and pepper. Top with bread crumbs and bake until crumbs are golden brown, about 10 minutes. Serve.

Easy Chocolate Pudding

Instant pudding has one thing going for it—speed. Without sacrificing that entirely, could we also have a pudding that tastes good, please? BY ERIKA BRUCE

A CRAVING FOR chocolate pudding can come on in a hurry. But when I reach for a box of instant pudding mix as a quick fix, I often regret it: The pudding it makes is cloyingly sweet, unpleasantly starchy, and right after sugar and cocoa on the ingredients list (so far, so good) comes a slew of preservatives, commercial thickeners, and artificial colors and flavors. No thank you. What I needed was a homemade pudding from recognizable ingredients that was fast, easy, and tasty.

But when I turned to cookbooks for guidance, I found labor-intensive recipes involving separated eggs, double-boilers, thermometers, strainers, and food processors. These recipes produced puddings that were impressively thick and creamy, but their flavor was like a high-end, single-origin, dark chocolate bar. Instead of the quick and easy treat I wanted to satisfy the Hershey-bar loving kid in me, I was eating fancy custards fit for a state dinner. But how would I get a creamy and chocolaty pudding without all that fussy work?

Leaving the eggs to the custards, I started with cocoa powder, sugar, cornstarch, and, of course, milk, ingredients for classic American stovetop pudding. With eggs out of the equation, I wouldn't have to strain the pudding at the end (which is done to get rid of any stray scrambled bits), so before I'd even begun much testing, I'd saved myself some time and trouble. Once I worked out the proper ratio of cornstarch to milk—1 tablespoon per cup—to get a texture that was neither too thick nor too thin, I gradually added cocoa powder for a good dose of chocolate flavor. But too much cocoa powder meant that, before long, the pudding developed a starchy texture. I found I had to stop at 3 tablespoons of cocoa powder (for 3 cups of milk), which meant a chocolate pudding with wimpy chocolate flavor.

Obviously, I needed to add some solid chocolate, and I opted for the convenience of chocolate chips. But when I melted a cup of semisweet chips into the pudding, it went to the opposite extreme: from a pudding with wan flavor to one that was just too rich and too thick—exactly what I was trying to avoid. Milk chocolate chips were next up. Thankfully, now the flavor was exactly right—homey, mild, creamy, and

caramel-y, without any of the edge of bittersweet chocolate. I added a small spoonful of vanilla extract to deepen the flavors and a dash of salt to bring them forward. Switching neutral granulated sugar for more rounded, molasses-y brown sugar also improved the pudding, and now its flavor was spot-on.

But tasters craved more creaminess. I did the obvious thing: I replaced some of the milk with a touch of heavy cream. When I tasted this batch several hours later after it had cooled, I knew right away that I'd reached the sweet spot. I was neither underwhelmed by insipid flavor nor overwhelmed by complexity and intensity, plus the pudding was luscious and creamy. Just as important, it had taken barely 10 minutes to make—a mere matter of stirring together a few commonplace ingredients on the stove. It really wasn't that much more difficult than opening a box of the instant stuff, but it was miles tastier. The hardest part, as it turned out, was waiting for the pudding to cool so I could eat it.

CHOCOLATE PUDDING
Serves 4
Hershey's Milk Chocolate Chips are our favorite brand. Using chips saves you the trouble of chopping, but 6 ounces of bar milk chocolate, chopped, works, too.

- ¼ cup packed light brown sugar
- 3 tablespoons Dutch-processed cocoa powder
- 3 tablespoons cornstarch
- ¼ teaspoon salt
- 2¾ cups whole milk
- ¼ cup heavy cream
- 1 cup milk chocolate chips
- ½ teaspoon vanilla extract

1. Combine brown sugar, cocoa, cornstarch, and salt in large saucepan. Whisk milk and cream into sugar mixture until smooth. Add chocolate chips and bring to simmer, whisking occasionally, over medium heat. Reduce heat to medium-low and cook, whisking constantly, until thickened and large bubbles appear at surface, 2 to 3 minutes. Off heat, stir in vanilla.

2. Transfer pudding to large bowl and place plastic wrap directly on surface of pudding. Refrigerate until completely cool, at least 4 hours. (Pudding can be refrigerated in airtight container for 3 days.) Serve.

Two chocolates and a little heavy cream create a quick pudding everyone wants to dig into.

Chill Faster, Eat Sooner
To some pudding lovers (especially little ones), waiting 4 hours to eat pudding seems like a lifetime. To speed the chilling, transfer the pudding to a 13 by 9-inch baking dish in step 2 and place plastic wrap directly on its surface. Place in freezer until completely cool, at least 45 minutes or up to 1 hour.

MOCHA PUDDING
Prepare Chocolate Pudding, adding 2 tablespoons instant espresso powder to saucepan with brown sugar in step 1.

CHOCOLATE-ALMOND PUDDING
Prepare Chocolate Pudding, replacing vanilla with ½ teaspoon almond extract. To serve, sprinkle with ½ cup toasted sliced almonds. (Toast the sliced almonds in a skillet over medium heat, stirring often, until lightly browned, about 5 minutes.)

Fairy Gingerbread Cookies

We brush off (and polish) a 118-year-old recipe for delicate, gingery wafers. They'll steal your heart.

BY ERIKA BRUCE

Centuries ago, gingerbread was so popular that cookbooks devoted entire chapters to it—exhaustive catalogs of passed-down recipes, each producing a confection a tad fluffier or chewier, a little thinner or crispier, than the one before. I'd always pegged the recipes as merely subtle variants, but one recipe in an old cookbook I was thumbing through caught my eye: Fairy Gingerbread. Amid the sober likes of Common Gingerbread, Hot Water Gingerbread, Sponge Gingerbread, and so on, the fanciful name stood out like a frivolous bauble. On closer inspection, the curious method—no eggs, no leavener, batter spread "no thicker than a visiting card" on an inverted baking pan—made me suspect there was more afoot than descriptive whimsy. This was no ordinary gingerbread. I had to try it.

It was in Jessup Whitehead's 1893 classic *Cooking for Profit* that I'd stumbled across the recipe. According to the book, it was a popular sweet served between rounds of the card game euchre—especially in Boston, where it was "held in high favor" and considered "a sort of social duty to know how to make it." Given that geographical shout-out, I wasn't surprised to find a similar recipe with the same name in Fannie Merritt Farmer's seminal *Boston Cooking-School Cook Book* (1896).

Following these recipes, I creamed light brown sugar with softened butter (in a roughly 2:1 ratio) until it was light and fluffy, and then slowly added the remaining ingredients (bread flour, milk, dried ground ginger). With some difficulty, I spread the stiff batter with the back of a knife into an ultra-thin layer across a cookie sheet. (Apparently, a "visiting card" was about as thick as a modern business card.) Then I baked it, as directed, in a "slack oven" (I went with a moderate 350 degrees). Fifteen

Don't let the cute name and slender profile of these cookies fool you: Fairy Gingerbread packs a significant ginger punch.

minutes later, I pulled the sheet from the oven and, working quickly, cut the result into rectangles.

These cookies came out unlike any gingerbread cookie I'd ever made. The crisp, feather-light texture shattered in a single bite, then the ginger wafer promptly melted in my mouth. The indulgent recipe title rang true: as delicate as fairy wings, indeed.

Once I got past the ethereal texture, however, the appeal faded. These cookies were pretty bland. Bumping up the ginger flavor was clearly in order, as was rounding out the overall flavor complexity. But the fairy-wing texture had me sold. I was going in.

Taking care of the easy stuff first, I added a bit of vanilla extract and salt, and the flavor started to sing. Then I tried doubling the amount of ground ginger (to 2 teaspoons). But without any competing flavors, the sharp, astringent quality of the dried spice dominated. I tried to mellow it by steeping it in the milk first—to no avail. Retreating to 1½ teaspoons, I toasted the ginger in a dry skillet, hoping to bring out more of its floral qualities. The kitchen quickly filled with a gingery aroma, which I took as a good sign: The resulting cookies now boasted a welcome aromatic punch. But they needed still more ginger flavor, so I went straight to the source, grating some fresh ginger root right into the batter. With this two-pronged ginger approach, I now had zesty ginger flavor in spades.

I also had heavy batter that was a bear to wrestle into a thin layer across the baking sheet. I'd been using bread flour, as called for in the vintage recipes. Could switching to softer, lower-protein all-purpose flour help? (Bread flour yields stiffer batters than all-purpose.) The batter was a little more malleable but still a struggle, so I reduced the amount of flour by 2 tablespoons (from the full cup I had been using). Now the batter was loose enough to coax over the cookie sheet without a fight, but stiff enough that it didn't drip over the edges.

But the flour adjustment robbed the cookies of some of their crunch and fairy-wing airiness. Adding a modest

amount of baking soda (½ teaspoon) made the cookies puff up in the oven just enough that they set with a lighter crumb, hence achieved a sublime crispiness once baked and cooled. Unfortunately, baking soda also promotes browning, and it made the edges of these thin cookies dark before their center was cooked. Thankfully, the solution to this problem was the easiest yet: lowering the oven temperature to 325 degrees. (Apparently, my "slack oven" wasn't quite slack enough.)

My "social duty" fulfilled, I vowed to serve these crisp, gingery, ethereally delicate wafers to whoever comes a-callin'. And I'm thinking of taking up euchre.

FAIRY GINGERBREAD COOKIES
Makes 5 dozen cookies
Use cookie or baking sheets that measure at least 15 by 12 inches. Don't be disconcerted by the scant amount of batter: You really are going to spread it very thin. Use the edges of the parchment paper as your guide, covering the entire surface thinly and evenly. For easier grating, freeze a 2-inch piece of peeled ginger for 30 minutes, then use a rasp-style grater.

1½	teaspoons ground ginger
¾	cup plus 2 tablespoons all-purpose flour
½	teaspoon baking soda
¼	teaspoon salt
5	tablespoons unsalted butter, softened
9	tablespoons packed light brown sugar
4	teaspoons grated fresh ginger
¾	teaspoon vanilla extract
¼	cup whole milk, room temperature

1. Adjust oven racks to upper-middle and lower-middle positions and heat oven to 325 degrees. Spray 2 cookie sheets (or inverted baking sheets) with cooking spray and cover each with 15 by 12-inch sheet parchment paper. Heat ground ginger in small skillet over medium heat until fragrant, about 1 minute. Combine flour, toasted ginger, baking soda, and salt in medium bowl.

2. With electric mixer on medium-high speed, beat butter and brown sugar until light and fluffy, about 2 minutes. Add fresh ginger and vanilla and mix until incorporated. Reduce speed to low and add flour mixture in 3 additions, alternating with 2 additions of milk.

3. Following photo 1, evenly spread ¾ cup batter to cover parchment on each prepared cookie sheet (batter will be very thin). Bake until deep golden brown, 16 to 20 minutes, switching and rotating sheets halfway through baking. Following photos 2 and 3, immediately score cookies into 3 by 2-inch rectangles. Cool completely, about 20 minutes. Using tip of paring knife, separate cookies along score mark. Serve. (Cookies can be stored in airtight container at room temperature for 3 days.)

TEST KITCHEN TECHNIQUE **Making Fairy Gingerbread Cookies**
While making several dozen batches of Fairy Gingerbread, we had time to perfect our technique. The cookies are made with an unusual method we'd never encountered before. Here's how:

1. SPREAD BATTER
To form cookies of the requisite thinness, use a small offset spatula to spread the batter to the edges of a 15 by 12-inch sheet of parchment paper.

2. SCORE COOKIES
Immediately after removing the cookies from the oven, use a chef's knife or pizza wheel to score 3 by 2-inch rectangles. Work quickly to prevent breaking.

3. SEPARATE COOKIES
Once the cookies are cool, trace over the scored lines with a paring knife and gently break the cookies apart along the lines.

RATING GROUND GINGER

A staple in bakers' pantries, ground ginger adds a warm, spicy flavor and aroma to baked goods and many Asian and Indian dishes. Since ginger is often used in combination with other pungent spices and strong flavors, such as molasses, would it matter which brand we used in recipes like gingerbread? We bought ground ginger by two top-selling national supermarket brands, McCormick and Spice Islands, and compared them with mail-order ground ginger from Penzeys Spices. We tasted each in gingerbread muffins and in our recipe for Fairy Gingerbread, a crisp, wafer-thin cookie in which ginger is the undisputed star.

In gingerbread muffins, where cinnamon and allspice muffled our perceptions of the ginger, all three brands received equivalent scores, although a few tasters singled out the more pungent profile of Penzeys for extra praise. But in Fairy Gingerbread, tasters showed decided preferences. Although we deemed all three brands acceptable, we gave the lowest marks to McCormick, which we found quite mild. Once again, a vocal minority strongly preferred Penzeys' potent ginger heat, but the highest scores went to Spice Islands Ground Ginger, which straddled the middle ground with full ginger flavor but more moderate heat than Penzeys.

– LISA McMANUS

HIGHLY RECOMMENDED		TASTERS' NOTES
SPICE ISLANDS Ground Ginger **Price:** $6.21 for 1.9 ounces		"Starts mild but builds to a nice pepperiness," said one taster. Others described it as "a little earthy," "spicy, toasty, and fragrant," and providing "just enough ginger" and "just the right amount of spice." "My favorite of the bunch," summed up one taster.
RECOMMENDED		TASTERS' NOTES
PENZEYS SPICES Powdered China #1 Ginger **Price:** $2.65 for 0.9 ounce		"Complex," "pleasing," and "assertive," Penzeys came across as "quite fiery," with a "black-peppery bite." Tasters liked the "pleasant burn" it provided but found it less "floral" than our winner.
McCORMICK GOURMET COLLECTION Ground Ginger **Price:** $5.29 for 1.62 ounces		"Mild and not especially gingery," tasters said, faulting the McCormick sample as "very delicate" and "a bit lackluster after [the others]." But they liked how it "lingers" and "lifts up" to a "stronger finish."

Popcorn Shrimp

Beachside seafood shacks churn out these crisp fried shrimp by the bucketful. But how do you make them at home without a Fry-o-lator and unlimited access to tiny shrimp? BY JEREMY SAUER

Eat these crispy shrimp with cocktail sauce, tartar sauce, or a squeeze of lemon.

SOME PREFER FRIED clams, others scallops or calamari. For my money, popcorn shrimp is the crown jewel of the seafood shack. When properly fried, these tiny shrimp are just as crunchy, salty, and addictive as their namesake. Unfortunately, a recent run through some recipes left me utterly disappointed. Pretty much every recipe produced something greasy and gummy, or featured so much coating that you could barely taste the shrimp.

When it comes to the coating, popcorn shrimp recipes are all over the map. There are batters, cornmeal dredges, egg and bread-crumb (fresh and dried) coatings—you name it. But most seafood shacks keep things simple: They dip impeccably fresh shrimp in a light batter and fry until golden and crisp. That was just what I intended to do.

The most basic fry batter whisks together equal parts water and flour until smooth; this seemed a decent place to start. However, I quickly found that this batter fries up soft and bready. While I didn't want a super-crunchy shell to overwhelm the delicate shrimp, with a name like popcorn shrimp, these puppies needed more texture. To this end, I used two tried-and-true test kitchen tricks. I replaced some of the flour with cornstarch (cornstarch makes the coating drier and crispier), ultimately settling on 1½ cups of flour and ½ cup of cornstarch for a solid crunch. And to turn the crunch toward crisp, I added a teaspoon of baking powder, which increases browning and "lift." That accomplished, I dropped the water by ½ cup so that the batter would have more cling.

But who says I had to use water in this batter at all? Some fry batters employ beer, milk, or buttermilk. I was disappointed to find that the bitterness of the beer distracted from the briny shrimp. Milk and buttermilk were both abject failures: The former was cloying, the latter tasted like shrimp gone bad. Chicken broth, often used to add savory nuance to recipes without tasting overtly chicken-y, worked surprisingly well, but not nearly as well as clam juice. It added a brininess to the batter that echoed the sweet ocean-y shrimp. A little Old Bay seasoning, along with a couple of teaspoons of black pepper, finished it off.

As for the shrimp, if there was one thing that most recipes could agree on, it was that the preferred size is small, smaller, and smallest. But small shrimp not only overcook quickly, they also tend to get lost in the batter coating. After testing every size I could get ahold of, I found that 31/40 (industry shorthand for 31 to 40 shrimp per pound) were best: These shrimp were large enough to withstand a good fry (two minutes in 375-degree oil) but small enough to stay true to their popcorn nature. Now that the shrimp were perfectly cooked and the coating well seasoned, I turned to bumping up the mild shrimp flavor.

A quick marinade seemed to be the best way to go. Wanting complementary—not overpowering—flavors, I tossed the shrimp with a little oil, minced garlic, lemon zest, and reliable Old Bay. Thirty minutes in the marinade made all the difference. The flavor popped. Now if I can just find my flip-flops…

POPCORN SHRIMP Serves 4
Leave plenty of space between the frying shrimp to prevent them from sticking.

- 1½ pounds medium/large (31 to 40 per pound) shrimp, peeled, deveined, and tails discarded
- 3 quarts peanut or vegetable oil
- 1 teaspoon grated lemon zest
- 1 garlic clove, minced
- 1½ tablespoons Old Bay seasoning
- 1½ cups all-purpose flour
- ½ cup cornstarch
- 2 teaspoons pepper
- 1 teaspoon baking powder
- 1½ cups bottled clam juice

1. Toss shrimp, 1 tablespoon oil, lemon zest, garlic, and ½ teaspoon Old Bay in large bowl. Refrigerate, covered, for at least 30 minutes or up to 1 hour.

2. Adjust oven rack to middle position and heat oven to 200 degrees. Heat remaining oil in large Dutch oven over medium-high heat to 375 degrees. Combine flour, cornstarch, remaining Old Bay, pepper, and baking powder in large bowl. Stir clam juice into flour mixture until smooth. Fold marinated shrimp into batter until evenly coated.

3. Working quickly, add quarter of shrimp, 1 at a time, to oil. Fry, stirring frequently, until golden brown, about 2 minutes. Drain on paper towel-lined plate, then transfer shrimp to wire rack set inside rimmed baking sheet. Place shrimp in oven. Bring oil back to 375 degrees and repeat with remaining shrimp. Serve.

Classic Tomato Soup

Bringing out the sweetness and tartness of tomatoes in a satiny soup is easier said than done. Until, that is, a surprising cupboard staple saves the day. BY JEREMY SAUER

CANNED TOMATO SOUP is convenient, sure, but it's strange how little it tastes like real tomatoes. Great recipes for classic tomato soup—where the sweet, tart, almost meaty flavors of tomato are enhanced (not overwhelmed) by milk or cream—are hard to find. Modern versions often include random vegetables (fennel?), fancy herbs (chervil?), and enough fat (quarts of cream, butter by the stick) to make Mario Batali blush. Older recipes are predictably simpler, consisting of little more than canned tomatoes, chopped onion, milk or cream, and sometimes flour to thicken. Simple sounded right for what I had in mind, so I began with the old-fashioned approach.

Because I crave this soup year-round and tomato season is fleeting, I chose canned tomatoes. Although some recipes just dump the tomatoes in the pot, my tasters much preferred it when I concentrated the flavor by first draining the can (reserving the juice to use as the soup base) and browning the tomatoes. Firmer diced tomatoes proved easier to caramelize than whole ones. To add savory depth, I softened a chopped onion in butter before adding the tomatoes. But while the browning deepened the flavor, the pureed soup now lacked freshness. To perk it up, I held back a few cups of tomatoes, stirring them into the soup toward the end of cooking.

As for the seasonings, I quickly learned that a light hand was best. Although herbs such as basil, oregano, and even thyme seemed a natural fit, they made the soup taste like marinara sauce. Likewise with garlic, red pepper flakes, anchovy paste, and Parmesan cheese. Ultimately, tasters thought that a single bay leaf was enough. With a bit of chicken broth to add a meaty backdrop, the soup was starting to take shape.

Every old-fashioned recipe I found used either milk or cream to smooth out the soup. Tasters preferred the richness of cream (nothing crazy, just half a cup), particularly when it was added at the last minute, but these same tasters also praised the texture of the milk-based soups. Why? Because every milk-based recipe included flour, which provides a satiny, "chowder-y" texture (the flour also prevents the milk from curdling). Thinking I could combine the best elements of both, I added flour to a cream-based soup. Unfortunately, the combination of flour and cream quashed the bright taste of the tomatoes. I reduced the flour to ¼ cup (most recipes call for ½ cup or more), then 3 tablespoons to no avail. Would cornstarch work better? No, it made the texture slippery. How about bread crumbs? They made the soup gummy. At last, the solution came to me: tomato paste. (Although it seems like a natural, I didn't find a single old recipe that included it.) Two tablespoons each of flour and tomato paste made the soup robust and smooth.

I buzzed the soup in the blender, stirred in the cream, and sat down with my spoon. What had gone wrong? The tomatoes had a harsh, almost metallic tang. A colleague suggested adding sugar (brown, ideally, for depth), and it helped, but not enough. Would more cream do it? Nope. More salt? Not that either. Stumped, I went back to the piles of recipes I'd gathered and found a clue. A few older recipes suggested adding baking soda to the canned tomatoes, supposedly to counteract their acidity. It sounded like an old wives' tale, but I had nothing to lose. I dutifully stirred ½ teaspoon of baking soda into the pot. The soup foamed a bit, but the bubbles dissipated quickly. When I tasted the soup, I was amazed. The soda eliminated the "off" taste and brought the flavor into focus. What's more, the pureed soup was ultra-satiny (baking soda breaks down the flesh of the tomatoes). I know it sounds like hyperbole, but this was a revelation.

CLASSIC TOMATO SOUP Serves 6 to 8
Use unseasoned canned tomatoes.

- 2 (28-ounce) cans diced tomatoes
- ¾ cup low-sodium chicken broth
- 3 tablespoons unsalted butter
- 1 onion, chopped
- 1 bay leaf
- 1 teaspoon brown sugar
- 2 tablespoons tomato paste
- 2 tablespoons all-purpose flour
- ½ teaspoon baking soda
- Salt and pepper
- ½ cup heavy cream

1. Drain tomatoes in colander set over large bowl, pressing lightly to release juices. Transfer tomato juice and chicken broth to large measuring cup (mixture should measure about 4 cups); reserve.

2. Melt butter in Dutch oven over medium heat. Add onion and cook until softened, about 5 minutes. Add two-thirds of drained tomatoes, bay leaf, and brown sugar and cook, stirring occasionally, until tomatoes begin to brown, about 15 minutes.

3. Add tomato paste and flour to pot and cook, stirring frequently, until paste begins to darken, 1 to 2 minutes. Slowly stir in reserved tomato juice–broth mixture, remaining tomatoes, baking soda, and ½ teaspoon salt and bring to boil. Reduce heat to medium-low and simmer until slightly thickened, about 5 minutes. Remove from heat.

4. Discard bay leaf. Puree soup in batches. Return pureed soup to pot and stir in cream. Season with salt and pepper. Serve. (Soup can be refrigerated in an airtight container for 3 days.)

A little technique elevates canned tomatoes into a soup far better than the condensed glop.

Are You Kidding Me?
You can use it to brush your teeth, scrub your counters, or make your refrigerator smell better. Still, we were shocked at the difference that a mere ½ teaspoon of baking soda made in our Classic Tomato Soup. It neutralized some of the acid in the tomatoes for a perfect sweet-tart balance. And its sodium ions weakened the pectin in the cells of the tomatoes, allowing them to puree into a silken soup.

JUST ½ TEASPOON BAKING SODA

Introducing Pastitsio

Hello Greek lasagna. This diner classic can rival its Italian cousin as long as you keep it light and flavorful.

BY ADAM RIED

THE CONSUMMATE GREEK comfort food, pastitsio is a rich ground meat and pasta casserole that is often described, even in Greek cookbooks, as "Greek lasagna." The flavors and components track—pasta, a tomatoey meat sauce (with a little cinnamon, which is common in Greek cooking), plenty of cheese, and a creamy white sauce, all layered and baked. Sounds great…Well, I sampled pastitsio in several Greek diners and to my dismay found it bland and heavy rather than rich and satisfying. The béchamel was uninspired, the meat sauce greasy and timid, and the pasta bloated and mushy. Certainly the test kitchen could improve matters.

Béchamel, a dairy-based white sauce thickened with a butter and flour roux, is the defining element of pastitsio. It's often used both to sauce the pasta and as a top layer, with eggs added to give it a firm, light, custardy texture. Since béchamel is usually seasoned mildly, I suspected that it was largely to blame for the blandness I encountered.

Reviving the béchamel had three important steps. First, I reduced the quantity. Many recipes called for up to 7 cups, which smothered the casserole. After testing different quantities, I scaled back to 5 cups—2 to sauce the pasta and the remaining 3 to top the casserole. Second, I scrutinized the dairy element, ultimately banishing the fatty heavy cream called for in many recipes. Whole milk produced a sauce that was plenty rich.

Third, and most critically, I had to boost the flavor. Using a full cup of grated Pecorino Romano cheese, the most common substitute for the traditional but hard-to-find Greek *kefalotyri* cheese, was a good start. (I divided a second cup of grated cheese between the meat sauce and the top of the casserole.) Next, I replaced the usual seasoning of mild onion with a tablespoon of pungent chopped garlic. Last, I took a tip from one Greek cookbook I consulted and added some thick Greek yogurt; just ⅓ cup added a welcome tang and extra complexity to the béchamel.

For the custardy béchamel topping, different recipes introduce eggs in various numbers and configurations. I tried from two to six whole eggs, and combinations of whole eggs with extra yolks, yolks alone, and yolks with whipped

For a Pastitsio recipe that doesn't end with "take a nap," we cut back on the pasta and béchamel, and upped the garlic and spices considerably.

whites. The simplest approach of whisking three whole eggs into the béchamel prevailed, providing a casserole cap that was both smooth and firm enough to slice neatly.

Though lamb is traditional in the meat sauce, it can be gamy, so not everyone likes it. I circumvented the debate by using beef instead, which is also common. The leanest choice in most supermarkets, 93 percent, kept the grease factor well in check. Tomatoes

are the second sauce ingredient, and plain tomato sauce, with some added tomato paste for punch, won out over canned diced, crushed, and pureed tomatoes. Onions, garlic, oregano, and cinnamon are the requisite flavorings: I ignored the advice in many cookbooks to use them sparingly. By the time I was done, I'd increased the garlic to 2 tablespoons and the oregano and cinnamon to a hefty 2 teaspoons each. Adding a half cup of red wine bolstered the acidity

enough to balance the rich meat sauce and béchamel.

Lastly, I turned to the pasta. A tubular shape is traditional, so the sauce can work its way inside. Purists insist on long, slender tubes, in Greece called simply "Number 2" pasta, with bucatini or perciatelli typical substitutes here. The bucatini and perciatelli, however, struck tasters as awkward to eat. Instead they favored short, small shapes, giving the nod to small elbow macaroni over shells, penne, ziti, and rigatoni because they were easy on the fork and compacted into a tidy layer. Boiling the macaroni just to parcook it, and allowing it to finish cooking in the oven, helped avoid mushy pasta. Since the pasta adds more substance than flavor, I also cut the quantity to just half a pound, which helped give both the custardy béchamel layer and the meat sauce stronger voices in the dish.

I still love Greek diners and restaurants, but now that I have this recipe I'll be eating pastitsio at home.

GREEK LASAGNA (PASTITSIO)
Serves 8 to 10
You will need a total of 4 ounces of Pecorino Romano cheese. Use whole milk Greek yogurt in this recipe.

MEAT SAUCE
- 1 tablespoon olive oil
- 1 onion, chopped fine
- 3 tablespoons tomato paste
- 6 garlic cloves, minced
- 2 teaspoons dried oregano
- 2 teaspoons ground cinnamon
- 1½ pounds 93 percent lean ground beef
  Salt and pepper
- ½ cup red wine
- 1 (15-ounce) can tomato sauce
- ½ cup grated Pecorino Romano cheese

PASTA AND BÉCHAMEL SAUCE
  Salt and pepper
- 8 ounces elbow macaroni
- 5 tablespoons unsalted butter
- ½ cup all-purpose flour
- 3 garlic cloves, minced
- 5 cups whole milk
- 1½ cups grated Pecorino Romano cheese
- 3 large eggs
- ⅓ cup Greek yogurt

1. Adjust oven rack to middle position and heat oven to 425 degrees. Heat oil in large skillet over medium heat

until shimmering. Add onion and cook until softened, about 5 minutes. Stir in tomato paste, garlic, oregano, and cinnamon and cook until paste begins to darken, 1 to 2 minutes. Add beef and 1 teaspoon salt and cook until beef is no longer pink, about 5 minutes. Stir in wine and cook until reduced to about 1 tablespoon, 2 to 4 minutes. Add tomato sauce and simmer until slightly thickened, about 10 minutes. Off heat, stir in Romano. Season with salt and pepper; set aside.

2. Bring 4 quarts water to boil in Dutch oven. Add 1 tablespoon salt and macaroni and cook until nearly al dente, 3 to 4 minutes. Drain in colander and rinse with cold water until cool. Drain again and transfer to large bowl.

3. Melt butter in now-empty Dutch oven over medium heat. Add flour and garlic and cook, stirring constantly, until golden and fragrant, about 1 minute. Slowly whisk in milk and bring to boil. Reduce heat to medium-low and simmer until thickened and reduced to 4 cups, about 12 minutes. Off heat, whisk in 1 cup Romano until smooth. Season with salt and pepper.

4. Stir 2 cups béchamel into macaroni until combined. Transfer sauced pasta to 13 by 9-inch baking dish. Beat eggs in now-empty pasta bowl until smooth. Whisk 1 cup béchamel into egg mixture. Slowly whisk tempered egg mixture into remaining béchamel. Stir in yogurt.

5. Spread meat sauce over macaroni and top with egg-béchamel mixture. Sprinkle with remaining Romano and bake until golden brown, 35 to 40 minutes. Let cool 10 minutes. Serve.

MAKE AHEAD Meat sauce can be refrigerated in airtight container for 3 days. Microwave, covered, until heated through, about 1 minute, before proceeding with step 2.

STEP BY STEP **Béchamel Two Ways**
Béchamel sauce makes many a pasta or potato casserole moist and creamy. But only in pastitsio is it used in two very different ways.

1. The parcooked elbows are combined with 2 cups béchamel sauce. The pasta finishes cooking to full tenderness in the oven.

2. Beaten egg and yogurt are combined with the rest of the béchamel. This modified sauce is poured over the assembled casserole for a custardy, golden topping.

ON THE SIDE
Greek Bread Salad

We weren't going to let soggy pita bread sully this vibrant chopped salad of Mediterranean ingredients.

BY KELLY PRICE

YOU MAY KNOW Italian bread salad, panzanella, which regularly shows up in the United States come summer, but do you know its Greek cousin? The Greeks call it *dakos*; after eating some in a local Greek restaurant, I call it delicious. I gathered the ingredients to try to make it at home: tomatoes, cucumbers, olives, chickpeas, onions, pepperoncini, feta cheese, and pita bread (but no lettuce). The pita adds substance and soaks up the highly seasoned vinaigrette. I chopped and dressed my salad and tasted a forkful. It wasn't terrible, but it was no gold medalist, either. The flavors were unexciting and the pita was soggy.

I had been serving the salad as soon as it was tossed, but I noticed that it became more flavorful as it sat. For my next test, I compared vegetables allowed to sit in the dressing for 15 minutes with those that sat for 30. Tasters preferred the longer "marinating" time, but not too long; more than 30 minutes and the vegetables got mushy. To add spicy pop to the dressing, I replaced some of the vinegar with brine from the jarred pepperoncini and added a spoonful of mustard.

To flavor the pita and head off the soggy situation, I tossed torn pieces with olive oil, garlic, and oregano and toasted them in a 400-degree oven for 10 minutes. I mixed them into the salad five minutes before I was ready to serve it so that they gently softened but didn't get soggy. Great bread salad was no longer Greek to me.

Slow down: Letting the dressed vegetables sit for 30 minutes gives the flavors a chance to meld.

GREEK BREAD SALAD Serves 4 to 6

- ¼ cup chopped jarred pepperoncini, plus 1½ tablespoons pepperoncini brine
- 1½ tablespoons red wine vinegar
- 1 teaspoon dried oregano
- ½ teaspoon Dijon mustard
- 6 tablespoons extra-virgin olive oil
- 1 pint cherry tomatoes, halved
- 1 (16-ounce) can chickpeas, drained and rinsed
- 1 cucumber, peeled, halved lengthwise, seeded, and sliced thin
- 1 cup crumbled feta cheese
- ¾ cup pitted kalamata olives, halved
- ½ small red onion, halved and sliced thin
- 2 (10-inch) pita breads, torn into 1-inch pieces
- 1 garlic clove, minced
- ⅓ cup chopped fresh parsley
  Salt and pepper

1. Adjust oven rack to upper-middle position and heat oven to 400 degrees. Combine pepperoncini brine, vinegar, ½ teaspoon oregano, and mustard in medium bowl. Slowly whisk 5 tablespoons oil into vinegar mixture. Add tomatoes, chickpeas, cucumber, feta, olives, onion, and pepperoncini and toss to combine. Let sit 30 minutes.

2. Meanwhile, toss pita, remaining oil, garlic, and remaining oregano in medium bowl. Bake pita on rimmed baking sheet until golden brown, about 10 minutes, stirring halfway through baking. Stir toasted pita and parsley into salad. Let stand 5 minutes. Season with salt and pepper. Serve.

MAKE AHEAD Toasted pita can be stored at room temperature in airtight container for up to 2 days.

The Best Weeknight Chicken

Sure, baked chicken pieces are convenient, but they're often disappointing. We wanted crisp skin and tender, well-seasoned meat—with no more than a "baked chicken" level of effort. BY DIANE UNGER

YOU'RE DRIVING HOME from work. You swing by the supermarket to grab a "family pack" of chicken parts for supper. You set the oven to 350, put the pieces in a baking dish with a few shakes of salt and pepper, and bake until done. This sounds like typical weeknight cooking, right? The kind of meal many of us grew up eating? I guess I didn't eat as well as I remember: When I tried this method recently, I found that baking at this moderate temperature meant that the fatty skin hadn't rendered and crisped by the time the meat was properly cooked.

I did the obvious thing: I raised the oven's heat to 450. Now I had two choices, neither good: meat that wasn't fully cooked by the time the skin was browned, or nicely cooked meat with burnt skin—and the sound of the smoke alarm filling the kitchen. I refused to choose between crisp skin and moist, tender, well-seasoned meat. And I refused to follow a long day at the office with a long night in the kitchen. The recipe would have to be fast and easy.

I decided to work with 3 pounds of chicken pieces—enough to feed a family of four. Restaurant cooks often start chicken on the stovetop, giving it a good sear for a head start on a nice, crisp skin. Next, they put the chicken, still in its skillet (no extra dishes!), in a hot oven—very hot, because restaurants are in a hurry to feed customers. I was all set: I'd simply steal this restaurant method for my home-cooked dinner. Too late, I remembered that when I'd used the technique as a line cook, the chicken had been brined first, which both protects it from drying out and gives it flavor. Since my goal was supper on the table fast, I ruled out brining. Ditto marinating. Yet without those techniques, the chicken was dry and flavorless.

After some consideration, I got the idea to add liquid to the pan: It was simple, fast, and would keep the chicken moist in the oven. Plus I'd have the opportunity to add flavor. I poured chicken broth and wine into the skillet before moving it to a 350-degree oven. I took care not to add too much, knowing that if I submerged the chicken, its skin would turn soggy. For more flavor, I sprinkled in fresh thyme and a few smashed garlic cloves. On the plus side, the flavor was much improved and the meat wasn't dry—not even the breasts, which are ready at a lower temperature

Browning the chicken pieces on the stovetop (before finishing them in the oven) creates the building blocks for an easy, flavorful sauce.

(160 degrees) than the thighs (175 degrees). The liquid acted as a helpful buffer to keep the white meat from drying out. Despite my precautions, though, the chicken emerged with soggy skin 25 minutes later. I theorized that at this moderate temperature, the skin had gently steamed in the bubbling broth.

I made the chicken again, as before, only this time I cranked the heat to 450 degrees. The skin crisped like a newly starched shirt, plus the high heat had the happy side effect of speeding along dinner. Meanwhile, the liquid had partly evaporated, hence had concentrated. It seemed crazy to throw it away. I decided to use it as a base for a flavorful sauce to dress up the chicken, but I set myself a single criterion first: Any sauce would have to be dead easy to make. I set the chicken aside, quickly defatted the juices, and returned them to the skillet to reduce and intensify further. Once they'd done so, I thickened them slightly with cornstarch and finished with a bit of butter for gloss and richness. (Even on a weeknight, who doesn't deserve a little gloss and richness?) About 30 minutes later, very little of which was hands-on time, I sat down to a satisfying and uncomplicated chicken dinner—one that was, truth told, worth eating any day of the week.

WEEKNIGHT CHICKEN Serves 4 to 6

Use any combination of white and dark meat. For even cooking, halve breasts crosswise and separate leg quarters into thighs and drumsticks.

- 1   cup low-sodium chicken broth
- 1½ teaspoons cornstarch
- 1   cup white wine
- 4   garlic cloves, peeled and smashed
- 2   teaspoons minced fresh thyme
- 3   pounds bone-in, skin-on chicken pieces
     Salt and pepper
- 1   tablespoon vegetable oil
- 2   tablespoons unsalted butter

1. Adjust oven rack to middle position and heat oven to 450 degrees. Whisk 2 tablespoons broth and cornstarch in small bowl until no lumps remain; reserve. Combine remaining broth, wine, garlic, and thyme in large measuring cup.

2. Pat chicken dry with paper towels and season with ½ teaspoon salt and ¼ teaspoon pepper. Heat oil in large oven-safe skillet over medium-high heat until just smoking. Cook chicken, skin side down, until well browned, 6 to 10 minutes. Flip and cook until lightly browned on second side, about 2 minutes.

3. Slowly pour broth mixture into skillet and bring to boil. Transfer skillet to oven and roast until white meat registers 160 degrees and dark meat registers 175 degrees, 12 to 18 minutes. Transfer chicken to platter and tent with aluminum foil. Discard garlic.

4. Pour pan juices into liquid measuring cup; skim and discard fat. Return 1½ cups defatted pan juices to now-empty skillet and bring to boil over medium-high heat. Reduce heat to medium-low and simmer until sauce is reduced to 1 cup, 5 to 7 minutes. Add reserved cornstarch mixture and simmer until sauce is slightly thickened, about 2 minutes. Off heat, whisk in butter. Season with salt and pepper. Serve, passing sauce at table.

TEST KITCHEN TECHNIQUE Poaching Meets Roasting

When we want fast weeknight chicken, there's no time for long marinating or brining. So how can we keep the chicken meat moist and the skin crisp? We cook it partly submerged in flavorful liquid.

THE MEAT stays moist and drinks in flavor from the poaching liquid, which combines chicken broth, wine, and seasonings. The liquid moderates temperature so that the dark-meat thighs can finish cooking without the white-meat breasts overcooking.

THE SKIN, which we've already seared on the stovetop, stays above the simmering cooking liquid, crisping further in the 450-degree heat of the oven.

THE BROTH evaporates and concentrates in the oven, making the base for a quick, elegant, and flavorful sauce.

ON THE SIDE

Maple-Glazed Acorn Squash

Many recipes leave the glaze in puddles in the pan. In order to taste the maple in every bite, we needed the syrup to stick. BY CAROLYNN PURPURA

IDEALLY, A SWEET, caramel-y maple glaze should highlight the earthy flavor of acorn squash. But most recipes just halve the squash, pour on some syrup, top with a pat of butter, and roast, which results in a thin pool of buttery syrup at the bottom of each half and absolutely no maple flavor within. I wanted every bite of flavorful roasted squash to be coated in a buttery, syrupy maple glaze.

I started by cutting the squash into eighths, so the increased surface area would provide room for ample amounts of maple glaze. The smaller pieces also resulted in a shorter roasting time.

While this was more efficient, it also meant the squash cooked so quickly that it was barely browning. To remedy this, I tossed the squash wedges with vegetable oil and a small amount of granulated sugar before roasting them in a hot oven, then flipped them before glazing so that both sides had time to brown. This approach gave the caramelization a boost and achieved the deep brown color and added flavor I desired.

I knew that I wanted a straightforward glaze of maple syrup and melted butter (with a little cayenne for kick). Although the glaze was thick at room temperature, it ran right off the squash in the hot oven. To give the glaze more gripping power, I tried reducing the syrup by half on the stovetop before glazing the squash. This did enable the glaze to stick to the squash better—but it also stuck to the pan, the serving spoon, and my teeth. No good. I tried reducing the syrup only slightly. Closer.

When the squash came out of the oven, I flipped the slices over and painted them with a little more glaze. Bull's-eye. Finally, I had tender, nicely caramelized squash with plenty of maple depth.

MAPLE-GLAZED ACORN SQUASH Serves 6

Don't even think about using pancake syrup—use pure maple syrup.

- 2   acorn squash
- 2   tablespoons vegetable oil
- 2   teaspoons sugar
- ¾   teaspoon salt
- ½   teaspoon pepper
- 5   tablespoons maple syrup
- 4   tablespoons unsalted butter
- ⅛   teaspoon cayenne pepper

1. Adjust oven rack to middle position and heat oven to 475 degrees. Halve squash through stem, seed, and cut each half into 4 wedges. Toss squash, oil, sugar, salt, and pepper in large bowl. Arrange squash cut side down in single layer on rimmed baking sheet. Bake until bottoms of squash are deep golden brown, about 25 minutes.

2. Meanwhile, bring syrup to boil in small saucepan over medium-high heat. Reduce heat to medium-low and simmer until slightly thickened, about 3 minutes. Off heat, whisk in butter and cayenne until smooth. Cover and keep warm.

3. When bottoms of squash are deep golden, remove from oven. Flip and brush with 6 tablespoons glaze. Bake, rotating baking sheet, until squash is tender and deep golden all over, about 15 minutes. Flip and brush with remaining glaze. Serve.

Cutting the squash into eighths promotes speedy cooking—and provides more surface area for the glaze to cling to.

Apple Fritters

You can't have apple fritters without apples. But apples caused a bushel of problems.

BY DIANE UNGER

I n 1880, Mark Twain, writing in "A Tramp Abroad," bellyached for more than 10 pages about the lousy food on his trip: "A man accustomed to American food and American domestic cookery would not starve to death suddenly in Europe; but I think he would gradually waste away, and eventually die." Twain proceeded to pen a lengthy list of dishes that he hoped would await him, hot, when he reached home: fried chicken, corn-pone, Boston bacon and beans, … and apple fritters. You wouldn't catch me grousing about the food in Europe. But maybe, just maybe, I'd cut my vacation a few days short if I knew a plate of warm, sweet apple fritters would be waiting for me when I got home.

Apple fritters should be crisp on the outside, moist within, and sing out apple flavor. I started my testing with a delicious recipe for drop doughnuts that the test kitchen developed several years back: I combined milk, eggs, flour, sugar, cinnamon, nutmeg, and baking powder, and then stirred in grated apples. (I figured the apple would distribute better if it was grated.) I heated the oil, scooped out batter, and got down to the business of frying.

When I pulled the fritters out of the oil, they looked pretty good. But when tasters bit in, it turned out the crispy exteriors enclosed heavy, wet goo—more raw batter than light, fluffy fritter. And so much for even distribution of the apples: If I hadn't stirred them in myself, I never would have known they were in there.

I made up a new batch of fritters using chopped apples, which I hoped would be drier and more conspicuous. My tasters weren't impressed as these fritters weren't much better. The apple chunks were identifiable, sure, but also crunchy and raw. And yet again the insides of the fritters hadn't cooked. "Fritter flops," a colleague announced to my embarrassment.

A cider glaze underlines the apple flavor in our fritters. We also use cider in the batter.

No matter what variety of apple I tried, the fruit caused trouble. Moist to begin with, the apple chunks became even wetter as the fritters fried. (As anyone who has ever baked a fruit pie knows, fruit oozes water as it cooks.) Consequently, the fritters were too wet on the inside to cook through.

I refused to cut back on the apples (two for 2 cups of flour)—these were apple fritters, after all. Instead, I tried both salting and sugaring the chopped apples to draw out their moisture before stirring them into the batter. Both methods did draw out liquid, but I couldn't seem to shut off the spigot, even after the fritters hit the hot oil. At that point, the weeping liquid prevented the insides from cooking through. If I simply fried the fritters longer, the outsides burned, yet the interiors still didn't cook. I was running out of ideas.

I dispiritedly blotted the chopped apples dry with paper towels and made a new batch. In all honesty, I didn't expect this to do much, but it did produce marginally drier fritters. Tossing the towel-dried apples with the dry ingredients had a bigger impact. Our science editor explained that the dry ingredients soaked up moisture that would otherwise migrate out from the inside of the finished fritters as they cooled, making them soggy.

Maybe I could get the insides to cook through if I made flatter fritters. I'd been deep-frying the fritters in 4 quarts of peanut oil, dropping in the batter, and getting big, round fritters. I cut back the oil to just 3 cups and tried shallow-frying the fritters in large scoopfuls, lightly pressing the batter against the bottom of the Dutch oven. With this method, the fritters (and the apple chunks) cooked through, and as a bonus produced beautifully crunchy, almost caramelized edges.

Now it was time to bump up the apple flavor. I replaced the milk in the batter with, in turn, apple juice, apple butter, and apple cider. The juice was wimpy and the apple butter weighed down the batter, but the apple cider got the nod of approval. I added dashes of nutmeg and cinnamon to the batter and stirred in 2 tablespoons of melted butter for richness. Serendipitously, the butter helped the fritters crisp.

I had one final decision to make: should I crown my fritters with a dusting of powdered sugar or a glaze? (Of such grueling decisions the life of a test cook is made.) The shell-like, translucent glaze gave a little snap to the fritter's craggy exterior, contrasting nicely with the fluffy interior, so I went with that. To make the glaze, I mixed confectioners' sugar with more spices and more apple cider, which gave these warm, sweet, apple-imbued fritters one final layer of apple flavor.

APPLE FRITTERS
Makes 10 fritters
We like Granny Smith apples in these fritters because they are tart and crisp. Apple juice doesn't have enough flavor—you really do need the cider. Penzeys Extra Fancy Vietnamese Cassia Cinnamon is the test kitchen's favorite brand.

FRITTERS
- 2 Granny Smith apples, peeled, cored, and cut into ¼-inch pieces
- 2 cups all-purpose flour
- ⅓ cup granulated sugar
- 1 tablespoon baking powder
- 1 teaspoon salt
- 1 teaspoon ground cinnamon
- ¼ teaspoon ground nutmeg
- ¾ cup apple cider
- 2 large eggs, lightly beaten
- 2 tablespoons unsalted butter, melted
- 3 cups peanut or vegetable oil

GLAZE
- 2 cups confectioners' sugar
- ¼ cup apple cider
- ½ teaspoon ground cinnamon
- ¼ teaspoon ground nutmeg

1. Spread prepared apples in single layer on paper towel–lined baking sheet and pat thoroughly dry with paper towels. Combine flour, granulated sugar, baking powder, salt, cinnamon, and nutmeg in large bowl. Whisk cider, eggs, and melted butter in medium bowl until combined. Stir apples into flour mixture. Stir in cider mixture until incorporated.

2. Heat oil in Dutch oven over medium-high heat to 350 degrees. Following step 1, use ⅓-cup measure to transfer 5 heaping portions of batter to oil. Press batter lightly with back of spoon to flatten. Fry, adjusting burner as necessary to maintain oil temperature between 325 and 350 degrees, until deep golden brown, 2 to 3 minutes per side. Transfer fritters to wire rack set inside rimmed baking sheet. Bring oil back to 350 degrees and repeat with remaining batter. Let fritters cool 5 minutes.

3. Meanwhile, whisk confectioners' sugar, cider, cinnamon, and nutmeg in medium bowl until smooth. Top each fritter with 1 heaping tablespoon glaze. Let glaze set 10 minutes. Serve.

STEP BY STEP **Forming Fab Fritters**

1. Use a ⅓-cup measure and a spoon to carefully and gently portion batter into the hot oil.

2. Use the spoon to gently press on each fritter. The flattened shape helps the interior cook through.

RATING SPIDER SKIMMERS

Trying to pull fritters from bubbling oil with a spoon or a pair of tongs may leave you with mangled pastries, an oily mess, burns—or all three. The best tool for the job is a type of skimmer that chefs call a "spider." Essentially a shallow basket at the end of a long handle, a spider lets boiling fat or water safely drain away while you lift food comfortably from a pot. We tested five spiders while boiling wontons and frying apple fritters and french fries. All were about 5 inches in diameter and cost from $6.95 to $19.95.

Each spider handled wontons and french fries with relative ease. But the fritters, which we shallow-fried, were another story. We like to fry in a deep Dutch oven to reduce splattering, but getting under the fritters posed a problem. Some skimmers were awkward to use and had us chasing finished fritters around the Dutch oven while the rest of the batch burned. We prefer longer metal handles with extreme angles that keep our hands away from hot edges and don't absorb odors. We also preferred woven wire baskets to solid perforated or slotted ones, which tend to bring oil with them, and we like baskets with shallower, flatter lips that get underneath food easily. The WMF Profi Plus strainer has all of these features, plus it's dishwasher-safe for easy cleanup.

—TAIZETH SIERRA

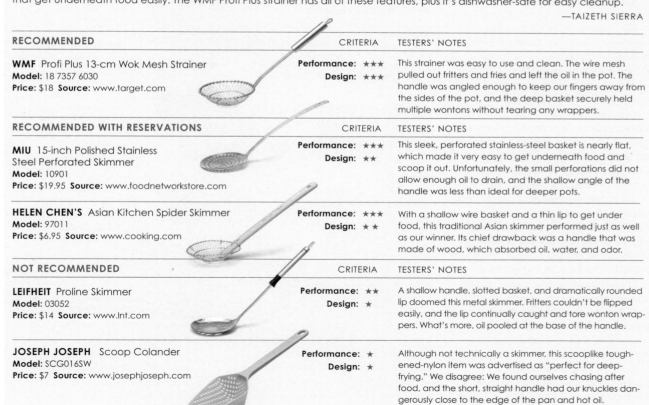

RECOMMENDED	CRITERIA	TESTERS' NOTES
WMF Profi Plus 13-cm Wok Mesh Strainer **Model:** 18 7357 6030 **Price:** $18 **Source:** www.target.com	Performance: ★★★ Design: ★★★	This strainer was easy to use and clean. The wire mesh pulled out fritters and fries and left the oil in the pot. The handle was angled enough to keep our fingers away from the sides of the pot, and the deep basket securely held multiple wontons without tearing any wrappers.
RECOMMENDED WITH RESERVATIONS	CRITERIA	TESTERS' NOTES
MIU 15-inch Polished Stainless Steel Perforated Skimmer **Model:** 10901 **Price:** $19.95 **Source:** www.foodnetworkstore.com	Performance: ★★★ Design: ★★	This sleek, perforated stainless-steel basket is nearly flat, which made it very easy to get underneath food and scoop it out. Unfortunately, the small perforations did not allow enough oil to drain, and the shallow angle of the handle was less than ideal for deeper pots.
HELEN CHEN'S Asian Kitchen Spider Skimmer **Model:** 97011 **Price:** $6.95 **Source:** www.cooking.com	Performance: ★★★ Design: ★★	With a shallow wire basket and a thin lip to get under food, this traditional Asian skimmer performed just as well as our winner. Its chief drawback was a handle that was made of wood, which absorbed oil, water, and odor.
NOT RECOMMENDED	CRITERIA	TESTERS' NOTES
LEIFHEIT Proline Skimmer **Model:** 03052 **Price:** $14 **Source:** www.lnt.com	Performance: ★★ Design: ★	A shallow handle, slotted basket, and dramatically rounded lip doomed this metal skimmer. Fritters couldn't be flipped easily, and the lip continually caught and tore wonton wrappers. What's more, oil pooled at the base of the handle.
JOSEPH JOSEPH Scoop Colander **Model:** SCG016SW **Price:** $7 **Source:** www.josephjoseph.com	Performance: ★ Design: ★	Although not technically a skimmer, this scooplike toughened-nylon item was advertised as "perfect for deep-frying." We disagree: We found ourselves chasing after food, and the short, straight handle had our knuckles dangerously close to the edge of the pan and hot oil.

Equipment Review Muffin Tins

Does a hefty price tag guarantee million-dollar muffins (and cupcakes)? BY ADAM RIED

BAD MUFFIN TINS are a nuisance. They can warp, rust, or stick, tearing your baked goods. If there's nowhere for your oven mitt to hold on, it will get gummed up with batter or dent your fresh-baked cupcakes. And have fun scrubbing out each one of those little cups afterward.

Six years ago, we tested muffin tins and decided that two "must-have" features were a nonstick coating and handles—or at least extended rims—for easy gripping. At that time, many muffin tins lacked handles or broad rims. This time I found eight, priced from $14 to $30. Over the next few weeks I turned into a muffin machine, cranking out more than 300 muffins (blueberry streusel and corn) and cupcakes (vanilla).

I watched how deeply and evenly the tins browned, how easily they gave up the goods, and whether form—how the muffins and cupcakes looked—reflected function. None of the muffins would have embarrassed us on a brunch table, but some looked more "professional" than others, with straighter sides and sharply creased bottom edges. The lightest-colored tins didn't brown the muffins and cupcakes, forcing us to extend baking times and hover by the oven to get the color we wanted. Other tins browned muffins unevenly, indicating that they were poor heat conductors.

How nonstick were these tins? With cooking spray, as our muffin recipes specify, corn muffins fell right out. Blueberry streusel muffins can be sticky with fruit and a sugary topping, yet all of the tins released them fairly easily (a few required a couple of brisk shakes, which wasn't a deal-breaker). Cupcakes, with ample sugar in the batter, proved more of a challenge, even though the cups were greased and floured. Only the Norpro tin released cupcakes perfectly.

A few tins sport silicone handle tabs, which we assumed would be the easiest to grip. Actually, tins with wide, angled rims or raised lips all around, such as those on the Wilton, Anolon, and Pyrex, proved easier to grab and hold with thick mitts than tins with small silicone tabs, such as those on the Rachael Ray pan. Anolon covered both bases: a raised lip plus large silicone handles.

You'd never pry a muffin out of a nonstick pan with a metal utensil, right? Just in case, we simulated such scratching by running a dinner knife around a cup in each tin 25 times. While light scratches were apparent, the damage was minimal and didn't affect any tin's ability to release baked goods. We shocked the pans by heating them empty to 500 degrees and then plunging them into ice water. A few warped slightly, indicating less sturdy construction. To simulate an overnight stay in the sink without washing (hand washing is recommended for all the tins), we smeared them with thick white sauce (béchamel)

and let it harden overnight. The next day, testers had to scrape and scrub the USA and Rachael Ray tins, yet on the Wilton and Pyrex tins, the hardened sauce came right off.

I had hoped to find a tough, slick tin that produced perfect muffins and cupcakes. Instead there were trade-offs. No tin scored high enough for us to rank it as Highly Recommended, nor

did any score low enough for us to rule it out. We found that you can economize on a tin without shortchanging your muffins—the expensive tins didn't wow us. For its handsome muffins, reliable release, durability, affordability, and excellent handles, we recommend the Wilton Avanti Everglide Metal-Safe Non-Stick 12-Cup Muffin Pan ($13.99)—which won last time, too.

RECOMMENDED		CRITERIA	TESTERS' NOTES
WILTON AVANTI EVERGLIDE Metal-Safe Non-Stick 12-Cup Muffin Pan **Model** 2105-3018 **$13.99** at www.wilton.com		Browning ★★ Baked Goods Shape ★★ Release ★★★ Handle Design ★★★ Durability ★★★	Wide, extended rims and a raised lip make this tin very easy to grip even with thick oven mitts. Its durable construction withstood abuse, and its nonstick coating consistently released. Browning was acceptably even, though not stellar—but the price sure is right.
NORPRO Nonstick 12-Muffin Cupcake Pan **Model** 3931 **$15.99** at www.amazon.com		Browning ★★★ Baked Goods Shape ★★★ Release ★★★ Handle Design ★ Durability ★★★	This tin had one big drawback: a single extended rim, on a long side, which sloped downward, making it hard to hang on to. However, it browned deeply, baked relatively evenly, and released perfectly.
ANOLON ADVANCED BAKEWARE 12-Cup Muffin Pan **Model** 54710 **$24.99** at www.cooking.com		Browning ★★ Baked Goods Shape ★★ Release ★★★ Handle Design ★★★ Durability ★★★	This comparatively expensive tin was a respectable performer, with good "grab-ability" thanks to generous, well-placed silicone handles and a raised lip around the perimeter.
BONJOUR COMMERCIAL NONSTICK BAKEWARE 12-Cup Muffin Pan **Model** 57086 **$24.99** at www.amazon.com		Browning ★★ Baked Goods Shape ★★★ Release ★★ Handle Design ★★ Durability ★★★	Two-toned finish (dark bottom, light top) earned high honors in the cupcake competition, turning out pert little cakes with well-defined edges and even tops. It stumbled releasing blueberry muffins (some berries burnt on), and the handles were not generous.

RECOMMENDED WITH RESERVATIONS		CRITERIA	TESTERS' NOTES
FARBERWARE SOFT TOUCH Nonstick 12-Cup Muffin Pan **Model** 52146 **$13.95** at www.cookware.com		Browning ★★ Baked Goods Shape ★★ Release ★★★ Handle Design ★★ Durability ★★	This tin was one of two pans to emerge from the thermal shock abuse test with a very slight warp. Its cupcakes were not impressive and the muffins a bit squat, although they baked fairly evenly and released well.
PYREX METAL BAKEWARE 12-Cup Muffin Pan with Cover **Model** 70950044973 **$25.99** at www.shopworldkitchen.com		Browning ★ Baked Goods Shape ★ Release ★★★ Handle Design ★★★ Durability ★★★	Browning was inconsistent. "They look boiled," one tester said about the mottled, pale cupcakes. A ridge line (described by the manufacturer as a "fill" line) marred the shape of the muffins and cupcakes. Too bad, because the wide, four-sided upturned rim was easy to grab. The optional carrying cover is too low to fit our blueberry muffins and frosted cupcakes.
RACHAEL RAY OVEN LOVIN' Nonstick 12-Cup Muffin Pan **Model** 54075 **$19.99** at www.bedbathandbeyond.com		Browning ★★ Baked Goods Shape ★★ Release ★ Handle Design ★★ Durability ★★	When the going got tough, this tin couldn't take it. Muffins released without incident, but cupcakes stuck. Hardened béchamel stuck so tenaciously we had to use a scraper. Heat discolored the orange silicone handle tabs. Very uneven performance.
USA PANS 12-Cup Muffin Pan **Model** 1200MF-3 **$29.95** at www.amazon.com		Browning ★ Baked Goods Shape ★★ Release ★★ Handle Design ★★ Durability ★	The highest-priced pan proved among the least durable. It warped slightly after thermal shock and clutched béchamel crusts for dear life in spots. The light-colored metal led to very light browning, so if you like deeper color, you will have to extend baking times in this tin.

Taste Test Milk Chocolate

Has trendy dark chocolate changed our taste for good old milk chocolate? BY DAVID PAZMIÑO

DARK CHOCOLATE HAS been in vogue for more than a decade. Now, milk chocolate manufacturers are taking their cue from dark chocolate, reformulating recipes and developing new milk chocolate bars complete with cacao percentages on the label. Is milk chocolate just getting fancy? Or is it getting better?

To find out, we bought ten national brands—find the full chart at Cooks Country.com—of top-selling milk chocolate (from a list compiled by the market research firm SymphonyIRI Group), including our previous favorite, Dove, and asked 21 staffers to taste them plain and in chocolate pudding. Colors ranged from tan to deep mahogany, and textures from waxy or gritty to lush and creamy. A few had the mild, sweet, milky taste we expected; others were deeper, cocoa-y, and less sweet—dead ringers for dark chocolate.

Why so different? Milk chocolate makers have lots of latitude. Federal standards require milk chocolate to contain at least 10 percent cacao, which is the actual chocolate in the candy bar. (Cacao, also called "chocolate liquor," is roasted, ground-up cacao beans, containing both cocoa solids and cocoa butter.) By comparison, dark chocolate, both bittersweet and semisweet, must have at least 35 percent cacao. Those percentages are the legal minimums, but most chocolate brands contain more. In fact, several brands of milk chocolate we tasted would qualify as dark chocolate if not for the presence of milk.

Beyond the amount of chocolate, manufacturers can choose among cream, whole or reduced-fat milk, powdered, condensed, or evaporated milk. The dairy ingredient is heated with sugar to caramelize it and remove water before it's blended with cacao. Manufacturers may add extra cocoa butter or milk fat, lecithin to keep the fat from separating, and flavors such as vanilla or malt. (Some even add a sour flavor compound that's present in spoiled milk.) The liquid chocolate goes into machines called conches, where heavy rollers grind it and coat the solids with fat. The longer chocolate is conched—from a few hours to days—the finer, creamier, and mellower it will be. Finally, the chocolate is tempered: heated and cooled to create a crystalline structure for the perfect "snap" when it's bitten or broken.

While chocolate makers never divulge recipes or methods, our tasters preferred smoother chocolate and downgraded classic Hershey's and Nestlé for grittiness. We sent samples to a lab and learned that the chocolates we liked were also higher in fat. Cocoa butter melts at body temperature, adding to the creamy sensation when you let chocolate melt in your mouth. But milk fat is also present in milk chocolate. Chocolates with less milk fat are firmer, to the point of being "hard," as one taster described Nestlé. Abundant milk fat creates a super-creamy softness, but can overwhelm chocolate flavor without proper balance. Tasters preferred plenty of both fats: Our recommended chocolates have at least 31 percent total fat.

But creamy texture wasn't everything. Our three top-ranked milk chocolates—Dove Silky Smooth, Endangered Species All-Natural, and Green & Black's Organic—shared one thing: intense chocolate flavor. Classic milk chocolate lovers praised Dove and Green & Black's. Those who secretly wanted dark chocolate in milk chocolate clothing singled out Endangered Species for its roasted-chocolate taste. Extra cacao was no guarantee, either. Case in point: Scharffen Berger, which had a high cacao percentage and low scores. Each maker processes cacao beans to create distinctive nuances. Scharffen Berger's characteristic fruity, acidic notes may suit dark chocolate, but apparently not milk chocolate. Finally, even in milk chocolate, too much sugar was a turn-off. The brand with the highest total sugar, Nestlé, fell to the bottom of our rankings.

Once again, Dove topped our taste tests for its full chocolate flavor, creamy texture, and moderate sweetness. But Endangered Species and Green & Black were close behind, introducing dark chocolate characteristics and scoring points with chocolate lovers.

RECOMMENDED | TASTERS' NOTES

DOVE SILKY SMOOTH MILK CHOCOLATE
$2.79 for 3.53-ounce bar
36% cacao
Sugars: 56.7%
Milk Fat: 7%
Cocoa Butter: 24%

Our old favorite won again. Tasters found Dove "very satisfying" and "super creamy" with a "surprisingly rich chocolate flavor" yet "not overwhelmingly sweet." This chocolate "tastes like more than just sugar and milk," one taster wrote. Said another: "Definitely would eat this, and I only buy dark chocolate."

ENDANGERED SPECIES ALL-NATURAL SMOOTH MILK CHOCOLATE
$2.99 for 3-ounce bar
56% cacao
Sugars: 36.6%
Milk Fat: 6%
Cocoa Butter: 33%

A relative newcomer, this brand was "not terribly creamy." But it had "great chocolate taste" that was "intense" with "hints of coffee"—perhaps not surprising given its 56 percent cacao, more than enough to qualify as dark chocolate (with which some tasters compared it). Tasters also praised its "bitter and sweet" but "not too sweet" taste.

GREEN & BLACK'S ORGANIC MILK CHOCOLATE
$3.69 for 3.5-ounce bar
37% cacao
Sugars: 55.5%
Milk Fat: 7%
Cocoa Butter: 27%

Tasters found this organic brand "very creamy and not too sweet" with "mild bittersweet notes," in which the "sweetness is balanced with chocolate flavor." It "does not try to hide the fact that it's milk chocolate," wrote one taster approvingly.

LINDT CLASSIC RECIPE MILK CHOCOLATE
$2.79 for 4.4-ounce bar
43% cacao
Sugars: 51.5%
Milk Fat: 5%
Cocoa Butter: 27%

Tasters liked Lindt (whose namesake invented conching) for its creaminess with a "caramel, nutty" flavor and "balanced sweetness." But a few criticized it as "lacking in chocolate oomph."

RECOMMENDED WITH RESERVATIONS | TASTERS' NOTES

GHIRARDELLI LUXE MILK CHOCOLATE
$3.19 for 3-ounce bar
36% cacao
Sugars: 56.3%
Milk Fat: 7%
Cocoa Butter: 26%

Tasters split: Some liked the creamy texture and milk flavor, calling it "the epitome of creamy, milky milk chocolate." Others said the "sweetness overpowered everything" and the bar tasted "more like caramel or toffee." Concluded one: "Not bad, but not worth the calories, either."

SCHARFFEN BERGER EXTRA RICH MILK CHOCOLATE
$3.99 for 3-ounce bar
47% cacao
Sugars: 46.8%
Milk Fat: 5%
Cocoa Butter: 26%

Despite its "deep chocolate flavor," tasters found Scharffen Berger to be "very bitter and acidic," with "burnt sugar," "kind of chemical-y" off-flavors, and a texture that "could be a little more creamy." Some disliked the "slightly fruity" taste. "Is this really milk chocolate?" one asked.

HERSHEY'S MILK CHOCOLATE
$1.99 for 4.4-ounce bar
36% cacao
Sugars: 56.5%
Milk Fat: 7%
Cocoa Butter: 23%

Tasters identified the iconic American brand as "a familiar friend," "like the milk chocolate I ate as a kid." They found it "chocolaty," "rich and pure," but also "a touch grainy" and "waxy." Several criticized it as too sweet. One speculated that it was "more appealing because of memories than quality."

NOT RECOMMENDED | TASTERS' NOTES

NESTLÉ MILK CHOCOLATE
$1.99 for 5-ounce bar
31% cacao
Sugars: 64.2%
Milk Fat: 4%
Cocoa Butter: 25%

Nestlé—the first milk chocolate, invented in 1875—was "very sugary" and "tastes thin," with "no real chocolate flavor," tasters said. It lost more points for its "sandy and gritty," even "waxy" texture. "Tastes like that cheap chocolate you get on sale the day after Easter."

Cooking Class How to Bake a Yellow Layer Cake

A layer cake is the crowning glory of American baking. Fortunately, making one needn't be intimidating. With our core techniques and recipe, you'll produce a moist, tender, fine-crumbed (and fabulous) cake time and again.

Prep School

Have Ingredients at the Right Temperature

SOFTENED BUTTER

Softened butter blends easily into the dry ingredients and coats the flour particles with fat. If the butter is too cold or too warm, the cake may turn out heavy or greasy. A properly softened stick of butter will bend without breaking.

ROOM-TEMPERATURE EGGS AND MILK

Likewise, room-temperature eggs and milk blend into cake batter more easily and produce a taller cake. To quickly warm the eggs and milk, place the measuring cup containing them in a bowl of warm water for 10 minutes.

Use the Right Measuring Cup

DRY MEASURING CUPS

LIQUID MEASURING CUP

We asked several test cooks to measure flour in liquid measuring cups. Because the shape of these cups does not allow leveling, the amounts of flour varied by as much as 26 percent. The takeaway? When measuring dry ingredients, use dry measuring cups. Also, remember to "dip and sweep"—scoop up the flour with the cup and then level it off with a flat utensil. Similarly, you can best gauge the volumes of liquid with a liquid measuring cup, which is transparent and, handily, has a spout.

Use the Right Mixing Method: REVERSE CREAMING

In "standard creaming," butter and sugar are beaten together (or "creamed"), eggs are beaten in one at a time, and then dry and liquid ingredients are added alternately. For our yellow and white layer cakes, we use a less well-known mixing method called "reverse creaming": First the dry ingredients are combined, next the softened butter is added bit by bit, and then the combined milk and eggs are incorporated in two additions. To finish, the batter is beaten until it's thick and fluffy. Since the fat is blended with the flour before any liquid is added, the flour proteins are well greased, so gluten formation is minimal. (Too much gluten development makes cakes tough.) Consequently, reverse creaming creates a tender, tight crumb with none of the air pockets that can occur in standard creaming, yet the cake is still sturdy enough to frost.

Portion the Batter Evenly

USE A SCALE...

...OR A RULER

An equal amount of batter in each pan yields even cake layers. Weighing the filled pan on a kitchen scale is the most accurate way to gauge even portions, but you can also use a ruler to measure the space between the top of the batter and the top of the pan

YELLOW LAYER CAKE

Makes two 9-inch cake rounds

Adding the butter 1 tablespoon at a time while the electric mixer is on low speed prevents the dry ingredients from flying out of the bowl. You can also use low-fat milk in this cake.

- ½ cup whole milk, room temperature
- 4 large eggs, room temperature
- 2 teaspoons vanilla extract
- 1¾ cups cake flour
- 1½ cups sugar
- 2 teaspoons baking powder
- ¾ teaspoon salt
- 16 tablespoons (2 sticks) unsalted butter, cut into 16 pieces and softened

1. Adjust oven rack to middle position and heat oven to 350 degrees. Grease, line with parchment paper, grease parchment, and flour two 9-inch cake pans. Whisk milk, eggs, and vanilla in large liquid measuring cup. Whisk flour, sugar, baking powder, and salt in bowl of electric mixer until combined. With mixer on low speed, add butter, 1 piece at a time, and beat until only pea-size pieces remain.

2. Pour in half of milk mixture and increase mixer speed to medium-high. Beat until light and fluffy, about 1 minute. Slowly add remaining milk mixture and beat until incorporated, about 30 seconds.

3. Using rubber spatula, give batter final stir. Scrape equal amounts of batter into prepared pans and smooth tops. Gently tap pans on counter to release any trapped air bubbles. Bake until toothpick inserted in center comes out clean, 20 to 25 minutes, rotating pans halfway through baking.

4. Cool cakes in pans 10 minutes, then turn out onto wire rack (see step 12). Cool completely, at least 1 hour. (Cooled cakes can be wrapped in plastic wrap and stored at room temperature for 2 days.)

TO TOP IT OFF...

Add the finishing touch to your cake with our easy chocolate (or vanilla) buttercream frosting. Find the recipe at **CooksCountry.com/extra**. Let the cake cool completely before you frost it or you'll regret it: The hot cake will melt the frosting.

Twelve Steps to Perfect Layer Cake

1. ADJUST OVEN RACK
Place the oven rack in the middle of the oven and heat the oven to 350 degrees. **WHY?** If baked on a rack that's too high, the cake will overbrown. Too low? No browning at all.

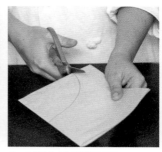

2. CUT PARCHMENT
Trace the outline of the cake pan on parchment paper. Then cut out parchment circles to line the pans. **WHY?** To ensure the baked cakes release easily from the pans.

3. GREASE AND FLOUR
Grease the pans. Line with parchment circles. Grease the parchment and flour the pans, shaking out extra flour. **WHY?** To doubly ensure that the cakes will not stick.

4. COMBINE LIQUIDS
Combine the eggs, milk, and vanilla in a measuring cup. **WHY?** Combined, the wet ingredients are easier to incorporate. Plus, it's easy to see how much liquid you've added in step 7.

5. WHISK DRY INGREDIENTS
Whisk the flour, sugar, baking powder, and salt together. **WHY?** For layer cakes, whisking aerates as effectively as sifting.

6. BEAT IN BUTTER
With the mixer on low speed, add the softened butter, one piece at a time, until only pea-size pieces remain. **WHY?** This "reverse creaming" ensures a cake with a tender but tight crumb.

7. ADD LIQUID IN 2 PARTS
Pour in half of the milk-egg mixture and beat until fluffy. Then add the remaining milk mixture. **WHY?** The liquid will be absorbed more efficiently, for a lighter cake with no streaks of flour.

8. SCRAPE INTO PANS
Divide the batter evenly between the greased, lined, and floured pans. **WHY?** The layers will bake evenly and be of equal height.

9. TAP ON COUNTER
Gently tap the pans on the counter to settle the batter. **WHY?** Tapping releases air bubbles that may have formed during mixing; they could cause tunnels in the cake.

10. BAKE AND ROTATE
Bake until a toothpick inserted in the center comes out clean, 20 to 25 minutes. Rotate the pans halfway through baking. **WHY?** Switching the pans ensures that the layers bake evenly despite any hot spots in the oven.

11. COOL IN PANS
Leave the hot cakes in the pans for 10 minutes. **WHY?** The cakes need a few minutes to cool and firm slightly, so they won't break apart when you remove them from the pans.

12. TURN OUT
Flip the cakes out of their pans onto a wire rack. Flip onto a second wire rack so that the cake layers are right side up. **WHY?** The rack lets air circulate underneath, so the cakes won't steam and get soggy as they cool.

Avoid These Mistakes

DOMED CAKE

Cake layers that are domed won't stack securely. Doming is caused by cake pans that are too small or an oven that's too hot; use an oven thermometer to check. If your cakes do dome, slice off the dome with a serrated knife.

UNEVEN BAKING

We tested our yellow layer cake baked side by side on one oven rack, on two racks with one pan directly above the other, and on two racks with one pan on the top left and the other on the lower right. Only the cakes on the same rack baked evenly. The reason? Although ovens heat differently, hot air can always circulate around cakes baked side by side. Switch the cakes once during baking so that each layer spends an equal amount of time in each position.

Extra Credit

What If I Don't Have Cake Flour?
Cake flour delivers a light, fine-crumbed cake. To approximate it, combine ⅞ cup of all-purpose flour with 2 tablespoons of cornstarch for each cup of flour. In this recipe, you'd use 1½ cups all-purpose flour and 3½ tablespoons cornstarch.

⅞ cup all-purpose flour   +   2 tablespoons cornstarch   =   1 cup cake flour

Is My Cake Done?
Keep your eye on the clock and do the toothpick test (see step 10). To be sure, also gently touch the cakes in the center with your finger; they should spring back, not dent. And use your nose. Does the kitchen smell delicious? Time to check your cake.

Note to Bakers: These techniques also apply to white cake, which is yellow cake with no egg yolks.

Looking for a Recipe

READER TO READER

Did you misplace a favorite recipe? Can you almost taste a chocolate cake from childhood, but the bakery—and the recipe—are long gone? Ask a *Cook's Country* reader. While you're at it, answer a reader. Visit the *Cook's Country* website both to post your requests and to answer those of fellow readers. Go to **CooksCountry.com** and click on **Looking for a Recipe**. We'll share all your submissions on the website (hundreds are already posted!) and print as many as we can fit in the magazine (see recipes at right). You may also write to us at Looking for a Recipe, Cook's Country, P.O. Box 470739, Brookline, MA 02447. Please include your name and mailing address with each request.

Raspberry Dumplings
Michelle Wagner, Collins, Wis.

My father's mother used to make a recipe for dumplings with raspberries that were mixed right into the dough. The dumplings were cut using a thread and served with butter on top. I would love to be able to make these for my dad. If anyone knows the recipe, I would be very grateful.

White Fruitcake
Delores Mischel, Minneapolis, Minn.

I am looking for a recipe my mom used to make called white fruitcake. It had yummy things in it: maraschino cherries and other colorful, tasty candied fruits, like orange slices and pineapple bits. It was not an ordinary cake; it had the heavier texture of a fruitcake without the dark molasses taste. Has anyone ever heard of such a recipe? Your help will be greatly appreciated.

Orange Bread
Kathy Hamilton, Metuchen, N.J.

I am trying to find a recipe for orange bread that my mother used to make in the late 1950s or early '60s. The very thick batter was baked in different size tin cans. The bread had intense orange flavor, maybe from the sugar syrup with orange rind. Can you help me celebrate my mother by finding this recipe?

Cheese Straws
Anne Beauchamp, Mansfield, Mass.

My grandmother grew up in West Virginia and later lived in Virginia. When I was growing up, we celebrated every visit to her house with a fresh batch of her cheese straws—buttery, flaky, a little spicy, and full of cheddar. My mother is sure that the recipe we have is missing some details. We would love to re-create them!

Chocolate Soufflé Pie
Mary Boyd, Portland, Ore.

I'm looking for a chocolate soufflé pie recipe that I had at a friend's house many years ago. You put half the batter in a pie pan and bake it. That falls and becomes the crust. Then you fill the "crust" with the rest of the batter and bake the pie again. It's foolproof (if I could just find the recipe).

Chicken and Cornmeal Dumplings
Mike Currie, DeFuniak Springs, Fla.

I am looking for a recipe for chicken and cornmeal dumplings that my great aunt used to cook back in the 1950s. I don't know of anyone else who makes this. It was an old recipe from the southern Alabama logging camps. With the added bulk of the dumplings, one chicken could serve a whole family, and it was quite tasty.

Graham Cracker Cream Pie
Pamela Williams, Denver, Colo.

I was volunteering at the Great American Pie Festival in Florida when a gentleman approached me and asked about graham cracker cream pie. He said the recipe used to be on the back of the graham cracker box. Has anyone heard of this recipe and can you help him find it?

Instant Chocolate Fudge
Karen Hamerski, West Mifflin, Pa.

I used to make a very fast recipe for chocolate fudge that called for Jell-O chocolate pudding and powdered sugar. I lost the recipe and was wondering if anyone else might have it? Please help.

Imperial Crab Cakes
William Thomas, Frackville, Pa.

Do you know imperial crab cakes? They're heavily breaded and then deep fried, which gives them a hard, crunchy crust that contrasts with the tender, creamy inside. They were popular in Lancaster, Pennsylvania, in the 1950s. I'd love to eat them again if anyone out there has got a recipe.

FIND THE ROOSTER!

DATE-NUT BREAD Makes two 8.5-inch loaves
Carolyn McCowan, Waltham, Mass.

"This recipe reminds my family of the Thomas' Date-Nut Bread that [reader] Michael Foster was looking for, only better! We like to serve slices with butter, cream cheese, or sometimes a smear of olive spread." You'll need 3 cups of pitted, chopped dates and 2 loaf pans.

2	(8-ounce) packages chopped dates
2	cups boiling water
2	cups sugar
3	tablespoons unsalted butter
1	teaspoon baking soda
3½	cups all-purpose flour
1	teaspoon baking powder
½	teaspoon salt
1	large egg
1	tablespoon vanilla extract
1	cup pecans, toasted and chopped

1. Adjust oven rack to middle position and heat oven to 350 degrees. Grease two 8½-inch loaf pans. Combine dates, water, sugar, butter, and baking soda in medium bowl. Let mixture cool until just warm to touch, about 20 minutes.

2. Combine flour, baking powder, and salt in large bowl. Whisk cooled date mixture, egg, and vanilla into flour mixture until combined. Stir in pecans.

3. Scrape equal amounts of batter into prepared pans and bake until toothpick inserted into center comes out with few dry crumbs attached, 45 to 50 minutes. Cool bread in pans for 15 minutes, then turn out onto wire rack. Serve warm or at room temperature. (Bread can be stored in airtight container at room temperature for up to 3 days.)

CORNFLAKE STUFFING Serves 10 to 12
Diana Simon, Wayland, Mass.

"My mom always served this stuffing with chicken, but it's good with turkey too. She sautéed the onions in chicken fat, but nothing's wrong with butter!" You can find rendered chicken fat with the kosher foods in the freezer section of most supermarkets. You will need 14 cups of cornflakes.

6	tablespoons unsalted butter or rendered chicken fat
4	onions, chopped fine
2	celery ribs, chopped fine
1	(18-ounce) box cornflakes
4	cups low-sodium chicken broth
½	cup chopped fresh parsley
3	large eggs, lightly beaten
1	teaspoon salt
1	teaspoon pepper

1. Adjust oven rack to middle position and heat oven to 400 degrees. Grease 3-quart baking dish. Melt butter (or chicken fat) in large skillet over medium heat. Cook onions and celery until softened and beginning to brown, 10 to 15 minutes. Remove from heat and let cool 5 minutes.

2. Combine cornflakes and warm onion mixture in large bowl. Stir in broth, parsley, eggs, salt, and pepper until combined. Transfer mixture to prepared baking dish and cover tightly with aluminum foil. Bake until set, about 30 minutes. Remove foil and continue to bake until surface is golden and crisp, about 10 minutes. Let cool 15 minutes. Serve.

Mint Chocolate Chip Cake

Transform a favorite ice cream into a cake that's perfect for St. Patrick's Day: Flavor the layers with mint, stud the cake with chocolate chips, and slather it with luscious chocolate buttercream.

To make this cake you will need:

- 1 recipe white layer cake*
- 2½ cups mini chocolate chips
- 1½ teaspoons mint extract
- 5 drops green food coloring
- 20 tablespoons (2½ sticks) unsalted butter, cut into 20 pieces and softened
- 8 ounces bittersweet chocolate, melted and cooled
- 1 teaspoon vanilla extract
- ⅛ teaspoon salt
- 2 cups confectioners' sugar

For the cake: Adjust oven rack to middle position and heat oven to 350 degrees. Grease and flour three 8-inch cake pans. Prepare white layer cake batter according to directions, stirring 1 cup chocolate chips, mint extract, and food coloring into batter until combined. Scrape equal amounts of batter into prepared pans and bake until toothpick inserted in center comes out clean, 20 to 25 minutes. Cool cakes in pans 10 minutes, then turn out onto wire rack. Cool completely, at least 1 hour.

For the frosting: With electric mixer fitted with whisk attachment, beat butter, melted chocolate, vanilla, and salt on medium-high speed until combined. Reduce speed to medium-low. With machine running, slowly add confectioners' sugar and mix until smooth, about 1 minute. Increase speed to medium-high and beat until light and fluffy, 3 to 5 minutes.

To assemble: Place 1 cake round on serving platter. Spread ¾ cup frosting over cake, then top with second cake round. Spread another ¾ cup frosting over cake, then top with third cake round. Spread remaining frosting evenly over top and sides of cake. Press remaining chocolate chips onto sides of cake. Serve.

* Go to **CooksCountry.com/extra** for our **White Layer Cake** recipe or use your own.

Recipe Index

RC = Recipe Card

Cook's Country

APRIL/MAY 2011

Fluffy Cream Cheese Biscuits

Slow-Cooker BBQ Steak Tips

Easy Glazed Picnic Ham

Jo Jo Potato Wedges
Light Inside, Crunchy Outside

Breakfast Casserole for 2
Easy Cheesy

Orange-Glazed Chicken
Simple Stovetop Method

Pineapple Upside-Down Cake
Low Fat, Full Flavor

Perfect Egg Salad
2 Secrets to Creaminess

Smothered Pork Chops
Which Chop Works Best?

Rating Kitchen Shears
Tiny Teeth Make the Cut

Funeral Potatoes
Comfort Food Updated

Tasting Boxed Mac & Cheese
We Actually Like Two

Chocolate-Walnut Pie
Not Just Sweet

www.CooksCountry.com
$4.95 U.S./$6.95 CANADA

*Biscuits are an American original, with regional favorites all over the country. In Charleston, South Carolina, folks favor **Cream Cheese Biscuits**, said to be particularly soft and fluffy. And they are—now that we've made dozens of batches in our test kitchen to figure out their secrets.* PAGE 10

Cook's Country

Dear Country Cook,

A bunch of locals were down at the country store and pretty much agreed that fear of a good licking, often with a switch, helps a youngster to learn. One man disagreed.

"I ain't sure of the value of a licking," he said. "Thinking back on it, I remember that the hardest licking I ever got was for telling the truth."

There was silence while his neighbors considered this statement. Then, quietly, one of them said, "Well, Sam, it cured you."

When it comes to the kitchen, I am all for lickings, from frostings to fillings, even soups and stews. When I do this on our public television show, Cook's Country, I often get angry letters saying, in effect, "Stop sticking your hand in the food, it's not sanitary!" Well, here are a few words to the contrary.

The ideal kitchen tool is the hand (preferably a clean one). It is perfectly designed for tossing salads, working dough, shelling peas, and countless other cooking tasks. And a lick or two in the kitchen is just fine by me.

Our obsession with sterilized foods began around 1900 when adulterated foods were a real menace to public health, from the poisons used for colorings (notably arsenic and lead) to the pollution in shellfish beds. But we have gone too far, prohibiting, for example, the sale of raw milk. (I grew up drinking it; some experts claim that it prevents or even cures childhood food allergies.) And then there are the ridiculous rules about importing fresh French cheeses.

Perhaps our digestive systems would be better off with a bit more bacteria. So go ahead, stick your finger in and have a lick.

Christopher Kimball
Founder and Editor, Cook's Country

Cook'sCountry

Founder and Editor Christopher Kimball
Editorial Director Jack Bishop
Executive Editor, Magazines John Willoughby
Executive Editor Peggy Grodinsky
Managing Editor Scott Kathan
Senior Editors Lisa McManus, Cali Rich, Diane Unger
Test Kitchen Director Erin McMurrer
Associate Editors Lynn Clark, Amy Graves
Test Cooks Sarah Gabriel, Kelly Price
Assistant Editor Taizeth Sierra
Assistant Test Cooks Rebeccah Marsters, Carolynn Purpura
Senior Copy Editor Catherine Tumber
Copy Editor Nell Beram
Editorial Assistant Shannon Hatch
Executive Assistant Christine Gordon
Assistant Test Kitchen Director Gina Nistico
Senior Kitchen Assistant Leah Rovner
Kitchen Assistants Maria Elena Delgado, Ena Gudiel, Ed Tundidor
TV Producer Melissa Baldino
Contributing Editors Erika Bruce, Eva Katz, Jeremy Sauer
Consulting Editor Meg Ragland
Science Editor Guy Crosby, Ph.D.
Executive Food Editor, TV, Radio & Media Bridget Lancaster

Online Managing Editor David Tytell
Online Editor Kate Mason
Online Assistant Editors Eric Grzymkowski, Mari Levine

Design Director Amy Klee
Art Director Julie Bozzo
Deputy Art Director Susan Levin
Art Director, Marketing & Web Christine Vo
Associate Art Directors, Marketing & Web Erica Lee, Jody Lee
Designers Elaina Natario, Mariah Tarvainen
Staff Photographer Daniel J. van Ackere

Director, Information Technology Rocco Lombardo
Systems Administrator Marcus Walser
Lead Developer Scott Thompson
Software Architect Robert Martinez
Senior Web Developer Christopher Candelora
Web Developers Bach Bui, James Madden, Alphonse Shiwala
Business Analyst Wendy Tseng
Quality Assurance Micquella Bradford
Web Production Coordinator Evan Davis
Web Production Assistant Debbie Chiang
IT Support Specialist Geoffrey Clark

VP, New Media Product Development Barry Kelly
Lead Developer, New Media Bharat Ruparel
Senior Information Architect Melissa MacQuarrie
Social Media Manager Steph Yiu
Web Programmer, New Media Anand Kumar
Graphic Designer Eggert Ragnarsson

Production Director Guy Rochford
Senior Projects Manager Alice Carpenter
Traffic & Production Coordinator Kate Hux
Asset & Workflow Manager Andrew Mannone
Production & Imaging Specialists Judy Blomquist, Heather Dube, Lauren Pettapiece

Vice President, Marketing David Mack
Circulation Director Doug Wicinski
Fulfillment & Circulation Manager Carrie Horan
Partnership Marketing Manager Pamela Putprush
Marketing Assistant Lauren Perkins
Database & Direct Mail Director Adam Perry
Senior Database Analyst Marina Sakharova
Products Director Steven Browall
Product Promotions Director Tom Conway
E-Commerce Marketing Director Hugh Buchan
E-Commerce Marketing Manager Laurel Zeidman
Marketing Copywriter David Goldberg
Customer Service Manager Jacqueline Valerio
Customer Service Representatives Jillian Nannicelli, Kate Sokol

Chief Financial Officer Sharyn Chabot
Human Resources Director Adele Shapiro
Controller Mandy Shito
Finance Director Wayne Saville
Senior Accountant Aaron Goranson
Staff Accountant Connie Forbes
Accounts Payable Specialist Steven Kasha
Office Manager Michael Pickett
Receptionist Henrietta Murray

Sponsorship Sales Director Marcy McCreary
Retail Sales & Marketing Manager Emily Logan
Sponsorship & Marketing Coordinator Bailey Vatalaro
Publicity Deborah Broide

COLOR FOOD PHOTOGRAPHY: Keller + Keller
STYLING: Mary Jane Sawyer
ILLUSTRATION: Greg Stevenson
ON THE COVER: Biscuits, Keller + Keller

Cook's Country magazine (ISSN 1552-1990), number 38, is published bimonthly by Boston Common Press Limited Partnership, 17 Station Street, Brookline, MA 02445. Copyright 2011 Boston Common Press Limited Partnership. Periodicals postage paid at Boston, Mass., and additional mailing offices. Publications Mail Agreement No. 40020778. Return undeliverable Canadian addresses to P.O. Box 875, Station A, Windsor, Ontario N9A 6P2. POSTMASTER: Send address changes to Cook's Country, P.O. Box 8382, Red Oak, IA 51591-1382. Customer Service: It's easy to subscribe, give a gift subscription, change your address, and manage your subscription online. Visit www.americastestkitchen.com/customerservice for all of your customer service needs or write to us at Cook's Country, P.O. Box 8382, Red Oak, IA 51591-1382. PRINTED IN THE USA

Contents

APRIL/MAY 2011

ASPARAGUS GRATIN, 11   GLAZED PICNIC HAM, 8   THOROUGHBRED PIE, 14

Features

In Every Issue

Watch Us on Television

Watch the folks behind our recipes test equipment, taste ingredients, perfect classic American recipes, and stroll through food history. Find out when *Cook's Country from America's Test Kitchen* airs on public television in your area at **CooksCountryTV.com**.

Holiday Cookie Contest

You can't have too many holiday cookie recipes. Submit your best to **CooksCountry.com/cookiecontest**. The deadline for entries is April 30, 2011. For details, see page 32.

GRAND PRIZE $1,000

 America's TEST KITCHEN America's Test Kitchen is a 2,500-square-foot kitchen located just outside of Boston. It is the home of *Cook's Country* and *Cook's Illustrated* magazines and is the workday destination for more than three dozen test cooks, editors, and cookware specialists. Our mission is to test recipes until we understand how and why they work and arrive at the best version. We also test kitchen equipment and supermarket ingredients in search of brands that offer the best value and performance. You can watch us work by tuning in to *Cook's Country from America's Test Kitchen* (CooksCountryTV.com).

Kitchen Shortcuts

Unsticking Pizza Dough
Scott Dudley, Norman, Okla.

I used to have problems with pizza dough sticking when I stretched it out to form a crust. A friend suggested that I lightly coat my hands and counter with nonstick cooking spray before I start shaping the dough. This works really well, and my pizza crusts have never looked better.

DOUBLE DUTY
Cake Layer Transport
Lauren Vincent, Simsbury, Conn.

I like to bake cakes with lots of layers, which means I often find myself slicing single layers in half horizontally to make two thin layers. As you might guess, these thin layers are delicate and prone to falling apart. I've found that sliding the layers onto the metal disk from the bottom of a tart pan (the kind with a removable bottom) supports those layers and keeps them from breaking when it's time to place them back together and frost the cake.

SPEEDY PREP
A Few Crumbs
John Fields, Charlestown, Mass.

When I need fresh bread crumbs but not a lot of them, I find that I can freeze a few slices of bread and then grate them on a box grater to get crumbs. It's easy and it saves me the trouble of having to pull out, and then clean, my food processor.

COOL TIP
Perfect Pie Crust in the Summer
Leslie Wilson, Albany, N.Y.

Summer is a mixed blessing for pie bakers. The best fruits—peaches! blueberries! plums!—are everywhere, but just try to roll out a nice pie crust on a hot, sticky day. The butter in the pastry melts, the dough becomes too soft to roll out, and there's a good chance that it'll stick to the counter and tear. A friend taught me a cool (pun intended) trick: Fifteen minutes before I plan to roll out the dough, I place a casserole dish filled with ice on the counter. The ice chills the counter briefly—just enough time for me to roll a pie crust.

TIDY TIP
Child-Friendly Spaghetti
Joanna McNamara, Chicago, Ill.

My kids love spaghetti, but they need it cut up into manageable bites. Instead of smearing my cutting board with saucy pasta (or breaking the strands before they go into the pot, which forces my husband and me to eat itty-bitty pieces), I've found a faster, neater way to cut the kids' portion: I use clean kitchen scissors to snip the cooked pasta into small bites right in their plastic bowls. This works for bite-sizing plenty of other foods as well.

CLEVER CLEANING
Natural Lemon Polish
Kristine Hunter, Baltimore, Md.

Instead of buying expensive polish for my copper pots, I simply sprinkle a cut lemon half with salt and polish away. It does a great job and smells nice, too.

DOUBLE DUTY
Tidy Blind Baking
Julia DeSimone, Natick, Mass.

I like using the disposable liners for my slow cooker: They make cleanup much faster. Recently, I found a new use for the liners: I use them instead of foil when I'm blind baking pie crusts. I place a liner on the raw pie shell, fill it with dried beans, and bake. When I'm done, I store the beans right in the liner to use the next time I need a blind-baked crust.

If you'd like to submit a tip, please e-mail us by visiting **CooksCountry.com/kitchenshortcuts** or send a letter to Kitchen Shortcuts, Cook's Country, P.O. Box 470739, Brookline, MA 02447. Include your name, address, and phone number. If we publish your tip, you will receive a free one-year subscription to *Cook's Country*. Letters may be edited for clarity or length.

Ask Cook's Country

I love the crunch that panko gives fried foods. Can I make it at home?
Alex Murphy, Milwaukee, Wis.

Yes. We've developed a method for approximating panko, the Japanese-style bread crumbs that have caught on in the United States in recent years. Feed crustless white sandwich bread through the largest grating disk of a food processor, then bake the crumbs on a rimmed baking sheet at 300 degrees until dry but not toasted (about six minutes). We tasted our homemade panko against commercial panko on fried pork cutlets. Tasters preferred store-bought panko by a hair, but they found the homemade panko perfectly acceptable.

THE BOTTOM LINE Make panko by grating white sandwich bread in a food processor and then drying it in the oven.

Why do my cakes sometimes turn out lopsided?
Robyn Empey, Carlsbad, Calif.

Cakes can come out lopsided for a few reasons. Naturally, if the oven or oven rack is not level, the batter will flow toward the lower side. So first check to make sure that the rack is seated properly in its grooves. If it is, use a carpenter's level to see if your oven itself is crooked (check for levelness both on a rack and on the floor of the oven). Most ovens have adjustable feet that allow you to correct for floor slant.

Cakes can also come out asymmetrical if your oven is hotter on one side, so lopsided cakes may indicate that it's time to have your oven serviced. You can mitigate the effects of sloping and uneven heat by rotating your cake pans midway through baking. And if your oven is drastically hotter on one side? If all else fails, bake only one layer at a time so you can put the pan in the center of the rack and rotate it midway through baking.

THE BOTTOM LINE Make sure that your oven and racks are level. Also, rotate the pans midway through baking to counteract uneven heating.

THE PROBLEM
A lopsided cake.

ONE SOLUTION
A bubble level.

Do I really need a food processor to make pie dough? Your recipes call for one.
Alexis Garland Waller, New York, N.Y.

Bakers were making pie dough long before the invention of the food processor, so we tested two low-tech tools: a pastry cutter and our bare hands. Cutting in the butter and shortening with a pastry cutter or rubbing it in with our fingers worked fine. Both methods did, however, take about five times longer than the processor method. Because of the added minutes and/or the warmth of our hands, the butter and shortening got a little greasy and warm before we were finished mixing. Freezing the fats for 30 minutes cooled them down sufficiently and bought us the time we needed to mix the dough without a machine before the butter melted.

THE BOTTOM LINE Of course you don't need a food processor to make pie dough. But you do need to chill the butter and shortening in the freezer for 30 minutes before you begin if you are mixing by hand or with a pastry cutter.

The big bags of onions I buy at Costco sometimes go bad before I can use them all. Can I freeze them?
Lou Lynch, Reedley, Calif.

Frozen diced onions are available in the freezer section of many grocery stores, so it stands to reason that you should be able to preserve your extra onions in the freezer. To find out how the texture and flavor of frozen onions stack up against fresh, we froze both whole peeled onions and diced onions in zipper-lock bags. But then we took it a step further. Commercial frozen goods are often individually quick frozen ("individually" to prevent the product from freezing into a solid mass, and "quick" to prevent textural damage by the formation of ice crystals). For our third batch of onions, we set out to simulate individual quick freezing by spreading diced onions in one layer on a rimmed baking sheet, freezing them, and only then loading them into zipper-lock bags for storage. We tested all three batches of onions against fresh in recipes that used them raw and cooked.

Whole onions came out of the freezer mushy and flavorless: They were unacceptable used either raw or cooked. Tasters found both sets of frozen diced onions acceptable in our cooked preparation of baked rice. (You don't need to thaw them.) The simply diced and bagged batch finished slightly ahead, so there's no need to freeze the diced

onions before bagging. The frozen diced onions didn't fare well, however, when we made salsa with them. Tasters panned all three salsas made with frozen onions for being "dull," "sulfuric," and "squishy."

THE BOTTOM LINE You can dice and store extra onions in zipper-lock bags in the freezer, but use them only for cooked preparations. Frozen onions simply aren't as good as fresh in raw dishes like salsas and salads.

What's the difference between bittersweet and semisweet chocolate?
Betsy Wickens, East Setauket, N.Y.

Legally speaking, there is no difference. In order for a chocolate to be called "bittersweet" or "semisweet," the FDA mandates that it contain at least 35 percent cacao, and manufacturers may use either term for chocolate that meets

that minimum. That said, most manufacturers use "bittersweet" for chocolates that are higher in cacao (and hence less sweet) than their "semisweet" offering. Thus, "bittersweet" and "semisweet" can be useful terms for comparing products within one brand but are imprecise across different brands. For example, Ghirardelli's bittersweet baking bar contains more cacao than its semisweet bar, but it has less cacao than semisweet bars by Guittard and Scharffen Berger.

THE BOTTOM LINE Legally speaking, manufacturers can call any chocolate with at least 35 percent cacao either bittersweet or semisweet, but bittersweet is usually darker, richer, and less sweet.

To ask us a cooking question:
Visit **CooksCountry.com/emailus**. You can also write to Ask Cook's Country, P.O. Box 470739, Brookline, MA 02447. Just try to stump us!

Can I substitute gluten-free flour for regular flour?
Mary Kate Smith-Despres, Salem, Mass.

To find out how gluten-free flour blends stack up against all-purpose flour, we tested the two most popular brands, King Arthur and Bob's Red Mill, against regular all-purpose flour in batter-fried onion rings, yellow cake, a cheese sauce thickened with flour, sugar cookies, and pie crust.

King Arthur's gluten-free blend is made from rice flour, tapioca starch, potato starch, and whole-grain brown rice flour. Bob's Red Mill makes its blend with garbanzo bean flour, potato starch, tapioca, whole-grain sweet white sorghum flour, and fava bean flour. The Bob's Red Mill substitute nearly passed for regular flour in the batter for onion rings; some tasters faulted onion rings made with King Arthur's gluten-free flour for being "too crunchy." Cakes made with these flours were a bit more crumbly and dry than those made with all-purpose flour, but tasters found them acceptable. Both blends worked well for thickening sauces.

The cookies, however, were a different story. With regular flour, sugar cookies were chewy and slightly domed. With gluten-free substitutes, they spread wide and thin and were sandy and brittle once cooled. Pie crusts were equally disastrous: They didn't hold their shape and came out dry and badly cracked.

Our science editor explained that gluten is an elastic protein, whereas the proteins in other cereal grains (like the rice, potato, and bean flours used in gluten-free blends) are brittle. In recipes for which the formation of gluten is essential for chewy texture or structure, the gluten-free blends just don't measure up.

THE BOTTOM LINE Gluten-free flours are acceptable in place of all-purpose flour when baking cakes and thickening sauces, but not in cookies and pie crusts, which need the elasticity of gluten. Bean-based flour blends can be used in batter for frying, while rice-based blends are too hard and brittle.

CAKES AND SAUCES
YES!
Gluten-free flours can be successfully substituted for all-purpose flour.

PIES AND COOKIES
NO!
Gluten-free flours can not achieve the elasticity needed for flaky crusts and chewy cookies.

ONION RINGS
MAYBE...
Bean-based gluten-free flours work well in batters for frying, while rice-based gluten-free flours do not.

Recipe Makeover Pineapple Upside-Down Cake

How do you cut calories in a cake known for its buttery base and sugary glazed pineapple? BY KRIS WIDICAN

PINEAPPLE UPSIDE-DOWN CAKE has been popular for about a century, since not long after a certain Mr. Dole figured out how to peel, core, and can pineapples really quickly. But one slice can pack more than 400 calories and almost 20 grams of fat. It was time for a makeover.

The handful of diet recipes I found scaled back drastically on the fat. As you'd expect, they baked up colorless and flavorless, so I opted to use a full-fat version as my jumping-off point. Most of the fat and calories came from the butter (full-fat recipes used anywhere from 8 to 12 tablespoons), the sugar (usually about 1½ cups), the canned pineapple (in a sugary, caloric syrup), and the milk or sour cream that recipes variously call for. Informed, I embarked on my calorie countdown.

Truth be told, we didn't love everything about that full-fat version. The canned pineapple rings, for instance, tasted metallic, not fruity; I switched to fresh fruit. Also, the maraschino cherries added calories but not flavor, so I left them out of future tests. With those decisions out of the way, I assessed the fat. In a series of tests, I was able to take the butter down to just 4 tablespoons without sacrificing much. To cut the fat further, I used low-fat sour cream in place of full-fat. Not hearing any complaints, I snuck fat-free into my next test cake. Nobody suspected, so it stayed.

I turned to sugar. Typically, pineapple upside-down cake uses brown sugar for the topping and white sugar in the cake batter. I exchanged a few tablespoons of the granulated sugar in the batter for brown sugar, eventually working my way up to ¼ cup. The brown sugar improved the color of the cake (with less butter, it had been otherwise quite pale). At the same time, because brown sugar is moister (and more flavorful) than white sugar, I could reduce the total sugar in the batter by ¼ cup without worrying the cake would be dry or under-sweetened.

Turning to the topping, I was tired of trimming, coring, and chopping the pineapple. Canned pineapple had been a dud, but that didn't rule out frozen. A cake topped with frozen pineapple tasted just as good as that with fresh. Not only that, but the frozen pineapple proved consistently sweeter (so sweet that I

added a squeeze of lemon to balance it). The fresh fruit, on the other hand, was a gamble, dependent on the season, the store, and the supply. With consistently sweet frozen pineapple, I confidently trimmed the brown sugar in the topping by half (to ⅓ cup).

To coax flavor from the pineapple, I cut it into smaller pieces. My idea was to give eaters a bite of pineapple with every forkful (to help them forget the missing fat). I mixed 5½ tablespoons of melted butter with the ⅓ cup of brown sugar in the bottom of the cake pan, and arranged the pineapple over it. But the pineapple didn't fully cook in the time it took the cake to bake, plus the juice it released in the oven made the cake soggy and the glaze runny. (I'd had the same problems with fresh pineapple.) Taking a cue from a past America's Test Kitchen recipe, I tried sautéing the fruit and sugar on the stovetop. In 15 minutes, the pineapple nicely caramelized, the juices concentrated, and the brown sugar thickened. Yet enough juices remained to let me cut back the butter to a scant 1½ tablespoons. I distributed the fruit-sugar-butter mixture in the cake pan, scraped the cake batter over it, and stuck the cake in the oven. When I turned out the cake 40 minutes later, the pineapple was tender, the syrup stayed put, and the topping glistened.

But tasters complained that the cake tasted a little flat, even with the fresh lemon. So I doubled the vanilla and divided it between the topping and the cake. When all was said and done, I'd cut more than 100 calories and 9 grams of fat per slice of cake, plus I'd put the focus back on the fruit.

The Numbers

All nutritional information is for one single-serving slice of cake.

Traditional Pineapple Upside-Down Cake
CALORIES **430**
FAT **18g** SATURATED FAT **13g**

Cook's Country **Reduced-Fat Pineapple Upside-Down Cake**
CALORIES **310**
FAT **9g** SATURATED FAT **6g**

We nixed the canned pineapple rings and day-glo cherries. Frozen pineapple made for a consistently sweeter cake (and let us trim sugar from the caramelized topping).

REDUCED-FAT PINEAPPLE UPSIDE-DOWN CAKE Serves 8

If you can't find frozen pineapple, substitute fresh.

PINEAPPLE TOPPING
- 4 cups frozen pineapple, thawed and cut into ½-inch pieces
- ⅓ cup packed dark brown sugar
- 1½ tablespoons unsalted butter
- 2 teaspoons lemon juice
- ½ teaspoon vanilla extract

CAKE
- 1 cup all-purpose flour
- 1 teaspoon baking powder
- ½ teaspoon salt
- ½ cup fat-free sour cream
- ½ cup granulated sugar
- ¼ cup packed dark brown sugar
- 2 large eggs
- 1½ teaspoons vanilla extract
- 4 tablespoons butter, melted and cooled slightly

1. For the topping, adjust oven rack to middle position and heat oven to 350 degrees. Grease 9-inch cake pan. Cook pineapple and brown sugar in large skillet over medium-high heat, stirring frequently, until pineapple is light brown and juices are nearly evaporated, 12 to 15

minutes. Off heat, stir in butter, lemon juice, and vanilla. Scrape pineapple mixture into bottom of prepared pan.

2. For the cake, combine flour, baking powder, and salt in medium bowl. Whisk sour cream, granulated sugar, brown sugar, eggs, and vanilla in large bowl until smooth. Slowly whisk butter into sour cream mixture until incorporated. Stir flour mixture into wet mixture until just combined.

3. Scrape batter over pineapple mixture, spreading to cover. Bake until cake is golden and toothpick inserted into center comes out clean, 25 to 30 minutes. Cool cake in pan 10 minutes, then turn out onto platter. Cool at least 1 hour. Serve. (Cake can be stored at room temperature, covered, for 2 days.)

Frozen Pineapple
More consistently sweet than fresh fruit—with none of the prep hassle.

This brunch dish is normally made a night ahead and baked in the morning. Great for a crowd, but suppose it's just the two of you? BY CAROLYNN PURPURA

WHEN YOU EXPECT a crowd for brunch, few dishes are as practical as breakfast casserole, a substantial all-in-one meal that combines eggs, milk or cream, stale bread, cheese, and extras like bacon or onion. You assemble the jumbo 13 by 9-inch casserole the night before and weight it with a heavy pot so that the custard soaks into and softens the bread. In the morning, you simply turn on the oven and wait for the casserole to bake.

Beyond offering convenience, breakfast casserole is a delicious, supremely satisfying contrast of custardy, savory interior and crisp, toasty top. I crave it even when there are just two of us at the table. But planning breakfast for two a day in advance, let alone making it a day in advance, borders on silly. I wanted to refashion breakfast casserole to make it suitable for two.

I started with four eggs, two slices of bread, and a quick pour of milk, which seemed reasonable proportions for feeding two. To jazz up my mixture, I tossed in shredded cheddar cheese, chopped scallions, and diced, cooked bacon. I stirred everything together, adding the (cubed) bread last. I poured the mixture into the smallest ovensafe dish I could put my hands on and baked it at 350 degrees. In the oven, the bread dissolved into nothingness, making for an altogether unsatisfactory texture. Exacerbating the problem was the lack of crunchy bits on top; because the bread had disintegrated, there was nothing to crisp. For this mediocre breakfast, I still had to wait more than 45 minutes. I knew I could do better.

To fix the texture problem, I tried toasting the bread in the oven (my effort to stale it) before folding it into the other ingredients. Now I had the opposite problem: all crunch and chew, with none of the necessary yielding, lighter, custardy component. On attempt No. 3, I split the difference, cubing and toasting one slice of bread and cubing the other slice but leaving it untoasted.

The texture and structure of the dish were much improved, but I was getting tired of the long wait for breakfast (a bowl of cold cereal was starting to look good). Maybe I could speed things along if I started the casserole on the stovetop. I combined the ingredients as before, but this time I poured the

Breakfast casserole usually has to sit, weighted, in the refrigerator overnight so the custard can soak into the bread. This version is on the table in about 30 minutes, start to finish.

mixture into a hot ovensafe skillet that I'd set on the stove. Within a minute, my "casserole" was starting to set, and I moved it into the oven to finish cooking. After a couple of tries, I realized that if I cranked the heat to 475, in less than 10 minutes I could get the same nice, crisp top that it took nearly an hour to create with a large breakfast casserole.

All along, tasters had grumbled that my casserole wasn't rich enough, so I switched from milk to cream. While I was at it, I upped the amount from 4 tablespoons of cream to 6—just enough to add creamy richness without slowing down the oven time. Next, tasters got on my case about flavor. The casserole was frontloaded with bacon, cheese, and scallions; why did it taste so flat? I surmised that since it didn't sit overnight, the flavors couldn't meld and deepen as they ordinarily would in a breakfast casserole. A colleague suggested that I reinforce the smoky, porky

flavor by toasting the bread right in the skillet in the fat that the bacon rendered as it cooked. Brilliant. Finally, my breakfast casserole was quick to make and simultaneously creamy and crisp. Plus, it had almost as much richness and depth as versions that soak overnight. All this, for just the two of us.

BREAKFAST CASSEROLE FOR TWO
Serves 2
You can substitute an equal amount of shredded Swiss, Gouda, or pepper Jack cheese for the cheddar.

- 3 slices bacon, chopped
- 2 slices hearty white sandwich bread, cut into ½-inch pieces
- 6 tablespoons heavy cream
- 4 large eggs
- ⅛ teaspoon salt
- ⅛ teaspoon pepper
- 2 scallions, sliced thin
- ½ cup shredded sharp cheddar cheese

1. Adjust oven rack to upper-middle position and heat oven to 475 degrees. Cook bacon in 8-inch nonstick, ovensafe skillet over medium heat until crisp, about 8 minutes. Using slotted spoon, transfer bacon to paper towel–lined plate. Pour off all but 1 tablespoon fat from pan.

2. Add half of bread to skillet and cook over medium heat, stirring frequently, until golden brown, 3 to 5 minutes. Transfer to medium bowl and toss with untoasted bread.

3. Whisk cream, eggs, salt, and pepper in another medium bowl until smooth. Stir in bacon, scallions, and cheddar. Add egg mixture to now-empty skillet and cook over medium heat, using spatula to scrape bottom of pan, until eggs are just beginning to set, about 1 minute. Fold in bread and lightly pat mixture into even thickness. Bake until puffed and golden brown, 7 to 9 minutes. Serve.

TEST KITCHEN DISCOVERY **Bread Two Ways**
Breakfast casserole should have a soft, custardy interior and a crisp, contrasting crust. To ensure the right texture when the dish is downsized for two, we combined toasted and untoasted bread cubes.

SOFT
Fresh bread cubes soak up the cream and eggs to make a custardy interior.

CRISP
Bread cubes toasted in bacon fat add flavor and crunch.

Slow Cooker Barbecued Steak Tips

It's easy to get juicy, saucy barbecued steak tips from a hot grill. But can you make them in the mellow heat and closed confines of a slow cooker? BY DIANE UNGER

STEAK TIPS HAVE great beefy flavor and just enough marbling to keep them moist and tender when quickly grilled. But I wanted to find a way to make "barbecued" tips in my slow cooker. I was surprised to find a bevy of recipes. Their general modus operandi was to drop the raw tips into the cooker, dump on bottled barbecue sauce, and cook for upwards of 12 hours. If it's true that you get out of something what you put into it, maybe I should have known that this no-effort method would lead to dry, stringy, bland meat and sauce so diluted by the ample meat juices that it tasted like meat-flavored water.

My first correction was simple: browning the tips in a skillet before they went into the cooker. This not only improved their flavor and texture, but it also gave me flavorful fond from which to build a concentrated sauce. To do that, I sautéed onion and garlic in the now-empty skillet, added a little tomato sauce and ketchup (no strangers to barbecue sauce recipes), and scraped up the bits of fond so they could dissolve in the sauce. I reduced the mixture to intensify and concentrate before scraping it into the slow cooker. After six hours the meat was cooked properly, but it was bobbing in a lake of liquid, so it tasted boiled: Steak tips throw off a lot of juice during long cooking. I needed to get the meat out of the juices.

A footed vegetable steamer–basket came to mind, and it did elevate the meat enough to keep it out of the beefy hot tub. But the chunks of meat cooked

Skewers in the slow cooker? Yes—they keep the tips above the liquid, so they don't taste boiled.

unevenly in the tight confines of the basket. Then I thought to apply a grilling technique: skewering the steak tips. I threaded the raw tips onto bamboo skewers, then browned the kebabs and laid them on top of the inverted steamer basket in the cooker. Hours later, the

texture of the cooked meat actually resembled that of grilled tips: tender and moist, with a nice seared crust. As the tips cooked, the meat juices had mingled with my concentrated sauce; I poured this mixture into a saucepan to tighten it. Once it had reduced to barbecue-sauce consistency, I brushed it on the meat. The meat's texture was good and the sauce had plenty of flavor, but the tips themselves needed more seasoning.

What if I brushed the raw tips with something clingy and flavorful up front? I rubbed a simple mixture of tomato paste, soy sauce, and brown sugar on the kebabs and tried to brown them. But the mixture was too wet, and it scorched in the pan. I had better luck rubbing the mixture onto the tips after I'd browned them: The potent wet rub seasoned the meat as it cooked above the liquid. Six hours later, I couldn't believe how far this recipe had come: The beef, bathed in a complex sweet-tangy sauce, was rich, meaty, and tender. Not the genuine, cooked-on-the-grill article, true, but they do taste surprisingly close.

STEP BY STEP **Getting Barbecue Flavor from the Slow Cooker. Really.**
To simulate the flavor of grilled steak tips in the slow cooker, you have to compensate for the juices released by the meat.

1. SEAR Brown the skewered steak tips in a skillet to intensify the flavor of both the meat and the sauce.

2. COAT Once the meat is browned, coat it with a potent wet rub.

3. ELEVATE Lay the skewers on an inverted steamer basket to keep them out of the liquid.

Caesar salad takes well to innovations—as long as the flavors are bold yet balanced. BY KELLY PRICE

OPEN THE MENU in any American family restaurant and chances are you'll find a variation on Caesar salad alongside the spinach-artichoke dip and the Asian chicken salad. And why not? The classic—romaine lettuce, Parmesan, anchovies, and croutons tossed in a creamy, garlicky dressing—provides lots of opportunity for reworking. But these "modern" Caesars rarely live up to their promise: The dressings burn with garlic; the hard, desiccated croutons threaten to crack your teeth; and the jumble of mismatched add-ins turns what should be interesting combinations into discombobulated messes. To breathe new life into Caesar, I wanted balanced dressings, bold add-ins that would mesh with the other components, and crunchy, flavorful croutons.

I decided to use the test kitchen's easy Caesar dressing, which enlists mayonnaise and oil instead of the raw egg required by the traditional dressing. Anchovies and Worcestershire sauce contribute complexity and depth. This dressing uses just a single clove of garlic for a solid backbone of flavor without the burn. Vinegar and lemon juice add brightness and balance. And our Caesar croutons are simple: Toss cubed French bread with oil and a second garlic clove and bake until light and crisp.

With my basic components locked down, it was time to tap into my culinary creativity. But developing salads that stood up to the assertive flavors of Caesar dressing proved harder than I'd anticipated: My tasters emphatically dismissed salads that featured subtle flavors. After a good bit of trial and error, I was able to provide them with the robust flavors they demanded.

This being *Cook's Country*, my tasters demanded … bacon. It took eight strips in the salad before they were satisfied. For buttery contrast and richness, I added two chopped avocados. Cherry tomatoes delivered acidity and color, and croutons seasoned with Dijon mustard and black pepper rounded out the flavors of my Bacon-Avocado Caesar.

For a Cajun Blue Caesar variation, I crumbled a full ½ pound of blue cheese into the salad—nothing meek about that. To give my croutons Cajun flair, I coated them with Old Bay, garlic, onion powder, and coriander before toasting. These croutons now

had bold "blackened" flavor.

It may sound odd, but I wanted a salad that incorporated the flavors of chili. Canned kidney beans fit the bill and gave my Cowboy Caesar plenty of substance. I turned up the heat by coating store-bought cornbread with smoky minced chipotle peppers for croutons with a kick. Extra chipotle in the dressing lent additional giddyap.

Finally, I fortified an Italian Deli Caesar with plenty of thick-cut salami and ham, Swiss cheese, and sliced pepperoncini (jarred, moderately spicy Italian peppers). Substituting pepperoncini brine for the vinegar reinforced the dressing's bite. I played up the deli theme by using rye bread (instead of French) for the croutons.

With a little creativity, I had four new, boldly flavored Caesar salads that were every bit as good as the original.

CLASSIC CAESAR SALAD

Serves 6 to 8
You can substitute two 10-ounce bags of chopped romaine lettuce for the hearts.

- ½ cup olive oil
- 2 garlic cloves, minced
- 1 (12-inch) piece French baguette, cut into ½-inch pieces (about 4 cups)
  Salt and pepper
- ½ cup mayonnaise
- ¼ cup grated Parmesan cheese, plus 1 cup shredded
- 2 anchovy fillets, rinsed and patted dry (optional)
- 1 tablespoon lemon juice
- 1 tablespoon white wine vinegar
- 1 tablespoon Worcestershire sauce
- 1 tablespoon Dijon mustard
- 3 romaine hearts, torn into bite-size pieces (about 12 cups)

1. Adjust oven rack to middle position and heat oven to 350 degrees. Whisk oil and garlic in large bowl; reserve ¼ cup. Toss bread with remaining oil mixture and season with salt and pepper. Bake bread on rimmed baking sheet until golden, about 20 minutes. Cool completely.

2. Process mayonnaise, grated Parmesan, anchovy (if using), lemon juice, vinegar, Worcestershire, mustard, ½ teaspoon salt, and ½ teaspoon pepper in blender until smooth. With machine running, pour in reserved oil and process

until thoroughly incorporated.

3. Toss romaine, shredded Parmesan, and dressing in large bowl. Add croutons and toss to combine. Season with salt and pepper. Serve.

BACON-AVOCADO CAESAR
Prepare Classic Caesar Salad, tossing 4 teaspoons Dijon and 1½ teaspoons pepper with bread and oil in step 1. Add 1½ cups halved cherry tomatoes; 8 slices cooked bacon, chopped into ½-inch pieces; and 2 pitted, skinned, and chopped avocados with croutons in step 3.

CAJUN BLUE CAESAR
Prepare Classic Caesar Salad, tossing 1 tablespoon Old Bay seasoning, 2 teaspoons onion powder, and ¾ teaspoon ground coriander with bread and oil in step 1. Omit shredded Parmesan. Add 2 cups crumbled blue cheese with croutons in step 3.

COWBOY CAESAR
Prepare Classic Caesar Salad, replacing baguette with 5 ounces prepared cornbread. Toss 2 teaspoons minced canned chipotle chiles in adobo with cornbread and oil in step 1. Add 1 teaspoon minced canned chipotle chiles in adobo

to blender in step 2. Add 1 (16-ounce) can drained and rinsed kidney beans with croutons in step 3.

ITALIAN DELI CAESAR
Prepare Classic Caesar Salad, replacing baguette with 5 slices rye bread, shredded Parmesan with 1 cup shredded Swiss cheese, and vinegar with 1 tablespoon pepperoncini brine. Add 6 ounces ¼-inch-thick deli ham, cut into ¼-inch strips; 6 ounces ¼-inch-thick deli salami, cut into ¼-inch strips; and 1 cup drained jarred sliced pepperoncini with croutons in step 3.

Our Bacon-Avocado Caesar (pictured here) features croutons seasoned with Dijon mustard.

ESSENTIAL GEAR **Garlic Press**
Our favorite garlic press has long, comfortable handles and an effortless action that make it live up to its "Easy-Squeeze" name.

KUHN RIKON EASY-SQUEEZE GARLIC PRESS

Glazed Picnic Ham

Picnic ham tastes like a cross between a rich pork shoulder and a salty, smoky ham.
But it takes a few tricks to transform this flavorful-but-fatty cut into a tender, juicy roast. BY DIANE UNGER

Your garden-variety supermarket ham—a lean cut from the rear leg of a pig—gets its complex salty savor from curing and smoking. But many cooks are unaware of an even more flavorful cut, the picnic ham, that's given the same treatment. Picnic hams, which come from the lower part of a hog's shoulder, are pleasantly smoky and salty like leg hams, but they taste richer and meatier because they have a lot more fat. Most of the recipes I found for picnic ham called for simmering the meat for hours. But boiling wasn't what I had in mind. I wanted to roast this exceptionally flavorful cut of meat to present as the centerpiece of my Easter table.

Since we've never cooked a picnic ham in the test kitchen, I started with our basic method for spiral-sliced ham: After trimming off most of the tough rind (a step not needed for spiral-sliced hams), I slipped the ham into an oven bag, cinched the bag shut, cut slits in the top to vent the steam, and baked the bagged ham in a 300-degree oven until the meat registered 100 degrees. A couple of hours later, I had high hopes as I carved samples for my tasters, but my optimism was short-lived. The meat was unpleasantly chewy, and it was riddled with pockets of fat. Lesson learned: Although picnic hams are technically fully cooked, the extra fat means they need extra cooking (not just heating through, like leg ham) to become palatable.

For my next test, I upped the cooking time to three hours (still in the oven bag) to give the connective tissue enough time to render. The outside of

We bake this "ham" in a low oven for 3 hours to tenderize it, then turn up the heat and brush on a glaze at the end of cooking.

the ham was leathery, and the meat was overcooked, dry, and still pocked with chunks of fat and gristle. Adding insult to injury, since the meat had dried out and concentrated, it was also too salty. Picnic ham was proving to be no picnic in the kitchen.

Was the oven bag actually hurting me here? Through years of smoking similarly large, fatty cuts on the grill, we've learned that collagen (the tough, fatty connective tissue) renders most

effectively in a moist, steamy environment (that's why we often use a drip pan when slow-smoking on the grill). But the vented oven bag, which traps enough moisture to keep a leg ham moist when reheating, wasn't trapping enough moisture to keep the picnic ham moist through the necessary "extra" cooking. I decided to bag the bag and instead placed the ham directly on a rack in a large roasting pan. To create a contained moist environment (akin

to covering the grill when smoking), I wrapped the whole roasting pan tightly with foil.

In a single test, the picnic ham improved dramatically. I sorted through the cooking details in subsequent tests and found that cooking the meat to 140 degrees in a 325-degree oven (which took anywhere from 2 to 3 hours, depending on the size of the ham) produced the best results—consistently moist, tender meat with much of the fat rendered out.

To balance the salty richness of the meat, I opted for a sweet, spicy glaze. As soon as I put the ham in the oven, I got to work simmering a simple mixture of brown sugar, Dijon mustard, clove, cayenne pepper, and apple cider vinegar. When the ham was almost done cooking, I carefully removed and discarded the foil, slathered the ham with the sticky glaze, and cranked the heat to 450 degrees so the glaze could caramelize (it took about 25 minutes). The glaze nicely countered the ham's salinity, but tasters wanted more depth. Switching from cider vinegar to balsamic did the trick (and had the added benefit of giving the glaze a deep, rich color), and I thinned out a little extra glaze to a pourable consistency for ladling on at the table. This ultra-savory ham was better than any I'd ever tasted—and is primed to be my Easter centerpiece for many years to come.

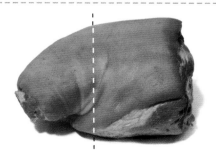
GLAZED PICNIC HAM (SMOKED SHOULDER)
Serves 12 to 16

We like the larger whole smoked picnic when we're cooking for a crowd, but you can also use a shankless roast (sometimes labeled "smoked shoulder picnic" or "smoked Boston butt"). Crimp the foil tightly around the roasting pan to keep the ham moist and help the collagen render.

- 1 (8- to 10-pound) bone-in smoked picnic ham
- 3 tablespoons dry mustard
- 1 teaspoon pepper
- 1 cup packed dark brown sugar
- ½ cup Dijon mustard
- ½ cup balsamic vinegar
- ¼ teaspoon cayenne pepper
- ⅛ teaspoon ground cloves
- 1 tablespoon apple cider or water

1. Adjust oven rack to lowest position and heat oven to 325 degrees. Line large roasting pan with aluminum foil. Remove skin from exterior of ham and trim fat to ¼-inch thickness. Score remaining fat at 1-inch intervals in crosshatch pattern. Combine 1 tablespoon dry mustard and pepper in small bowl. Rub ham all over with spice rub. Set ham on V-rack set inside prepared roasting pan. Cover pan tightly with foil. Bake until internal temperature registers 140 degrees, 2 to 3 hours.

2. Meanwhile, bring brown sugar, Dijon mustard, vinegar, remaining dry mustard, cayenne, and cloves to boil in medium saucepan. Reduce heat to low and simmer until reduced to 1 cup, 15 to 20 minutes. (Glaze can be refrigerated in airtight container for 3 days. Microwave glaze until bubbling around edges before using.)

3. Remove ham from oven and let sit for 5 minutes. Increase oven temperature to 450 degrees. Discard foil and brush ham evenly with ½ cup glaze. Return ham to oven and bake until dark brown and caramelized, 25 to 30 minutes. Stir cider (or water) into remaining glaze. Transfer ham to carving board, loosely tent with foil, and let rest 30 minutes. Carve (see Test Kitchen Technique box) and serve with cider-thinned glaze.

WHAT TO DO WITH LEFTOVERS

Lentil Soup with Ham

The leftover ham bone helped, but for great lentil soup, we also had to figure out the best way to cook the lentils.

BY DIANE UNGER

WHEN I WRAPPED up my testing for Glazed Picnic Ham, I was given another, more immediate challenge by my colleagues: clearing the test kitchen refrigerators of all those leftover ham bones. As any good cook knows, when life gives you ham bones, you make soup. In this case, I decided on a hearty lentil soup fortified with leftover ham and greens.

To start my soup, I followed the lead of most recipes and sautéed chopped carrot, onion, and garlic in olive oil, then added a pound of dried brown lentils (the most common variety in supermarkets), the ham bone, and enough chicken broth to just cover the bone. (Some recipes use water, not broth, but since lentils are relatively quick-cooking, the ham bone wouldn't have time to give up all its flavor; I'd supplement with broth.)

After the soup gently simmered for about an hour, I stirred in a couple of cups of cubed ham and called tasters over to dip in their spoons. The flavor was pretty good (if a little plain), but the lentils were unevenly cooked: Some were blown out to mush, while others were firm and underdone.

I happened to come across a recipe that required sautéing the lentils right in with the vegetables. In a side-by-side test, the soup made with this unusual method had superior texture, with uniformly soft but not blown-out lentils. Taking it one step further, I let the lentils brown slightly in the oil to deepen their flavor. I added the broth and stirred in a bay leaf, thyme, and red pepper flakes to bump up the flavor even more. The soup tasted delicious, and the lentils were perfectly cooked, but it was a little thin. To give it a thicker, rustic texture, I buzzed a few cups of the soup in a blender, then added the puree back to the pot. Chopped kale (stirred in with the ham chunks at the end of cooking) put this warming soup over the top.

Kale gives this soup heartiness and color.

LENTIL SOUP WITH HAM
Serves 6 to 8

Snap the ham bone into 2 pieces to fit into the Dutch oven.

- 2 tablespoons olive oil
- 2 cups dried brown lentils, rinsed and picked over
- 2 carrots, peeled and chopped
- 1 onion, chopped fine
- 3 garlic cloves, minced
- ½ cup white wine
- 7 cups low-sodium chicken broth
- 1 teaspoon minced fresh thyme
- 1 bay leaf
- ¼ teaspoon red pepper flakes
- 1 ham bone, plus 2 cups leftover chopped ham
- ½ pound kale, stemmed and leaves chopped
- Salt and pepper

1. Heat oil in Dutch oven over medium heat until shimmering. Add lentils, carrots, and onion and cook until vegetables are softened and lentils are beginning to brown, about 5 minutes. Stir in garlic and cook until fragrant, about 30 seconds. Add wine and cook until reduced by half, about 1 minute. Stir in broth, thyme, bay leaf, and pepper flakes and bring to boil.

2. Add ham bone, reduce heat to medium-low, and simmer, covered, until thickened and lentils are completely tender, about 1 hour. Discard ham bone and bay leaf. Puree 2 cups soup until smooth. Return pureed soup to pot and stir in kale and ham. Simmer, covered, until kale is tender, about 10 minutes. Season with salt and pepper. Serve.

Cream Cheese Biscuits

Everyone told us that cream cheese made the lightest, fluffiest biscuits ever. That proved true—after we figured out a cool trick and a new cutting method. BY CAROLYNN PURPURA

IN THE TEST KITCHEN, we've never met a biscuit we didn't like—from buttermilk to cathead, from refrigerator to Quaker bonnet. One sort we hadn't yet tackled was cream cheese biscuits. A particular favorite in Charleston, South Carolina, they're made like ordinary biscuits—with flour, leavener, and buttermilk—but cream cheese substitutes for some of the butter. That swap produces biscuits that are moist, incredibly fluffy, and downy soft—or that's what I'd heard. I tried an assortment of recipes, and while they were definitely in the fluffy (not flaky) camp, I didn't get the full-on lightness, tenderness, and height I expected.

These recipes called for a range of ratios of cream cheese to butter. Since these were cream cheese biscuits, why use butter at all? I picked a recipe from among those I'd tested and ejected the butter whole hog, replacing it with cream cheese. Dumb idea, I admitted half an hour later as I tossed a dozen bricks into the trash. (Flakes of butter melt and steam in the oven, creating lightness; the cream cheese resolutely refused to flake or melt.) I eased up, adding back butter tablespoon by tablespoon while subtracting the equivalent amount of cream cheese. At 4 tablespoons of butter and 8 tablespoons of cream cheese (to 3 cups of flour), my biscuits melded a slight cream cheese tang with plenty of buttery flavor. (I tested shortening with the cream cheese, too, but as usual we found that we like butter in our biscuits.)

Flavor? Check. Texture? Still problematic. The biscuits remained short and a little tough. Many of the recipes I'd found called for White Lily flour, a low-protein flour that's famous (it has a fanatical following in the South) for producing notably tender baked goods. Because it's not easy for everybody to find White Lily, I replaced the all-purpose flour I'd been using with cake flour—another low-protein flour, but one you can buy in most grocery stores. Alas, the biscuits had a slight chemical flavor from the flour. For my next test, I used equal amounts of all-purpose flour and cake flour. Now the biscuits had a tender crumb, and the flavor was back on track.

Something had struck me as really peculiar about several of the recipes I'd started with: They called for softened butter and cream cheese, and—against

my better judgment—that's what I'd been using. Ordinarily, biscuits call for cold fat: You cut the fat into the flour until you have coarse crumbs. These create the aforementioned pockets of steam in the oven. I thought that these old recipes might know something I didn't. Apparently not. My biscuits with softened fat were heavy and short. Refrigerating the fat proved to be a step in the right direction. But because cream cheese is soft and smushy by nature, the biscuits came out best—tall and light—when I thoroughly chilled the fat in the freezer.

One problem remained. I had been using the standard method for shaping biscuits: Roll out the dough, cut rounds with a biscuit cutter, then reroll the

scraps and cut as many more biscuits as possible. The rerolled biscuits were tough—a problem that all biscuits share, but with cream cheese biscuits, the rerolled remainders bordered on inedible. Our science editor explained that the water content in cream cheese is significantly higher than in butter (57 percent compared with 14 percent). Kneading/rolling develops gluten. The extra water was producing even more gluten, making cream cheese biscuits especially susceptible to being overworked. The next time I got to work, I avoided rerolling altogether. Instead, I rolled out the dough into a rectangle, sliced 12 cut-to-fit squares, and baked a dozen moist, tender, perfect cream cheese biscuits.

All-purpose flour gives these biscuits structure, while "softer" cake flour makes them fluffy.

CREAM CHEESE BISCUITS
Makes 12 biscuits

- 1½ cups all-purpose flour
- 1½ cups cake flour
- 1 tablespoon sugar
- 1 tablespoon baking powder
- 1 teaspoon salt
- ¾ teaspoon baking soda
- 4 ounces cream cheese, cut into ½-inch pieces and frozen 30 minutes
- 4 tablespoons unsalted butter, cut into ½-inch pieces and frozen 30 minutes
- 1 cup plus 1 tablespoon buttermilk

1. Adjust oven rack to middle position and heat oven to 450 degrees. Line baking sheet with parchment paper. Pulse all-purpose flour, cake flour, sugar, baking powder, salt, baking soda, cream cheese, and butter in food processor until mixture resembles coarse meal. Transfer flour mixture to large bowl. Stir in buttermilk until combined (dough may appear slightly dry).

2. Turn dough onto lightly floured surface and knead briefly until dough comes together. Roll dough into 8 by 6-inch rectangle, about ¾ inch thick. Cut into twelve 2-inch squares and transfer to prepared baking sheet. Bake until light brown, 12 to 15 minutes. Transfer to wire rack and let cool 5 minutes. Serve warm.

MAKE AHEAD Unbaked cut biscuits can be refrigerated on baking sheet, covered with plastic wrap, for 1 day. To finish, heat oven to 450 degrees and bake as directed.

TEST KITCHEN TECHNIQUE
Square Is the New Round
Instead of rolling the dough, cutting round biscuits, then rerolling the scraps to cut more, we roll the dough into a rectangle and cut 12 square biscuits.

Asparagus Gratin

Asparagus can taste as bright and sunny as a spring afternoon. So why do so many gratins load it up and bog it down with masses of cream and cheese? BY SARAH GABRIEL

A TRADITIONAL GRATIN swaddles vegetables in a creamy, cheesy sauce. This approach works wonders for hardy potatoes and cauliflower. The mild vegetables get a boost from the strong cheese sauce while providing starch that thickens the sauce as they slowly bake and soften. Asparagus, by contrast, has a bright flavor and takes mere minutes to cook, so I wasn't surprised when I dug into an asparagus gratin and pulled out a brown, lifeless stalk. What a shame to smother this delicate spring vegetable. For a dish more like a light spring jacket than a bulky woolen coat, I'd approach the asparagus and sauce separately, and then bring them together for a quick broil to brown the top.

I trimmed the tough bottom ends off two bunches of asparagus, steamed the stalks until barely tender, and then set to work on the sauce. I made a roux with 2 tablespoons each of butter and flour and whisked in a cup of half-and-half (heavy cream was stifling), followed by Parmesan and Gruyère, two classic gratin cheeses. The sauce was slightly gritty and squelched the vegetable's flavor. Tests showed that the Gruyère was to blame for the grit, so I traded it for milder, smoother Monterey Jack. I poured this new sauce over steamed asparagus and summoned tasters. The grit was gone and the cheese flavor was well calibrated. Unfortunately, the half-and-half still muffled the fresh asparagus flavor.

To give the asparagus more breathing room, I made three different sauces: my working recipe (with the half-and-half), a version that replaced half of the half-and-half with water, and a third that used all water. "A cheese sauce with no milk or cream?" asked some incredulous tasters. But much to our surprise, we liked that version best. For the first time in weeks, we could really taste the asparagus. True, the sauce was now anemic, but I could fix that: I'd replace the water with vegetable stock. Scrounging around the test kitchen for scraps to make stock, I remembered the asparagus trimmings. Perfect—I'd use those.

For clean, pure asparagus flavor, I'd make the stock with nothing but the trimmings. After just five minutes of simmering, I had a decidedly asparagus-flavored stock. I made a new sauce using one cup of my five-minute stock in place of the original half-and-half and was pleased by how it brought the asparagus

and cheese flavors into balance.

At this point I happened to notice that when I drained the water from cooking the asparagus, it was pale green—I had been pouring flavor down the drain. To harness it, I first simmered the asparagus ends in water to make my five-minute stock, and then simmered the spears in the stock instead of in plain water. After the spears were cooked, I reserved the now double-concentrated stock and used it to make the sauce. I sauced the asparagus, sprinkled extra Parmesan on top, and broiled the gratin to crisp the cheese. This asparagus gratin was dressed for spring.

ASPARAGUS GRATIN Serves 8
For even cooking, buy asparagus spears between ¼ and ½ inch in diameter.

- 2 pounds thin asparagus
- 2½ cups water
- Salt and pepper
- 2 tablespoons unsalted butter
- 2 tablespoons all-purpose flour
- ¾ cup grated Parmesan cheese
- ½ cup shredded Monterey Jack cheese

1. Adjust oven rack to upper-middle position and heat broiler. Line broiler-safe baking dish with paper towels. Trim 1½ inches from stem end of asparagus and reserve ends. Bring water to boil in large skillet over medium-high heat. Add asparagus ends and ¼ teaspoon salt and cook, covered, for 5 minutes. Using slotted spoon, remove asparagus ends and discard. Add asparagus stalks to skillet, cover, and cook, stirring occasionally, until nearly tender, 2 to 4 minutes. Transfer asparagus to paper-lined baking dish. Pour asparagus water into liquid measuring cup; reserve 1 cup.

2. Melt butter in now-empty skillet over medium heat. Add flour and cook, stirring constantly until golden, about 1 minute. Whisk in reserved asparagus water and bring to boil. Reduce heat to medium-low and simmer until thickened, 3 to 5 minutes. Off heat, whisk in ½ cup Parmesan and Monterey Jack until smooth. Season with salt and pepper. Cover and let stand for 5 minutes.

3. Remove paper towels from baking dish. Drizzle sauce over center of asparagus and top with remaining Parmesan. Broil until cheese is golden and asparagus is tender, 6 to 8 minutes. Serve.

Asparagus calls for a light touch. Instead of baking for an hour, we steam the asparagus in a quick asparagus broth and finish the dish under the broiler.

TEST KITCHEN SECRET Making a Lighter, Livelier Sauce
To highlight the flavor of delicate asparagus, we make a five-minute vegetable stock from the woody ends. The asparagus spears simmer in the stock, and we reserve the now double-concentrated liquid to use in our cheese sauce in place of the usual (smothering) heavy cream.

TREASURE NOT TRASH
The asparagus ends make a flavorful stock in which to cook the spears.

ASPARAGUS STOCK
The stock is now double-concentrated. We use it (instead of cream) in the sauce.

Funeral Potatoes

This gooey, cheesy casserole classic is usually made with convenience products.
We wanted to keep the convenience but inject some "from scratch" flavor. BY SARAH GABRIEL

This cheesy shredded potato casserole is one of those American folk dishes that are so popular everyone claims them. Mormons call it "funeral" or "Ward Party" potatoes. In the South, it's "hash brown casserole," but I've heard it called "neighborhood potatoes" in Massachusetts and "cheesy potatoes" in Washington. Mormons will tell you it's a Mormon recipe, Southerners will tell you it's a Southern recipe, and half a dozen people have told me that their mom invented it. But too many versions prioritize convenience over flavor, using condensed-soup sauces and cornflake toppings. I hoped to upgrade the flavor without sacrificing ease.

I started by making five different casseroles. They all followed the same basic formula: Mix grated, parcooked potatoes or frozen hash browns with cream of chicken soup, cheddar cheese, sour cream, and chopped onion. Scrape the mixture into a casserole dish, top with cornflakes (in some cases), and bake. Easy? Check. Delicious? Not exactly.

Sure, the creamy texture was nice, but the potatoes were bland and the whole assemblage too rich. The canned soup I opposed on principle: Its lengthy list of unpronounceable ingredients barely sounded edible. As for the cornflake toppings, they resembled soggy cardboard. Yet despite these drawbacks, I knew that the casserole's many fans weren't wrong. If I seasoned the casserole properly, tempered its richness, replaced the canned soup with real food, and found something better to top it all

Plenty of casseroles are topped with potato chips. We up the ante—and reinforce the casserole's flavors—by using sour-cream-and-onion chips.

off, I could get onboard with a one-dish, easy, cheesy, creamy, crunchy, and uncommonly comforting casserole.

To begin, I pitted frozen hash browns against fresh potatoes. Parcooking, peeling, and grating the potatoes took too long; plus, the frozen hash browns made for a less starchy, gloppy casserole. But though the frozen hash browns were easy to work with, baking times approached two hours. I'd have to find a quicker way to cook them.

Thawing was a quick fix—at least in theory. In actual fact, it took at least an hour, even when the hash browns sat out on the counter. Since I knew I'd be making my own sauce, maybe, I thought, I could thaw the potatoes right in it. To test my idea, I mixed up a basic cheese sauce (cheddar whisked into milk that I'd thickened with a butter-flour roux) and then emptied a bag of frozen hash browns into the pot. I turned down the heat, covered the pot,

and—yes!—the potatoes thawed in just 10 minutes, and the casserole baked in a reasonable 45 minutes.

My quickie cheese sauce didn't yet resemble the real thing; also, the sauce curdled and separated in the oven. I fixed that problem by switching from milk to half-and-half (which has more fat, so the protein in it is less prone to curdling). For my next test, I replaced some of the half-and-half with chicken broth, creating a savory backbone that nodded to the cream of chicken soup that's in the original casserole. Sour cream is a signature flavor in funeral potatoes, so I stirred 2 cups into the pot, as called for in many recipes. Ugh. Sour cream overload. Ultimately, just half a cup lent plenty of tang and richness.

My dish still lacked a crunchy topping. Since we'd rejected cornflakes, I browsed the grocery store aisles for possibilities, grabbing crackers, panko (Japanese-style bread crumbs), and potato chips—hey this is comfort food, after all. The crackers were sandy. The panko needed buttering and seasoning. The potato chips, however, I simply crushed and sprinkled over the casserole. And when I switched to sour-cream-and-onion-flavored chips (to echo the flavors in the body of the casserole), the crunchy-salty payoff was irresistible. As was the casserole.

FUNERAL POTATOES Serves 8 to 10
You'll need one 30-ounce bag of frozen shredded (not cubed) hash brown potatoes.

- 3 tablespoons unsalted butter
- 2 onions, chopped fine
- ¼ cup all-purpose flour
- 1½ cups low-sodium chicken broth
- 1 cup half-and-half
- 1¾ teaspoons salt
- ½ teaspoon dried thyme
- ¼ teaspoon pepper
- 2 cups shredded sharp cheddar cheese
- 8 cups frozen shredded hash brown potatoes
- ½ cup sour cream
- 4 cups sour-cream-and-onion potato chips, crushed

1. Adjust oven rack to middle position and heat oven to 350 degrees. Melt butter in Dutch oven over medium-high heat. Cook onion until softened, about 5 minutes. Add flour and cook, stirring constantly, until golden, about 1 minute. Slowly whisk in broth, half-and-half, salt, thyme, and pepper and bring to boil. Reduce heat to medium-low and simmer, stirring occasionally, until slightly thickened, 3 to 5 minutes. Off heat, whisk in cheddar until smooth.

2. Stir potatoes into sauce, cover, and cook, stirring occasionally, over low heat until thawed, about 10 minutes. Off heat, stir in sour cream until combined.

3. Scrape mixture into 13 by 9-inch baking dish and top with potato chips. Bake until golden brown, 45 to 50 minutes. Let cool 10 minutes. Serve.

MAKE AHEAD Potato mixture can be refrigerated in baking dish, covered with aluminum foil, for 2 days. To finish, bake potatoes 20 minutes. Remove dish from oven and uncover. Top with potato chips and bake until golden brown, 45 to 50 minutes.

Not All Processed Foods Are Created Equal

LOSE
Instead of gloppy condensed soup, make your own cream of chicken base.

USE
Frozen hash browns keep prep time short. Sour-cream-and-onion potato chips add flavor and crunch.

Spinach Salad with Raspberry Vinaigrette

Bottled raspberry vinaigrette is usually too sweet. To make this '80s classic relevant again, we knew we'd have to start from scratch.

BY CAROLYNN PURPURA

Whole raspberries in the salad reinforce the dressing's berry flavor.

IF YOU WERE frequenting nice restaurants in the 1980s, you would have found it hard to avoid raspberry vinaigrette—chefs used it to dress anything from artichokes to lamb. We see a lot less of this condiment these days, but the one place where it has stood the test of time is in spinach salad. It's a winning concept: The sweet-tart vinaigrette pairs well with the earthy, mineral-y spinach, and soft goat cheese, pistachios, and fresh raspberries add interest and texture. Since store-bought raspberry vinaigrette can be cloying, I set out to make an easy homemade version that would bring this salad back into good graces.

I started with our basic red wine vinaigrette, which includes olive oil, Dijon mustard, and shallots. To this I added pureed fresh raspberries. The flavor was excellent, but tasters disliked the seeds in their salad dressing. Straining was a non-starter: too much work. Using seedless jam was an easier approach. Now the seeds were gone, but the vinaigrette was too sweet—exactly what I'd hoped to avoid. I added extra mustard and vinegar and restored the balance—almost. The shallots fought with the raspberry flavor, so I lost them.

For the salad, baby spinach and fresh raspberries were must-haves. My tasters, however, insisted I deviate from tradition when it came to the goat cheese, which they felt became unpleasantly squishy as it soaked up the dressing. I tried a dozen other cheeses, and, honestly, most of them were pretty good. In the end, we settled on the salty tang and creamy texture of shredded Gouda. A scattering of peppery, crunchy radishes completed the recipe. This salad is definitely ready for a comeback.

SPINACH SALAD WITH RASPBERRY VINAIGRETTE
Serves 4 to 6
Avoid chunky preserves and super-sweet jams.

- 2 tablespoons seedless raspberry jam
- 2½ teaspoons red wine vinegar
- 1 teaspoon Dijon mustard
  Salt and pepper
- 3 tablespoons olive oil
- 8 cups baby spinach
- 1 cup fresh raspberries
- ¾ cup shredded Gouda cheese
- ½ cup thinly sliced radishes
- ⅓ cup pistachios, toasted

1. Whisk jam in medium bowl until smooth. Add vinegar, mustard, ⅛ teaspoon salt, and ⅛ teaspoon pepper, whisking until combined. Slowly whisk in oil until thoroughly incorporated. (Dressing can be refrigerated in airtight container for 4 days.)

2. Toss spinach and dressing in large bowl. Add raspberries, Gouda, radishes, and pistachios and toss to combine. Season with salt and pepper. Serve.

Thoroughbred Pie

What better way to top off the Kentucky Derby than with a slice of chocolate-walnut-bourbon pie? None, as long as you rein in the runaway sweetness. BY ERIKA BRUCE

In the final stretch of any properly hosted Kentucky Derby party—trailing behind the mint juleps, burgoo, and hot browns—comes a slice of gooey, rich, chocolate-nut pie. Although you can find countless recipes for it, the Kern family created the standard-bearer. They began baking it at their inn in Prospect, Kentucky, in 1954 and subsequently trade-marked it as "Derby-Pie." It's soft and very sweet, and studded with walnuts and chocolate chips; the top of the pie has a sugary, slightly crackly crunch. To this day, the recipe remains a closely guarded Kern family secret, but I was determined to crack the code—or at least create an equally winning pie.

I mail-ordered a "Derby-Pie" from the original makers and, when it arrived, called my fellow test cooks to the table. The pie fell decisively into the classic Southern category of homey, soft, and super-sweet pies; other examples include pecan, chess, vinegar, and transparent pies. All use butter and eggs, as well as flour, cornstarch, or cornmeal to thicken, and all go heavy on the sweetener (variously white or brown sugar, molasses, or Karo syrup). There they diverge. Among the characteristics that distinguish this pie (generically called thoroughbred pie) is its use of bourbon (usually), chocolate, and walnuts, not to mention that signa-ture crackle layer at the top.

I rounded up recipes, dusted off my rolling pin, and rolled up my sleeves. It was hard to imagine how anything

Our version of this Kentucky Derby classic uses browned butter to add depth of flavor.

made from these tempting ingredients could taste bad, but a few hours later, I found myself surveying a disappoint-ing bunch. As a group, the pies were sweeter than a John Denver tune, and with all that sugar going on, you barely noticed the nuts or the chocolate. On top of that (or, more accurately, below that), the crusts were pale, soggy, and underdone. Well, at least my goals were clear: more flavor, less sugar, and a nicely browned, crisp crust.

As my starting point, I used tasters'

top pick from the recipes in my initial test and gradually reduced the amount of sugar, pie by pie, until I was using not much more than half of what many recipes call for. (Thoroughbred pies by definition don't call for liquid sweeten-ers like corn syrup or molasses.) Next, I did side-by-side tests of pies made using all white sugar, all brown sugar, and a combination (other recipes went in all directions). Brown sugar contributed a hint of spice and depth; more neu-tral white sugar ensured that the nuts

and the chocolate weren't eclipsed. Ultimately, I used a bit of both. The chocolate was also helping to push the sugar level into the stratosphere. To bring more balance, I replaced the semisweet chips with chopped bitter-sweet chocolate. (For more information on the differences between semisweet and bittersweet chocolate, see Ask Cook's Country on page 3.)

Now that I had a handle on the sugar, I could actually taste the other elements. For the first time I noticed that as the pie baked, the layer of walnuts that floated to the top got nice and crisp while those underneath were soggy and bland. So I toasted the nuts (stirring often in a skillet over medium heat for about 5 minutes) before stirring them into the filling, which kept them crisp no matter their location. At the same time, I went up to 1½ cups from the 1 cup called for in most recipes.

But the pie took a giant leap forward when I got the idea to brown the butter. When you brown butter—melting it in a skillet until the milk solids toast—you get a heady, nutty aroma and flavor. You can stop the process when the butter turns golden, but I took it a step further, cooking the butter to a light brown. Now the pie tasted deeply nutty.

The top of my pie had none of the appealing faint crunch that we'd tasted in the trademarked pie. Our science editor gave me a couple of helpful hints: Increase the carbohydrates and decrease the protein. In plain English: I switched the flour (which contains protein) that I'd been using for thickener to cornstarch (which is a carbohydrate). At the same time, I lost an egg white (protein again, and also moist, so it was softening the top) and tested a pie with two whole eggs plus one yolk. Right on cue, that distinctive sugary crunch presented itself.

To avoid underbaking, many pie recipes require parbaking the crusts. But doing so would require that I refrigerate and then freeze the shell to keep it from shrinking, slumping, and toughening, all before I even turned on the oven. Hoping to avoid these steps, I tried a favorite test kitchen method: starting the pie on a low shelf in a very hot oven to take advantage of the blast of heat from the bottom of the oven, then immediately lowering the heat to bake the pie through.

Unfortunately, while this method succeeds beautifully for pecan pie, thoroughbred pie simply didn't stay in the oven long enough for it to work. I made my peace with blind baking. As

I was taking a warm, golden, parbaked shell from the oven, I got a good idea. I sprinkled the chopped chocolate over the still-warm crust, where it gently melted. I spread the softened chocolate evenly over the bottom crust. Now the pie had a flavorful, browned crust plus a hit of intense chocolate in every bite— an improvement on the usual random smattering of chips.

I baked one last pie. Its delicately crisp top layer contrasted nicely with the soft yet nutty center, and the whole pie had layers of flavor. I called tasters over and watched happily as slices left the gate as fast as any Churchill Downs thoroughbred.

THOROUGHBRED PIE Serves 8

Use your favorite pie dough or go to CooksCountry.com/extra for our Single Crust Pie Dough recipe.

- 1 (9-inch) unbaked pie shell
- 3 ounces bittersweet chocolate, chopped fine
- 8 tablespoons (1 stick) unsalted butter, cut into 8 pieces
- 3 tablespoons bourbon
- ¾ cup granulated sugar
- ½ cup packed light brown sugar
- 2 tablespoons cornstarch
- ½ teaspoon salt
- 2 large eggs plus 1 yolk, lightly beaten
- 1 teaspoon vanilla extract
- 1½ cups walnuts, toasted and chopped

1. Cover pie shell with plastic wrap and refrigerate 40 minutes, then freeze 20 minutes. Adjust oven rack to lower-middle position and heat oven to 375 degrees. Line chilled pie shell with two 12-inch squares parchment paper, letting parchment hang over edges of dough. Top with pie weights and bake until surface of dough no longer looks wet, 20 to 25 minutes.

2. Remove pie from oven and reduce oven temperature to 325 degrees. Carefully remove parchment and weights and sprinkle chocolate over bottom of hot crust. Let sit 5 minutes, then spread chocolate into even layer; set aside.

3. Melt butter in small saucepan over medium-low heat. Cook, stirring constantly, until butter is nutty brown, 5 to 7 minutes. Off heat, slowly stir in bourbon (mixture will bubble strongly) and let cool 5 minutes.

4. Whisk granulated sugar, brown sugar, cornstarch, and salt in large bowl until combined. Add eggs, yolk, and vanilla, whisking until smooth. Slowly whisk in warm butter mixture until incorporated. Stir in walnuts and pour filling into chocolate-lined crust. Bake until filling is puffed and center jiggles slightly when pie is gently shaken, 35 to 40 minutes. Cool on wire rack 4 hours. Serve with Bourbon Whipped Cream. (Pie can be refrigerated, covered, for 2 days.)

TEST KITCHEN TECHNIQUE Keys to Blue-Ribbon Thoroughbred Pie Crust
Our chill, freeze, and weight method of blind-baking prevents the crust from slumping. For chocolate in every bite, we spread softened chocolate over the entire bottom.

1. COOL IT
Refrigerate the unbaked crust for 40 minutes, then freeze it for 20 more.

2. BAKE IT
Line the chilled crust with parchment paper, fill with pie weights, and bake.

3. LINE IT
Sprinkle chopped chocolate on the warm crust, then spread it evenly.

Getting to Know Asian Vegetables

Asian vegetables used to be relegated to ethnic markets—if you could find them at all. Now many sit alongside the carrots and tomatoes at ordinary supermarkets. Here's how to store, cook, and enjoy some of our favorites.

Shiitake Mushrooms
NATURAL SPONGE

We prize shiitakes for their earthy-sweet flavor and pleasantly chewy texture. Like many other types of mushrooms, they act like a sponge, soaking up the flavor of sauces and dressings. That's why we particularly like them in stir-fries and salads, although you can also use them in place of white mushrooms in many recipes. However you cook with them, remove the woody stems first (unless they are very fresh and tender).

Daikon
MEGA RADISH

Dai means "big" in Japanese, and this bulbous Japanese radish lives up to its name: It can grow to be well over a foot long. (A common insult in Japan is to compare a woman's stocky legs to daikon.) Daikon tastes more sweet than spicy, with a "peppery finish" and a texture like that of water chestnuts. You may know daikon as the small, white (raw, grated) pile on your sushi plate. You can also stir-fry or pickle it.

Lotus Root
PRETTY ON THE INSIDE

Lotus root is not a root at all. Rather, it's the underwater stem (or rhizome) of the lotus plant. It looks like a fat, cream-colored sausage until you cut into it—surprise! The pretty pattern of circles makes each slice look like a snowflake. Our tasters noted the root's "slippery but crisp" texture and its "subtle mushroom" flavor. Lotus root should be peeled before stir-frying, boiling, braising, steaming, or deep-frying.

Bamboo Shoots
FRESH IS BEST

Fresh bamboo shoots taste a little like crunchy asparagus. To prepare them, peel off the outer leaves and parboil the shoots for 20 minutes in an uncovered pan so compounds that cause bitterness in the shoots can dissipate. Then slice the shoots and add them to soups and dumplings. Avoid canned bamboo shoots, which have little flavor—and what flavor there is tinny.

Chinese Broccoli
MUSTARD POWER

Like traditional broccoli, Chinese broccoli (sold as *gai lan* in Asian markets) is a member of the mustard family. It resembles broccoli rabe. We boil or steam it—in order to cook the thick stems—before sautéing it with seasonings (commonly garlic, ginger, and chiles). Our tasters found it "somehow both sweeter and more bitter" than ordinary broccoli.

Chinese Eggplant
KISSING COUSINS

Chinese eggplants are sweeter than the more familiar globe eggplants, and their skin is thinner. Despite these differences, you can usually use them interchangeably, although Chinese eggplant's slender shape makes it a poor candidate for stuffing or use in eggplant Parmesan. Salting and draining is unnecessary with Chinese eggplants, which are mild. Slice them lengthwise and grill or quickly braise; slice them crosswise and sauté.

Bok Choy
CHINESE CABBAGE

Bok choy has crisp, juicy stalks and leafy greens. When cooked (bok choy is usually stir-fried or quickly braised), the stalks become creamy, with an underlying sweetness, while the leaves soften; what our tasters call its "earthy, robust" flavor brings to mind chard. To evenly cook bok choy, separate the stalks and greens and give the former a head start. With baby bok choy, you can cook both at once.

Napa Cabbage
PICKLE PARTNER

Napa cabbage is milder and slightly sweeter than ordinary green cabbage. It's delicious raw or cooked; you can use it in place of regular cabbage in most recipes. Koreans use it for kimchi, a fiery fermented condiment; other Asian nations also pickle it. We like napa cabbage in soups, dumplings, stir-fries, braises, or Asian-flavored slaws.

Snow Peas
STIR-FRY SWEETHEART

Both the pea and the pod are edible—hence the French name *mange-tout* ("Eat it all"). Snow peas are crunchy, slightly sweet, and delicious. When shopping, pick up a pea and try to bend it until it breaks: Fresh peas will snap cleanly. Snap off the stem end and remove the string before eating snow peas raw, or stir-fry them quickly. If you overcook them, their nice crunch will disappear.

Edamame
JAPANESE BAR FOOD

Beer-drinking Japanese snack on boiled, heavily salted edamame in much the way we eat peanuts. And like peanuts, edamame, which are fresh soybeans, taste "nutty." Our tasters also noted their "firm, dense texture." Sold fresh or frozen, edamame should be boiled in their pods, then salted and eaten out of hand, in salads, or mixed into stir-fries or rice dishes. (But don't eat the fibrous, fuzzy pod.)

Mung Bean Sprouts
SEVENTIES HIT

Although the Chinese have cultivated them for thousands of years, in this country, mung bean sprouts gained popularity during the health food craze of the 1970s, finding their way into sandwiches and many a stir-fry. Asians use them in egg rolls, in soups, or to top such dishes as pad thai. Cook sprouts quickly to maintain their snappy crunch and use them quickly. They don't store well.

Long Beans
LANKY LEGUME

These skinny, dense beans can grow to nearly three feet in length and are often sold in coiled, knotted ropes. Our tasters reported that they are more pliable than string beans, with a "mellow earthiness" and a "meaty, slightly chewy" texture. Cut into lengths, they are a traditional choice in Asian stir-fries and braises, but they can also be blanched or steamed like "regular" green beans.

LINGUINE WITH CHICKEN AND MUSHROOMS

FLANK STEAK WITH HERBED POTATOES
AND GREEN BEANS

PAN-SEARED HALIBUT WITH ARUGULA-BASIL AIOLI

TEX-MEX CHICKEN AND RICE

FLANK STEAK WITH HERBED POTATOES AND GREEN BEANS
Serves 4

WHY THIS RECIPE WORKS: A vinaigrette made with red wine vinegar and mustard doubles as marinade for the steak and dressing for the salad.

- 2 medium Yukon Gold potatoes, scrubbed and sliced ¼ inch thick
- 7 tablespoons olive oil
- 1 flank steak (about 1½ pounds)
  Salt and pepper
- 3 tablespoons red wine vinegar
- 1 tablespoon Dijon mustard
- 8 ounces green beans, trimmed and cut into 2-inch pieces
- 1 shallot, minced
- 2 tablespoons finely chopped fresh parsley
- 2 tablespoons finely chopped fresh dill

1. Toss potatoes and 1 tablespoon oil in large bowl and wrap tightly with plastic wrap. Microwave until potatoes are translucent, 4 to 7 minutes, shaking bowl (without removing plastic) to redistribute halfway through cooking. Drain well.

2. Pat steak dry with paper towels and season with salt and pepper. Combine vinegar and mustard in medium bowl. Slowly whisk in 5 tablespoons oil. Coat steak with 2 tablespoons vinaigrette. Heat remaining oil in large skillet over medium-high heat until just smoking. Cook steak until well browned, 5 to 7 minutes per side. Transfer to cutting board and tent with foil.

3. Cook potatoes and beans in now-empty skillet over medium heat until browned and tender, about 5 minutes. Off heat, stir in remaining vinaigrette, shallot, parsley, and dill. Season with salt and pepper. Slice steak thinly against grain. Serve with potato and bean salad.

TEST KITCHEN NOTE: You can use tarragon or chives in place of the dill.

LINGUINE WITH CHICKEN AND MUSHROOMS Serves 4 to 6
WHY THIS RECIPE WORKS: Sautéed cubed chicken and quartered mushrooms add flavor and heft to this hearty pasta.

- 8 slices prosciutto (about 4 ounces), chopped
- ⅓ cup pine nuts
- 4 boneless, skinless chicken breasts (about 1½ pounds), cut into 1-inch pieces
  Salt and pepper
- 4 tablespoons unsalted butter
- 10 ounces cremini mushrooms, quartered
- 3 garlic cloves, minced
- ¼ cup white wine
- 1 pound linguine
- 4 cups baby spinach

1. Bring 4 quarts water to boil in large pot. Toast prosciutto and pine nuts in large skillet over medium heat, stirring frequently, until nuts are golden and prosciutto is crisp, about 5 minutes; set aside. Pat chicken dry with paper towels and season with salt and pepper. Melt 1 tablespoon butter in now-empty skillet over medium-high heat. Cook half of chicken until no longer pink, 3 to 5 minutes. Transfer to plate. Repeat with additional 1 tablespoon butter and remaining chicken.

2. Cook mushrooms, remaining butter, ½ teaspoon salt, and ¼ teaspoon pepper in now-empty skillet until browned, 6 to 8 minutes. Add garlic and cook until fragrant, about 30 seconds. Stir in wine and simmer until reduced to 1 tablespoon, about 1 minute.

3. Meanwhile, add 1 tablespoon salt and pasta to boiling water and cook until al dente. Reserve 1 cup cooking water. Drain pasta and return to pot. Stir in chicken, spinach, mushrooms, and ½ cup reserved water, adding additional reserved water as needed. Add nuts and prosciutto. Serve.

TEX-MEX CHICKEN AND RICE Serves 4
WHY THIS RECIPE WORKS: We precook the rice in the microwave to help get this skillet supper on the table in 30 minutes.

- 1½ cups low-sodium chicken broth
- 1 cup long-grain white rice
  Salt and pepper
- 4 boneless, skinless chicken breasts (about 1½ pounds)
- 1 tablespoon vegetable oil
- 1 (10-ounce) can Ro-Tel tomatoes
- 1 (16-ounce) can black beans, drained and rinsed
- 3 cups Fritos, crushed
- 1 cup shredded Mexican cheese blend
- ⅓ cup finely chopped fresh cilantro

1. Adjust oven rack to upper-middle position and heat broiler. Combine 1 cup broth, rice, and ½ teaspoon salt in large bowl. Cover with plastic and microwave until liquid is absorbed, 6 to 8 minutes. Pat chicken dry with paper towels and season with salt and pepper. Heat oil in large ovensafe skillet over medium-high heat until just smoking. Cook chicken until golden brown, about 3 minutes per side. Transfer to plate.

2. Add remaining broth, rice, tomatoes, and beans to now-empty skillet and bring to boil. Return chicken and juices to skillet and cook, covered, over medium-low heat until chicken is cooked through and rice is tender, 12 to 15 minutes. Transfer chicken to cutting board and tent with foil. Let rest 5 minutes, then cut into ½-inch slices. Meanwhile, let rice mixture stand, covered, for 5 minutes. Combine Fritos, cheese, and cilantro in bowl. Stir chicken and juices into rice mixture. Sprinkle Frito mixture over chicken-rice mixture and broil until golden, 2 to 3 minutes. Serve.

TEST KITCHEN NOTE: Ro-Tel tomatoes have chiles added: If you can't find them, substitute 1 cup diced tomatoes and 1 diced jalapeño.

PAN-SEARED HALIBUT WITH ARUGULA-BASIL AIOLI Serves 4
WHY THIS RECIPE WORKS: Classic aioli is a garlicky mayonnaise. We've added a twist with peppery arugula, tart lemon, and fragrant basil.

- ¾ cup finely chopped arugula
- ½ cup mayonnaise
- ¼ cup finely chopped fresh basil
- 1 teaspoon grated zest plus 1 tablespoon juice from 1 lemon
- 1 garlic clove, minced
  Salt and pepper
- ½ cup all-purpose flour
- 4 skinless halibut fillets (about 6 ounces each), about 1 inch thick
- 2 tablespoons vegetable oil

1. Combine arugula, mayonnaise, basil, lemon zest, lemon juice, garlic, ¼ teaspoon salt, and ¼ teaspoon pepper in medium bowl.

2. Place flour in shallow dish. Pat fish dry with paper towels and season with salt and pepper. Coat fish lightly with flour. Heat oil in large nonstick skillet over medium-high heat until just smoking. Cook fish until golden and thickest part of fillets flake easily, 6 to 8 minutes. Serve, passing aioli at table.

TEST KITCHEN NOTE: To prevent the raw garlic from overpowering the aioli, use a medium-size clove, yielding about 1 teaspoon when minced.

FARMHOUSE CHICKEN CHOWDER

HONEY MUSTARD CRUMB-COATED PORK CUTLETS

ROASTED RED PEPPER SHRIMP AND PASTA SALAD

MINUTE STEAKS WITH PAN GRAVY

HONEY MUSTARD CRUMB-COATED PORK CUTLETS Serves 4

WHY THIS RECIPE WORKS: Instead of making a sauce, we add flavor early on by seasoning the egg wash with honey and mustard.

- ½ cup all-purpose flour
- ¼ cup coarse-grain mustard
- 2 tablespoons honey
- 1 large egg
- 1¼ cups panko bread crumbs
- 1 large pork tenderloin (about 1 pound), cut into 4 equal pieces and pounded ¼ inch thick
  Salt and pepper
- ½ cup vegetable oil

1. Adjust oven rack to middle position and heat oven to 200 degrees. Place flour in shallow dish. Beat mustard, honey, and egg in second shallow dish. Place bread crumbs in third shallow dish.

2. Pat cutlets dry with paper towels and season with salt and pepper. One at a time, coat cutlets lightly with flour, dip in egg mixture, and dredge in bread crumbs, pressing to adhere. Transfer pork to platter and let rest 5 minutes.

3. Heat ¼ cup oil in large nonstick skillet over medium-high heat until just smoking. Cook 2 cutlets until golden, about 3 minutes per side. Transfer to wire rack set inside rimmed baking sheet and keep warm in oven. Wipe out skillet with paper towels and repeat with remaining oil and remaining cutlets. Serve.

TEST KITCHEN NOTE: After cutting the tenderloin into equal pieces, stand each piece on a cut side before pounding to ¼ inch thickness.

FARMHOUSE CHICKEN CHOWDER Serves 4

WHY THIS RECIPE WORKS: Rotisserie chicken is the key to streamlining this hearty soup.

- 6 slices bacon, chopped
- 6 scallions, white parts chopped fine and green parts sliced thin
- 2 carrots, peeled and sliced thin
- 1 celery rib, sliced thin
  Salt and pepper
- 6 tablespoons all-purpose flour
- 5 cups low-sodium chicken broth
- 1 pound red potatoes, scrubbed and cut into ½-inch pieces
- 1 rotisserie chicken, skin discarded, meat shredded into bite-size pieces (about 3 cups)
- 1 cup half-and-half

1. Cook bacon in Dutch oven over medium heat until crisp, about 8 minutes. Using slotted spoon, transfer bacon to paper towel–lined plate. Pour off all but 1 tablespoon fat from pot. Cook scallion whites, carrots, celery, and ½ teaspoon salt in bacon fat until vegetables are softened, about 5 minutes. Add flour and cook until golden, 1 to 2 minutes.

2. Stir in broth and potatoes and bring to boil. Reduce heat to medium-low and simmer, covered, until vegetables are tender, 10 to 12 minutes. Add chicken and half-and-half and simmer until chicken is heated through, about 2 minutes. Season with salt and pepper. Sprinkle with bacon and scallion greens. Serve.

TEST KITCHEN NOTE: For a richer soup, use cream instead of half-and-half.

MINUTE STEAKS WITH PAN GRAVY Serves 4

WHY THIS RECIPE WORKS: Pounding the steaks to ¼ inch thickness guarantees quick, even cooking.

- ¾ cup plus 1 tablespoon all-purpose flour
- 1 teaspoon garlic powder
  Salt and pepper
- 4 cube steaks (about 6 ounces each), pounded ¼ inch thick
- 3 tablespoons vegetable oil
- 2 tablespoons unsalted butter
- 1 small onion, chopped fine
- 1 cup beef broth
- 1 tablespoon Worcestershire sauce
- ¼ teaspoon dried thyme

1. Adjust oven rack to middle position and heat oven to 200 degrees. Combine ¾ cup flour, garlic powder, 1 teaspoon salt, and 1 teaspoon pepper in shallow dish. Pat steaks dry with paper towels. One at a time, dredge steaks in flour. Transfer steaks to platter and let rest 5 minutes.

2. Heat 1½ tablespoons oil in large nonstick skillet over medium-high heat until just smoking. Add 2 steaks and cook until well browned, 2 to 3 minutes per side. Transfer to wire rack set inside rimmed baking sheet and keep warm in oven. Repeat with remaining oil and remaining steaks.

3. Melt butter in now-empty skillet over medium heat. Add onion and cook until softened, about 5 minutes. Stir in remaining flour and cook until golden, about 1 minute. Add broth, Worcestershire, and thyme and simmer (scraping up any browned bits) until slightly thickened, about 3 minutes. Season with salt and pepper. Pour gravy over steaks. Serve.

TEST KITCHEN NOTE: Don't be put off by cube steak's mottled appearance. These steaks are machine tenderized.

ROASTED RED PEPPER SHRIMP AND PASTA SALAD Serves 4

WHY THIS RECIPE WORKS: To save time and dishes, we cook the pasta, shrimp, and asparagus all in the same pot.

- Salt and pepper
- 12 ounces rotini pasta
- 2 pounds extra-large (21 to 25 per pound) shrimp, peeled, deveined, and tails discarded
- 1 pound asparagus, trimmed and cut into 1-inch pieces
- ¾ cup crumbled feta cheese
- ½ cup mayonnaise
- ½ cup drained jarred roasted red peppers, chopped
- 2 teaspoons grated zest plus 2 tablespoons juice from 1 lemon
- 1 garlic clove, minced
- 1 pint grape or cherry tomatoes, halved

1. Fill large bowl with ice water. Bring 4 quarts water to boil in large pot. Add 1 tablespoon salt and pasta to boiling water and cook until nearly al dente, 6 to 8 minutes. Add shrimp and asparagus and simmer until cooked through, about 2 minutes. Reserve ¼ cup cooking water. Drain pasta mixture, then transfer to ice bath. Once cool, drain again and pat dry with paper towels.

2. Meanwhile, process feta and reserved hot water in food processor until combined. Add mayonnaise, roasted peppers, lemon zest, lemon juice, garlic, ½ teaspoon salt, and ½ teaspoon pepper and process until smooth. Stir dressing into pasta mixture. Add tomatoes and toss to combine. Season with salt and pepper. Serve.

TEST KITCHEN NOTE: Feta cheese sold in blocks is better quality than the pre-crumbled variety.

Chicken Bonne Femme

This classic Creole dish has great flavors and plenty of down-home appeal. For today's cook, though, it also has too many steps and way too much fat. We figured we could fix that. BY ADAM RIED

CHICKEN BONNE FEMME, a Creole classic combining browned chicken with bacon, onions, garlic, and potatoes, has an honored place in Louisiana's culinary repertoire. But while its name suggests the home kitchen—bonne femme, or "good woman," once referred to dishes made by housewives rather than by chefs—the way we cook at home today has changed considerably since this dish first saw the light of day.

The differences became clear after I cooked five promising chicken bonne femme recipes. Most were deathly rich, some containing a full pound of bacon (with directions to use all the fat) plus 2 sticks of butter—for six servings. And although the dish calls for few ingredients, most versions were complicated and time-consuming to prepare, requiring that we butcher the chicken(s) and dredge and fry the pieces, then fry the potatoes, then make the sauce, and then, finally, combine the three. Two hours and a mountain of dishes later, dinner was served. Clearly, I needed to slim down and speed up this Creole stalwart while keeping its basic flavors and homey appeal intact.

First, I tackled the procedure. Looking to turn this into an easy, one-pot wonder, I immediately ruled out frying the chicken and potatoes separately. My thoughts turned to braising, which would allow me to brown the chicken and potatoes sequentially, finish cooking them in a bit of liquid, and then make the sauce from that flavorful liquid, all in the same pot.

The decision to braise rather than fry the chicken pointed me toward chicken thighs, which are moist, rich, and stand up well to long, slow cooking. Next, I had to decide between skinless and skin-on. I knew the skin would protect the outer layer of meat from drying out during browning, a procedure that was essential to the dish's flavor. But I also knew that the rendered skin would lose its crispness in the braising liquid. Eventually, I worked out a compromise by browning the thighs skin-on, then removing the skin before braising. The bits left in the pan during browning, plus the fat rendered from the skin, gave me the flavor I wanted without any leathery skin in the finished dish.

Bacon is a key flavor in bonne femme, but the pound required by many recipes is overkill. I made batches reducing the quantity slice by slice until I reached a reasonable five slices, which provided plenty of smoky-sweet richness. Turning to the potatoes, I was surprised that only a few recipes specified a particular type, so I tried high-starch russets, medium-starch Yukon Golds and "all-purpose," as well as low-starch baby red-skinned potatoes. The red-skinned potatoes stood up best to braising, becoming tender and creamy without breaking down.

Last up was the sauce. The rather greasy, flour-thickened sauces I encountered in the original recipes would have to go; I pictured a lighter version that would be easy to build from the pan drippings left after browning the chicken. I added dry white wine to counter the rich bacon, then poured in a little chicken broth to balance the wine. On top of the onion and a healthy four cloves of garlic, I added fresh thyme, hot sauce, scallions, and parsley to bolster my bonne femme's Creole credentials.

Modernized but not wimpified, this chicken bonne femme is just right for a home kitchen on a busy weeknight.

CHICKEN BONNE FEMME
Serves 4 to 6
To ensure even cooking and browning, use baby red potatoes no larger than 1½ inches round.

- 3 **pounds bone-in, skin-on chicken thighs, excess fat trimmed**
  Salt and pepper
- 5 **slices bacon, chopped**
- 1½ **pounds baby red potatoes, scrubbed and halved**
- 1 **onion, chopped fine**
- 4 **garlic cloves, minced**
- 2 **teaspoons minced fresh thyme**
- ¾ **cup white wine**
- ½ **cup low-sodium chicken broth**
- 1 **teaspoon hot sauce**
- 3 **scallions, sliced thin**
- 2 **tablespoons chopped fresh parsley**

1. Pat chicken dry with paper towels and season with salt and pepper. Cook bacon in Dutch oven over medium heat until crisp, about 8 minutes. Using slotted spoon, transfer bacon to paper towel–lined plate. Pour off all but 1 tablespoon fat from pot. Heat bacon fat over medium-high heat until just smoking. Cook chicken until well browned all over, about 10 minutes; transfer to plate. When chicken is cool enough to handle, remove and discard skin.

2. Pour off all but 1½ tablespoons fat from pot. Arrange potatoes, cut-side down, in pot and cook over medium heat until golden brown, about 10 minutes. Stir in onion and cook until softened, about 5 minutes. Add garlic and thyme and cook until fragrant, about 30 seconds. Stir in wine, broth, half of bacon, and hot sauce and bring to boil.

3. Return chicken and any accumulated juices to pot. Reduce heat to medium-low and cook, covered, until potatoes are tender and meat registers 175 degrees, about 25 minutes. Sprinkle with scallions, parsley, and remaining bacon. Season with salt and pepper. Serve.

This deeply seasoned chicken braise is flavored with garlic, bacon, wine, and herbs.

Griddled Patty Melts

This big burger with caramelized onions and Swiss cheese on rye is a diner classic.
So can you make it without a flat-top griddle and a skilled short-order cook? BY JEREMY SAUER

There's nothing fancy about patty melts: juicy burgers smothered with sweet onions and gooey cheese, all sandwiched between buttery griddled rye bread. In your local diner, a patty melt is ready five minutes after you order it. But without a big griddle, a tray of caramelized onions on the back burner, and the practiced hand of a short-order cook, making patty melts at home can become an hours-long odyssey. Sorry, but even one hour is too long for burgers, however tasty. I set out to streamline the process.

The big problem is that the meat is cooked twice: It's first browned in butter, then cooked a second time as the sandwich is griddled. It's no surprise that this double-cooking can result in burgers with the texture of dried-up hockey pucks. To compensate, I tried slightly undercooking the patties in a skillet, then piling on the cheese and onions and letting the meat finish cooking while the bread was grilling. But the results were unpredictable: The patties came out overdone and dry as often as they came out perfect.

To improve my odds, I employed a technique the test kitchen often uses to keep burgers, meatloaf, and meatballs moist: mixing a panade (or paste) of milk and bread into the raw meat. The paste keeps even well-done meat moist. While I was at it, I'd use the panade to bump up the flavor. At diners, patty melts get depth of flavor from onions that simmer and steam for hours on the flat-top. At home, my patty melts were wan. To reinforce their rye and onion flavors, I used rye bread and onion powder in the panade. These patties tasted positively robust.

Soft, sweet onions play an essential role in patty melts. Unfortunately, caramelizing onions can take close to

Our novel cooking method maximizes flavor transfer between the beef and the onions.

an hour—I needed a way to enrich and soften them more quickly. To boost their flavor, I cooked them in the flavorful patty drippings. The taste, but not the timing, improved. I tried covering the skillet, and although the trapped steam did help the onions soften in just 15 minutes, it also washed out their flavor. Could I use the patties themselves to partly cover the onions and speed their cooking? I browned the patties on one side and then set them aside. I added the onions to the pan and

let them get started in the burger fat for a good 10 minutes. Then I put the burgers on top of them (browned side up) to almost finish cooking; I wanted to slightly undercook them at this stage. As I'd hoped, the patties trapped some, but not all, of the steam, accelerating the softening without diluting the onion flavor. And the flavor exchange between the meat and onions was significant: The onions took on big, meaty taste while the beef was perfumed with awesome oniony flavor.

Once the onions were tender and the meat just cooked through, I sandwiched each patty and a pile of onions between slices of Swiss and rye. Working two at a time, I toasted the melts in melted butter in a skillet. Now I had four crisp, buttery melts with juicy, well-seasoned patties, but where was the cheese? We could barely taste it. Thicker slices didn't melt quickly enough. Shredded cheese, however, melted easily, and with ½ cup per sandwich, there was no question that the cheese had joined the party.

PATTY MELTS Serves 4

To make sure the melts hold together, use rye bread that's sliced about ½ inch thick.

- 10 slices hearty rye sandwich bread
- 2 tablespoons whole milk
- ¾ teaspoon onion powder
- 1¼ teaspoons salt
- ½ teaspoon pepper
- 1½ pounds 85 percent lean ground beef
- 3 tablespoons unsalted butter
- 2 onions, halved and sliced thin
- 2 cups shredded Swiss cheese

1. Adjust oven rack to middle position and heat oven to 200 degrees. Tear 2 pieces of bread into ½-inch pieces. Using potato masher, mash torn bread, milk, onion powder, ¾ teaspoon salt, and pepper in large bowl until smooth. Add beef and gently knead until well combined. Divide meat into 4 equal portions. Following photo 2, shape each portion into 6 by 4-inch oval.

2. Melt 1 tablespoon butter in large nonstick skillet over medium-high heat. Cook 2 patties until well browned on first side, about 5 minutes. Transfer to large plate, browned-side up, and repeat with remaining patties.

3. Pour off all but 1 teaspoon fat from pan. Add onions and ½ teaspoon salt and cook, stirring occasionally, until golden brown, 8 to 10 minutes. Arrange patties, browned-side up, on top of onions, pouring any accumulated juices into pan. Reduce heat to medium and cook, shaking pan occasionally, until onions are tender and burgers are cooked through, about 5 minutes.

4. Divide 1 cup cheese among 4 slices bread. Top with patties, onions, remaining cheese, and remaining bread. Wipe out skillet with paper towels. Melt 1 tablespoon butter in now-empty skillet over medium heat. Cook 2 sandwiches until golden brown and cheese is melted, 3 to 4 minutes per side. Transfer to rimmed baking sheet and keep warm in oven. Repeat with remaining butter and remaining sandwiches. Serve.

KEY STEPS Patty Melts at Home

1. USE RYE IN BURGERS
The burgers are twice cooked, so use a panade to keep them moist. To boost the flavor, use rye bread in the panade.

2. SHAPE INTO OVALS
Form the patties into ovals that mirror the shape of the rye slices to avoid those disappointing bites of sandwich without any meat.

3. COOK OVER ONIONS
Brown one side of the patties. Cook the second side over the sizzling onions to maximize flavor exchange.

RATING ONE-HANDED PEPPER GRINDERS

One-handed pepper mills hold one obvious advantage over the usual two-handed twist styles: They free up the other hand to stir a sauce or turn a whole raw chicken for seasoning. One-handed pepper mills can cost well over $100: We set a ceiling of $50, which allowed us to include mills in many styles and sizes, both manual and electric. We put six to a range of tests (visit CooksCountry.com for the full results), focusing on the quality of each grind (from fine to coarse), the output of each mill (the efficiency in producing 1 teaspoon of ground pepper), and ease of use.

To win us over, any one-handed pepper grinder would have to match the output of our favorite two-handed mill, the Unicorn Magnum Plus, which produces plenty of perfectly ground pepper with minimal effort. Alas, only a few electric models and just one manual version matched the output of the Unicorn; the rest took twice as long, or longer, to produce the same amount. One electric model, the PepperMills Supreme ($39.95), produced uniformly ground pepper at five settings as quickly as our winning two-handed mill. And one manual model, the Chef'n Pepper Ball, proved easy to fill and adjust for different grinds, and it operated one-handed with no need for batteries or electricity. Neither model would compel us to retire our favorite Unicorn, but at just $11.95, the Chef'n Pepper Ball is worth picking up—with one hand, of course. BY AMY GRAVES

RECOMMENDED	CRITERIA		TESTERS' NOTES
CHEF'N Pepper Ball **Model:** 101-035-001 **Price:** $11.95 www.chefsresource.com	Ease of Use Grind Quality Output Design	★★★ ★★ ★★ ★★★	This sturdy, compact manual grinder gave us 1 teaspoon of ground pepper in just 45 seconds of easy squeezing. The clearly marked, easy-to-adjust grind mechanism yielded uniform-size pepper grinds in three textures—but only very coarse, coarse, and medium (not fine). 
PEPPERMILLS Supreme **Model:** 2000 **Price:** $39.95 www.peppermills.com	Ease of Use Grind Quality Output Design	★★ ★★★ ★★★ ★½	This large electric mill produced perfectly ground pepper in five textures from fine to coarse—and more of it more quickly than our favorite two-handed grinder. Although it's heavy, it was surprisingly easy to manipulate. It ran on one charge throughout testing; still, we'd rather not have to plug in our pepper mill.

RECOMMENDED WITH RESERVATIONS			
TRUDEAU Duo **Model:** 0716450 **Price:** $49.42 www.mycuisina.com	Ease of Use Grind Quality Output Design	★★½ ★★ ★★ ★★	This dual model grinds both salt and pepper quickly and proved easy to handle—once we mastered the trick of twisting it open to fill the battery chamber and hoppers. Changing grinds was straightforward. But there was a problem: Trace amounts of salt sometimes trickled down when we hit the button for pepper. 

NOT RECOMMENDED			
WILLIAM BOUNDS Titan Battery Pepper Mill **Model:** HM Titan **Price:** $49.95 www.cooking.com	Ease of Use Grind Quality Output Design	★★ ★ ★ ★	This battery-powered model looks impressive. But it took four times as long as our favorite manual model to grind a teaspoon of pepper, and holding down the grind button became taxing. Worse, a loose tracking mechanism both on the model and a replacement did not let us adjust the grind settings for anything other than coarse or fine. 
TRUDEAU Graviti **Model:** 0716900 **Price:** $26.95 www.cooking.com	Ease of Use Grind Quality Output Design	★ ★½ ★½ ½	This electric grinder turns on automatically whenever it is tipped just past 90 degrees, which had us scattering ground pepper around the test kitchen. It also lost points on grind quality: Whenever we tipped it upright, we could see bits of ground pepper filtering back into the hopper with the whole peppercorns. Finally, and fatally, its loud, whining grind sounds like a dentist's drill. 

Orange-Glazed Chicken

It may seem like the perfect weeknight dinner, but getting nicely rendered skin and plenty of orange flavor can take a little doing. BY MARÍA DEL MAR SACASA

TYPICALLY, RECIPES FOR orange-glazed chicken require searing bone-in, skin-on breasts in a skillet, roasting them in the oven, and then painting them with an orangey glaze to finish. That approach wins points for simplicity but loses them when judged on flavor or texture. As I learned when I road-tested several recipes, the chicken can suffer from painfully sweet glazes, soggy and/or chewy skin, dry meat, and superficial orange flavor. I was looking for nicely rendered skin, juicy meat, and balanced, fresh orange flavor—all while staying in the realm of the uncomplicated and quick.

To begin, I stirred together a basic glaze (a quickly reduced mixture of orange juice and sugar) based on those in my test recipes; I'd perfect mine later. I then got to work on technique. Rather than simply searing the breasts (skin side down, of course), I dredged the breasts in cornstarch to help them crisp. I poured the glaze over the chicken and stuck the pan in the oven for 30 minutes. The results were fine but not fantastic: The meat was a tad dry, the skin a tad chewy. I knew I could do better.

Do you remember chicken under a brick? I suddenly did. For this technique, a whole chicken is butterflied, so that it lies flat, and then weighted with a brick while it cooks. The weight presses out the fat, and the skin crisps up and gets a serious tan. Also, the flattened chicken cooks quicker—a bonus on a weeknight. The test kitchen has sometimes mimicked the technique by weighting chicken with a large, heavy pot. I tried it, placing a Dutch oven on top of the browning breasts. Then I removed the Dutch oven, flipped the chicken, added the glaze, and baked. The skin had rendered nicely and was in no way chewy.

A few days later, I was headed toward the oven with some browned chicken when I suddenly wondered if baking was really necessary. I switched course and let the chicken finish cooking on the stovetop. It was ready in less than 10 minutes, and the skin, I am happy to report, was as crisp as a fall day.

I turned to getting orange flavor into the bird. I figured I'd brine (soak in saltwater) to kill two birds with one stone, so to speak: increasing both flavor and moisture in the chicken. But replacing the water in the brine with orange juice produced chicken with absolutely

It takes both juice and zest to create a bold yet balanced orange glaze.

no orange flavor. Stumped, I added lots of (powerful) orange zest to the brine and tried again, but I can't say it helped. It finally occurred to me to process the salt with the zest before dissolving it in water. Processing zest releases its flavorful oils, which the salt then carries into the meat. This time, the chicken drank up the orange flavor.

The glaze was but a minute's work: I set aside the chicken pieces, discarded the fat from the skillet, and poured in orange juice, more zest, cornstarch (to thicken), sugar, and a touch of cayenne. I returned the chicken, skin side up, to the skillet and let the glaze thicken and the chicken absorb a final bit of flavor. Just before serving the chicken, I gave the pieces a quick turn—enough to coat them with the bright, flavorful glaze but not so much that I'd wilt the skin I'd worked so hard to crisp.

TEST KITCHEN TECHNIQUE
Press for Success
For well-rendered chicken skin that can stand up to a glaze, we set a weight (a foil-lined Dutch oven) on the chicken as it browned. It flattened the breasts and helped press out the fat.

ORANGE-GLAZED CHICKEN
Serves 4
The fat will render best if you pat the chicken thoroughly dry after you remove it from the brine.

- 3 tablespoons grated zest plus ½ cup juice from 3 to 4 oranges
- 2 tablespoons sugar
- 1 teaspoon cornstarch
- ⅛ teaspoon cayenne pepper
- ¼ cup salt
- 1 quart water
- 4 bone-in, skin-on, split chicken breasts (about 3 pounds), ribs removed and halved crosswise
- 1 tablespoon vegetable oil

1. Whisk orange juice, ½ teaspoon orange zest, sugar, cornstarch, and cayenne in medium bowl until no lumps remain; set aside. Process salt and remaining zest in food processor until finely ground. Whisk water and orange salt in large bowl until salt dissolves. Add chicken and refrigerate, covered, for 30 minutes or up to 1 hour.

2. Cover bottom of Dutch oven with aluminum foil. Remove chicken from brine and discard brine. Pat chicken dry with paper towels. Heat oil in large non-stick skillet over medium-high heat until just smoking. Place chicken skin-side down in skillet and weight with prepared Dutch oven. Cook until very well browned and crisp, 10 to 15 minutes. Remove pot and flip chicken skin-side up. Reduce heat to medium and cook until meat registers 160 degrees, 5 to 10 minutes. Transfer chicken to plate and let rest 5 minutes.

3. Pour off fat from pan and discard. Add orange juice mixture to now-empty skillet and bring to boil over medium heat. Return chicken, skin-side up, and any accumulated juices to skillet and simmer until sauce is thick and glossy, 2 to 3 minutes. Turn chicken to coat. Serve.

DIY Orange Salt
Processing orange zest with the salt for the brine breaks down the zest and releases the fruit's natural oils. The orange flavor enters the chicken meat with the brine.

Miracle Carrots

We rediscover an old technique for cooking carrots without any liquid whatsoever. Can it possibly work? BY DIANE UNGER

CARROTS ARE ALWAYS on my Easter table, right next to the ham, asparagus, and a lemon dessert of some sort. Over the years, I've glazed them with marmalade; simmered them with chicken stock, honey, and butter; and roasted them in a very hot oven. As I put together this year's holiday menu, I found myself thinking "been there, done that." That's when I remembered reading about an intriguing method for "waterless carrots." It's an adaptation of a French technique in which finely sliced, or "ribboned," carrots are cooked in a covered saucepan with butter, salt, pepper, and nothing else. While I liked the idea of a simple recipe showcasing the natural sweetness and earthiness of carrots, I admit I was skeptical. Was it possible to cook this hard root vegetable well with no liquid at all? I decided to find out.

Following an old recipe, I peeled and "scraped" 2 pounds of medium carrots with a vegetable peeler, into what resembled a pile of carrot ribbons. I put them in a saucepan with 4 tablespoons butter and the seasonings, and then covered the pot. After they'd cooked 10 minutes over low heat, I lifted the lid and was surprised to find the carrot ribbons simmering in very buttery, orange liquid. The salt was apparently drawing out the natural moisture as they cooked. I dipped a spoon into the carrot liquid and was delighted by its sweet, concentrated flavor. Unfortunately, the carrots themselves had cooked down into a greasy mound of vegetable mush.

For my next test, I abandoned the ribbons (they were labor intensive and, truth be told, a little too frou-frou for my tastes) and instead sliced the carrots into ¼-inch pennies. I also cut the butter back to 3 tablespoons—enough to coat the carrots without making them greasy. To speed things along, I started cooking them over medium heat. When steam began coming from the saucepan, indicating the carrots were producing their own liquid (after about 5 minutes), I reduced the heat to low and let them simmer in those juices until tender, 15 to 20 minutes more. Now I helped myself to a bowl: Utterly undiluted by any water or chicken broth, the sweet, pure carroty flavor was intense—and the very essence of

carrot. Some of the slices remained slightly crunchy, however, so I transferred the operations to a skillet for my next test. Spread out on the larger surface, the carrot pennies could cook more evenly.

At this point, the carrots were really good, especially considering that I'd hardly done any work. There was still carrot liquid left in the skillet, so I uncovered it and turned up the heat. As the carrot juices reduced and concentrated, the milk solids in the butter began to brown. What luck! The browning butter added an unexpected and utterly delicious, nutty, caramelized dimension to the dish.

These carrots were so naturally concentrated and sweet, they needed almost no seasoning: just a hit of fresh chive, and they tasted fantastic. Still, variety is the spice of life, and my tasters demanded some. I developed three simple variations. To one batch of carrots, I added sliced shallots and tarragon. To a second, I added freshly grated ginger and cilantro. And to a third, a bit of orange zest and parsley. I'd have gone on, but the magazine had to go to print. The technique is so simple that I'd urge all home cooks to come up with their own variations.

BUTTERED CARROTS
Serves 6 to 8

Slice the carrots as evenly as you can so they cook at the same rate.

- 3 tablespoons unsalted butter
- 2 pounds carrots, peeled and cut diagonally into ¼-inch-thick slices
  Salt and pepper
- 2 tablespoons finely chopped fresh chives

1. Melt butter in large skillet over medium heat. Add carrots and ½ teaspoon salt and cook, covered, until steam begins to escape from under the lid, about 5 minutes. Reduce heat to low and continue to cook covered, stirring occasionally, until carrots are just tender, 15 to 20 minutes.

2. Remove lid, add ¼ teaspoon pepper, and cook, stirring occasionally, until liquid is evaporated and butter begins to brown, about 5 minutes. Sprinkle with chives and season with salt and pepper. Serve.

These carrots taste deeply sweet and, well, carroty because they steam in their own juices with just a little butter.

BUTTERED CARROTS WITH GINGER AND CILANTRO
Prepare Buttered Carrots, adding 2 teaspoons grated fresh ginger with carrots in step 1. Replace chives with 1 tablespoon finely chopped fresh cilantro.

BUTTERED CARROTS WITH ORANGE AND PARSLEY
Prepare Buttered Carrots, adding 1 teaspoon grated orange zest with carrots in step 1. Replace chives with 1 tablespoon finely chopped fresh parsley.

BUTTERED CARROTS WITH SHALLOTS AND TARRAGON
Prepare Buttered Carrots, adding 2 peeled, thinly sliced shallots with carrots in step 1. Replace chives with 1 tablespoon finely chopped fresh tarragon.

Smothered Pork Chops

Smothered pork chops may sound like Grandma's best dish, but they often taste like dinner discards. Because no matter how you smother them, you can't hide badly cooked pork chops. BY ERIKA BRUCE

In the abstract, recipes for smothered pork chops sound utterly appealing: Generously season and sear bone-in chops and remove them from the skillet, fry lots of sliced onions in the fat, add flour and broth, return the chops to braise in the flavorful, oniony liquid for 30 minutes until tender, and reduce the liquid to a porky, full-bodied gravy. But the handful of recipes I tried were deeply disappointing. The chops, most commonly meaty rib or loin chops, were dry and tough, while the "gravy" was watery and bland. How could such a simple, straightforward recipe—a staple of Southern cooking, at that—fly so far off the rails?

How do you get these? Choose the right chops and the right seasoning, and figure out just the right time to thicken the rich onion gravy.

Getting smothered chops right meant starting with the right cut of pork. Bone-in chops were a must because I knew the bone would help keep the meat moist and add flavor to the sauce. Lean, meaty rib or loin chops are the standard choices for this dish, but in test after test (using a working recipe of 2 sautéed onions, ¼ cup flour, and a cup of chicken broth), lean chops came out dry and tough.

Most braised meats are fatty cuts that cook for hours; would fattier chops be less apt to dry out? I tried a batch with fattier blade chops and was happy when the meat emerged tender and moist—but it did take a full hour and a half. Since I was braising the pork for so long, the gentle, even heat of a 300-degree oven made more sense than the stovetop. Now that I had tender, succulent chops, I could work on the onions and sauce.

Given the mound of onions I started with, it surprised me how little they brought to the sauce. I tried caramelizing them before adding the broth, but this made the sauce too sweet (and took almost an hour). I had better luck cooking the onions in butter over medium heat until they were lightly browned. I further improved the sauce by using muscular beef broth instead of the wimpier chicken broth and adding dried thyme, a bay leaf, and a splash of cider vinegar. For even more pop, I seasoned the chops with a mixture of onion powder, paprika, and cayenne before searing. Now all three components—the chops, the sauce, and the onions—were boldly seasoned.

Although the sauce was nice and thick when the chops went into the oven, it wasn't always that way when the dish came out. During braising, the chops and onions gave up a lot of liquid. The hitch was that it was almost impossible to gauge exactly how much "a lot" was from batch to batch, which meant that sometimes I made perfect gravy but other times it was thin and washed out. For more reliable results, I tried waiting until the end and then thickened only the amount of sauce I needed for my chops (exactly 1 cup) with an easy cornstarch-and-broth slurry. Now the sauce consistency was consistently good.

I may have added an hour to the usual cooking time for smothered pork chop, but as I ladled the rich gravy over the moist, tender chops, I knew that it was time well spent.

SMOTHERED PORK CHOPS Serves 4

Chops thicker than ½ inch won't be fully tender in the allotted cooking time.

- 1 teaspoon onion powder
- ½ teaspoon paprika
  Salt and pepper
- ¼ teaspoon cayenne pepper
- 4 bone-in blade-cut pork chops, about ½ inch thick
- 1½ tablespoons vegetable oil
- 1 tablespoon unsalted butter
- 2 onions, halved and sliced ¼ inch thick
- 2 garlic cloves, minced
- ¼ teaspoon dried thyme
- ¾ cup plus 1 tablespoon beef broth
- 1 bay leaf
- 1 teaspoon cornstarch
- 1 teaspoon cider vinegar

1. Adjust oven rack to middle position and heat oven to 300 degrees. Combine onion powder, paprika, ½ teaspoon salt, ½ teaspoon pepper, and cayenne in small bowl. Pat chops dry with paper towels and rub with spice mixture.

2. Heat oil in large skillet over medium-high heat until just smoking. Brown chops, 3 to 4 minutes per side, and transfer to plate. Melt butter in now-empty skillet over medium heat. Cook onions until browned, 8 to 10 minutes. Add garlic and thyme and cook until fragrant, about 30 seconds. Stir in ¾ cup broth and bay leaf, scraping up any browned bits, and bring to boil. Return chops and any accumulated juices to pan, cover, and transfer to oven. Cook until chops are completely tender, about 1½ hours.

3. Transfer chops to platter and tent with foil. Discard bay leaf. Strain contents of skillet through fine mesh strainer into large liquid measuring cup; reserve onions. Let liquid settle, then skim fat. Return 1½ cups defatted pan juices to now-empty skillet and bring to boil. Reduce heat to medium and simmer until sauce is reduced to 1 cup, about 5 minutes.

4. Whisk remaining broth and cornstarch in bowl until no lumps remain. Whisk cornstarch mixture into sauce and simmer until thickened, 1 to 2 minutes. Stir in reserved onions and vinegar. Season with salt and pepper. Serve.

SHOPPING **Don't Get Hoodwinked**
Markets sometimes mislabel pork chops. This photo shows what a blade chop really looks like.

BLADE CHOP
Your best bet for braising.

ON THE SIDE

Foolproof Baked Rice

The oven is more dependable than the stovetop for cooking rice. But the method isn't perfect—not until we worked out the details. BY KELLY PRICE

I'M A CHEF by training and trade, but I'll admit that making perfect rice can be a challenge—and I have the scorched pots to prove it. Looking for an alternative to stovetop simmering, I turned to the oven's immersive heat, which cooks more evenly than bottom-up stovetop burners do. Oven-baked rice is not without its pitfalls, though. More than one recipe I tried yielded mushy, sticky glop—a distant relation to the fluffy, flavorful grains I wanted.

I started by adapting the test kitchen's techniques and ratios for stovetop rice to the oven. I rinsed 1½ cups of long-grain rice (to feed 4 to 6) in a colander to wash away the exterior starch and thus minimize clumping. I quickly toasted the grains in butter (for flavor and a further hedge against clumping), then, using our 1:1½ ratio of rice to liquid, I added 2¼ cups water, threw on the lid, and slid the pot into a 350-degree oven.

After 15 minutes, the rice had absorbed the water. I pulled the pot from the oven and let it sit for 10 minutes (our standard technique to help ensure even cooking) before calling my tasters to sample it. The grains were separate but had a slight unpleasant crunch; a little more liquid was clearly in order. After a few tests, I determined that adding another ½ cup water—for a total of 2¾ cups—produced baked rice with the best texture.

Tasters wanted more flavor, so I sautéed a little chopped onion in the melted butter before toasting the rice. More importantly, I swapped the water, which contributed zilch for flavor, for savory, meaty chicken broth. First-rate rice—fluffy and flavorful, with distinct, clump-free grains—has never been so foolproof.

For the most flavorful rice, start by sautéing onion and use broth instead of water.

FOOLPROOF BAKED RICE
Serves 4 to 6
Lundberg Organic Long-Grain White Rice is our favorite brand.

- 1½ cups long-grain white rice
- 2 tablespoons unsalted butter
- 1 small onion, chopped fine
- 2¾ cups low-sodium chicken broth
  Salt

1. Adjust oven rack to middle position and heat oven to 350 degrees. Place rice in fine-mesh strainer set over large bowl. Rinse under running water until water runs clear, about 1 minute. Drain rice well.

2. Melt butter in Dutch oven over medium heat. Add onion and cook until lightly browned, about 6 minutes. Stir in rice and cook, stirring frequently, until edges begin to turn translucent, about 2 minutes. Add broth and ½ teaspoon salt and bring to boil.

3. Cover and bake until liquid is absorbed and rice is tender, about 15 minutes. Let stand 10 minutes. Fluff with fork and season with salt. Serve.

TEST KITCHEN TECHNIQUE
Rinse Your Rice
Rinse raw rice in a colander under cold running water until the water runs clear. This washes away the excess starch on the exterior of the grains, resulting in lighter, fluffier cooked grains.

Click on Us
Which rice should you buy? To read our taste-test of long-grain white rice, visit CooksCountry.com/extra.

Creamy Egg Salad

It's an easy recipe, yes, but it's also easy to make less-than-perfect egg salad.
The secret? Divide (the eggs) and conquer. BY CAROLYNN PURPURA

EGG SALAD IS about as simple as recipes come: Mix together chopped hard-boiled eggs, mayonnaise, onion, salt, and pepper, and serve. Do you even need a recipe? Turns out you do—if you can find a good one. The five recipes I prepared were described variously as greasy, bland, watery, rubbery, or chalky. It's a simple recipe, yes, but one with plenty of problems.

If I were going to fix this recipe—and I was going to fix this recipe—I would have to begin with the eggs. Starting with the test kitchen's foolproof method for hard-cooked eggs, I made two batches, covering 10 eggs (for four generous servings) with an inch of water in each pot, bringing them to a boil, then covering the pots and letting them sit off the heat for 10 minutes. I drained the eggs and chilled them in an ice bath, then peeled and chopped the eggs finely for one batch, roughly for the other. Finally, I mixed each with a half cup of mayonnaise and a few tablespoons of chopped onion and celery.

Tasters had strong opinions about how the eggs were chopped. Too small and they missed the chunks of egg whites. Too large and they complained about the chalky bits of yolk. What to do? For my next batch, I separated the yolks and whites and treated them as separate elements. I chopped the whites into ¼-inch pieces and then finely mashed the yolks before combining both with the mayo. I was making progress, but tasters thought the salad could be creamier. Next I tried mixing the mashed yolks directly into the mayonnaise. This new approach not only

reduced the overall amount of mayonnaise needed to bind the salad, it also helped smooth out most of the yolk bits.

But some small bits of yolk remained, and since I was after the creamiest possible egg salad, this wouldn't do. I tried an old kitchen trick: adding boiling water to the yolks. This made the yolks ultra-smooth, but it also diluted their flavor (no surprise there). I reconsidered my cooking method: The test kitchen technique I'd been using produces perfect hard-cooked eggs, but would slightly undercooking the eggs make for creamier, smoother yolks? Yes. After a few tests, I landed on eight minutes (and an immediate bath in ice to stop the cooking) as the right cooking time for firm whites and yolks that blended easily into the mayonnaise.

I did some final fine-tuning: Replacing the chopped onion with chives gave the salad better balance—and eliminated the onion water leached by the juicy onions. A tablespoon of Dijon mustard lent kick. Tasters wanted acid to cut the richness, so I tried a handful of different vinegars. In the end, we preferred lemon juice for its fresh taste, the same reason we liked a few pinches of chopped parsley.

CREAMY EGG SALAD Makes about 3½ cups, enough for 4 sandwiches

We prefer Hellmann's Real Mayonnaise (also known as Best Foods). You can substitute Hellmann's Light, but avoid Hellmann's Low-Fat Mayonnaise. If you like, replace the chives with scallions.

- 10 large eggs
- ⅓ cup mayonnaise
- 1½ tablespoons lemon juice
- 1 tablespoon Dijon mustard
  Salt and pepper
- 1 celery rib, chopped fine
- 2 tablespoons finely chopped fresh chives
- 1 tablespoon finely chopped fresh parsley

1. Combine 4 cups water and 4 cups ice cubes in large bowl; set aside. Place eggs in large saucepan, cover with 1 inch water, and bring to boil over high heat. Remove pan from heat, cover, and let stand 8 minutes. Pour off water from saucepan and gently shake pan back and forth to crack egg shells. Transfer eggs to ice water and cool 5 minutes.

2. Peel eggs and halve lengthwise.

Transfer yolks to large bowl. Using potato masher, mash yolks with mayonnaise, lemon juice, mustard, ¼ teaspoon salt, and ⅛ teaspoon pepper. Whisk mixture until smooth; set aside.

3. Chop whites into ¼-inch pieces. Fold whites, celery, chives, and parsley into yolk mixture and refrigerate for 30 minutes. Season with salt and pepper. Serve. (Salad can be refrigerated in airtight container for 2 days.)

MAKE AHEAD Eggs can be made through step 1 and refrigerated in airtight container for 1 day. To finish, proceed with step 2.

DEVILED EGG SALAD
Prepare Creamy Egg Salad, reducing mayonnaise to ¼ cup. Replace Dijon

with 2 tablespoons spicy brown mustard. Add ½ teaspoon paprika and ¼ teaspoon hot sauce to yolk dressing in step 2. Omit celery and parsley.

OLIVE AND OREGANO EGG SALAD
Prepare Creamy Egg Salad, omitting celery, chives, and parsley. Add ¼ cup chopped pitted kalamata olives and 3 tablespoons finely chopped fresh oregano with egg whites in step 3.

RADISH AND ARUGULA EGG SALAD
Prepare Creamy Egg Salad, omitting celery, chives, and parsley. Add ½ cup thinly sliced radishes and ½ cup chopped baby arugula with egg whites in step 3.

For the best egg salad, treat the hard-cooked yolks and whites differently.

TEST KITCHEN TIP A Good Egg
Great egg salad requires precision. "Undercooking" the eggs by two minutes and immediately shocking them in ice water (to prevent carry-over cooking) yields the creamiest egg salad possible.

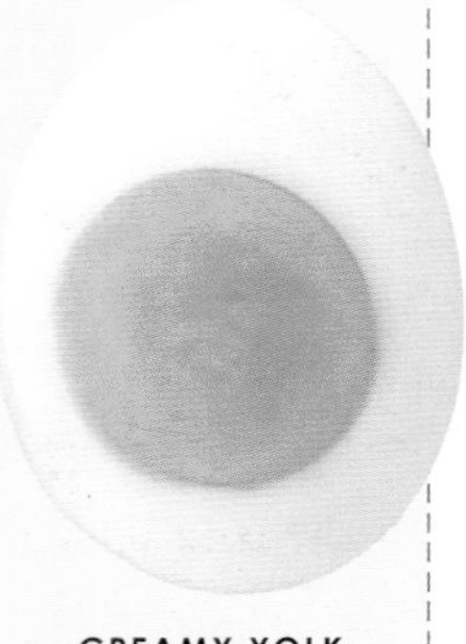

CREAMY YOLK
The yolk should be slightly soft in the center.

Jo Jo Potato Wedges

Fluffy inside with a shaggy, crunchy shell, Jo Jo Potatoes are popular in taverns and roadside joints. What would it take to reproduce them at home? BY JEREMY SAUER

JO JO POTATOES are common at taverns, gas stations, and takeout counters from Puget Sound to Pensacola, but I've never seen them in the Northeast, where I now live. And that's a shame, because Jo Jos are an old favorite of mine; they're shaggy and crunchy with seasoned bread crumbs, yet fluffy and tender in the middle. Since I can't find them here, I figured I'd make my own. But none of the recipes I unearthed delivered the real deal. In lieu of using the commercial pressure fryer traditionally employed to cook the spuds, recipes called for either deep-frying or baking. Deep-fried Jo Jos were more like no-no's: burnt on the outside and raw inside. Baked versions were slightly better—sure, they were greasy, dense, and leaden, but at least they were cooked through. I decided to go back to the drawing board and create my own recipe for baked Jo Jo potatoes.

Every recipe agreed that Jo Jos start with russet potatoes; the russet's high starch content is key to both fluffiness and crispiness (which is why it's the spud of choice for french fries). Most recipes require baking the potatoes at 375 degrees or so, but I cranked the dial to 450 in hopes that a hotter oven would give me a better crust. I cut each potato into fat wedges and, following the lead of most recipes, dipped them in melted butter and then in bread crumbs (tasters preferred the big crunch of panko, Japanese-style bread crumbs, to homemade or standard canned crumbs) seasoned with paprika, dried thyme, garlic powder, mustard powder, cayenne, and salt. I placed the breaded wedges on a baking sheet and slid it into the oven. After baking them for 15 minutes on each side, the potatoes were golden brown and crisp. Alas, the interiors were dense and lacking fluffiness. Extending the baking time meant that the exteriors burned. Lowering the temperature to 400 degrees helped a little, but any lower gave me soggy spuds.

Classic french fries get their crisp-on-the-outside, fluffy-on-the-inside texture from a double fry (first in moderate oil to cook them through, then in hot oil to crisp). Might a dual cooking method help me out here? For my next test, I microwaved the potatoes (covered) until they were barely softened before I breaded them. After 30 minutes in the oven, these Jo Jos had a fluffy interior.

But the exterior, though crisp, lacked deep-fried crunch. A couple of tests showed me that I could introduce serious crunch by preheating the baking sheet and then brushing it with oil before arranging the breaded wedges on it. But now the melted butter I was using to get the seasoned panko to adhere to the wedges scorched on the hot baking sheet. Substituting vegetable oil prevented the scorching, but the Jo Jos didn't taste as good. Fortunately, adding a good handful of grated Parmesan cheese to the panko allowed me to reclaim the flavor. After a few tests, I settled on equal parts Parm and panko.

My last task: upping the signature shaggy factor, which I'd never been entirely satisfied with. Instead of fiddling with additional ingredients to try to glue on extra crumbs, I wondered if I could deploy the potato starch to do the work for me. After the potatoes came out of the microwave, I tossed them with oil as usual. I continued to toss them, and toss them, and toss them some more, hoping to draw out the starch. In about a minute, the potatoes were coated in a starchy paste. I dredged the sticky wedges in the crumb mixture and let them sit for a few minutes to affix the coating before baking. It worked—with an extra benefit: The potato starch not only held the ample breading in place, but the baked wedges were crispier than ever (potato starch promotes crisping). Finally, Jo Jo potatoes had reached the Northeast in all their shaggy, crunchy, fluffy glory.

Jo Jo Potatoes are often served with ranch dressing for dipping.

JO JO POTATOES Serves 4 to 6
Panko adds a big crunch. Standard store-bought bread crumbs are too heavy.

- 3 medium russet potatoes (about 8 ounces each), scrubbed
- 5 tablespoons vegetable oil
- ⅔ cup panko bread crumbs
- ⅔ cup grated Parmesan cheese
- 1 tablespoon paprika
- 2 teaspoons dry mustard
- 1 teaspoon salt
- ¾ teaspoon garlic powder
- ¾ teaspoon dried thyme
- ⅛ teaspoon cayenne pepper

1. Adjust oven rack to middle position, place rimmed baking sheet on rack, and heat oven to 400 degrees. Cut each potato lengthwise into 6 wedges. Place potatoes in large bowl and wrap tightly with plastic wrap. Microwave until edges of potatoes are translucent but centers remain slightly firm, 6 to 8 minutes, shaking bowl (without removing plastic) to redistribute potatoes halfway through cooking. Carefully remove plastic and drain potatoes well. Return potatoes to bowl, add 3 tablespoons oil, and stir until potatoes are coated with starchy film, about 1 minute.

2. Combine panko, Parmesan, paprika, dry mustard, salt, garlic powder, thyme, and cayenne in shallow dish. Dredge one-quarter of potatoes in panko mixture, pressing gently to adhere. Transfer to platter and repeat with remaining potatoes. Let sit 15 minutes.

3. Remove hot baking sheet from oven and brush with remaining oil. Arrange potatoes, cut side down, in single layer. Bake, flipping halfway through cooking, until crisp and golden brown, 25 to 30 minutes. Serve.

Morning Glory Muffins

Fruits, vegetables, seeds, nuts, and enough spices to fill a rack—clearly, you *can* have too much of a good thing. For more glorious results, we trimmed this muffin back. BY SARAH GABRIEL

A cousin to carrot cake, morning glory muffins are cinnamon-scented breakfast treats, chockablock full of carrots, nuts, raisins, coconut, apples, pineapple, and, sometimes, seeds. The muffin was "invented" (and certainly given its name) by Pam McKinstry, who owned a café by the same name in Nantucket, and it soon spread to bakeries across the country, with recipes appearing regularly in magazines and cookbooks. This was in the 1970s, when wholesome, hippie cooking was in ascendence. Since then, many such recipes have gathered dust along with our Captain and Tennille records. But morning glory muffins had legs—and no wonder. They're spicy, moist, and bursting with flavor... maybe too much of all three.

Most recipes use oil to make Morning Glory Muffins. What's up with that? We use butter *in* them, not just *on* them.

I baked the original recipe and a handful of others. The muffins all shared problems of excess: too much sugar, too much oil, too many spices, too many soggy nuts and coconut bits, and way too much juicy fruit; in short, too much, period. (Unsurprisingly, several recipes also produced too much batter—more than could possibly fit in 12 muffin cups.) As a result, the muffins as a group veered toward greasy, gummy, heavy, too sweet, and just plain confusing. Still, if excess had taken its toll, it hadn't shaken my faith. Underneath the glut, I could almost taste the pared-down, more refined morning glory muffins waiting to take shape—moist, tender, fruity, and balanced.

Judging by the greasy fingerprints my tasters left behind after the first round of tests, morning glory muffins could stand to lose a little fat. The original recipe contained 1 cup of vegetable oil for a mere 2¼ cups of flour, and the other recipes weren't far behind. I inched down to ¾ cup oil. Still greasy. Ten tablespoons? Not yet. At a half cup (or 8 tablespoons), the telltale counter fingerprints had vanished, and I was ready to move on.

Not so fast, said my tasters, who urged me to switch to butter. Granted, butter tastes better, but I also knew that many muffin recipes use oil to maintain a moist crumb. Could I make the switch without any unintended consequences? I exchanged the ½ cup of oil for an equal amount (1 stick) of melted butter (melted, so I could stick with the ease of simply stirring it into the batter). The flavor improved by leaps and bounds and, luckily, the texture was unaffected:

The combined carrots, apples, and pineapple contributed plenty of moisture to the muffins, oil or no.

So much moisture, actually, that even minus half the fat, the muffins remained gummy and wet. Blaming the crushed pineapple (canned, for ease) and grated apple, I drained the fruits in a fine-mesh strainer, then pressed out (and tossed out) the juice before mixing the fruit into the batter. As I had hoped, this method produced moist muffins, not soggy ones. Unfortunately, the missing fruit juice also resulted in missing fruit flavor.

When we make sauces in the test kitchen, we often boil down stock or wine to concentrate the flavor and thicken the liquid—this was exactly what I needed. After pressing the fruit, this time I boiled the cup of juices down to ¼ cup and added the now syrupy juice back to the batter. At the same time, I cut back on the sugar by ¼ cup; although crystalline at room temperature, sugar adds moisture to baked goods. Using less sugar had the secondary benefit of making the muffins less sweet, which, in turn, let the fruit flavors come to the forefront.

But tasters still complained about limp, stringy coconut and mealy nuts. I tried toasting them for heightened flavor and crunch, but once they hit the batter they soaked up moisture and got soggy all over again. Texture aside, toasting did wonders for the flavor. I tried sprinkling the coconut and nuts on top of the muffin where they'd stay dry, instead of mixing them into the batter, but the muffins came out squat and flat-topped. In addition to adding flavor, the coconut and nuts had been providing the infrastructure for my muffin tops. If only I could make the coconut and nuts invisible. What's the next best thing? Very, very tiny. The next time I made the muffins, I toasted the coconut and nuts as before, then ground them finely in the food processor and mixed the meal into the dry ingredients. The result? Deep, nutty flavor and nicely domed muffins with no mealy bits.

My muffins almost done, I quickly took stock of the flavors, ejecting the ground ginger and clove found in some of the recipes I'd tried—there was enough going on here—and reducing the cinnamon to a manageable 1 teaspoon (some recipes include three times that much). Toning down the cinnamon helped showcase the fruit and nuts.

Granted, these muffins take more work than the recipes I'd started with, but when we tasted them side by side, there was no question they were worth the effort. With a cup of coffee in one hand and a balanced, tender, perky-domed muffin in the other, I was all set up to take in a glorious morning.

MORNING GLORY MUFFINS
Makes 12 muffins

Don't throw away the juice from the can of pineapple; you'll need it. To toast the coconut and walnuts, place them in a dry skillet over medium heat and cook, stirring occasionally, until they're golden, about 5 minutes. Cool before grinding them. We prefer golden raisins here, but ordinary raisins will work, too.

- ¾ cup sweetened shredded coconut, toasted
- ½ cup walnuts, toasted
- 2¼ cups all-purpose flour
- ¾ cup sugar
- 1½ teaspoons baking soda
- 1 teaspoon ground cinnamon
- ½ teaspoon baking powder
- ¾ teaspoon salt
- 1 (8-ounce) can crushed pineapple
- 1 Granny Smith apple, peeled, cored, and shredded
- 8 tablespoons (1 stick) unsalted butter, melted and cooled slightly
- 3 large eggs
- 1 teaspoon vanilla extract
- 1½ cups shredded carrots (2 to 3 medium)
- 1 cup golden raisins

1. Adjust oven rack to middle position and heat oven to 350 degrees. Grease 12-cup muffin tin. Process coconut and walnuts in food processor until finely ground. Add flour, sugar, baking soda, cinnamon, baking powder, and salt and pulse until combined. Transfer mixture to large bowl.

2. Place pineapple and shredded apple in fine-mesh strainer set over liquid measuring cup. Press fruit dry (juice should measure about 1 cup). Bring juice to boil in large skillet over medium-high heat and cook until reduced to ¼ cup, about 5 minutes. Let cool slightly. Whisk melted butter, cooled juice, eggs, and vanilla until smooth. Stir wet mixture into dry mixture until combined. Stir in pineapple-apple mixture, carrots, and raisins.

3. Divide batter evenly among muffin cups. Bake until toothpick inserted in center of muffin comes out clean, 24 to 28 minutes. Cool in tin for 10 minutes, then turn out onto wire rack. Serve warm. (Muffins can be stored in airtight container for 3 days.)

WILTON AVANTI EVERGLIDE METAL-SAFE NON-STICK 12-CUP MUFFIN PAN

ESSENTIAL GEAR **Muffin Tin**
The four important qualities for muffin tins are how evenly and thoroughly the muffins or cupcakes brown, how they release (we like nonstick), the design of their handles (or extended lip), and durability. In a recent testing of muffin tins, our old favorite (from Wilton) once again beat all contenders. It costs about $14.

KEY STEPS **Secrets to Morning Glory Muffins**
Many of the recipes we tested produced muffins that were wet and overloaded. Three steps proved key as we worked to simplify the flavor and repair the texture.

1. PROCESS We toasted the coconut and walnuts to heighten their flavor, then ground them up to avoid soggy, stringy coconut and mealy nuts.

2. PRESS The juicy apple and pineapple made the muffins soggy. We pressed the juice out of the fruit and only then stirred the fruit into the batter.

3. CONCENTRATE Finally, we reduced the fruit juices on the stovetop (down from 1 cup to ¼ cup) before stirring them, too, into the batter.

TASTING GOLDEN RAISINS

When a recipe calls for golden raisins, your choices are surprisingly limited. Only a few brands are available nationwide; they are processed practically the same way, and from the same grapes usually grown in the same region (California). Thompson Seedless green grapes (which are also the source for dark brown raisins) are dehydrated in ovens and treated with sulfur dioxide. This preservative keeps them golden yellow and moist.

A handful of specialty-food purveyors carry organic golden raisins, which are sun-dried Black Monukka or Sultana seedless grapes. They aren't processed with sulfur dioxide, so the raisins turn pale green or a very light tan. We mail-ordered organic golden raisins called Hunza (the grapes are grown in a Himalayan valley), to see if they differ from the golden raisins we found at the supermarket (Sun-Maid and Champion). The Hunza cost nearly twice as much.

The first thing we noticed about the organic raisins, apart from their color, was that they tended to be drier and less plump than the national brands. Sampled plain, we liked the organic raisins fine, but not as much as we liked the plump sugariness of conventional golden raisins. A stalwart minority preferred the organic raisins over both conventional brands, praising their "lively" and "kiwi-like" taste, but most tasters found the "malted" and "honeyed" flavors and tender texture of conventional golden raisins more to their liking. Would it matter which kind of golden raisin we used in Morning Glory Muffins? No: All three brands passed muster in this round. BY AMY GRAVES

RECOMMENDED		**TASTERS' NOTES**
SUN-MAID CALIFORNIA Golden Raisins **Price:** $3.49 for 15-ounce box **Ingredients:** Raisins, sulfur dioxide		These raisins had a pleasing sweet flavor "with just enough tang," and "moist, substantial" texture in the muffins, but more than a few tasters noticed fluctuations in size, texture (from soft to gritty), and color (from dark to light) when sampling them plain. "Some are good, several are dry and leathery."
CHAMPION Golden Raisins **Price:** $3.59 for 15-ounce canister **Ingredients:** Raisins, sulfur dioxide		Although glistening and golden (one lyrical taster called them "sparkling topaz gems"), these raisins were "nice, but not mind-blowing" and "like honey-flavored raisins" in the plain tasting. In the muffins, they were "nice and soft, with a sweet flavor."

RECOMMENDED WITH RESERVATIONS

HIMALAYAN HARVEST Organic Hunza Golden Raisins **Price:** $5.99 for 8-ounce bag (www.igourmet.com) **Ingredients:** Organic raisins | | For tasters who got past their pale green color, "these really taste like fruit." Others couldn't warm up to their texture, "like leather." In muffins, "these seemed more shrunken and chewy than the others," but their flavor was "a bit stronger—I can taste the raisins more."

Taste Test Macaroni and Cheese

We tasted 25 boxed and frozen versions of mostly clumpy, gloppy, wimpy mac and cheese. Were there any we'd actually eat? BY TAIZETH SIERRA

ALTHOUGH MAKING MACARONI and cheese from scratch isn't hard, many busy parents (and hungry, budget-conscious college students) still opt for the convenience of box mixes and frozen dinners—and their numbers are growing. Sales are up 25 percent over the past four years, according to SymphonyIRI Group, a Chicago-based market research firm. New brands and varieties (Kraft alone has more than 50 kinds) have exploded onto the market. Are they any good?

To narrow down our choices, we conducted two preliminary taste-offs of Kraft and Annie's, companies that offer a dizzying profusion of styles. We plucked the winners from among 19 of their best sellers and added other brands to round out our list, including two brands of frozen dinners; after all, what's more convenient than heat and serve? We carefully followed package instructions, microwaving the frozen dinners (far quicker than baking), and asked 22 cooks and editors at America's Test Kitchen to weigh in.

"Revolting." That's how they judged most of the brands in our blind tasting. We found just three brands we would even consider eating.

The so-called "cheese sauce" was one of several features that distinguished winners from losers. Our favorite reinforced its sauce with blue and cheddar cheeses, and all our top choices used liquid sauce, which was creamy and suitably clingy. Brands that relied on a cheese powder packet (to which the cook adds milk and/or margarine) tasted "artificial" and were "chalky" and "thin." Also, dry noodles triumphed; frozen dinners turned pasta into mush. Both elbows and shells were acceptable (confession: we skipped Kraft's "SpongeBob SquarePants" shape).

Our winner, Kraft Homestyle Macaroni & Cheese Dinner with Classic Cheddar Cheese Sauce, requires the cook to make a milk-based cheese sauce, substituting Kraft's seasoning packet for flour and Kraft's cheese sauce for grated cheese. The effort is slightly less than from-scratch, and so is the flavor (but we did like the crumb topping). Only one other brand, Velveeta Original Shells & Cheese, earned a recommended rating. We found a third acceptable, with reservations. The other five brands are not worth eating, even if the kids are screaming.

RECOMMENDED	TASTERS' NOTES
KRAFT HOMESTYLE MACARONI & CHEESE DINNER Classic Cheddar Cheese Sauce **$2** for 12.6-ounce bag **Total Cooking Time:** Approximately 20 minutes **Type of Cheese Sauce:** Liquid **The Cook Adds:** 2% milk, unsalted butter	The best of the 11 Kraft varieties we tried and the best overall, this creamy, flavorful macaroni tasted the most like homemade. Tasters really liked the breadcrumb topping and praised the "thick" sauce for its "real" cheese flavor.
**KRAFT VELVEETA ORIGINAL SHELLS & CHEESE** **$2** for 12-ounce box **Total Cooking Time:** Approximately 10 minutes **Type of Cheese Sauce:** Liquid **The Cook Adds:** Nothing	This cheese flavor was strong and rich, the sauce nice and thick. Many of our tasters instantly recognized the distinct taste of Velveeta. Some complained that the cheese became waxy if it sat around even briefly.

RECOMMENDED WITH RESERVATIONS	
**ANNIE'S DELUXE SHELLS & REAL AGED CHEDDAR** **$3.99** for 11-ounce box **Total Cooking Time:** Approximately 12 minutes **Type of Cheese Sauce:** Liquid **The Cook Adds:** Nothing	The small shells sometimes clumped, cooking unevenly and leaving some rubbery. Tasters liked the initial cheddar flavor, but many detected an off-putting aftertaste.

NOT RECOMMENDED	
STOUFFER'S MACARONI & CHEESE FAMILY SIZE **$5.99** for 40 ounces **Total Cooking Time:** 23 minutes in the microwave, 75 minutes in a 375°F oven **Type of Cheese Sauce:** Already incorporated **The Cook Adds:** Nothing	Some tasters praised the good cheddar flavor; others tasted only salt. But our biggest gripe was the "smushy," "gloppy" texture. We cooked it in the microwave for speed.
BACK TO NATURE MACARONI & CHEESE **$2.19** for 6.5-ounce box **Total Cooking Time:** Approximately 8 minutes **Type of Cheese Sauce:** Powdered **The Cook Adds:** Low-fat milk, unsalted butter	Despite the addition of milk and butter, tasters found this brand "pasty" and "powdery," with cheese that was "chemical-y," strangely "sweet," and wan. As one taster put it, "It was as if the mac and cheese was depressed."
KRAFT MACARONI & CHEESE DINNER Original **$1.15** for 7.25-ounce box **Total Cooking Time:** Approximately 8 minutes **Type of Cheese Sauce:** Powdered **The Cook Adds:** Margarine, 2% milk	"The Cheesiest" was plastered across the box, but this classic mac and cheese was everything but. Tasters jotted down "sweet," "bitter," "fake," "fishy," "sour," and more—but nary a "cheesy." Kraft may eat up 80 percent of the dry macaroni-and-cheese market, but this blue box we all know from childhood was just plain awful.
PASTA RONI CHEDDAR MACARONI **$1.59** for 5.3-ounce box **Total Cooking Time:** Approximately 16 minutes **Type of Cheese Sauce:** Powdered **The Cook Adds:** Nothing	Easy-peasy to make: You bring water to a boil, add the pasta and seasoning packet, simmer, and let stand. No draining, no fuss, and . . . oops, no flavor! The cream-colored powder turned a disturbing neon yellow. Also disturbing—the flavorless, "rubbery, mushy mass" of "hideous orange elbows."
BANQUET: MACARONI & CHEESE MEAL **$1.25** for 8 ounces **Total Cooking Time:** 6 minutes in the microwave, 28 minutes in a 350°F oven **Type of Cheese Sauce:** Already incorporated **The Cook Adds:** Nothing	This heat-and-eat frozen dinner was "bland" and "squishy" with a "weird plastic" aftertaste. Described as "flabby" and with zero cheese flavor, the closest it came to getting a compliment was "Tastes like a Cheez Doodle."

Sharp, comfortable shears are a kitchen essential. But do you need to spend $75 for a good pair? BY AMY GRAVES

DON'T IGNORE YOUR kitchen shears. They're the best all-around tool on the counter, useful for butterflying or quartering chicken, trimming pie dough, shaping parchment to line cake pans, snipping herbs, or cutting lengths of kitchen twine. We set out to find a pair that aced all of these tasks, with powerful, sharp blades that are easy to maneuver; slip-resistant, comfortable handles; and easy cleanup. We wanted shears that would work for most cooks whatever their hand size or strength—and preferred a design that would also work for lefties.

We gathered seven promising pairs priced from $9.95 to $75—including the favorite from our 2006 testing (the Messermeister Take-Apart Shears) and an ambidextrous model from Messermeister—and started snipping. Our testers cut whole raw chickens, twine, parchment, woody fresh rosemary stems, and tender pie dough. They scissored away with hands both large and small, and included a left-handed tester.

Some shears sacrifice comfort for style, with snazzy-looking handles that made our hands ache or slipped once they got wet or greasy. The Wüsthof Come-Apart Kitchen Shears and Kuhn Rikon Household Shears both had cramped handles made of uncomfortably hard material. Also, we didn't feel safe with pull-apart blades unless we knew they wouldn't separate spontaneously, as happened with the ambidextrous model from Messermeister and that Kuhn Rikon pair, which both fell apart when spread just 90 degrees. Nor should it take Herculean strength to open and close the shears. Testers with weaker or smaller hands were fatigued by a model with spring-loaded handles (the clipper-like Kuhn Rikon 8-Inch Kitchen Shears), which kept threatening to pop out of our grasp, making precision work difficult.

Also critical to comfort and precision was the tension of the shears. If the tension was too tight, cutting became halting and laborious; if too loose, the shears felt flimsy. We preferred models that allowed us to adjust the tension at the stud fastening the blades. Kuhn Rikon's Household Shears, which began with ideal calibration, felt looser by the end of testing, but since neither Kuhn Rikon model was adjustable we could do nothing about it. Blade length and overall balance proved important as well.

Longer shears meant fewer strokes; our top-ranked pair was a full inch longer than most in the lineup, yet it felt balanced in the hand.

The shears we considered all stayed perfectly sharp throughout testing. This was not entirely surprising, since many are made of the same high-carbon stainless steel used in chef's knives. But what made the most difference to cutting performance was the presence of micro-serrations. They anchor the blades to what you are cutting, helping the scissor action glide effortlessly without slipping and sliding off target. Most pairs had them on one or both blades, but only Shun and Wüsthof offered dual serrations, with fine teeth along one blade and deeper grooves along the other. These really prevented slippage—it felt like they had a death grip on slippery raw poultry bones and stems of rosemary.

Our new favorite is the Shun Classic Kitchen Shears ($39.99). Testers praised them for their precision and economy of motion. While they separate for cleaning, the blades stayed together until opened to 120 degrees. They work for both right- and left-handed users and feel sturdy and well engineered. Although these shears aren't cheap, their lifetime guarantee salves some of the sting.

KEY **Good ★★★** **Fair ★★** **Poor ★**

HIGHLY RECOMMENDED

SHUN CLASSIC Kitchen Shears
Model 1120M **Price:** $39.99
Source: www.bedbathandbeyond.com
Extras: Jar gripper, bottle opener, screwdriver, nutcracker
Cleanup: Separable blades. Washing by hand highly recommended.

CRITERIA
Cutting: ★★★
Comfort: ★★★

TESTERS' NOTES
Thanks to 9-inch, very sharp blades (one with fine micro-serrations; the other deeply grooved ones), breaking down a chicken felt effortless. Large, rubbery handles were comfy, and blades were symmetrical for right- and left-handed use. They come with a lifetime guarantee.

RECOMMENDED

J. A. HENCKELS INTERNATIONAL (BEST BUY)
Kitchen Shears—Take Apart
Model 11517-100 **Price:** $14.95
Source: www.sears.com
Extras: Jar and screw cap gripper, nutcracker
Cleanup: Separable blades. Dishwasher-safe.

Cutting: ★★★
Comfort: ★★½

Cutting through branches of fresh rosemary or poultry bones felt effortless with these solid, sharp shears. Fine serrations on one side helped blades stay in place when breaking down a chicken. But the handles fit only three fingers, and the blade tension is not adjustable.

MESSERMEISTER
8-Inch Take-Apart Kitchen Shears
Model DN-2070 **Price:** $9.95
Source: www.cutleryandmore.com
Extras: Jar gripper, bottle opener, screwdriver, nutcracker
Cleanup: Separable blades. Dishwasher-safe.

Cutting: ★★½
Comfort: ★★★

The short blades on this ambidextrous model lack serrations, so they sometimes slid on slippery poultry bones and rosemary branches. Their separable blades fell apart unexpectedly when opened to as little as 90 degrees. Still, the rubbery handles are roomy and symmetrical, and thus suited to a variety of hand types.

WÜSTHOF Come-Apart Kitchen Shears
Model 5557 **Price:** $74.95
Source: www.cutleryandmore.com
Extras: Jar gripper, bottle opener, screwdriver, notch for cutting bones
Cleanup: Separable blades. Washing by hand recommended.

Cutting: ★★★
Comfort: ★

Thanks to their heft and sharpness, these pricey shears butchered a chicken with powerful, sure strokes. A notch and serrated edge on one blade got a grip on bigger bones. But their weight (nearly a half pound) and blade-heavy balance wore some testers out, and tight stainless-steel handles felt slippery in greasy hands.

RECOMMENDED WITH RESERVATIONS

MESSERMEISTER Take-Apart Shears
Model DN-1070 **Price:** $14.95
Source: www.cutleryandmore.com
Extras: Jar gripper, bottle opener, screwdriver
Cleanup: Separable blades. Dishwasher-safe.

Cutting: ★★
Comfort: ★★

These sharp, slim shears (our old favorite) felt secure in our hands thanks to rubber-wrapped handles for a comfortable, sure grip. Our gripes? The nonserrated blades sometimes slipped, and left-handed testers found them unsatisfying, if not impossible, to use.

KUHN RIKON Household Shears
Model 2722 **Price:** $16
Source: www.surlatable.com
Extras: Herb stripper, rounded "safety" blade tips
Cleanup: Separable blades. Washing by hand recommended.

Cutting: ★★½
Comfort: ★

These colorful, lightweight shears cleaved poultry bones easily thanks to ultra-fine, barely visible serrations on one blade. However, the hard plastic-wrapped handles proved uncomfortable, the thumbhole pinched, and the tension (which is not adjustable) loosened slightly over the course of testing.

NOT RECOMMENDED

KUHN RIKON 8-Inch Kitchen Shears
Model 2705 **Price:** $19.99
Source: www.bedbathandbeyond.com
Extras: Bottle opener, herb stripper
Cleanup: Not separable. Dishwasher-safe.

Cutting: ★★
Comfort: ★

These shears are spring-loaded: The cutting action only involves squeezing them closed. Testers with large, strong hands found them liberating (no holes to shove your fingers into), but smaller, weaker testers struggled. A plastic safety sheath is necessary to keep them closed.

Cooking Class How to Make Dinner Rolls

Not much can top a warm, soft, yeasty roll straight from your oven. But even many accomplished home cooks find the prospect of making rolls intimidating. Use our recipe and techniques to conquer your fears.

SOFT AND CHEWY ROLLS
Makes 12 rolls

- 1¼ cups water, heated to 110 degrees
- 2 tablespoons extra-virgin olive oil
- 1 tablespoon sugar
- 3 cups all-purpose flour
- ½ cup instant potato flakes
- 2¼ teaspoons rapid-rise or instant yeast
- 2 teaspoons salt
- 1 egg, lightly beaten

1. Adjust oven rack to middle position. Heat oven to 200 degrees and turn it off. Line baking sheet with parchment paper. Grease large, clear, straight-sided container.

2. Whisk water, oil, and sugar in large liquid measuring cup until sugar dissolves. In bowl of stand mixer fitted with dough hook, mix flour, potato flakes, yeast, and 1½ teaspoons salt until combined. With mixer on low, slowly add water mixture and mix until dough comes together, about 1 minute. Increase speed to medium and mix until dough is smooth and comes away from sides of bowl, about 6 minutes.

3. Turn dough onto lightly floured counter and knead briefly to form smooth, cohesive ball. Transfer dough to prepared container and turn to coat. Cover with plastic wrap and place in turned-off oven until dough has doubled in size, about 45 minutes.

4. Gently press down on dough on lightly floured counter. Divide dough into quarters and cut each quarter into 3 equal pieces. Form each piece into rough ball by pinching and pulling dough edges under so that top is smooth. On clean counter, cup each ball with your palm and roll into smooth, tight ball. Transfer to prepared baking sheet. Cover loosely with plastic and let rest in turned-off oven until doubled in size, about 20 minutes. (Unbaked, formed rolls can be refrigerated for up to 24 hours.)

5. Remove unbaked rolls from oven and discard plastic. Heat oven to 400 degrees. Brush rolls with egg and sprinkle evenly with remaining salt. Bake until golden brown and 200 degrees in the middle, about 15 minutes, rotating sheet halfway through baking. Cool rolls on sheet 10 minutes. Serve.

Click on Us
Wake up your bread basket with our flavorful variations on Soft and Chewy Dinner Rolls. For recipes for **Cranberry-Pecan Rolls**, **Herbed Sun-Dried Tomato Rolls**, and **Rosemary-Olive Rolls**, visit CooksCountry.com/extra.

What You Need: The Goods and the Gear

RECOMMENDED INGREDIENTS

Instant Yeast Yeast comes in three forms: fresh, active dry, and instant. Fresh yeast, which is used by professional bakers, has plenty of power. But it's hard for home bakers to find, and even when stored in the refrigerator, it loses its power within two weeks. Active dry yeast lasts much longer and is sold at any supermarket, but it must be dissolved in water for several minutes to activate. In the test kitchen, we like instant yeast best. It combines the potency of fresh yeast with the availability of active dry yeast, and it can be mixed in with the dry ingredients. Don't let the labels confuse you: Yeasts labeled "Instant," "Rapid Rise," and "Bread Machine" are one and the same. And remember, keep yeast in the refrigerator, where it will last longer.

TEST KITCHEN CHOICE
Faster, stronger, simpler

All-Purpose Flour It's called all-purpose for a reason. We tested our Soft and Chewy Rolls with all-purpose flour and bread flour; the latter promotes gluten development, generally a good thing for yeast breads. But made with all-purpose flour, our rolls were soft, chewy, and delicious. Save bread flour for crusty, artisanal loaves.

Instant Potato Flakes It's a well-known bakers' trick: Add mashed potato to yeast dough for moist, tender rolls and breads. To avoid the extra step of boiling and mashing a potato, however, we use dehydrated potato flakes (the stuff that comes in a box and is normally used to make instant mashed potatoes).

RECOMMENDED EQUIPMENT

Instant-Read Thermometer No guesswork for us. We rely on a thermometer to take the temperature of the water for the dough and to gauge whether the rolls have finished baking.

TEST KITCHEN BEST BUY
ThermoWorks Super-Fast Waterproof Pocket Thermometer

Bench Scraper Use it to cut unbaked dough into portions, pry dough loose from the counter, and—come cleanup time—push extra flour into the trash.

TEST KITCHEN FAVORITE
OXO Good Grips Stainless Steel Multi-Purpose Scraper and Chopper

Stand Mixer We prefer to knead bread dough in a mixer to avoid mixing in excess flour and, consequently, producing tough rolls. A hand mixer lacks a dough hook and isn't strong enough to knead dough; don't use it.

TEST KITCHEN BEST BUY
KitchenAid Classic Plus Stand Mixer

A Dozen Steps to Homemade Dinner Rolls

1. HEAT OVEN Bring the oven to a gentle 200 degrees, then turn it off. **WHY?** A warm oven provides a perfect, draft-free home for the dough to rise and coaxes the best performance from yeast.

2. COMBINE LIQUIDS Whisk the water, oil, and sugar in a large liquid measuring cup until combined. **WHY?** Combined, they can be more easily incorporated into the dry ingredients.

3. COMBINE DRY INGREDIENTS Mix the flour, potato flakes, yeast, and salt in a standing mixer fitted with a dough hook. **WHY?** To evenly distribute the yeast and the salt.

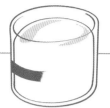

4. ADD LIQUID Add the liquid in a slow, steady stream and mix until the dough comes together. **WHY?** Adding the liquid slowly distributes the water more evenly, hydrates the flour, and begins gluten development.

5. KNEAD IN MIXER Knead at medium speed until the dough is elastic and smooth and forms a ball, about 6 minutes. **WHY?** The machine mixes more uniformly than you can by hand, so you're less likely to add extra flour.

6. GREASE DOUGH Lightly coat a large, straight-sided container with oil. Place the kneaded dough inside and turn it to lightly coat in oil. **WHY?** Otherwise, the dough will stick to the sides of the container, which would impede rising.

7. LET RISE Cover the container with plastic wrap and place it in the (turned-off) oven until the dough doubles. **WHY?** The dough is releasing carbon dioxide. The trapped gas makes the dough, and subsequently the bread, rise.

8. PRESS DOWN On a lightly floured counter, push down gently on the dough. **WHY?** Pressing down, or degassing, removes large air bubbles and will give the rolls a more uniform crumb.

9. FORM ROLLS Divide the dough into 12 pieces. Form each into a rough ball. On a clean counter, cup each with your palm and roll taut. **WHY?** Because the dough can grip the flour-free surface, it can be formed into smoother, tighter rolls.

10. LET RISE AGAIN Cover the shaped rolls with plastic and let them rise in the (turned-off) oven until they've doubled, about 20 minutes. **WHY?** The live active yeast continues to release carbon dioxide gas, further increasing the volume of the rolls.

11. BRUSH ROLLS Heat the oven to 400 degrees. Brush the rolls with lightly beaten egg and sprinkle them lightly with salt. **WHY?** The egg wash helps the rolls brown and gives them a pretty, glossy sheen.

12. BAKE ROLLS Bake the rolls about 15 minutes, until they register 200 degrees on an instant-read thermometer. **WHY?** The most accurate way to know when the rolls are done is to take their temperature.

Tips and Techniques

How Do I Gauge the Rise?

FIRST RISE
In step 6, we put the dough in a 4-cup liquid measure for rising. If you don't have one, put the dough in a clear, straight-sided container and mark its height on the container with tape. It's easy to see when the dough has doubled.

SECOND RISE
After the rolls have been shaped, the dough rises a second time. To test its progress, poke it gently with a finger. When it's ready, the dough feels springy, and the indentation briefly holds its shape.

What If I Don't Have a Mixer?

Then you'll need to knead by hand. In step 2 of the recipe, whisk the water, oil, and sugar together, as instructed. Now mix the flour, potato flakes, yeast, and 1½ teaspoons salt in a large bowl. Make a well in the middle of these dry ingredients, pour in the liquid mixture, and stir until it's difficult to stir. Dump the dough onto a lightly floured counter, push it away from you with the heel of your hand, and fold it over itself. Repeat until the dough is smooth and elastic, about 10 minutes.

Nifty Make-Ahead Trick
Steal a technique from commercial bakeries: par-bake. When the rolls are just beginning to brown (about 5 minutes), remove them from the oven, cool, and freeze for up to a month. To finish, let the parbaked rolls sit on a parchment-lined baking sheet at room temperature for 1 hour. Bake in a 400-degree oven until they're golden brown, about 10 minutes.

Looking for a Recipe

READER TO READER

Did you misplace a favorite recipe? Can you almost taste a chocolate cake from childhood but the bakery—and the recipe—are long gone? Ask a reader. While you're at it, answer a reader. Post queries and finds at **CooksCountry.com**; click on **Looking for a Recipe** (or write to Looking for a Recipe, Cook's Country, P.O. Box 470739, Brookline, MA 02447.) We'll share all of your submissions online—hundreds are already posted—and print several on this page. Include your name and mailing address with each submission.

Apple Flan
Mark Scibbe, Elyria, Ohio

One of our "must do" stops whenever we visited Epcot Center at Disney World was the Fountain View Café, which we learned this spring had closed. The café served an apple flan like no other flan I had ever seen or tasted—it was absolutely delicious. I asked for the recipe but managed to lose it. One thing I remember was that the crust was made from sugar-cookie dough. Any help finding or re-creating this recipe for the home kitchen would be greatly appreciated.

Chocolate-Coconut Shortbread Cookies
Martha B. Harris, Dallas, Texas

More than 30 years ago, I lived in Springfield, Illinois. A bakery around the corner from the Senate Theatre sold a shortbread cookie that included coconut, chocolate chips, and chopped pecans. I'd sure appreciate getting the recipe.

Coca-Cola Cake
Catherine Lucas, Ft. Lauderdale, Fla.

Do you have a World War II–era recipe for Coca-Cola cake? I think the recipe made creative use of soft drinks to deal with the sugar rationing of the time.

Swiss Crab Casserole
Lilia Claude, Washington, D.C.

Years ago I was invited to a classmate's home for dinner. Her mom served Swiss crab casserole, and I remember it still. What I can recall is fresh crabmeat, almonds, and rice. I'd appreciate it if you could find this recipe for me.

President's Pie
Andrea McCormick, Harrisburg, Pa.

I'd love to find a recipe for what I know as President's pie. A graham cracker crust is blind-baked and then filled with a white pudding-like mixture, with pineapple and nuts mixed in. The pie had to be stored in the refrigerator and was served cold. I grew up in the 1970s in western Pennsylvania, and I remember my grandmother making this all the time.

Hasty Pudding
Joe Malone, Chatham, Mass.

I'm looking for a reliable recipe for Hasty Pudding. It's an old-fashioned dessert made with cornmeal and maple syrup or honey. My grandmother used to make it every Thanksgiving for me and my seven siblings. It was delicious served warm with a scoop of vanilla ice cream. I'd love to bring it back.

Jell-O Cake
Rindy Hrad, Des Plaines, Ill.

The recipe for a cake my mother used to make in the 1960s has been lost. It used a cake mix to which you added a box of Jell-O, along with oil and eggs. Then you beat it with a mixer for 10 minutes. A topping made from bread crumbs and other ingredients was pressed into a Bundt pan before the cake batter was scraped in. My favorite variation was chocolate cake with raspberry Jell-O, but my mother loved yellow cake with orange Jell-O. Thanks for your help.

Amazing Applesauce
John Carter, Lincoln, Neb.

My saintly grandmother, who died just short of her 100th birthday, made an amazing applesauce using fresh apple slices and cinnamon (pretty standard), but it also included whole pearl tapioca—the big ones, not Minute Tapioca. Served hot with real cream, it made life worth living. The trick, as I recall, was cooking it in a double boiler. Done right, the tapioca is firm, almost rubbery, and the apples crisp and tart. I would love to know if readers have this recipe. It is a family tradition, of German and Danish origin.

SPOT THE ROOSTER!

A tiny version of this rooster has been hidden in the pages of this issue. Write to us with its location and we'll enter you in a random drawing. The first correct entry drawn will win a pair of Shun Classic Kitchen Shears (see page 29), and each of the next five will receive a free one-year subscription to Cook's Country. To enter, visit **CooksCountry.com/emailus** by May 31, 2011, or write to Rooster, Cook's Country, P.O. Box 470739, Brookline, MA 02447. Include your name and address. Keen-eyed Anna Miner of Skamania, Wash., found the rooster in the December/January 2011 issue in the Homemade Stuffing Mix photo and won our favorite toaster. Cock-a-doodle-doo.

Holiday Cookie Contest
$1,000 Grand Prize

Start the holidays very early: Submit your best holiday cookie recipes to CooksCountry.com/cookiecontest or Cookie Contest, Cook's Country, P.O. Box 470739, Brookline, MA 02447. Include your name, address, telephone, and email. The deadline for submissions is April 30, 2011. All entries become property of Cook's Country. Grand Prize is $1,000; six finalists get $100 each.

MATZO BRITTLE Makes about 15 pieces
Hillary Kolosky, Cambridge, Mass.

"I make this brittle every year for Passover, and it's always a hit."

- 3 (6½-inch) squares matzo
- 12 tablespoons (1½ sticks) unsalted butter, cut into 12 pieces
- 1 cup packed light brown sugar
- 1 teaspoon vanilla extract
- 1 cup semisweet chocolate chips
- ½ teaspoon kosher salt
- 1 cup slivered almonds, toasted

1. Adjust oven rack to middle position and heat oven to 350 degrees. Line 13 by 9-inch metal baking pan with aluminum foil, allowing foil to hang over pan edges. Spray foil with cooking spray. Place 2 matzo squares in bottom of pan. Cut remaining matzo into two 6½ by 2½-inch rectangles and fit into empty space of pan.

2. Bring butter and brown sugar to boil in medium saucepan over medium heat and cook, stirring constantly, until thickened, 2 to 3 minutes. Off heat, stir in vanilla. Pour caramel over matzo, spreading to coat completely. Bake until deep golden brown, about 10 minutes.

3. Remove pan from oven and let cool 5 minutes. Sprinkle chocolate chips over caramel and let sit 5 minutes. Spread chocolate in even layer and sprinkle with salt and almonds. Refrigerate until firm, at least 30 minutes. Invert brittle onto cutting board, discard foil, and break into large pieces. Serve. (Brittle can be stored in airtight container at room temperature for up to 4 days.)

RHUBARB CUSTARD PIE Serves 8
Bill Swarthout, Avon, Ohio

"I make this pie for my daughter every spring when the rhubarb in my garden turns bright red. A lattice-top crust looks beautiful, too." Use your favorite pie dough or go to **CooksCountry.com/extra** for our Double-Crust Pie Dough recipe.

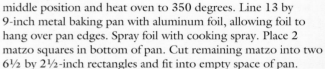

- 2 (9-inch) pie dough rounds
- 1 cup sugar
- 2 large eggs
- 2 tablespoons all-purpose flour
- ½ teaspoon salt
- 1 pound rhubarb, trimmed, halved lengthwise, and chopped

1. On lightly floured surface, roll 1 dough round into 12-inch circle. Transfer to 9-inch pie plate, cover with plastic wrap, and refrigerate 30 minutes. Roll second dough into 12-inch circle and refrigerate, covered, on large plate for 30 minutes.

2. Adjust oven rack to lowest position and heat oven to 375 degrees. Whisk sugar, eggs, flour, and salt in large bowl. Stir in rhubarb. Scrape filling into prepared pie shell. Brush border of dough with water, then arrange top crust over filling. Crimp edges of pie. Cut four 1-inch slits near center of pie.

3. Bake until juices are bubbling and crust is golden brown, about 50 minutes. Cool completely on wire rack, about 4 hours. Serve.

Strawberry Shortcake Roll

Celebrate spring: Peepers sing, daffodils sprout, warm breezes waft,
and we roll fresh strawberries and cream into a soft, light sponge cake.

To make this cake you will need:

- 1½ **pounds fresh strawberries,
  hulled and halved**
- ½ **cup granulated sugar**
- 1 **tablespoon water**
- 1 **tablespoon lemon juice**
- 1½ **teaspoons unflavored gelatin**
- 1 **recipe 18 by 13-inch jellyroll cake***
  Confectioners' sugar
- 1 **cup heavy cream, chilled**
- 4 **ounces mascarpone cheese**
- ½ **teaspoon vanilla extract**

FOR THE STRAWBERRY FILLING: Cook straw-berries and 6 tablespoons granulated sugar in large saucepan over medium heat, mashing occasionally with potato masher, until thick and jamlike, 10 to 15 minutes (mixture should measure 2¼ cups). Meanwhile, combine water, 2 teaspoons lemon juice, and gelatin in small bowl and let stand until gelatin softens, about 5 minutes. Stir gelatin mixture into hot strawberry mixture until dissolved. Transfer to large bowl and refrigerate until set, at least 4 hours.

FOR THE CAKE: Bake cake according to recipe instructions in parchment-lined pan. Before cooling, run knife around pan edges to loosen. Turn out cake onto fresh sheet of parch-ment that has been dusted with confectioners'

sugar. Gently peel off parchment attached to cake and discard. Starting at short edge, roll cake and fresh parchment into log and cool completely, seam side down, about 1 hour.

TO FINISH: With electric mixer fitted with whisk attachment, whip cream, mascarpone, remaining granulated sugar, remaining lemon juice, and vanilla on medium speed until stiff peaks form, about 3 minutes. Gently unroll cake and spread with strawberry mixture, leaving 1-inch border around edges. Top with whipped cream and reroll cake snugly, leaving parchment behind. Wrap in plastic wrap and refrigerate until firm, at least 4 hours. Dust with confectioners' sugar. Serve.

---

*Go to **CooksCountry.com/extra** for our Easy Jellyroll Cake recipe.

Follow us on **Twitter:** twitter.com/TestKitchen
Find us on **Facebook:** facebook.com/CooksCountry

Cook's Country

JUNE/JULY 2011

Peaches and Cream Pie

Steakhouse-Style Steak Tips

Guide to Perfect Barbecued Ribs

Dill Potato Salad
Triple Dill Flavor

Barberton Fried Chicken
Moist Meat, Big Crunch

Strawberry Dream Cake
Move Over, Chocolate Cake

Slow-Cooker Brunswick Stew
Southern Barbecue Classic

Low-Fat Lemon Squares
Even Better Than Full-Fat

Carolina Red Slaw
Spicy Slaw Gets Crisp

Grilled Pork Chops
Honey Glaze That Sticks

Chicken Chimichangas
No-Fuss, No-Fail Recipe

Grilled Vegetable Salad
Marinating Is the Key

Baltimore Pit Beef
Juicy Beef, Spicy Sauce

Rating Ice-Cream Bars
The Coating Matters Most

www.CooksCountry.com
$4.95 U.S./$6.95 CANADA

0 74470 05251 7

07>

*Leafing through old cookbooks, we found **Peaches and Cream Pie**. Sounded fantastic. And it is—now that we've spent a few weeks in the test kitchen making adjustments for things like the difference between cream today and 100 years ago.* PAGE 17

Cook's Country

Dear Country Cook,

I grew up knowing a trace from a whippletree because the local farmer Floyd Bentley used a team for mowing and tedding.★ We used mules for cutting cow corn, and once in a while, Charlie Bentley hooked up a team to haul sap for sugaring. These were big workhorses, their flanks higher than my head, their hooves large and spread, like a camel's. They were also used for horse pulls at the late-summer fairs. The blue ribbons still hang in Charlie's house, the one up on SE Corners Road.

On a small farm, agriculture wasn't a business. It was what you did from before breakfast until suppertime. Food was local—store-bought was the exception. You knew where everything came from: the corn, the lettuce, the berries (from bushes down around the abandoned corn crib), the maple syrup, the beef, the green beans, and the potatoes, that last stored in large plastic buckets on an unheated porch. But we didn't study food, or compare it, or set out to find the best this or the best that. It was just our food, the stuff that we cooked and ate.

It's hard to explain all this to someone used to the aisles of Whole Foods. Choices give life possibilities but also complications. Sometimes it's nice to know what's for dinner simply by peeking into the root cellar, the garden, or the freezer. It's also nice to spend a summer's afternoon sitting on a horse-drawn wagon.

That's why the woman in the photo below is smiling. She knows where she's come from and where she's going. How many of us today can say the same?

Christopher Kimball, Founder and Editor

★ If you don't know a trace from a whippletree or have no idea what the heck tedding is, find out on **Facebook.com/CooksCountry**.

Cook's Country

Founder and Editor Christopher Kimball
Editorial Director Jack Bishop
Executive Editor, Magazines John Willoughby
Executive Editor Peggy Grodinsky
Managing Editor Scott Kathan
Senior Editors Lisa McManus, Cali Rich, Diane Unger
Test Kitchen Director Erin McMurrer
Associate Editors Lynn Clark, Amy Graves
Test Cooks Sarah Gabriel, Kelly Price
Assistant Editors Hannah Crowley, Taizeth Sierra
Assistant Test Cooks Rebeccah Marsters,
Carolynn Purpura
Senior Copy Editor Catherine Tumber
Copy Editor Nell Beram
Editorial Assistant Shannon Hatch
Executive Assistant Christine Gordon
Assistant Test Kitchen Director Gina Nistico
Senior Kitchen Assistant Leah Rovner
Kitchen Assistants Maria Elena Delgado,
Ena Gudiel, Ed Tundidor
TV Producer Melissa Baldino
Contributing Editors
Erika Bruce, Eva Katz, Jeremy Sauer
Consulting Editors Anne Mendelson, Meg Ragland
Science Editor Guy Crosby, Ph.D.
Executive Food Editor, TV, Radio & Media
Bridget Lancaster

Design Director Amy Klee
Art Director Julie Bozzo
Deputy Art Director Susan Levin
Staff Photographer Daniel J. van Ackere
Color Food Photography Keller + Keller
Styling Mary Jane Sawyer

Art Director, Books Greg Galvan
Associate Art Director, Books Matthew Warnick
Designer, Books Beverly Hsu

Art Director, Marketing & Web Christine Vo
Associate Art Directors, Marketing & Web
Erica Lee, Jody Lee
Designers Elaina Natario, Mariah Tarvainen

Production Director Guy Rochford
Senior Projects Manager Alice Carpenter
Traffic & Production Coordinator Kate Hux
Asset & Workflow Manager Andrew Mannone
Production & Imaging Specialists
Judy Blomquist, Heather Dube, Lauren Pettapiece

Online Managing Editor David Tytell
Online Editor Kate Mason
Online Assistant Editors
Eric Grzymkowski, Mari Levine

Executive Editor, Books Elizabeth Carduff
Executive Food Editor, Books
Julia Collin Davison
Senior Editors, Books Louise Emerick, Lori Galvin,
Suzannah McFerran
Associate Editors, Books Kate Hartke,
Chris O'Connor, Adelaide Parker, Dan Zuccarello
Test Cooks, Books Rebecca Morris,
Christie Morrison, Kate Williams
Editorial Assistant, Books Alyssa King

ON THE COVER:
Peaches and Cream Pie, Keller + Keller
ILLUSTRATION: Greg Stevenson

Cook's Country magazine (ISSN 1552-1990), number 39, is published bimonthly by Boston Common Press Limited Partnership, 17 Station Street, Brookline, MA 02445. Copyright 2011 Boston Common Press Limited Partnership. Periodicals Postage paid at Boston, Mass., and additional mailing offices. Publications Mail Agreement No. 40020778. Return undeliverable Canadian addresses to P.O. Box 875, Station A, Windsor, Ontario N9A 6P2. POSTMASTER: Send address changes to Cook's Country, P.O. Box 8382, Red Oak, IA 51591-1382. Customer Service: It's easy to subscribe, give a gift subscription, change your address, and manage your subscription online. Visit www.AmericasTestKitchen.com/customerservice for all of your customer service needs or write to us at Cook's Country, P.O. Box 8382, Red Oak, IA 51591-1382. PRINTED IN THE USA

JUNE / JULY 2011

Contents

DILL POTATO SALAD, 11

BALTIMORE PIT BEEF, 12

CHOCOLATE ÉCLAIR CAKE, 24

Features

In Every Issue

Watch Us on Television
Watch the folks behind our recipes test equipment, taste ingredients, perfect classic American recipes, and stroll through food history. Find out when *Cook's Country from America's Test Kitchen* airs on public television in your area at **CooksCountryTV.com**.

Ask Cook's Country

Pie recipes call for egg washes of all sorts. Does it matter what I brush my pie crust with?
Lisa Unangst, Brighton, Mass.

Bakers brush double-crust pies with egg wash to improve browning and lend a shiny finish. As you've noticed, different recipes call for different formulations. We made a list of the typical methods and put them all to the test. We started by making three double-crust pies and brushing the top crust of one with a beaten egg, one with a beaten egg white, and one with beaten yolk. The crust brushed with egg white was still dull and pale when the pie was done. Yolk alone made the crust very shiny, but by the time the pie was fully cooked, it was too dark. Moreover, the yolk was too thick to spread evenly, leaving deep brush marks and bald spots. A whole egg spread evenly and browned well but lacked the shine of the yolk-brushed crust. Some recipes call for thinning egg wash with water, milk, or cream. We tried each of these in combination with yolks, whites, and whole eggs. None produced the glossy crust we were looking for, although both milk and cream sped browning. In the end, we found that brushing the crust with a whole egg plus one yolk gave us both a glossy finish and perfect browning.

THE BOTTOM LINE: Brushing pie crust with a whole egg and one yolk, lightly beaten, yields a shiny finish and moderate browning speed.

WHITE ONLY
Underbrowned

YOLK ONLY
Overbrowned

WHOLE EGG PLUS YOLK
Perfect browning

What are the differences between old-fashioned, quick-cooking, and instant oatmeal?
Richard Weiner, Hanover, N.H.

All three varieties of oats are flattened between rollers to speed cooking. For even faster cooking, both instant and quick oats are steamed, toasted, and cut into smaller pieces (instant are smaller than quick) before packaging.

We prepared instant oatmeal, quick oats, and old-fashioned rolled oats and found that they all tasted fine. Both instant and quick oats were "mushy," tasters said. In the microwave, both of these oat types take 90 seconds to cook, while the old-fashioned oats take about a minute longer. One serving of instant oatmeal costs about 32 cents—more than double the cost of the other two. So if you're buying the instant packets, you're paying for all sorts of flavorings and additives. We recommend that you buy old-fashioned oats.

THE BOTTOM LINE: Old-fashioned rolled oats have the best texture and take only a minute longer to cook.

Does the amount of time I soak wood chips affect smoke flavor on the grill?
Noah Hull-Diamond, Seward, Alaska

Wood chips are soaked for smoking because they produce much more smoke than dry chips do. To investigate the effects of soaking time, we soaked batches of relatively mild oak chips for 15 minutes, one hour, four hours, and 24 hours before smoking halved chickens for one hour, and large pork shoulders for two hours (we finished cooking the pork in the oven) in a standard kettle grill.

We noticed something interesting right away: After about two hours of soaking, the chips started to saturate and sink. At the four-hour mark, all lay at the bottom of the bowl. And whether the chips were saturated or not made a big difference in the flavor of the chicken. The chicken we smoked using chips soaked for 15 and 60 minutes tasted nice and smoky, but the chicken smoked using chips that had soaked for four and 24 hours tasted like "a wet ashtray," in the words of one taster. What was going on here?

Saturated chips produce steam until they dry out, at which point they begin smoking. The culprit here is not the smoke but the steam, which carries malodorous molecules from the wood to the surface of the food. When smoking for a short period, saturated chips produce impure steam for a greater proportion of the total smoking time, so the off-flavors dominate. In longer-smoked pulled pork,

however, tasters couldn't detect a difference between pork that was smoked with short-soaked versus saturated chips. When food is left on the grill long after the soaked chips stop producing impure steam, any off-flavors are covered up by the additional smoke.

THE BOTTOM LINE: Fifteen minutes is sufficient for soaking wood chips—and longer soaking can be a problem.

What's the best fat to use for greasing the pan for pancakes?
Matt Swarthout, Cuyahoga Falls, Ohio

To answer your question, we tested butter and vegetable oil side by side on our pancake griddle. For the sake of consistency—and to guarantee properly cooked pancakes—we followed our recipe to a "T" and flipped all the pancakes when the bottoms were set and the batter on the top was beginning to bubble (after about one minute over medium heat).

When we greased the griddle with butter, the pancakes overbrowned: The milk solids in the butter brown more quickly than the pancake batter cooks. (The butter may burn, too.) But the pan greased with vegetable oil produced perfectly golden pancakes.

THE BOTTOM LINE: For perfectly cooked, golden-brown pancakes, cook them over medium heat and grease the pan with vegetable oil.

Is grocery store ground bison healthier than beef? And how do the two compare?
Beth Golay, Seattle, Wash.

Most bison meat is labeled 90 percent lean, but it's actually healthier than 90 percent lean beef because of the type of fat that each meat contains. Commercially raised bison are typically grass-fed, which results in relatively low levels of saturated fat in the meat. By contrast, most commercial beef cows are fed a grain-based diet, which leads to higher levels of unhealthy saturated fat in the meat.

We grilled 90 percent lean buffalo burgers alongside both 85 percent and 90 percent lean beef burgers (our burger recipe calls for 85 percent lean beef) to see how they compared. The bison burgers were slightly drier, and some tasters found them "gamy" or "iron-y," but we liked them nonetheless.

THE BOTTOM LINE: Ground beef is milder and slightly juicer than bison, but bison is a fine—and healthier—substitute.

To ask us a cooking question:
Visit **CooksCountry.com/emailus**. Or write to Ask Cook's Country, P.O. Box 470739, Brookline, MA 02447. Just try to stump us!

Cook's Country

VP, New Media Product Development Barry Kelly
Lead Developer, New Media Bharat Ruparel
Senior Information Architect Melissa MacQuarrie
Social Media Manager Steph Yiu
Web Programmer, New Media Anand Kumar

Director, Information Technology Rocco Lombardo
Systems Administrator Marcus Walser
Lead Developer Scott Thompson
Software Architect Robert Martinez
Senior Web Developer Christopher Candelora
Web Developers Bach Bui, James Madden, Alphonse Shiwala
Business Analyst Wendy Tseng
Quality Assurance Micquella Bradford
Web Production Coordinator Evan Davis
Web Production Assistant Debbie Chiang
IT Support Specialist Geoffrey Clark

Vice President, Marketing David Mack
Circulation Director Doug Wicinski
Fulfillment & Circulation Manager Carrie Horan
Partnership Marketing Manager Pamela Putprush
Marketing Assistant Lauren Perkins
Database & Direct Mail Director Adam Perry
Senior Database Analyst Marina Sakharova
Products Director Steven Browall
Product Promotions Director Tom Conway
E-Commerce Marketing Director Hugh Buchan
E-Commerce Marketing Manager Laurel Zeidman
Marketing Copywriter David Goldberg
Customer Service Manager Jacqueline Valerio
Customer Service Representatives Jillian Nannicelli, Kate Sokol

Chief Financial Officer Sharyn Chabot
Human Resources Director Adele Shapiro
Controller Mandy Shito
Finance Director Wayne Saville
Senior Accountant Aaron Goranson
Staff Accountant Connie Forbes
Accounts Payable Specialist Steven Kasha
Office Manager Michael Pickett
Receptionist Henrietta Murray

Sponsorship Sales Director Marcy McCreary
Retail Sales & Marketing Manager Emily Logan
Sponsorship & Marketing Coordinator Bailey Snyder
Publicity Deborah Broide

Visit us online at CooksCountry.com

Follow us on **Twitter:** twitter.com/TestKitchen
Find us on **Facebook:** facebook.com/CooksCountr

America's TEST KITCHEN

America's Test Kitchen is a 2,500-square-foot kitch located just outside of Boston. It is the home of Cook Country and Cook's Illustrated magazines and the workday destination of more than 50 test coo editors, and cookware specialists. Our mission is to te recipes until we understand how and why they we and to arrive at the best version. We also test kitch equipment and supermarket ingredients in search brands that offer the best value and performance. Y can watch us at work by tuning in to Cook's Coun from America's Test Kitchen (CooksCountryTV.co on public television.

Kitchen Shortcuts

COMPILED BY CAROLYNN PURPURA

TIDY TIP
Splatter Guard
Erica Zito, Cedar Rapids, Iowa

I don't have a splatter guard, but there are times when I wish I did. Rather than buy yet another one-use-only kitchen gadget, I discovered that I could substitute a colander as a splatter guard when I'm frying something. It fits over the pan and keeps my kitchen cleaner.

DOUBLE DUTY
Shaken Not Stirred
Lawrence Tetterson, Albuquerque, N.M.

Rather than going out to a coffee shop and spending nearly five bucks for a single iced-coffee drink, I make them at home. I've found that shaking the ice, coffee, and milk in my cocktail shaker works much better than simply stirring everything together in a glass. I get a light, frothy, delicious drink for pennies. Who needs a barista?

HANDY TIP
Easy Chicken Soup
Janine Chase, Independence, Ohio

When I'm making chicken soup, I tie the chicken up in a cheesecloth bag before putting it in the pot. After a few hours, when the soup is done, I easily and neatly fish the chicken bag out with tongs. I find this method much less cumbersome than trying to pour a big, hot pot of chicken and vegetables into a colander.

BETTER BAKING
Cupcake Decorating
LeeAnne Shoenfeld, Hampton, N.H.

I found a great new use for packages of hot cocoa. I empty one envelope into a strainer and use it to dust the tops of frosted cupcakes. It makes the cupcakes look nice and adds flavor, too.

TIDY TIP
Cookbook Page Holder
Karla Sartor, Los Alamos, N.M.

I use a clear glass baking dish as a page holder for my cookbooks, so they don't flip shut as I'm trying to cook from them. Open the cookbook to the page you need and set the baking dish on top. You can read the recipe through the dish, and the book is safe from kitchen splatter.

TIMESAVER
Instant Defrosting
Nancy Petrie, Stanley, N.Y.

I often use frozen vegetables in my pasta salads. I put the frozen vegetables right in the colander and then drain the hot pasta over them. The vegetables are instantly defrosted.

DOUBLE DUTY
Kernel Catcher
Elise Peters, Bangor, Maine

Removing the kernels from an ear of corn can be a messy task, as the cobs tend to slide on the cutting board and the kernels fly all over the place. To avoid the mess, I steady each cob on the center of a tube pan before slicing off the kernels. This keeps the cob stable, plus the kernels fall directly into the tube pan.

EASY CLEANUP
Cleaning Small Tupperware
Loretta Michalczak, Clinton Township, Mich.

I know a great way to wash small, lightweight plastic containers in the dishwasher without their flipping over and filling with water—one of life's small annoyances. Place the containers on the top rack of the dishwasher and secure them by placing a wire cooling rack on top.

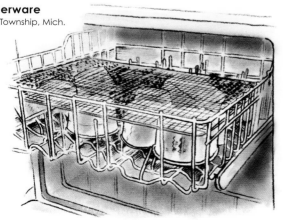

Submit a tip by e-mail at **CooksCountry.com/kitchenshortcuts** or send a letter to Kitchen Shortcuts, Cook's Country, P.O. Box 470739, Brookline, MA 02447. Include your name, address, and phone number. If we publish your tip, you will receive a free one-year subscription to *Cook's Country*. Letters may be edited for clarity or length.

Recipe Makeover Lemon Squares

Our challenge? Reducing the fat in the ultra-buttery crust yet making a bar cookie we'd still want to eat.

BY KRIS WIDICAN AND CAROLYNN PURPURA

EVEN WHEN WE'RE counting calories, we're not into deprivation. That's why we wanted a slimmed-down lemon bar that didn't announce the fact. Standard recipes pack 16 grams of fat and 330 calories per bar—and that's assuming you can stop at one. We collected several full-fat recipes and discovered that while the lemon topping was not all that fattening, the crust had so much butter that we probably put on pounds just thinking about it.

We looked around to see what diet recipes have tried. Not a heck of a lot, it turns out, beyond replacing the butter in the shortbread with either vegetable oil or margarine. We vetoed margarine, which tastes bad. That left us with oil. Following one recipe, we topped the oil-based crust with a basic lemon curd (a mixture of lemon juice, sugar, and eggs) and baked them. We had no shortage of tasters—or critics. Shortbread, they told us curtly, is all about butter. They were right: The bars had zero flavor and were mealy. To add insult to injury, the calorie and fat counts had barely budged.

Clearly, our chief challenge would be to cut back on the butter while retaining its flavor and the "short," tender texture it traditionally gives the crust. We took a recipe for full-fat lemon bars and got to work. Following it, we set 12 tablespoons of butter, ½ cup of confectioners' sugar, and 1¼ cups of flour on the counter for the (8 by 8-inch) crust.

Market Report: Butter Down Almost 70 Percent

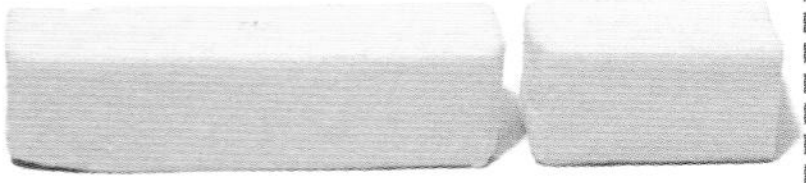

FULL-FAT CRUST
12 tablespoons

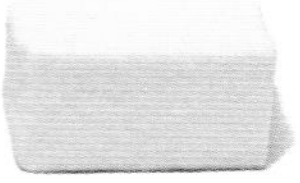

OUR REDUCED-FAT CRUST
4 tablespoons

Cornstarch, baking powder, and milk work together to keep the crust tender (despite the drastic cut in butter), while lemon zest adds bright lemon flavor.

The Numbers

All nutritional information is for a single lemon square.

Traditional Lemon Squares
CALORIES **330**
FAT **16g**   SATURATED FAT **11g**

**Cook's Country
Reduced-Fat Lemon Squares**
CALORIES **190**
FAT **6g**   SATURATED FAT **4g**

We did an inordinate amount of testing in an attempt to replace the butter with lower-calorie Neufchâtel cream cheese. But no matter how much we tinkered, the crusts tasted pasty, gummy, and underbaked. Eventually, we rejected this approach. On the plus side, we learned that just 4 tablespoons of butter still provided acceptable buttery flavor.

But butter contributes moisture to the crust as well; with such a drastic cutback, the crust didn't hold together. We "glued" it with an egg yolk and used a bit less flour, but the crust still crumbled when we tried to cut it into bars. We ditched the yolk (we hadn't been thrilled with the fat that it added anyhow) and reached for milk. Now the crust held together, but it was dense, tough, and tasteless. To bring back tenderness, we replaced some of the flour with cornstarch, which gives baked goods a melt-in-your-mouth quality. We added lemon zest and extra salt for flavor. Finally, to lighten the crust, we tested baking powder, eventually landing on ½ teaspoon. We also found that we could trim the sugar and not miss the sweetness. With the crust under control, we moved on to the filling.

We had been using two eggs in the filling, but we quickly ejected one of the yolks, and no one was the wiser. Next, we cut back the sugar a tablespoon at a time until we'd lost ¼ cup. Tasters actually liked these lemon bars better because the lemon flavor really popped. (That, in turn, helped the crust: We now barely noticed the missing butter.) At this point, each bar was down nearly 150 calories and 10 grams of fat yet tasted terrific. we'd lowered the calories and fat, but we'd raised the (ahem) bar.

Thin? Yes. Wimpy? No. Each bite of these reduced-fat squares explodes with bright lemon flavor.

REDUCED-FAT LEMON SQUARES
Makes 9 lemon squares
Press the crust dough snugly against the pan edges to keep the lemon topping from running beneath the crust. Cool the crust for at least 15 minutes before pouring on the lemon topping.

CRUST
- ¾ cup (3¾ ounces) all-purpose flour
- ⅓ cup (1⅓ ounces) confectioners' sugar
- 3 tablespoons cornstarch
- 1½ teaspoons grated lemon zest
- ½ teaspoon baking powder
- ¼ teaspoon salt
- 4 tablespoons unsalted butter, cut into ½-inch pieces and chilled
- 1 tablespoon whole milk

LEMON TOPPING
- ¾ cup (5¼ ounces) granulated sugar
- 1 large egg plus 1 large egg white, lightly beaten
- 2 tablespoons all-purpose flour
- ⅛ teaspoon salt
- 1 tablespoon grated lemon zest plus 6 tablespoons juice (2 lemons)
- 1 tablespoon confectioners' sugar

1. Adjust oven rack to middle position and heat oven to 350 degrees. Line 8-inch-square baking pan with aluminum foil, allowing foil to hang over pan edges. Spray foil lightly with vegetable oil spray.

2. For the crust: Process flour, sugar, cornstarch, lemon zest, baking powder, and salt in food processor until combined. Add butter and milk and pulse until mixture resembles coarse meal, about 10 pulses. Transfer mixture to prepared pan and press into even layer. Bake until edges are lightly browned, 16 to 20 minutes. Cool crust on wire rack for 15 minutes.

3. For the lemon topping: Reduce oven temperature to 325 degrees. Whisk granulated sugar, egg, egg white, flour, and salt together in bowl until smooth. Stir in lemon juice and zest until combined. Pour filling over cooled crust and bake until filling is set, 15 to 20 minutes. Cool completely in pan on wire rack, about 1 hour. Dust with confectioners' sugar. Using foil overhang, lift lemon squares from pan and cut into 9 squares. Serve.

Cooking for Two Lasagna

It's a perfect dish for a crowd but too much work for only two. We'd have to find a way to cut back the labor, not just the proportions. BY ADELAIDE PARKER

LASAGNA IS A dynamite dish for a crowd: Recipes make enough to feed hungry hordes. Boiling the noodles, making both long-simmered meat sauce and white sauce, layering the components, then baking—sure, it's time-consuming to prepare, but that's not a deal breaker given the substantial (and delicious) result. Making this deeply satisfying dish for two, though, is another story. Scaling down the recipe was a given. So was simplifying it.

To that end, when I decided to downsize a recipe for lasagna, no-boil noodles were a no-brainer. They're far more convenient than the traditional dried noodles, which require boiling, draining, and careful separating (as they tend to stick and tear). I tested baking dishes of varying sizes as well as some random, off-size ceramic casseroles. I soon settled on a standard loaf pan—everybody has one. It makes a lasagna that generously serves two, and a single lasagna noodle fit inside perfectly.

For the meat sauce, I wanted a version as rich and thick as is traditional, but I refused to simmer it for an hour or two to achieve that flavor. For help, I turned to meatloaf mix, which combines ground beef, pork, and veal, hence adds complexity by its very nature. I sautéed onion and garlic in oil and then stirred in the meat and cooked it until it was no longer pink. Because no-boil noodles chiefly rely on the liquid in the sauce to rehydrate and soften, I knew that I'd need to get the moisture content just right. If the sauce was too thick, the noodles would be crunchy; too loose and they would be limp and lifeless. It took a number of tests to nail down the correct proportions. Ultimately, I combined the meat-onion mixture with one (14.5-ounce) can of drained tomatoes (including ¼ cup of the liquid from the can), plus a small can of tomato sauce. After just a few more minutes of simmering, the sauce was done.

Classic lasagna also uses béchamel sauce, a white sauce made from butter, flour, and milk. I vetoed it without a second thought: Two sauces for two people is too much work. Instead, to get complex flavor without complex cooking, I relied on three classic lasagna cheeses: ricotta, Parmesan,

and mozzarella. All I'd need to do was grate the latter two. An egg helped thicken and bind the cheeses. Since it was summer, I also added a flavor that practically defines the season: chopped fresh basil.

A few final tests showed that covering the lasagna with foil prevented moisture from escaping during baking, offering extra insurance that the no-boil noodles would soften. I removed the foil for the last 10 minutes to let a top layer of cheese brown. With all the time I'd saved preparing lasagna for two, maybe I could get started on some cannoli for dessert.

LASAGNA FOR TWO
Serves 2
If your store doesn't carry meatloaf mix, substitute equal parts 85 percent lean ground beef and ground pork. You'll need vegetable oil spray to grease the inside of the foil.

SAUCE
- 1 tablespoon olive oil
- 1 small onion, chopped fine
  Salt and pepper
- 2 garlic cloves, minced
- 8 ounces meatloaf mix
- 1 (14.5-ounce) can diced tomatoes, drained, with ¼ cup juice reserved
- 1 (8-ounce) can tomato sauce

FILLING, NOODLES, AND CHEESE
- 4 ounces whole-milk or part-skim ricotta cheese
- 1 ounce Parmesan cheese, grated (½ cup), plus 2 tablespoons
- 3 tablespoons chopped fresh basil
- 1 large egg, lightly beaten
- ⅛ teaspoon salt
- ⅛ teaspoon pepper
- 4 no-boil lasagna noodles
- 4 ounces whole-milk mozzarella cheese, shredded (1 cup)

1. Adjust oven rack to middle position and heat oven to 400 degrees.
2. For the sauce: Heat oil in large saucepan over medium heat until shimmering. Add onion and ⅛ teaspoon salt and cook until softened, 3 to 5 minutes. Stir in garlic and cook until fragrant, about 30 seconds. Add meatloaf mix and cook, breaking up meat into small pieces, until no

We lost one sauce and simplified the other for meaty lasagna that's easy enough for two.

longer pink, about 4 minutes.
3. Stir in tomatoes, reserved juice, and tomato sauce and cook until slightly thickened, about 2 minutes (sauce should measure about 3 cups). Season with salt and pepper to taste.
4. For the filling, noodles, and cheese: Combine ricotta, ½ cup Parmesan, basil, egg, salt, and pepper in bowl. Cover bottom of 8½ by 4½-inch loaf pan with ½ cup sauce. Top with 1 noodle and spread one-third of ricotta mixture evenly over noodle. Sprinkle with ¼ cup mozzarella and cover with ½ cup sauce. Repeat twice, beginning with noodle and ending with sauce. Top with remaining 1 noodle, remaining 1 cup sauce, remaining ¼ cup mozzarella, and remaining 2 tablespoons Parmesan.
5. Cover pan tightly with foil sprayed with vegetable oil spray and bake until bubbling around edges, 25 to 30 minutes. Discard foil and continue to bake until browned, about 10 minutes. Cool on wire rack for 20 minutes. Serve.

ESSENTIAL GEAR **Loaf Pan**
While developing our recipe for Lasagna for Two, we tested several types of pans. In the end, we found that an ordinary loaf pan accommodates this lasagna as if it were built for the job. It easily fits a stack of four no-boil lasagna noodles layered with sauce and cheese. And we bet you've already got a loaf pan in your kitchen.

NOT JUST FOR BREAD
The Williams-Sonoma Goldtouch Nonstick Loaf Pan is the test kitchen's favorite.

Slow Cooker Brunswick Stew

This long-cooking Southern stew seemed a natural for the slow cooker. But it turned out as a big mush. The right timing—and a trick—helped us fix that. BY DIANE UNGER

BRUNSWICK STEW SHOULD be tailor-made for the slow cooker. It's a rustic mix of assorted meats (chicken, pork, squirrel, rabbit, or whatever else you happened to shoot while out hunting) and vegetables (corn, lima beans, tomatoes, potatoes, peas, okra) in a tomato-based broth. In the South, where the stew originated, it's often cooked for fund-raisers in giant batches that simmer for hours. But when I moved the stew into the slow cooker—I tested a range of recipes supposedly engineered for the appliance—the results weren't pretty.

These recipes required dumping a hodgepodge of cubed ingredients into the cooker and hitting "start." After as many as 12 hours, no wonder the meats were dry, the vegetables were mushy, and the potatoes had disintegrated entirely. The seemingly random ingredients in many recipes (mustard, canned beans, whole bottles of ketchup, the contents of the vegetable drawer) exacerbated the problem. At least, my goals were crystal clear: correctly cooked vegetables; moist, tender

meats; and a pared-down stew that tasted bright, not dreary.

I made two decisions up front: I opted for supermarket-friendly chicken and pork, and I limited the cooking time to roughly six hours to give the stew a fighting chance. Then I dove in, testing cuts of meat to see which could handle the (still) lengthy cooking time. Blade chops, moist and consistently tender, won the pork face-off (with country-style ribs a close second). Bone-in, skin-on chicken thighs beat out breasts, but even they overcooked by the time the chops were tender. To slow the thighs' cooking, I used a favorite test kitchen technique: I wrapped them in foil before adding them to the slow cooker. After six hours, I removed the foil packet, chopped up the (now moist) chicken, and stirred it back into the slow cooker along with the pork, which I'd also fished out, boned, and chopped.

For the base, I settled on a combination of chicken broth and tomato. Ketchup—in moderation—added body and sweet-tart balance. The stew really turned the corner when I browned the pork and sautéed the onions and garlic in the rendered fat. Both meat and sauce were now so robust that I could dispense with browning the chicken. I retained the skin, however, to help flavor the chicken as it cooked.

Turning to the vegetables, I added a bit of everything from my initial tests and asked tasters to weed out. Potatoes, corn, and lima beans made the grade. For convenience, I opted for frozen corn and limas, stirring them in toward the end of cooking. But the limas were tough. Added at the beginning of cooking, they turned out tender, creamy, and intact. (Our science editor explained that the limas needed extra time to soften because the acidic tomato-based sauce strengthened the pectin that holds their cell walls together.) And the potatoes? Initially, they were trouble. Added at the start, they turned to sludge. Added at the end, they never cooked. In the foil packet with the chicken, however, they softened yet held their shape.

Two Brunswicks—a town in Georgia and a county in Virginia—famously vie for this stew. With my version, I'd staked a claim for the test kitchen, too.

Brunswick Stew has none of the wintry associations of many other stews: It's a barbecue classic.

TEST KITCHEN DISCOVERY **Two Meats, Two Treatments**

PORK Before adding the blade chops to the slow cooker, we browned them to add savory depth to the stew.

POULTRY To prevent the chicken from overcooking, we cooked it (with the potatoes) in a foil packet on top of the stew.

SLOW-COOKER BRUNSWICK STEW Serves 6 to 8

You can substitute 2 pounds of bone-in, country-style pork ribs for the blade chops. Add the lima beans frozen.

1½	pounds Yukon Gold potatoes, peeled and cut into ¾-inch pieces Salt and pepper
2	pounds bone-in, skin-on chicken thighs, trimmed
3	(10-ounce) bone-in pork blade chops, about 1 inch thick, trimmed
1	tablespoon vegetable oil
2	onions, chopped fine
4	garlic cloves, minced
½	teaspoon cayenne pepper
1	(29-ounce) can tomato sauce
2½	cups low-sodium chicken broth
⅓	cup ketchup
20	ounces frozen lima beans
10	ounces frozen corn, thawed
1	tablespoon cider vinegar

1. Place potatoes over half of 24 by 18-inch sheet of heavy-duty aluminum foil and season with salt and pepper. Pat chicken dry with paper towels. Top potatoes with chicken and season with salt and pepper. Fold foil over chicken and crimp edges to seal; set aside.

2. Pat pork dry with paper towels and season with salt and pepper. Heat oil in 12-inch skillet over medium-high heat until just smoking. Brown chops, 3 to 4 minutes per side; transfer to slow cooker.

3. Add onions to now-empty skillet and cook over medium heat until browned, 6 to 8 minutes. Stir in garlic and cayenne and cook until fragrant, about 30 seconds. Add tomato sauce, broth, ketchup, and ½ teaspoon salt and bring to boil. Pour sauce into slow cooker. Stir in lima beans and place foil packet on top of pork. Cover and cook on low until pork is tender, 6 to 7 hours (or cook on high for 4 to 5 hours).

4. Transfer foil packet and pork to carving board and carefully open packet. Stir potatoes, any accumulated juices, and corn into slow cooker. Cover and cook on high for 30 minutes.

5. When chicken and pork are cool enough to handle, chop into bite-size pieces, discarding skin, fat, and bones. Stir meat and vinegar into slow cooker and season with salt and pepper to taste. Serve. (Stew can be refrigerated for up to 2 days.)

Don't let the basil get lost in the shuffle. BY KELLY PRICE

THERE ARE GOOD reasons why pesto has gone from obscure Italian sauce to American favorite. It's incredibly delicious and incredibly easy. Too often, though, this bright summer sauce is overloaded with cheese and oil and bludgeoned by harsh garlic.

I put together a recipe of standard ratios to dress a pound of pasta—2 cups of basil, 3 cloves of garlic, ¼ cup of pine nuts, and ¾ cup of olive oil—and pureed everything in the food processor. Most recipes stir in the grated Parmesan at the end (to preserve its texture), and I followed suit. Just as I'd feared, the garlic manhandled the basil. In the test kitchen we occasionally toast individual cloves in their skins on the stovetop to soften their flavor. Here, that technique mellowed the potent paste. As I watched the garlic soften and sweeten, I got the idea to toss the pine nuts into the skillet for the opposite reason—to bring out their flavor. It worked nicely, as long as I gave the garlic a good head start (pine nuts toast quicker).

Tasters, continuing to demand that basil be the focus, now asked me to cut back from the standard ½ cup of grated Parmesan. Ultimately, I used half that amount. And was it really necessary to stir it in at the end? I skipped that step, and we couldn't taste the difference.

Finally, a series of olive oil tests showed that just under ½ cup loosened and enriched the pesto without making it greasy. With a simple, balanced recipe in hand, variations came easily.

TEST KITCHEN TECHNIQUE
Toasty Treatment
We toast the raw garlic to soften its bite, but the pine nuts to heighten their flavor.

Stick with the classic pesto (basil and pine nuts) or try our four fresh variations.

CLASSIC PESTO
Makes ¾ cup pesto, enough for 1 pound of pasta
Use medium-size garlic cloves. Thoroughly dry the basil leaves before processing them (as oil and water don't mix). You may associate pesto with pasta, but it's also good in a sandwich, on fish, or stirred into soup.

3	garlic cloves, unpeeled
¼	cup pine nuts
2	cups fresh basil leaves
7	tablespoons extra-virgin olive oil
¼	cup grated Parmesan cheese Salt and pepper

1. Toast garlic in 10-inch skillet over medium heat, stirring occasionally, until fragrant and skins are just beginning to brown, about 5 minutes. Add pine nuts and continue to cook until garlic is spotty brown and nuts are golden, 2 to 3 minutes. When it's cool enough to handle, peel garlic.

2. Process garlic, nuts, basil, oil, Parmesan, and ½ teaspoon salt in food processor until smooth, scraping down bowl as needed, about 1 minute. Season with salt and pepper to taste. (Pesto can be covered with 1 tablespoon oil and refrigerated for up to 4 days or frozen for up to 1 month.)

CILANTRO-LIME PESTO
Replace pine nuts with ¼ cup shelled pistachios, basil with 2 cups fresh cilantro leaves, and Parmesan with ¼ cup grated Pecorino Romano. Add ½ teaspoon grated lime zest and 1 tablespoon lime juice to food processor in step 2.

OREGANO-LEMON PESTO
Reduce basil to 1¾ cups and replace Parmesan with 1 ounce crumbled feta cheese. Add ¼ cup fresh oregano leaves, ½ teaspoon grated lemon zest, and 2 tablespoons lemon juice to food processor in step 2.

ROMESCO PESTO
Replace pine nuts with ¼ cup slivered almonds and basil with 2 cups fresh parsley leaves. Add ½ cup jarred roasted red peppers, rinsed, patted dry, and chopped coarse, and 2 teaspoons red wine vinegar to food processor in step 2.

SUN-DRIED TOMATO-ARUGULA PESTO
Replace basil with 1 cup baby arugula and 1 cup fresh parsley leaves. Add ½ cup sun-dried tomatoes, rinsed, patted dry, and chopped coarse, to food processor in step 2.

Barberton Fried Chicken

What defines Ohio's famous fried chicken? A bread-crumb coating and an old-fashioned frying fat that adds deep flavor. BY DIANE UNGER

For a lover of fried chicken like me, the fact that the small Akron suburb of Barberton, Ohio, is known as "the chicken capital" of the state is an irresistible lure. So one day I hopped into my car and drove the 12 hours from Boston to Barberton on a fried chicken pilgrimage. Once there, I ate my way through chicken dinners—chicken, fries, slaw, and a bowl of the signature "hot sauce"—in five of the town's most famous chicken joints. The chicken was definitely worth the trip. The meat was tender and juicy, the coating thick and crunchy beyond belief and infused with a subtle nutty flavor from having been fried in 100 percent lard. I was determined to re-create this delicious chicken back home in the test kitchen.

From my conversations with the gracious cooks and owners of various chicken houses—and in particular with Milos Papich of Belgrade Gardens, the king of chicken houses—I had a pretty good idea of how Barberton chicken is made. Fresh small chickens are cut into pieces (including the backs and wings) and then salted and hand-breaded via successive dips in seasoned flour, beaten egg, and dried bread crumbs. At Belgrade Gardens, the chicken is breaded in huge batches and chilled for up to two days. (I was told that this resting time ensures that the shaggy coating sticks to the chicken when it's fried.) My Barberton fried chicken had to be tender, juicy, and well seasoned, with a crunchy coat-

The crunchy, deep mahogany crust of this chicken beautifully contrasts with the tender, juicy meat inside.

ing that stuck to the bird through thick and thin—but a two-day rest was out.

In the test kitchen, we often brine chicken (that is, soak it in salt water) before frying to ensure a moist, deeply seasoned bird. I'd learned that Barberton chicken was salted, which achieves a similar outcome and, although it takes longer than brining, is more practical for restaurants serving thousands of pounds of chicken per week (think of the huge tank they'd need to submerge all those birds). In a side-by-side test, tasters

actually preferred the brined chicken. And so did I, because brining took only an hour (30 minutes will do in a pinch).

As for the coating, the seasoned flour and beaten egg were business as usual, but finding the right bread crumbs took some investigation. I set up a breading assembly line and tested homemade fresh, homemade dried, and store-bought panko (coarse, dry Japanese-style crumbs). The fresh crumbs had burned in the fryer by the time the chicken was cooked. The dried crumbs fared better,

but required me to dry them first. So the winner was the incredibly crunchy panko. For more consistent chicken coverage, I pulverized them before coating the chicken.

I still faced the question of how long to let the chicken sit for the coating to adhere. To cover my bases, I tested a range of times, from none at all, to 30 minutes, to up to two days. Waiting was indeed required, but 30 minutes was plenty. While testing these coatings, I made a surprising discovery:

Whenever I brought the oil to 350 degrees, our usual temperature for frying flour-coated chicken, the crumb coating burned. Fortunately, maintaining a temperature of about 300 degrees let the chicken cook through without incinerating the panko crust.

As for the lard, don't discard the idea before you give it a chance. Lard imparts a meaty, nutty flavor that I grew to really like as I ate my way through Barberton. I had to try it in the test kitchen, so I pitted lard against pure peanut oil (our usual choice), as well as against a combination of the two. My tasters liked the flavor imparted by the lard, but using all lard was a little much. After several tests, I found that 2 quarts of peanut oil combined with 1 pound of lard imparted the right amount of porky flavor. My chicken was tender and moist and had the same crisp, mahogany coating that I'd enjoyed at the best chicken house in Barberton. Mission accomplished.

BARBERTON FRIED CHICKEN
Serves 4 to 6
If using breasts, halve crosswise for even cooking. Wings require about 10 minutes of frying. If you can't find lard, use 2 cups extra peanut or vegetable oil.

BRINE
- ½ cup salt
- 3 pounds bone-in chicken pieces, trimmed

COATING
- 3 cups panko bread crumbs
- 1 tablespoon pepper
- 1 teaspoon salt
- 1 cup all-purpose flour
- 3 large eggs
- 2 quarts peanut or vegetable oil
- 1 pound lard

1. For the brine: Whisk 2 quarts cold water and salt together in large container until salt dissolves. Add chicken and refrigerate, covered, for 30 minutes to 1 hour.

2. For the coating: Pulse panko in food processor until finely ground, about 5 pulses. Place ground panko, 2 teaspoons pepper, and ½ teaspoon salt in shallow dish. Combine flour, remaining 1 teaspoon pepper, and remaining ½ teaspoon salt in second shallow dish. Beat eggs in third shallow dish.

3. Remove chicken from refrigerator and pour off brine. Pat chicken dry with paper towels. Dredge chicken pieces, 2 at a time, in flour mixture. Shake excess flour from chicken. Dip chicken in egg, then dredge in panko mixture, pressing crumbs to adhere. Place chicken on wire rack set in rimmed baking sheet and refrigerate, uncovered, for 30 minutes to 2 hours.

4. Adjust oven rack to middle position and heat oven to 200 degrees. Heat

oil and lard in large Dutch oven over medium-high heat until 325 degrees. Fry half of chicken, adjusting burner as necessary to maintain oil temperature between 275 and 300 degrees, until deep golden brown and breasts register 160 degrees and thighs/drumsticks register 175 degrees, 14 to 18 minutes. Drain chicken on clean wire rack set in rimmed baking sheet and place in oven. Bring oil back to 325 degrees and repeat with remaining chicken. Serve with Barberton Hot Sauce.

ON THE SIDE
Barberton Hot Sauce

This hot sauce comes in a bowl, not a bottle.

BY DIANE UNGER

IN BARBERTON, OHIO, it's not a proper fried chicken dinner without a mildly spicy side of stewed Hungarian hot peppers, tomatoes, and onions that the locals call "hot sauce" (though it's not all that hot). Based on a Serbian sauce called *satarash*, what makes this sauce unusual is what's used to thicken it: white rice. Barberton hot sauce isn't really a condiment. Instead, it serves as both a dip for the chicken and a side dish. I'd already re-created the town's famous fried chicken, so I'd finish the job by developing a recipe for the sauce.

I started by sautéing onion and peppers in olive oil. I couldn't find Hungarian hot peppers at the supermarket, but a red bell pepper, two jalapeños, and a smidge of red pepper flakes offered a similar ratio of sweetness to heat. To this mix I added paprika, a can of diced tomatoes, garlic, and a little brown sugar.

I knew from sampling plates of Barberton chicken all over town that you should barely notice that the rice is there—too much and the sauce turns into gruel. After some trial and error, I found that a single tablespoon of raw rice was enough to give the sauce its distinctive silky, jammy quality. To help the rice break down and do its thickening work, I added water to the pot, and I cooked everything over low heat for about 45 minutes.

When I tasted the sauce with a fresh batch of crispy Barberton Fried Chicken, I knew that I'd hit the mark. Though tasters were a little perplexed ("This is hot sauce?"), it didn't stop them from coming back for seconds.

The heat is relatively mild: This "hot sauce" is really more of a side dish.

BARBERTON HOT SAUCE
Makes about 2½ cups
Try leftover sauce with quesadillas or fish, or use it to fill an omelet.

- 3 tablespoons olive oil
- 1 onion, chopped fine
- 2 jalapeño chiles, stemmed, seeded, and minced
- 1 red bell pepper, stemmed, seeded, and chopped fine
- 2 teaspoons paprika
- 1 garlic clove, minced
- 1½ cups water
- 1 (14.5-ounce) can diced tomatoes
- 1 tablespoon long-grain white rice
- 2 teaspoons packed brown sugar
- ¼ teaspoon red pepper flakes

1. Heat oil in medium saucepan over medium heat until shimmering. Add onion, jalapeños, and bell pepper and cook until softened, about 5 minutes. Stir in paprika and garlic and cook until fragrant, about 30 seconds. Add water, tomatoes, rice, sugar, and pepper flakes and bring to boil.

2. Reduce heat to low, cover, and simmer, stirring occasionally, until thickened and vegetables are completely softened, about 45 minutes. (Hot sauce can be refrigerated for up to 3 days.)

Who Knew?
Barberton Hot sauce, a stewed mixture of peppers and tomatoes, gets its thickened, slightly silky texture from a spoonful of rice.

LONG-GRAIN RICE
A surprising addition

Grilled Salmon Steaks

For moist, flavorful fish, we used the grill in a surprising way.

BY ERIKA BRUCE

CHOOSING SALMON STEAKS for the grill is a no-brainer: Their bone and thickness make them a far sturdier cut than a fillet. That's good news for a laid-back summer cook like me. I'd rather turn on my oven on a 90-degree day than try to scrape bits and pieces of salmon off the grill grate. Unfortunately, that thickness can also work against grilled salmon steaks: By the time the interior is cooked through, what was a nicely charred exterior can become blackened and dry. Also overcooked and dry are the two thin strips of flesh that come down on either side of the bone (the fish's belly flaps). And no matter how much seasoning goes on the outside, it never seems to permeate the whole steak.

My quest began with a much needed tummy tuck (for the salmon, not me). I gently removed the skin from one of the belly flaps and tucked it in toward the center of the steak, and then wrapped the other flap around it and secured the steak with kitchen twine. Now I had neat medallions that cooked evenly and could be easily maneuvered around the grill.

As fun as it is to grill with serious fire, I knew that I would have to take a more gentle approach: Grilling over medium-low heat produced moist, tender cooked interiors—but at the steep cost of a good, flavorful sear. I needed a two-level fire: high heat to sear the steaks, low heat to finish the job. This method took up to 20 minutes total for a 1½-inch steak, but the steaks were now both moist and nicely browned.

Turning to flavor, I thought wistfully about how another common

Our tuck-and-tie method (see below) makes neat and sturdy medallions.

cooking method for salmon steaks—broiling—solves the problem of bland flesh. The steaks are slathered with some sort of sauce and absorb its flavor as they cook. How could I transfer this technique to the grill without risking flare-ups and burnt, stuck-on fish? Got it: I'd replace the broiling pan with a disposable aluminum roasting pan and finish cooking the steaks in a sauce over low heat.

A sucker for classics, I made a simple lemon-and-shallot butter sauce directly in the roasting pan while the steaks seared on the hot part of the grill. Then I transferred the browned fish steaks to the pan, coating them with sauce. When they were done, they were flavorful, juicy, and moist. But the delicate sauce needed a boost to compete with the charred grill flavor; more lemon juice, the addition of zest and capers, plus a sprinkling of fresh parsley gave it the necessary fortification. Now I had zesty, succulent salmon steaks, plus built-in insurance against overcooking if I happened to get distracted by my lawn chair and a glass of chilled white wine.

GRILLED SALMON STEAKS WITH LEMON-CAPER SAUCE Serves 4

Before eating, lift out the small circular bone from the center of each steak.

- **4** (10-ounce) salmon steaks, 1 to 1½ inches thick
  Salt and pepper
- **2** tablespoons olive oil
- **1** teaspoon grated lemon zest and 6 tablespoons juice (2 lemons)
- **1** shallot, minced
- **3** tablespoons unsalted butter, cut into 3 pieces
- **1** tablespoon capers, rinsed
- **2** tablespoons minced fresh parsley
- **1** (13 by 9-inch) disposable aluminum pan

1. Pat salmon steaks dry with paper towels. Working with 1 steak at a time, carefully trim 1½ inches of skin from 1 tail. Tightly wrap other tail around skinned portion and tie steaks with kitchen twine. Season salmon with salt and pepper and brush both sides with oil. Combine lemon zest, lemon juice, shallot, butter, capers, and ⅛ teaspoon salt in disposable pan.

2A. For a charcoal grill: Open bottom vent completely. Light large chimney starter filled with charcoal briquettes (6 quarts). When top coals are partially covered with ash, pour evenly over half of grill. Set cooking grate in place, cover, and open lid vent completely. Heat grill until hot, about 5 minutes.

2B. For a gas grill: Turn all burners to high, cover, and heat grill until hot, about 15 minutes. Leave primary burner on high and turn off other burner(s).

3. Clean and oil cooking grate. Place salmon on hot part of grill. Cook until browned, 2 to 3 minutes per side. Meanwhile, set pan on cool part of grill and cook until butter has melted, about 2 minutes. Transfer salmon to pan and gently turn to coat. Cook salmon (covered if using gas) until center is still translucent when checked with tip of paring knife and registers 125 degrees (for medium-rare), 6 to 14 minutes, flipping salmon and rotating pan halfway through grilling. Remove twine and transfer salmon to platter. Off heat, whisk parsley into sauce. Drizzle sauce over steaks. Serve.

MORE FLAVORS ONLINE

For **Lime-Cilantro** and **Orange-Ginger** variations, visit **CooksCountry.com/extra**.

KEY STEPS Prepping Salmon Medallions

1. For salmon steaks that are sturdy enough to grill easily, remove 1½ inches of skin from one tail of each steak.

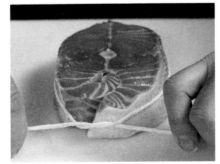

2. Next, tuck the skinned portion into the center of the steak, wrap the other tail around it, and tie with kitchen twine.

Dill Potato Salad

A dusting of fresh dill isn't enough to wake up potato salad.
Our goal was to get dill flavor into the potatoes, not just on them. BY CALI RICH

JUST THROWING A tablespoon of fresh dill into any old potato salad recipe does not a dill potato salad make. I know this for a fact because when I tested a bunch of recipes that advertised themselves as Dill Potato Salad, they all fell short. In each case, the rich, mayonnaise-heavy dressing swallowed up the superficial sprinkling of fresh dill. For a dill potato salad with emphasis on the dill, I'd need to pump up the dressing and get dill flavor into the potatoes themselves.

First, the potatoes. I set out five large pots of water filled with diced potatoes and seasoned them with dill in every possible form. To one, I added fresh dill sprigs; to the second and third, dill seeds (raw and toasted, respectively); to the fourth, dill pickle juice; and to the last pot—call me crazy—whole dill pickles. Once the potatoes were tender, I drained them and called over my fellow cooks. Three of my attempts—the potatoes boiled in pickle brine, those cooked with raw dill seeds, and those cooked with several pickles bobbing in the water—had no discernible dill flavor. The toasted dill seeds had added

flavor—"musky" flavor, according to tasters. The clear winner was the fresh dill sprigs, which gave the potatoes a clean, clearly dilly taste.

This was a road worth traveling. For that initial test, I'd simply tossed a handful of dill fronds into the water, but the dill clung to the drained potatoes like wet paper towels. I didn't want these soggy, spent fronds in my salad, so for the next test I chopped a generous ½ cup of leaves, stems included, and tied them inside a paper coffee filter, making a homespun version of what the French call a *bouquet garni*. The dill sachet seasoned the potatoes as they cooked—and it kept them clean.

It was time to fine-tune my dressing. I met tasters' demands for a tangier, zippier dressing by replacing some of the mayonnaise with sour cream and adding more vinegar than required in other recipes (I landed on ¼ cup). A little Dijon mustard rounded things out, and for clear and present fresh dill flavor, I used 2 tablespoons of chopped dill. I summoned my tasters and prepared to hang up my apron. But their refrain— "More dill! More dill!"—sent me back to the chopping board.

I made two new batches of my recipe, adding dill relish to one and chopped dill pickles to the other. Both were tasty but (unsurprisingly) tasted of pickled stuff. For this recipe, I wanted the emphasis squarely on the dill. Next, I tried stirring the brine from the dill pickle jar into the salad. Nothing wrong with that either, if garlic and salt were what I was after.

Fortunately, I had a sudden inspiration: Commercial herb vinegars are often used to add flavor to dressings. I'd never heard of a dill version, so I decided to make one. I microwaved the vinegar I had been using in the dressing with a tablespoon of chopped fresh dill and let it steep (at least 15 minutes worked much better than five). I could have stirred the seasoned vinegar right into the dressing, but instead I applied a favorite test kitchen technique and drizzled some of it over the hot potatoes. They drank in the seasoned vinegar, which, in turn, seasoned them to the core. I added the remaining 2 tablespoons of vinegar to the creamy dressing. I let everything chill to meld the flavors and then dipped in a tasting fork. Give it up for dill power.

TEST KITCHEN TECHNIQUE
Dill Three Ways
Three rounds of fresh dill season our Dill Potato Salad.

INFUSE
We add a packet of chopped dill to the water in which the potatoes simmer.

MARINATE
We steep vinegar with minced dill and use it to dress the hot potatoes.

MINCE
We sprinkle extra minced dill over the dressed potato salad.

With a trio of techniques to bring the herb front and center, we finally got our fill of dill.

DILL POTATO SALAD Serves 8

Use both dill stems and chopped leaves (sometimes called fronds) in the herb sachet. Grey Poupon is our favorite brand of Dijon mustard.

- ¼ cup white wine vinegar
- 3 tablespoons minced fresh dill plus ½ cup leaves and stems, chopped coarse
- 3 pounds Yukon Gold potatoes, peeled and cut into ¾-inch pieces
  Salt and pepper
- ½ cup mayonnaise
- ¼ cup sour cream
- 1 tablespoon Dijon mustard
- 3 scallions, green parts only, sliced thin

1. Combine vinegar and 1 tablespoon minced dill in bowl and microwave until steaming, 30 to 60 seconds. Set at room temperature until cool, 15 to 20 minutes.

2. Meanwhile, place chopped dill inside disposable coffee filter and tie closed with kitchen twine. Bring potatoes, dill sachet, 1 tablespoon salt, and enough water to cover by 1 inch to boil in large pot over high heat. Reduce heat to medium and simmer until potatoes are just tender, about 10 minutes.

3. Drain potatoes thoroughly, then transfer to large bowl; discard sachet. Drizzle 2 tablespoons dill vinegar over hot potatoes and gently toss until evenly coated. Refrigerate until cooled, about 30 minutes, stirring once.

4. Whisk mayonnaise, sour cream, remaining dill vinegar, mustard, ½ teaspoon salt, and ¼ teaspoon pepper together until smooth. Add dressing to cooled potatoes. Stir in scallions and remaining 2 tablespoons minced dill. Cover and refrigerate to let flavors meld, about 30 minutes. Season with salt and pepper to taste. Serve. (Salad can be refrigerated for up to 2 days.)

Baltimore Pit Beef

Forget low and slow. Baltimore's "barbecue" tradition pits a mammoth cut of beef against the direct heat of the grill. We set out to unlock the secrets of this beloved sandwich. BY JEREMY SAUER

*P*it beef, Baltimore's signature sandwich, is a high-heat, fast-paced answer to the slow smoking that takes place farther south. Pit beef starts as a massive spice-rubbed beef roast that's grilled over a hot fire until it's thoroughly charred on the outside and a juicy medium-rare on the inside. The meat is sliced paper-thin, piled on a big squishy bun, and topped with a few rings of raw onion. For added zip, locals spoon on plenty of Baltimore's ubiquitous tiger sauce (a horseradish-spiked mayonnaise). The end result is a sloppy, spicy, savory mess of an absolutely perfect sandwich.

Since there's not a pit beef sandwich shop to be found in Boston, I figured I'd attempt to make my own. Unfortunately, each recipe I tried featured meat that was blander and chewier than the last. Since my recipes were a bust, I got on the horn with a handful of well-loved Baltimore pit beef joints and found out that most start with whole top or bottom rounds, both monstrous cuts from the hindquarters of the steer. Meat from the round is flavorful, but it's also notoriously tough when cooked medium-rare—unless you have a meat slicer to slice it very thin. What were my other options? Premium cuts from the short loin (rib eye, strip steak, and tenderloin) are tender, but I refuse to spend $15 per pound on sandwich meat. Instead, I looked to top sirloin roast. This cut—a test kitchen favorite for roast beef—is affordable, tender, and flavorful. But how would it do on the grill? In a side-by-side test, the top sirloin (hand-sliced reasonably thin) easily outpaced both top and bottom round.

Tiger Sauce, a horseradish mayonnaise that takes only seconds to make, gives Pit Beef its signature kick.

What really sets apart pit beef is the salty, spicy, nearly blackened crust. Every recipe uses a paprika-based rub that includes some combination of herbs and spices, most often black pepper, cayenne, garlic powder, dried oregano, and salt. The components are nothing fancy, but getting the right ratios took more time than I care to admit. When I finally nailed it, I found that even with that savory exterior, the meat's interior was still undeniably bland. A few restaurants rub the meat two or three days in advance to let the seasonings take hold. It works, but who's got the time? Instead, I cut the roast in half. The seasonings permeated these two smaller roasts more quickly, which meant that I could get good flavor in six hours' time (although longer is even better). What's more, two roasts meant twice the smoky, spicy crust.

To develop that signature heavy char, I grilled the mini roasts over a hot fire, rolling them around until they were nice and dark. But the first slice revealed a thick band of overcooked gray meat surrounding a small core of medium-rare beef. To shrink the gray ring, I tried searing the roasts over direct heat and then finishing them with gentle indirect heat. This improved the interior but left me with a subpar crust. What to do? A colleague suggested that I slowly bring the meat up to temperature using indirect heat and then quickly sear the meat over the hot fire. Although this was a step in the right direction, that gray band stubbornly stayed put.

I had a hunch that the ambient heat of the grill was the culprit: On a small backyard grill, "indirect" heat is a relative term. For my next test, I loosely wrapped the roasts in aluminum foil to protect the meat nearest the burner from overcooking. My improvised foil shield did the trick. I removed the roasts once they reached about 100 degrees and let them rest while I cranked the heat on the grill. Since the roasts released some juices as they sat, I gave them another dusting with seasoning to reinforce the crust and then rolled the roasts on the hot grill for about 15 minutes, at which point they were charred on the outside and uniformly rosy within. After slapping together a simple version of tiger sauce, I piled my sandwich high with my own homemade pit beef and enjoyed it in the comfort of my own backyard.

BALTIMORE PIT BEEF Serves 10
Buy brined (not creamy) prepared horse-radish and, if necessary, drain it.

TIGER SAUCE
- ½ cup mayonnaise
- ½ cup hot prepared horseradish
- 1 teaspoon lemon juice
- 1 garlic clove, minced
  Salt and pepper

PIT BEEF
- 4 teaspoons kosher salt
- 1 tablespoon paprika
- 1 tablespoon pepper
- 1 teaspoon garlic powder
- 1 teaspoon dried oregano
- ¼ teaspoon cayenne pepper
- 1 (4- to 5-pound) boneless top sirloin roast, trimmed and halved crosswise
- 10 kaiser rolls
- 1 onion, sliced thin

1. For the tiger sauce: Whisk mayonnaise, horseradish, lemon juice, and garlic together in bowl. Season with salt and pepper to taste. (Sauce can be refrigerated for up to 2 days.)

2. For the pit beef: Combine seasonings in bowl. Pat roasts dry with paper towels and rub with 2 tablespoons seasoning mixture. Wrap meat tightly with plastic wrap and refrigerate for 6 to 24 hours.

3A. For a charcoal grill: Open bottom vent halfway. Light large chimney starter filled with charcoal briquettes (6 quarts). When top coals are partially covered with ash, pour evenly over half of grill. Set cooking grate in place, cover, and open lid vent halfway. Heat grill until hot, about 5 minutes.

3B. For a gas grill: Turn all burners to high, cover, and heat grill until hot, about 15 minutes. Leave primary burner on high and turn off other burner(s).

4. Clean and oil cooking grate. Unwrap roasts and place end to end on long side of 18 by 12-inch sheet of aluminum foil. Loosely fold opposite long side of foil around top of roasts. Place meat on cool part of grill with foil-covered side closest to heat source. Cover (positioning lid vents over meat if using charcoal) and cook until meat registers 100 degrees, 45 to 60 minutes.

5. Transfer roasts to plate and discard foil. Turn all burners to high if using gas. If using charcoal, carefully remove cooking grate and light large chimney starter three-quarters full with charcoal briquettes (4½ quarts). When top coals are partially covered with ash, pour evenly over spent coals. Set cooking grate in place and cover. Heat grill until hot, about 5 minutes.

6. Pat roasts dry with paper towels and rub with remaining spice mixture. Place meat on hot part of grill. Cook (covered if using gas), turning occasionally, until charred on all sides and meat registers 120 to 125 degrees (for medium-rare), 10 to 20 minutes. Transfer meat to carving board, tent loosely with foil, and rest 15 minutes. Slice meat thin against grain. Transfer sliced beef to buns, top with onions, and drizzle with sauce. Serve.

TEST KITCHEN TECHNIQUE **Cooking Baltimore Pit Beef**

1. SHIELD Even with indirect heat, the sides of the roasts closest to the fire can overcook. A simple foil shield protects them.

2. RE-SEASON After about one hour of grill roasting, we remove the roasts, rub them with more seasoning, and turn up the heat.

3. BLAST With a hot fire and a fresh coating of spices, it's easy to create a flavorful seared crust on the roasts.

WHAT TO DO WITH LEFTOVERS
Hearty Beef and Potato Hash

Who needs corned beef when you've got Pit Beef? BY JEREMY SAUER

Starting the potatoes in the microwave gives this breakfast a jump start.

I'M ALWAYS LOOKING for an opportunity to turn yesterday's dinner into this morning's breakfast, and a leftover chunk of Baltimore Pit Beef gave me just such a chance. Since I'm a big fan of corned beef hash, I figured I'd try my hand at pit beef hash.

For the potatoes, russets are typical—and for good reason. Their high starch content makes for a cohesive—and crisp—hash. Diners make their hash with precooked potatoes, and most recipes call for boiled. But when I wake up, I'm ready to eat. Instead of boiling the spuds, I microwaved them, which took less than 10 minutes.

While the potatoes were in the microwave, I softened some onions in a skillet with a pat of butter. Then in went garlic, thyme, and the chopped pit beef. Next, I packed the softened potatoes into the pan to ensure that the hash would develop a thick crust. To get crisp morsels throughout, I turned over the hash in bits and pieces after it had spent a few minutes over medium heat, and I continued to let it cook.

After a few more turns, I gave the hash a taste. The flavor was right, but the hash was crumbly. I tried adding more butter, but it made the hash greasy. Instead, heavy cream gave the hash a creamy, cohesive quality with no hint of greasiness. To finish it off, I topped the hash with four eggs, reduced the heat to medium-low, and covered the pan. Five minutes later, my pit beef hash was ready to eat. And I was ready to eat it.

HEARTY BEEF AND POTATO HASH Serves 4
We developed this recipe with a large nonstick skillet, but a seasoned cast-iron skillet works great, too. For well-distributed crisp bits, crush the hash while turning and stirring it (in step 3).

- 2 pounds russet potatoes, peeled and cut into ½-inch pieces
- 2 tablespoons unsalted butter
- 1 onion, chopped fine
- 2 garlic cloves, minced
- ½ teaspoon minced fresh thyme
- 2½ cups chopped leftover roast beef
- ½ cup heavy cream
- 1 teaspoon hot sauce
  Salt and pepper
- 4 large eggs

1. Place potatoes in large bowl, cover, and microwave until potatoes are nearly tender, 7 to 9 minutes, stirring halfway through cooking.

2. Meanwhile, melt butter in 12-inch nonstick skillet over medium heat. Add onion and cook until browned, 6 to 8 minutes. Stir in garlic and thyme and cook until fragrant, about 30 seconds. Add potatoes, beef, cream, hot sauce, ½ teaspoon salt, and ½ teaspoon pepper, mashing to combine.

3. Increase heat to medium-high and cook, without stirring, until bottom begins to brown, 3 to 4 minutes. Turn hash, one scoop at a time, until browned bits are distributed. Repeat turning and mashing several times, until potatoes are deep golden brown and completely tender, 6 to 8 minutes.

4. Make 4 indentations on top of hash. Crack 1 egg into each indentation and season with salt and pepper. Reduce heat to medium-low, cover, and cook until egg whites are just set, about 5 minutes. Cut hash into wedges. Season with salt and pepper to taste. Serve.

Quicker Boston Baked Beans

This cookout classic has been around for ages, but does it have to take ages to make?

BY REBECCAH MARSTERS

BOSTON BAKED BEANS—THAT familiar long-cooked combination of beans, molasses, and pork—has been a pillar of New England home cooking for hundreds of years. So why does the canned version show up on so many picnic tables? The truth is, keeping the oven on all day in the middle of the summer, not to mention devoting the entire day to a side dish, are dealbreakers for many modern cooks (me included). I wanted authentic-tasting baked beans that I'd be proud to bring to a barbecue, and I didn't want to wake up at the crack of dawn to make them.

My biggest challenge was reducing that long baking time: Most recipes require 6 (or so) hours at 250 or 300 degrees. I needed to give my beans a head start, but soaking them overnight was contrary to my accelerated timetable. Working with a basic recipe (I'd refine it later) of molasses, mustard, chopped onion, and a hunk of salt pork, I tried a common shortcut: simmering the beans on the stovetop before they went into the oven. After several tests, I found that 45 minutes of simmering saved considerable baking time, especially when I bumped up the oven temperature to 350 degrees. After two hours in the oven, the beans were perfectly cooked—not exactly speedily, but it was a big improvement. To ensure beans of the proper consistency with this shorter cooking time, I decreased the amount of liquid in the recipe and removed the lid for the last half-hour of baking, which let some of the liquid cook down.

With such a simple dish, I had to make every single ingredient count. To get the most out of the salt pork, I used a test kitchen technique of chopping and browning it before adding it to the beans; this ensured that the salt pork rendered some of its fat and was actually edible, as opposed to simply flavoring the dish before being fished out and discarded.

Chopped onion and prepared brown mustard are standard, but more than one staunch New Englander told me that tomato products have no place in Boston baked beans (contrary to many recipes). I tested tomato paste, ketchup, diced tomatoes, and tomato sauce anyway, but my tasters, New Englanders by residence if not by birth, just said "no" to tomato—its flavor

Canned beans can't hold a candle to the robust flavor of these homemade baked beans.

simply wasn't right here.

I was making progress, but the beans' flavor was a little weak with less time to deepen. Replacing half the molasses with the same amount of dark brown sugar softened and rounded the former's bitter edge. Cider vinegar provided acidity, Worcestershire sauce brought complexity, and Dijon mustard (in place of the spicy brown I had been using) added sharpness. I reserved some of the molasses and mustard to stir in at the very end, which both boosted flavor and helped thicken the sauce. At last, tasters were satisfied with the complex, long-cooked flavor of these beans.

But it wasn't party time quite yet. Call me greedy or impatient, but I wanted the same results faster. A little

research unearthed a lot of buzz about baking soda's ability to speed up bean cooking, so I turned to our science editor. He explained that in addition to containing sodium (which helps soften the exterior of the beans so they hydrate faster), baking soda is alkaline, which breaks down large starch molecules. Call me skeptical (and I'm paid to be so), but I needed proof. I measured out the water and beans, added baking soda, and simmered away. After 20 minutes (less than half the time it had required previously), I proceeded with the recipe as before. The end result? The beans were tender and creamy. In under three hours, I had baked beans that would make any Bostonian proud.

Carolina Red Slaw

In Carolina barbecue restaurants, customers can't get enough of this spicy slaw. Once we tasted it, we had to figure out how to make it. BY CAROLYNN PURPURA

MY FIRST MISTAKE was calling it coleslaw. The pulled-pork sandwich I ordered at Lexington Barbecue #1 (known as Honey Monk's locally) in Lexington, North Carolina, came with a vinegary, red-tinged slaw, spicy but sweet and as good as any I'd ever tasted. It was so good, in fact, that I had to have the recipe. I politely asked my waitress for the information. She told me the cabbage was shredded in a food processor and dressed with the restaurant's vinegar-based barbecue sauce and a few secret ingredients. That was all I could get out of her. Back in Boston, I kept thinking about that slaw. I finally phoned the restaurant and asked to speak to the kitchen.

"Hi. I'd like to ask you about your coleslaw."

There was a long pause on the line.

"We don't have coleslaw. We have barbecue slaw."

Not surprisingly, they weren't too interested in divulging their house secrets to a Northerner who didn't even know the dish's proper name. I took the information I already had and resolved to re-create red slaw on my own.

In the test kitchen, we used to prepare cabbage for coleslaw by shredding it, then salting it, letting it sit for an hour, rinsing off the salt, and draining the cabbage again. The technique draws liquid out of the cabbage beforehand so the dressed coleslaw won't weep and become watery. But a fellow test cook recently discovered a faster way to achieve the same result: microwaving the shredded cabbage with salt and sugar. The sugar helps the salt, and the heat weakens the cabbage's cell walls, prompting it to shed more water and to do so faster. What's more, subsequent tests showed that slaw made with this technique keeps longer than ordinary slaws.

Having settled on a technique, I turned to duplicating the flavor. Before going any further, I paused to look up recipes for Carolina red slaw. Most contained vinegar, ketchup, salt, sugar, and red pepper flakes—a lot like Lexington barbecue sauce, come to think of it. I quickly prepared a batch of the test kitchen's recipe for Lexington Barbecue Sauce, tossed it with the drained, microwaved cabbage, and offered it to my tasters. Wa-a-ay too much vinegar, they protested. And where was the pretty pinkish color I remembered?

I cut down on the vinegar and went up on the ketchup.

Even without any secret ingredients, the slaw tasted good right away, but it was even better a few hours later after the flavors had a chance to marry. Could I speed it along? I was already using the microwave for the cabbage; maybe I could also use it to give the vinegar and red pepper flakes a head start at melding. I zapped them together for barely two minutes and, just like that, the spice flavor deepened and permeated the slaw, helping it meld more quickly. Now the slaw tasted great after just 30 minutes, and lucky for you, I'm more than happy to share the recipe. Just don't call it "coleslaw" if a Carolinian is within earshot.

CAROLINA RED SLAW Serves 8 to 10

If any large pieces of cabbage slip by the shredding blade of the food processor, chop them by hand.

- ½ cup cider vinegar
- ½ teaspoon red pepper flakes
- ⅔ cup ketchup
- 2 teaspoons salt
- 1 head green cabbage, cored
- ¼ cup sugar

1. Microwave vinegar and pepper flakes until mixture is bubbling around edges, 1 to 1½ minutes. Whisk ketchup and 1 teaspoon salt into vinegar mixture until combined.

2. Cut cabbage into 2-inch-thick wedges and shred in food processor fitted with shredding disk. Toss cabbage, sugar, and remaining 1 teaspoon salt in large bowl. Cover bowl and microwave until cabbage is just beginning to wilt, 1½ to 2 minutes, stirring halfway through. Transfer cabbage mixture to colander set over bowl. Let cool to room temperature, about 15 minutes, stirring occasionally.

3. Press cabbage to release excess moisture; discard liquid (it should measure about ⅓ cup). Toss cabbage and dressing in clean large bowl until combined. Cover and refrigerate for 30 minutes or up to 2 days. Serve.

CLICK ON IT

Have some pork with your coleslaw. For our recipe for **Lexington-Style Pulled Pork**, go to CooksCountry.com/extra.

The cabbage in this tangy, decidedly non-creamy slaw is shredded finer than for ordinary slaw.

KEY STEPS Faster Shredding and Draining

To prevent soggy slaw, you could chop a head of cabbage by hand, salt it, and let it drain for an hour before rinsing and pressing it dry. Or not.

1. Push the cabbage wedges through the feed tube of a food processor fitted with a shredding disk.

2. Together, heat (from the microwave), salt, and sugar quickly draw moisture from shredded cabbage.

Getting to Know Shellfish

Despite the name, shellfish are not fish (and they don't all have shells, either). They come in two basic models: mollusks, such as clams, oysters, snails, scallops, and mussels; and crustaceans, such as lobster, shrimp, crayfish, and crab. Both can confuse shoppers; both are easy to overcook. Here are some tips from the test kitchen.

Clams
SAND TRAP
Clams are sold as hard-shell or soft-shell. Because hard-shell clams stay shut, they are less sandy and better suited to serving raw (smaller cherrystones and littlenecks) or baked and stuffed (larger quahogs). By contrast, soft-shell clams (steamers and razor clams) gape when they are alive, so they contain a lot of sand. If you're making clam broth, strain the sand out through a paper coffee filter.

Mussels
SEABEARD
Whether you've got North Atlantic blue (found mostly on the East Coast) or "Mediterranean" mussels, scrub them with a stiff brush to remove any grit and debeard them (pull on the strands extending from the shell) before cooking. You can refrigerate mussels for one day in a colander covered with a damp kitchen towel. If the mussels won't close when tapped, discard them.

Oysters
BICOASTAL
East or West? Each coast has die-hard fans. As a rule, Atlantic oysters are briny with an intense hit of fresh, cold sea salt. (All Atlantic oysters are the same species: *Crassostrea virginica*.) They range from 2 inches long to nearly 6 inches long. Pacific oysters are rarely as salty and often taste complex and fruity.

Snails
FRENCH FAVORITE
Surprise! Not all shellfish live in the ocean. The snail is a mollusk, therefore a shellfish, but many of those that we eat live on land. In this country, intrepid eaters will likely find only frozen or canned (already cooked) snails.

Lobster
HARD BODIES
The quality of lobster meat depends to a large extent on where the crustacean is in its molting cycle, during which the old, hard shell is replaced with a soft, new one. Hard-shell lobsters taste better and are meatier. To determine the stage of your lobster, just squeeze: A soft-shell lobster will yield to pressure. Like the roe? Look for a female. Her soft "swimmerets" (appendages under the lowest legs) give her away.

Dungeness Crab
LEFT COAST RESIDENT
The Dungeness is a Pacific crab with a range from Alaska to Baja, California. Only adult males at least 6¼ inches long can be legally harvested, so Dungeness crabs typically weigh at least 2 pounds. Their rich, firm meat is often compared to lobster meat. Boil live Dungeness crabs in water or in seasoned crab boil. If you don't live on the West Coast and can't get live crabs, buy cooked, frozen whole crabs. Defrost, crack, dress with vinaigrette, and toss with salad greens.

Blue Crab
CHESAPEAKE BAY CELEB
Such classic American dishes as crab imperial and crab Louis are best with blue crab (or its close cousin, the blue swimmer crab from the Pacific Rim). The Chesapeake Bay is famous for its blue crabs, although demand now outstrips supply. In that region, the crabs are typically steamed with vinegar and Old Bay seasoning, then cracked with mallets and slurped with melted butter. Soft-shell crabs are blues that have just shed their hard shells and not yet grown new ones.

King Crab
LONG LEGGED
Fishing for king crab, mostly done in Alaska, is seriously scary business. The peak season is winter, when all too often fishermen die of exposure (or drowning). Among the three species of king (red, blue, and golden), red is best, and the leg meat is prized above all else. The legs are meaty, sweet, mild, and big—10 to 12 inches long. Most king crab is sold cooked and frozen. To reheat the legs, we like to steam them, which preserves their firm texture.

Crayfish
LOBSTER KIN
Crayfish—also known as crawfish, crawdads, or (our favorite) mudbugs—are closely related to lobsters. They live in fresh water, though. North America, particularly Kentucky and Louisiana, is home to more than half of the world's species. Soups, bisques, and étouffées use the tail portion of the crayfish, but at crawfish boils (great, messy fun in Louisiana and Texas), people eat the whole body (including the head) with gusto.

Shrimp
SIZE MATTERS
Shrimp are sorted by size. Look for the letter U (for "under") followed by a number. One pound contains fewer shrimp than that number, so the smaller the number, the bigger the shrimp. To remove the unsightly vein and peel the shrimp in one easy step, snip along the crustacean's back with scissors. Save the shells to make a quick, flavorful stock.

Bay Scallops
SMALL AND RARE
Bay scallops, harvested from North Carolina to Maine, are small, cork-shaped scallops (they're also sold as Nantucket scallops). Since their season is limited—fall through mid-winter—they're pricey. One pound may include as many as 90 scallops. Chefs prize them for their sweet taste and use them in soups, stews, and stir-fries.

Sea Scallops
DON'T GET WET
Unlike bay scallops, the larger sea scallops are in markets year-round. Before cooking, remove the small crescent-shaped muscle that attaches the scallop to the shell. Avoid "wet" scallops (ask at the store), which are treated with a chemical preservative. If wet is all you can find, soak them in 1 quart of cold water, ¼ cup of lemon juice, and 2 tablespoons of salt for 30 minutes to mask any off flavors.

THAI PORK TENDERLOIN WITH CUCUMBER SALAD

SPICY CHICKEN AND BROCCOLINI

PENNE ALLA VODKA

GRILLED RIB EYE WITH ROASTED RED PEPPER BUTTER

SPICY CHICKEN AND BROCCOLINI Serves 4

WHY THIS RECIPE WORKS: Cooking the chicken skin side down, covered, ensures well-rendered skin and evenly cooked meat in about 20 minutes.

- 1 pound broccolini, trimmed
- 3 tablespoons olive oil
- ½ teaspoon red pepper flakes
- 1 tablespoon minced fresh parsley
- 1½ pounds bone-in chicken thighs, trimmed
  Salt and pepper
- 2 garlic cloves, minced

1. Place broccolini in bowl, cover, and microwave until nearly tender, about 5 minutes; set aside. Microwave oil and pepper flakes in bowl until fragrant, about 1 minute. Combine 2 tablespoons pepper oil and parsley in bowl.

2. Pat chicken dry with paper towels and season with salt and pepper. Heat remaining 1 tablespoon pepper oil in 12-inch skillet over medium-high heat until just smoking. Cook chicken skin side down until well browned, about 5 minutes. Reduce heat to medium, cover, and cook until meat registers 175 degrees, 15 to 18 minutes. Transfer chicken to platter and tent loosely with foil.

3. Pour off all but 1 tablespoon fat from skillet. Add broccolini and cook over medium-high heat until lightly browned and tender, about 2 minutes. Add garlic and cook until fragrant, about 30 seconds. Drizzle parsley-pepper oil over chicken and serve with broccolini.

TEST KITCHEN NOTE: Broccolini, a hybrid of broccoli and Chinese kale, is also sold as baby broccoli or Asparation.

THAI PORK TENDERLOIN WITH CUCUMBER SALAD Serves 4

WHY THIS RECIPE WORKS: Coconut milk is traditional in creamy Thai sauces; we use it to balance a tart cucumber salad as well.

- 1 seedless English cucumber, peeled, halved lengthwise, seeded, and sliced thin
- ¼ cup thinly sliced red onion
- 3 tablespoons rice vinegar
- 1 tablespoon plus 1¼ cups unsweetened coconut milk
- 5 tablespoons minced fresh cilantro
  Salt and pepper
- 2 (12-ounce) pork tenderloins, trimmed
- 1 tablespoon vegetable oil
- 1 tablespoon grated fresh ginger
- 1 teaspoon sambal oelek chili paste

1. Combine cucumber, onion, vinegar, 1 tablespoon coconut milk, 1 tablespoon cilantro, ½ teaspoon salt, and ¼ teaspoon pepper in bowl. Refrigerate until chilled, about 15 minutes. Meanwhile, pat pork dry with paper towels and season with salt and pepper. Heat oil in 12-inch skillet over medium-high heat until just smoking. Cook pork until browned, 3 to 4 minutes per side. Transfer to plate.

2. Add ginger to now-empty skillet and cook over medium heat until fragrant, about 30 seconds. Stir in remaining 1¼ cups coconut milk and chili paste, scraping up any browned bits, until incorporated. Add pork and any accumulated juices and cook, turning occasionally, until sauce is thickened and meat registers 145 degrees, 8 to 10 minutes. Transfer pork to carving board, tent loosely with foil, and rest for 5 minutes. Off heat, stir remaining ¼ cup cilantro into sauce. Season with salt and pepper to taste. Slice pork and serve with cucumber salad.

TEST KITCHEN NOTE: Serve over rice.

GRILLED RIB EYE WITH ROASTED RED PEPPER BUTTER
Serves 4

WHY THIS RECIPE WORKS: We dress up steak with a compound butter that takes just moments to prepare.

- 4 tablespoons unsalted butter, softened
- 2 tablespoons finely chopped roasted red pepper, patted dry
- 1 garlic clove, minced
  Salt and pepper
- ⅛ teaspoon cayenne pepper
- 4 (12-ounce) rib-eye steaks, about 1½ inches thick, trimmed

1. Combine butter, roasted pepper, garlic, ¼ teaspoon salt, ¼ teaspoon pepper, and cayenne in bowl; set aside.

2. Pat steaks dry with paper towels and season with salt and pepper. Grill steaks over hot fire until well browned and register 120 to 125 degrees (for medium-rare), about 4 minutes per side. Transfer to platter, top with roasted red pepper butter, tent loosely with foil, and rest for 5 minutes.

TEST KITCHEN NOTE: Dry the jarred roasted red pepper well so that the compound butter blends together easily.

PENNE ALLA VODKA Serves 4

WHY THIS RECIPE WORKS: Instead of the usual fresh tomatoes, we use sun-dried tomatoes to get assertive flavor fast.

- 1 tablespoon olive oil
- 3 garlic cloves, minced
- ¼ teaspoon red pepper flakes
- 1 (28-ounce) can crushed tomatoes
- ½ cup oil-packed sun-dried tomatoes, rinsed and chopped fine
- ½ cup vodka
- ¾ cup heavy cream
  Salt and pepper
- 1 pound penne
- ⅓ cup minced fresh basil

1. Bring 4 quarts water to boil in large pot. Meanwhile, heat oil in 12-inch skillet over medium heat until shimmering. Add garlic and pepper flakes and cook until fragrant, about 30 seconds. Add crushed tomatoes and sun-dried tomatoes and cook until slightly thickened, about 5 minutes. Off heat, add vodka. Bring sauce to boil, reduce heat to medium, and simmer until thickened, 12 to 15 minutes. Off heat, stir in cream. Season with salt and pepper to taste; cover and keep warm.

2. Add pasta and 1 tablespoon salt to boiling water and cook, stirring often, until al dente. Reserve ¼ cup cooking water, then drain pasta and return it to pot. Toss sauce and basil with pasta, adding reserved pasta water as needed. Serve.

TEST KITCHEN NOTE: Use decent-quality vodka; the cheap stuff will make the sauce harsh. To avoid flare-ups, add the vodka off the heat.

MEDITERRANEAN GRILLED CHICKEN
WITH TOMATO-FETA SALAD

SPANISH-STYLE FRITTATA

CASHEW PORK WITH SNOW PEAS AND GINGER

FLANK STEAK TACOS WITH GRILLED CORN SALSA

SPANISH-STYLE FRITTATA Serves 4

WHY THIS RECIPE WORKS: Spicy chorizo and nutty Parmesan give this simple egg dish heft and richness.

- 10 large eggs
- 1 ounce Parmesan cheese, grated (½ cup)
- 3 tablespoons half-and-half
- 2 scallions, sliced thin
- ½ teaspoon salt
- ¼ teaspoon pepper
- 6 ounces chorizo, halved lengthwise and sliced thin
- 1 onion, chopped fine
- 1 red bell pepper, stemmed, seeded, and chopped

1. Adjust oven rack to upper-middle position and heat oven to 475 degrees. Whisk eggs, ¼ cup Parmesan, half-and-half, scallions, salt, and pepper together in bowl.

2. Cook chorizo in 10-inch nonstick skillet over medium-high heat until beginning to brown, 2 to 3 minutes. Add onion and red pepper and cook until browned, 6 to 8 minutes.

3. Stir in egg mixture and cook over medium heat, using spatula to scrape bottom of skillet, until large curds form but eggs are still very wet, about 2 minutes. Shake skillet to distribute eggs evenly and cook, without stirring, until bottom is set, about 30 seconds. Sprinkle remaining ¼ cup Parmesan over top and bake until golden brown, about 5 minutes. Serve.

TEST KITCHEN NOTE: You can substitute linguiça for the chorizo.

MEDITERRANEAN GRILLED CHICKEN WITH TOMATO-FETA SALAD Serves 4

WHY THIS RECIPE WORKS: A yogurt dressing doubles as a marinade and a finishing sauce for the chicken.

- 1 teaspoon grated lemon zest plus 3 tablespoons juice
- 3 garlic cloves, minced
- 1 tablespoon minced fresh oregano
  Salt and pepper
- 4 tablespoons olive oil
- 1 pound cherry tomatoes, halved
- 4 ounces feta cheese, crumbled (1 cup)
- ¼ cup thinly sliced red onion
- ¼ cup plain yogurt
- 1½ pounds boneless, skinless chicken breasts, trimmed and cut into 1-inch pieces

1. Whisk lemon juice, garlic, oregano, lemon zest, ½ teaspoon salt, and ½ teaspoon pepper together in medium bowl. Slowly whisk in oil until thoroughly incorporated. Reserve half of dressing. Add tomatoes, feta, and onion to remaining dressing and toss to coat. Season with salt and pepper to taste.

2. Whisk yogurt into reserved dressing. Reserve half of yogurt dressing. Add chicken to remaining yogurt dressing and toss to coat. Thread chicken onto four 12-inch skewers. Grill chicken over hot fire, turning occasionally, until lightly charred and registers 160 degrees, about 10 minutes. Transfer skewers to platter and brush with reserved yogurt dressing. Tent loosely with foil and rest for 5 minutes. Serve with tomato salad.

TEST KITCHEN NOTE: We like Norpro's 12-Inch Stainless Steel Skewers.

FLANK STEAK TACOS WITH GRILLED CORN SALSA Serves 4 to 6

WHY THIS RECIPE WORKS: Microwaving the corn before grilling ensures that the corn and beef will be ready at the same time.

- 2 ears corn, husks and silk removed
- ¼ cup finely chopped red onion
- 1 jalapeño chile, stemmed, seeded, and minced
- ¼ cup lime juice (2 limes)
- 1 tablespoon minced fresh cilantro
  Salt and pepper
- 1 teaspoon ground cumin
- 1 (1½- to 2-pound) flank steak, trimmed
- 12 (6-inch) corn tortillas
- ½ cup sour cream

1. Place corn in large bowl and microwave, covered, until nearly tender, 3 to 5 minutes. Stir onion, jalapeño, 2 tablespoons lime juice, cilantro, ½ teaspoon salt, and ¼ teaspoon pepper together in bowl; set aside.

2. Combine cumin, ¾ teaspoon salt, and ½ teaspoon pepper in bowl. Pat steak dry with paper towels and rub with cumin mixture. Grill corn over hot fire, turning often, until lightly charred and tender, about 10 minutes. Grill steak over hot fire until well browned and registers 120 to 125 degrees (for medium-rare), 5 to 7 minutes per side. Transfer steak and corn to carving board and tent loosely with foil. Grill tortillas until lightly charred, 1 to 2 minutes per side. Transfer to plate and tent loosely with foil.

3. Combine sour cream and remaining 2 tablespoons lime juice in bowl. Season with salt and pepper to taste. Cut kernels from cob and add to reserved onion mixture. Slice steak thinly against grain. Serve with corn salsa, tortillas, and sour cream mixture.

TEST KITCHEN NOTE: You can use flour tortillas instead of corn.

CASHEW PORK WITH SNOW PEAS AND GINGER Serves 4

WHY THIS RECIPE WORKS: Coating the raw pork in cornstarch gives it a velvety texture. It also keeps the meat moist and helps the sauce adhere.

- ½ cup raw cashews, chopped
- 1 cup low-sodium chicken broth
- ¼ cup mirin
- ¼ cup soy sauce
- 3 tablespoons cornstarch
- 1 (16-ounce) pork tenderloin, trimmed
- 3 tablespoons vegetable oil
- 8 ounces snow peas, strings removed
- 6 garlic cloves, minced
- 1 tablespoon grated fresh ginger

1. Toast cashews in 12-inch nonstick skillet over medium heat until golden, about 5 minutes. Whisk broth, mirin, soy sauce, and 1 tablespoon cornstarch together in bowl until no lumps remain; set aside. Cut pork crosswise into ½-inch-thick slices, then cut each slice into ½-inch-thick strips. Toss pork and 1 tablespoon oil in large bowl. Add remaining 2 tablespoons cornstarch and toss to coat. Heat 2 teaspoons oil in 12-inch skillet over medium-high heat until just smoking. Brown half of pork, 3 to 5 minutes. Transfer pork to plate and tent with foil. Repeat with 2 teaspoons oil and remaining pork.

2. Cook snow peas and remaining 2 teaspoons oil in now-empty skillet until bright green, about 1 minute. Add garlic and ginger and cook until fragrant, about 30 seconds. Whisk broth mixture to recombine and add to skillet. Cook until thickened, about 2 minutes. Return pork, any accumulated juices, and cashews to skillet and cook until heated through, about 1 minute. Serve.

TEST KITCHEN NOTE: Mitoku Organic is our favorite brand of mirin.

Peaches and Cream Pie

The name made it sound delicious, but unfortunately the historic recipes we tried didn't pan out. Custard to the rescue. BY ERIKA BRUCE

"PEACHES AND CREAM" is a common expression, so I wasn't surprised to find the two words combined in several recipes that I recently came across in 100-year-old cookbooks. Those recipes instruct the baker to arrange peach halves in a buttery pie shell; sprinkle sugar and flour over the fruit; pour "thick, sweet" or "thick, yellow" cream into the crust; and then bake the pie until the peaches are rendered tender in the bubbling filling. Yum.

Well, that's what I imagined I would say. In reality, the old recipes were too simple to be true. Or, more likely, cream has changed so much over the past century (from straight from the cow to today's homogenized, ultra-pasteurized, often-weeks-old factory product) that it ruined the recipes of yore. Unwieldy peach hunks sat in a milky, lumpy puddle that ran as soon as I cut into the pie, and the bottom crust was raw and sodden. Mind you, once I worked my fork around the bits of raw dough and managed to snare a bite of peach in the rich, syrupy filling, it was pretty delicious (if slightly bland). With a little refining, I was sure that this pie would eventually make the cut.

For the filling, I whisked together the sugar, flour, and cream before pouring the mixture into the crust over the peaches. While I had succeeded in banishing clumps of flour, the filling remained unacceptably runny. I was facing the perennial peach problem: The fruit lets off an inordinate amount of liquid as it bakes. Fortunately, I knew what to do. I halved the peaches, sprinkled them with sugar, placed them on a broad baking sheet, and slipped them into the oven so that the peach juices could evaporate. The pie made with these prebaked peaches was markedly less soupy and had a concentrated, honeyed peach flavor. But the large chunks of fruit remained cumbersome. I tried slicing the peaches thin before roasting them; they turned to mush in the pie. It was back to roasting them in halves, but now I cut them into quarters after they had baked and slightly cooled. This snug layer of quartered fruit held up to the second round of baking.

But the pie was still too loose to slice. I figured the addition of more flour would help, but the amount required to set the filling made the pie heavy and dense. Cornstarch, for its part, made the filling gelatinous. Looking for something that would thicken the filling without compromising its creamy quality, I thought of baked custard—eggs! Two yolks later, I was in business. For flavor, I added a bit of salt and vanilla extract. Then I turned to the crust.

I've baked enough pies to know that with such a wet filling, the crust would never cook through without a head start. Prebaking the crust was a must, and just as I'd hoped, the baked shell stayed crisp even after the filling was added. Handily, I found that I could bake the empty pie crust at the same time that I roasted the peaches. My homey pie had a flaky, buttery crust; caramelized peach flavor; and a luscious juxtaposition of creamy dairy and bright fruit.

The last words in a "Cream Peach Pie" recipe that I'd run across in the 1884 cookbook *The Successful Housekeeper* (by Milon W. and Tinnie Ellsworth) were "eat fresh." My tasters needed no encouragement to do so.

PEACHES AND CREAM PIE Serves 8

Use your favorite pie dough or go to CooksCountry.com/extra for our Single-Crust Pie Dough recipe. Keep an eye on the peaches at the end of their baking time to ensure that they don't scorch.

- 1 (9-inch) unbaked pie shell
- 2 pounds ripe but firm peaches, peeled, halved, and pitted
- 2 tablespoons plus ½ cup (3½ ounces) sugar
- 3 tablespoons all-purpose flour
- ¼ teaspoon salt
- ⅓ cup heavy cream
- 2 large egg yolks
- ½ teaspoon vanilla extract

1. Cover pie shell with plastic wrap and refrigerate for 40 minutes, then freeze for 20 minutes. Adjust oven racks to upper-middle and lower-middle positions and heat oven to 375 degrees. Line chilled pie shell with two 12-inch squares aluminum foil, letting foil lie over edges of dough. Top with pie weights.

2. Place peach halves cut side up on aluminum foil–lined rimmed baking sheet and sprinkle with 2 tablespoons sugar. Bake peaches on upper-middle rack until softened and juice is released, about 30 minutes, flipping halfway through baking.

3. Place crust on lower-middle rack and bake until edges are lightly browned, about 15 minutes. Remove crust from oven and carefully remove foil and weights. Continue to bake until bottom of crust is light brown and peaches are caramelized, about 5 minutes. Cool crust and peaches for 15 minutes.

4. Reduce oven temperature to 325 degrees. Cut peaches lengthwise into quarters. Arrange peaches in single layer over crust. Combine remaining ½ cup sugar, flour, and salt in bowl. Whisk in cream, egg yolks, and vanilla until smooth. Pour cream mixture over peaches. Bake until filling is light golden brown and firm in center, 45 to 55 minutes. Cool pie on wire rack for at least 3 hours. Serve.

Buttery crust, deep caramelized peach flavor, and creamy custard—now that's a perfect slice.

TEST KITCHEN DISCOVERY
Twice-Baked Peaches
Eat a peach out of hand and its juiciness is no small part of what makes it so good. But cook the fruit and that same high water content can ruin peach pie, especially when coupled with cream. To evaporate the peach juices and concentrate the peach flavor, we roasted the fruit before filling the pie. A sprinkle of sugar helps the peach halves caramelize.
PLUS Save time: While you're roasting the fruit on one shelf of the oven, you can prebake the crust on another.

Grilled Honey-Glazed Pork Chops

Char, chops, and honey—the combination is a natural.
But the glaze refused to stay put. BY CAROLYNN PURPURA

Cayenne pepper, cider vinegar, and mustard keep the honey glaze from tasting cloying.

PORK CHOPS AND honey is a natural pairing, and grilling should enhance the combination, with the honey glaze complementing the smoky char. Recipes for the dish abound, so I started by testing the different approaches. Some dip raw chops in a glaze of honey, sugar, and liquid (vinegar, apple juice, and brandy are common) and then grill them. These glazes melted right off. Others grill the chops naked and subsequently paint them with honey glaze. These chops never developed lacquered exteriors. The third method, painting the chops with glaze partway through cooking, showed the most promise.

Using the best glaze from my initial tests (honey, brown sugar, cider vinegar, and cornstarch), I tried the test kitchen's standard method for grilling pork chops: Cook over direct heat to sear, brush on the glaze, and finish the chops over indirect heat. Despite the cornstarch, the glaze ran off; although honey is sticky at room temperature, heat causes it to thin and melt away. I reversed our method, cooking the chops over indirect heat, glazing, and then finishing with a quick sear on direct heat. I hoped the honey would caramelize before it had a chance to melt. Instead, the indirect heat released the meat's moisture, which meant I had to leave the chops over the high heat longer so the moisture could evaporate and then the chops could brown. The result? Overcooked chops.

I turned to sugar, which increases browning. The chops cooked over low heat until, aided by a sugar rub, they were deep brown. Moreover, the crackly, sugared surface gave the glaze something to cling to. I'd use the brief time on high heat simply to set the glaze.

At this point, my tasters demanded more honey flavor. I compared the glaze I had been using (equal parts honey and brown sugar) with one made entirely with honey. Unsurprisingly, the latter had better honey flavor, but subsequent testing revealed why recipes usually combine honey with sugar. Brown sugar has a much lower water content (2 percent or less versus honey's 17 percent), so the honey-only glaze was watery, and a watery glaze doesn't adhere to a chop. I reached for a pot and concentrated the glaze at a fast boil for a few minutes, effectively removing the moisture.

I added Dijon mustard, thyme, and cayenne pepper to the glaze. Then I grilled, glazed, and seared until the chops were crusty and caramelized and smelled fantastic. Minutes later, tasters proclaimed it a honey of a grilled pork chop and a honey of a recipe, too.

GRILLED HONEY-GLAZED PORK CHOPS Serves 4

- 4 (10-ounce) bone-in pork rib or center-cut chops, about 1 inch thick, trimmed
- ¼ cup sugar
- 1 teaspoon salt
- 1 teaspoon pepper
- 2 tablespoons cider vinegar
- ½ teaspoon cornstarch
- ¼ cup honey
- 1½ tablespoons Dijon mustard
- ½ teaspoon minced fresh thyme
- ⅛ teaspoon cayenne pepper

1. Cut 2 slits about 2 inches apart through fat and connective tissue around outside of each chop. Combine sugar, salt, and pepper in bowl. Pat chops dry with paper towels and rub with sugar mixture.

2. Whisk vinegar and cornstarch in small saucepan until no lumps remain. Stir in honey, mustard, thyme, and cayenne and bring to boil. Reduce heat to medium-low and simmer until glaze is reduced to ¼ cup, 5 to 7 minutes.

3A. For a charcoal grill: Open bottom vent completely. Light large chimney starter filled with charcoal briquettes (6 quarts). When top coals are partially covered with ash, pour two-thirds evenly over grill, then pour remaining coals over half of grill. Set cooking grate in place, cover, and open lid vent completely. Heat grill until hot, about 5 minutes.

3B. For a gas grill: Turn all burners to high, cover, and heat grill until hot, about 15 minutes. Leave primary burner on high and turn other burner(s) to medium-low.

4. Clean and oil cooking grate. Place chops on cool part of grill and cook (covered if using gas) until meat registers 140 degrees, 3 to 5 minutes per side. Brush chops with glaze and grill, glazed side down, over hot part of grill until caramelized, about 1 minute. Repeat with second side of chops. Transfer chops to platter, tent loosely with aluminum foil, and rest for 5 to 10 minutes. Brush with remaining glaze. Serve.

TEST KITCHEN TECHNIQUE **Getting the Glaze to Cling**

REDUCE Thin glaze runs off the chop in the heat of the grill. Simmering the glaze until it's thick and sticky helps it cling.

RUB Smooth chops offer nothing for a glaze to grab. A sugar rub melts into a bumpy, caramelized crust as the chops grill, which gives the glaze a hold.

BRUSH The chops cook over indirect heat until almost done. Then they're brushed with glaze and get a fast, hot sear; the glaze never has time to melt off.

Grilled Vegetable Salad

After many tests, we finally cracked the code:
Don't treat all the vegetables the same. BY CAROLYNN PURPURA

GRILLED VEGETABLE SALADS are just that: a combination of smoky grilled vegetables tossed in a dressing. I tracked down several recipes and got busy chopping, whisking, and grilling. Some were unnecessarily complicated, adding ingredients like nuts, segmented citrus, and grated cheese, all of which took the focus off the fresh summer vegetables. Other recipes had the opposite problem: nothing but chunks of grilled vegetables drizzled with oil and vinegar. Several included wan dressings that couldn't stand up to the flavor of the grill. Recipes that grilled bite-size pieces were hard to maneuver on the grill and mushy by the time they were cooked through.

Most of the recipes I tried used some combination of eggplant, bell pepper, zucchini, and red onion. Tasters liked this variety. I liked the fact that (as I discovered with a few rounds of testing) if I sliced the eggplant and onion into easy-to-maneuver half-inch rounds and simply halved the zucchini and peppers lengthwise, all the vegetables took the same amount of time to cook—about five minutes per side. A colleague suggested marinating the vegetables before grilling, so I made two batches of salad. In one, all the vegetables were marinated for an hour (in a potent, acidic vinaigrette of 2 parts olive oil, 1 part white wine vinegar) before being grilled and dressed with more of the same vinaigrette. In the other, I skipped the marinade and simply dressed the vegetables after grilling them. Tasters preferred the flavor of the salad for which the vegetables had been marinated, but they took issue with the squishy, fall-apart texture of the eggplant.

I thought that reducing the marinating time to 30 minutes would fix the problem, but now the eggplant was alternately either squishy or under-cooked. Cutting it thicker didn't help, since the rounds were absorbing the marinade unevenly and thus cooking unevenly. After testing marination times for the eggplant—from 15, to 10, to five minutes—I came to the conclusion that the eggplant simply didn't take well to marinating. I also discovered that without the acidic marinade to start its "cooking," the eggplant needed a few extra minutes on the grill. With these adjustments, the texture of all the grilled vegetables was perfect.

From there, the recipe came together quickly and easily. Dijon mustard and minced garlic gave the marinade deeper flavor; a sprinkling of chopped parsley and basil at the back end dressed the salad for summer.

GRILLED VEGETABLE SALAD
Serves 4 to 6

Keep the onion rounds together when you add them to the marinade or they'll be difficult to grill.

- 3 tablespoons white wine vinegar
- 1½ teaspoons Dijon mustard
- 3 garlic cloves, minced
  Salt and pepper
- 6 tablespoons olive oil
- 3 zucchini (8 ounces each), halved lengthwise
- 1 red onion, sliced into ½-inch-thick rounds
- 1 red bell pepper, stemmed, seeded, and halved lengthwise
- 1 pound eggplant, sliced into ½-inch-thick rounds
- 3 tablespoons minced fresh basil
- 1 tablespoon minced fresh parsley

1. Whisk vinegar, mustard, garlic, ½ teaspoon salt, and ½ teaspoon pepper together in large bowl. Slowly whisk in oil until thoroughly incorporated. Reserve 2 tablespoons dressing. Add zucchini, onion, and bell pepper to remaining dressing and turn to coat. Marinate vegetables for 15 minutes, tossing occasionally.

2A. For a charcoal grill: Open bottom vent completely. Light large chimney starter three-quarters full with charcoal briquettes (4½ quarts). When top coals are partially covered with ash, pour evenly over grill. Set cooking grate in place, cover, and open lid vent completely. Heat grill until hot, about 5 minutes.

2B. For a gas grill: Turn all burners to high, cover, and heat grill until hot, about 15 minutes. Turn all burners to medium-high.

3. Clean and oil cooking grate. Place eggplant and marinated vegetables on grill, beginning with eggplant. Grill (covered if using gas) until charred and tender, 4 to 6 minutes per side, removing eggplant last. Chop vegetables into 1-inch pieces and toss with reserved dressing, basil, and parsley. Cool 10 minutes. Season with salt and pepper to taste. Serve.

Vegetable planks are easy to handle and won't fall through the grill grates. Before dressing the cooked planks, cut them into bite-size pieces.

TEST KITCHEN DISCOVERY **Not All Vegetables Are Created Equal**
Marinating the vegetables before grilling and then dressing them afterward gave us a dish flavored from the inside out. But the marinated eggplant cooked unevenly. Ultimately, we left the eggplant out of the initial marinade. It absorbed plenty of vinaigrette, and thus flavor, after grilling.

MARINATE EARLY
Most vegetables can hold up to a pregrilling marinade.

DRESS LATE
Spongy eggplant cooks unevenly and falls apart if marinated before grilling.

Easier Chicken Chimichangas

Could we streamline the filling, forming, and frying so that these deep-fried burritos were a realistic weeknight option? BY LYNN CLARK

Chimichangas were invented in Tucson, Arizona, in the 1950s, when the owner of a Mexican restaurant accidentally dropped a burrito in the deep-fryer and hollered "Chimichanga!" to keep from cussing in front of children. Or they were invented in Phoenix in the 1940s, when a restaurant cook repurposed leftover lunchtime burritos as a dinner special. Or Mexican cowboys tucked cooked meat into tortillas so they could eat on the go, later crisping them over the campfire. If you're expecting a final word on this, you're out of luck. And if you're thinking you can just whip up a few "chimis" for dinner, you're also out of luck. Why? Do you have seasoned meat, rice, and beans at the ready, to say nothing of a commercial fry-o-lator to make fast work of frying?

We like to serve our crunchy chimichangas with guacamole, salsa, sour cream, and lime wedges.

One fact is indisputable: The chimichanga is a staple in Mexican American restaurants from coast to coast—and for good reason. It's basically a burrito taken to the next level. It has the same hearty meal's worth of tender meat, rice, cheese, beans, heat, and spice rolled into a flour tortilla. What gives it the edge is deep-frying: The shell becomes exquisitely crisp and flaky, and the cheese oozes into gooey nirvana. Add the parade of toppings—guacamole, salsa, sour cream, enchilada sauce—and it's no wonder people are passionate about chimichangas.

First things first: Chimichangas can be made with beef or chicken. We opted for chicken (we'd save a beef recipe for another time). I spent a long day boiling rice in one pot, sautéing bone-in, skin-on chicken pieces in a pan, and soaking and boiling dried beans in another pot, as classic recipes suggest. Know what? I wasn't even close to being done. I still had to pile the filling into each tortilla and roll it into a cylinder, tucking in the edges as I went. After several hours of preparation, I dropped these oversize

burritos into pot number four, this one filled with hot oil. A few minutes later, I fished them out. Their exterior was crisp, even buttery, but the folded edges had unsealed in the oil, letting the filling escape and burn. As I collapsed in an exhausted heap at my desk, I resolved to repair and streamline this recipe.

First, the easy decisions: I would use canned beans instead of dried, specifically pinto beans, which had trumped red kidney and black beans in early tests. Next, I'd start with boneless, skinless

chicken breasts so that I could avoid the steps of skinning and boning.

Dismayed by the sink full of dirty dishes, I tried cooking everything in a single pot. I sautéed onions and garlic in a little oil; stirred in chili powder and cumin; and tossed in whole, raw chicken breasts (I'd chop the meat after it was cooked), raw rice, and the canned, drained beans. To poach the chicken and cook the rice, I poured in flavorful chicken broth, covered the pot, and waited. My one-pot plan had mixed results. On the plus side, the chicken was nicely cooked. On the minus side, the rice was crunchy, and overall the dish was lackluster. I knew who was to blame: me. The quicker-cooking boneless, skinless chicken and canned beans for which I'd opted were convenient, sure, but I'd sacrificed flavor and texture. This would not do.

The chicken cooked faster than the rice, and since I couldn't slow down the bird's cooking speed, I'd help the rice get a move on. I tried using Minute Rice and then precooked, microwavable Ready Rice. Both were chalky and sticky. I cycled back to ordinary long-grain rice. To give it a head start, I microwaved it with some chicken broth until the broth was absorbed. I added this partially cooked rice to the pot with the other ingredients. In just 15 minutes, the rice was tender.

To give the filling depth and flavor, I added extra spices to the rice and broth as they parcooked in the microwave, hoping that the rice would drink up the flavors. Not so much. Too late, I remembered that ground dried spices need to be cooked in fat to release their flavor compounds. Happily, minced, canned chipotle peppers yielded a smoky, well-seasoned broth that flavored the rice nicely.

I combined my now tasty and easy filling with cheddar cheese and cilantro, rolled up the chimichangas, and dropped these 1-pound burritos into 2 quarts of scalding oil. What a nightmare. Not only was the potential for pain scary, but once again the filling leaked out and burned. My first solve? Switching from deep- to shallow-frying. Frying with just 3 cups of oil let me ease the unwieldy chimichangas into the pan without splashing oil. I secured the ends with toothpicks. No luck—the picks burned and broke into shards, and the filling leaked out in every direction. What I needed was … glue. Bingo! I mixed up a homemade food "glue" of equal parts flour and water, brushing the paste on the edges of the tortilla before rolling and frying each chimichanga. This time, the chimichangas stayed in one piece.

Unfortunately, the tightly tucked edges had created folds of extra tortilla at the end of the chimichangas that came out of the oil doughy, not crisp. Back to the cutting board. A test kitchen colleague and I spent an afternoon doing tortilla origami. We tried and rejected several shapes and folding strategies before hitting on the idea of folding each tortilla as though we were wrapping a present (see "Glue and Fold") and, as before, sealing the edges with the flour-water paste. In the oil, these thinner edges became decidedly crunchy—a perfect match for the rest of the big, golden, crisp tortilla and its spicy, delicious, and easy-to-make filling.

CHICKEN CHIMICHANGAS Serves 4

If using a cast-iron Dutch oven, increase the broth to 1¾ cups, adding 1¼ cups in step 2.

- 1¼ cups low-sodium chicken broth
- 1 tablespoon minced canned chipotle chile in adobo sauce
- ½ cup long-grain white rice
  Salt and pepper
- 2 (6-ounce) boneless, skinless chicken breasts, trimmed
- 1 tablespoon plus 3 cups peanut or vegetable oil
- 1 onion, chopped fine
- 2 garlic cloves, minced
- 1 teaspoon chili powder
- ½ teaspoon ground cumin
- 1 (15-ounce) can pinto beans, rinsed
- 4 ounces sharp cheddar cheese, shredded (1 cup)
- ⅓ cup chopped fresh cilantro
- 1 tablespoon all-purpose flour
- 1 tablespoon water
- 4 (10-inch) flour tortillas

1. Whisk broth and chipotle together in 2-cup liquid measuring cup. Combine ½ cup chipotle broth, rice, and ¼ teaspoon salt in bowl. Cover bowl and microwave until liquid is completely absorbed, about 5 minutes. Meanwhile, pat chicken dry with paper towels and season with salt and pepper.

2. Heat 1 tablespoon oil in Dutch oven over medium-high heat until just smoking. Add onion and cook until softened, about 5 minutes. Stir in garlic, chili powder, and cumin and cook until fragrant, about 30 seconds. Add remaining ¾ cup chipotle broth, parcooked rice, and beans and bring to boil.

3. Reduce heat to medium-low, add chicken, and cook, covered, until chicken registers 160 degrees and rice is tender, about 15 minutes, flipping chicken halfway through. Transfer chicken to cutting board and rest for 5 to 10 minutes. Cut chicken into ½-inch pieces and combine with rice and bean mixture, cheddar, and cilantro in large bowl. Wash now-empty pot.

4. Whisk flour and water together in bowl. Stack tortillas on plate and microwave, covered, until pliable, about 1 minute. Working 1 at a time, place one-quarter of chicken mixture in center of warm tortilla. Brush edges of tortilla with flour paste. Wrap top and bottom of tortilla tightly over filling. Brush ends of tortilla with paste and fold into center, pressing firmly to seal.

5. Heat remaining 3 cups oil in clean pot over medium-high heat until 325 degrees. Place 2 chimichangas, seam side down, in oil. Fry, adjusting burner as necessary to maintain oil temperature between 300 and 325 degrees, until chimichangas are deep golden brown, about 2 minutes per side. Drain on wire rack set inside rimmed baking sheet. Bring oil back to 325 degrees and repeat with remaining chimichangas. Serve.

Smoky Salsa Verde

Salsa verde, a.k.a. tomatillo salsa, is the lesser-known sibling of tomato salsa. It's time to remedy that: Its bright, bracing flavor perks up many a chimichanga (or scrambled eggs or tortilla chips). Sometimes, though, the highly acidic tomatillos wreak havoc. For my recipe, I sought balance.

To begin, I tested fresh versus canned tomatillos; the canned tasted (guess what?) canned. Having settled on fresh, I heeded the advice of many recipes and boiled the (husked) tomatillos to soften them. I combined the softened fruit with the traditional seasonings—jalapeño, onion, garlic, cilantro, lime juice, and salt—and buzzed everything in the food processor. The salsa tasted clean and fruity but, as I'd feared, too tart.

To soften its acidity, I turned to the broiler. I tossed the tomatillos with the jalapeño, onion, garlic, and a bit of oil. Then I spread them out on a baking sheet and broiled them until just charred, about 10 minutes. I then pureed them with the remaining ingredients and assembled a team of tasters. We spooned the salsa over chimichangas and dug in. The broiling had tempered the tart tomatillos, sweetened the onion, and mellowed the jalapeño and garlic, while the char gave the salsa a subtle smokiness. All was in balance. —LYNN CLARK

SMOKY SALSA VERDE
Makes 1¼ cups

- 1 pound tomatillos, husked
- 1 small onion, quartered
- 1 jalapeño chile, stemmed, halved, and seeded
- 1 garlic clove, peeled
- 1 teaspoon olive oil
- ½ cup fresh cilantro leaves
- 1 tablespoon lime juice
  Salt

1. Adjust oven rack 5 inches from broiler element and heat broiler. Toss tomatillos, onion, jalapeño, and garlic with oil and place on aluminum foil–lined rimmed baking sheet. Broil, shaking pan occasionally, until vegetables are lightly charred, 10 to 12 minutes. Cool slightly, about 5 minutes.

2. Add vegetables, cilantro, lime juice, and ¼ teaspoon salt to food processor and pulse until coarsely ground, 5 to 7 pulses. Season with salt to taste. Serve. (Salsa can be refrigerated for up to 3 days.)

TEST KITCHEN TECHNIQUE **Glue and Fold**
The usual burrito-style wrapping method left us between the devil and the deep blue sea: Either the filling leaked out in the pot of oil or the ends of the tortilla never crisped. Our new chimichanga folding technique solves both problems.

GLUE Place the filling in the middle of the tortilla. Brush the tortilla's circumference with a flour-and-water paste. The paste will act as a glue, letting you securely seal the chimichanga.

FOLD After you've folded two opposing sides toward the center and pressed them to seal, brush the open flaps with more paste. Fold the flaps in and again press firmly to seal the chimichanga shut.

Grilled Steakhouse Steak Tips

Most recipes for these are awful, despite the "secret" ingredients they tout. We set out to find (and spill) their real secrets. BY SARAH GABRIEL

We prick the steak tips with a fork before marinating them to help tenderize this chewy cut.

YOU CAN SMELL them coming from the kitchen before your server even sets the plate in front of you: a pile of big chunks of beef sirloin flap meat, loaded with flavor from both a potent marinade and a high-sear crust. I wanted to re-create this steakhouse classic for home cooks, so I phoned a few steakhouses and rooted around our cookbook library for recipes. Most sources stressed the importance of two things: high heat (for maximum char) and a "secret" marinade ingredient—beer, ketchup, barbecue sauce, Italian dressing, or cola. Intrigued, I was eager to put these recipes to the test.

The beer-based marinade produced bitter, soggy tips; Italian dressing sour, mushy tips. Both ketchup and barbecue sauce produced significant char because they contain sugar, but these distinctively seasoned condiments produced tips that tasted as though they belonged in a barbecue joint, not a steakhouse. The only "secret" ingredient that promoted the right sort of char was cola, but the cola marinade was a drippy mess, necessitating messy drying before grilling.

While none of these marinades was very good, at least I'd learned that sugar would play an important role in my recipe. I whisked together a working marinade of garlic, paprika, cayenne, black pepper, vegetable oil, soy sauce (which helps boost meaty flavors), and a tablespoon each of light brown sugar and (sugary) tomato paste. I cut a large flap steak into 2½-inch chunks: A few tests had already shown that smaller chunks overcooked by the time they were well charred, and larger chunks were more like mini roasts than like tips. I marinated the chunks for an hour—the minimum time called for in many recipes.

We generally like our steak cooked medium-rare, so I pulled the tips off the grill when they reached 120 degrees. They were OK, but the char needed a boost and the tips were a little chewy. Flap meat has more connective tissue than other steaks, so it can be tough when cooked rare or medium-rare. I found that cooking the tips to medium (about 130 degrees) provided the best meeting point of tenderness and juiciness. The combination of slightly longer cooking (to medium) and upping the brown sugar to 3 tablespoons gave me the smoky, crusty char I'd been looking for. Trading the light brown sugar for dark brown lent extra flavor.

The tips tasted great, but more than one taster joked about jaw fatigue—the meat was still a little tough. I tried the common trick of poking the meat with a fork before cutting it into chunks. It worked: The poking breaks long, tough muscle fibers into shorter, more tender pieces. Fork-tenderizing had the added advantage of exposing more surface to soak up the marinade. Before hanging up my tongs, I did a final round of time tests. They revealed that two hours of marinating was far superior to one, but also that there was no harm (though no great advantage, either) in soaking the tips for up to one day.

GRILLED STEAKHOUSE STEAK TIPS
Serves 4 to 6

Flap meat is sold as whole steaks, strips, and pieces. For even pieces, buy a whole steak of uniform size and cut it up yourself.

- ⅓ **cup soy sauce**
- ⅓ **cup vegetable oil**
- 3 **tablespoons packed dark brown sugar**
- 5 **garlic cloves, minced**
- 1 **tablespoon tomato paste**
- 1 **tablespoon paprika**
- ½ **teaspoon pepper**
- ¼ **teaspoon cayenne pepper**
- 1 **(2½-pound) beef flap steak**

1. Whisk soy sauce, oil, sugar, garlic, tomato paste, paprika, pepper, and cayenne together in bowl until sugar dissolves; transfer to zipper-lock bag. Pat beef dry with paper towels. Prick beef all over with fork and cut into 2½-inch pieces. Add meat to bag with soy mixture and refrigerate for 2 to 24 hours, turning occasionally.

2A. For a charcoal grill: Open bottom grill vents completely. Light large chimney starter filled with charcoal briquettes (6 quarts). When top coals are partially covered with ash, pour evenly over grill. Set cooking grate in place, cover, and open lid vents completely. Heat grill until hot, about 5 minutes.

2B. For a gas grill: Turn all burners to high, cover, and heat grill until hot, about 15 minutes.

3. Clean and oil cooking grate. Cook beef (covered if using gas) until charred and registers 130 to 135 degrees (for medium), 8 to 10 minutes. Transfer meat to platter, tent loosely with foil, and rest for 5 to 10 minutes. Serve.

Common Ingredients, Uncommon Results

We engineered our marinade to give the steak tips maximum meaty flavor and satisfying texture. These familiar ingredients make a strong team, each with its own part to play.

DARK BROWN SUGAR
Delivers depth, complexity, and a caramelized, crusty char.

TOMATO PASTE
Adds background savor and enough body to help the marinade cling.

VEGETABLE OIL
Distributes flavors and activates oil-soluble flavor compounds, such as those found in garlic.

SOY SAUCE
Its salt penetrates to deeply season the meat. Its glutamates boost meaty flavor.

The Best Sautéed Mushrooms

What's the best way to infuse mushrooms with the flavor of garlic and herbs?

BY KELLY PRICE

GRILLED MUSHROOMS ARE fast becoming a summer staple, but for me, they can't hold a candle to their sautéed cousins. Why? Because you can sauté mushrooms in butter. Deeply browned and redolent of herbs, garlic, and butter, the best versions are the perfect sidekick. I decided to make these mushrooms in the test kitchen, thinking it would be as easy as browning mushrooms and stirring in a knob of butter, some garlic, and herbs. Instead, I prepared a handful of recipes and found myself staring, dejected, at mounds of shriveled mushrooms that were either bland as Muzak or slicked with grease (some recipes called for as many as two sticks of butter for 2 pounds of mushrooms). These were a far cry from the earthy, deeply flavorful specimens I craved.

My first decision was to limit myself to mushrooms that I could pick up at the local supermarket. In addition to button and cremini mushrooms, most markets now stock shiitakes and portobellos, so I test-drove a handful of each of the four in my sauté pan. Portobellos, which are fantastic grilled, were springy and slimy when sautéed. Buttons were fine, as were cremini (these are actually immature portobellos), which have slightly heartier flavor. Tasters also liked the rich-yet-delicate shiitakes. After several tests, I settled on a roughly 2:1 ratio of cremini or button (halved) to shiitakes (cut into ½-inch slices).

The number one rule of mushroom cookery is to give them plenty of space. The idea is that crowding impedes the evaporation of the plentiful liquid that mushrooms release as they cook; consequently, the mushrooms never brown. Because I was working with 2 pounds of mushrooms (to feed six), that would mean cooking in batches on the stovetop. To avoid cumbersome batch cooking, I turned to the oven. A rimmed baking sheet easily accommodated all of the mushrooms, and I thought I was on to something. But several tests showed that the mushrooms needed more than 40 minutes (with vigilant stirring) in a very hot oven, which, on reflection, was too much time for a relatively simple side dish.

Stovetop cooking was starting to look like a better option after all. Since I couldn't fit 2 pounds of mushrooms in a single layer in a skillet, which would allow them to brown, I split up the

We use shiitakes and cremini or button mushrooms. You can find all of them at the supermarket.

mushrooms, starting the cooking with the cremini. Once they had released their liquid and shrunk, there was room in the skillet for the shiitakes. But the shiitakes soaked up the cremini liquid and never browned. If I let the liquid cook off before adding the shiitakes, the cremini overcooked. For the next test, I reversed the order: I browned the shiitakes first and then added the cremini. This time, the cremini were undercooked and slightly spongy while the shiitakes bordered on overcooked.

Running out of ideas, I decided to challenge the law of overcrowding. I melted butter in the skillet (I'd landed at 4 tablespoons for richness without grease) and, feeling like a defiant teen, tossed all 2 pounds of mushrooms into

my pan at once, and then popped on the lid. After 10 minutes of covered cooking, all of the mushrooms had thrown off their liquid and shrunk. With another 10 minutes of uncovered cooking, the liquid evaporated and the mushrooms—no longer crowded—browned beautifully. Easy.

It was time to refine the seasonings: Shallot and garlic added a backbone of flavor, while thyme provided an herbal note. Half a cup of white wine stirred in at the end not only contributed a welcome acidic punch, but also helped dissolve the flavorful mushroom fond (the brown stuff on the pan floor) back into the buttery "sauce," adding flavor.

So what's the secret to great sautéed mushrooms? Break the rules.

Forget What You've Heard

The cardinal rule for well-browned mushrooms is "Don't crowd the pan." Not this time.

STEAM
Cooking the heaping skillet full of mushrooms covered encourages them to release their juices.

BROWN
Once the liquid is gone, the now-much-smaller mushrooms have enough room to brown.

Creamy Chocolate Éclair Cake

We made an instant dessert classic slightly less instant and considerably more delicious.

BY SARAH GABRIEL

C hocolate éclair cake, although virtually nonexistent in traditional cook-books, is one of those odd items that, like the video of Belgian commuters dancing to "The Sound of Music" in Antwerp Central Station, has gone viral on the Internet. Confronted with a deluge of electronic recipes and a comparable number of rave reviews, I wondered how it was possible that I hadn't encountered éclair cake before. I soon learned that, despite its name, it's neither an outsize éclair nor a typical baked cake. It more closely resembles a classic easy icebox cake—and practically from the moment I began testing in earnest, I succumbed to its mysterious allure.

To construct Chocolate Éclair Cake, spread creamy pudding between layered graham crackers and glaze with rich chocolate ganache.

Of the hundreds of éclair cake recipes I found online, nearly all proceed the same way: Make an ersatz mousse filling by folding Cool Whip into instant vanilla pudding; line a casserole dish with graham crackers; top the graham crackers with half of the "mousse," more grahams, the remaining mousse, and one final layer of grahams. To finish, gild the lily with canned chocolate frosting.

I was skeptical but put together a few chocolate éclair cakes to see for myself what the online hubbub was all about. I predicted that my tasters would be scornful of this junk food assemblage, but then I noticed them eyeing the pans, forks in hand, poised like runners toeing the starting line, as I frosted the last one. I dug in right alongside them. The filling was creamy yet light, the

graham crackers just soft enough to scoop with a spoon. This cake was hard to stop eating. It quickly vanished, plates practically licked clean by a mob of former restaurant chefs and alleged food experts. When we finally did stop eating, however, we paid for our enthusiasm—with toothaches and an aftertaste best described as "plasticky." I knew that if I could reform this dessert using home-made substitutions for the processed-food components, chocolate éclair cake would live up to the hype.

To bring this dish a little more in line with its namesake, the éclair, I traded the graham crackers for pâte à choux, the French pastry that's used to make éclairs and cream puffs. My tasters laughed me out of the kitchen. I got the point: This was supposed to be a simple icebox cake. The graham crackers would stay. Next, I replaced the instant pudding with classic egg yolk–thickened pastry cream. This time, I didn't need tasters to tell me that using a sensitive egg-thickened cream,

necessitating a fine-mesh strainer and an ice bath to prevent lumps of curdled egg, was too much hassle for this for-merly instant dessert.

To simplify, I tried a classic corn-starch-thickened vanilla pudding. I combined 6 tablespoons of cornstarch with 1¼ cups of sugar, poured in 5 cups of milk, and simmered everything in a pot until thick. Then, off the heat, I added butter and vanilla extract. The pudding was perfectly creamy, with subtle vanilla flavor. I assembled the cake, this time using real whipped cream in place of the plasticky Cool Whip. But rather than a perky mousse, I had a runny pool that nearly dissolved the grahams. Fixing flavor, it seemed, was as simple as tossing out the packaged junk food, but getting the filling to set up was proving trickier.

Doubling the cornstarch in the pudding made a stiffer filling and restored the soft (not soggy) crackers in the assembled cake. Unfortunately, the pudding was now stodgy and chalky rather than rich and creamy. I had to back down on the cornstarch and find another way to set the filling. Cool Whip is packed with stabilizers; maybe reinforcing the homemade whipped cream would help. Gelatin was an obvious choice. After about a dozen tests, during which I slowly decreased the cornstarch in the pudding from 12 tablespoons and increased the gelatin from ½ teaspoon in the whipped cream, I eventually found the sweet spot: 6 tablespoons of cornstarch and 1¼ teaspoons of gelatin. Any more cornstarch and a film clung to my tongue. Any more gelatin and the filling was rubbery. Any less of either and the filling didn't set.

Having tossed out the packaged ingredients in the filling to make this already barely resistible dessert downright addictive, I couldn't settle for canned frosting. Ganache—the French way of saying chocolate melted into hot cream—had too strong a flavor for such a mild and creamy cake. Instead, I tried a glaze made of cocoa powder, confectioners' sugar, and milk. It had a shine reminiscent of a true éclair glaze, but now tasters missed the rich melted chocolate. I circled back to the ganache, this time thinning it out and taming the bitterness with extra cream and adding corn syrup for a smooth, shiny finish.

Tasters were coming back for thirds, and colleagues from other departments

were sidling up to me in the hallways and asking in hushed tones, "What *was* that thing? And when are you making another one?" Finally, I had a homemade treat with junk food appeal, only without the junk.

CHOCOLATE ÉCLAIR CAKE

Serves 15

You can use 6 ounces of finely chopped semisweet chocolate in place of the chips.

- 1¼ cups sugar
- 6 tablespoons cornstarch
- 1 teaspoon salt
- 5 cups whole milk
- 4 tablespoons unsalted butter, cut into 4 pieces
- 5 teaspoons vanilla extract
- 2 tablespoons water
- 1¼ teaspoons unflavored gelatin
- 2¾ cups heavy cream, chilled
- 14 ounces graham crackers
- 1 cup semisweet chocolate chips
- 5 tablespoons light corn syrup

1. Combine sugar, cornstarch, and salt in large saucepan. Whisk milk into sugar mixture until smooth and bring to boil, scraping bottom with rubber spatula, over medium-high heat. Immediately reduce heat to medium-low and cook, continuing to scrape bottom, until thickened and large bubbles appear on surface, 4 to 6 minutes. Off heat, whisk in butter and vanilla. Transfer pudding to large bowl and place plastic wrap directly on surface of pudding. Refrigerate until cool, about 2 hours.

2. Stir water and gelatin together in bowl and let sit until gelatin softens, about 5 minutes. Microwave until mixture is bubbling around edges and gelatin dissolves, 15 to 30 seconds. Using stand mixer fitted with whisk, whip 2 cups cream on medium-low speed until foamy, about 1 minute. Increase speed to high and whip until soft peaks form, about 2 minutes. Add gelatin mixture and whip until stiff peaks form, about 1 minute.

3. Whisk one-third whipped cream into chilled pudding, then gently fold in remaining whipped cream, 1 scoop at a time, until combined. Cover bottom of 13 by 9-inch baking dish with layer of graham crackers, breaking crackers as necessary to line bottom of pan. Top with half of pudding–whipped cream mixture (about 5½ cups) and another layer of graham crackers. Repeat with remaining pudding–whipped cream mixture and remaining graham crackers.

4. Microwave chocolate chips, remaining ¾ cup cream, and corn syrup in bowl, stirring occasionally, until smooth, 1 to 2 minutes. Cool glaze to room temperature, about 10 minutes. Cover graham crackers with glaze and refrigerate cake for 6 to 24 hours. Serve. (Éclair cake can be refrigerated for up to 2 days.)

RATING GRAHAM CRACKERS

The original graham crackers, developed by Sylvester Graham some 200 years ago, were more like hardtack than like the sweet wafers we know today. Marketed as "Dr. Graham's Honey Biskets," the dense crackers were made largely from coarse whole-wheat flour. Graham might be faintly horrified by what's become of them: Yes, supermarket grahams still incorporate graham (or whole-wheat) flour, but white flour is now the primary ingredient with sugar of some sort not far behind. They also contain oil, salt, and leaveners.

We tasted three top-selling national brands—Honey Maid Honey Grahams, Keebler Grahams Crackers Original, and Nabisco Grahams Original—sampling them plain, in Chocolate Éclair Cake, and in the crust of Key lime pie. All brands fared well enough to earn our recommendation. For straight snacking, we prefer Nabisco Grahams Original for their wheaty flavor and tempered sweetness. These crackers have the highest percentage of graham flour, which contributes to their flavor but could also account for their less substantial structure (they turned to mush in the Éclair Cake); graham flour forms less gluten than white flour. Keebler's grahams, which held up in both pie crust and cake, are best for baking. —HANNAH CROWLEY

RECOMMENDED		TASTERS' COMMENTS
KEEBLER GRAHAMS CRACKERS ORIGINAL $4.19 for 15 ounces		Sampled plain, Keebler's grahams struck some tasters as "fake" and "artificial." In both cake and pie, however, these crackers held up well. Tasters praised their "tender and light" and "robust" texture, which made them "definitely a winner—great graham cracker taste and smooth texture."
HONEY MAID HONEY GRAHAMS $4.29 for 14.4 ounces		While the other brands excelled in one area and fell short in another, Honey Maid's grahams earned consistent praise, whether sampled plain or in baked goods. Tasters found them "very pleasing," "butterscotch-y," and "very soft, fine, fresh-textured."
NABISCO GRAHAMS ORIGINAL $3.99 for 14.4 ounces		Eaten plain, Nabisco's grahams were "wheaty," "grainy," "hefty," "nutty," and "earthy." In the cake tasting, however, the crackers turned to mush, prompting comments like "Tastes like wet cardboard—ew" and "Just a ghost of crumbs." They were fine in the pie crust.

Strawberry Dream Cake

The name aside, getting real fruit flavor into a strawberry layer cake took some wide-awake testing. BY LYNN CLARK

I first ran into it at a birthday party for a little girl: a bubble-gum pink layer cake with fluffy, pale-pink frosting. The cake was shaped like a dome, which formed a skirt for the Barbie doll stuck in its center. When I looked for a recipe, I found a single one duplicated ad infinitum on the Internet. That recipe called itself Strawberry Dream Cake, although the closest it came to a real berry was the picture on the box of strawberry Jell-O. To make the cake, the contents of that box were stirred together with white cake mix and baked. But I dreamed of a cake made from scratch with real berries and real strawberry flavor. Recipes for chocolate, yellow, and lemon layer cakes abound. Where were the recipes for strawberry cake?

We sandwich fresh summer berries between the layers and use a few to decorate the cake.

I finally uncovered a few from home cooks who, like me, couldn't believe a recipe for real strawberry cake didn't exist, so they had developed their own. One afternoon in the test kitchen, I tested their recipes alongside the Jell-O-and-box-mix version. The latter, not surprisingly, tasted about as much like real strawberries as fake tans look like real ones. But the from-scratch versions didn't measure up either. Some used strawberry jam in the batter—as much as a cupful—but the cakes lacked fresh berry flavor. Others called for stirring in lots of chopped fresh berries. This approach sounded promising, but the layers came out dense and soggy. The frostings, while pink, lacked even the merest hint of berry, and most were too sweet. I was beginning to understand why original recipes were hard to come by, yet I remained determined to fill in the gap.

To develop my own recipe, I chose frozen strawberries over fresh. I'd be baking them anyway, plus I wanted to be able to bake this cake year-round. I started with the test kitchen's foolproof white layer cake recipe, which (because it uses an unusual reverse creaming method) produces a very tender cake with a notably fine crumb. Also, I hoped that the lack of rich egg yolks would allow the delicate strawberry flavor to shine.

I began by pureeing thawed, frozen berries and adding them to the cake in place of some of the milk. As in my initial tests, the berry solids made the cake soggy and dense. On the bright side, the puree did add flavor. Thinking the puree was too wet, I tried cooking it into a thicker, homemade "jam." (Since I was cooking it quickly and in a small batch, my jam retained the fresh berry flavor.) This yielded better flavor still but the same gummy layers.

To extract the berry flavor while leaving the pulp behind, I once again thawed the berries (the microwave made quick work of the job) and pressed them through a fine-mesh strainer. (It takes a bit of elbow grease.) I discarded the pulp that was in the strainer and stirred the strawberry juice into the batter. Now the cake was light and tender again, but the strawberry

flavor was faint. To get supercharged berry flavor, I reduced the juice by more than half on the stovetop until it was thick and syrupy—it took about eight minutes. The cake I made using that syrup had "berrylicious" flavor, as one taster put it, and the syrup turned the cake a pretty shade of pink.

Even the Jell-O-and-cake-mix recipes usually called for from-scratch frosting, in most cases a classic American icing made from confectioners' sugar, butter, and chopped fresh berries. It wasn't bad, but the cream cheese icing used by a few of the recipes was better. Its tang offset the sweet, fruity cake. The final piece of the icing puzzle came together one day while I was pressing juice out of the berries for some additional batter testing. Why, I suddenly wondered, was I discarding the pulp? I tried beating it into the frosting and found that in one pressing, I could flavor both cake and frosting.

I'd come to believe that any self-respecting strawberry cake needed a few fresh berries, so as a final touch I laid fresh, sliced berries over the bottom layer. But when I placed the second cake layer over the first, it slid off the slick berries. I was able to prevent the problem by sandwiching the berries between thin coats of frosting.

To confirm that my Strawberry Dream Cake was now in perfect working order, I baked and iced one last one. The cake was tender and light. Its pale tint was the color of a June rose and its subtle berry flavor was as soft and alive as a June day. It may not have been Barbie's strawberry dream cake, but it was definitely mine.

STRAWBERRY DREAM CAKE
Serves 8 to 10

CAKE
- 10 ounces frozen whole strawberries (2 cups)
- ¾ cup whole milk, room temperature
- 6 large egg whites, room temperature
- 2 teaspoons vanilla extract
- 2¼ cups (9 ounces) cake flour
- 1¾ cups (12¼ ounces) granulated sugar
- 4 teaspoons baking powder
- 1 teaspoon salt
- 12 tablespoons unsalted butter, cut into 12 pieces and softened

FROSTING
- 10 tablespoons unsalted butter, softened
- 2¼ cups (9 ounces) confectioners' sugar
- 12 ounces cream cheese, cut into 12 pieces and softened
  Pinch salt
- 8 ounces fresh strawberries, hulled and sliced thin (about 1 ½ cups)

1. For the cake: Adjust oven rack to middle position and heat oven to 350 degrees. Grease two 9-inch round cake pans, line bottoms with parchment, grease parchment, and flour.

2. Transfer strawberries to bowl, cover, and microwave until strawberries are soft and have released their juice, about 5 minutes. Place in fine-mesh strainer set over small saucepan. Firmly press fruit dry (juice should measure at least ¾ cup); reserve strawberry solids. Bring juice to boil over medium-high heat and cook, stirring occasionally, until syrupy and reduced to ¼ cup, 6 to 8 minutes. Whisk milk into juice until combined.

3. Whisk strawberry milk, egg whites, and vanilla in bowl. Using stand mixer fitted with paddle, mix flour, sugar, baking powder, and salt on low speed until combined. Add butter, 1 piece at a time, and mix until only pea-size pieces remain, about 1 minute. Add half of milk mixture, increase speed to medium-high, and beat until light and fluffy, about 1 minute. Reduce speed to medium-low, add remaining milk mixture, and beat until incorporated, about 30 seconds. Give batter final stir by hand.

4. Scrape equal amounts of batter into prepared pans and bake until toothpick inserted in center comes out clean, 20 to 25 minutes, rotating pans halfway through baking. Cool cakes in pans on wire rack for 10 minutes. Remove cakes from pans, discarding parchment, and cool completely, about 2 hours. (Cooled cakes can be wrapped with plastic wrap and stored at room temperature for up to 2 days.)

5. For the frosting: Using stand mixer fitted with paddle, mix butter and sugar on low speed until combined, about 30 seconds. Increase speed to medium-high and beat until pale and fluffy, about 2 minutes. Add cream cheese, one piece at a time, and beat until incorporated, about 1 minute. Add reserved strawberry solids and salt and mix until combined, about 30 seconds. Refrigerate until ready to use, up to 2 days.

6. Pat strawberries dry with paper towels. When cakes are cooled, spread ¾ cup frosting over 1 cake round. Press 1 cup strawberries in even layer over frosting and cover with additional ¾ cup frosting. Top with second cake round and spread remaining frosting evenly over top and sides of cake. Garnish with remaining strawberries. Serve. (Cake can be refrigerated for 2 days. Bring to room temperature before serving.)

RATING CAKE LIFTERS

Handling cakes can be tricky, whether you're stacking fragile, split layers as you frost them or moving an iced cake to a serving platter. In the past, we've pressed other kitchen gear into service, such as rimless cookie sheets, the bottoms of tart pans, or pizza peels. Now bakeware companies have created cake lifters—large spatula-like devices designed to slip under and support cakes, preventing breakage. We put six lifters, priced from $9.99 to $29, to the test. (Read the full story at CooksCountry.com/extra.)

Moving the two un-iced layers of Strawberry Dream Cake posed no problem for any cake lifter. But as we transferred each of the thin, fragile, split layers to assemble a four-layer lemon cake, we were grateful for the extra support. Large lifters got in the way as we tried to line up the layers' edges. Smaller lifters let us see what we were doing. The greater challenge, however, was moving cakes after they were assembled and frosted. Thin cake lifters, though easy to slide under cakes, flexed and bounced under the weight. Lifters that were too large or unbalanced felt awkward and heavy, straining our wrists. Poorly designed handles provided no leverage.

Fat Daddio's Cake Lifter fell right in the middle. It's slightly flexible, small enough to maneuver for stacking cake layers, and sturdy enough to let us hoist finished cakes with confidence. Plus, we like the comfortable offset handle. Do you need a cake lifter? Not really, but it's a nice addition to the avid baker's bag of tricks. —TAIZETH SIERRA

	CRITERIA		TESTERS' COMMENTS
HIGHLY RECOMMENDED			
FAT DADDIO'S CAKE LIFTER Model: SPAT-JCS Price: $11.88 Source: www.bridgekitchenware.com	 Assembling ★★★ Lifting ★★★		This square-shaped cake lifter felt very sturdy for its small size, particularly when moving a finished cake. Plus, it has a comfortable offset handle. Its rounded edges made for good visibility when stacking layers, while still fully supporting them.
RECOMMENDED			
WILTON CAKE LIFTER Model: 2103-307 Price: $9.99 Source: www.wilton.com	 Assembling ★★ Lifting ★★★		Its compact size works well for assembling cake layers, while its sturdiness allowed us to move a decorated cake with ease. An ergonomic handle gave us plenty of control. Our only quibble was its square edges, which obstructed our view slightly.
RECOMMENDED WITH RESERVATIONS			
NORDIC WARE CAKE LIFTER Model: 02600 Price: $13 Source: www.nordicware.com	 Assembling ★ Lifting ★★★		This brand was sturdy and compact and had a comfortable handle. That strong construction stood it in good stead for moving decorated cakes, but most testers found it too stiff and too thick to slip between layers to assemble a cake.
FOX RUN LARGE COOKIE SPATULA Model: 7272 Price: $9.99 Source: www.bedbathandbeyond.com	 Assembling ★★★ Lifting ★		The manufacturer says that the Cookie Spatula doubles as a cake lifter. True, its compact design and weight made it perfect for assembling layers. But the small size proved problematic for moving iced cakes.
NOT RECOMMENDED			
PADERNO WORLD CUISINE STAINLESS STEEL CAKE LIFTER Model: 4794-30 Price: $29 Source: www.sears.com	Assembling ★★ Lifting ★		This expensive model was the least successful. It adequately maneuvered cake layers, but the lifter is so flexible that it buckled under the weight of a whole decorated cake.

Taste Test Ice-Cream Bars

Is it the vanilla ice cream or the milk chocolate coating that matters most? BY TAIZETH SIERRA

KEY   **Good** ★★★   Fair ★★   Poor ★

AMERICANS HAVE BEEN eating ice-cream bars for some 90 years (lucky us). Today dozens of brands, styles, and flavors compete in a crowded market-place. Among the array, the classic milk-chocolate-coated vanilla ice-cream bars are the most popular. Wondering what separates the champs from the flops, we bought six brands—both with sticks and without—and we asked 21 tasters from America's Test Kitchen to eat and evaluate them.

And people call this work? tasters joked. How bad could even the worst of these possibly be? As it turns out, ice-cream bars are not pure chocolate and ice cream: Most brands use stabilizers, dyes, and artificial flavors in the ice-cream portion, and every brand uses coconut oil in the coating. (The oil reduces chocolate bloom—that gray, chalkiness that otherwise develops when the coating is frozen). Most brands even list the oil as the first coating ingredient, which means the coating contains more of it than any other ingredient. Because of that, many of the bars we tasted had weak or muddled chocolate flavor. By contrast, our two favorite bars list milk chocolate as the first ingredient in the coating, and our top choice supplements it with semisweet chocolate.

Interestingly, while prominent chocolate flavor was important to our tasters, vanilla flavor wasn't. Neutral or scant vanilla flavor was fine as long as it was clean. Only a single bar (Häagen-Dazs) contained vanilla extract in its ice cream; all the rest listed natural or artificial flavors only.

The first bite of an ice-cream bar is telling. Shards of too-thin chocolate can splinter off, leaving plain ice cream on a stick and throwing off the ice cream–chocolate ratio of subsequent bites. Or the sides might collapse as you bite down, squeezing the ice cream out of the middle (and depositing it on your napkin—or your shirt). The best chocolate shells snap readily without splintering, just like a properly tempered chocolate bar.

The texture of the ice cream also needs to be just right. Thicker, denser ice cream stands up to a thicker shell, both of which we preferred, whether the bar had a stick or did not. Light, fluffy ice cream seemed thin and wan to many tasters, and it melted too quickly. We didn't mind the use of some stabilizers as long as the ice cream was dense and creamy.

So what makes a great ice-cream bar? Good ice cream and even better chocolate. The Häagen-Dazs bar (which came in second in this tasting) uses premium ice cream made from cream, skim milk, sugar, egg yolks, and vanilla extract—just like you might make at home, and the very same ingredients found in its vanilla ice cream. (The brand, not incidentally, took second place in our vanilla ice cream tasting in June 2010.)

When we tallied the results, we found that the other winning brands were no strangers to the top of previous America's Test Kitchen rankings either. Our winner, Dove Bar Vanilla Ice Cream with Milk Chocolate ($4.39 for a package of three), is the same brand that won our milk chocolate tasting in March.

		CRITERIA		TASTERS' NOTES
HIGHLY RECOMMENDED				
DOVE BAR Vanilla Ice Cream with Milk Chocolate **Price:** $4.39 for three **Serving size:** (1 bar) 74g **Chocolate shell thickness:** 1.77 mm		Coating Ice Cream	★★★ ★★	It's no surprise that the winner of *Cook's Country*'s March milk chocolate tasting took top honors: Tasters liked the "very chocolaty" and "thick, crunchy chocolate coating," which also happened to be the thickest coating of those we tested. The "thick, creamy ice cream" is "not too sweet," and it complemented the chocolate.
RECOMMENDED				
HÄAGEN-DAZS Vanilla Milk Chocolate All Natural Ice Cream Bars **Price:** $4.39 for three **Serving size:** (1 bar) 83g **Chocolate shell thickness:** 1.33 mm		Coating Ice Cream	★★ ★★★	Häagen-Dazs was the only brand that listed vanilla extract in its ice-cream ingredients. That list, incidentally, was the shortest among all the brands we tested and included no gums or stabilizers. No wonder "the ice cream was great!" as more than one taster concluded. Unfortunately, full-flavored ice cream overshadowed the weak chocolate flavor.
BLUE BUNNY BIG ALASKA BAR **Price:** $2 each **Serving size:** (1 bar) 95g **Chocolate shell thickness:** .98 mm		Coating Ice Cream	★★ ★★	Tasters praised this thick ice-cream bar for its "light, crisp chocolate shell" and "creamy, sweet" and "rich" vanilla ice cream. Although the texture was good, the flavor of the chocolate coating was off—perhaps because coconut oil, not chocolate, comes first on the ingredient list.
GOOD HUMOR MILK CHOCOLATE BAR **Price:** $2.50 for six **Serving size:** (1 bar) 59g **Chocolate shell thickness:** .88 mm		Coating Ice Cream	★★ ★	Tasters were familiar with this style of bar from ice-cream trucks: "light, fluffy, airy ice cream," "light, crispy chocolate," very sweet, and a "very clean flavor." While we preferred a thicker, richer bar, most tasters found the Good Humor bar generally acceptable.
RECOMMENDED WITH RESERVATIONS				
KLONDIKE ORIGINAL VANILLA BAR **Price:** $2.99 for six **Serving size:** (1 bar) 86g **Chocolate shell thickness:** 1.6 mm		Coating Ice Cream	★ ★★	"Thick chocolate shell" with "creamy" ice cream that had the right texture. So what was wrong? The flavor of both the ice cream and, especially, the chocolate was ambiguous, our tasters noted. Coffee, butterscotch, toffee, and mocha were among the competing flavors they detected.
NOT RECOMMENDED				
HOOD ICE CREAM BARS **Price:** $4.39 for 12 **Serving size:** (1 bar) 46g **Chocolate shell thickness:** .75 mm		Coating Ice Cream	★ ★	This "thin, sad, and foamy" bar won few fans. Tasters labeled it "generic" and "wimpy" for flavor and texture. The Hood bar was roughly half the size of our winner, and it "melted too fast to taste anything."

An Oldie But Not a Goodie

In 1921, a shopkeeper in Iowa noticed a young customer struggling to choose between ice cream and a chocolate bar. The boy's dilemma (he couldn't afford to buy both) gave the shopkeeper an idea: a chocolate-covered ice cream bar. And so the "I-Scream-Bar," the original ice cream bar, was born (the name soon changed to Eskimo Pie). We pitted the bars in our lineup against the Eskimo Pie (which has a dark chocolate coating). Tasters found the chocolate coating "waxy" and "plasticky," while the ice cream reminded many of Cool Whip. The Eskimo Pie came in dead-last, failing the test of time.

Equipment Review Portable Charcoal Grills

Can smaller, portable charcoal grills match the performance of their full-size cousins? BY TAIZETH SIERRA

WHETHER YOU GRILL for two, take your grilling on the road, or just lack the space for a full-size grill, a portable charcoal grill offers the smoky flavors of charcoal grilling in a convenient size. Portable grills come in two styles: Some look like smaller versions of full-size kettle grills; others collapse flat for easy storage. We gathered six portable grills with prices ranging from just over $20 to $140 and tested them with burgers, flank steak, and butterflied whole chickens.

A portable grill should be just that: portable. It practically goes without saying that grills that fold flat are handy for fitting into the trunk of a car. But dismantling and reassembling greasy grates and ash-covered panels that must be folded just so turned out to be more trouble than the grills were worth. Weight also hindered portability. Most of the grills that we tested weighed less than 15 pounds, but a 32-pound cast-iron model was difficult to lift, let alone move. We came to appreciate lightweight grills that don't require assembly every time we want to cook, as well as features like clips to secure the lid for easy transport.

Cooking over an open flame is the most basic, and probably the oldest, culinary technique. So it may not be news that we were able to cook burgers and flank steak on all of the grills. But when it came to capacity and design, we found significant differences among the models. We preferred grills that fit at least six burgers and three-quarters of a chimney's worth of briquettes—enough to cook two rounds of burgers and steak back-to-back. We also saw the value of a raised lip, which kept the food from falling off; otherwise, we had to chase burgers that were dangerously close to (or partway off) the edge. You don't need a cover for basic grilling, but you do for grill-roasting. The technique, which in effect creates a small oven, is ideal for larger cuts, like a butterflied chicken. To get low, steady heat, you bank the coals on one side and use a cover to trap the warmth. Excepting one very small grill, we had no trouble building the fire this way on all the models. But only one of the two grills that had covers could actually fit the chicken under the lid.

Between enduring high heat, grease, grime, and getting banged around in the back of a car, portable grills undergo a lot of heavy-duty use. They need to be made of sturdy stuff. We downgraded a few grills for their flimsy construction; one model even buckled as we were cooking on it. To simulate the grill being knocked over while unpacking a picnic, we dropped the models from the back of an SUV onto hard pavement. All grills passed this test, although not without a few dents.

So, which portable grill should you buy? It depends on what you need it for. If you don't intend to lug it on trips, the cast-iron Lodge Logic Sportsman's Grill is the high-heat cooking champ. Remember, though, that it lacks a lid, so you can't grill-roast. For the best all-around portable grill, we recommend the Weber Smokey Joe Gold, which offers an ample cooking surface, a cover that can be secured for travel, a convenient raised lip, and a reasonable price.

		CRITERIA	TESTERS' NOTES
HIGHLY RECOMMENDED			
WEBER SMOKEY JOE GOLD **Model:** 40020 **Price:** $34.70 **Coal Capacity:** ¾ chimney **Cooking Surface:** Round, 13½ inches in diameter **Source:** www.homedepot.com		**Cooking** ★★★ **Portability** ★★ **Durability** ★★★ **Design** ★★★	This smaller version of our favorite Weber One Touch Gold Charcoal Grill shares many of its attributes. The ample cooking surface fit six to eight burgers at a time or a 1½-pound flank steak. The domed cover allowed us to grill-roast a butterflied chicken perfectly. Adjustable vents on the cover and on opposite sides of the grill's body gave us plenty of control over the fire.
RECOMMENDED			
FYRKAT CHARCOAL PICNIC GRILL BY BODUM **Model:** 10630 **Price:** $49.95 **Coal Capacity:** ¾ chimney **Cooking Surface:** Round, 13¾ inches in diameter **Source:** www.target.com		**Cooking** ★★½ **Portability** ★★ **Durability** ★★★ **Design** ★★½	Compact and lightweight for easy transport, this colorful little grill is similar in design to our winner. While the cooking surface easily accommodated a whole butterflied chicken, the lid's dome was too shallow for it. But for high-heat grilling, such as steaks and burgers, this grill performed as well as the winner.
RECOMMENDED WITH RESERVATIONS			
LODGE LOGIC SPORTSMAN'S GRILL **Model:** L410 **Price:** $139.95 **Coal Capacity:** ¾ chimney **Cooking Surface:** 17½ by 9-inch oval **Source:** www.lodgemfg.com		**Cooking** ★★½ **Portability** ★ **Durability** ★★★ **Design** ★★	This grill easily fit six burgers but was a little too narrow to accommodate a butterflied chicken. We couldn't grill-roast, either, because the grill has no cover. We did, however, like the draft door to regulate heat, and a flip-down door made it easy to access coals. Made entirely of cast iron, this grill seared beautifully. If only it didn't weigh 32 pounds. Portable, yes—if you're Arnold Schwarzenegger.
SON OF HIBACHI **Model:** B003G73SBW **Price:** $69.99 **Coal Capacity:** ½ chimney **Cooking Surface:** Two 10 by 8-inch rectangles **Source:** www.cooking.com		**Cooking** ★½ **Portability** ★★★ **Durability** ★★★ **Design** ★	This grill is a chimney starter and a grill in one: Fill it with coals and use it as a chimney when folded; unfold it to reveal two adjustable cast-iron grates, albeit very small ones. When you're done, fold it up and place the hot grill in its heat-resistant snuff-out pouch—very clever. Unfortunately, this grill held the fewest briquettes and could not fit a whole chicken, nor does it have a cover. Only for small batches of food.
FIRE SENSE HOTSPOT NOTEBOOK PORTABLE CHARCOAL GRILL **Model:** 60508 **Price:** $27 **Coal Capacity:** Full chimney **Cooking Surface:** Rectangular, by 17 by 12¾ inches **Source:** www.buy.com		**Cooking** ★★ **Portability** ★★★ **Durability** ★ **Design** ★	This grill stands 13½ inches tall but collapses to just 1 inch thick. It has plenty of cooking surface and a high coal capacity, and it easily fit eight burgers. But it doesn't have a cover, making it ill suited for anything other than high-heat grilling, nor does it have a lip, so we found ourselves chasing burgers off the edge of the grill. This model dented and warped during testing.
NOT RECOMMENDED			
BAYOU CLASSIC FOLD AND GO CHARCOAL GRILL **Model:** 400-402 **Price:** $20.43 **Coal Capacity:** Full chimney **Cooking Surface:** Rectangular, 19¼ by 14¼ inches **Source:** www.sears.com		**Cooking** ★ **Portability** ★★★ **Durability** ★ **Design** ★	This grill has the largest cooking surface of all the grills we tested, but no lip or lid. It folds down to just 2½ inches wide, which is nice for portability, but all the hinges required to collapse it proved cumbersome. More than once, the sides buckled while we were cooking, making the grilling surface unsteady (to say the least). What's more, the grill's sharp edges tore the carrying case it came with.

Cooking Class How to Barbecue Ribs

For lip-smacking good ribs with juicy, fall-off-the-bone texture, master our surefire techniques.

SHOPPING

Choose the Right Ribs

Butchers get three different cuts from the ribs of a pig (pigs can have anywhere from 13 to 17 sets of ribs). You can barbecue any of these cuts, but in the test kitchen, we usually reach for St. Louis cut spareribs. Because they've been trimmed of the brisket bone and surrounding meat, they fit nicely on a standard-size backyard grill and they give us consistent results. Ordinary spareribs, which come from near the pig's belly, include that brisket bone and meat; their size and irregular shape make them unwieldy on a backyard grill. Among the three, baby back ribs are smallest and leanest; they come from nearest the pig's back (and, despite the name, from an adult pig). Baby backs cook comparatively quickly, which means they tend to dry out more easily than the other cuts.

ST. LOUIS CUT SPARERIBS
Manageable size and consistent results.

SPARERIBS
Unwieldy on a backyard grill.

BABY BACK RIBS
These smaller, leaner ribs can dry out quickly.

BARBECUED RIBS Serves 4 to 6

The longer you leave the ribs with the spice rub the better (we recommend up to 2 days) their flavor, so try to plan ahead. We suggest homemade barbecue sauce (our recipe follows), but if you're short on time, Bull's-Eye is the test kitchen favorite among supermarket brands. This recipe uses the oven, as well as a charcoal grill.

- 3 tablespoons paprika
- 2 tablespoons packed brown sugar
- 1 tablespoon salt
- 1 tablespoon pepper
- ¼ teaspoon cayenne pepper
- 2 (2½- to 3-pound) racks pork spareribs, preferably St. Louis cut, trimmed and membrane removed
- 2 cups wood chips, soaked in water for 15 minutes and drained
- 3 cups barbecue sauce

1. Combine paprika, sugar, salt, black pepper, and cayenne pepper in bowl. Pat ribs dry with paper towels and rub with spice mixture. Wrap meat tightly with plastic wrap and refrigerate for 1 to 48 hours. Using large sheet of heavy-duty aluminum foil, wrap soaked chips in foil, crimp to make packet, and cut several vent holes in top.

2. Open bottom vent halfway. Light large chimney starter three-quarters full with charcoal briquettes (4½ quarts). When top coals are partially covered with ash, pour into steeply banked pile against one side of grill. Place wood chip packet on coals. Set cooking grate in place, cover, and open lid vent halfway. Heat grill until hot and wood chips are smoking, about 5 minutes.

3. Clean and oil cooking grate. Unwrap ribs and place, meat side down, on cool part of grill (ribs may overlap slightly). Place sheet of aluminum foil on top of ribs. Cover, positioning lid vent over meat, and cook until ribs are deep red and smoky, about 2 hours, flipping and rotating racks halfway through grilling. During last 20 minutes of grilling, adjust oven rack to middle position and heat oven to 250 degrees.

4. Remove ribs from grill, brush with 1 cup barbecue sauce, and wrap tightly with foil. Place foil-wrapped ribs on rimmed baking sheet and bake until tender and fork inserted into meat meets no resistance, 1½ to 2½ hours. Rest ribs, still wrapped, for 30 minutes. Unwrap and brush with 1 cup sauce. Slice meat between bones and serve with remaining 1 cup sauce.

BARBECUE SAUCE

Makes 3 cups

This recipe was developed using relatively mild Frank's RedHot hot sauce.

- ¼ cup vegetable oil
- 2 onions, chopped fine
- 2 garlic cloves, minced
- 2 teaspoons chili powder
- ½ teaspoon cayenne pepper
- 2 cups ketchup
- 10 tablespoons molasses
- ¼ cup cider vinegar
- ¼ cup Worcestershire sauce
- ¼ cup Dijon mustard
- 2 teaspoons hot sauce

1. Heat oil in large saucepan over medium heat until shimmering. Add onions and cook until softened, about 5 minutes. Stir in garlic, chili powder, and cayenne and cook until fragrant, about 30 seconds.

2. Add ketchup, molasses, vinegar, Worcestershire, mustard, and hot sauce and simmer, stirring occasionally, until sauce is thickened and reduced to 3 cups, about 30 minutes. (Sauce can be refrigerated for up to 1 week or frozen for up to 1 month.)

KEY SUPPLIES AND GEAR

Aluminum Foil

When we're making barbecue ribs, we always keep a box of foil at hand. After we've soaked the wood chips, we wrap them tightly in foil and cut a few vent holes in the packet. Otherwise, they'll quickly combust, and their smoke will dissipate just as fast. We cover the grilling ribs loosely with more foil to trap enough steam to tenderize the meat yet still let it develop a good crust. Finally, we keep the ribs from drying out in the oven by wrapping them tightly in—yep—more foil.

Grill Thermometer

Pork ribs have lots of fat and sinew, so they require long, slow cooking, ideally at a steady 300 degrees. To monitor the heat inside a covered grill, insert a grill thermometer into the lid's vents. You can read it without opening the lid. That's key if you're cooking over charcoal, as you can't simply crank a burner to bring the temperature up if the heat escapes.

TEST KITCHEN FAVORITE
Polder Dual Sensor Thermometer

Perfect Ribs in 12 Easy Steps

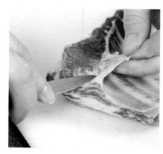

1. LOOSEN MEMBRANE
Use the tip of a paring knife to loosen the edge of the membrane on each rack.
WHY? The papery membrane on the underside is chewy and unpleasant to eat.

2. REMOVE MEMBRANE
Pull the membrane off slowly, using a paper towel. It should come off in a single piece.
WHY? The paper towel will give you a good grip.

3. SEASON RIBS
Rub the ribs with a spice mixture, wrap them in plastic wrap, and refrigerate for 1 to 24 hours.
WHY? To give the rub plenty of time to season the ribs.

4. PREPARE COALS
Pour the hot coals into a steeply banked pile on one side of the grill.
WHY? By banking the coals, you're transforming your grill into a slow, low oven, perfect for cooking ribs.

5. ADD WOOD CHIPS
Place a foil packet of soaked wood chips over the coals, cover the grill, and let them smoke for 5 minutes.
WHY? If you start the meat immediately, it will taste acrid from too much harsh smoke.

6. PLACE RIBS Clean and oil the cooking grate, unwrap the ribs, and set them on the cool side of the grill.
WHY? So the ribs can cook low and slow without the exterior burning before the interior is tender.

7. COVER WITH FOIL
Cover the ribs loosely with aluminum foil, close the grill, and cook until the ribs are deep red, about 2 hours.
WHY? The foil will trap steam to aid in tenderizing the ribs.

8. BRUSH WITH SAUCE
Remove the ribs from the grill, brush with 1 cup of barbecue sauce, and wrap tightly in foil.
WHY? The ribs will cook for several more hours in the oven, drinking up the smoky, sweet flavor.

9. BAKE RIBS Lay the foil-wrapped ribs on a rimmed baking sheet and move them to a preheated oven.
WHY? So the ribs can fully tenderize without your having to rebuild the charcoal fire.

10. FORK TEST Insert a fork into the ribs and lift. If the fork pulls right out, the ribs are done. If not, the meat needs to cook longer.
WHY? To check if the ribs are truly fork-tender.

11. LET REST Remove the ribs from the oven and let them rest, wrapped in foil, for 30 minutes.
WHY? The juice will redistribute. What does that mean? Moist ribs.

12. BRUSH, SLICE, EAT
Unwrap the ribs, brush with more barbecue sauce, slice between the bones, and eat.
WHY? We sauce the ribs twice, but not on the grill, where the sauce would burn.

Q&A

How do the vents work?
Charcoal grills have both bottom and lid vents, which affect airflow and thus how fast and how hot the charcoal burns. For long-cooking barbecued ribs, open the top and bottom vents halfway to let enough oxygen into the grill to fuel the fire without the coals burning out too fast. Control the grill temperature by changing the position of the top vents; always keep them slightly open to keep soot from building up on the food. Position the vents directly over the food so the smoke must pass over it as it exits.

Why put the ribs in the oven?
For tender meat, ribs must remain over low, indirect heat for hours on end. After 2 hours, we'd need to rebuild the fire with freshly lit charcoal to maintain that temperature. By this point, the meat is plenty crusty and smoky. We move it to the oven to tenderize at a consistent temperature and avoid extra hours tending a finicky fire.

Gas Grill Method

We prefer charcoal for barbecuing: Wood chips smoke better on charcoal. Still, you can make respectable ribs on a gas grill. First, a vocabulary lesson—the burner that will stay on during grilling is called the primary burner. Substitute these steps for steps 4 to 6 at left.

While the grill is off, remove the grill grate. Now place the packet of wood chips on the primary burner.

Next, replace the grate and turn both of the burners to high.

After the chips have been smoking for 5 minutes, turn the primary burner to medium-high. Turn the other burner off and place the ribs over it. Adjust as needed to keep the heat at 300 degrees.

Looking for a Recipe

COMPILED BY DIANE UNGER

READER TO READER

Did you misplace a favorite recipe? Can you almost taste a chocolate cake from childhood but the bakery—and the recipe—are long gone? Ask a reader. While you're at it, answer a reader. Post queries and finds at **CooksCountry.com**; click on **Looking for a Recipe** (or write to Looking for a Recipe, Cook's Country, P.O. Box 470739, Brookline, MA 02447). We'll share all of your submissions online—hundreds are already posted—and print several on this page. Include your name and mailing address with each submission.

Date-Nut Bars
Doris Bartsch, Waltham, Mass.

I have fond memories of my mom making date-nut bars when I was little. After they baked, she cut them into bars, which she rolled in powdered sugar. They were moist, sweet, and the perfect after-school snack. I'd love to be able to make them, but I don't have her recipe. Can anyone help?

Biscuits with Chocolate Gravy
Trisha Kruse, Eagle, Idaho

My husband grew up in Oklahoma, where every Christmas morning his aunt Pauline would bake biscuits with chocolate gravy. He looked forward to this treat as much as he did to opening presents. I've questioned every family member, but not a single one knows the secret to her fluffy biscuits and thin (but rich) chocolate gravy. I've found some recipes, but they've yielded thick, pudding-like topping on heavy biscuits. Please help me revive this holiday tradition.

Bailey's Hot Butterscotch Sauce
Lisa Wheeler, Cambridge, Mass.

When I was a kid, Saturdays meant shopping in Boston with my mom—and a trip to Bailey's ice cream parlor for a hot butterscotch sundae. It was served in a footed metal cup with so much molten sauce that it overflowed the melting vanilla ice cream and stuck to the chilled plate underneath like candy. Bailey's has long since gone the way of the trolley car, but I'd sure love to revive happy memories with a recipe for its famous sauce.

Idaho Potato-Chicken Pie
Ann Cueva, Heyburn, Idaho

Many years ago, I purchased a recipe booklet titled *A Pie from Every State*. Idaho's contribution was a delicious potato and chicken pie with both a top and bottom crust. I've lost the booklet and recipe and can't find a similar recipe anywhere. I hope someone can help.

Soft-Sided Cream Puffs
Josephine Mullane, Moncton, New Brunswick, Canada

I am in search of a recipe for soft-sided cream puffs that I used to buy in the 1940s and '50s at a bake shop in my hometown in Ontario. They were not made with the typical choux pastry. The dough was soft and sweet, and the buns were the shape of hamburger buns. They were cut in half, filled with sweetened whipped cream, and dusted with powdered sugar. If anyone knows what I'm talking about and has a recipe, please let me know.

Soufflé Crackers
Carolyn Roberts, Natchitoches, La.

A colleague of mine made what he called soufflé crackers for a party recently. They were delicious. He told me that it was a very old recipe that began with saltines. Does anyone know how to make these?

Amish Friendship Bread
Janet Carroll, Greenfield, Mass.

Years ago, our local paper published a recipe for Amish Friendship Bread. Unfortunately, I've misplaced the recipe. The bread was great to give as a gift, along with the recipe and a bit of the yeast starter. I'd love to be able to make it again.

"Schnitzeled" Green Beans
Holly Shaffer, Los Angeles, Calif.

An elderly family friend remembers his mother making "schnitzeled" green beans. I have looked for a recipe by this name but have had no luck. He was raised in Ohio, so perhaps this is an Amish or Mennonite dish? It would be such fun to surprise him with it. Thanks for your help.

Peanut-Butter Pie
Edward Butler, Cocoa, Fla.

When I was in my 20s, I used to go to a small family diner called the Suncrest Restaurant. They made the best peanut-butter pie I have ever eaten. Their pie had a flaky pie crust. (Most recipes that I know of use graham cracker crust.) The pie had at least 1½ inches of creamy peanut-butter filling and another 1½ inches of firm, sweet cream topping. They sprinkled crushed nuts on top. Do you know of a recipe that would fit the bill?

FIND THE ROOSTER!

A tiny version of this rooster has been hidden in the pages of this issue. Write to us with its location and we'll enter you in a random drawing. The first correct entry drawn will win our top-rated portable charcoal grill (see page 29), and each of the next five will receive a free one-year subscription to *Cook's Country*. To enter, visit CooksCountry.com/emailus by July 31, 2011, or write to Rooster, Cook's Country, P.O. Box 470739, Brookline, MA 02447. Include your name and address. Keen-eyed Elaine Blaufuss of Fargo, N.D., spotted the rooster in the February/March 2011 issue in the Pastistio photo and won our favorite muffin tin. Cock-a-doodle-doo.

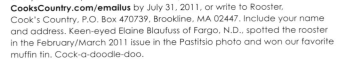

TOMATO CASSEROLE Serves 6 to 8
Marla Friedmann, Augusta, Ga.

"My family adores this casserole with baked ham or eggs. It's economical and easy to put together, too."

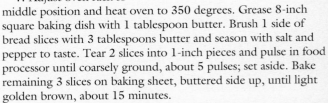

- 5 tablespoons unsalted butter, softened
- 5 slices hearty white sandwich bread
- Salt and pepper
- 1 (28-ounce) can whole peeled tomatoes
- 1 onion, chopped fine
- 4 teaspoons packed brown sugar
- ¼ teaspoon cayenne pepper

1. Adjust oven rack to middle position and heat oven to 350 degrees. Grease 8-inch square baking dish with 1 tablespoon butter. Brush 1 side of bread slices with 3 tablespoons butter and season with salt and pepper to taste. Tear 2 slices into 1-inch pieces and pulse in food processor until coarsely ground, about 5 pulses; set aside. Bake remaining 3 slices on baking sheet, buttered side up, until light golden brown, about 15 minutes.

2. Pulse tomatoes in food processor until coarsely ground, 3 to 5 pulses. Melt remaining 1 tablespoon butter in 12-inch skillet over medium-high heat. Add onion and cook until browned, 6 to 8 minutes. Stir in tomatoes, sugar, ½ teaspoon salt, and cayenne and bring to boil.

3. Quarter toasted bread slices and arrange over bottom of prepared baking dish. Pour tomato mixture over bread and top with bread crumbs. Bake until golden brown, 25 to 30 minutes. Cool on wire rack for 10 minutes. Serve.

BOSTON BROWN BREAD Makes two 8½-inch loaves
Barbara Brandel, Simpsonville, S.C.

"I tried this recipe for a picnic when I was also serving baked beans. By the time I had made sure everything was on the table, all that was left of the bread was crumbs! (And even the crumbs were very good!)" Use a mild molasses, such as Grandma's Original. Serve with Quicker Boston Baked Beans (see page 14).

- 1½ cups (7½ ounces) all-purpose flour
- 1½ cups (8 ounces) raisins
- 1 cup (5½ ounces) whole-wheat flour
- 1 cup (5 ounces) cornmeal
- 1½ teaspoons baking soda
- ¼ teaspoon salt
- 2 cups buttermilk
- 1 cup molasses
- ⅓ cup vegetable oil
- 1 large egg, lightly beaten

1. Adjust oven rack to middle position and heat oven to 350 degrees. Grease two 8½ by 4½-inch loaf pans. Whisk all-purpose flour, raisins, whole-wheat flour, cornmeal, baking soda, and salt together in bowl. Whisk buttermilk, molasses, oil, and egg together in another bowl. Whisk buttermilk mixture into flour mixture until combined.

2. Scrape equal amounts of batter into prepared pans and bake until toothpick inserted in center comes out with few crumbs attached, 40 to 45 minutes, rotating pans halfway through baking. Cool bread in pans on wire rack for 15 minutes. Remove from pans and cool for at least 30 minutes before serving warm or at room temperature. (Bread can be stored at room temperature for up to 3 days.)

Margarita Cake

Skip cocktail hour. Instead, enjoy a slice of this tart icebox cheesecake, with its salty-sweet pretzel crust and gelatin glaze "shot."

To make this cake you will need:

- **1** cup sweetened shredded coconut
- **1** teaspoon grated lime zest plus 1 lime, sliced thin (2 limes)
- **3** cups pretzels
- **6** tablespoons unsalted butter, melted
- **¾** cup water
- **4** teaspoons unflavored gelatin
- **1** (10-ounce) can frozen margarita mix, thawed
- **¼** cup tequila
- **¼** cup triple sec
- **1½** cups heavy cream, chilled
- **1** (14-ounce) can sweetened condensed milk
- **4** ounces cream cheese, softened

FOR THE CRUST: Place oven rack in middle position and heat oven to 350 degrees. Grease 9-inch springform pan and line perimeter with 3-inch-wide strip of parchment paper. Process coconut and lime zest in food processor until coarsely ground; reserve ½ cup. Add pretzels to remaining coconut mixture and process until finely ground. Add melted butter and pulse to combine. Press mixture into bottom of prepared pan. Bake until edges are golden, 10 to 12 minutes. Cool completely.

FOR THE FILLING: Combine ¼ cup water and gelatin in small saucepan and let sit until gelatin softens, about 5 minutes. Add margarita mix, tequila, and triple sec and cook over low heat, stirring frequently, until gelatin dissolves, about 5 minutes. Cool 15 minutes. Using mixer fitted with whisk, whip cream on medium-low speed until foamy. Increase speed to high and whip until soft peaks form. Using clean bowl, whip sweetened condensed milk and cream cheese until combined. Add 1 cup margarita mixture and whip until incorporated. Fold in one-third whipped cream, then gently fold in remaining whipped cream. Pour filling into crust. Refrigerate until just set, about 1 hour.

FOR THE TOPPING: Stir remaining ½ cup water into remaining margarita mixture. Pour mixture through fine-mesh strainer into 2-cup liquid measuring cup. Pour over filling and refrigerate until set, about 4 hours. Remove sides of pan and parchment. Press reserved coconut mixture onto sides of cake and top with lime slices. Serve.

Recipe Index

Visit us online at CooksCountry.com

Cook's Country

AUGUST/SEPTEMBER 2011

Texas-Style Fruit Cobbler

All-American Steak Burgers

The Best Grilled Chicken Wings

Slow-Cooker Stuffed Peppers
Flavorful, Not Soggy

BBQ Country-Style Ribs
Quick Trick for Even Cooking

Low-Fat Potato Salad
No One Will Know

Quick Collard Greens
15 Minutes to Table

Shoestring Onions
Fried and Gone to Heaven

Grilled Citrus Chicken
Juicy and Full of Flavor

Italian Cream Cake
Showstopper Gets Tasty

Ketchup Taste Test
New Formula Wins

How to Grill Pork Chops
Everything You Need to Know

Chiles Rellenos Casserole
Southwest Favorite Updated

www.CooksCountry.com
$4.95 U.S./$6.95 CANADA

In the Texas Hill Country, **Texas-Style Fruit Cobbler** *is the pride of every barbecue joint and roadside café. Its thick, pancake-like batter makes it very different from traditional cobbler, but now that we've perfected this blueberry version, it's become a test kitchen summertime favorite.* PAGE 17

Cook's Country

Dear Country Cook,

Many of our summer friends were "refugees" from New York, stranded with their mothers without a car or even running water during the week, their fathers driving up to our small Vermont town only on weekends. Bathing was done at the Saturday night sauna. We cranked out ice cream made with an old White Mountain freezer, pressed wildflowers, built toy canoes out of birch bark, melted wax to make our own candles, and spent most hot summer days exploring the hills and hollows much like Tom Sawyer and Huck Finn. We also did our share of haying, milking, and barn cleaning, but the fun jobs included shooting barn rats with a .22 or exploring abandoned cabins, finding old jam jars or bits of blue-edged crockery amid the weeds.

Summers were filled with fishing expeditions to the small dark pool below the waterfall in the pines, all-day hikes to the cemetery on Egg Mountain, small brown bags of penny candies that were made to last, and tucking into a half-dozen ears of hot boiled butter-and-sugar corn on a warm August evening.

Life back then was much like going to an ice-cream parlor. There were so many choices within reach of a young boy or girl, in the woods or in the high meadows: the smell of sweat from the haunches of the workhorses, a tight bunch of Indian paintbrushes, or a running jump into a pond that felt as cold as the North Sea.

Food contains memories, as do places. The best of it is when food and place meet in the telling as well as in the memory.

Christopher Kimball
Founder and Editor, Cook's Country

Cook'sCountry

Founder and Editor Christopher Kimball
Editorial Director Jack Bishop
Executive Editor, Magazines John Willoughby
Executive Editor Peggy Grodinsky
Managing Editor Scott Kathan
Senior Editors Lisa McManus, Cali Rich, Diane Unger
Test Kitchen Director Erin McMurrer
Associate Editors Lynn Clark, Amy Graves
Test Cooks Sarah Gabriel, Kelly Price
Assistant Editors Hannah Crowley, Taizeth Sierra
Assistant Test Cooks Rebeccah Marsters,
Carolynn Purpura
Senior Copy Editor Catherine Tumber
Copy Editor Nell Beram
Editorial Assistant Shannon Hatch
Executive Assistant Christine Gordon
Assistant Test Kitchen Director Gina Nistico
Senior Kitchen Assistants Meryl MacCormack,
Leah Rovner
Kitchen Assistants Maria Elena Delgado,
Ena Gudiel, Ed Tundidor
TV Producer Melissa Baldino
Contributing Editors
Erika Bruce, Eva Katz, Jeremy Sauer
Consulting Editors Anne Mendelson, Meg Ragland
Science Editor Guy Crosby, Ph.D.
Executive Food Editor, TV, Radio & Media
Bridget Lancaster

Design Director Amy Klee
Art Director Julie Bozzo
Deputy Art Director Susan Levin
Staff Photographer Daniel J. van Ackere
Online Photo Editor Steve Klise
Color Food Photography Keller + Keller
Styling Mary Jane Sawyer

Art Director, Books Greg Galvan
Associate Art Director, Books Matthew Warnick
Designer, Books Beverly Hsu

Art Director, Marketing & Web Christine Vo
Associate Art Directors, Marketing & Web
Erica Lee, Jody Lee
Designers Elaina Natario, Mariah Tarvainen

Production Director Guy Rochford
Senior Projects Manager Alice Carpenter
Traffic & Production Coordinator Kate Hux
Asset & Workflow Manager Andrew Mannone
Production & Imaging Specialists
Judy Blomquist, Heather Dube, Lauren Pettapiece

Online Managing Editor David Tytell
Online Editor Kate Mason
Online Assistant Editors
Eric Grzymkowski, Mari Levine

Executive Editor, Books Elizabeth Carduff
Executive Food Editor, Books
Julia Collin Davison
Senior Editors, Books Louise Emerick, Lori Galvin,
Suzannah McFerran
Associate Editors, Books Molly Birnbaum,
Kate Hartke, Chris O'Connor, Adelaide Parker,
Dan Zuccarello
Test Cooks, Books Rebecca Morris,
Christie Morrison, Kate Williams
Editorial Assistant, Books Alyssa King

ON THE COVER:
Texas-Style Blueberry Cobbler, Keller + Keller
ILLUSTRATION: Greg Stevenson

Cook's Country magazine (ISSN 1552-1990), number 40,
is published bimonthly by Boston Common Press Limited
Partnership, 17 Station Street, Brookline, MA 02445. Copyright
2011 Boston Common Press Limited Partnership. Periodicals
Postage paid at Boston, Mass., and additional mailing
offices. Publications Mail Agreement No. 40020778. Return
undeliverable Canadian addresses to P.O. Box 875, Station A,
Windsor, Ontario N9A 6P2. POSTMASTER: Send address changes
to Cook's Country, P.O. Box 8382, Red Oak, IA 51591-1382.
Customer Service: It's easy to subscribe, give a gift subscription,
change your address, and manage your subscription online.
Visit AmericasTestKitchen.com/customerservice for all of your
customer service needs or write to us at Cook's Country, P.O.
Box 8382, Red Oak, IA 51591-1382. PRINTED IN THE USA

AUGUST/SEPTEMBER 2011

Contents

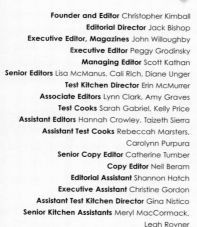

FRESH CORN SALADS, 5　　　GRILLED STEAK BURGERS, 10　　　MAGIC STRAWBERRY ICE CREAM, 27

Features

In Every Issue

Watch Us on Television

Watch the folks behind our recipes
test equipment, taste ingredients,
perfect classic American recipes, and
stroll through food history. Find out
when *Cook's Country from America's
Test Kitchen* airs on public television in
your area at **CooksCountryTV.com.**

Ask Cook's Country

BY SARAH GABRIEL

What's the best way to store chewy cookies so they don't dry out?
Matt Schraut, Waltham, Mass.

Even though it sounds weird, many people swear by storing cookies with a slice of apple or bread to keep them chewy. Are these old wives' tales or useful kitchen tips? To find out, we made three batches of chewy chocolate chip cookies and stored each in a cookie jar at room temperature, one with a slice of bread, one with a slice of apple, and the third holding nothing but the cookies. The cookies stored alone kept well for about a day but after that gradually toughened and dried out. The cookies packed with a slice of bread stayed chewy for three days, and although tasters could distinguish them from fresh cookies in a side-by-side tasting, they were perfectly acceptable. But the cookies stored with a slice of apple were definitely not. The apple gave off so much moisture that the cookies were soggy after barely a day. On day two, tasters noticed a distinctive apple flavor—an odd addition, to say the least, to a chocolate chip cookie.

THE BOTTOM LINE To keep your chewy cookies chewy longer, store them in an airtight container along with a slice of bread.

NO APPLES ALLOWED...TRY BREAD, INSTEAD

I've heard buzz about the health benefits of coconut oil. Can I sauté with it in place of vegetable oil?
Denise Cubano-Lausell, Somerville, Mass.

Coconut oil is high in saturated fat, so what's this about health benefits? It turns out that coconut oil is also high in lauric acid, which proponents tout for antimicrobial and antioxidant properties, among other things. Leaving the health issues to the health experts, we grabbed a few jars of oil and headed into the test kitchen.

Unlike most oils, coconut oil is solid at room temperature (like butter, it turns liquid when heated) and keeps in that environment for up to a year. We began by examining both refined and virgin (unrefined) coconut oil. The minute we unscrewed the jar, the unrefined oil revealed its powerful coconut presence. The food we cooked with it tasted like Coppertone. Stick with the refined oil, which has a neutral flavor. (The jars aren't always labeled clearly, but the aroma is a giveaway.) We continued our testing with refined coconut oil only.

We sautéed green beans and breaded pork chops in refined coconut oil, and tasted them side by side with beans and chops that we'd cooked in the same amount of vegetable oil. Our tasters couldn't tell the difference.

THE BOTTOM LINE Skip the unrefined coconut oil—it adds potent coconut flavor to whatever you sauté in it. Go ahead and try refined coconut oil as a replacement for vegetable or canola oil for sautéing.

Cake recipes call for different pan preparations (greasing, flouring, papering). Which is best?
Erin Schroeder, Port Jefferson Station, N.Y.

Greasing the pan before baking a cake ensures that the cake won't stick. To figure out the best greasing method, we baked nearly 30 cakes in pans greased alternately with butter, vegetable oil spray, and baking spray (vegetable oil spray with flour added). Next, we dusted some pans with flour, lined some with parchment paper, and left some alone, trying every possible combination of grease, flour, and paper. What did we discover? Greasing alone works well for ordinary layer cakes baked in pans that are in good condition (cakes are more likely to stick and break when pans are scratched). Flouring provides a little extra protection for delicate cakes or those that are prone to sticking (say, a moist gingerbread or molten chocolate cake). But for a foolproof regimen, grease the cake pan (vegetable oil spray, baking spray, and butter all work fine), line it with a parchment circle, grease the parchment, and then flour it. Also, most cakes benefit from cooling in the pan for 10 to 15 minutes after they've come out of the oven before being turned out.

THE BOTTOM LINE If you're going to the trouble of baking a cake, prevent it from sticking by greasing the cake pan, lining it with parchment paper, and then greasing the parchment and flouring the inside of the pan.

Meatloaf and burger recipes often call for panades made with milk. Can I use another liquid?
Sandy Guermantes, Bennington, Vt.

Panade is a paste, usually made from bread and milk, that keeps ground meat moist when it's cooked above 130 degrees. As you observed, our recipes for meatloaf and well-done hamburgers, as well as meatballs, often call for panades. (Burgers cooked to rare or medium usually remain moist without any help.) To determine whether panade can be created with liquids other than milk, we made four batches of hamburgers and four meatloaves: one with the classic milk-and-bread combination, and one each substituting chicken broth, beef broth, and water for the milk. Tasters liked all of the burgers; some even preferred the burger made with the chicken broth panade, describing it as savory and especially well seasoned. Likewise, all of the meatloaves passed muster.

THE BOTTOM LINE Water and broth are fine substitutes for milk in panade. Use them when cooking for people with a milk allergy, to keep ground meat dishes kosher, or to boost seasoning in burgers and meatloaf. Bear in mind that the broth will add salt to the mixture.

Your grilling recipes call for a charcoal chimney starter. Why can't I use "matchlight" briquettes?
Eugenia Hamilton, Tucson, Ariz.

We always light charcoal in a chimney starter; it's fast and easy, and we don't want to taste lighter fluid on our food. But we decided to give matchlight charcoal (briquettes that come saturated with lighter fluid) another look. We fired up four grills—two with regular briquettes lit in a chimney, and two with matchlight briquettes lit with a match—and grilled both chicken and hamburgers over each.

The chicken cooked over the matchlight charcoal had an unpleasant taste, especially the skin; this "chemical-y" flavor was less noticeable in the burgers, but the petroleum odor that persisted during cooking was a big turnoff. Matchlight's instructions say the coals will be ready to cook in 10 minutes, but it took nearly 15. With the chimney starter, the coals were ready in about 20 minutes.

THE BOTTOM LINE Matchlight charcoal doesn't save much time, and it can give food unpleasant flavors. Buy a chimney starter and use regular charcoal.

Ask us a cooking question:
Visit **CooksCountry.com/AskCooksCountry**. Or write to Ask Cook's Country, P.O. Box 470739, Brookline, MA 02447. Just try to stump us!

Cook's Country

VP, New Media Product Development Barry Kelly
Lead Developer, New Media Bharat Ruparel
Senior Information Architect Melissa MacQuarrie
Social Media Manager Steph Yiu
Associate Editor, Social Media Christine Liu
Web Programmer, New Media Anand Kumar

Director, Information Technology Rocco Lombardo
Systems Administrator Marcus Walser
Lead Developer Scott Thompson
Software Architect Robert Martinez
Senior Web Developer Christopher Candelora
Web Developers Bach Bui, James Madden, Alphonse Shiwala
Business Analyst Wendy Tseng
Quality Assurance Micquella Bradford
Web Production Coordinator Evan Davis
Web Production Assistant Debbie Chiang
IT Support Specialist Geoffrey Clark

Vice President, Marketing David Mack
Circulation Director Doug Wicinski
Fulfillment & Circulation Manager Carrie Horan
Partnership Marketing Manager Pamela Putprush
Marketing Assistant Lauren Perkins
Database & Direct Mail Director Adam Perry
Senior Database Analyst Marina Sakharova
Products Director Steven Browall
Product Promotions Director Tom Conway
E-Commerce Marketing Director Hugh Buchan
E-Commerce Marketing Manager Laurel Zeidman
Marketing Copywriter David Goldberg
Customer Service Manager Jacqueline Valerio
Customer Service Representatives Jillian Nannicelli, Kate Sokol

Chief Financial Officer Sharyn Chabot
Human Resources Director Adele Shapiro
Controller Mandy Shito
Finance Director Wayne Saville
Senior Accountant Aaron Goranson
Staff Accountant Connie Forbes
Accounts Payable Specialist Steven Kasha
Office Manager Michael Pickett
Receptionist Henrietta Murray

Retail Sales & Marketing Manager Emily Logan
Sponsorship & Marketing Coordinator Bailey Snyder
Publicity Deborah Broide

Visit us online at **CooksCountry.com**

Follow us on **Twitter:** twitter.com/TestKitchen
Find us on **Facebook:** facebook.com/CooksCountry

America's TEST KITCHEN

America's Test Kitchen is a 2,500-square-foot kitchen located just outside of Boston. It is the home of *Cook's Country* and *Cook's Illustrated* magazines and is the workday destination of more than 50 test cooks, editors, and cookware specialists. Our mission is to test recipes until we understand how and why they work and to arrive at the best version. We also test kitchen equipment and supermarket ingredients in search of brands that offer the best value and performance. You can watch us at work by tuning in to *Cook's Country from America's Test Kitchen* (CooksCountryTV.com) on public television.

Kitchen Shortcuts

COMPILED BY CAROLYNN PURPURA

HANDY TIP
Quick-and-Dirty Fat Separator
Paul McLain, Olympia, Wash.

I dropped and cracked my fat separator long ago, but I decided not to bother replacing it after a friend showed me a great trick: Cool the liquid (stock, meat juices, whatever) to room temperature and then pour it into a zipper-lock freezer bag. After the fat floats to the top, snip a small hole in the bottom of the bag. Use your hand to keep the flow under control and simply stop letting liquid out once it gets down to the fat.

HANDY TIP
Oil Storage
Nancy Goeke Whiting, Columbia, Pa.

I use lidded 8-ounce canning jars to hold olive and canola oil in a cabinet near my stove. I fill each jar halfway with oil, and place a plastic tablespoon measuring spoon in each one. I can easily measure the amount of oil I need for any recipe without messily pouring from the large containers. The jars sit on a plastic lid to minimize any mess from drips.

RECYCLE IT
Rubber Band "Name Tags"
Kelly Beck Plishka, Munroe Falls, Ohio

I found a great use for the rubber bands that are wrapped around lots of super-market produce. When I have a bunch of kids over for a party, I put a different colored band around each child's cup. Now we always know which drink belongs to which kid.

HANDY TIP
Processor Whipped Cream
Taylor Cook, New York, N.Y.

Recently, I needed whipped cream for a dessert, but the bowl for my mixer was in the dishwasher in the middle of the wash cycle. What the heck? I tried making the whipped cream in my food processor and hoped for the best. The processor made perfect whipped cream in under a minute. (Just watch carefully so that the cream doesn't overwhip and turn into butter.)

DOUBLE DUTY
Strainer Substitute
Betsy Gell, Ridgefield, Conn.

Whenever I squeeze fresh lemons for lemon juice (something I do just about every day in my kitchen), seeds fall into the juice or whatever I'm cooking. It's annoying—and more difficult than you'd think—to have to chase the seeds around to retrieve them. One day, I figured out that I could squeeze the lemon over a flat-plane cheese grater. Now the juice goes right through the holes but the seeds rest on top, so I can just throw them out.

STORAGE SOLUTION
Neater Freezer
Sandra Arbogast Butler, Via Facebook

I was always hunting in my freezer for this or that, and no matter how hard I tried to stack my food items, they eventually slid all over the place. To get the freezer organized, I bought three clear plastic shoe boxes at the local dollar store. I placed them side by side, without the lids, in the bottom half of the freezer. I use one box for vegetables, one for meat, and the third for fish. I can easily lift them out to clean them or to search for an item more quickly. Now there's no more free-for-all in my freezer.

BETTER BAKING
Cookie Saver
Leah Hobert, Framingham, Mass.

When I was baking cookies, the parchment paper used to roll up at the corners and mar the cookies it touched. Now I weigh down the edge of the parchment with a butter knife: Every cookie turns out perfect (and the knife isn't harmed by its short stay in the oven).

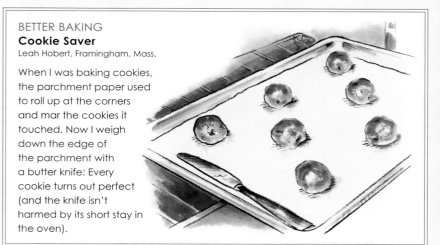

Submit a tip by e-mail at **CooksCountry.com/KitchenShortcuts** or send a letter to Kitchen Shortcuts, Cook's Country, P.O. Box 470739, Brookline, MA 02447. Include your name, address, and phone number. If we publish your tip, you will receive a free one-year subscription to *Cook's Country*. Letters may be edited for clarity or length.

Recipe Makeover Creamy Potato Salad

You can replace the sour cream and mayonnaise with low-fat equivalents and have passable "healthier" potato salad. We set our sights a little higher. BY CAROLYNN PURPURA

IF YOU'RE LIKE me, you don't think too much about how much mayonnaise is in creamy potato salad because you don't really want to know. But when forced to take a good, hard look at this salad's nutritional profile, I found it a little unnerving that the price for just one serving is a whopping 380 calories and 30 grams of fat. I decided to make it my personal mission to create a lighter potato salad that tasted just as good as the rich original.

I collected and prepared a selection of promising diet recipes. They used the usual reduced-fat or fat-free suspects to replace the full-fat mayonnaise: cottage cheese, yogurt, sour cream, and mayonnaise. None produced potato salad that most of us would willingly eat. The dressings were runny, chunky, or tasted just plain wrong—failings that were only compounded by potent ingredients meant to mask their taste, such as curry powder, caraway seed, and even two heads of garlic (yes, for one batch of potato salad). The various mayonnaises made salads with the best texture, but too much low-fat or nonfat mayonnaise can produce nasty flavors. I wanted unadulterated, classic creamy potato salad—just boiled potatoes, mayonnaise, and maybe some celery, herbs, relish, and mustard.

I knew my first step would be to use at least some lower-calorie mayonnaise. But which kind? I did a side-by-side comparison of reduced-fat (the highest in calories and fat), light, low-fat, and fat-free mayonnaise (the lightest). Tasters preferred light mayonnaise for its combination of clean flavor and creamy texture. It also reduced the calories per serving to 200 and the fat to 10 grams. But there was a downside: The light mayonnaise introduced unwelcome sweetness to the potato salad. I tried adding lemon juice and different kinds of vinegar for balance, but they tasted too assertive in the quantity needed to offset the sweetness. I had better luck replacing half of the mayonnaise with naturally tangy plain fat-free Greek yogurt. A little Dijon mustard and pickle relish added depth with little nutritional damage.

At this point, the potato salad tasted good, but I hoped to reduce the fat and calories even further. I tried thinning

You'd never know it because this potato salad tastes so creamy and flavorful, but our recipe has just a single gram of fat (and no saturated fat at all).

the dressing with some of the potato cooking water (so I could use less of the dressing), but this trick made the flavor wan and the texture watery. What if I tried using the potatoes themselves in place of some of the light mayonnaise? I reserved some of the cooked potatoes and mashed them smooth with a little of their cooking water. Then, to make the dressing, I whisked the remaining ingredients together and stirred in the mashed potatoes. My tasters were impressed. One even complimented this version for its "great potato flavor."

I tallied up the numbers and was thrilled. I had managed to cut the calories in each serving by 250 and the fat by 29 grams, and yet I still had a beautifully creamy, flavorful potato sala d. Now I can use the savings in fat and calories for a burger and dessert.

Click On Us
End your meal with a healthy dessert.
Visit **CooksCountry.com/extra** for our recipe for
Reduced-Fat Key Lime Pie.

TEST KITCHEN TECHNIQUE
Do the Mashed Potato
Some reduced-fat potato salads simply replace full-fat mayonnaise with a lighter variety, but 1 cup of light mayonnaise still had more calories and fat than we were comfortable with. Instead, we used fat-free Greek yogurt and potatoes mashed with a little of their cooking water in place of some of the mayonnaise.

The Numbers
All nutritional information is for a 1-cup serving of potato salad.

Traditional Potato Salad
CALORIES **380**
FAT **30g** SATURATED FAT **4g**

Cook's Country **Reduced-Fat Potato Salad**
CALORIES **130**
FAT **1g** SATURATED FAT **0g**

REDUCED-FAT POTATO SALAD
Serves 6
We recommend Hellmann's mayonnaise (known as Best Foods west of the Rockies) and prefer the light version to the low-fat one. Dill pickle relish can stand in for the sweet pickle relish.

2	pounds red potatoes, cut into ¾-inch pieces
	Salt and pepper
2	tablespoons white vinegar
¼	cup light mayonnaise
¼	cup nonfat Greek yogurt
1	celery rib, chopped fine
1½	tablespoons sweet pickle relish
1	tablespoon Dijon mustard
2	scallions, green parts only, sliced thin

1. Bring potatoes, 2 teaspoons salt, and enough water to cover by 1 inch to boil in large saucepan over high heat. Reduce heat to medium and simmer until potatoes are just tender, about 10 minutes.

2. Reserve ¼ cup cooking water. Drain potatoes thoroughly, then transfer to large bowl. Drizzle vinegar over hot potatoes and gently toss until evenly coated. Transfer ¾ cup potatoes to medium bowl; reserve. Refrigerate remaining potatoes until cooled, about 30 minutes.

3. Using potato masher, mash reserved hot potatoes with 3 tablespoons reserved cooking water until smooth, adding remaining cooking water as needed. Stir mayonnaise, yogurt, celery, relish, mustard, ½ teaspoon salt, and ¼ teaspoon pepper into mashed potato. Refrigerate mixture until cooled, about 15 minutes.

4. Add cooled potato dressing to cooled potatoes, stirring until evenly coated. Stir in scallions, cover, and refrigerate for 30 minutes. Season with salt and pepper to taste. Serve. (Salad can be refrigerated for up to 2 days.)

For a corn salad that was full of flavor and not waterlogged, we got out our frying pan and salt shaker. BY KELLY PRICE

IT'S NOT HARD to find recipes for corn salad, but, as I recently learned after making several of them, it's hard to find a good one. The standard method—stripping kernels off the cob, adding vegetables (usually tomatoes, onions, and/or peppers), and tossing with dressing—produced salads that were not up to snuff. Some were too sweet and meek. Others were so tart that you couldn't taste the corn through the pucker. And some were waterlogged, overwhelmed by the juices the vegetables released as they sat. I wanted a simple recipe that was nonetheless bold, balanced, and full of corn flavor.

My initial tests showed that raw corn is very sweet, yes, but its delicate taste can disappear in a salad. I hoped to heighten the flavor of the kernels by browning them lightly in a skillet for a few minutes. It worked, giving the corn—even inferior, out-of-season corn—a complex, nutty dimension. I learned the hard way, though, that using a nonstick pan was crucial. Otherwise, the corn's milky starch burned and stuck to the skillet.

When it came time to dress the salad, the sweetness of the corn still proved challenging. A standard vinaigrette (3 parts oil to 1 part vinegar) wasn't acidic enough to bring the salad into balance. Retooling the ratios, I found it took equal parts oil and vinegar to create a dressing that offset the sugary corn. When we make potato salad in the test kitchen, we often sprinkle the hot cooked potatoes with vinegar, which seasons them deeply. I decided to borrow the technique to heighten the flavor of my corn salad further. As I'd hoped, the hot, thirsty kernels absorbed the vinaigrette beautifully.

When incorporated into salads like these, tomatoes (and other juicy summer produce, like the watermelon and cucumber in our variations) weep water and make the salads soggy. Using another test kitchen technique, I tossed the tomatoes with ½ teaspoon salt and let them sit in a colander for 30 minutes to draw out some of their liquid, which I then discarded. Unfortunately, as soon as I added the drained tomatoes to the warm corn, the tomatoes broke down and wept more water. To prevent a soupy salad, I waited until the corn had

cooled in the dressing before stirring in the tomatoes (or other juicy vegetables). At last, my corn salad was tasty and crunchy. But I found that it improved greatly if I let it sit for at least 30 minutes before serving so that the flavors could meld.

This corn salad was so good that I developed four easy variations of it—you can enjoy some version of the dish all summer long without ever tiring of it.

FRESH CORN SALAD
Serves 4 to 6
Don't add the tomatoes to the toasted corn until it is cool, as the heat from the corn will partially cook the tomatoes.

- 2 tomatoes, cored and cut into ½-inch pieces
  Salt and pepper
- 2 scallions, sliced thin
- 1½ tablespoons white wine vinegar
- 2½ tablespoons olive oil
- 5 ears corn, kernels cut from cobs
- ¼ cup finely minced fresh parsley

1. Toss tomatoes and ½ teaspoon salt in bowl. Transfer to colander set over bowl and let drain for 30 minutes. Combine scallions, vinegar, ¾ teaspoon salt, and ½ teaspoon pepper in large bowl. Slowly whisk in 1½ tablespoons oil.
2. Meanwhile, heat remaining 1 tablespoon oil in 12-inch nonstick skillet over medium-high heat until shimmering. Add corn and cook, stirring occasionally, until spotty brown, 5 to 7 minutes. Transfer corn to bowl with vinaigrette, tossing to coat, and cool to room temperature, about 20 minutes. Stir in drained tomatoes and parsley. Let sit until flavors meld, about 30 minutes. Season with salt and pepper to taste. Serve. (Salad can be refrigerated for up to 2 days.)

ARUGULA-GOAT CHEESE FRESH CORN SALAD
Replace white wine vinegar with 1½ tablespoons lemon juice. Stir in 2 ounces coarsely chopped baby arugula and 4 ounces crumbled goat cheese with tomatoes. Omit parsley.

CHICKPEA-AVOCADO FRESH CORN SALAD
Replace white wine vinegar with 1½ tablespoons red wine vinegar. Add ¾

teaspoon smoked paprika, 1 minced garlic clove, and ⅛ teaspoon cayenne pepper to skillet with corn for last 30 seconds of cooking. Toss 1 (15-ounce) can rinsed chickpeas with vinaigrette and hot corn. Stir in 1 avocado, pitted and cut into ½-inch pieces, with tomatoes.

TUSCAN FRESH CORN SALAD
Replace white wine vinegar with 1½ tablespoons red wine vinegar. Toss 1 (15-ounce) can rinsed cannellini beans with vinaigrette and hot corn. Replace parsley with 2 tablespoons chopped fresh basil.

WATERMELON-FETA FRESH CORN SALAD
Replace tomatoes with 2 cups watermelon, cut into ½-inch pieces, and 2 cucumbers, peeled, quartered lengthwise, seeded, and cut into ½-inch pieces. Stir 4 ounces crumbled feta cheese into cooked and cooled corn. Replace parsley with ¼ cup minced fresh mint.

Our Watermelon-Feta variation (pictured here) is brightened by fresh mint.

TEST KITCHEN TIP
Easy Corn off the Cob
Trying to cut the kernels off a wobbly, unsteady ear of corn is asking for trouble. To keep the cob stable as you slice off the kernels, cut each ear of corn in half crosswise then turn each half on its cut side. Use a large cutting board because the loose kernels tend to scatter.

Slow Cooker Stuffed Peppers

Low and slow proved to be the perfect path to tender peppers. The filling was another story. BY REBECCAH MARSTERS

STUFFED PEPPERS BAKED in tomato sauce is a classic Italian-American dish that I thought would adapt well to the slow cooker. The peppers would slowly simmer in the sauce, and when it was time for supper, I'd just open the lid and serve them up. To establish a starting point, I made a standard recipe. I put together a simple tomato sauce and poured it into the insert. I also made a basic filling of cooked, long-grain rice; sautéed ground beef; and grated cheese. Then I stuffed a few bell peppers, set them in the sauce, and set the slow cooker to low.

Not quite five hours later, I stared in dismay at the results. The stuffing had formed a dense mass inside each pepper. I could barely distinguish blown-out rice mush from sodden meatball mash. Not only that, but the slow cooker had drained away most of the flavor. The one good piece of news was that, while traditional recipes require you to stand over a pot of boiling water, dropping in and fishing out the peppers to soften them before they are stuffed, the long,

low heat of the slow cooker eliminated this tiresome task. The peppers were tender, almost silken, but still whole.

Before doing anything else, I borrowed an idea from a recipe I'd run across while researching this project: I stirred some of the tomato sauce into the filling. It would make the filling wetter than ever, but I hoped that what it cost me in texture would be made up in flavor. Then I embarked on a series of rice tests, since repairing its texture would be critical to my recipe. To take advantage of the moist, wet heat of the slow cooker, I tried using raw rice (and tried and tried). By the time the rice cooked through, the peppers had disintegrated. Next, I parcooked the rice with water in the microwave before using it in the pepper filling. These grains emerged from the slow cooker tender at their core but blown out at the edges. Hoping that better circulation inside the peppers would promote even cooking, I poked holes in the peppers. Now the rice cooked evenly, but it remained wet and heavy. Frankly, I was beginning to doubt the wisdom of pairing stuffed peppers with slow cookers.

As my hopes faded, I reluctantly considered removing the tomato sauce I'd added to the filling to such flavorful effect. But then a colleague suggested I try Arborio, the classic risotto rice. It cooks in lots of liquid. Even better, unlike long-grain rice, Arborio absorbs liquid very slowly (as you know if you've ever made risotto), kind of like…hey, the timetable of a slow cooker. I retained the rice-parcooking and the pepper-poking steps from previous tests, filled the peppers with an Arborio-based stuffing, and waited several anxious hours. To my relief, Arborio turned creamy and delectable in the moist filling.

Now that the rice was finally on target, I looked for ways to boost flavor in the other ingredients. To begin, I replaced the ground beef with hot Italian sausage. (The flavorful sausage added so much oomph that I had to gradually cut down on the amount before attaining lighter, brighter stuffed peppers.) Next, I presided over a cheese face-off: Mozzarella made the filling gummy without injecting much flavor. Cheddar wasn't bad, but Parmesan hit the ball out of the park, giving the

peppers Italian credibility and a jolt of flavor without adding much moisture. For even more flavor, I used chicken broth to parcook the Arborio, instead of water. Much better. And in a final bit of tweaking, I added extra garlic at the start and fresh basil at the finish.

SLOW-COOKER STUFFED PEPPERS
Serves 4

- 4 red, yellow, or orange bell peppers
- 1½ cups low-sodium chicken broth
- ¾ cup Arborio rice
- 8 ounces hot Italian sausage, casings removed
- 2 onions, chopped fine
- 6 garlic cloves, minced
- ½ teaspoon dried oregano
  Salt and pepper
- ⅛ teaspoon red pepper flakes
- 1 (28-ounce) can crushed tomatoes
- 2½ ounces Parmesan cheese, grated (1¼ cups)
- 2 tablespoons chopped fresh basil

1. Working one at a time, cut off top ½ inch of bell peppers. Discard stem and seeds. Chop pepper tops into ¼-inch pieces; reserve pepper cups. Microwave broth and rice in covered large bowl until liquid is absorbed and rice is nearly tender, 13 to 15 minutes.

2. Meanwhile, cook sausage in 12-inch nonstick skillet over medium-high heat, breaking up meat into small pieces, until browned, 6 to 8 minutes. Using slotted spoon, transfer sausage to paper towel-lined plate.

3. Pour off all but 1 tablespoon fat from skillet. Add onions and chopped pepper and cook until browned, 8 to 10 minutes. Stir in garlic, oregano, ½ teaspoon salt, ¼ teaspoon pepper, and pepper flakes and cook until fragrant, about 30 seconds. Add tomatoes, bring to boil, and remove from heat.

4. Combine 1 cup sauce, sausage, and 1 cup Parmesan with parcooked rice. Transfer remaining sauce to slow cooker. Using skewer, poke 4 holes in bottom of each reserved pepper cup. Fill each pepper with one-quarter of rice mixture and place upright in slow cooker. Top peppers with remaining ¼ cup Parmesan. Cover and cook on low until peppers and rice are tender, 4 to 4½ hours.

5. Transfer peppers to plate. Stir basil into sauce and season with salt and pepper to taste. Spoon sauce over peppers. Serve.

What you can't see: Our robust tomato sauce also seasons the cheesy sausage and rice filling.

DON'T MAKE THIS MISTAKE
Mushy Filling

While long-grain white rice is ideal for light and fluffy pilafs, it couldn't handle the wet, slow environment of the slow cooker combined with a wet, tomato-heavy stuffing. The grains turned into blown-out mush. Starchy, short-grained Arborio rice, by contrast, produced a creamy filling.

PROBLEM
Long-grain rice turned to mush.

SOLUTION
Use Arborio rice for a creamy filling.

Cooking for Two Spaghetti Bolognese

Long simmering is out of the question when making dinner for two on a rushed weeknight. We searched for a way to get deep flavor—fast. BY REBECCAH MARSTERS

BOLOGNESE IS USUALLY reserved for weekends at home, when a big pot of the aromatic, long-simmering sauce means Sunday supper with the family. But its comforts shouldn't be out of reach on busy weeknights with just two to feed. The keys to Bolognese sauce are melding its components so that no one ingredient stands out, and cooking it long enough to impart depth of flavor. My challenge was to downsize the yield, simplify the procedure, keep all in balance, and produce a sauce that tasted complex—all in a fraction of the time it usually takes to prepare.

I began with the test kitchen's basic Bolognese recipe: Mince and lightly brown onions and garlic; add meatloaf mix (a beef-veal-pork combo often used in Bolognese); add milk, wine, and tomatoes and bring to a boil; reduce; simmer and simmer and . . . simmer. To uncover what that long simmer is supposed to achieve, I made a bold first move and slashed the time to just 20 minutes, about how long I'd be willing to wait for a weeknight dinner for two. I also cut down the proportions. Otherwise, I followed the recipe as directed.

What a disappointment. The sauce was flat and wan. To make up for it, I looked for ingredients I could add to the sauce that would provide a fast beefy boost. A series of tests led me to a combination of pancetta (an unsmoked Italian bacon called for in some Bolognese recipes), dried porcini mushrooms,

Our steamlined Spaghetti Bolognese is on the table in less than an hour.

and anchovies. Amazingly, though each is strongly flavored, if I pulsed them in the food processor with the onions and carrots I not only made short work of mincing, but they added intense meatiness without announcing themselves. Dried porcini usually must rehydrate in hot water for 20 minutes before they are usable. I was unwilling to spend the time so I simply tossed the porcini bits into the simmering sauce, where—fortuitously—they softened.

As I pulled out a colander and filled a pot with water for boiling the spaghetti, I glanced at the vigorously simmering sauce. Why not add the dry noodles directly to the skillet with the sauce? I thinned the sauce with lots of water for the pasta to absorb as it softened, covered the pan, and held my breath. Fifteen minutes later, I had a skillet full of tender noodles and full-bodied sauce. True, the water had diluted the tomato flavor, but a dollop of tomato paste soon revived it.

In less than an hour, I had achieved much of the incredible complexity for which Bolognese is known. Finished with fresh basil and grated Parmesan cheese, my version was good enough for the family table—even if it was set for two.

SPAGHETTI BOLOGNESE FOR TWO
If you can't find meatloaf mix, substitute equal parts of 85 percent lean ground beef and ground pork. Take the time to thoroughly rinse the dried porcini mushrooms to remove any grit. Serve with grated Parmesan cheese.

- 1 small onion, chopped coarse
- 1 carrot, peeled and chopped coarse
- 1½ ounces pancetta, chopped coarse
- ¼ ounce dried porcini mushrooms, rinsed
- 1 anchovy fillet, rinsed
- 1 (14.5-ounce) can diced tomatoes
- 1 tablespoon unsalted butter
- 1 tablespoon tomato paste
- 2 garlic cloves, minced
- ½ teaspoon sugar
- ⅛ teaspoon red pepper flakes
- 6 ounces meatloaf mix
- ¾ cup whole milk
- ¼ cup dry white wine
- 2 cups water
- 6 ounces spaghetti
- 2 tablespoons chopped fresh basil
  Salt and pepper

1. Pulse onion, carrot, pancetta, mushrooms, and anchovy in food processor until finely ground, 10 to 15 pulses; transfer to bowl. Pulse tomatoes with their juice until coarsely ground, about 8 pulses.

2. Melt butter in 12-inch nonstick skillet over medium heat. Add processed onion mixture and cook until browned, 6 to 8 minutes. Stir in tomato paste, garlic, sugar, and pepper flakes and cook until paste begins to darken, about 1 minute. Add meatloaf mix, breaking up meat into small pieces, and cook until just no longer pink, 2 to 3 minutes.

3. Stir in milk and bring to simmer, scraping up any browned bits. Cook until liquid is nearly evaporated, 5 to 8 minutes. Stir in wine, bring to boil, and simmer until liquid is nearly evaporated, 2 to 3 minutes.

4. Add water, processed tomatoes, and pasta and bring to boil. Cover, reduce heat to medium, and simmer, stirring occasionally, until pasta is tender and sauce is thickened, 15 to 18 minutes. Off heat, stir in basil and season with salt and pepper to taste. Serve.

Aloha, Kalua Pork

Wrapping a suckling pig in banana leaves and roasting it in a hole in the ground was a non-starter.
But to replicate the flavors of this luau dish, we tried just about everything else. BY ADAM RIED

I first encountered kalua pork—the succulent, smoked suckling pig that's the centerpiece of Hawaiian luaus—on a trip to Oahu. It was fantastic, but it was clear why I'd never run into it before. The word kalua refers to the traditional Hawaiian pit-cooking method using an imu, a deep hole in the ground with a native kiawe wood fire and a lining of hot rocks and banana leaves. The leaves flavor the meat and help keep it moist. Seasoned with only local pink sea salt, the pork roasts at low heat in the pit for hours, emerging tender, juicy, and smoky and bearing the unique flavor stamp of the leaves. How could I ever make that happen at home—minus the whole pig, the banana leaves, and (sigh) the Hawaiian beaches?

Understandably, recipes in most modern Hawaiian cookbooks skip the imu, too. They use the oven, rely on bottled liquid smoke for the essential smoky flavor, and bypass the vegetation altogether. Imu aside, in terms of cooking method, true kalua pork resembles any barbecued pork in that it cooks "low and slow"—in other words, at a low temperature for a long time. The test kitchen has plenty of experience using a grill to barbecue pork, so I was confident that we could employ that technique here, too. Mimicking the elusive, herbaceous flavor of the banana leaves, however, would be another matter entirely.

To start, in place of the traditional but obviously impractical whole pig, I opted for boneless pork shoulder roast, often labeled "pork butt" or "Boston butt" in supermarkets. Comprising several well-exercised muscles with plenty of fat and connective tissue that melts during cooking to keep the meat moist, the rich, flavorful shoulder roast stands up well to long, slow cooking (it's the cut usually used for pulled pork).

Unlike most pulled pork and other types of barbecue, though, kalua pork is not sauced, so it wasn't a surprise

Kalua Pork is a close cousin to classic pulled pork. What makes it different is the distinct flavor that comes from its unusual wrapper.

that the first time I attempted to make it, some tasters found it a bit dry and bland. I decided to capture the flavorful juices that were dripping into the fire by placing the pork in a disposable aluminum pan on top of the grill grate. This allowed me to moisten the finished pork by adding back some of the collected—and defatted—juices, which, of course, are rich in porky flavor. A few tests showed me that it was also necessary to loosely cover the pan with foil in order to replicate the steamy environment of the imu. I poked holes in the foil to let the smoke through.

The test kitchen's first choice for building smoky flavor is a charcoal fire topped with a packet of wood chips. While developing a recipe for Hawaiian Huli Huli Chicken a couple of years ago, we learned that mesquite is related to Hawaiian kiawe wood, so it was the natural choice for this recipe (both types of wood produce smoke that is more assertive than hickory or oak). Refueling the fire to keep it burning (and smoking) for an extended cooking time is inconvenient to say the least (you have to remove the roast, then the hot grill grate to add more charcoal, then replace the grate and meat), which is why we've developed a terrific hybrid method: Start by smoking the meat with gentle indirect heat and then, when after two hours the coals and chips have burned out, move the meat to a 325-degree oven to cook (covered or wrapped in foil) until it's fork-tender, another two to three hours.

To remind myself of the flavor imparted by the banana leaves, I ordered some online, wrapped a pork butt in the leaves, and slow-smoked it. The herbal, mineral-y flavor played off the smoke perfectly and really was unusual. Thinking about how to re-create that flavor, I paced the produce department for inspiration, picking up various large, leafy greens to try wrapping around the pork.

I wrapped each of seven pork butts with a different type of leaf: collard greens, kale, Swiss chard, green cabbage, napa cabbage, savoy cabbage, and corn husks. It was an interesting experiment but not a successful one. The corn husks burned, and the rest of these vegetables infused the smoked pork with cabbage-y, sulphuric flavors. Yuck. I rubbed more pork butts with pastes made from parsley, watercress, and spinach. These flavors weren't unpleasant; they were just plain wrong for kalua pork.

Back to the supermarket produce aisle. This time I focused on the tropical nature of the banana leaves and chose bananas and pineapple. It took some doing (and fellow test cooks looked at me as if I'd lost my mind), but I used kitchen twine to lash pork roasts with fancy patchworks of banana peels and pineapple rind. I got—no surprise—pork that tasted like bananas and pineapples. Not what I was going for, either. I was running out of steam.

I had one last banana leaf in the freezer, so I tried it again to jog my memory and further analyze the flavor: aromatic, earthy, and mildly grassy, with a tea-like quality. Ding, ding, ding! I hit the tea aisle at the market, bringing home smoky Lapsang Souchong, a few herbal tea blends, and green tea, each of which I made into seasoning rubs. Several more test porks later, I was delighted to find that a rub made from 3 tablespoons of crumbled green tea and 4 teaspoons of kosher salt hit very close to the mark, and rubbing it on was far easier than tying leaves or peels around a large pork roast. A little brown sugar helped the rub caramelize and made the meat's crust a more attractive (and delicious) shade of deep brown.

Luau or not, now I can enjoy kalua pork wherever I want.

HAWAIIAN-STYLE SMOKED PORK (KALUA PORK) Serves 8

You'll need 10 to 15 tea bags. If your pork butt comes with an elastic netting, remove it before you rub the pork with the tea. To eat Kalua Pork as the Hawaiians do, serve it with steamed rice, macaroni salad, and cabbage salad.

- 3 tablespoons green tea
- 4 teaspoons kosher salt
- 1 tablespoon packed brown sugar
- 2 teaspoons pepper
- 1 (4- to 5-pound) boneless pork butt roast, trimmed
- 1 (13 by 9-inch) disposable aluminum roasting pan
- 6 cups mesquite wood chips, soaked in water for 15 minutes and drained

1. Combine tea, salt, sugar, and pepper in bowl. Pat pork dry with paper towels and rub with tea mixture. Wrap meat tightly with plastic wrap and refrigerate for 6 to 24 hours. Place pork in pan and cover pan loosely with aluminum foil. Poke about twenty ¼-inch holes in foil. Using large sheet of heavy-duty foil, wrap 2 cups soaked chips into foil packet and cut several vent holes in top. Make 2 more packets with additional foil and remaining 4 cups chips.

2A. For a charcoal grill: Open bottom vent halfway. Light large chimney starter three-quarters full with charcoal briquettes (4½ quarts). When top coals are partially covered with ash, pour into steeply banked pile against side of grill. Place wood chip packets on coals. Set cooking grate in place, cover, and open lid vent halfway. Heat grill until hot and wood chips are smoking, about 5 minutes.

2B. For a gas grill: Place wood chip packets over primary burner. Turn all burners to high, cover, and heat grill until hot and wood chips are smoking, about 15 minutes. Turn primary burner to medium-high and turn off other burner(s). (Adjust primary burner as needed to maintain grill temperature at 300 degrees.)

3. Place pan on cool part of grill. Cover (positioning lid vent over meat if using charcoal) and cook for 2 hours. During last 20 minutes of grilling, adjust oven rack to lower-middle position and heat oven to 325 degrees.

4. Remove pan from grill. Cover pan tightly with new sheet of foil, transfer to oven, and bake until tender and fork inserted into meat meets no resistance, 2 to 3 hours. Let pork rest, covered, for 30 minutes. Unwrap and, when meat is cool enough to handle, shred into bite-size pieces, discarding fat. Strain contents of pan through fine-mesh strainer into fat separator. Let liquid settle, then return ¼ cup defatted pan juices to pork. Serve. (Pork can be refrigerated for up to 3 days.)

TEST KITCHEN INGENUITY Bringing the Luau Stateside

Traditional kalua pork is wrapped in banana leaves and smoked for hours in a pit. Here's how we've re-created its distinctive flavor and texture:

1. Rub pork with **green tea** mixture.

2. Place meat in **aluminum pan** on cool side of grill.

3. Cover meat with **perforated foil.**

Grill Set-Up
Pile coals on one side of the grill and top with vented foil packets of soaked mesquite chips to create smoke. The covered meat cooks on the cool side of the grill for 2 hours, then finishes in the oven so you don't have to rebuild the fire.

TASTING SUPERMARKET GREEN TEA

The Japanese and Chinese have sipped green tea for more than a millennium. Suddenly, Westerners are drinking it, too, and even using it to give astringent, slightly bitter flavor to custard, ice cream, and even pork roast. (It's made from the same plants as black tea but is unfermented, which accounts for its distinctive flavor.) Connoisseurs have their pick among high-end selections, but cooking with $14-an-ounce tea makes about as much sense as cooking with a $100 bottle of wine. We wanted a tea we could both sip and cook with on occasion. Supermarket green teas are affordable, but would any suit our two needs? We set the tea kettles a-boiling and gathered 21 tasters to sample five nationally available supermarket brands of bagged green tea, tasting each on its own (following manufacturers' brewing instructions) and in green-tea infused custard. None dazzled us, but we did identify a few that were both drinkable and imparted nice flavor to recipes. We liked the mild grassiness of Celestial Seasonings best, sipped, infused, and rubbed on Kalua Pork. —TAIZETH SIERRA

RECOMMENDED

		TASTERS' NOTES
CELESTIAL SEASONINGS Authentic Green Tea $4.99 for 40 bags		"Clean" green tea flavor with a "nice grassy quality," "mild, toasty aromas," and just "a bit astringent," tasters said. In custard, those flavors offset the richness.

RECOMMENDED WITH RESERVATIONS

TWININGS Green Tea $3.69 for 20 bags		Tasters found the brewed tea "bitter," "astringent," and "funky." It was the strongest tea we tasted. But in custard, this "harsh" tea mellowed and imparted a "pleasant, smoky" taste.
BIGELOW Green Tea $2.99 for 20 bags		While interesting, this tea's "floral," "mellow," "herbal" flavors are atypical of green tea. In the custard, we couldn't even taste it.
LIPTON Green Tea $3.79 for 40 bags		What a few tasters described as "subtle grassy notes," most characterized as "weak," "bland," and "watery without much green tea flavor." Unsurprisingly, the tea imparted scant flavor to custard. It squeaked into its "Recommended with Reservations" ranking.

NOT RECOMMENDED

TAZO China Green Tips Green Tea $3.69 for 20 bags		This tea's "harsh," "strong," "soapy," "tinny" flavor earned it low marks as brewed tea. It fared only slightly better in custard, with many tasters finding it bitter.

Grilled Steak Burgers

Most so-called steak burgers are plain beef patties drowning in A1. We wanted what the best steakhouses would be proud to serve: robust steak-like burgers with a deep, crusty char. BY SARAH GABRIEL

MOST STEAKHOUSES FEATURE a burger on their menus. The meat is usually ground from intensely beefy steak trimmings, cooked on a ripping-hot grill (or under the broiler) to crusty perfection, and served with steak sauce. In essence, the steak experience on a bun. I wanted the same results from my backyard grill.

Fancy burger recipes call for grinding various cuts of beef at home. For an easier route to similarly big flavor, I started by grilling burgers made with ground beef readily available in markets (chuck, round, and sirloin), seasoned with salt and pepper, and grilled over high heat to medium-rare. Round was fine, chuck was better, but neither tasted as "steak-y" as the robust sirloin (from which steaks are cut). But sirloin is about 90 percent lean, so these burgers were a little dry. I decided to add butter to the meat. Melted butter blended easily and took on a texture similar to beef fat. Perfect.

But I wanted more flavor. In the test kitchen, we often add soy sauce to beef recipes because it contains a lot of savory, meaty-tasting glutamates. Two teaspoons increased meatiness without tasting like soy. Onions and garlic, of course, also add baseline flavor, so I sautéed some in the butter before mixing it into the meat. But the moisture from the chopped onions made the burgers mushy. I kept the minced garlic but

switched to onion powder for depth without dampness.

I moved on to the sauce. We found that all commercial steak sauces (yes, even A1) tasted harsh. I'd have to make my own. Following the lead of most recipes, I sautéed garlic and onion in butter, added tomato paste, water, raisins, vinegar, Worcestershire, and mustard. This sauce got better when I added a few tablespoons of soy sauce and traded white vinegar for balsamic, and water for beef broth. I let it simmer for a few minutes, then buzzed the sauce in the blender and was good to go.

These burgers still lacked serious steakhouse char. I was grilling them over high heat but if I left them on longer, they overcooked. I looked for something sweet to brush on the raw patties to encourage char. With tomato paste, raisins, and balsamic, my homemade sauce fit the bill, so I tried that. These burgers came off the grill still a perfect medium-rare but with a deeper charred crust than before.

As a final flourish, I brushed steak sauce mixed with butter onto rolls and toasted them on the grill. I was almost done, but before I put this recipe to bed, I realized I could streamline it by starting with a big batch of garlic and onion powder sautéed in melted butter, then divide it for triple use in the burgers, sauce, and buns. These burgers require nothing but a big appetite—and plenty of napkins.

It all starts with the meat: Ground sirloin tastes "steakier" than chuck or round.

Butter Makes It Better

Why are our steakhouse burgers so good? Yep, butter. Ground sirloin has great flavor, but it's a little dry: Butter helps keep the burgers moist. Butter also gives richness and body to our homemade steak sauce. And we slather butter on the buns before toasting them on the grill.

FLAVORED BUTTER
For the meat, sauce, and buns.

GRILLED STEAK BURGERS Serves 4
Use Kaiser rolls or other hearty buns.

BURGERS
- 8 tablespoons unsalted butter
- 2 garlic cloves, minced
- 2 teaspoons onion powder
- 1 teaspoon pepper
- ½ teaspoon salt
- 2 teaspoons soy sauce
- 1½ pounds 90 percent lean ground sirloin
- 4 hamburger buns

STEAK SAUCE
- 2 tablespoons tomato paste
- ⅔ cup beef broth
- ⅓ cup raisins
- 2 tablespoons soy sauce
- 2 tablespoons Dijon mustard
- 2 tablespoons balsamic vinegar
- 1 tablespoon Worcestershire sauce

1. For the burgers: Melt butter in 8-inch skillet over medium-low heat. Add garlic, onion powder, pepper, and salt and cook until fragrant, about 1 minute. Pour all but 1 tablespoon butter mixture into bowl and let cool slightly, about 5 minutes.

2. For the steak sauce: Meanwhile, add tomato paste to skillet and cook over medium heat until paste begins to darken, 1 to 2 minutes. Stir in broth, raisins, soy sauce, mustard, vinegar, and Worcestershire and simmer until raisins plump, about 5 minutes. Process sauce in blender until smooth, about 30 seconds; transfer to bowl.

3. Add 5 tablespoons cooled butter mixture and soy sauce to ground beef and gently knead until well combined. Shape into four ¾-inch-thick patties and press shallow divot in center of each. Brush each patty all over with 1 tablespoon steak sauce. Combine remaining 2 tablespoons cooled butter mixture

with 2 tablespoons steak sauce; set aside.

4A. For a charcoal grill: Open bottom vent completely. Light large chimney starter filled with charcoal briquettes (6 quarts). When top coals are partially covered with ash, pour evenly over grill. Set cooking grate in place, cover, and open lid vent completely. Heat grill until hot, about 5 minutes.

4B. For a gas grill: Turn all burners to high, cover, and heat grill until hot, about 15 minutes. Leave burners on high.

5. Clean and oil cooking grate. Grill burgers (covered if using gas) until meat registers 120 to 125 degrees (for medium-rare), 3 to 4 minutes per side, or 130 to 135 degrees (for medium), 4 to 5 minutes per side. Transfer burgers to plate, tent loosely with aluminum foil, and let rest 5 to 10 minutes. Brush cut side of buns with butter–steak sauce mixture. Grill buns, cut side down, until golden, 2 to 3 minutes. Place burgers on buns. Serve with remaining steak sauce.

Shoestring Onion Rings

What does an apple have to do with preventing mushy onion rings?

BY SARAH GABRIEL

LET'S BE HONEST: Thick beer-battered rings are more about the puffy, crunchy coating than about the onions themselves. Shoestring onions, on the other hand, have a thinner, crisp coating that highlights the onions. At their best, shoestrings arrive at the table a salty, crunchy tangle of feathery fried onions that are hard to stop eating. At their worst, they're a greasy, soggy pile of breading.

My initial task was to determine what variety of onion had the sweet-yet-robust flavor that would work best here. I started with a simple recipe that called for tossing thinly sliced onions in flour seasoned with salt and pepper. I sliced red, white, yellow, and sweet onions, tossed each in the flour, fried them separately in peanut oil, and called over my colleagues. Red onions browned faster than the flour coating did, while sweet onions were (duh) too sweet and didn't have much oniony oomph. White onions were a little flat and lacked sweet-savory balance, but yellow onions were identifiably "onion" without being offensively pungent. Now I had the correct onions, but the seasoned flour coating was limp and greasy.

In search of something that would give these onions more crunch, I dug through dozens of recipes for fried foods. Baking soda and cornstarch were the most common dredge additives, so I gave them a try. Cornstarch did improve the crunch, but it made the coating a bit pasty. Baking soda sped up the browning too much, making for burnt coating and underdone onions. Shifting gears, I decided to look at wet ingredients. Some recipes call for soaking the sliced onions in milk or buttermilk for about 30 minutes before dredging in flour. I soaked one batch in milk and another in buttermilk and then dredged and fried them alongside a batch that

hadn't been soaked. Only the buttermilk-soaked onions were really crisp, but they held on to so much flour that the onion flavor was diminished. Before I could solve this problem, I first had to figure out why the buttermilk improved crunch.

Buttermilk is made by adding live cultures (friendly bacteria of the sort used to produce yogurt or cheese) to milk; the cultures produce lactic acid, which gives buttermilk its signature tang. Our science editor explained that the acid in the buttermilk was helping the coating fry up crisper by speeding up the gelatinization of the starch and drawing more amylose out of the starch granules in the flour (see "Waiter, There's an Apple in My Onions!"). I wondered if another acidic liquid would yield the same crunch yet release more of the flour. Soaking the onions in white vinegar did just that.

Unfortunately, while the vinegar made for a super-crunchy coating, the shoestring onions were now way too sour. Cider vinegar, while also too tart, improved matters, so I tried diluting it with an equal amount of water. That worked pretty well, but what worked even better was trading the water for apple juice. The juice contributed more acid (hence more crunch) than water did, plus it added sweetness to balance the vinegar. As a bonus, I discovered that the onions didn't need to soak for 30 minutes—a quick dip did the trick.

Having unlocked the secret to maximum crunch (acid), I wondered if I could take it one step further. The wet ingredients were working hard to create crunch, but what about the flour? Was there a dry acidic ingredient that I could add to the flour to promote even more crispness? Searching the test kitchen pantry, I came across cream of tartar, which is often used as an acidic activator in baked goods leavened with baking soda (the soda requires an acid to release its lift-giving bubbles). A few tests of cream of tartar in varying amounts determined that ¾ teaspoon added a crunchy boost without leaving a flavor trail.

You don't have to understand the science of why apple cider vinegar, apple juice, and cream of tartar make for the crispest, tastiest fried onions ever. All you have to do is try to stop eating them.

Waiter, There's an Apple in My Onions!

Apple juice and apple cider vinegar are both flavorful and acidic. Their acid is key here, because it draws more amylose out of the starch granules as they gelatinize (or absorb water). The amylose makes the coating crisp when the gelatinized starch is fried in oil.

Our thin, shatteringly crisp coating doesn't obscure the sweet onion flavor.

SHOESTRING ONIONS Serves 4

You will need a Dutch oven with a capacity of at least 6 quarts for this recipe. We prefer yellow onions here, but white onions will also work. Do not use red or sweet onions.

- 2 quarts peanut or vegetable oil
- 1½ cups all-purpose flour
  Salt and pepper
- ¾ teaspoon cream of tartar
- 1 pound onions, sliced into ¼-inch-thick rings
- ½ cup apple juice
- ¼ cup apple cider vinegar

1. Adjust oven rack to middle position and heat oven to 200 degrees. Heat oil in Dutch oven over medium-high heat until 350 degrees.

2. Meanwhile, combine flour, 1 teaspoon salt, cream of tartar, and ½ teaspoon pepper in large bowl. Toss onions, apple juice, and vinegar to coat in another bowl. Drain onions and transfer to flour mixture, tossing to coat.

3. Fry half of onion rings, stirring occasionally and adjusting burner as necessary to maintain oil temperature between 325 and 350 degrees, until golden brown and crisp, 3 to 4 minutes. Drain onions on wire rack set in rimmed baking sheet and place in oven. Bring oil back to 350 degrees and repeat with remaining onions. Season with salt and pepper to taste. Serve.

Easy New England Clam Chowder

We had no time to prepare clams in their shells, so how would we get good clam flavor?

BY DIANE UNGER

CLAM CHOWDER FROM scratch is fantastic, but it's sure not quick: To serve six, you have to soak, scrub, steam, shuck, and mince some seven pounds of clams, then collect and strain the seafood broth—all this before you so much as chop a single potato or onion. Also, if you don't hover over the (expensive) simmering clams, chances are good they'll turn to rubber. I wanted to develop a recipe that only tasted like I'd spent hours in the kitchen.

I collected and prepared a smattering of New England clam chowder recipes that claimed to accelerate the usual process. As a group, they sacrificed straight-from-the-sea flavor for speed and ease. Some were bland and milky. Others were very thin. A few called for canned clams—my tasters firmly vetoed those. Also, none nailed the delicate dance of cream, clam, and pork that defines good chowder. I cherry-picked features from among the test group to put together a basic working recipe: sauté pork product for its fat; sauté onions in said fat; add milk, potato chunks, and seasonings; simmer until the potatoes are tender, stir in clams.

New England clam chowders typically start with either salt pork or bacon. Each had its merits, so I let the clock determine the winner. I found I could chop, sauté, and extract flavor from diced bacon twice as fast as with salt pork (plus it gave me crispy bacon to sprinkle on

Bottled clam juice and fresh, pre-shelled clams stand in for homemade clam stock.

at the end). Bacon it would be. Since we'd nixed fresh clams (too much work) and canned clams (nothing like the real deal), I went to the supermarket, returned with a tub of fresh chopped clams, and cooked a batch of soup. Fresh, shucked, chopped clams, stirred in at the end to quickly cook them, proved an excellent compromise between haste and taste.

But even with 2 pounds of clams, the soup tasted wan. It needed some supporting players. In a series of tests, I tried liquid bases of many sorts, alone and in combination: Milk, which I'd been using (that, or water, is traditional in older recipes), made for pallid chowder while an all-cream version was over-the-top rich. Plus, neither registered the sea. Some quicker chowder recipes call for bottled clam juice, so I pulled a

bottle out of the pantry. In the end, a combination of bottled clam juice, heavy cream, and plain water actually fooled a couple of tasters into thinking I'd gone to the trouble of making homemade clam stock. For seasonings, I stayed simple and classic, using fresh minced thyme and a single bay leaf.

My quicker chowder still had one serious drawback—it was as thin as skim milk. I tried thickening it with flour, as many recipes do—stirring in flour with the sautéing onions. But the amount I needed to get the full-bodied texture I sought turned the chowder pasty. In search of ideas, I returned to the recipes I'd gathered, including some from the 19th-century. These early recipes used crackers and potatoes as thickeners. The modern practice of floating a few crackers in chowder stems from these

early thickeners. Curious, I made a new batch, this time adding roughly a sleeve of crushed saltines with the simmering potatoes. In 20 minutes, they disappeared into the soup, leaving behind body and a subtle, salty depth. It was a revelation (and surprising, too, that the path to speedy chowder came from a slower time). When the potatoes were tender, I fished out a few chunks and crushed them into the chowder for even more body.

Not even 40 minutes after I'd planted my cutting board in the kitchen, I ladled out a thick, fragrant bowl of chowder. Happily, I had managed to shortcut the work of clam chowder without short-changing the flavor.

EASY CLAM CHOWDER Serves 6
If you buy frozen clams, thaw them before using. You can substitute 9 *Cook's Country* Common Crackers for the saltines.

- 4 slices bacon, chopped fine
- 1 onion, chopped fine
- 3 (8-ounce) bottles clam juice
- 2 cups water
- 1½ pounds russet potatoes, peeled and cut into ½-inch pieces
- 20 saltines, crushed
- 1 teaspoon minced fresh thyme
- 1 bay leaf
- 2 pounds chopped clams, rinsed, drained, and chopped fine
- 1 cup heavy cream
- Salt and pepper

1. Cook bacon in large saucepan over medium heat until crisp, 6 to 8 minutes. Using slotted spoon, transfer bacon to paper towel–lined plate. Pour off all but 1 tablespoon fat from saucepan. Add onion and cook over medium heat until softened, about 5 minutes. Stir in clam juice, water, potatoes, saltines, thyme, and bay leaf and bring to boil. Reduce heat to medium and simmer, stirring occasionally, until potatoes are tender, about 20 minutes.

2. Using slotted spoon, transfer ½ cup potatoes to bowl and mash with potato masher until smooth. Return mashed potatoes to pot. Reduce heat to low. Stir clams into pot and simmer until cooked through, 3 to 5 minutes. Off heat, stir in cream. Season with salt and pepper to taste. Sprinkle with bacon. Serve.

Common Crackers

We hoped to revive this delicious old-fashioned cracker, but could we speed up its production for a faster world? BY DIANE UNGER

COMMON CRACKERS WERE once as common in New England as great schools of cod off the coastline. Whalers carried close kin to the plain, yeasty crackers as provisions since, unlike bread, they were sturdy enough to last the length of their expeditions. On land, women bought them from barrels at general stores and used them to thicken chowders, or to eat (buttered and toasted) crumbled in their soups and stews. Today, these crunchy, layered crackers—the direct descendents of hardtack—are anything but common, and recipes for them are few and far between.

The few recipes I was able to find called for flour, shortening (early versions used lard), yeast, sugar, salt, and water. To develop flavor, these recipes required long, overnight fermentation or used starters. Then the dough was rolled and stamped into circles about the size of a half-dollar. In the oven, the crackers puffed and hollowed, browned, and then dried. To bring back this forgotten staple, so I set to work in the test kitchen, keeping one eye on the clock.

The obvious way to gain speed was to use chemical leaveners rather than yeast and to bake the crackers as soon as I'd formed them. Though baking soda overbrowned one batch I tried, baking powder showed promise. It had a drawback, too: Tasters missed the yeasty flavor. To address that, I tried replacing the water with beer, which the test kitchen sometimes uses to add yeasty, well-developed character to baked goods. It worked nicely here. (At the same time, I ejected the sugar, as it was no longer necessary to kick-start the yeast.)

To get the requisite layered structure, I borrowed a technique sometimes used to produce light and flaky scones: I rolled the dough into a rectangle, brushed it with melted shortening, and folded it in thirds, like a business letter. I rolled it out again and only then stamped out the crackers. When they came out of the oven, they had beautiful flaked layers.

My version of the common cracker was improving, but the latest batch lacked the big crunch of the real thing. After a few failed experiments with time and temperature, I realized that all I needed to do was to bake them on a wire baking rack set over a sheet tray. That way, the air could circulate both above and below, drying out and crisping up my crackers nicely. The method worked even better after I poked each raw cracker several times with a fork, which let steam escape as they baked.

I set a basket of my crackers out, alongside a big pot of clam chowder, and called my team of tasters to try a combination that New Englanders have loved for almost two centuries. The crackers may be named common crackers, tasters told me, but they're uncommonly good.

The difference between these crisp, flaky homemade crackers and the ones you can buy at the store is like night and day.

KEY INGREDIENT **Mild Lager**

Traditionally, Common Crackers were made from yeast dough that sat overnight before the crackers were shaped. To mimic its fermented, yeasty flavor without the wait, we turned to beer.

HIT OF HOPS
Instant flavor

COMMON CRACKERS

Makes about 3 dozen crackers
Use mild lager, such as Budweiser, to make this recipe.

- 2½ cups (12½ ounces) all-purpose flour
- 2 teaspoons baking powder
- 1¼ teaspoons salt
- 3 tablespoons vegetable shortening cut into ½-inch pieces and chilled, plus 2 tablespoons melted and cooled
- 1 cup beer, chilled

1. Adjust oven rack to lower-middle position and heat oven to 350 degrees. Set wire rack in rimmed baking sheet. Pulse flour, baking powder, and salt in food processor until combined, about 5 pulses. Add chilled shortening and pulse until just combined, about 5 pulses.

2. Transfer flour mixture to large bowl. Stir in beer until combined. Turn dough onto lightly floured surface and knead briefly until dough comes together. Roll dough into 10 by 7-inch rectangle. Brush dough with melted shortening, then fold as you would a letter: Working from short edge, fold dough over itself, leaving ⅓ of dough uncovered. Fold opposite uncovered short edge over dough. Roll folded dough into 18 by 7-inch rectangle, about ¼ inch thick.

3. Using 2-inch biscuit cutter dipped in flour, cut out rounds and arrange on rack-lined baking sheet. Gather remaining dough and roll into ¼-inch-thick circle. Cut rounds from dough and transfer to rack. Prick dough rounds twice using fork.

4. Bake until light golden brown and firm, 50 to 55 minutes. Let crackers cool completely, about 1 hour. Serve. (Crackers can be stored in closed paper bag for up to 3 days.)

Citrus-and-Spice Grilled Chicken

When this popular Latin dish migrated north to Mexican restaurants across the states, it left its citrus flavor behind. We went looking for it. BY ADAM RIED

I'D WAGER that almost every Mexican taqueria in America serves grilled citrus- and spice-marinated chicken. For a standard dish, the range in quality is dramatic. Sometimes you luck out with chicken that is juicy and full of flavor from the marinade of citrus juices, onions, garlic, oregano, and spices like cinnamon, cumin, and cloves. More often, though, the chicken is as dry, leathery, bland, and lifeless as it is at the taco joint around the corner from my house (where it's served with a side of ear-splitting Mexican karaoke). To give my ears some relief and my tastebuds something to celebrate, I decided that I needed to come up with a great version to grill at home.

Recipes often call for marinating chicken halves in a combination of orange and lime juices (to substitute for the juice of sour oranges, the fruit that's authentic to the dish but hard to come by), along with the aromatics, spices, and herbs. Using chicken parts, which are easier to find than halves, I tried these recipes, but none delivered bold flavors, even after I tinkered with the seasonings, the ratio of juice, the marinating times, and the techniques, such as toasting the garlic or charring the onion.

Since the juices did little on their own, I offered them a helping hand: grated zest. The zest is, after all, home to the oils that give citrus fruits much of their fragrance and flavor. A teaspoon of grated lime zest with a tablespoon of orange zest worked so well that I did away with the orange juice entirely. Into the food processor went the onion, garlic, lime juice, and orange and lime zest, along with the spices. I added just enough olive oil to make a paste that could cling to the chicken. Grilled after an hour's rest in the pungent paste, this chicken had the best flavor yet.

But I still needed a grilling technique that would fix the chewy, leathery texture. With a gas grill, cooking the pieces over medium-low heat was just the ticket. But a medium-low charcoal fire was dicey: If the fire were a little too hot, flare-ups burned the chicken. If the fire were a little too cool, the fat didn't render properly by the time the meat was cooked. The solution for cooking over charcoal was

This succulent grilled chicken is known in Mexico as pollo asado al carbon.

using indirect heat—that is, positioning the meat away from (and not directly over) the fire. The most foolproof way to set this up is to place a disposable aluminum pan in the center of the bottom grill grate, then pour half the lit charcoal on either side. Grilling the pieces with indirect heat with the skin side up allowed the paste to cook gently until the end, when I flipped the chicken and moved it over the fire for a few minutes of direct heat, crisping the skin and giving the paste a substantial char (on a gas grill, just turn up the heat to sear the pieces at the end of cooking). Finally, no more flare-ups, and I got the succulent meat, crisp skin, and nicely caramelized seasonings I'd been aiming for. Now I can have citrus chicken whenever I want—and I get to choose the soundtrack.

TEST KITCHEN TIP
Sour Orange Substitute

THE ORIGINAL
Bright, tart sour oranges can be hard to find.

THE FACSIMILE
Orange zest, lime zest, and lime juice mimic the sour orange flavor.

CITRUS-AND-SPICE GRILLED CHICKEN Serves 4 to 6

- 1 onion, chopped coarse
- 1 teaspoon grated lime zest plus ¼ cup juice (2 limes)
- 6 garlic cloves
- 2 tablespoons olive oil
- 1 tablespoon grated orange zest (2 oranges)
- 2 teaspoons dried oregano
- 1½ teaspoons salt
- ½ teaspoon pepper
- ½ teaspoon ground cinnamon
- ½ teaspoon ground cumin
- ⅛ teaspoon ground cloves
- 3 pounds bone-in chicken pieces, trimmed (breasts halved crosswise)
- 1 (13 by 9-inch) disposable aluminum roasting pan (for charcoal grill only)

1. Process onion, lime juice, garlic, oil, orange zest, oregano, salt, lime zest, pepper, lime juice, cinnamon, cumin, and cloves in food processor until smooth, about 30 seconds; transfer to zipper-lock bag. Pat chicken dry with paper towels and add to bag, turning to coat. Refrigerate for 1 to 24 hours, turning occasionally.

2A. For a charcoal grill: Open bottom vent completely and place pan in center of grill. Light large chimney starter filled with charcoal briquettes (6 quarts). When top coals are partially covered with ash, pour into 2 even piles on either side of pan. Set cooking grate in place, cover, and open lid vent completely. Heat grill until hot, about 5 minutes.

2B. For a gas grill: Turn all burners to high, cover, and heat grill until hot, about 15 minutes. Turn all burners to medium-low. (Adjust burners as needed to maintain grill temperature around 350 degrees.)

3. Clean and oil cooking grate. Place chicken skin side up on grill (in center of grill if using charcoal). Cover and cook until bottom is browned and chicken registers 155 degrees, about 25 minutes.

4. Flip chicken skin side down. If using charcoal, slide chicken to hot part of grill. If using gas, turn all burners to high. Cook until well browned and breasts register 160 degrees and thighs/drumsticks register 175 degrees, 5 to 10 minutes. Transfer chicken to platter, tent loosely with aluminum foil, and let rest for 5 to 10 minutes. Serve.

Chiles Rellenos Casserole

Too often, this Tex-Mex casserole is a gloppy mess. We wanted to replicate the roasted chile flavor, hearty filling, and crisp fried shell of the original—without all the work. BY KELLY PRICE

AH, CHILES RELLENOS: roasted poblano (or Anaheim) peppers stuffed with cheese and often meat, and then deep-fried in a light batter to a delicate crunch. The mild heat of the chiles, the heft of the filling, and the crispness of the coating make them crunchy, cheesy, spicy flavor bombs.

But between roasting, preparing the filling, stuffing, and frying, making chiles rellenos is truly a labor of love. Enter the chiles rellenos casserole, through which the cook can (hopefully) achieve the payoff of traditional chiles rellenos without the work. Unfortunately, the recipes that I tried were either too eggy or more like dips than casseroles. Most recipes included convenience products, like condensed milk and canned peppers. I insisted that my casserole mirror the original dish, with a crisp crust, flavorful peppers, and a substantial filling.

Step one: Use fresh chiles instead of the drab canned variety. Step two: Let my tasters decide whether to use poblano or Anaheim chiles. Working with a basic filling of 2 pounds of ground beef and 2 cups of shredded Monterey Jack cheese, I made a batch using each chile. My tasters preferred the smokier poblanos. To emulate the traditional roasting, I broiled the peppers and then carefully peeled them. These chiles were terrific, but took too long. Since I'd need to use a skillet to brown the beef anyway, I tried sautéing the chopped peppers until nicely browned. Baked into separate casseroles, the roasted and sautéed peppers were indistinguishable.

We usually use 85 percent lean ground beef because it has the most flavor, but in this case it made the casserole wet and greasy. Switching to 90 percent lean ground beef and draining it after sautéing solved that problem. For flavor, I settled on the classic Tex-Mex mix of garlic, cumin, oregano, and cayenne. A can of spicy Ro-Tel tomatoes contributed acidic punch.

A standard chiles rellenos batter is just water and flour lightened with whipped egg whites. That's fine for deep-frying, but not for a baked casserole. A few tests showed that I could get color by replacing the water with skim milk. The sugars in the milk encouraged the topping to brown (without weighing it down). For flavor, I sprinkled extra cheese over the casserole several minutes before taking it out of the oven. Perfect.

CHILES RELLENOS CASSEROLE
Serves 6 to 8

If you can't find Ro-Tel tomatoes, use 1 cup of drained diced tomatoes combined with 1 finely chopped, stemmed, and seeded jalapeño.

- 1 tablespoon vegetable oil
- 1 onion, chopped fine
- 2 pounds 90 percent lean ground beef
- 4 poblano (or 6 Anaheim) chiles, stemmed, seeded, and chopped
- 2 garlic cloves, minced
- 2 teaspoons ground cumin
- 1¼ teaspoons salt
- 1 teaspoon dried oregano
- ¾ teaspoon pepper
- ¼ teaspoon cayenne pepper
- 1 (10-ounce) can Ro-Tel tomatoes, drained
- 10 ounces Monterey Jack cheese, shredded (2½ cups)
- ½ cup all-purpose flour
- ¾ cup skim milk
- 2 large egg whites

The contrast between the light, crisp, cheesy topping and the hearty filling is part of the appeal.

1. Adjust oven rack to upper-middle position and heat oven to 450 degrees. Heat oil in 12-inch nonstick skillet over medium heat until shimmering. Add onion and cook until softened, about 5 minutes. Stir in beef, breaking up meat into small pieces, and cook until no longer pink, 8 to 10 minutes. Using slotted spoon, transfer beef mixture to paper towel–lined plate. Pour off all but 2 tablespoons fat from skillet.

2. Add poblanos and cook over medium-high heat until browned, 8 to 10 minutes. Stir in beef mixture, garlic, cumin, ¾ teaspoon salt, oregano, ½ teaspoon pepper, and cayenne and cook until fragrant, about 30 seconds. Add tomatoes and cook until beef mixture is dry, about 1 minute. Off heat, stir in 2 cups Monterey Jack.

Scrape mixture into 13 by 9-inch baking dish, pressing into even layer.

3. Combine flour, remaining ½ teaspoon salt, and remaining ¼ teaspoon pepper in bowl. Slowly whisk milk into flour mixture until smooth; set aside. Using stand mixer fitted with whisk, whip egg whites on medium-low speed until foamy, about 1 minute. Increase speed to medium-high and whip until stiff peaks form, about 3 minutes. Whisk one-third whipped egg whites into batter, then gently fold in remaining whites, 1 scoop at a time, until combined.

4. Pour batter over beef mixture. Bake until topping is light golden and puffed, about 15 minutes. Sprinkle with remaining ½ cup cheese and bake until golden brown, about 10 minutes. Let cool on wire rack for 10 minutes. Serve.

A Restaurant Classic Becomes a Casserole
There are a lot of things to love about traditional chiles rellenos, but the work required to make them is not among them. We duplicated their appeal in an easier, faster casserole.

ROASTED PEPPER
Roasting and peeling whole chiles is a pain. We got a similar deep, sweet flavor by simply sautéing chopped poblanos.

CRISP SHELL
We skip battering and deep-frying for a light, crisp topping made with flour, milk, egg whites, and cheese.

SPICY SAUCE
Instead of serving our casserole with spicy tomato sauce, we added spicy tomatoes to the meaty filling.

Getting to Know Sweet Peppers

The spectrum of peppers is vast, including everything from bell peppers with no heat to "ghost peppers" that are so incendiary, it's a challenge to handle them safely. Here is a selection of peppers, a New World discovery, incidentally, in the "sweet" category. They are mostly mild with just the occasional trace of heat.

Green Bell Pepper
CALLOW FELLOW

All peppers, whether sweet or hot, start out green on the vine; green bell peppers are harvested before they fully ripen. If a recipe asks for green peppers, it almost certainly means green bell peppers. The easiest way to prepare any bell pepper is to lop off the top and bottom, then cut through the flesh to open the pepper flat on the cutting board; from there simply trim off the white ribs, discard the seeds, and cut the pepper as desired.

Red Bell Pepper
AMERICA'S SWEETHEART

Let a green bell pepper ripen (and sweeten) and you'll have a red bell pepper. In the test kitchen we enjoy them roasted, grilled, or charred over the open flame of a gas burner, which concentrates the sugars and makes them sweet. Homemade roasted red peppers (char thoroughly over a flame, steam in a paper bag for 10 minutes, and then peel) will keep for weeks if covered in olive oil and refrigerated.

Orange/Yellow Bell Pepper
SONS OF GREEN

These varieties start out as green bell peppers, but they've been bred to ripen into a rainbow of colors. Orange and yellow peppers taste like red bell peppers (and can be substituted for them in most recipes), but they are slightly less sweet and more expensive. Most cooks use them as much for their color as for their flavor. They maintain their bright hues through cooking.

Anaheim
SEMI-HOT STUFF

A Mexican farmer first planted these very mild chiles in Anaheim, California, in the early 1900s—hence the name—though the pepper is thought to have originated in New Mexico. (Red Anaheims are called chile Colorado.) Today, they are common in supermarkets nationwide. Anaheims taste like a milder version of the hot poblano pepper; use them anywhere you'd use poblanos: chiles rellenos, salsa, or enchiladas. They're also delicious in stir-fries.

Cubanelle
ITALIAN WORKHORSE

Sweet, yet mildly pungent, Cubanelles are a mainstay of Italian cooking; they're often called "Italian frying peppers." Early explorers of the Caribbean brought them back to Italy, where cooks eventually took to frying, stuffing, and pickling them. Cubanelles are thin-walled and usually sold when they're chartreuse. As they mature, orange and red streaks may appear on their skin. You might see them mislabelled as banana peppers—the two look similar, though Cubanelles tend to be less tapered.

Shishito
BAR SNACK

You can identify shishitos, which come from Japan, by their wrinkled, polished, green skin. Our tasters described them as "earthy," "musky," and slightly "tangy." Japanese often skewer and grill these peppers (as bar food) or dip them in tempura batter and fry them. We also like them tossed in a stir-fry. Their heat can surprise you—most are mild, but about one in 10 has a kick.

Banana Pepper
NOT AFRAID TO PLAY SECOND

There is no doubt about how this yellow pepper got its name—just look at the picture. (It is also sometimes called a yellow wax pepper). "Fruity with a gentle heat," the banana pepper plays well in salsas and salads or stuffed and roasted. Be careful: Banana peppers look almost identical to Hungarian wax peppers, which can be quite hot.

Juanita
PICKLED PEPPER

Did Peter Piper pick a peck of these? While fresh ones can be found in some specialty and farmers' markets, juanita peppers—which were discovered growing wild in South Africa in 1993—are most often seen in the United States pickled and sold under the Peppadew brand. We found that fresh juanitas tasted "fruity with a little kick." Fill these bite-size peppers (either fresh or pickled) with cream cheese for an easy appetizer.

Pimento
CHEESE CHUM

Ever wonder about that red stuffing in your green olive? It comes from this sweet, meaty pepper, which is usually sold jarred and pickled. Pimento peppers (also spelled "pimiento") are a key ingredient—and the namesake—of pimento cheese, the beloved Southern spread eaten with crackers or squishy white bread. There are many varieties of both pimento peppers and chiles. The latter have mild heat.

GREEK BEEF KEBABS

**PAN-ROASTED CHICKEN
WITH CHEESY-HERB MASHED POTATOES**

THAI SHRIMP SALAD SANDWICHES

SPAGHETTI WITH SUMMER VEGETABLE SAUCE

PAN-ROASTED CHICKEN WITH CHEESY-HERB MASHED POTATOES Serves 4

WHY THIS RECIPE WORKS: The microwave greatly reduces the cooking time for mashed potatoes.

- 2 pounds small red potatoes, scrubbed and cut into 1-inch pieces
- 1¼ cups low-sodium chicken broth
- 1 (5-ounce) package Boursin cheese
- ¼ cup minced fresh chives
- 4 (12-ounce) bone-in split chicken breasts, trimmed and halved crosswise
  Salt and pepper
- 1 tablespoon vegetable oil
- 1 shallot, minced
- ¼ cup dry white wine

1. Microwave potatoes and ½ cup broth in large covered bowl until potatoes are tender, 10 to 12 minutes. Add ⅓ cup Boursin and 2 tablespoons chives and, using potato masher, mash mixture. Meanwhile, pat chicken dry with paper towels and season with salt and pepper. Heat oil in 12-inch skillet over medium-high heat until just smoking. Cook chicken, skin side down, until well browned, 5 to 10 minutes. Reduce heat to medium, cover, and cook until meat registers 160 degrees, 12 to 15 minutes. Transfer chicken to platter and tent loosely with foil.

2. Pour off all but 1 tablespoon fat from skillet. Add shallot and cook until softened, about 1 minute. Add remaining ¾ cup broth, wine, and any accumulated chicken juices and simmer until slightly thickened, about 3 minutes. Off heat, whisk in remaining 2 tablespoons Boursin and remaining 2 tablespoons chives. Season with salt and pepper to taste. Pour sauce over chicken and serve with potatoes.

TEST KITCHEN NOTE: For easy prep, buy 2-inch red potatoes.

GREEK BEEF KEBABS Serves 4 to 6

WHY THIS RECIPE WORKS: A potent vinaigrette including lemon, garlic, and oregano seasons each component of this dish separately.

- 2 tablespoons lemon juice
- 3 garlic cloves, minced
  Salt and pepper
- ½ teaspoon dried oregano
- 6 tablespoons olive oil
- 8 ounces block feta cheese, sliced ½ inch thick
- 6 (10-inch) pita breads
- 1 (1½-pound) flank steak, trimmed, halved lengthwise, and sliced ¼ inch thick
- 2 ounces baby arugula (2 cups)
- ½ cup pitted kalamata olives, halved

1. Combine lemon juice, garlic, ¾ teaspoon salt, ½ teaspoon pepper, and oregano in bowl. Slowly whisk in oil until thoroughly incorporated. Brush feta slices and pita with 2 tablespoons vinaigrette.

2. Toss steak with 5 tablespoons vinaigrette. Thread steak onto six 12-inch skewers. Grill skewers over hot fire until lightly charred, 1 to 2 minutes per side. Transfer steak to platter and tent loosely with foil.

3. Grill feta and pita over hot fire until lightly charred, about 1 minute per side. Transfer to platter with steak. Toss arugula and olives with remaining 1 tablespoon vinaigrette. Season with salt and pepper to taste. Serve greens with steak, feta, and pita.

TEST KITCHEN NOTE: The test kitchen recommends Norpro's 12-inch Stainless Steel Skewers.

SPAGHETTI WITH SUMMER VEGETABLE SAUCE Serves 4

WHY THIS RECIPE WORKS: Store-bought pesto gives this light summer pasta extra oomph.

- 3 tablespoons unsalted butter
- 1 onion, chopped
- 1 large summer squash, halved lengthwise and sliced thin
- 1 large zucchini, halved lengthwise and sliced thin
- 2 garlic cloves, minced
- 12 ounces cherry tomatoes, halved
- ½ cup dry white wine
  Salt and pepper
- 1 pound spaghetti
- 6 tablespoons basil pesto

1. Bring 4 quarts water to boil in large pot. Melt butter in 12-inch skillet over medium-high heat. Add onion and cook until softened, about 5 minutes. Stir in squash and zucchini and cook until softened, 3 to 5 minutes. Add garlic and cook until fragrant, about 30 seconds. Stir in tomatoes, wine, ¾ teaspoon salt, and ½ teaspoon pepper and cook until liquid is reduced by half, about 2 minutes. Season with salt and pepper to taste; cover and keep warm.

2. Meanwhile, add pasta and 1 tablespoon salt to boiling water and cook, stirring often, until al dente. Reserve ½ cup cooking water, then drain pasta and return it to pot. Toss vegetable mixture and pesto with pasta, adding reserved pasta water as needed. Serve.

TEST KITCHEN NOTE: Serve with grated Parmesan cheese.

THAI SHRIMP SALAD SANDWICHES Serves 4

WHY THIS RECIPE WORKS: Sweet shrimp get dressed in a bright, lively mayonnaise-based dressing.

- 1½ pounds extra-large (21 to 25 per pound) shrimp, peeled, deveined, and tails removed
- 1 tablespoon salt
- 6 tablespoons mayonnaise
- 1 carrot, peeled and shredded
- 3 scallions, sliced thin
- 1 tablespoon minced fresh mint
- 1 tablespoon soy sauce
- 1 tablespoon lime juice
- 2 teaspoons sriracha sauce
- 4 (6-inch) sub rolls, split partially open lengthwise

1. Fill large bowl with ice water. Bring 4 quarts water to boil in large pot. Add shrimp and salt and simmer until cooked through, about 2 minutes. Drain shrimp, then transfer to ice bath. Once cool, drain again, and pat dry with paper towels. Cut shrimp into ½-inch pieces.

2. Combine mayonnaise, carrot, scallions, mint, soy sauce, lime juice, and sriracha in large bowl. Stir in shrimp. Divide shrimp mixture among rolls. Serve.

TEST KITCHEN NOTE: Sriracha is a hot sauce found in the Asian section of most markets. If you can't find it, substitute an equal amount of Frank's RedHot. This dressing also works well with cooked-and-diced chicken breast.

BUFFALO CHICKEN QUESADILLAS

COWBOY STEAKS

GRILLED CHICKEN CAPRESE

SKILLET PORK CHOPS AND RICE

COWBOY STEAKS Serves 4

WHY THIS RECIPE WORKS: These hearty steaks take less than 10 minutes to cook, but our rub gives them the complex flavor profile of slow-smoked barbecue.

- ¼ cup wood chips, soaked in water for 15 minutes and drained
- 2 tablespoons paprika
- 1 tablespoon packed light brown sugar
- 1 tablespoon chili powder
- 1 teaspoon garlic powder
- ¾ teaspoon salt
- ½ teaspoon pepper
- ¼ teaspoon cayenne pepper
- 4 (8-ounce) boneless strip steaks, 1 to 1½ inches thick

1. Using sheet of heavy-duty aluminum foil, wrap soaked chips into foil packet and cut several vent holes in top. Combine paprika, sugar, chili powder, garlic powder, salt, pepper, and cayenne in bowl.

2. Pat steaks dry with paper towels and rub with spice mixture. Place wood chip packet on coals (or over primary burner) and cover until chips begin to smoke. Grill steaks over hot fire until well browned and meat registers 120 to 125 degrees (for medium-rare), about 4 minutes per side. Transfer to platter, tent loosely with foil, and let rest for 5 to 10 minutes. Serve.

TEST KITCHEN NOTE: Use hickory wood chips for this recipe.

BUFFALO CHICKEN QUESADILLAS Serves 4

WHY THIS RECIPE WORKS: Poaching strips of chicken in a butter-laced hot sauce opens a quick path to potent flavor.

- 4 ounces blue cheese, crumbled (1 cup)
- 1 celery rib, sliced thin
- ¼ cup sour cream
- 2 scallions, sliced thin
- 3 tablespoons unsalted butter
- 1½ pounds boneless, skinless chicken breasts, trimmed and cut into 1-inch-thick strips
- ⅓ cup hot sauce
- 4 (10-inch) flour tortillas
- 1 tablespoon vegetable oil

1. Combine blue cheese, celery, sour cream, and scallions in bowl. Melt butter in 12-inch nonstick skillet over medium heat. Add chicken and hot sauce and simmer until chicken is cooked through, 6 to 8 minutes. Transfer chicken mixture to bowl. Using 2 forks, shred chicken into bite-size pieces. Wipe out skillet.

2. Working one at a time, spread one-quarter of blue cheese mixture over half of tortilla, leaving ½-inch border around edges. Top with one-quarter of chicken mixture. Fold tortilla over filling, pressing firmly to seal.

3. Heat 1½ teaspoons oil in now-empty skillet over medium-high heat until shimmering. Cook 2 quesadillas until golden brown and crisp, 1 to 2 minutes per side. Transfer to cutting board. Repeat with remaining 1½ teaspoons oil and remaining 2 quesadillas. Cut into wedges. Serve.

TEST KITCHEN NOTE: The test kitchen prefers the mild burn of Frank's RedHot hot sauce. If you are using a spicier brand (like Tabasco), use less and supplement it with water to equal ⅓ cup.

SKILLET PORK CHOPS AND RICE Serves 4

WHY THIS RECIPE WORKS: We give the rice a head start in the microwave to ensure that it's ready at the same time as the pork chops.

- 4 tablespoons unsalted butter, softened
- 2 tablespoons minced fresh parsley
- 2¼ cups low-sodium chicken broth
- 1 cup long-grain white rice
- 4 (6- to 8-ounce) boneless pork chops, ¾ to 1 inch thick, trimmed Salt and pepper
- 1 onion, chopped fine
- 1 garlic clove, minced
- ½ teaspoon dried thyme

1. Combine 2 tablespoons butter and parsley in bowl; reserve. Microwave 1 cup broth and rice in covered large bowl until liquid is absorbed, 6 to 8 minutes.

2. Meanwhile, pat pork chops dry with paper towels and season with salt and pepper. Melt 1 tablespoon butter in 12-inch skillet over medium-high heat. Brown chops, 3 to 4 minutes per side. Transfer to plate and tent loosely with foil. Melt remaining 1 tablespoon butter in now-empty skillet over medium-high heat. Cook onion until browned, 6 to 8 minutes. Add garlic and thyme and cook until fragrant, about 30 seconds.

3. Stir in parcooked rice and remaining 1¼ cups broth and bring to boil. Return pork chops and any accumulated juices to skillet and cook, covered, over medium-low heat until pork registers 145 degrees and rice is tender, 12 to 15 minutes. Serve pork with reserved parsley butter.

TEST KITCHEN NOTE: To keep these quick-cooking chops from curling, cut two slits about 2 inches apart through the fat around the outside of each chop.

GRILLED CHICKEN CAPRESE Serves 4

WHY THIS RECIPE WORKS: We introduce heft to the classic combination of tomato and mozzarella by adding grilled chicken cutlets, and we boost flavor by grilling the tomatoes.

- 2 tablespoons chopped fresh basil
- 1 tablespoon red wine vinegar
- 2 garlic cloves, minced Salt and pepper
- 3 tablespoons olive oil
- 6 ounces fresh mozzarella, cut into ¼-inch slices, halved, and patted dry
- 1½ pounds chicken cutlets, trimmed
- 2 tomatoes, cored and cut into ½-inch slices

1. Combine basil, vinegar, garlic, ½ teaspoon salt, and ¼ teaspoon pepper in bowl. Slowly whisk in oil until thoroughly incorporated. Transfer 2 tablespoons vinaigrette to bowl and toss with mozzarella; reserve remaining vinaigrette.

2. Pat chicken dry with paper towels and season with salt and pepper. Grill chicken and tomatoes over hot fire until chicken is well browned and tomatoes are lightly charred, about 2 minutes per side. Transfer chicken to platter. Top with tomato slices and drizzle with reserved vinaigrette. Cover with even layer of mozzarella and tent loosely with foil. Let rest for 5 to 10 minutes. Serve.

TEST KITCHEN NOTE: Purchase ripe but still firm tomatoes so they will hold their shape when grilled.

Texas-Style Blueberry Cobbler

A cobbler made with a thick, pancake-like batter? *Really?*

BY REBECCAH MARSTERS

IN MOST OF America, cobbler means lots of sweet, jammy fruit under a biscuit topping. But at many a barbecue joint in the Hill Country region of central Texas, the same word applies to a very different dessert, one with a moist, tender interior and a crisp, craggy top. As the cobbler bakes, the fruit (which starts out on top) sinks and forms juicy pockets throughout. Whatever you call it, it tastes delicious.

Working my way through a stack of Texas community cookbooks, I found a version of the homey recipe in almost every one. They went under several different names, but the techniques and ingredients were nearly identical. "Don't Stir Cobbler" seemed particularly apt, since you melt lots of butter in a baking dish; pour a simple batter of milk, flour, baking powder, and sugar over it; scatter on fruit; and then simply bake. In Texas, peaches are standard cobbler fare, but summer in New England means blueberries, so I made a handful of the recipes that I'd found, substituting berries for the sliced peaches. It was very easy, but I did uncover a few problems: The cobblers were thin and a little bland, and the tops were underbaked. I rolled up my sleeves and got to work.

All the versions that I'd tested were skimpy, barely reaching halfway up the sides of 13 by 9-inch baking dishes. So my first alteration was to increase all the ingredients by 50 percent for a more ample amount. The adjustment meant that I was melting 12 tablespoons of butter in the baking dish, so it was no surprise when tasters complained that the bottom was greasy. I found I could cut the grease if I divided the butter between the pan and the batter. I settled on half a stick of butter melted in the dish and twice that amount stirred into the batter. A bonus: Now the cobbler's crisp brown edges were so good that my tasters fought over them.

To turn the berries into a more cohesive filling, I realized that I needed to get their juices flowing before the fruit went into the oven. I grabbed a potato masher and went to work. Adding a little sugar helped further break down the berries, and for a bright note, I stirred in grated lemon zest. But in the baked cobbler, the zest was barely discernible. Processing the lemon zest with the sugar in the food processor released the zest's flavorful oils.

To get a crisp, nicely browned top, I knew what I had to do: I sprinkled the cobbler with sugar to help it caramelize. It occurred to me that I had another chance to reinforce the lemon flavor. I mashed a portion of the lemon-sugar mixture with the berries, as before, but set some aside to sprinkle over the unbaked assembled cobbler.

A couple of hours later, I was contentedly eating a cobbler that was nothing like the sort I'd grown up with. No complaints there.

TEXAS-STYLE BLUEBERRY COBBLER
Serves 8 to 10

Keep a close eye on the butter as it melts in the oven so that it doesn't scorch. Place the hot baking dish with butter on a wire rack after removing it from the oven. Avoid untreated aluminum pans here. If using frozen blueberries, thaw them first.

- 4 tablespoons unsalted butter cut into 4 pieces, and 8 tablespoons melted and cooled
- 1½ cups (10½ ounces) sugar
- 1½ teaspoons grated lemon zest
- 15 ounces (3 cups) blueberries
- 1½ cups (7½ ounces) all-purpose flour
- 2½ teaspoons baking powder
- ¾ teaspoon salt
- 1½ cups milk

1. Adjust oven rack to upper-middle position and heat oven to 350 degrees. Place 4 tablespoons cut-up butter in 13 by 9-inch baking dish and transfer to oven. Heat until butter is melted, 8 to 10 minutes.

2. Meanwhile, pulse ¼ cup sugar and lemon zest in food processor until combined, about 5 pulses; set aside. Using potato masher, mash blueberries and 1 tablespoon lemon sugar together in bowl until berries are coarsely mashed.

3. Combine flour, remaining 1¼ cups sugar, baking powder, and salt in large bowl. Whisk in milk and 8 tablespoons melted, cooled butter until smooth. Remove baking dish from oven, transfer to wire rack, and pour batter into prepared pan.

4. Dollop mashed blueberry mixture evenly over batter, sprinkle with remaining lemon sugar, and bake until golden brown and edges are crisp, 45 to 50 minutes, rotating pan halfway through baking. Let cobbler cool on wire rack for 30 minutes. Serve warm.

The crispy brown edges push this cobbler to another level.

STEP BY STEP **A Different Kind of Cobbler**

Many of us know cobbler as a jammy fruit base with a baked biscuit topping. In the Lone Star State, they start with the batter on the bottom and the fruit on top.

MELT BUTTER
First, melt butter right in the baking pan. It gives the finished cobbler rich, crisp edges.

SPREAD BATTER
Next, pour the batter into the baking pan over the melted butter.

DOLLOP FRUIT
Finally, scatter on the mashed berries. In the oven, the batter rises over the berries.

Barbecued Country-Style Ribs

They're inexpensive and flavorful, but these ribs are hard to cook evenly.
We'd have to either speed up the dark meat or slow down the white. BY CAROLYNN PURPURA

COUNTRY-STYLE PORK RIBS are a misnomer: They aren't ribs. A more accurate (but probably less marketable) name would be hybrid loin/shoulder pork chops. This affordable cut contains both tender loin (light) and flavorful shoulder (dark) meat, meaning that each rib represents the best of both worlds. These ribs sound grand for the grill, I thought. I set out to infuse country-style ribs with smoky, tangy barbecue flavor.

Recipes for barbecued country-style ribs don't agree on much. For starters, some call for boneless ribs; some call for bone-in. Bone-in ribs were harder to find, and when I did find them, often many in the package were actually boneless. To keep things more consistent, I went with boneless ribs. Next, grilling methods ranged from searing them over a hot fire for eight minutes, to smoking them with indirect heat for two hours, to everything in between—and I tried them all. I quickly realized that country-style ribs are finicky. Long cooking times were great for the dark meat, but they made the light meat dry and chalky. Short cooking times meant tender light meat, but this left the dark meat chewy. My big challenge, then, would be to somehow manipulate the ribs so that both white and dark meat were done at the same time.

Since I was after smoky barbecue flavor, I decided to start with a low-and-slow method (which was, again, great for the dark meat) and figure out how to fix the white meat. My first thought was to try to simultaneously insulate the white meat and add smoky flavor by wrapping each rib in bacon. Fabulous idea, right? Although the flavor was good and the light meat was slightly less dry than before, it was still a long way from moist. For once, bacon wasn't the solution. Brining the ribs (soaking them in a saltwater solution) helped them stay somewhat juicier but still not sufficiently so. After attempting dozens of batches of ribs, I came to the conclusion that I couldn't keep the white meat moist through long cooking. I'd have to do the opposite: find a way to get the dark meat to become tender on the white meat's timetable.

Obviously, thinner cuts cook more quickly than thicker cuts do, so I tried pounding the boneless ribs into ¼-inch-thick cutlets before brining. When the ribs were out of the brine, I

We pound and brine these country-style ribs and then cook them in less than 15 minutes.

dried them off and seasoned them with a simple barbecue dry rub of brown sugar, chili powder, paprika, onion powder, dry mustard, and pepper and then grilled the ribs (using smoke and indirect heat) until cooked but still tender, about 15 minutes. The brining and the shorter cooking time meant that the white meat was juicy; the pounding meant that the dark meat finally cooked to tenderness at the same rate as the white meat. Disappointingly, the finished product looked more like cutlets than like ribs. But pounding a little less, to about ¾ inch, fixed that.

From here, the recipe came together easily. To get a nice saucy, caramelized lacquer on the meat, I mixed half of

the dry rub spices with ketchup and vinegar for an easy barbecue sauce that I could sear onto the ribs (over high heat) at the end of cooking. I had been using 1 cup of soaked wood chips to impart smoke flavor, but my tasters had complained through every test that the ribs tasted too smoky (even with the short cooking time). I reduced the chips to ½ cup—still too smoky. One-quarter cup of wood chips was plenty for this quick smoke.

Country-style ribs may be oddly and inaccurately named, and my method may not technically be "barbecue," but who's quibbling? This recipe is a terrific weeknight alternative to slow-smoked ribs.

BARBECUED COUNTRY-STYLE RIBS
Serves 4 to 6

For easier pounding, cut any ribs that are longer than 5 inches in half crosswise.

- 1 tablespoon salt
- 2 pounds boneless country-style pork ribs, trimmed
- ¾ cup packed dark brown sugar
- 2 tablespoons chili powder
- 2 tablespoons paprika
- 1 tablespoon dry mustard
- 1 tablespoon onion powder
- ¾ teaspoon pepper
- ¼ teaspoon cayenne pepper
- 6 tablespoons ketchup
- 1 tablespoon cider vinegar
- ¼ cup wood chips, soaked in water for 15 minutes and drained

1. Dissolve salt in 2 cups cold water in large container. Place ribs, cut side down, between 2 sheets of plastic wrap and pound to ¾ inch thickness. Submerge pork in brine, cover, and refrigerate for 30 minutes to 1 hour.

2. Combine sugar, chili powder, paprika, dry mustard, onion powder, pepper, and cayenne in shallow dish. Transfer half of mixture to bowl and stir in ketchup and vinegar; set aside.

SHOPPING **Country-Style Ribs**
Country-style ribs aren't ribs at all. They're well-marbled pork chops cut from the blade end of the loin. We bought dozens of these chops while testing this recipe and found that they were inconsistently shaped and sized. What's more, these "ribs" had widely varying proportions of light and dark meat. To help level the culinary playing field and ensure even cooking, we pounded each piece into an even ¾ inch thickness.

MISMATCHED MEAT
Each "rib" contains both light and dark meat.

Quick Collard Greens

Traditionally, collards cook for hours. We perfected a method that gets these greens on the table in less than 15 minutes. BY KELLY PRICE

3. Remove pork from brine and pat dry with paper towels. Dredge pork in remaining spice mixture and transfer to plate. Using large piece of heavy-duty aluminum foil, wrap soaked chips in foil packet and cut several vent holes in top.

4A. For a charcoal grill: Open bottom vent halfway. Light large chimney starter filled with charcoal briquettes (6 quarts). When top coals are partially covered with ash, pour evenly over half of grill. Place wood chip packet on coals. Set cooking grate in place, cover, and open lid vent halfway. Heat grill until hot and wood chips are smoking, about 5 minutes.

4B. For a gas grill: Place wood chip packet over primary burner. Turn all burners to high, cover, and heat grill until hot and wood chips are smoking, about 15 minutes. Leave primary burner on high and turn off other burner(s).

5. Clean and oil cooking grate. Place pork on cool part of grill, cover (positioning lid vent over meat if using charcoal), and cook until meat registers 125 degrees, 3 to 5 minutes. Brush pork with ketchup mixture and grill, brushed side down, over hot part of grill until lightly charred, 2 to 3 minutes. Brush second side of pork and grill until lightly charred and meat registers 145 degrees, 2 to 3 minutes. Transfer pork to platter, tent loosely with foil, and let rest for 5 to 10 minutes. Serve.

I'M A SOUTHERNER, and the collard greens that I know spend the better part of a day languishing in a hot bath with a ham bone until the bitterness is gone and the leaves are almost silken. But recently I've come across recipes for quick-cooked collard greens. Skeptical but curious, I wanted to see what these recipes had to offer.

Collard greens have tough stems. This isn't an issue in the recipes that I grew up with since the greens simmer long enough to tenderize a tractor tire. But quick-cooking recipes usually cut out and discard the stems before slicing the leaves into strips and sautéing them. A few recipes also instruct the cook to blanch the sliced leaves in boiling water first. The blanching proved key; otherwise, the leaves were bitter and chewy. But if I simply blanched, drained, and put the sliced leaves in a hot pan, they steamed into a soggy mess. I'd have to wring the water out first to get some browning.

I had been rolling the de-stemmed leaves into a cigar shape, slicing them into strips, and then boiling. It turned out it was simpler to blanch halved leaves. After five minutes of blanching, I drained the leaves, rinsed them with cold water to stop the cooking, and wrung them out. The blanched leaves were easy to roll into a log (especially inside a clean kitchen towel). I chopped this neat log into thin ribbons that were now dry and ready to sauté.

These collards were a big departure for my Southern relatives, but they loved them. Southerners will just have to file this recipe under "New South."

Get to know a whole new side of collards with this fast, fresh-tasting recipe.

QUICK COLLARD GREENS
Serves 4 to 6
If you use mustard or turnip greens instead of collards, reduce boiling time to 2 minutes.

	Salt and pepper
2½	pounds collard greens, stemmed and leaves halved lengthwise
3	tablespoons olive oil
2	garlic cloves, minced
¼	teaspoon red pepper flakes

1. Bring 4 quarts water to boil in large pot over medium-high heat. Add 1 tablespoon salt and collard greens, 1 handful at a time. Cook until tender, 4 to 5 minutes. Drain and rinse with cold water until greens are cool, about 1 minute. Press greens with rubber spatula to release excess liquid. Place greens on top of kitchen towel and compress into 10-inch log. Roll tightly, then remove from kitchen towel. Cut greens crosswise into ¼-inch slices.

2. Heat oil in 12-inch nonstick skillet over medium-high heat until just smoking. Scatter greens in skillet and cook, stirring frequently, until just beginning to brown, 3 to 4 minutes. Stir in garlic and pepper flakes and cook until greens are spotty brown, 1 to 2 minutes. Season with salt and pepper to taste. Serve.

MAKE AHEAD
Collards can be prepared through step 1 and refrigerated for up to 2 days. To finish, proceed with step 2.

TEST KITCHEN TECHNIQUE Collard Prep

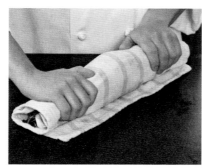

ROLL Using a clean kitchen towel, roll the greens into a tight log.

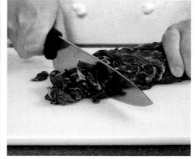

SLICE Cut the log into ¼-inch slices. The greens are dry and ready to sauté.

Fried Green Tomatoes, Y'all

For this delightful Southern classic, it's just dip, dredge, and fry. But dip in what? And dredge in what? And how do you get the coating to stay put? BY SARAH GABRIEL

FRIED GREEN TOMATOES are just that—slices of tart, unripe tomato coated in mellow, savory cornmeal (or flour, or both) and shallow-fried until crisp. But this prosaic description doesn't do them justice. If you've eaten them, you probably understand why novelists, movie directors, and many an ordinary Southerner wax lyrical (or at least nostalgic) about this homespun dish. Delicious as they are, though, fried green tomatoes still languish in relative obscurity north of the Mason-Dixon Line. I hoped to bring them into the (northern) sun.

Unfortunately, the first crop of recipes I tested—despite their bona fide Southern-cookbook roots—was disappointing. One called for dipping slices of tomato in a mixture of flour and cornmeal; with no wet ingredients to cement the coating, it was soggy, thin, and patchy. Other recipes more sensibly required dipping the slices in milk or buttermilk combined with egg before dredging, a method that yielded more substantial coatings, yes, but they were soggy or slid off—or both. These initial tests also revealed that green tomatoes dredged in flour alone were lackluster while those dredged in cornmeal alone were delicious but gritty. It became clear that a combination of the two would work best.

But before turning to the coating, I took a hard look at the frying medium, pitting bacon fat, which some Southern cooks swear by, against peanut oil, the test kitchen's usual choice for frying. Some tasters complained that the porky, smoky bacon fat overwhelmed the green tomatoes. Since using peanut oil meant I could skip the step of cooking bacon, I stuck with it and turned to finding the right cornmeal-to-flour ratio.

We all liked the flavor of 2 parts cornmeal to 1 part flour; with any less cornmeal, the flavor lacked backbone. Unfortunately, even with finely ground cornmeal, this ratio made the coating gritty. No problem. I dumped the cornmeal into the blender and hit start. Eventually, I found that by grinding just half of the cornmeal, I achieved the right balance of full cornmeal flavor and subtle grit.

But my perfected coating continued to slip off the tomato slices somewhere between frying pan and mouth. To determine the function of each adhesion ingredient (buttermilk, milk, egg),

Compensation for the long winter ahead? Come first frost, we'll fry up the unripe tomatoes.

I tested each separately, dipping and then dredging. The egg dip gave me a coating that stuck like white on rice. Too bad it was rubbery and tasted like overcooked eggs. The milk dip yielded a soggy coating that slipped off. The buttermilk didn't improve adhesion, but made for a coating so crunchy tasters gobbled up the sloughed-off bits. (Our science editor explained that the acid in the buttermilk sped the gelatinization—or absorption of moisture—of the starchy coating, making it especially brittle and crunchy when fried.) To get it to stick, I embarked on another series of ratio tests, eventually learning that one egg beaten with ⅔ cup of buttermilk produced a crunchy, not eggy coating that stayed put. Almost.

Part of what makes fried green

tomatoes a beloved Southern staple is the contrast between tart tomato and crunchy coating in every bite. "Almost" wouldn't cut it. The problem was that the green tomatoes released moisture while they fried. Despite my best efforts to make the coating stick, the moisture accumulated beneath the coating and loosened its grip. Just dry off the tomatoes, a practical colleague suggested. Good thinking. I pressed the slices between paper towels, dipped them in the egg-buttermilk mixture, and then dredged and fried them.

This time, the crunchy, sweet-tart tomatoes were so good, I actually found myself looking forward to the first frost with its bonanza of green (never-to-ripen) tomatoes.

FRIED GREEN TOMATOES
Serves 4

You'll need 4 to 5 green tomatoes. We recommend finely ground Quaker cornmeal for this recipe.

- 1½ **pounds green tomatoes, cored and sliced ¼ inch thick**
- ⅔ **cup cornmeal**
- ⅓ **cup all-purpose flour**
- 1½ **teaspoons salt**
- ½ **teaspoon pepper**
- ⅛ **teaspoon cayenne pepper**
- ⅔ **cup buttermilk**
- 1 **large egg**
- 2 **cups peanut or vegetable oil**

1. Place tomatoes on paper towel–lined rimmed baking sheet. Cover with more paper towels, let sit for 20 minutes, and pat dry. Meanwhile, process ⅓ cup cornmeal in blender until very finely ground, about 1 minute. Combine processed cornmeal, remaining ⅓ cup cornmeal, flour, salt, pepper, and cayenne in shallow dish. Whisk buttermilk and egg together in second shallow dish.

2. Working one at a time, dip tomato slices in buttermilk mixture, then dredge in cornmeal mixture, pressing firmly to adhere; transfer to clean baking sheet.

3. Heat oil in 12-inch skillet over medium-high heat until 350 degrees. Fry 4 tomato slices until golden brown, 2 to 3 minutes per side. Drain on wire rack set in baking sheet. Bring oil back to 350 degrees and repeat with remaining tomato slices. Serve.

KEY STEP **Dry Before You Fry**

To keep the tomatoes from weeping as they fry (which will loosen the coating), let them sit between paper towels for 20 minutes and then press dry.

Dilly Casserole Bread

Unusual ingredients give this homey loaf a chewy, airy crumb.
But did they also cause the big hole in its center? BY LYNN CLARK

FOR LEONA SCHNUELLE of Crab Orchard, Nebraska, the ninth time was the charm. After years of trying, she took home the $25,000 grand prize in the 1960 Pillsbury Bakeoff for her Dilly Casserole Bread, an easy yeast bread that requires no kneading. The ingredients, including onion and dill seed, are quickly mixed, and the dough rises twice before being baked in a round casserole dish. The loaf emerges large-crumbed, distinctly chewy, and amazingly moist. The very first loaf I baked rose to form a perfect golden-brown dome, and the fragrance of dill and onion filled the test kitchen—a winner. But as we nibbled on wedges a while later, we could barely taste the dill and onion. Also, a strange hole the size of a golf ball lurked in the middle of the loaf. I couldn't understand. This was a famous, prize-winning recipe. What had gone wrong?

I quickly homed in on the baking soda and cottage cheese, the two oddball ingredients in Dilly Bread. The baking soda, in tandem with the yeast, produces gas bubbles that create the bread's signature network of uneven holes. The cottage cheese keeps the bread moist and adds chew. Were they to blame?

To make Dilly Bread, you warm the cottage cheese with a little water. You add this to flour, egg, butter, the yeast and baking soda mix, and the seasonings to form sticky dough. Since the bread already uses yeast to rise, was the baking soda over-leavening it? I tried using less baking soda, none at all, and baking powder in its place. I experimented with yeast every which way. Some loaves came out dense. Others lost their mesh of small holes. The giant central hole mostly stayed put.

I turned to the other atypical ingredient. At the time the recipe for Dilly Bread was created, manufacturers made cottage cheese by allowing milk to sour and slowly thicken from naturally occurring bacteria. Today, they speed the process by adding acid to milk. Our science editor told me that the large, very strong curds this shortcut creates don't break down as easily as those smaller, weaker curds of yore did. So as the Dilly Bread dough heats, the large curds create channels that the gas bubbles can move through. Gases naturally migrate to the coolest spot, he said, in this case the center of the dough, where they were meeting and forming a large hole.

Skip the dried and dehydrated stuff: Fresh dill and real onion bring this recipe up to date.

For my next loaf, I used small-curd cottage cheese. Smaller curds equals smaller hole, right? Wrong. Next, I tried mashing the curds with a potato masher before adding the cheese to the dough. Later that afternoon, I nervously cracked open the cooled loaf. To my immense relief, the hole was gone.

It was time to freshen up the spices. True to its mid-century roots, the original recipe called for shelf-stable dried dill seed and dehydrated minced onion. I replaced them with minced fresh dill and grated onion, but the onion tasted harsh. Heating the onion in the microwave along with the cottage cheese softened its flavor. For a finishing touch, I mixed more fresh dill with butter, which I brushed on the loaf after it baked. This easy, homey loaf was back in the winner's circle.

TEST KITCHEN TIP
Mash the Cheese

Because of changes over the years in the manufacturing process of cottage cheese, the classic recipe for Dilly Bread repeatedly produced a loaf with a large hole in the center. Happily, the fix was simple: Mash the cheese before mixing it into the dough.

HOLE IN ONE
Don't let this happen to you.

DILLY CASSEROLE BREAD
Serves 8

You can use either small- or large-curd cottage cheese in this recipe. If you don't own a 1½-quart soufflé dish, use a loaf pan.

- 8   ounces (1 cup) cottage cheese
- ¼   cup water
- 2   tablespoons sugar
- 1   tablespoon plus 1 teaspoon unsalted butter, softened
- 1   tablespoon grated onion
- 1   large egg, room temperature
- 2¼   cups (11¼ ounces) all-purpose flour
- 2¼   teaspoons instant or rapid-rise yeast
- 2½   tablespoons minced fresh dill
- 1   teaspoon salt
- ¼   teaspoon baking soda

1. Adjust oven rack to lower-middle position and heat oven to 200 degrees. When oven reaches 200 degrees, turn it off. Grease large bowl and 1½-quart soufflé dish. Using potato masher, mash cottage cheese until no large lumps remain. Combine cottage cheese, water, sugar, 1 tablespoon butter, and onion in 2-cup liquid measuring cup. Microwave until mixture registers 110 degrees, about 30 seconds. Whisk in egg until combined.

2. Using stand mixer fitted with paddle, mix 1¼ cups flour, yeast, 2 tablespoons dill, salt, and baking soda on low speed until combined. Slowly add cottage cheese mixture and mix until dough just comes together, about 1 minute. Using rubber spatula, stir in remaining 1 cup flour until just combined.

3. Transfer dough to prepared bowl. Cover with plastic wrap and place in turned-off oven until dough has doubled in size, about 45 minutes. Stir dough to remove air bubbles and transfer to prepared soufflé dish. Cover loosely with plastic and let rest in turned-off oven until doubled in size, about 20 minutes.

4. Combine remaining ½ tablespoon dill and remaining 1 teaspoon butter in bowl. Remove dough from oven and discard plastic. Heat oven to 350 degrees. Bake loaf until deep golden brown, about 25 minutes. Brush bread with dill butter and let cool in dish on wire rack for 20 minutes. Remove bread from dish and let cool completely, about 2 hours. Serve.

The Best Grilled Chicken Wings

Fat and fire don't mix. We wanted pleasantly smoky wings—not sooty ones.

BY JEREMY SAUER

CHICKEN WINGS ARE my thing, but deep-frying them in the summertime is most definitely not. So I decided to try grilling them. I found plenty of recipes for grilled wings, each selling the idea that the fat and connective tissue render and drip away through the grill grate, leaving the skin crisp and lightly charred, the meat succulent and smoky.

But I've grilled enough skin-on chicken to foresee the problem with grilling wings: The fat drips away over a fire—and fat mixed with fire means flare-ups. The recipes I rounded up used three basic strategies to get around this problem, and I gave all three a go. The "firefighter" approach: Grill over high heat and hose down the flare-ups with a spray bottle of water. Well, the flare-ups were impossible to control and I ended up with burnt, sooty wings. The "par-cook" approach: Start the wings in the oven to render the fat and then finish them on a hot grill to crisp the skin. Although successful, this technique was a bother. And finally, the "low-and-slow" approach: Grill the wings using indirect heat and wait for them to cook to about 170 degrees. With this method, the fat easily rendered with no flare-ups. But the skin was more leathery than crisp, plus the wings took almost two hours to cook.

Determined to come up with a better strategy, I started with a riff on the low-and-slow approach. Instead of using indirect heat, I placed the wings directly over the low fire to accelerate the cooking. There were no flare-ups and the fat did render. So far, so good. But the fire was so weak that the chicken never developed any char, and the skin stuck to the grill grate like bubble gum to hot asphalt. I tested varying heat levels, ultimately finding that a medium-low fire was just hot enough to prevent stickups yet cool enough to avoid a conflagration as the fat rendered.

But the wings still lacked proper char. Turning up the heat was a non-starter—even a medium-hot fire brought back the flare-ups. Could I just leave the wings on the grill longer? A little extra time on the grill meant a marked improvement for the char, but it also left the wings overcooked—about 180 to 185 degrees, well above the 170 degrees most recipes suggest. Still, I was intent on getting feedback so I brought the "overcooked" wings to the tasting table.

As I guessed, tasters complained that the wings were dry, but that wasn't the end of the story. They also thought the meat was significantly more tender than previous batches cooked to 170 degrees. I was confused by these seemingly contradictory contentions—until I spoke with our science editor. Apparently, the tasters were experiencing two separate phenomena. First, as the internal temperature of a piece of meat rises, protein fibers within the meat constrict and force out juices. The higher the internal temperature, the more juices are expelled. The result, as noted by my tasters, was that the 180-degree wings were drier than those cooked to 170 degrees. But the second phenomenon dictated that an internal temperature of 180 degrees actually worked to my advantage.

You see, wings contain a large amount of collagen. Collagen is naturally chewy until it starts breaking down into gelatin, which happens most efficiently at temperatures above 170 degrees. So if wings are grilled to only 170 degrees, the collagen has barely had any time to denature and the result is chewy wings. At 180-plus degrees, much of the collagen has turned to gelatin. The result is more tender wings. How could I fix the dry meat yet keep the tenderness?

From past experience, I knew that brining (soaking meat in a saltwater solution) helps meat retain moisture even if it is overcooked. But most recipes call for brining for an hour, and I didn't want to wait that long. Cutting the wings into sections (called drumettes and flats in restaurants—some wings are sold already sectioned) and piercing the pieces all over with a fork allowed the brine to soak down to the bone in just 30 minutes. Now the wings cooked to 180 degrees were tender and juicy.

This approach had one downside, though: The moisture from the brine made the wings steam and stick to the grill again. A colleague suggested tossing the wings with a little cornstarch before grilling to discourage sticking. The thin layer of cornstarch worked like a charm—no more sticking. Whether tossed with salt and pepper or rubbed with a sophisticated spice blend, these grilled wings were good enough to make me forget the fryer forever. Or at least until winter rolls around.

Enjoy these tender, crispy wings as they are, or try one of our three flavor variations.

TEST KITCHEN TECHNIQUE Prepping Grilled Chicken Wings

PRICK Use a fork to puncture each wing all over. This lets the brine easily penetrate and gives the rendered fat an escape route.

BRINE A quick saltwater brine seasons the wings and keeps them juicy, even when cooked to the 180 degrees called for in this recipe.

DUST Right before grilling, dust the wings with a mixture of cornstarch (to prevent sticking) and black pepper.

GRILLED CHICKEN WINGS

Makes 2 dozen wings

If you buy whole wings, cut them into 2 pieces before brining. Don't brine the wings for more than 30 minutes or they'll be too salty.

- ½ cup salt
- 2 pounds chicken wings, wingtips discarded
- 1½ teaspoons cornstarch
- 1 teaspoon pepper

1. Dissolve salt in 2 quarts cold water in large container. Prick chicken wings all over with fork. Submerge chicken in brine, cover, and refrigerate for 30 minutes.

2. Combine cornstarch and pepper in bowl. Remove chicken from brine and pat dry with paper towels. Rinse and dry bowl. Transfer wings to now-empty bowl and sprinkle with cornstarch mixture, tossing until evenly coated.

3A. For a charcoal grill: Open bottom vent completely. Light large chimney starter half filled with charcoal briquettes (3 quarts). When top coals are partially covered with ash, pour evenly over grill. Set cooking grate in place, cover, and open lid vent completely. Heat grill until hot, about 5 minutes.

3B. For a gas grill: Turn all burners to high, cover, and heat grill until hot, about 15 minutes. Turn all burners to medium-low. (Adjust burners as needed to maintain grill temperature around 350 degrees.)

4. Clean and oil cooking grate. Grill wings (covered if using gas), thicker skin side up, until browned on bottom, 12 to 15 minutes. Flip chicken and grill until skin is crisp and lightly charred and meat registers 180 degrees, about 10 minutes. Transfer chicken to platter, tent loosely with aluminum foil, and let rest for 5 to 10 minutes. Serve.

BBQ GRILLED CHICKEN WINGS

Reduce pepper to ½ teaspoon. Add 1 teaspoon chili powder, 1 teaspoon paprika, ½ teaspoon garlic powder, ½ teaspoon dried oregano, and ½ teaspoon sugar to cornstarch mixture in step 2.

CREOLE GRILLED CHICKEN WINGS

Add ¾ teaspoon dried oregano, ½ teaspoon garlic powder, ½ teaspoon onion powder, ½ teaspoon white pepper, and ¼ teaspoon cayenne pepper to cornstarch mixture in step 2.

TANDOORI GRILLED CHICKEN WINGS

Reduce pepper to ½ teaspoon. Add 1 teaspoon garam masala, ½ teaspoon ground cumin, ¼ teaspoon garlic powder, ¼ teaspoon ground ginger, and ⅛ teaspoon cayenne pepper to cornstarch mixture in step 2.

Sweet Potato Salad

Sweet potatoes cook differently from ordinary potatoes. To create a really good dish, we had to learn this tuber's secrets. BY CAROLYNN PURPURA

I GREW UP on ordinary American potato salad—the kind with mayonnaise, celery, and sometimes hard-cooked egg—but I've since fallen for the sweet potato version. Unlike classic potato salad, it's tossed with vinaigrette. I found a handful of recipes in our cookbook library and headed into the test kitchen with my trusty peeler to get to work.

All the recipes I prepared required boiling and then dressing sweet potato cubes. Terrible idea—the boiled sweet potatoes were mushy and waterlogged. I scrapped the recipes without ceremony and switched to steaming, which immediately produced fluffy, flavorful potatoes—until I stirred in a basic vinaigrette. Suddenly, the sweet potato salad turned oily. I was baffled until our science editor explained that steaming damages the cell walls of sweet potatoes, so they absorb oil more easily. I made a few additional batches, comparing ratios of oil to vinegar, before deciding on a vinaigrette that reduced the usual amount of oil by one-third.

When we make ordinary potato salad in the test kitchen, we often toss the warm potatoes with a little vinegar—they drink it up and become deeply seasoned. I did the same with the sweet potatoes, but their edges broke down. The problem this time, our trusty science editor explained, was that there's less pectin to hold cells together in sweet potatoes than in white potatoes. When the sweet potatoes are hot, the pectin begins to lose its grip. Cooling them lets the pectin re-bond slightly. Could I get the same flavor impact without compromising texture by tossing cold potatoes with hot dressing? Happily, yes.

Now that I had the technique down, I turned to flavor. The sweet potato salad cried out for a little heat, bite, and crunch. I added those with, respectively, cayenne pepper, Dijon mustard, and chopped red bell pepper. A common refrain at *Cook's Country* is "Bacon makes it better," and it certainly did here: crisp, salty, meaty bacon. We liked this sweet potato salad so well, I developed a variation that sent the dish on a trip to Asia.

Our Asian-Style Sweet Potato Salad includes snow peas, scallions, and peanuts.

SWEET POTATO SALAD Serves 4 to 6

- 2 pounds sweet potatoes, peeled and cut into ¾-inch pieces
- 1 red bell pepper, stemmed, seeded, and cut into ½-inch pieces
- 2 tablespoons cider vinegar
- 1 tablespoon Dijon mustard
  Salt and pepper
- ⅛ teaspoon cayenne pepper
- 5 slices bacon, chopped
- 3 tablespoons vegetable oil
- 3 scallions, sliced thin

1. Fill Dutch oven with 1 inch water. Bring water to boil. Place steamer basket in Dutch oven and fill with sweet potatoes. Reduce heat to medium-low and cook, covered, until potatoes are nearly tender, 16 to 20 minutes. Add bell pepper and cook, covered, until sweet potatoes and pepper are tender, 2 to 4 minutes. Drain vegetables and rinse with cold water until cool, about 2 minutes. Drain again briefly and transfer to large bowl.

2. Combine vinegar, mustard, ½ teaspoon salt, ¼ teaspoon pepper, and cayenne in bowl. Transfer half of vinegar mixture to small bowl and microwave until steaming, about 30 seconds. Drizzle hot vinegar mixture over vegetables and gently toss until evenly coated. Set at room temperature until flavors meld, about 15 minutes.

3. Meanwhile, cook bacon in 10-inch skillet over medium heat until crisp, 6 to 8 minutes. Using slotted spoon, transfer bacon to paper towel–lined plate. Slowly whisk oil into remaining vinegar mixture until thoroughly incorporated.

4. Pour dressing over vegetables and gently toss until evenly coated. Stir in bacon and scallions. Cover and refrigerate until chilled, about 30 minutes. Season with salt and pepper to taste. Serve. (Salad can be refrigerated for up to 2 days.)

ASIAN-STYLE SWEET POTATO SALAD

Replace bell pepper with 4 ounces snow peas, strings removed and sliced ½ inch thick on bias. In step 2, replace cider vinegar with 1 tablespoon lime juice and 1 tablespoon rice vinegar, mustard with 1 tablespoon grated fresh ginger, and salt with 1 tablespoon soy sauce. Replace 1 tablespoon vegetable oil with 1 tablespoon toasted sesame oil and replace bacon with ⅓ cup salted, dry-roasted peanuts, chopped.

Introducing Italian Cream Cake

Chockablock full of nuts and coconut, this gorgeous Southern layer cake isn't as well known as it deserves to be. It's time to spill its secrets. BY ERIKA BRUCE

Other than its name, there isn't anything remotely Italian about Italian cream cake (and for the record, it doesn't contain cream, either). Its name be damned, for more than 40 years this moist coconut-pecan layer cake swathed in cream cheese frosting has been a favorite in the American South—a region that knows a thing or two about gorgeously showy layer cakes. You may find it sitting on bakery shelves, big and tempting, easily holding its own right next to the red velvet and caramel cakes. (The name remains mostly a mystery.) A cake this enticing I had to learn how to make.

There was scant disagreement among recipes: 1 cup of fat (usually made up of half butter and half shortening) beaten with 2 cups of sugar; 5 eggs (with the whites separated); 2 cups of all-purpose flour mixed with 1 teaspoon of baking soda; 1 cup of buttermilk; and, finally, shredded coconut and chopped pecans. The frosting called for cream cheese, butter, and a lot of confectioners' sugar.

The results were disappointing. While plenty sweet, the cake was bland; if I hadn't stirred in the coconut and pecans myself, I wouldn't have known they were there. (And those nuts that I *could* detect were soggy.) Although I had taken the trouble to whip and fold in the egg whites, the cake was heavy and gummy and sank slightly. To top it off, the frosting was too sweet. I got to work simplifying, balancing, and boosting.

Because I am firmly pro-butter, I immediately ditched the shortening. But due to all the nuts and coconut, my all-butter cake was even denser than before. Shortening, I learned, has small

Cream of coconut makes this cream cheese frosting especially velvety and flavorful.

fat crystals that trap air bubbles and make a higher (less dense) cake. Butter's larger fat crystals, in contrast, tend to rise in the batter and escape. Eventually, I found that a ratio of three-quarters butter to one-quarter shortening balanced buttery flavor with lightness. At the same time, I switched from all-purpose to cake flour to return the cake to its original tenderness. (I added a little extra flour for structural support.) I made a few more flavor adjustments—adding salt, upping the vanilla extract,

and cutting back on the sugar—before turning my attention to a recurring problem: gummy cake.

The recipe called for baking soda, which produces gas bubbles upon contact with the buttermilk, but no baking powder, a leavener that reacts to heat for a longer, more gradual rise. Cakes that rely solely on baking soda are unusual. Was that the source of the trouble? The cake was collapsing before the structure could set (and the whipped whites weren't picking up the slack). I skipped

the steps of separating and whipping the whites (saving me trouble and dirty dishes) and supplemented the baking soda with baking powder. Now the cake had an even, airy crumb.

To bring out the coconut and pecans, I added more, and I toasted them. The nuts now had lots of presence. But while the toasted coconut gave the cake a fabulous, macaroon-like flavor, it was dry and fibrous. I pulverized the toasted strands, but even the crumbs made the cake dry. To remoisten them, I soaked

Tall, frosted layer cakes may seem the epitome of homemade, but it was actually the convergence of (mostly American) technological innovations that made them possible. Baking a cake used to require scrubbing butter, working it until it was firm, and draining it; breaking up and crushing a solid chunk of sugar; sifting flour through muslin; and whipping egg whites for (gasp) two hours—all by hand, of course. But in a roughly 60-year period spanning the late-19th and early-20th centuries, manufacturers figured out how to make refined white sugar and soft white flour. They perfected confectioners' sugar, which made frostings a snap. They began to produce reliable baking soda and powder, as well as good butter. (Until then, butter had a season, like peaches; when the cows weren't producing milk, the butter was either rancid or encrusted with salt preservative.) Factories churned out better, more efficient beaters and gas and electric stoves that let homemakers control oven temperatures. In the young, rapidly industrializing nation, the cost of ingredients and kitchen equipment dropped. Taken together, these advancements made cake baking, once laborious, time-consuming, and expensive, (ahem) a piece of cake.

them in the buttermilk while I readied the other ingredients. To my relief, this fixed the problem. The cake was ready for its cream cheese cap.

After doubling the amount of cream cheese called for in most recipes and cutting back on the confectioners' sugar, I had a rich, tangy frosting. To make it a vehicle for extra coconut flavor, I added some potent canned cream of coconut. After pressing a cup of chopped pecans onto the sides of the cake, I was ready to dish out some genuine Southern hospitality.

ITALIAN CREAM CAKE
Serves 8 to 10

Toast the coconut and nuts in a 350-degree oven until golden brown, 10 to 12 minutes. Watch carefully and stir occasionally to prevent burning.

CAKE

1½	cups sweetened shredded coconut, toasted
1	cup buttermilk, room temperature
2	teaspoons vanilla extract
2½	cups (10 ounces) cake flour
2	teaspoons baking powder
¾	teaspoon salt
½	teaspoon baking soda
12	tablespoons unsalted butter, cut into 12 pieces and softened
4	tablespoons shortening, cut into 4 pieces
1¾	cups (12¼ ounces) sugar
5	large eggs, room temperature
2	cups (8 ounces) pecans, toasted and chopped

FROSTING

12	tablespoons unsalted butter, softened
2¼	cups (9 ounces) confectioners' sugar
½	cup cream of coconut
½	teaspoon vanilla extract
	Pinch salt
16	ounces cream cheese, cut into 8 pieces and softened

1. For the cake: Adjust oven rack to middle position and heat oven to 350 degrees. Grease two 9-inch round cake pans, line with parchment paper, grease parchment, then flour pans. Process coconut in food processor until finely ground, about 1 minute. Combine coconut, buttermilk, and vanilla in 2-cup liquid measuring cup and let sit until coconut is slightly softened, about 10 minutes; reserve.

2. Combine flour, baking powder, salt, and baking soda in bowl. Using stand mixer fitted with paddle, beat butter, shortening, and sugar on medium-high speed until pale and fluffy, about 3 minutes. Add eggs, one at a time, and beat until combined. Reduce speed to low and add flour mixture in 3 additions, alternating with 2 additions of reserved coconut-buttermilk mixture, scraping down bowl as needed. Add ¾ cup pecans and give batter final stir by hand.

3. Scrape equal amounts of batter into prepared pans and bake until toothpick inserted in center comes out clean, 28 to 32 minutes. Cool cakes in pans on wire rack for 10 minutes. Remove cakes from pans, discarding parchment, and cool completely, about 2 hours. (Cooled cakes can be wrapped with plastic wrap and stored at room temperature for up to 2 days.)

4. For the frosting: Using stand mixer fitted with paddle, mix butter and sugar on low speed until com-

bined, about 30 seconds. Increase speed to medium-high and beat until pale and fluffy, about 2 minutes. Add cream of coconut, vanilla, and salt and beat until smooth, about 30 seconds. Add cream cheese, one piece at a time, and beat until incorporated, about 1 minute. Refrigerate until ready to use.

5. When cakes are cooled, spread 1½ cups frosting over 1 cake round. Top with second cake round and spread remaining frosting evenly over top and sides of cake. Press remaining pecans onto sides of cake. Serve. (Cake can be refrigerated for up to 2 days. Bring to room temperature before serving.)

RATING MANUAL NUT CHOPPERS

Could a simple manual nut chopper work faster and better than a chef's knife or food processor? We pitted five choppers, from $7 crank-style jars to almost $30 mills, against our favorite food processor (the KitchenAid 750) and timed ourselves chopping pecans, hazelnuts, almonds, and walnuts. The highest-priced chopper fared the worst, processing nuts into gritty, mushy bits, but only one did much better: the Progressive International Heavy Duty Nut Chopper ($8.89). Its sharp stainless-steel tines pushed the nuts through slats that gave us a coarse texture as we turned the handle in one direction, a slightly finer texture in the other. It is the only manual nut chopper worth buying. Not only that, but chopping with our chef's knife actually took twice as long for worse results, plus we had to corral scooting nuts. Nor did we love the food processor. In thirty 1-second pulses, it pulverized some nuts, left others whole, and coated all in a fine, sticky nut dust. —AMY GRAVES

HIGHLY RECOMMENDED

		CRITERIA		TESTERS' NOTES
PROGRESSIVE INTERNATIONAL Heavy Duty Nut Chopper **Model:** Pri1018 **Price:** $8.89 **Source:** www.walmart.com 	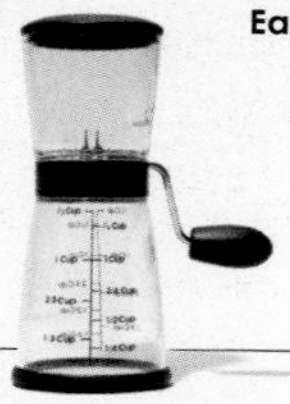	Chop quality Ease of use Design Cleanup	★★★ ★★★ ★★★ ★★★	In 90 seconds, we chopped a cup of pecans into mostly even-size pieces—with minimal dust. The chopper can handle harder, fatter nuts but will crank more slowly. It disassembles easily to clean by hand or dishwasher.

NOT RECOMMENDED

		CRITERIA		TESTERS' NOTES
ZYLISS "EASY CHOP" Food Chopper with Smart Base **Model:** 10700 **Price:** $19.95 **Source:** www.surlatable.com		Chop quality Ease of use Design Cleanup	★ ★★★ ★★ ★★★	This slap-chop model chops nuts and other foods. It's easy to use and neatly catches the nuts. But the pieces were too variable, and it produced too much dust. Dishwasher-safe.
BLACK & DECKER ERGO 3-Cup Chopper **Model:** EHC650 **Price:** $22 **Source:** www.walmart.com		Chop quality Ease of use Design Cleanup	★ ★★★ ★ ★★★	This mini food processor claims to chop nuts. It easily accommodated a large load but gave us dust interspersed with whole nuts and every size in between. It was easy to operate and clean, though.
NORPRO 576 Nut Chopper **Model:** NPW576 **Price:** $6.99 **Source:** www.norprowebstore.com 		Chop quality Ease of use Design Cleanup	★★★ ★ ★ ★★★	All went well with this chopper until it jammed on raw almonds and its tines twisted out of alignment. It balked at chopping hazelnuts, plus its glass base felt fragile. Dishwasher-safe.
WESTON ALL-PURPOSE Seed, Nut, and Spice Grinder **Model:** 7582 **Price:** $29.99 **Source:** www.fantes.com		Chop quality Ease of use Design Cleanup	★ ★ ★ ★	Nuts bounced around the hopper and didn't get chopped. Despite repeated cleaning, the grinder left machine grease on the nuts.

TEST KITCHEN DISCOVERY
Coconut: Toast, Grind, Soak

To bring out the flavor of the shredded coconut, we toast it in a 350-degree oven until it is golden brown (about 10 minutes). To help the coconut flavor permeate the cake, we grind it to meal in the food processor. But toasted, ground coconut is hard and dry, a real problem in such a deliciously soft, moist cake. To moisten and soften the coconut meal, we soak it in buttermilk before adding it to the cake batter.

Melting Moments

We searched high and low to find the formula for these meltingly tender butter cookies.
Was the solution in the cereal aisle? BY SARAH GABRIEL

Melting moments are simple, sweet, and indulgently buttery cookies. While closely related to short-bread and similar in their tidy, blond appearance, what makes them special is their impossibly delicate texture. I baked eight examples, the best of which one taster praised for "self-destructing in your mouth," but they all had the same problem: Far from disappearing without a trace, the cookies left starchy trails on our tongues. The culprit? The very ingredient responsible for their melt-away texture: cornstarch.

I knew my cookies would need a fair amount of cornstarch because it is key to their delicate structure. (Unlike flour, cornstarch does not form structure-reinforcing gluten when mixed with water.) But how much cornstarch was too much? To figure that out, I created a hybrid of the most promising recipes. I mixed confectioners' sugar (which, because it's very fine and contains some cornstarch, aids the "short" texture) with two sticks of butter and a teaspoon of vanilla extract in the food processor and added 1 cup each of flour and cornstarch. I rolled the dough into a log, chilled it, and then sliced and baked the cookies. The starchy film was as bad as ever. I repeated the recipe, subtracting 2 tablespoons of cornstarch each go-around. By the time the film disappeared, just ¼ cup of cornstarch was left—and the cookies were totally flat. I'd have to add back some bulk, but it couldn't leave behind a trail (like cornstarch), nor contribute chewy gluten (like flour).

Before turning to that matter, I reconsidered the all-purpose flour I'd been using. In baked goods, higher-

You can simply slice and bake this buttery dough into rounds, or use a pastry bag for shapes like jam thumbprints and spritz cookies.

protein flour produces chewier results, so I switched to lower-protein cake flour, baked a batch of cookies, and called the tasters. Better? Absolutely. Melt-away tender? "Not yet," they said.

Racking my brain for a cornstarch stand-in, I remembered that Scottish shortbread recipes use rice flour to achieve their famed tenderness. Rice, like cornstarch, does not form gluten. I dashed off to the grocery store but rice flour was nowhere to be found. Instead, I returned to the kitchen with a host of

other rice products. I ground these rice snacks, one after another, into powder, which I used to replace the missing cornstarch. I found that rice cakes refused to blend into a fine powder, while puffed rice "flour" tasted like cardboard. But ½ cup of Rice Krispies had a toasty, pleasantly sweet flavor and delivered tender, tasty cookies.

Alas, there was a catch. Tasters griped about "gritty, crystalline bits" and hearing that characteristic "Snap, crackle, pop!" I sieved my homemade

Rice Krispie "flour," but even the tiniest particles crackled in our mouths. I was on the verge of snapping and popping myself: Were Rice Krispies really so resilient? Leave your bowl to refill a juice glass and you come back to limp kernels floating listlessly in milk—that's it! Maybe soggy Rice Krispies was the key.

But I'd soak the ground cereal in cream. Cream has less water than milk, and water promotes gluten development —just what I needed to avoid. Three tablespoons of cream gave the cookies the right delicate texture. But the thick cereal-cream paste was almost impossible to incorporate into the soft cookie dough. So I melted some of the butter I was already using and added it to the cream as a paste thinner. I mixed in the ground cereal and, a few minutes later, the confectioners' sugar, remaining butter, and dry ingredients. I chilled and sliced the dough and loaded the cookies into a 300-degree oven. Some 45 minutes later, I nibbled my way through a perfectly shaped cookie, listening for that telltale crackle. The cookie melted away, leaving behind only silence and pure satisfaction.

MELTING MOMENTS
Makes about 6 dozen cookies
If the dough gets too soft to slice, return it to the refrigerator to firm up.

- ½ cup Rice Krispies cereal
- 16 tablespoons unsalted butter cut into 16 pieces and softened
- 3 tablespoons heavy cream
- 1 teaspoon vanilla extract
- 1¼ cups (5 ounces) cake flour
- ¼ cup (1¼ ounces) cornstarch
- ⅛ teaspoon salt
- ⅔ cup (2⅔ ounces) confectioners' sugar

1. Process Rice Krispies in blender until finely ground, about 30 seconds. Combine 4 tablespoons butter and cream in large bowl and microwave until butter is melted, about 30 seconds. Whisk in processed Rice Krispies and vanilla until combined. Let cool slightly, 5 to 7 minutes.

2. Combine flour, cornstarch, and salt in medium bowl; reserve. Whisk sugar into cooled butter mixture until incorporated. Add remaining 12 tablespoons butter, whisking until smooth. Stir in flour mixture until combined.

3. Working with half of dough at a time, dollop dough into 8-inch strip down center of 14 by 12-inch sheet of parchment paper. Fold 1 long side of

parchment over dough. Using ruler, press dough into tight 1-inch-wide log. Repeat with remaining dough and another sheet of parchment. Refrigerate dough until firm, about 1 hour. (Dough can be wrapped in plastic wrap and aluminum foil and frozen for up to 1 month.)

4. Adjust oven racks to upper-middle and lower-middle positions and heat oven to 300 degrees. Line 2 baking sheets with parchment. Cut dough into ¼-inch slices and place 1 inch apart on prepared baking sheets. Bake until set but not brown, 18 to 22 minutes, switching and rotating sheets halfway through baking. Let cool completely on sheets, about 15 minutes. Repeat with remaining dough. Serve. (Cookies can be stored at room temperature for up to 2 days.)

CRESCENT COOKIES
After step 2, transfer dough to pastry bag fitted with ½-inch star tip. Pipe 1½-inch-long crescents onto prepared baking sheets. Refrigerate dough until firm, about 30 minutes. Bake as directed.

JAM THUMBPRINT COOKIES
After step 2, transfer dough to pastry bag fitted with ½-inch plain tip. Pipe 1-inch-wide and ½-inch-high dough rounds onto prepared baking sheets. Using back of ¼ teaspoon measuring spoon dipped in water, make indentation in center of each round. Refrigerate dough until firm, about 30 minutes. Bake until set, 18 to 20 minutes, switching and rotating sheets halfway through baking. Fill each dimple with ½ teaspoon jam and bake for 5 minutes.

ROUND SPRITZ COOKIES
After step 2, transfer dough to pastry bag fitted with ½-inch star tip. Pipe 1-inch-wide and ½-inch-high dough rounds onto prepared baking sheets. Refrigerate dough until firm, about 30 minutes. Bake as directed.

TEST KITCHEN TECHNIQUE **Handling Soft Dough**
The high proportion of butter to flour makes the dough for these cookies very soft and challenging to handle. With this technique, you can easily roll it into a log.

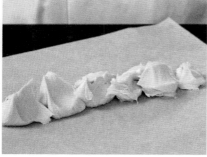
Dollop half of the dough in a strip down the center of a sheet of parchment.

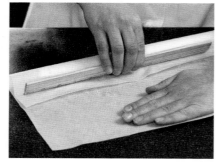
Pulling the parchment taut, use a ruler to press the dough into a tight log.

Magic Strawberry Ice Cream

We expected it to be a walk in the park: Simply stir strawberries into our no-machine vanilla ice cream. But the berries formed icy crystals. BY LYNN CLARK

Even without an ice-cream machine, our strawberry ice cream is rich and creamy.

WE DID CHOCOLATE (in 2009), and we did vanilla (in 2010). And now, in response to reader demand, we embarked on yet another "magical" challenge: how to make delicious, creamy strawberry ice cream without an ice-cream machine.

Ice-cream machines both freeze the typical mixture of cream, milk, eggs, sugar, and flavorings very aggressively (to prevent ice crystals) and incorporate air (for a light texture). Our previous recipes achieve a similar light, creamy texture with a dead-simple base of sweetened condensed milk, melted chocolate chips (either semisweet or white), and whipped cream. I went into the test kitchen sure this one was in the bag: I'd add pureed strawberries to our Magic Vanilla Ice Cream recipe and be done. Not so fast. Fresh berries contain a lot of water, so the berry chunks crystallized into shards of ice.

OK then, I'd just cook down the pureed strawberries in a saucepan before stirring the puree into the base. But the reduced puree gave the ice cream an odd gelatinous texture (the cooking activated the natural pectin in the strawberries), and it still tasted like spoons of frost instead of cream. I asked our science editor for help. He suggested adding a small amount of strawberry liqueur to the berry puree. Because alcohol doesn't freeze, he reasoned, the liqueur should prevent the strawberry solids from icing up.

It worked, but I still wasn't satisfied. True, the texture of the ice cream was worlds better, but I had to make a special trip to the liquor store. On top of that, the strawberry liqueur didn't taste like fresh berries; instead, it made the ice cream taste fake. I fixed that by exchanging the liqueur for a tablespoon of neutral-tasting vodka. Now the ice cream froze beautifully and had plenty of bright berry flavor. Looks like we've pulled another rabbit out of our hat.

MAGIC STRAWBERRY ICE CREAM Makes 1 quart ice cream
You can use 6 ounces of thawed, frozen berries in place of fresh ones and bar white chocolate in place of the chips—chop it finely before melting it. If you plan to store the ice cream for more than a few days, place plastic wrap directly on its surface.

- 8 ounces strawberries, hulled (1½ cups)
- ½ cup sweetened condensed milk
- 1 ounce white chocolate chips
- 1 tablespoon vodka
- ½ teaspoon vanilla extract
- Pinch salt
- 1¼ cups heavy cream, chilled

1. Process strawberries in food processor until smooth, about 30 seconds (puree should measure about ¾ cup). Microwave sweetened condensed milk, white chocolate chips, and vodka in large bowl until chocolate melts, about 1 minute, whisking halfway through cooking. Whisk in strawberry puree, vanilla, and salt.

2. Using stand mixer fitted with whisk, whip cream on medium-low speed until foamy, about 1 minute. Increase speed to high and whip until soft peaks form, 1 to 3 minutes. Whisk one-third of whipped cream into strawberry mixture, then gently fold in remaining whipped cream, 1 scoop at a time, until combined. Freeze in airtight container until firm, 6 hours or up to 2 weeks. Serve.

Taste Test Ketchup

Responding to public demands, many manufacturers have ditched high-fructose corn syrup for other sweeteners. Do these new ketchups taste better? BY HANNAH CROWLEY

IT'S NO SECRET that Americans love ketchup. We spend almost half a billion dollars on it every year, according to Chicago-based market research firm SymphonyIRI Group. Since the 1980s, most ketchup has been made with high-fructose corn syrup (HFCS); manufacturers like this ingredient because it's cheap and easy to mix with other ingredients. But in the past few years, HFCS has been blamed (loudly) for rising obesity rates and other health problems, so many manufacturers now offer alternatives, such as ketchup made with white sugar.

When we last tasted ketchup, in 2006, Hunt's finished on top. Last year this ketchup was reformulated, with sugar replacing the HFCS. In 2010, Heinz—America's bestselling ketchup by an overwhelming margin—launched Simply Heinz, its own sugar spinoff. (It still sells its classic version, sweetened with corn syrup and HFCS.) Agave nectar, derived from the agave plant (the spiky succulent from which tequila is also distilled), sweetens Organicville ketchup, now the ninth bestselling national brand. All this sweetener swapping means that it's time for us to taste and rate ketchup again.

In choosing eight national brands, we focused on classic tomato ketchups—no curried or spicy riffs. Then we gathered 21 editors and test cooks from America's Test Kitchen to try each sample plain and with fries. We also sent an unopened bottle of each brand to the lab for analysis, so we could get to the bottom of our results. At the tasting table, it became clear that our tasters wanted ketchup that tasted the way they remembered it from childhood: salty and boldly seasoned, with all the flavor elements—salt, sweet, tang, and tomato—assertive yet harmonious. Offending samples were scolded: "Does not please my inner child." (Our in-house poll revealed that the majority of tasters grew up with Heinz.)

After we tallied up the scores, we noticed that, sure enough, our top three winners—Heinz Organic Tomato Ketchup, Hunt's Tomato Ketchup, and Simply Heinz Tomato Ketchup—were all sweetened with sugar, not corn syrup. Corn syrup is a thick liquid sweetener made by putting wet cornstarch through a process that converts starches to sugar. HFCS undergoes additional processing to convert

dextrose to sweeter fructose. It is then mixed with regular corn syrup until the desired sweetness is reached.

Whether HFCS really is the culprit for obesity is a subject of fierce debate. But it was clear that, given a choice (and assuming the ketchups' balance and general tastiness), our tasters preferred sugar. Why? Maybe because people perceive that sugar has a cleaner, purer sweetness, according to our science editor. Corn syrup (and HFCS), he added, can exhibit off-flavors from the cornstarch and from the manufacturing process. The two ketchups that included corn syrup, classic Heinz and Del Monte, sat right in the middle of the pack.

So how to understand that two of the lowest-ranking brands (Annie's and Muir Glen) were also sweetened with sugar? In those cases, other factors had more impact: The low-rankers were pasty or watery, they had too little salt, or they had too much clove.

As for agave nectar, it was a "no go" for our tasters. Organicville, the brand sweetened with agave, scored dead last in our lineup. Tasters found it "cloyingly sweet" and undersalted, with a "funky" texture.

Tasters also liked ketchups that had enough acid to balance the sugar. Our lab tested each ketchup for salt and pH; the latter measures the acidity—the higher the number, the less acidic the ketchup. Our two lowest-ranked ketchups had the least acidity. Our favorite had the highest percentage of salt.

Our two top-rated ketchups, Heinz Organic and Hunt's, were virtually tied for first place. Tasters ever-so-slightly preferred Heinz Organic for its "bright and fresh" flavor, calling it "tangy, salty, smooth" and "full bodied." It is almost three times as expensive as Hunt's, though, which lost by a nose and also uses sugar. Hunt's is our Best Buy; it offers flavor—and value.

We wondered how our winner, Heinz Organic, differs from our third place finisher, Simply Heinz. But for the organic ingredients, they are the same, a company spokesman told us. So how to account for their different rankings, given that many studies have found no definitive difference in the taste of organic versus ordinary tomatoes? Our lab results indicated that the organic version was actually slightly saltier and slightly tangier.

RECOMMENDED

TASTERS' NOTES

HEINZ ORGANIC TOMATO KETCHUP
$2.49 for 15 ounces (17 cents per ounce)
Sweetener: Sugar, 4 grams per 1-tablespoon serving
Salt: 3.14 percent **pH:** 3.69

Tasters praised the "bright and fresh," "well rounded ketchup-y flavor" of Heinz Organic. Its bold, harmonious punch of saltiness, sweetness, tang, and tomato flavor nudged it into first place. Altogether, "like ketchup should be."

HUNT'S TOMATO KETCHUP   BEST BUY
$1.39 for 24 ounces (6 cents per ounce)
Sweetener: Sugar, 4 grams per 1-tablespoon serving
Salt: 2.79 percent **pH:** 3.54

The word "classic" popped up more than once to describe Hunt's ketchup. Tasters found it "perfectly aggressive" (meant in the nicest possible way) and "balanced." It won points for smoothness and color, too. "Love it. Classic. Tastes like ketchup should."

SIMPLY HEINZ TOMATO KETCHUP
$2.59 for 32 ounces (8 cents per ounce)
Sweetener: Sugar, 4 grams per 1-tablespoon serving
Salt: 2.92 percent **pH:** 3.64

This sugar version of classic Heinz fooled several tasters into thinking it was their old (corn syrup) favorite: "Tastes the way I remember—nostalgia," wrote one. "Great balance, very classic-tasting. Heinz?" asked another.

HEINZ TOMATO KETCHUP
$2.79 for 36 ounces (8 cents per ounce)
Sweetener: High fructose corn syrup, corn syrup, 4 grams per 1-tablespoon serving
Salt: 2.53 percent **pH:** 3.6

For the second time, America's number-one selling ketchup fell in the middle of the pack. Tasters praised its "tangy, sharp, a little zippy" flavor. They also liked the strong tomato presence. While it got respectable scores, it was edged out of the top because it "lack(ed) oomph and complexity."

DEL MONTE KETCHUP
$2.95 for 24 ounces (12 cents per ounce)
Sweetener: High fructose corn syrup, corn syrup, 4 grams per 1-tablespoon serving
Salt: 2.61 percent **pH:** 3.74

Our tasters found Del Monte acidic. Some liked that quality, praising the ketchup as "zippy" and "bright" with a "nice tangy flavor." A minority registered that latter quality as sour.

RECOMMENDED WITH RESERVATIONS

ANNIE'S NATURALS ORGANIC KETCHUP
$3.99 for 24 ounces (17 cents per ounce)
Sweetener: Cane sugar, 4 grams per 1-tablespoon serving
Salt: 2.09 percent **pH:** 3.59

Annie's does not taste like classic ketchup. That appealed to a few tasters, who liked its "roasted" and "darker, richer" flavors and described it as "gourmet" ketchup. Others disagreed, finding the ketchup unbalanced: "Way too sweet. Okay tomato flavor but sugar overwhelms it all."

MUIR GLEN ORGANIC TOMATO KETCHUP
$3.49 for 24 ounces (15 cents per ounce)
Sweetener: Naturally milled sugar, 3 grams per 1-tablespoon serving
Salt: 2.84 percent **pH:** 3.77

Tasters split on this brand, which, again, didn't taste like "classic" ketchup; the critics found it closer to barbecue sauce, cocktail sauce, or marinara. Some praised it as "thick and flavorful." Others faulted both texture ("lumpy") and taste ("too much spice"). Summed up a taster, "Complex but weird."

NOT RECOMMENDED

ORGANICVILLE ORGANIC KETCHUP
$3.50 for 24 ounces (15 cents per ounce)
Sweetener: Agave nectar, 3 grams per 1-tablespoon serving
Salt: 2.11 percent **pH:** 3.83

This brand hit rock bottom for its "gritty" texture and off-flavors. Tasters faulted the spiced flavor and "overwhelming sweetness." It uses agave nectar to sweeten. Although it had less sweetener per serving than our winning ketchups, it wasn't offset by salt and acidity. Tasters bellowed: "Impure ketchup! Impostor!"

Equipment Review Inexpensive Stockpots

Can you get a serviceable jumbo-size stockpot for under $40? BY TAIZETH SIERRA

KEY **Good** ★★★ **Fair** ★★ **Poor** ★

WHAT'S THE POINT in plunking down $70 for a stockpot that can both simmer chili and boil pasta if you already own a Dutch oven that can ably handle both? No point. (Incidentally, we didn't pluck that number from thin air; $70 is the price of the Cuisinart Chef's Classic Stockpot, the Best Buy from our 2007 testing.) But when you're cooking for a crowd, it's handy to have a really big pot for mulling cider or boiling water for, say, a double batch of pasta, steamed lobsters, or corn on the cob. (Dutch ovens typically hold 6 to 8 quarts.) A large pot dedicated to such tasks wouldn't require the well-constructed (and expensive) bottom that keeps foods like chili from scorching. Our mission? Find a decent, truly cheap stockpot for boiling. We gathered seven 12-quart stockpots, each less than $40.

To test them, we boiled a double batch of spaghetti and a dozen ears of corn in each. We quickly developed a preference for short, wide pots. With more surface area in contact with the heat, a wide bottom heats water faster. Wider pots accommodated the corn more comfortably, and pots with lower, shorter sides let us see the contents and stir without burning our knuckles. Our top-ranking pots were both under 9 inches tall, with bottoms more than 10 inches wide.

A good stockpot should be easy to handle. Our recipes call for 8 quarts of water to boil 2 pounds of pasta: That's about 18 pounds of boiling water plus pasta that you need to haul from stovetop to sink. Empty, our stockpots weighed between 1.5 and 4.7 pounds. None was unmanageable, even when full. The handles were more important: Big, sturdy, protruding handles gave us a good grip, even with oven mitts. We also demanded pots have lids, which confine the steam and thus expedite boiling; one brand charged an extra $8.50 for the lid, a deal-breaker.

So could any of these cheap pots handle a double batch of chili in a pinch? After getting some degree of scorching in every one, we confirmed our suspicion that you're better off using a thick, heavy Dutch oven (or a heavier, pricier stockpot), which can simmer without burning. That said, our higher-ranked pots performed slightly better; some had thicker bottoms; others were made of heat-responsive materials that cooled fast when we lowered the heat.

Our winner, the Alpha Heavy Gauge 12 QT Stainless Steel Stock Pot with Glass Lid, costs just $28. With a low, wide profile, easy-to-grasp handles, generous capacity, sturdy construction, and affordable price, it's our favorite for a big pot devoted to boiling.

	CRITERIA		TESTERS' NOTES
RECOMMENDED			

ALPHA HEAVY GAUGE 12 QT
Stainless Steel Stock Pot with Glass Lid
Model: S-5512 **Price:** $26
Source: www.savezoneusa.com
Dimensions: 8¼ inches tall, 10¼ inches wide
Bottom thickness: 4.8mm **Weight:** 4.7 pounds
Material: Stainless steel with encapsulated aluminum disk bottom

Handling ★★
Boiling ★★★
Simmering ★★
Durability ★★★

The wide bottom of this heavy pot accommodated corn easily, and water boiled rapidly. Large handles made it easy to carry, though its heft presented a challenge when we went to pour from it. Chili scorched a little around the edges of the pot, where the sides bulged over the encapsulated aluminum disk bottom.

RECOMMENDED WITH RESERVATIONS

VASCONIA 12-QUART
Aluminum Stock Pot with Lid
Model: 5032030 **Price:** $14.99
Source: www.target.com
Dimensions: 8½ inches tall, 10¼ inches wide
Bottom thickness: 1.6mm **Weight:** 1.5 pounds
Material: Aluminum (with satin exterior finish)

Handling ★★★
Boiling ★★★
Simmering ★★
Durability ★

This aluminum stockpot, the lightest and least expensive we tested, was easy to carry thanks to long handles with plastic grips that stayed cool. Chili barely scorched, because the aluminum was so responsive (turning down the heat instantly cooled the pot). But the pot discolored on the inside, and the bottom warped slightly.

ONEIDA 12 QUART STOCK POT
Model: 62592 **Price:** $39.99
Source: www.oneida.com
Dimensions: 9¼ inches tall, 9¾ inches wide
Bottom thickness: 4.8mm **Weight:** 3.97 pounds
Material: Stainless steel with encapsulated aluminum disk bottom

Handling ★★
Boiling ★★★
Simmering ★
Durability ★

This pan felt flimsy and bottom-heavy. It was a little too tall and skinny to maneuver easily, even though its handles were large and easy to grasp. Cooking chili, we found several hotspots where food stuck, plus it scorched around the edges of the pot.

PAULA DEEN 12 QT COVERED STOCKPOT
Model: 51654 **Price:** $39.95
Source: www.cooking.com
Dimensions: 9 inches tall, 10¼ inches wide
Bottom thickness: 3.2mm **Weight:** 4.4 pounds
Material: Porcelain enameled steel

Handling ★★
Boiling ★★★
Simmering ★
Durability ★

Water boiled quickly and the pot was easy to lift and pour—but beware of the searing hot lid and handles. It failed at making chili, cooking way too fast. Turning the heat down didn't help: A big scorch spot required a metal scrubber to clean. Enamel chipped inside the lid.

NOT RECOMMENDED

NORDIC WARE 12 QUART
Stock Pot without Cover
Model: 22120 **Price:** $29.89
Source: www.csnstores.com
Dimensions: 9¾ inches tall, 10⅛ inches wide
Bottom thickness: 1.6mm **Weight:** 3.7 pounds
Material: Aluminized steel with a nonstick interior

Handling ★
Boiling ★★
Simmering ★
Durability ★★

The only pot sold without a lid—it costs an extra $8.50—is at a disadvantage, since covering pots of water makes them boil faster. Once the water was finally rolling, stubby handles close to the sides of the pot made it difficult to carry. The nonstick interior was helpful when cleaning a large spot of charred chili.

T-FAL SPECIALTY 12-QUART
Nonstick Stock Pot
Model: A9228064 **Price:** $27.69
Source: www.ourcrave.com
Dimensions: 10¼ inches tall, 9½ inches wide
Bottom thickness: 3.2mm **Weight:** 3.8 pounds
Material: Aluminum with nonstick coating, inside and out

Handling ★
Boiling ★
Simmering ★
Durability ★★

We had to stick our hands deep inside this tall skinny pot to stir; more than once we burned our knuckles. The bottom scorched the chili, and while the nonstick coating made it easy to clean, its presence on the exterior of the pot gave off awful fumes. (Eventually, the fumes abated, but it was too late. They'd put us off the pot for good.)

M.E. HEUCK 12 QT. STOCKPOT
Model: 36110 **Price:** $28.30
Source: www.cometsupply.com
Dimensions: 9⅛ inches tall, 9¾ inches wide
Bottom thickness: 3.2mm **Weight:** 2.4 pounds
Material: Stainless steel with encapsulated aluminum disk bottom

Handling ★
Boiling ★★
Simmering ★
Durability ★

The handles of the pot were too small and became very hot, but otherwise its performance was not out of line with the others we tested. What landed it at rock bottom was poor construction: The second time we cooked in it, the disk began to separate from the pot.

Cooking Class How to Grill Pork Chops

Thick chops are relatively easy to grill. But thin chops are hard—if you leave them on the grill long enough to get good char, they become overcooked and dry. Our technique saves the day...and your dinner.

These thin chops have a beautiful sear yet are tender and juicy.

The Best Pork Chop for Grilling

At the supermarket, pork chops may be labeled "loin chops," a term that can apply to sirloin, blade, center-cut, or rib chops. Sirloin chops are tough and tasteless; blade chops are best cooked long and slow. Center-cut chops have a bone that divides the chop into meat from the loin and a small portion of the tenderloin. The tenderloin portion cooks more quickly, so center-cut chops can be challenging to cook evenly. That leaves rib chops—our favorite for grilling.

Thin vs. Thick-Cut Pork Chops

What's the difference? About an inch. Thin-cut pork chops are more common and are often sold in family packs.

SIZE MATTERS
This measurement is about ½ inch for thin chops and 1½ inches for thick ones.

Bone-In vs. Boneless Chops

To settle this debate, we boned several rib pork chops, grilled them, and then compared them with their bone-in counterparts. The meat that was cooked on the bone had better flavor and was undeniably juicier. Why? First, the bone insulates the meat closest to it, protecting it from exposure to the air so that less of the flavorful juice can evaporate during cooking. Second, deposits of fat are generally located next to the bone. Fat is both a crucial source of flavor and, as it melts during cooking, a source of perceived juiciness. When the bone is removed, some of the fat (hence flavor and juiciness) goes with it.

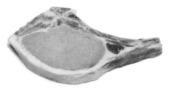

RIB CHOP
This test kitchen favorite stays moist.

CENTER-CUT CHOP
Our runner-up is more difficult to cook evenly.

Buy Natural Pork. Avoid Enhancements.

Pigs today are bred to be 50 percent leaner than they were 50 years ago—a response to market demand. But less fat equals drier, less flavorful pork. Enter "enhanced pork," which processors inject with a solution of water, salt, and sodium phosphate. In the test kitchen, we much prefer natural pork, which has far better flavor and won't dry out if you cook it correctly. You won't find the terms "enhanced" or "natural" on package labels, but if the package has an ingredient list, the pork has been enhanced. How is commercially enhanced pork different from pork that you brine yourself in a saltwater solution (a step that we recommend for thick-cut pork chops)? With brining, *you* get to control the salt level as well as how long the pork stays in the brine.

GRILLED THIN-CUT PORK CHOPS

Serves 4 to 6
Don't freeze the chops for more than an hour or they will cook unevenly.

- 6 (3-ounce) bone-in pork rib or center-cut chops, ½ inch thick, trimmed
- ¾ teaspoon salt
- 4 tablespoons unsalted butter, softened
- 1 teaspoon packed brown sugar
- ½ teaspoon pepper
- 1 teaspoon minced fresh chives
- ½ teaspoon Dijon mustard
- ½ teaspoon grated lemon zest

1. Pat chops dry with paper towels, cut slits about 2 inches apart through the fat around each chop, and rub with salt. Arrange chops on wire rack set in rimmed baking sheet and freeze until firm, 30 to 60 minutes. Combine 2 tablespoons butter, sugar, and pepper in bowl; set aside. Mix remaining 2 tablespoons butter, chives, mustard, and lemon zest in another bowl and refrigerate until firm, about 15 minutes. (Chive butter can be refrigerated, covered, for up to 1 day.)

2. Pat partially frozen chops dry with paper towels. Spread 1 teaspoon softened butter mixture evenly over both sides of each chop.

3A. For a charcoal grill: Open bottom vent completely. Light large chimney starter filled with charcoal briquettes (6 quarts). When top coals are partially covered with ash, pour evenly over grill. Set cooking grate in place, cover, and open lid vent completely. Heat grill until hot, about 5 minutes.

3B. For a gas grill: Turn all burners to high, cover, and heat grill until hot, about 15 minutes. Leave burners on high.

4. Clean and oil cooking grate. Grill chops (covered if using gas) until well browned and meat registers 145 degrees, 3 to 4 minutes per side. Transfer chops to platter and top with chilled chive butter. Tent loosely with aluminum foil and let rest for 5 to 10 minutes. Serve.

Banish Tough Chops

This past spring, the U.S. Department of Agriculture changed its pork safety guidelines, shaving 15 degrees off its prior "done" temperature for chops and roasts to 145 degrees, and instructing cooks to allow the meat to rest for 3 minutes before eating. (The temperature of the chop will continue to rise slightly after it comes

145 DEGREES
Pink, Perfect, and Safe to Eat

off the heat.) It's about time. The test kitchen has long recommended that pork be cooked to 145 degrees to keep it tender and juicy. The U.S.D.A. standard was established to protect against trichinosis, a dangerous parasite that once tainted the U.S. pork supply. But improved farming practices have all but obliterated trichinosis. According to the U.S.D.A., ground pork should still be cooked to 160 degrees.

Twelve Steps to Perfect Thin-Cut Chops

1. CUT SLITS
Using a knife, cut slits about 2 inches apart through the fat and connective tissue.
WHY? So the pork chops won't buckle and curl when exposed to high heat.

2. RUB WITH SALT
Dry the chops, then rub them on both sides with salt.
WHY? Surface moisture is the enemy of char. Rubbing the pork chops with salt draws out excess moisture so we can remove it.

3. SET ON RACK Arrange the chops on a wire rack set in a rimmed baking sheet.
WHY? The chops won't brown unless their surfaces are dry. The rack lets air circulate so that both sides of the chop dry out.

4. FREEZE BRIEFLY
Freeze until the chops are firm—no more than an hour.
WHY? The cold, dry air of the freezer both evaporates exterior moisture and chills the chops' interior so that they can stay on the grill longer.

5. FLAVOR FINISHING BUTTER Combine butter, chives, mustard, and lemon zest and refrigerate until firm.
WHY? After the chops are grilled, the butter and seasonings will add fat and flavor to otherwise lean chops.

6. PAT DRY Wipe off any remaining exterior moisture with paper towels.
WHY? In case the freezer missed a spot. The drier the chops are, the better crust they'll have.

7. SPREAD WITH BUTTER Spread softened, sweetened butter on both sides of the chops. The butter will harden on the frozen chops.
WHY? The protein in the butter, combined with the sugar, accelerates browning.

8. HEAT GRILL
Pour hot coals evenly over the bottom of the grill and heat for five minutes. For a gas grill, heat all burners on high for 15 minutes.
WHY? The fire must be hot to char the chops without overcooking them.

9. CLEAN GRILL Use a grill brush to give your grill a good scrub and then oil it.
WHY? A clean grill grate won't impart off-flavors to the chops. Plus, it helps prevent the meat from sticking.

10. GRILL AND TEMP Grill the chops until they are well browned, 3 to 4 minutes per side. The chops are done when they register 145 degrees.
WHY? Precision—in this case determined by a thermometer—guarantees the best results.

11. TOP WITH BUTTER
Place some compound butter on each chop.
WHY? When the cold butter hits the hot chops, you'll have an instant bright, buttery sauce.

12. LET REST
Tent the chops with foil and let them sit for a few minutes.
WHY? The foil tent keeps the chops warm, while the rest allows the meat juices to redistribute, which translates into juicier chops.

Thick-Cut Chops

Less Prep, Different Grill Setup

Now that we've taught you how to grill thin pork chops, here's the lowdown on thick ones: In brief, they're much easier to grill. But we do like to brine them to keep the meat juicy. (We don't brine thin chops because their extra moisture would slow down the browning.) We use a two-level fire for thick chops, searing them over high heat and then moving them to the cooler side to gently cook through. Thick chops take more than twice as long to cook.

GRILLED THICK-CUT PORK CHOPS
Serves 4

If you're using enhanced pork, skip the brining and season the chops with salt along with the pepper in step 1.

- 3 tablespoons salt
- 4 (12-ounce) bone-in pork rib or center-cut chops, 1½ inches thick, trimmed
  Pepper
- 2 tablespoons unsalted butter, softened
- 1 teaspoon minced fresh chives
- ½ teaspoon Dijon mustard
- ½ teaspoon grated lemon zest

1. Dissolve salt in 1½ quarts cold water in large container. Submerge pork in brine, cover, and refrigerate for 1 hour. Remove pork from brine, pat dry with paper towels, and cut slits about 2 inches apart through fat around each chop. Season with pepper. Mix butter, chives, mustard, and lemon zest in bowl and refrigerate until firm, about 15 minutes. (Chive butter can be refrigerated, covered, for up to 1 day.)

2A. For a charcoal grill: Open bottom vent completely. Light large chimney starter filled with charcoal briquettes (6 quarts). When top coals are partially covered with ash, pour two-thirds evenly over grill, then pour remaining coals over half of grill. Set cooking grate in place, cover, and open lid vent completely. Heat grill until hot, about 5 minutes.

2B. For a gas grill: Turn all burners to high, cover, and heat grill until hot, about 15 minutes. Leave primary burner on high and turn other burner(s) to medium-low.

3. Clean and oil cooking grate. Grill chops (covered if using gas) on hot part of grill until browned, about 3 minutes per side. Slide chops to cool part of grill and cook until meat registers 145 degrees, 7 to 9 minutes, flipping halfway through grilling. Transfer chops to platter and top with chilled chive butter. Tent loosely with aluminum foil and let rest for 5 to 10 minutes. Serve.

Looking for a Recipe

READER TO READER

Did you misplace a favorite recipe? Can you almost taste a chocolate cake from childhood, but the bakery—and the recipe—are long gone? Ask a reader. While you're at it, answer a reader. Post queries and finds at CooksCountry.com/Magazine. (Or write to Looking for a Recipe, Cook's Country, P.O. Box 470739, Brookline, MA 02447.) We'll share all your submissions online—hundreds are already posted— and print several on this page. Include your name and mailing address with each request.

Corn Dogs
Tim Preheim, Kalama, Wash.

I've never come across a recipe for corn dogs in any of the America's Test Kitchen books that I've looked through. My own attempts at making them have been pretty sad. Any help would be appreciated.

Best Buttermilk Pie
Connie Holmes, Evart, Mich.

The Wild Flower Tea Room at Loafers Glory in Blanchard, Michigan, makes the best buttermilk pie. It's creamy, cinnamony, and definitely worth the trip. They won't share their recipe, and I can't find a good one. Does anyone have a similar recipe? Thanks.

Salt-Rising Bread
Melissa Ostrom, Holley, N.Y.

Growing up in Jamestown, New York, I enjoyed many treats over the years from Jones Bakery. Now it is closed. More than anything I miss their salt-rising bread, a unique yeast bread with a subtle salty-sour tang. It was particularly good for toasting. It depresses me to think that I may never eat this bread again. Does anyone have a beloved salt-rising bread recipe that he or she is willing to share?

Potato Frosting (Really)
Ann Ball, St. James, N.Y.

When I was a child in the 1960s, birthday parties for kids almost always included homemade cakes. I still long for the wonderful frosting on one particular birthday cake from my childhood. It was vanilla frosting, not too sweet, and I remember being told that it was made with potatoes! I'd love to find a recipe for it.

Biscuit Tortoni
Stacey Griffin, Boston, Mass.

When I was a kid, the old Café Marliave on Bosworth Street in downtown Boston used to serve a terrific dessert called frozen biscuit tortoni. It came in a fluted paper cup, was creamy and rich, and had crushed amaretti cookies inside and a maraschino cherry on top. The restaurant has long since changed hands, and I'd love to find this recipe to make for my family.

Zucchini-Banana Bread
Shelley Conti, Kent, Wash.

I'm trying to find a recipe for zucchini-banana bread that uses a fair amount of zucchini, with a banana or two for added flavor. Most recipes take too long to bake or use very little zucchini. Does anyone have the perfect recipe?

Deep-Fried Pickles
William C. Lohse, Philadelphia, Pa.

I have been looking for a recipe for deep-fried pickles like the ones I've eaten at a restaurant in Gettysburg, Pennsylvania. The pickle spears are bathed in a coating that holds in all the juices when they're fried. To eat, you dip the deep-fried pickles into ranch dressing and get a double crunch from both coating and pickle. I'd love to learn how to make them.

Southern Egg Custard Pie
Ashley Indhara, Dallas, N.C.

My family has grown up loving egg custard pie. We usually just buy it from a local restaurant, but I would sure like to make it at home. Recipes I've tried make either a lumpy filling or one that weeps. Can someone help?

S'Mores Pie
Katie Snyder, San Francisco, Calif.

The first time I tasted this pie I loved it so much that it has become a birthday tradition to go and eat it at the Buckeye Roadhouse, which is just north of the Golden Gate Bridge. I'd love to have the recipe (or a similar one) so I can make it myself, but I don't believe the Buckeye would shake it loose!

Gorditas
Sandy Drawbond, Jacksonville, Fla.

There's a stand at the edge of El Marcado (Market Square) in San Antonio that makes the most mouthwatering gorditas. The shells are cooked in front of you from masa dough that's hand-flattened into a circle and placed on the hot griddle, where it puffs. After both sides have browned, the vendor cuts the shell to form a pocket for the delicious seasoned beef. The shells have a crisp outside and a slightly chewy inside, and they don't fall apart, even though they're quite thin. Wonderful! I've tried to duplicate the gorditas at home, without success, as have several of my friends. Can you help?

Tamari Almonds
Beth Iverson, Rapid City, S.D.

While attending school on the East Coast, my son sent me a lovely goodie basket. One of my favorite things in it was the tamari almonds that he said he bought at a Whole Foods Market. I'd love to be able to make them myself, but the results of the recipes I've attempted haven't tasted nearly as good. Does anyone have a recipe that produces dark brown, salty, crunchy almonds?

HAM LOAF Serves 6 to 8
Rachael Hartman, Elysburg, Pa.

"Ham loaf is a favorite at our family dinners and church socials. I love the saltiness of the ham with the sweet glaze. Because the loaf is rich, I usually serve it with simple baked or boiled potatoes." The test kitchen recommends that you line the rimmed baking sheet with foil for easy cleanup.

GLAZE
- ¾ cup packed brown sugar
- ¼ cup cider vinegar
- ¼ cup ketchup
- ¼ cup water
- 2 tablespoons spicy brown mustard
- ⅛ teaspoon cayenne pepper

HAM LOAF
- 2 tablespoons vegetable oil
- 1 onion, chopped fine
- 36 saltine crackers
- 2 pounds boneless ham steak, rind removed, cut into 1-inch pieces
- 1 pound ground pork
- 1 cup whole milk
- 3 large eggs
- 1 tablespoon spicy brown mustard
- 1 teaspoon pepper
- ¼ teaspoon cayenne pepper

1. For the glaze: Whisk sugar, vinegar, ketchup, and water together in small saucepan and simmer over medium heat until thickened, 15 to 18 minutes. Off heat, whisk in mustard and cayenne; set aside.

2. For the ham loaf: Adjust oven rack to upper-middle position and heat oven to 375 degrees. Line rimmed baking sheet with aluminum foil and spray with vegetable oil spray.

3. Heat oil in 12-inch skillet over medium heat until shimmering. Add onion and cook until softened, about 5 minutes. Transfer to large bowl. Process saltines in food processor until finely ground, about 1 minute; transfer to bowl with onion. Pulse ham in food processor until finely ground, about 10 pulses; transfer to saltine-onion mixture. Add pork, milk, eggs, mustard, pepper, and cayenne to bowl and knead gently until well combined. Transfer mixture to prepared baking sheet and shape into 11 by 6-inch loaf.

4. Brush glaze over top and sides of loaf. Bake until loaf registers 160 degrees, 55 to 65 minutes. Transfer to carving board, tent loosely with foil, and let rest for 20 minutes. Slice and serve.

FIND THE ROOSTER!
A tiny version of this rooster has been hidden in the pages of this issue. Write to us with its location and we'll enter you in a random drawing. The first correct entry drawn will win our top-rated inexpensive stockpot (see page 29), and each of the next five will receive a free one-year subscription to Cook's Country. To enter, visit CooksCountry.com/emailus by September 30, 2011, or write to Rooster, Cook's Country, P.O. Box 470739, Brookline, MA 02447. Include your name and address.
Rowena Sjovall of Lithia, Fla., spotted the rooster in the April/May 2011 issue in the Smothered Pork Chops photo and won our favorite kitchen shears. Cock-a-doodle-doo.

Fruit Cocktail Cake

If Carmen Miranda were a cake, she'd look like our vivid version of the 1950s Del Monte classic recipe.

To make this cake you will need:

- 1 **(20-ounce) can pineapple slices in syrup, drained**
- 1 **(15-ounce) can peach halves in syrup, drained**
- 1 **(15-ounce) can pear halves in syrup, drained**
- 1 **(10-ounce) jar maraschino cherries, drained and stemmed**
- 3 **cups (15 ounces) all-purpose flour**
- 4 **teaspoons baking powder**
- ¾ **teaspoon salt**
- 2 **cups (14 ounces) sugar**
- 4 **large eggs, room temperature**
- 12 **tablespoons unsalted butter, melted and cooled**
- 3 **cups lightly sweetened whipped cream ***

FOR THE CAKE: Place oven rack in middle position and heat oven to 325 degrees. Grease and flour 16-cup tube pan. Reserve 5 pineapple slices, 2 peach halves, 2 pear halves, and 20 cherries for decorating. Pulse remaining fruit in food processor until finely ground, about 5 pulses. Combine flour, baking powder, and salt in bowl. Using stand mixer fitted with whisk, whip sugar and eggs on medium-high speed until pale and thick, about 3 minutes. Decrease speed to low and slowly add butter until incorporated. Add processed fruit and flour mixture until just combined. Scrape into prepared pan and smooth top. Bake until toothpick inserted in center comes out clean, about 1 hour.

Let cake cool in pan on wire rack for 25 minutes. Remove cake from pan and let cool completely, about 3 hours.

TO DECORATE: Transfer cooled cake to serving platter. Spread whipped cream evenly over cake. Cut reserved pineapple in half, thinly slice reserved peaches, and cut reserved pears into thirds. Starting from outer edge, shingle pineapple, peaches, and pears over top of cake. Place cherries in center of pineapple halves and around inner edge. Serve.

----

* Visit CooksCountry.com for our recipe for **Lightly Sweetened Whipped Cream.**

Recipe Index

RC = Recipe Card

Cook's Country

OCTOBER/NOVEMBER 2011

Lost Recipe: Danish Kleiners

Make-Ahead Turkey and Gravy

Slow-Cooker Glazed Ham

Old-Fashioned Bread Stuffing
Back to (Delicious) Basics

Scalloped Potatoes for Two
Quick Cheesy Spuds

Classic Meatloaf with Mushroom Gravy
Diner Favorite Comes Home

Honey–Whole Wheat Rolls
Secrets to Fluffy Texture

Creamy Root Vegetable Soup
Rich and Silky Smooth

Crispy Potato Tots
Not Just for Kids

Indoor BBQ Ribs
More Smoke Flavor

Rating Tomato Soups
Do Any Taste Homemade?

Ohio Buckeyes
Easiest Candy Ever

www.CooksCountry.com
$4.95 U.S./$6.95 CANADA

*The recipe for these delicious, distinctive cookies, called **Danish Kleiners**, was brought to the U.S. from Denmark by a reader's great-grandmother. The family kept the recipe alive. We simplified it, yet stayed true to its spirit, and now we pass it on to you.* PAGE 25

Cook's Country

Dear Country Cook,

On a glorious October day last fall, I drove to the Tunbridge World's Fair in central Vermont. One of the last agricultural fairs, it still offers pig races, oxen pulls, chicken barns, pie contests, and, of course, the giant vegetable competition. Last year's largest pumpkin weighed in at more than 700 pounds—a towering achievement compared with what the gents in the photo below had to show. Our affinities remain constant. At the end of the growing season, we still rush to display our fruit pies and weigh our pumpkins; to eat funnel cake, watch a horse pull, down a beer at the demolition derby, or cheer for one of the kids as they race barrels in the gymkhana.

A farmer I know, Charlie Bentley, is the essence of a Vermonter: quiet and unassuming. Fifteen years ago, he gave me a tour of his farm "museum," a small room off of his kitchen. There he displayed a photo of his favorite team from the 1960s, Duke and Dan, with the blue ribbons that they had won at late August horse draws from Wells to Rutland.

We are storytellers, through our photos and ribbons, by the flotsam hung on our walls and by what we tell our kids at night. A prize pumpkin may lack gravitas, but it shows that we are in the game, that we care enough to win, that we are part of the human parade.

I often think of Duke and Dan. I saw them pull a stoneboat in Wells in late August a half century ago. Charlie was younger then. The world was smaller. The fireflies of August were brighter and more numerous. My mother had brought a picnic to the fairgrounds. Teenagers tried to climb a greased pole. We went home sunburned, our shirtfronts stained with maple ice cream.

A photo of that day was never taken, but it hangs on the wall of memory, where Duke and Dan live on, in a world seen through the eyes of one who remains a child at heart.

Christopher Kimball

Christopher Kimball
Founder and Editor, Cook's Country

Cook's Country

Founder and Editor Christopher Kimball
Editorial Director Jack Bishop
Executive Editor, Magazines John Willoughby
Executive Editor Peggy Grodinsky
Managing Editor Scott Kathan
Senior Editors Lisa McManus, Cali Rich, Diane Unger
Test Kitchen Director Erin McMurrer
Associate Editors Lynn Clark, Amy Graves
Test Cooks Sarah Gabriel, Kelly Price
Assistant Editors Hannah Crowley, Taizeth Sierra
Assistant Test Cooks Nick Iverson,
Rebeccah Marsters, Carolynn Purpura
Copy Editor Nell Beram
Executive Assistant Christine Gordon
Assistant Editor Shannon Friedmann Hatch
Assistant Test Kitchen Director Gina Nistico
Senior Kitchen Assistants Meryl MacCormack,
Leah Rovner
Kitchen Assistants Maria Elena Delgado,
Andrew Straaberg Finfrock, Ena Gudiel
Executive Producer Melissa Baldino
Associate Producer Stephanie Stender

Contributing Editors
Erika Bruce, Eva Katz, Jeremy Sauer
Consulting Editors Anne Mendelson, Meg Ragland
Science Editor Guy Crosby, Ph.D.
Executive Food Editor, TV, Radio & Media
Bridget Lancaster

Online Managing Editor David Tytell
Online Editor Kate Mason
Online Assistant Editors
Eric Grzymkowski, Mari Levine
Video Operations Manager Peter Tannenbaum
Media Producer Alexandra Pournaras
Associate Editor/Camera Operator Nick Dakoulas
Assistant Editor/Camera Operator Jesse Prent

Design Director Amy Klee
Art Director, Magazines Julie Bozzo
Deputy Art Director Susan Levin
Designer Lindsey Timko
Staff Photographer Daniel J. van Ackere
Color Food Photography Keller + Keller
Styling Mary Jane Sawyer, Kelly Upson

Art Director, Marketing/Web Christine Vo
Associate Art Directors, Marketing/Web
Erica Lee, Jody Lee
Designers, Marketing/Web
Elaina Natario, Mariah Tarvainen
Online Photo Editor Steve Kilse

Vice President, Marketing David Mack
Circulation Director Doug Wicinski
Circulation & Fulfillment Manager Carrie Horan
Partnership Marketing Manager Pamela Putprush
Marketing Assistant Lauren Perkins
Customer Service Manager Jacqueline Valerio
Customer Service Representatives
Jessica Amato, Morgan Ryan

Retail Sales & Marketing Manager Emily Logan
Client Service Manager, Sponsorship Bailey Snyder

Production Director Guy Rochford
Senior Project Manager Alice Carpenter
Production & Traffic Coordinator Kate Hux
Asset & Workflow Manager Andrew Mannone
Production & Imaging Specialists Judy Blomquist,
Heather Dube, Lauren Pettapiece

Technology Director Rocco Lombardo
Systems Administrator Marcus Walser
Lead Developer Scott Thompson
Software Architect Robert Martinez
Software Project Manager Michelle Rushin
Business Analyst Wendy Tseng
Senior Web Production Coordinator Evan Davis

VP New Media Product Development Barry Kelly
Social Media Manager Steph Yiu

Chief Financial Officer Sharyn Chabot
Human Resources Manager Adele Shapiro
Publicity Deborah Broide
ON THE COVER:
Genuine Danish Kleiner, Keller + Keller
ILLUSTRATION: Greg Stevenson

Cook's Country magazine (ISSN 1552-1990), number 41, is published bimonthly by Boston Common Press Limited Partnership, 17 Station Street, Brookline, MA 02445. Copyright 2011 Boston Common Press Limited Partnership. Periodicals Postage paid at Boston, Mass., and additional mailing offices. Publications Mail Agreement No. 40020778. Return undeliverable Canadian addresses to P.O. Box 875, Station A, Windsor, Ontario N9A 6P2. POSTMASTER: Send address changes to Cook's Country, P.O. Box 8382, Red Oak, IA 51591-1382. Customer Service: It's easy to subscribe, give a gift subscription, change your address, and manage your subscription online. Visit www.americastestkitchen.com/customerservice for all of your customer service needs or write to us at Cook's Country, P.O. Box 8382, Red Oak, IA 51591-1382. PRINTED IN THE USA

OCTOBER/NOVEMBER 2011

Contents

HONEY-WHEAT ROLLS, 12

HOLIDAY GREEN BEANS, 5

MAKE-AHEAD THANKSGIVING TURKEY, 8

Features

In Every Issue

▶ **We've Remodeled Our Website**
CooksCountry.com has a brand new look. Go online to search for every recipe ever published in the pages of the magazine and watch every episode from all four seasons of our television show, the Emmy-nominated *Cook's Country from America's Test Kitchen.* Check it out!

America's TEST KITCHEN

RECIPES THAT WORK

America's Test Kitchen is a 2,500-square-foot kitchen located just outside of Boston. It is the home of *Cook's Country* and *Cook's Illustrated* magazines and is the workday destination of more than 50 test cooks, editors, and cookware specialists. Our mission is to test recipes until we understand how and why they work and arrive at the best version. We also test kitchen equipment and supermarket ingredients in search of brands that offer the best value and performance. You can watch us work by tuning in to *Cook's Country from America's Test Kitchen* (CooksCountryTV.com) on public television.

Ask Cook's Country

BY SARAH GABRIEL

After Halloween, I roast the seeds from our jack-o'-lanterns. Can I do the same with the seeds from butternut and acorn squashes?
John Navarro, Arlington, Mass.

Pumpkins, squashes, and melons all belong to the botanical family *Cucurbitaceae*, and their seeds are not poisonous. But "won't kill you" and "tastes good" are different criteria, so we roasted butternut and acorn squash seeds alongside pumpkin seeds to see if we'd like to snack on them, too. We roast seeds from any squash or pumpkin at 350 degrees in a lightly oiled rimmed baking sheet for 10 to 15 minutes, stirring a few times, and then season the seeds with salt and pepper while they are hot. Some tasters liked all three, but a few of us found the butternut squash seeds unpleasantly grassy.

THE BOTTOM LINE Squash seeds are not poisonous, so suit yourself and eat the ones you like. We prefer seeds from acorn squash to those from butternut.

ACORN SQUASH SEEDS
As tasty as pumpkin seeds but a little tougher.

The other day I saw red jalapeños in the grocery store. Do they have the same heat as the green ones?
Norman Scott, Seattle, Wash.

A red jalapeño is simply a jalapeño that has been allowed to ripen before harvest. To determine whether color makes a difference in the kitchen, we prepared two batches of our Green Chile Cheeseburgers, some with red jalapeños and some with green. With the competing beef and cheese flavors, tasters were hard-pressed to tell the difference between the red and green jalapeños. To see if red and green could stand in for each other in foods without such strong competing flavors, we grilled a few of each and had tasters try them plain. Some found the red jalapeños more "fruity" and the green more "vegetal." Still, all tasters felt that the jalapeños would make fine substitutes for each other. The factors responsible for a pepper's heat are genetic makeup and growing conditions (hot, dry conditions usually make for spicier peppers), not color.

But maybe our tasters were influenced by what they saw, not what they tasted. To correct for that possibility, we devised a third test: We pureed equal weights of each type of pepper with equal weights of water and then added food coloring to make the green pepper mixture appear red and the red pepper mixture appear green. (Sneaky, huh?) This time, the results split down the middle: Half of the tasters found the disguised red pepper mixture slightly fruitier and "spicier," but the other half, perhaps influenced by its apparent color, called it "green-tasting" and "flatter."

THE BOTTOM LINE You may use red and green jalapeños interchangeably. Heat is not determined by color.

Recently, a friend recommended "converted rice," saying that it always comes out perfect and is healthier than white rice. True?
Barb Bond, Amity, Ore.

Converted rice is either parboiled or steamed (in the husk) and then dehydrated before milling and packaging. The advantage of this extra processing is that converted rice holds its shape better than regular rice. Because it has less surface starch, it is less likely to stick to the bottom of pots.

As for your second question—is it healthier?—our digestive enzymes can't break down converted rice easily because (in simple terms) its starches have been partially crystallized through the precooking process. So converted rice causes a slower rise in blood sugar than regular rice does. These hardened starches also reach the large intestine intact, fueling beneficial bacteria, whereas other starches are broken down before they get that far.

However, these benefits still didn't convince us to switch from regular long-grain rice. When we cooked a batch of converted rice side by side with regular long-grain white rice, our tasters had no trouble telling the difference, and all preferred the regular rice. The converted rice turned yellowish brown, and tasters described its aftertaste as "sharp" or "sour." And while the converted rice sample had perfectly distinct, less sticky grains, tasters also found them "heavier" and "less fluffy."

THE BOTTOM LINE Converted rice holds its shape well and has a few health benefits, but its flavor and texture don't measure up to traditional rice. If you're concerned about rice sticking to the pot, rinse the rice well and use a nonstick pot.

What exactly is lemon oil? The package instructions say to use it in place of lemon zest.
Lyman Johnson, Pinehurst, N.C.

Lemon oil is not lemon-infused oil, but rather highly aromatic oil that is pressed from lemon rinds; as such, it is used in recipes to

replace lemon zest (and not juice). Lemon oil is much more potent than lemon extract, which is lemon oil diluted in alcohol.

LEMON OIL
A fine stand-in for lemon zest, but beware— it's potent.

We bought a few bottles of lemon oil and tried it out alongside fresh zest in the test kitchen's Lemon Pound Cake (the recipe calls for 2 tablespoons of zest). Boyajian, the leading brand of lemon oil here in Massachusetts, doesn't offer a conversion factor for zest to oil. After much trial and error, we found that ½ teaspoon of lemon oil provided the same lemony kick as 2 tablespoons of zest. We prepared our Roast Lemon Chicken using that same conversion; although a few tasters detected "something different" about the chicken made with oil, all found it acceptable.

At first glance, lemon oil seems pricey ($16.75 for a 5-ounce bottle). But at our conversion level of ½ teaspoon of oil for every 2 tablespoons of zest, each lemon's worth of oil costs around 14 cents—a pretty good deal when you consider that lemons often sell for around a dollar. (Admittedly, with the bottle, you don't get the juice.) A bottle of lemon oil should last a year in the refrigerator.

THE BOTTOM LINE Lemon oil is extremely potent; we found that ¼ teaspoon of lemon oil is equivalent to 1 tablespoon of lemon zest in recipes. We'll still be calling for fresh zest in our recipes, but lemon oil is an acceptable substitute.

Why do the cookies I make burn on the bottom and look undercooked on the top?
Alessandra Peters, via email

A number of factors can lead to overbrowned or unevenly browned cookies and if one (or worse, more than one) of these factors is at play in your oven, the results can be disappointing. The possible culprits are the pan (it should be sturdy, rimmed, and not dark-coated), the oven (monitor its temperature with an oven thermometer and if you find that it isn't maintaining the correct temperature, call a repair service), the positioning of the oven racks (the closer to the bottom, the browner the bottoms of your cookies will be relative to the tops), and whether or not you rotate the pans midway through baking (do so). For evenly baked cookies, we recommend the Wear-Ever Half-Size Heavy-Duty Sheet Pan by Vollrath. The test kitchen's favorite oven thermometer, made by Cooper-Atkins, sells for $6, a small price to pay for accuracy. Here in the test kitchen, we develop cookie recipes with the oven racks set to specific positions, so when you use our recipes, adjust the racks as directed. When baking two sheets at a time, at the same time you rotate the pans 180 degrees, also swap them, moving the one on the upper rack to the lower rack and vice versa. If recipes from other sources don't specify an oven position, try a test pan with just a few cookies on the middle rack before gambling with a whole batch of dough.

THE BOTTOM LINE Many factors can turn good cookies bad. Ensure even cooking by using heavy-gauge, uncoated pans lined with parchment paper. Adjust the oven racks and rotate the pans in accordance with the recipe, and be sure that your oven thermostat is accurate by monitoring it with an oven thermometer.

UNDERCOOKED TOP
This is the same cookie in both shots—the rack was too low in the oven...

UNEVEN AND OVER-BROWNED BOTTOM
...plus the flimsy baking sheet wasn't rotated halfway through baking.

To ask us a cooking question:
Visit **CooksCountry.com/askcookscountry**. Or write to Ask *Cook's Country*, P.O. Box 470739, Brookline, MA 02447. Just try to stump us!

Kitchen Shortcuts

COMPILED BY CAROLYNN PURPURA

NEAT TRICK
Fat Buster
Katie Kuber, Tahoe City, Calif.

I don't have a fat separator, but I've found that I can use my turkey baster to defat liquids from roasts or braises. I pour the pan drippings into a large measuring cup and wait about 5 minutes until the fat rises to the top. Then I use the baster to easily remove it to make gravies and sauces that aren't greasy.

NEAT TIP
Rust Buster
June Cottingham, Axson, Ga.

After cleaning pots and pans with steel wool, I store the pads in a plastic bag in the freezer to prevent them from making a rusty mess of the sink area. It takes only a few minutes to thaw them when I'm ready to use the steel wool again.

HANDY TIP
Zest 'n' Freeze
Wyatt Lovering, Boulder, Colo.

Some recipes call for lemon or lime juice but not the zest. Instead of throwing away the spent fruit, I zest it (it's easier to zest before juicing) and freeze the zest in a zipper-lock bag. I always have "fresh" zest at the ready.

HANDY TIP
Measuring Aid
Maureen Glynn, Kenosha, Wis.

I keep a plastic knife in my flour and sugar canisters. Whenever I'm measuring these ingredients for cakes or cookies, I can use the handy knife to neatly sweep the excess off the top of the measuring cup (or spoon) for a level cup. It makes my baking precise.

HANDY TIP
Auto Dryer
Maggie Arnold, Grafton, Mass.

Once I've washed my roasting pan after dinner, instead of drying it with a towel, I return it to the turned-off oven. There, the residual heat dries it in no time. This works with cookie sheets, too.

DOUBLE DUTY
Seed Remover
Mary Anne Hills, Melbourne, Fla.

My mother gave me a set of specialized serrated grapefruit spoons, which always seemed a little fussy to me (don't tell Mom I said that). But I've discovered a handy new use for them. There's no better tool for fishing out the stray seeds that fall into your food when you squeeze a lemon or lime over what you're cooking. The tines net the little seeds fast, so no more chasing them around the bowl.

ON THE GO
Transporting Soup
Danielle MacLean, Philadelphia, Pa.

I often bring soup to work, and lunch used to be a mess. That's because the plastic container I carried it in never sealed well, leaking soup all over my lunch bag. One day, I poured my soup into a wide-mouth canning jar I had in the cupboard. I screwed on the lid, packed my lunch, and it worked: I haven't had a problem with spilling since. Plus, once I remove the lid, I can microwave the soup right in the jar.

COOL TRICK
One Burner, Two Skillets
Nanci York, Liberty Township, Ohio

When I'm frying bacon in a 12-inch skillet, I place a heavy 10-inch skillet over the slices (with the bottom of the pan covered with foil to make cleanup easier). My trick prevents the bacon from curling. Plus, if I am frying eggs, I cook them, covered, in the top skillet at the same time.

Submit a tip by e-mail at **CooksCountry.com/kitchenshortcuts** or send a letter to Kitchen Shortcuts, Cook's Country, P.O. Box 470739, Brookline, MA 02447. Include your name, address, and phone number. If we publish your tip, you will receive a free one-year subscription to *Cook's Country*. Letters may be edited for clarity or length.

Recipe Makeover Chicken Tetrazzini

Cheese, butter, heavy cream . . . This hundred-year-old recipe cried out for an overhaul that actually tasted good. BY CAROLYNN PURPURA

TETRAZZINI IS THE ULTIMATE comfort food—noodles, poultry, and vegetables baked in cream sauce, with a crumb topping and loads of cheese and butter. Although I could swear my grandmother invented it, it was actually created in the early 1900s, long before the age of calorie counting and concern about fat. No surprise, then, that just a single serving contains almost 450 calories and as much as 25 grams of fat. (It's even named after a famously full-figured opera star.)

And no surprise, either, that many low-fat recipes exist. I gathered a handful and got to work. For the sauce, these recipes variously combined egg whites, cornstarch, canned evaporated milk, and margarine or vegetable oil—which were fine if you like bland, tinny flavors and punishingly lean, pasty sauces.

I switched to a high-fat recipe, opting to whittle it down myself: I sautéed mushrooms and onions in butter, made a white sauce (melting more butter, whisking in flour for a roux, and pouring in heavy cream), and stirred in sherry—a classic Tetrazzini flavor—and Parmesan cheese. I combined the sauce, vegetables, boiled noodles, and cubed leftover chicken (which I'm more likely to have on hand than leftover turkey), dumped everything into a casserole dish, and baked.

Before I cut so much as a single calorie or gram of fat, I noticed that the chicken was chalky. Chicken tends toward dryness under the best of circumstances. Cooked twice, it didn't stand a chance. A few tests showed I could use diced raw chicken (boneless, skinless breasts for ease), if I let it begin cooking in the sauce on the stovetop. A quick marinade in soy sauce both added flavor and helped keep the chicken juicy (a soak in salty soy sauce mimics a saltwater brine). Then I turned to my main concern—fat and calories.

The cream would have to go. Borrowing an idea from a low-fat recipe I'd seen, I replaced it with low-fat milk and low-fat mozzarella. As the mild cheese melted, it gave the sauce body (good) and made it stringy (bad). Searching for a mild, low-fat cheese that could perform the same function more smoothly, I tried Neufchâtel (cream cheese with one-third less fat). It yielded a full-bodied, less caloric sauce. To cut down

further, I replaced part of the milk with some of the starchy water in which the noodles had boiled; this helped thicken the sauce. Come to think of it, was that roux absolutely necessary? I skipped the butter and whisked the flour right into the pasta water—with excellent results.

The consistency of the sauce was on target, but it tasted bland. We test cooks put our heads together, and someone suggested I toast the flour. Well, nothing to lose by trying. In fact, toasting added a pleasant, nutty dimension. Next, since the Neufchâtel provided creaminess to spare, I replaced the remaining milk with more flavorful chicken broth. The sauce

went from blah to bright.

Finally, I reconsidered the vegetables. Recipes for full-fat Tetrazzini sauté the mushrooms and the chopped onion in as much as a stick of butter. I cut back tablespoon by tablespoon, and remarkably I found that just a single tablespoon offered enough buttery presence.

Altogether, I had reduced the recipe by 160 calories and 18 grams of fat. The numbers were so good that I was able to leave the crunchy (and, all things considered, only moderately caloric and fatty) bread crumb topping alone. This reduced-fat Tetrazzini is so satisfying that it is destined to become a weeknight staple.

Some people know Tetrazzini only as a leftover dish, but starting with raw chicken breasts solves the problem of dried-out, chalky meat.

The Numbers
All nutritional information is for a single 1-cup serving of chicken Tetrazzini.

Traditional Chicken Tetrazzini
CALORIES **440**
FAT **25 g** SATURATED FAT **16 g**

***Cook's Country* Reduced-Fat Chicken Tetrazzini**
CALORIES **280**
FAT **7 g** SATURATED FAT **4.5 g**

REDUCED-FAT CHICKEN TETRAZZINI Serves 6

You can substitute 2 cups of cooked chopped turkey for the chicken, omitting the marinade and the simmer in step 4.

- 12 ounces boneless, skinless chicken breasts, trimmed of all visible fat and cut into ¾-inch pieces
- 2 tablespoons soy sauce
- 1 slice hearty white sandwich bread, torn into quarters
- 7 tablespoons grated Parmesan cheese
- 2¼ teaspoons salt
- ¾ teaspoon pepper
- 5 ounces spaghetti, broken in half
- 2 tablespoons all-purpose flour
- 1 tablespoon unsalted butter
- 8 ounces white or cremini mushrooms, trimmed and sliced thin
- 1 onion, chopped fine
- 1 cup frozen peas
- 1 cup low-sodium chicken broth
- 2 tablespoons dry sherry
- 3 ounces Neufchâtel cream cheese

1. Combine chicken and soy sauce in zipper-lock bag and refrigerate for 30 minutes to 1 hour. Pulse bread, 2 tablespoons Parmesan, ¼ teaspoon salt, and ¼ teaspoon pepper in food processor until finely ground, 8 to 10 pulses.

2. Meanwhile, adjust oven rack to upper-middle position and heat oven to 400 degrees. Bring 2 quarts water to boil in large saucepan. Add pasta and 1½ teaspoons salt and cook, stirring often, until just al dente. Reserve ½ cup cooking water, then drain pasta and return it to saucepan. Toast flour in 12-inch skillet over medium heat, stirring constantly, until just beginning to brown, about 5 minutes. Whisk flour into reserved cooking water; set aside.

3. Melt butter in now-empty skillet over medium-high heat. Add mushrooms, onion, remaining ½ teaspoon salt, and remaining ½ teaspoon pepper and cook until browned, 6 to 8 minutes. Stir in peas and add mixture to saucepan with pasta.

4. Add broth and sherry to now-empty skillet, scraping up browned bits. Stir in reserved flour mixture, cream cheese, and remaining 5 tablespoons Parmesan and bring to boil, whisking until smooth. Add chicken and simmer until exterior of chicken is opaque, about 1 minute. Add chicken mixture to pasta mixture and toss until combined. Scrape into 8-inch-square baking dish and top with bread crumb mixture. Bake until golden brown, 12 to 14 minutes. Let cool on wire rack for 10 minutes. Serve.

The American Table
Why Is It Called That?

Luisa Tetrazzini

The tradition of naming dishes for famous people was originally associated with European aristocracy, whose chefs honored their masters by affixing their names to dishes. Sauce Soubise, for instance, is named for Charles de Rohan, Prince of Soubise, an exceptionally unsuccessful general under Louis XV. He was respected by the French in spite of his failings because of his dedication to feeding his troops well. (He once saved his chef and *batterie de cuisine* while losing 600 of his troops.) As the power of the aristocracy declined and chefs began to cook for the general public, they turned to naming dishes after artists and entertainers (like opera sensation Luisa Tetrazzini). Today, names on menus are often the farmers who grew the ingredients. —MEG RAGLAND

Refuse to settle for limp, washed-out green beans. With our one-pot method and varied flavors, they can be the surprise star of the meal. BY KELLY PRICE

AT A TYPICAL holiday dinner, my family keeps the dishes moving. "Please pass the potatoes." "May I have the rolls?" "More carrots, please." The one stationary, less-loved item? The sautéed green beans. I figured if I could guarantee a perfect crisp-tender texture and come up with interesting variations, green beans would finally get some respect.

Most recipes call for a two-part, two-pan cooking process: parboiling the beans in a saucepan, halting the cooking in ice water, drying them with kitchen towels, and then (finally) sautéing the beans in butter in a skillet. The test kitchen has found a way to cook green beans that avoids most of that rigmarole: We soften chopped shallot in butter and briefly sauté the beans until they're spotty brown but not fully cooked through; then we add ¼ cup of water, turn down the heat, and cover the skillet so the beans can steam. When they're almost done, we remove the cover so the liquid can evaporate as the beans finish cooking. Easy—both on the stove and in the sink at cleanup time.

With my basic method set, now I could focus on dressing up the basic recipe. As a nod to New England, I created a maple and apple variation where I replaced 2 tablespoons of the water with 2 tablespoons of maple syrup. A bit of rosemary and crunchy toasted pecans rounded out the dish.

A variation with an Italian theme featured sage, toasted hazelnuts, and browned butter. For a salty-sweet angle, I combined bacon and caramelized onions. I liked it so much that I tried a second salty-sweet riff, this time adding dried cranberries (plumped in the pan while the beans steamed); pungent, salty blue cheese; and walnuts.

SAUTÉED GREEN BEANS Serves 8

- 2 tablespoons unsalted butter
- 1 large shallot, sliced thin
- 2 pounds green beans, trimmed
- ¼ cup water
- Salt and pepper

1. Melt butter in 12-inch skillet over medium heat. Add shallot and cook until softened, 1 minute. Add beans and increase heat to medium-high. Cook, stirring occasionally, until beans are spotty brown, 8 to 10 minutes.

2. Stir in water and ½ teaspoon salt, cover, and reduce heat to medium-low. Cook until beans are nearly tender, 3 to 5 minutes. Remove lid and cook until liquid evaporates and beans are tender, about 1 minute. Season with salt and pepper to taste. Serve.

GREEN BEANS WITH APPLES, PECANS, AND ROSEMARY
Increase butter to 3 tablespoons. In step 1, add 2 Golden Delicious apples, cored and cut into ½-inch pieces, to melted butter and cook until light golden, 3 to 5 minutes, then stir in shallot. Replace 2 tablespoons water with 2 tablespoons maple syrup. After removing lid in step 2, add 2 teaspoons minced fresh rosemary. Top cooked beans with ¾ cup pecans, toasted and chopped.

GREEN BEANS WITH BROWNED BUTTER, HAZELNUTS, AND SAGE
Increase butter to 4 tablespoons. Cook butter, stirring constantly, until nutty brown, about 5 minutes, before adding shallot. After removing lid in step 2, add 1 tablespoon minced fresh sage. Top cooked beans with ¾ cup hazelnuts, toasted, skinned, and chopped.

GREEN BEANS WITH CARAMELIZED ONIONS AND BACON
Replace shallot with 2 halved and thinly sliced onions. In step 1, add onions to melted butter and cook until just beginning to brown, about 5 minutes. Stir in 2 teaspoons packed brown sugar and cook, stirring frequently, until light golden brown, about 5 minutes. Add ¾ cup water and cook until golden brown and sticky, about 5 minutes. Transfer onions to bowl and wipe out skillet with paper towels. Melt additional 2 tablespoons butter in now-empty skillet over medium-high heat and add beans. Top cooked beans with caramelized onions and 8 slices crumbled cooked bacon.

GREEN BEANS WITH CRANBERRIES, WALNUTS, AND BLUE CHEESE
Add ¾ cup dried cranberries with water in step 2. Top cooked beans with 4 ounces crumbled blue cheese and ¾ cup walnuts, toasted and chopped.

Dried cranberries, blue cheese, and toasted walnuts dress up green beans in this variation.

Slow Cooker Glazed Ham

The moist environment of the slow cooker guaranteed tender, juicy "baked ham."
But the glaze spelled trouble. BY CAROLYNN PURPURA

COOKING A BIG ham dinner presents a serious real estate problem: My oven is pressed to the max as I try to juggle the ham with all the pies, sides, and biscuits that also require baking. Expanding the cooking environment with a slow cooker seemed like the perfect solution. And sure enough, recipes abound for slow-cooker ham. These recipes called for a variety of hams: spiral and uncut, boneless and bone-in, and even ham steaks. Among the techniques they called for were spice rubs, jelly glazes, sugar smears, and juice braising.

After making seven of these recipes that represented all the various cuts and techniques, I was dispirited by the array of dry, pale, sorry-looking hams they produced. If I wanted moist ham with a dark, burnished glaze, I'd have to figure out the method myself.

Anyone who has ever cooked a ham knows its two main challenges: keeping the ham from drying out and getting a flavorful, caramelized glaze. At the test kitchen, we usually solve the first problem by oven-cooking the ham in the closed, steamy confines of an oven bag. The small, enclosed space of the slow cooker inherently replicates the moisture-retaining capability of an oven bag—to a degree. My early tests taught me a few keys to creating really moist slow-cooker ham: First, use a good-size (at least 6 pounds) bone-in, uncut ham to minimize moisture loss (smaller cuts, boneless, and spiral-sliced hams were more apt to dry out). Second, when placing the ham in the cooker, add about a cup of liquid to the cooker insert to ensure moist meat (recipes without this liquid emerged much drier).

Since I knew I had to add liquid, I hoped I could add flavor at the same time. I tried cooking hams with plain apple and pineapple juice, and with juice seasoned with vegetables and spices, but the meat picked up scant flavor. Water it would be.

As for getting the glaze right, I had already learned that rubs and glazes melted right off the ham over many hours in the slow cooker—even when I crosshatched the ham's exterior for more traction—so I knew I'd need a differ-

> ▶ Shopping for a slow cooker? Find out which one we like best by searching for "slow cooker testing" at CooksCountry.com.

ent approach. I tried making a simple, thick, and clingy glaze on the stovetop and then brushing it on the pale cooked ham. I started with brown sugar cooked down in a saucepan with a little water and butter. But once I brushed it on the cooked ham and let it set up, it became crystalline and gritty. One taster described it as "ham praline." Not exactly what I was aiming for.

Thinking that honey would be both smoother and stickier, I replaced some of the brown sugar with honey and again reduced the mixture slightly before brushing it on the cooked ham. But if the first glaze was praline, this one was caramel: It stuck to the pot, the stove, and even our teeth, and it sheared off the ham in one large sheet. I tried swapping the honey for another common glaze ingredient, apple jelly. Now I was getting somewhere, as tasters appreciated the sweet, fruity dimension of this glaze. But although the glaze seemed to be the right consistency in the saucepan, it was too loose to completely adhere to the ham. A tablespoon of cornstarch fixed that,

making the glaze thick enough to cling. The addition of Dijon mustard and black pepper rounded out the glaze's flavor. Now this ham would look (and taste) great as the centerpiece of any holiday dinner.

No matter what we tried, the glaze ran off the ham in the slow cooker. To fix the problem, we painted an extra-thick glaze onto the ham after it was cooked.

SLOW-COOKER HOLIDAY GLAZED HAM
Serves 16 to 20

Do not substitute spiral-cut ham, as it dries out during slow cooking. Let the glaze cool for 5 minutes before applying (it should be just warm to the touch). For a hint of spiciness, add ¼ teaspoon cayenne to the sugar mixture at the beginning of step 2.

- 1 (6- to 7½-pound) cured bone-in ham
- ½ cup packed dark brown sugar
- ½ cup apple jelly
- 2 tablespoons Dijon mustard
- 1 tablespoon cornstarch
- 1 teaspoon pepper

1. Remove skin from exterior of ham and trim fat to ¼-inch thickness. Score remaining fat at 1-inch intervals in crosshatch pattern. Place ham, cut side down, into slow cooker. Add 1 cup water, cover, and cook on low until fat is rendered and meat registers 100 degrees, 5 to 6 hours. Transfer to carving board and let rest for 15 to 20 minutes.

2. Bring sugar, jelly, mustard, cornstarch, and pepper to boil in small saucepan over medium-high heat. Cook, whisking until smooth, until glaze begins to darken and is slightly thickened, 2 to 3 minutes. Off heat, let glaze cool for 5 minutes in saucepan. Brush ham evenly with glaze and let sit for 5 minutes. Carve and serve.

STEP BY STEP Ham Prep

Spiral-sliced hams dry out in the slow cooker. Bone-in, uncut hams turn out moist and succulent, but they do require some upfront work.

TRIM Use a chef's knife to remove the tough skin or rind. Then carefully trim the fat to about a ¼-inch thickness.

CROSSHATCH Slice a grid pattern into the ham's exterior fat. The ham shrinks as it cooks, deepening the score marks, so the glaze adheres better.

Cooking for Two Cheesy Scalloped Potatoes

Our challenge? Scale down and speed up the rich, creamy casserole that's designed to serve a crowd. BY REBECCAH MARSTERS

IN MANY HOUSEHOLDS, scalloped potatoes are reserved for a large crowd. I suspect it's because the dish bakes for as long as 90 minutes, so people think the time commitment isn't worth it for a smaller group. I disagree: I say this bubbling casserole of sliced potatoes in a luscious, creamy sauce oozing with cheese is too good to save for company. I set out to both scale down and speed up this satisfying dish.

I made several versions to figure out my starting point. All of the recipes required layering thinly sliced raw potatoes in a casserole dish, pouring cream or milk (sometimes mixed with chicken broth) over the slices, sprinkling the dish with cheese, and setting it in the oven to bake. After assimilating tasters' comments, I cherry-picked aspects of the different versions to put together a basic dish. Mine used a combination of cream and chicken broth, with cheddar for the cheese. Now I whittled down the proportions to serve two; the potatoes and sauce fit neatly in a pie plate.

I expected that with so much less bulk, the dish would cook faster, but my just-for-two scalloped potatoes still required an hour of baking time to tenderize. Clearly, the spuds needed a head start. For my next test, I parcooked the sliced potatoes in boiling water before following the recipe as usual. These potatoes were tender after just 15 minutes in the oven. But they tasted watery, and the sauce was now thin. Too late, I realized that I'd forgotten a key advantage of the traditional method: The potatoes release starch into the liquid as they bake, which helps thicken it. By parboiling and then draining the potatoes, I was pouring all that starch—and thickening power—down the drain. I had a better idea.

It's a technique that the test kitchen has used that not only takes advantage of the potatoes' natural starch but also gets flavor deep inside the spuds. I pulled out a saucepan and simmered the raw potatoes on the stovetop right in the cream and broth. After about 10 minutes, I emptied everything into the pie plate and baked the scalloped potatoes. Barely 15 minutes later, I had tender potatoes nestled in velvety sauce. Since I was now using a saucepan to get the potatoes started, it seemed like an easy opportunity to introduce more flavor. I sautéed chopped onion, garlic, and thyme in butter for a few minutes, only then adding the potatoes, cream, and broth. Delicious.

As I was dumping the mix into the pie plate, I suddenly wondered why I was bothering. I ditched the pie plate and exchanged the saucepan for a small ovensafe skillet to allow the potatoes to bake more quickly and evenly. As I'd hoped, the skillet proved a talented multitasker, letting me sauté the vegetables, simmer the potatoes and cream, bake, and serve—all in a single dish.

For me, half of the pleasure of scalloped potatoes is the cheese. The ¼ cup of cheddar I'd been sprinkling on top wasn't adding much, so I doubled that amount and mixed it right into the sauce. Then, for nutty flavor, I sprinkled on Parmesan. The flavor was great, the grease not so much. Here in the test kitchen, we know how to solve that problem: tossing the cheese with cornstarch, which absorbs the fat (or grease) that the melting cheese releases.

Because my scalloped potatoes were baking comparatively quickly, they didn't have time to develop a deep golden crust. Not to worry: I raised the oven rack so that the top potatoes could brown where the oven was warmest. I baked one final test batch—the potatoes were tender, the sauce creamy and oozing, the top golden and gurgling, and the smell out of this world. All this in roughly 30 minutes.

KEY STEP Potato Jump Start
To get dinner on the table faster (and infuse the potatoes with flavor), we simmer the raw slices in the creamy sauce on the stovetop. Then we move everything to the oven, where the potatoes finish baking in less than 15 minutes.

The potatoes start on the stove and finish in the oven, so use an ovensafe, nonstick skillet.

CHEESY SCALLOPED POTATOES FOR TWO

Don't use preshredded cheese, which contains added starch to prevent caking. By adding cornstarch yourself, you can control the dish's texture. You'll need 2 small or 1 extra-large potato.

- 2 ounces mild cheddar cheese, shredded (½ cup)
- 1½ teaspoons cornstarch
- 1 ounce Parmesan cheese, grated (½ cup)
- 1 teaspoon vegetable oil
- ½ cup finely chopped onion
- 1 garlic clove, minced
- ¼ teaspoon dried thyme
- ⅓ cup low-sodium chicken broth
- ⅓ cup heavy cream
- 12 ounces russet potatoes, peeled and sliced ¼ inch thick
- ½ teaspoon salt
- ¼ teaspoon pepper

1. Adjust oven rack to upper-middle position and heat oven to 425 degrees. Toss cheddar and 1 teaspoon cornstarch together in bowl until well combined. Toss Parmesan and remaining ½ teaspoon cornstarch together in second bowl until well combined.

2. Heat oil in 8-inch nonstick, ovensafe skillet over medium heat until shimmering. Add onion and cook until browned, about 5 minutes. Stir in garlic and thyme and cook until fragrant, about 30 seconds. Add broth, cream, potatoes, salt, and pepper and bring to boil. Reduce heat to medium-low, cover, and simmer until potatoes are nearly tender, 10 to 12 minutes.

3. Off heat, stir in cheddar mixture and press potatoes into even layer. Sprinkle Parmesan mixture evenly over top and bake until golden brown, 12 to 14 minutes. Let potatoes cool on wire rack for 10 minutes. Serve.

Make-Ahead Turkey and Gravy

Restaurant kitchens manage the bustle of Thanksgiving dinner by cooking the turkey on Wednesday. Could we adapt that method for the home cook? BY DIANE UNGER

Wouldn't it be great if Thanksgiving actually felt like a holiday—a time to relax, visit with friends and family, and even enjoy dinner? But it rarely does, especially if you're the cook. You're more likely to spend the day running around, carving this, chopping that, and baking (or burning) the other as your entire extended family descends on your dinner table. Luckily, I know something most harried hosts don't: Turkey that's roasted ahead of time can still taste great.

In many restaurants, including one where I used to work, raw turkeys are carved into parts, sorted into white and dark meat, lined up on sheet pans, and cooked separately ahead of the holiday. This technique neatly solves the biggest problem of turkey cookery—the timing. All too often when the entire bird is cooked at once, the white meat is dry and overdone by the time the dark meat cooks through.

Since few home cooks want to spend the day before Thanksgiving breaking down a large, unwieldy raw turkey, I knew I'd need to start with parts. Most supermarkets carry packages of turkey legs and breasts, and, in many cases, the parts are "enhanced," an industry term that means they've been injected with salt water so they are juicier when cooked (similar to brining). I opted for these to boost my odds of ending up with a moist bird. Without the neck and giblets that come with the whole bird, I'd buy a couple of extra legs to simmer to make a stock for the gravy.

Going with turkey parts meant that I couldn't stuff the turkey. Frankly, I didn't consider that a downside, since you can rarely cook enough stuffing inside the bird for the usual number of guests, anyway (plus, baked

Starting with turkey parts makes the cooking more even. Just as important, it makes the reheating faster and more efficient on Thanksgiving Day.

in a casserole dish outside of the bird, the stuffing can get a nice, crisp brown top). As for the parts, was it really necessary to roast the slower-cooking legs and the faster-cooking breasts on separate trays? Could I streamline this restaurant method for the home cook?

I tried putting two legs and the bone-in breast together in a roasting pan, thinking that the smaller legs and larger breast might cook at about the same rate since the legs were no longer insulated under the breast, as they are

on a whole bird. In fact, it worked. But anywhere that the turkey touched the hot roasting pan cooked too fast. To even out the cooking, I placed the parts on an elevated roasting rack so the hot air could better circulate. As a bonus, I now had the opportunity to fill the roasting pan with onions, carrots, celery, and garlic, all of which could slowly roast, caramelize, and soak up flavorful drippings, eventually adding maximum flavor to the stock for the gravy.

After some trial and error, I arrived

at just over 2 hours in a 325-degree oven as the right cooking time and temperature. I'd cracked the code of turkey cookery, getting the legs and breast to cook perfectly at the same rate. At this point, it occurred to me that I could deepen the flavor of the gravy stock by roasting the extra legs that were destined for it in a separate baking dish.

While the meat cooled, I got busy making the stock for the gravy. I dumped the saturated roasted vegetables and the

COOK TURKEY PARTS THE DAY BEFORE: 2 to 2½ hours at 325 degrees

Fill the bottom of the roasting pan with chopped vegetables. Set breast, skin side up, on V-rack with larger end toward edge. Nestle two leg quarters against small end.

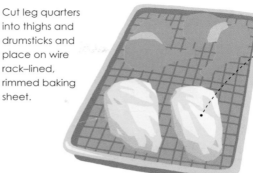

Place two extra leg quarters in a 13 by 9-inch baking dish. (These will be used to make the gravy.)

REHEAT ON THE HOLIDAY: 20 to 25 minutes at 500 degrees

Cut leg quarters into thighs and drumsticks and place on wire rack–lined, rimmed baking sheet.

Cut each half of breast from bone. Remove and save skin. Slice each breast crosswise into ¼-inch slices. Hold slices together and place on foil. Drizzle with stock and cover with skin, then wrap in foil. Place foil packets on the rack with the dark meat.

---

extra legs into a large pot, added chicken broth and water, and simmered the mixture on the stovetop. After the liquid had boiled down for about an hour and a half, I strained and chilled it. By this time, the meat was cool too, so I refrigerated it as well. I hoped my careful prep would pay off big the next day.

I began Day 2 (Thanksgiving Day) by working on the gravy. I scraped off the flavorful fat that had hardened on top of the stock overnight and then cooked some of that fat in a saucepan with flour to make a roux. I warmed the stock, poured it in, and simmered everything until it had reduced to a full-bodied, super-tasty gravy. Done—the gravy required no chopping, straining, or hassle on the big day. (Plus I could make it hours ahead, if I wanted to.)

Now I faced the challenge of reheating the meat. I worked my way through a pile of parts before I determined that a fast blast in a hot oven was the best way to keep the meat from drying out. Reheating the dark meat, which has more fat and is naturally more moist than the white meat, was easy: I separated the thighs from the drumsticks and placed them in a 500-degree oven for about 20 minutes.

The delicate breast meat, however, required a little more technique. Here's the neat trick I came up with: Cut the whole breast in two, remove the skin from each breast in one piece, cut the meat off the bone and slice it, sprinkle on a little reserved broth, then replace the skin over the sliced meat to insulate it during reheating. Next, I wrapped each breast in foil, placed the bundles on a rack-lined baking sheet (the rack ensures even heating), and put them in the hot oven with the thighs and drumsticks. The reserved stock, the skin, the foil, and the fast, hot oven combined to ensure that the breast meat stayed moist and juicy. Plus, there's no (anxiety-producing) carving to be done at the table. With a little foresight and effort the day before, this turkey and gravy make for a headache-free holiday.

MAKE-AHEAD ROAST TURKEY AND GRAVY
Serves 10 to 12

Check the label when you're shopping for turkey. If there's an ingredient list, the bird has been enhanced and will work in this recipe. If you prefer natural, unenhanced parts, we recommend brining. (Dissolve 1 cup of salt in 2 gallons of cold water. Submerge the turkey in the brine, cover, and refrigerate for 3 to 6 hours. Proceed with step 1 of Day 1, omitting the salt for seasoning.)

- 2 onions, chopped
- 2 carrots, peeled and chopped
- 2 celery ribs, chopped
- 2 garlic cloves, peeled
- 2 teaspoons minced fresh thyme
- 4 (1½- to 1¾-pound) turkey leg quarters, trimmed
- 1 (6- to 7-pound) whole bone-in turkey breast, trimmed
- 4 tablespoons unsalted butter, melted
  Salt and pepper
- 4 cups low-sodium chicken broth
- 4 cups water
- 1 bay leaf
- ½ cup all-purpose flour

DAY 1

1. Adjust oven racks to middle and lowest positions and heat oven to 325 degrees. Place onions, carrots, celery, garlic, and thyme in large roasting pan. Set V-rack inside pan. Pat turkey legs and breast dry with paper towels. Arrange 2 legs and breast, skin side up, in V-rack. Brush turkey with butter and season with salt and pepper. Place remaining 2 legs in 13 by 9-inch baking dish and season with salt and pepper.

2. Place roasting pan on middle rack and baking dish on lower rack. Roast until breast registers 160 degrees and thighs register 175 degrees, 2 to 2½ hours. Transfer 2 legs and breast to wire rack set in rimmed baking sheet and let cool to room temperature, about 2 hours.

3. Transfer vegetables in roasting pan and remaining 2 legs to large pot,

scraping up any browned bits. Add broth, water, bay leaf, and 1 teaspoon pepper and bring to boil. Simmer over medium-low heat until reduced to 5 cups, 1¼ to 1½ hours. Pour through fine-mesh strainer into large container, discarding solids. Let cool for 1 hour, cover, and refrigerate for 4 hours or up to 2 days. Wrap cooled legs and breast tightly in plastic wrap and refrigerate for up to 2 days.

DAY 2

1. Scrape fat from top of chilled stock and reserve 5 tablespoons. Bring stock to simmer in medium saucepan. Set aside ¼ cup stock. Heat reserved fat in large saucepan over medium heat. Add flour and cook, whisking constantly, until golden, 3 to 4 minutes. Slowly whisk in remaining 4¾ cups stock and bring to boil. Reduce heat to medium-low and simmer until slightly thickened and reduced to 4 cups, 12 to 14 minutes. Season with salt and pepper to taste.

2. Meanwhile, adjust oven rack to middle position and heat oven to 500 degrees. Transfer legs and breast to carving board. Separate legs into thighs and drumsticks and arrange on wire rack set in rimmed baking sheet. Cut breast meat from bone into 2 single breasts. Working one at a time, remove skin from breast in 1 piece; reserve. Slice breast crosswise into ¼-inch slices and place on 18 by 12-inch sheet of aluminum foil, keeping slices together. Pour 2 tablespoons reserved stock over each breast and top with reserved skin. Wrap tightly and place on rack with legs.

3. Roast until turkey is heated through and thighs and drumsticks are crisp, 20 to 25 minutes. Discard breast skin. Season with salt and pepper to taste. Serve with gravy.

▶ Curious about what other delicious turkey recipes we've developed in the past? Visit us online at **CooksCountry.com** and search for "turkey."

Back-to-Basics Bread Stuffing

To bring our bread stuffing back to its humbler roots, we subtracted ingredients— and then we had to figure out how to multiply flavor. BY SARAH GABRIEL

IN RECENT YEARS, there's been a proliferation of bread stuffing recipes with delusions of grandeur. Sure, stuffing with a dozen or more ingredients (wild rice, dried cherries, Italian sausage, fennel seeds, pine nuts, eggs, cream…) can be delicious, but I wanted to revisit an older, simpler style of stuffing to counter both the excess of the Thanksgiving table and the stress of preparing it. I wanted purer flavors and no fussy custard that could curdle or break.

My nostalgia evaporated as soon as I started cooking. Most 19th- and early-20th-century recipes called for cooking the stuffing inside a bird to ensure moisture and meaty flavor, but the big batch I planned wouldn't fit inside the cavity. Plus, trading the rougher loaves of yore for today's supermarket sandwich bread rendered much of the century-old stuffing wisdom useless. Two popular older methods—soaking sliced bread in milk and using moistened bread crumbs—turned my more-delicate modern bread into sludge.

But one batch had promise. The pared-down flavors and ingredient list were exactly what I had in mind—nothing but cubed, toasted bread; onions and celery sautéed in butter; poultry seasoning; and water. But this stuffing wasn't perfect. Despite the water, it was dry, plus it lacked poultry flavor (no surprise, since the bird was gone).

This recipe called for toasting the bread and then dicing it, but others did the reverse or simply used up stale bread. In tests, toasting cubed bread yielded the maximum toasty-flavored surface area and proved most resistant to sogginess. Great—but the recipe I was using suffered from the opposite problem. With a mere 1½ cups of water for 2 pounds of bread, the stuffing was dry and crumbly.

To moisten it, I doubled the original amount of water. Not enough. Four cups? Still dry. At 5 cups, moist patches were interspersed with dry, cottony patches. I learned that if I let the mixture rest for 10 minutes (so the water could permeate) and gave the mix a stir halfway through, things evened out.

Without the turkey to flavor the stuffing as it cooked, I needed to trade the water for chicken broth. But that alone didn't give me deep roasted flavor. I tried doubling the usual amount of onions, and instead of merely sautéing

Our secrets to no-frills stuffing with big flavor? Cooking extra onions and celery until really brown, concentrating some of the broth, and drizzling brown butter over the top before baking.

them with the celery until translucent, I took them all the way to brown. For more pervasive herb flavor, I "bloomed" the poultry seasoning, cooking it briefly with the butter and vegetables. Now I reconsidered the broth: Could I get more out of it? I used some to deglaze the pan that I'd cooked the vegetables in and let it boil down. (To make up for the volume of liquid lost to evaporation, I added an extra cup of broth to the recipe.) As I'd hoped, scraping the flavorful, browned bits from the pot and concentrating some of the broth deepened meatiness…but I still wasn't satisfied. If browned vegetables and toasty bread helped, what about browned butter? Cooking butter until the milk proteins began to brown finally

gave the stuffing all the roasted, nutty flavor I was after.

"Now, how about a crunchy top?" tasters asked. Can do. Unlike many modern stuffings, mine contained no eggs. That meant I could go from the moderate 350 degrees I'd been using to 425 degrees, without any fear that I'd scramble a custard. While I was at it, I moved the stuffing to a higher rack, where it would brown better. I reserved 3 tablespoons of browned butter to drizzle over the top before baking, guaranteeing that the top stayed moist. I had transformed this stuffing by browning the bread, vegetables, butter, and finished stuffing. It seemed that the key to successfully dusting off this classic wasn't more ingredients, but more cooking.

BACK-TO-BASICS
BREAD STUFFING Serves 10 to 12

Use a hearty white sandwich bread, such as Arnold Country Classics White Bread (our taste-test winner).

- 2 pounds hearty white sandwich bread, cut into ½-inch pieces
- 16 tablespoons unsalted butter, cut into 16 pieces
- 4 onions, chopped fine
- 4 celery ribs, chopped fine
- 4 teaspoons poultry seasoning
- 1¾ teaspoons salt
- 1 teaspoon pepper
- 6 cups low-sodium chicken broth

1. Adjust oven racks to upper-middle and lower-middle positions and heat oven to 325 degrees. Divide bread between 2 rimmed baking sheets and bake until golden brown, 50 to 55 minutes, stirring bread and switching and rotating sheets halfway through. Cool completely on baking sheets, then transfer to large bowl.

2. Melt butter in 12-inch skillet over medium-low heat. Cook, stirring constantly, until butter is nutty brown, 5 to 7 minutes. Reserve 3 tablespoons browned butter in small bowl. Add onions and celery to skillet, increase heat to medium, and cook until browned, 12 to 15 minutes. Stir in poultry seasoning, salt, and pepper and cook until fragrant, about 30 seconds. Add vegetable mixture to bowl with toasted bread.

3. Increase oven temperature to 425 degrees. Add 2 cups broth to now-empty skillet and cook over high heat, scraping up any browned bits, until reduced to 1 cup, 6 to 8 minutes. Combine remaining 4 cups broth and reduced broth with vegetable-bread mixture and let sit for 10 minutes, stirring once. Transfer stuffing to 13 by 9-inch baking dish and press into even layer. Drizzle reserved browned butter evenly over top and bake on upper-middle rack until golden brown and crisp, 35 to 45 minutes. Let cool for 15 minutes. Serve.

MAKE AHEAD

Stuffing without butter topping can be refrigerated in baking dish, covered with aluminum foil, for up to 1 day. To finish, remove foil, drizzle with melted reserved browned butter, re-cover, and bake for 10 minutes. Uncover and bake until stuffing is heated through and top is golden brown, 35 to 40 minutes.

Creamy Root Vegetable Soup

With a cup (or more) of cream in the pot, who can taste the root vegetables?
But with less cream, how could we keep the silkiness? BY JEREMY SAUER

ALL WINTER LONG I make friends with root vegetables: I roast, glaze, and fry potatoes, carrots, onions, and the occasional turnip. I slice them into salads and stir them into stew. But inevitably, they end up playing sidekick. This winter I was determined to make root vegetables the star of the show, so I sautéed some aromatics and added cupfuls of the chopped roots, a few glugs of chicken broth, and a heavy dose of heavy cream. After everything had simmered 20 minutes and been spun in the blender, I sat down with a bowl of soup, eager to taste the (ahem) roots of my labor. All I tasted was cream.

To see where I'd gone wrong, I hit the books. Classic soups like potato-leek or carrot-ginger focused on a single vegetable, letting that one root shine, whereas I wanted a mix of mellow, sweet, earthy vegetables. I started with the usual suspects—carrots, onion, and celery—plus some potato for its mild, earthy flavor. Then I ran through celery root, turnips, beets, even rutabaga, before landing on a couple of parsnips, which added a gentle, haunting sweetness. Now I needed a cooking technique that would accentuate the vegetables.

Most recipes followed the same generic soup method: sauté onions (and sometimes garlic); add chopped root vegetables; simmer in water, broth, or milk until tender; puree. A few recipes, however, called for browning the roots by either sautéing them with the aromatics or roasting them in the oven. Both approaches nicely brought out the vegetables' natural sweetness and concentrated their flavors. I chose sautéing, which was faster than roasting, plus it left me with fewer dishes to clean.

I browned everything in butter (tasters preferred its nutty taste to oil). Once the vegetables were golden brown, I stirred in four cups of chicken broth (water was "too watery" and milk "bland and sweet") and simmered the soup until the vegetables were tender. Next, I pureed the soup, added ¾ cup of cream (25 percent less than in my initial test), and seasoned it with salt and pepper. I dipped in a spoon, but instead of the complex mix of flavors I'd anticipated, I was again eating generic "cream of whatever." I added herbs. Thyme and sage were too strong; a bay leaf was just right. I then included garlic, smashed, at the start. Still, the soup lacked depth.

From experience, I knew that dairy products mute flavors. But I'd already cut the cream in half. Just to see what would happen, I dropped the cream down to a mere ½ cup. What do you know? The subtle complexity of the root vegetables did return. Unfortunately, with less cream, the soup was wan. It was a catch-22: More cream obliterated the flavor of the vegetables. Less cream damaged the texture of the soup. To fix the texture, I turned to an old test kitchen trick, replacing the onion with a leek. As I'd hoped, it added silkiness. It was a start. Next, I added extra potatoes, thinking that the additional starch might simulate "creamy" texture. Although the starch helped, the soup now tasted like mashed potato soup (or maybe *vichyssoise*). That gave me an idea.

In the test kitchen, whenever we mash potatoes, we take great care not to overwork them since a heavy hand with mashing activates the starches and results in gluey potatoes. Could I turn this to my advantage? This time, after I browned the other root vegetables, I added the lesser amount of potatoes to the pot and stirred the mixture for two minutes straight. In that time, the potato starches turned the vegetables sticky and glossy. I added the broth and kept stirring periodically. When the vegetables were tender, I pureed the soup, added in the ½ cup of cream, and tasted. The soup was silky smooth, earthy, flavorful, and sweet.

For a slightly chunkier soup, you can puree it right in the pot with an immersion blender.

CREAMY ROOT VEGETABLE SOUP
Serves 4 to 6
You'll need 2 medium parsnips here.

- 4 tablespoons unsalted butter
- 2 carrots, peeled and chopped
- 6 ounces parsnips, peeled and chopped
- 1 leek, white and light green parts only, halved lengthwise, sliced thin, and washed thoroughly
- 1 celery rib, chopped
- 1 garlic clove, peeled and smashed
  Salt and pepper
- 12 ounces russet potatoes, peeled and cut into ½-inch pieces
- 4¼ cups low-sodium chicken broth
- 1 bay leaf
- ½ cup heavy cream

1. Melt butter in Dutch oven over medium-high heat. Add carrots, parsnips, leek, celery, garlic, and ½ teaspoon salt and cook until browned, 6 to 8 minutes. Stir in potatoes and cook, stirring constantly, until starch begins to release and vegetables begin to stick together, about 2 minutes. Add broth and bay leaf and bring to boil.

2. Reduce heat to low and simmer, stirring occasionally, until vegetables are tender, 15 to 20 minutes. Discard bay leaf. Working in batches, process soup in blender until smooth, 1 to 2 minutes. Return soup to clean pot and stir in cream. Season with salt and pepper to taste. Serve. (Soup can be refrigerated for up to 2 days.)

Honey-Wheat Dinner Rolls

We wanted tender, fluffy dinner rolls that actually tasted of whole wheat and honey. Surely that wasn't too much to ask. BY LYNN CLARK

For whole wheat rolls with the fluffiness of classic dinner rolls, we found that we needed to include some white flour as well.

IN MY EXPERIENCE, there are two types of honey–whole wheat dinner rolls, and neither hits the mark: Commercially produced versions are light and fluffy, but they're usually too sweet and taste only faintly of wheat. Commercial bakeries rely on chemical dough softeners to lighten their rolls and use more artificial sweeteners than honey. Homemade honey-wheat rolls present a different set of problems. The ones I tried tasted wheaty and nutty, all right, but they were as dense as wet sand. In both cases, these rolls are often honey in name only. I wanted tender, fluffy honey-wheat rolls that actually tasted like their namesake ingredients.

Since I love the texture of the test kitchen's favorite white dinner roll, I decided to start with that recipe and reverse engineer it into a whole wheat roll (I'd worry about the honey later). Our recipe calls for all-purpose flour, yeast, milk, butter, honey, and salt. As a starting point, I exchanged all the white flour for an equal amount of whole wheat flour. Our resident test kitchen bread-baking expert warned me that I'd need more liquid than usual, so I dutifully added an extra ¼ cup of milk. Then I kneaded the dough, let it rise, shaped it into rolls, let it rise again, and baked. A few hours later, I stared unhappily at the tray of tough, dense honey-wheat rolls I'd produced. Also, using all whole wheat flour had made the rolls almost bitter.

I thought that adding more butter (I was working with 4 tablespoons) would yield softer, more tender rolls. Instead, it made them greasy and even denser than before. Some recipes for rolls add eggs: The protein in the egg whites traps air bubbles in the dough, helping the bread to rise, while the fat in the yolks tenderizes the dough. Adding an egg did help to lighten the dough a bit, so I tried adding a second. I'd gone too far. Now the crumb was crumbly instead of soft.

Several more tests showed that no matter what I added, the rolls were heavy, coarse, and bitter. I finally admitted to myself that a 100-percent wheat dinner roll wasn't going to work. That's because wheat flour and white flour function differently. The bran in whole wheat flour inhibits gluten development, which is why wheat rolls don't rise as well as white flour rolls. To get a light, fluffy roll, I'd have to put some all-purpose white flour back into the dough, letting more gluten develop. I gradually removed wheat flour and replaced it with all-purpose, at the same time cutting back on the milk I'd only just added. I could take it only so far before the nuttiness that defines whole grains disappeared. After a few tests, I figured out that a volume ratio of about 3 to 2 wheat to white flour was where I had to stop. At this point, while the texture of the rolls had improved, they still didn't wow me. I needed another idea.

On a particularly rainy day, as I poured the liquid ingredients into the dry, I noticed that the dough was much wetter than usual. I attributed it to the weather: The dough seemed to be absorbing extra moisture from the humid air. I figured my test was ruined, but, not wanting to have wasted time, I went ahead and shaped the loose dough rounds into rolls anyway. Because the dough was so floppy and wet, in the oven the rolls spread out, not up. But it wasn't all bad news. The interiors were decidedly lighter and fluffier than in my other tests thus far. Why?

Our science editor explained that whole wheat flour has a lot more bran than white flour. Big deal, I knew that. What I didn't know was that bran is sharp, so sharp that it can slice right through the gluten strands that give height and structure to bread (and cakes, for that matter). To stop the bran from doing so, I needed to soften it. How? By letting it absorb a lot of water. (Alternatively, I could let the bran soak for a long time, but I was unwilling to wait around any longer than necessary

---

STEP BY STEP **Shaping Honey-Wheat Rolls**

1. To get evenly sized rolls, cut the dough into quarters and then quarters again.

2. Shape each piece of dough into a ball by pulling the edges under and pinching to seal.

3. Working on a clean counter, cup the dough with your palm and roll it into a taut ball.

4. Nestle the balls closely in the dish for maximum rise: 6 down the center and 5 on either side.

for these rolls.) By sheer good luck (and bad weather), I'd found the key to fluffy wheat rolls—a super-wet (or "super-hydrated") dough.

With this in mind, I once again increased the amount of liquid called for in my recipe (we couldn't rely on rain) to make an especially sticky dough. To force the loose dough to rise up, not spread out, I snuggled the shaped rolls against one another in a baking dish. Placing them close together also translated into less crust and a more fluffy interior. Indeed, these rolls were the best yet: tall and soft yet still unequivocally wheaty.

I still wanted to bump up the honey flavor, though. Most recipes used just 2 tablespoons of honey, basically replacing the sugar that's usual in yeast dough with honey. I needed to increase the honey to 6 tablespoons before we could actually taste it. For a second hit of honey flavor, I mixed another teaspoon with some melted butter and brushed the honey butter on the rolls after they came out of the oven.

After several weeks of testing, I'd finally learned that honey-wheat rolls

---

TEST KITCHEN TECHNIQUE
Wet? You Bet.

Whole wheat flour contains a lot of bran, while white flour contains only trace amounts. While bran adds flavor and nutrients, it also causes problems for the bread baker. Bran is so sharp that it actually cuts the strands of gluten that should give rising bread its height and structure. To soften the bran so that it can't wreck havoc, we learned to make an especially hydrated (wet) honey-wheat dough.

JUST COMBINED
The dough looks very wet. Relax and trust us. It will come together.

AFTER KNEADING
The dough still looks comparatively wet. You may see a sticky ring around the bowl. That's good.

---

come in three types, and one of them is something you'd actually enjoy eating. My rolls were simultaneously fluffy and wheaty, plus the taste of honey came through loud and clear.

HONEY-WHEAT DINNER ROLLS
Makes 16 rolls
Expect this dough to be sticky.

- 1¾ cups whole milk, heated to 110 degrees, plus 1 tablespoon
- 6 tablespoons plus 1 teaspoon honey
- 5 tablespoons unsalted butter, melted and cooled
- 1 large egg
- 2½ cups (13¾ ounces) whole wheat flour
- 1¾ cups (8¾ ounces) all-purpose flour
- 1 tablespoon instant or rapid-rise yeast
- 2¼ teaspoons salt

1. Adjust oven rack to lower-middle position and heat oven to 200 degrees. When oven reaches 200 degrees, turn it off. Grease large bowl and 13 by 9-inch baking dish. Combine 1¾ cups milk, 6 tablespoons honey, 4 tablespoons butter, and egg in 4-cup liquid measuring cup.

2. Using stand mixer fitted with dough hook, mix whole wheat flour, all-purpose flour, yeast, and salt on low speed until combined. Slowly add milk mixture and mix until dough comes together, about 1 minute. Increase speed to medium and mix until dough is smooth and almost clears sides of bowl yet still sticks to bottom, 6 to 8 minutes.

3. Transfer dough, scraping sides of bowl, to greased bowl. Cover with plastic wrap and place in turned-off oven until dough has doubled in size, about 45 minutes.

4. Punch down dough on lightly floured counter. Divide dough into quarters and cut each quarter into 4 equal pieces. Form each piece into rough ball by pinching and pulling dough edges under so that top is smooth. On clean counter, cup each ball with your palm and roll into smooth, tight ball. Arrange in prepared baking dish and cover loosely with plastic. Let rolls rest in turned-off oven until doubled in size, about 20 minutes.

5. Remove rolls from oven and discard plastic. Heat oven to 400 degrees. Combine remaining 1 tablespoon butter and remaining 1 teaspoon honey in bowl. Brush rolls with remaining 1 tablespoon milk. Bake rolls until golden brown and register 200 degrees, about 20 minutes, rotating dish halfway through baking. Brush with honey butter and let cool in dish on wire rack for 10 minutes. Remove rolls from dish. Serve.

MAKE AHEAD
Instead of 20-minute rise in step 4, baking dish with formed rolls can be refrigerated, covered, for 24 hours. Let dough sit at room temperature for 30 minutes before brushing with milk and baking.

ON THE SIDE
Cranberry-Waldorf Relish

Bored by the same old relish, we married cranberry sauce with the flavors of Waldorf salad.

BY CAROLYNN PURPURA

SOME PEOPLE LOVE tradition. Year after year, they serve the identical Thanksgiving feast. Not me. I prefer to change it up. This year, I got the idea to jazz up my cranberry sauce with the flavors of Waldorf salad: apples, walnuts, grapes, and celery (skipping the mayonnaise, thank you very much).

I started with the test kitchen's basic cranberry sauce recipe, which uses 12 ounces of cranberries, 1 cup of sugar, and ¾ cup of water. My first move was to replace the water with an equal amount of apple juice. Next, I chopped up an apple, a rib of celery, some toasted walnuts, and a few grapes and tossed them into the pot as the cranberries cooked. This chunky sauce was OK, but the assertive cranberries overpowered the other ingredients. Also, the apple juice, grapes, and apples combined to make the relish too sweet. In order to taste the Waldorf flavors, I doubled the quantities of add-ins. Oops. I'd inadvertently made the relish sweeter than ever. Easy to fix—I cut back on the sugar.

The texture remained a problem, however. It was watery and the nuts were mushy. To thicken the sauce, I shredded the apples. Shredded apples, I figured, would break down faster and release their pectin, which, in turn, would bind the sauce. It worked as planned, but tasters missed the apple chunks from earlier tests. I split the difference, grating one apple and dicing the other. Next, I traded the grapes for pleasantly chewy golden raisins (also common in Waldorf salad), which helped soak up the excess liquid. As for the nuts, I waited until the relish was done cooking before I added them. They were still soft. Cooling the relish completely and only then stirring in the nuts let them retain more of their crunch.

My cranberry Waldorf creation was delicious. All my tasters agreed. But I'm already plotting something new for next year.

This sweet-tart relish pairs well with pork, as well as turkey.

CRANBERRY-WALDORF RELISH
Makes about 3½ cups
If you're using frozen cranberries, cook for 1 to 2 minutes longer. Use the large holes of a box grater to shred 1 apple. Don't worry if the relish looks thin—it thickens significantly as it cools. If you're making the relish ahead of time, add the walnuts when you're ready to serve it.

- ¾ cup apple juice
- ½ cup sugar
- ½ teaspoon salt
- 12 ounces (3 cups) fresh or frozen cranberries
- 2 apples, peeled and cored, 1 cut into ½-inch pieces and 1 shredded
- 2 celery ribs, chopped fine
- ¼ cup golden raisins
- ½ cup walnuts, toasted and chopped

1. Bring apple juice, sugar, and salt to boil in medium saucepan. Add cranberries, chopped apple, shredded apple, celery, and raisins and simmer over medium heat until slightly thickened and two-thirds of berries have burst, about 5 minutes.

2. Transfer to serving bowl and let cool completely, about 1 hour. Stir in walnuts. Serve. (Relish can be refrigerated for up to 1 week.)

Carolina Sweet Potato Sonker

Is pumpkin pie your default dessert for Thanksgiving? Shake things up with this little-known, homey treat. (And did we mention it comes with its own sauce?) BY REBECCAH MARSTERS

Sonker, a generous, old-fashioned North Carolina dessert that's kin to slump, grunt, cobbler, and buckle, is a riddle wrapped in a mystery inside a pastry crust. The recipe itself barely shows up in cookbooks. Culinary historians can't figure out how old the dessert is, or even the origins of the funny-sounding name. (The Shetland Isles in Scotland? An Appalachian dialect?) One thing we do know: Since 1980, the small, once remote town of Lowgap, in the foothills of the Blue Ridge Mountains, has hosted an annual festival in its honor. There, sonker comes in many styles and flavors. Nothing wrong with either the peach or the blackberry, but the most popular is sweet potato sonker. Taste it and you'll see there's no mystery about that.

Classic sweet potato pie calls for mashed sweet potatoes. For sonker, the sweets are sliced like apples.

Sweet potatoes, of course, have a long history in the South. Everybody knows about sweet potato pie, with its creamy filling and single crust, but sonker is a different kettle of fish. For one thing, the sweet potatoes aren't mashed—they're sliced (like apples for apple pie). These slices are boiled and then tossed with brown sugar, spices, and butter. Next, they're piled into the enormous crust, topped with a lattice, and baked to earthy, buttery, cinnamon-scented perfection. A sweet, spiced, milky sauce—"dip" in Lowgap, Surry County speak—is the usual accompaniment.

In the past, Surry County cooks used the biggest pans they owned, as sonker is meant to feed a crowd (of farm hands, historians say). To test a basic recipe, I used a 13 by 9-inch baking dish. After calculating that I'd need a quadruple batch of homemade pie dough, I opted for store-bought crust and proceeded to make and bake a sonker.

What a disappointment: The sweet potatoes were mushy and tasted washed out. The top crust was doughy wherever the strips of lattice intersected, plus the sides caved in. And while the store-bought pie dough simplified the recipe considerably, it tasted merely serviceable. Obviously, the residents of Surry County know something that I didn't.

I began with the filling. Boiling the potatoes had let the flavor leach out. Since recipes for apple or peach pie usually use raw fruit, why cook the potatoes at all? I filled the pastry crust with raw sweet potato slices, but in the oven the crust darkened long before the slices softened. Back to parcooking. Given such a big batch of sweet potatoes (4 pounds), I wasn't entirely surprised that the microwave failed to cook the slices evenly. My next strategy—steaming the sweet potatoes on the stovetop—worked well. And when I dumped the slices into the crust and baked off a sonker, they held their shape and texture.

The flavor, however, remained underwhelming. One recipe for sonker that I'd found (from cookbook writer and North Carolinian Jean Anderson) steamed the potatoes over apple juice in place of water. I modified the idea, steaming the slices over apple cider, which the test kitchen has found has better flavor. I set the potatoes aside and let the cider boil away until just ½ cup of deeply concentrated juice was left. I tossed it with the sweet potato slices. That, combined with the apple-infused steam that the sweet potatoes had cooked in, produced a very tasty sonker that improved further when I reinforced the standard cinnamon with allspice, vanilla extract, and lemon juice.

Fixing the slumping crust was a simple matter of letting the sweet potatoes cool before I filled it. I spread them on a baking sheet so they'd do so quicker. To boost the flavor, I used an old baker's trick: brushing the raw lattice with egg and sprinkling on cinnamon sugar. In the test kitchen, we usually bake pies on the lowest rack to ensure a nicely browned bottom crust. In this case, though, the double thickness of the lattice clearly required more heat from above in order to cook through. I experimented with temperatures and oven arrangements and found the sonker did best right in the middle at 375 degrees. I also needed to shield the sonker with foil at the start of baking.

Residents of Surry County say that a sonker just isn't the same without the sauce—er, dip. Some recipes thicken it with cornstarch; others call for an egg-based custard. In a side-by-side tasting, we didn't find the trickier egg-based sauce worth the trouble. So while the sonker was baking, I simmered milk, sugar, cinnamon, and cornstarch in a pot on the stove, later adding vanilla. The plain, old-fashioned sauce suggested that sonker goes back many generations.

Many of my colleagues were skeptical when I started testing. Blame it on the oddball star ingredient, the funny name, or the mediocre results early on. Whichever, I endured more than a few (lame) jokes that rhymed "sonker" with "bonkers." Just four weeks later, though, my colleagues were lining up for slices and demanding dip. I told them they were eating humble pie.

SWEET POTATO SONKER Serves 12

SONKER

- 2 (15-ounce) boxes Pillsbury Just Unroll! Pie Crust
- 1 large egg, beaten
- 2 cups apple cider
- 4 pounds sweet potatoes, peeled, quartered lengthwise, and sliced ¼ inch thick
- 1 cup (7 ounces) packed light brown sugar
- 4 tablespoons unsalted butter, softened
- 2½ tablespoons all-purpose flour
- 2 tablespoons lemon juice
- 1 teaspoon vanilla extract
- ¾ teaspoon ground cinnamon
- ½ teaspoon ground allspice
- ¼ teaspoon salt
- 1 tablespoon granulated sugar

CUSTARD DIP

- 2 cups whole milk
- ¼ cup (1¾ ounces) sugar
- 2 teaspoons cornstarch
- ¼ teaspoon ground cinnamon
- ⅛ teaspoon salt
- 1½ teaspoons vanilla extract

1. FOR THE SONKER: Working on lightly floured counter, unroll 2 dough rounds. Brush half of 1 round with egg and overlap with second round. Roll out dough to 17 by 13-inch rectangle and fit into 13 by 9-inch baking dish. Cover with plastic wrap and refrigerate for 30 minutes. Repeat shaping and rolling with remaining 2 dough rounds; reserve beaten egg. Trim dough into rectangle and cut into ten 1-inch strips. Transfer dough strips to parchment-lined rimmed baking sheet, cover with plastic, and refrigerate for 30 minutes.

2. Meanwhile, adjust oven rack to middle position and heat oven to 375 degrees. Bring cider to boil in Dutch oven. Place steamer basket in Dutch oven and fill with sweet potatoes. Reduce heat to medium and cook, covered, until potatoes are nearly tender, 20 to 30 minutes. Remove and reserve sweet potatoes, leaving cider in pot.

3. Cook cider over high heat until reduced to ½ cup, about 5 minutes. Combine drained sweet potatoes, brown sugar, reduced cider, butter, flour, lemon juice, vanilla, ½ teaspoon cinnamon, allspice, and salt in large bowl. Spread out sweet potato mixture on rimmed baking sheet and let cool to room temperature, about 20 minutes.

4. Scrape cooled sweet potato mixture into dough-lined dish and press into even layer. Brush edges of dough with reserved egg. With long side of dish facing you, lay 4 dough strips lengthwise over sweet potato mixture. Weave remaining 6 strips into lattice pattern. Press dough strips into bottom crust and trim excess. Fold dough sides inward under lip of baking dish and crimp with fork.

5. Combine granulated sugar and remaining ¼ teaspoon cinnamon in bowl. Brush dough with reserved egg and sprinkle with cinnamon sugar. Cover with aluminum foil and bake for 15 minutes. Uncover and bake until deep golden brown, 55 to 60 minutes, rotating dish halfway through baking. Let sonker cool on wire rack for at least 1½ hours before serving. (Sonker can be refrigerated, covered, for up to 1 day. Bring to room temperature before serving.)

6. FOR THE CUSTARD DIP: Meanwhile, bring milk, sugar, cornstarch, cinnamon, and salt to simmer in medium saucepan over medium heat. Reduce heat to medium-low and cook, whisking frequently, until slightly thickened, about 15 minutes. Off heat, add vanilla. Transfer to bowl and let cool to room temperature, about 30 minutes. Serve with sonker.

⏵ Feeling ambitious? Make your own pie dough. Go to CooksCountry.com/extra for our Double-Crust Pie Dough recipe. (You'll need to double that recipe to make the sonker.)

The American Table
Tuber Technology

George Washington Carver

Today, we think of sweet potatoes as ingredients in side dishes or desserts. But for hundreds of years they were a staple food in much of the United States, particularly in the South. During hard times, many people survived primarily on these tubers. One major problem was that sweet potatoes bruise easily during harvest, and bruised potatoes quickly rot. In her book *Dori Sanders' Country Cooking*, the African American novelist describes farmhands wearing cotton gloves while harvesting sweet potatoes as a way to avoid bruising. Farmers had better luck curing the potatoes, drying them out so that they would be less fragile. George Washington Carver, the scientist famous for his work with peanuts, devised a viable curing technique sometime in the late 1910s. After that, not only was much less of the crop wasted, but sweet potatoes became available year-round. One sweet potato practice that's probably not worth reviving? Using dried, ground sweet potatoes as a substitute for coffee, which was common during the Civil War.

Rounds into Rectangles

It takes a big sheet of pie dough to line a 13 by 9-inch baking dish. We make it easy by using store-bought pie crust. Take two rounds, overlap them by half, bind with beaten egg, and roll into a rectangle. Repeat, cutting the second rectangle into strips for the sonker's lattice top.

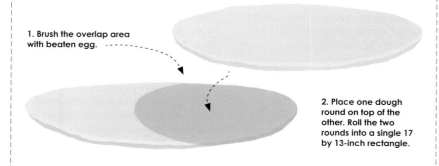

1. Brush the overlap area with beaten egg.

2. Place one dough round on top of the other. Roll the two rounds into a single 17 by 13-inch rectangle.

TEST KITCHEN TECHNIQUE How to Weave a Lattice

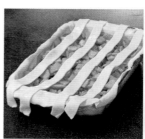  

1. Evenly lay four dough strips over the filled sonker parallel to the long side of the dish. The strips will be longer than the dish.

2. Fold the first and third strips back and lay a perpendicular strip across the other two. Unfold the folded strips to cover the perpendicular one.

3. Continue adding perpendicular strips, alternating between folding and unfolding the first and third and the second and fourth strips.

Getting to Know Baking Spices

To make the most of your baking spices, follow our tips: Preground spices are convenient, but their flavor fades fast. Label them with the purchase date and then store them in a cool, dry place and use them within a year. Otherwise, buy whole spices and grind them yourself in a coffee grinder devoted to this purpose. (P.S.: Many of these baking spices are good in savory foods, too.)

Cinnamon
AMERICAN CLASSIC

Americans love cinnamon and use it freely in favorites like apple crisp, sticky buns, and pumpkin pie. Most cinnamon sold in this country is actually cassia, not true Ceylon cinnamon (pictured above and also known as canela). Both are the dried bark of tropical evergreen trees, but the bolder, spicier cassia is cheaper to process. Our favorite mail-order brand of ground cinnamon is Penzeys; at the supermarket, buy Adams (both are cassia).

Nutmeg
EGGNOG ESSENTIAL

Heady and powerful, nutmeg is a hard, brown seed from a tropical tree. It's often used in dairy-based savory dishes, like quiche and creamed spinach, or for sweets such as spice cake. We compared fresh with preground and found that in dishes in which nutmeg is the sole spice, grinding it yourself (we like to use a rasp-style grater) is important. But in foods with lots of spices, preground nutmeg is fine.

Mace
NUTMEG'S OTHER HALF

Ground mace tastes like a more pungent nutmeg (and that's saying something), and for good reason: It's made from the lacy membrane, or aril, that surrounds the nutmeg seed inside the fruit. Dried, whole mace comes in "blades," but the ground form is more common. We pitted mace against nutmeg and found that you can substitute one for the other by using half as much of the more potent mace as you would nutmeg, or twice as much nutmeg in recipes that call for mace.

Allspice
ISLAND FAVORITE

Allspice tastes like a combination of cinnamon, clove, and nutmeg, hence its name. Ground allspice is used in sweets such as mincemeat pie and gingerbread, and it's a hallmark of Caribbean cooking and jerk seasoning. In the test kitchen, we sometimes cook (or "bloom") ground allspice in butter and then add the spiced butter to dough or batter; the technique brings out the flavor of the spice.

Cloves
NAIL-BITER

Pungent, peppery cloves are the dried, unopened buds of an Indonesian tree. They resemble nails—in fact, the word "clove" comes from the Latin word for nail, *clavus*. Ground cloves are potent, so the test kitchen uses them sparingly in baked goods. Add whole cloves to the poaching liquid for fruit or, on the savory side, employ them to flavor stocks and to stud holiday hams.

Star Anise
LICORICE KNOCKOFF

As the name suggests, these pods are star-shaped and they taste like anise. The warm, licorice-like flavor of star anise works well in foods both sweet and savory (Asian marinades, custards). It's an essential element of five-spice powder. Try flavoring sugar syrup with whole pods and drizzling the syrup over citrus fruits.

Cardamom
CHAI MATE

Fragrant cardamom comes in pods, either green or black, each holding many tiny seeds. Seeds from the more common green pods are used in many Scandinavian baked goods, Indian sweets, and chai tea. Although the whole pod can be toasted and ground or steeped, most of the highly aromatic flavors live in the seeds. The flavor doesn't stick around, so buy whole pods and then remove and grind the seeds, as needed.

Ground Ginger
ROBUST ROOT

Yes, ground ginger comes from the dried fresh root, but don't substitute one for the other. They taste different (fresh is more floral, dry is spicier), work differently in baking (fresh is moister), plus fresh is less potent. We do, however, sometimes reinforce ground ginger with fresh grated in the test kitchen, for instance to make gingerbread.

Vanilla Beans
POTENT POD

These fragrant beans are the dried, fermented pods of orchids. They need to be hand-harvested, which accounts for their high price. Freshness is the key to good flavor, so look for pods that are plump, shiny, and moist. Enlist whole, split beans to flavor poaching liquids. Scrape out the seeds with a paring knife to use them in ice cream and pudding. Fresh beans versus extract? In our tasting of custard, the bean swept the field.

Mahleb
MIDDLE EASTERN DARLING

This one's probably not in your pantry. Made from the dried, ground seed kernels found inside the pits of sour black cherries, mahleb tastes like bitter almonds with a hint of cherry. It's used to flavor many sweets in the Middle East and Greece. To add it to your repertoire, try introducing 2 to 4 teaspoons to sugar cookies or pound cake. Our tasters found it "herbal" and "floral" and compared it to vanilla and even anise.

Lavender
FLOWER POWER

Don't relegate lavender to soaps and perfumes. It's actually a relative of mint, and the dried buds give sweets an exotic floral quality. (It's also a component in the spice blend herbes de Provence, often used to flavor fish and poultry.) Try the buds infused into ice cream, custards, and syrups. Or pair lavender with chocolate—you'll be happily surprised. Remember that a little lavender goes a long way.

Black Pepper
DARK HORSE

What's pepper doing here? Actually, black pepper is more versatile than you may know: It makes an intriguing addition to many spiced baked goods. Don't be tempted to buy preground, though. The flavor doesn't compare with fresh ground. The test kitchen's favorite supermarket peppercorns are from Morton & Bassett. Try a pinch or two in caramel sauce, gingerbread, or spice cookies.

MEXICAN STEAK TIPS WITH CRISPY POTATOES

SESAME CHICKEN WITH BROCCOLI AND RED PEPPER

CHICKEN, ARTICHOKE, AND SPINACH CALZONE

SKILLET PENNE WITH OLIVES AND CAPERS

SESAME CHICKEN WITH BROCCOLI AND RED PEPPER Serves 4

WHY THIS RECIPE WORKS: Potent sesame oil and fresh ginger add quick punch to this stir-fry.

- ¾ cup low-sodium chicken broth
- ¼ cup soy sauce
- 2 tablespoons cornstarch
- 2 teaspoons toasted sesame oil
- 12 ounces boneless, skinless chicken breasts, trimmed and cut into 1-inch pieces
- 3 tablespoons vegetable oil
- 1 pound broccoli, florets cut into 1-inch pieces, stalks peeled and sliced ¼ inch thick
- 1 red bell pepper, stemmed, seeded, and cut into 2-inch-long matchsticks
- 1 tablespoon grated fresh ginger
- 1 tablespoon sesame seeds, toasted

1. Whisk together ½ cup broth, 3 tablespoons soy sauce, 1 tablespoon cornstarch, and sesame oil in medium bowl. Toss chicken, remaining 1 tablespoon soy, remaining 1 tablespoon cornstarch, and 1 tablespoon vegetable oil to coat in large bowl.

2. Heat 1 tablespoon vegetable oil in 12-inch nonstick skillet over medium-high heat until just smoking. Brown chicken, about 5 minutes. Transfer to plate and tent loosely with foil.

3. Add broccoli and remaining ¼ cup broth to now-empty skillet and cook, covered, until broccoli begins to soften, about 2 minutes. Uncover and cook until liquid evaporates, about 1 minute. Stir in remaining 1 tablespoon vegetable oil and bell pepper and cook until spotty brown, 3 to 4 minutes. Add ginger and cook until fragrant, about 30 seconds. Whisk sauce to recombine and add to skillet with chicken and any accumulated juices. Cook until thickened, about 1 minute. Sprinkle with sesame seeds. Serve.

MEXICAN STEAK TIPS WITH CRISPY POTATOES Serves 4

WHY THIS RECIPE WORKS: To speed along dinner, we use the microwave to jumpstart the potatoes.

- 2 pounds small red potatoes, quartered
- 7 tablespoons vegetable oil
- 3 tablespoons minced fresh cilantro
- 2 scallions, minced
- 1 tablespoon white wine vinegar
- 1 garlic clove, minced
- 1½ pounds sirloin steak tips, trimmed and cut into 2-inch pieces
  Salt and pepper
- 2 shallots, sliced thin

1. Microwave potatoes and 2 tablespoons oil in covered large bowl until edges of potatoes are translucent, 4 to 7 minutes. Whisk 3 tablespoons oil, cilantro, scallions, vinegar, and garlic together in medium bowl; reserve.

2. Meanwhile, pat steak dry with paper towels and season with salt and pepper. Heat 1 tablespoon oil in 12-inch nonstick skillet over medium-high heat until just smoking. Brown beef on all sides, 6 to 8 minutes. Transfer to plate and tent loosely with foil.

3. Heat remaining 1 tablespoon oil in now-empty skillet over medium-high heat until shimmering. Cook potatoes and shallots until golden, 5 to 7 minutes. Drizzle steak with reserved cilantro oil and serve with potatoes and shallots.

TEST KITCHEN TIP: Use potatoes that are between 1 and 2 inches in diameter.

SKILLET PENNE WITH OLIVES AND CAPERS Serves 4 to 6

WHY THIS RECIPE WORKS: Cooking the penne in the pasta sauce infuses the pasta with flavor and streamlines the cooking with a single pan.

- 1 tablespoon vegetable oil
- 1 pound hot Italian sausage, casings removed
- 2 garlic cloves, minced
- 1 (28-ounce) can crushed tomatoes
- 2 cups water
- 12 ounces penne
- ⅓ cup pitted kalamata olives, halved
- ¼ cup capers, rinsed
- ¼ cup chopped fresh basil
- 6 ounces Italian cheese blend, shredded (1½ cups)

1. Adjust oven rack to upper-middle position and heat oven to 450 degrees. Heat oil in 12-inch nonstick ovenproof skillet over medium heat until shimmering. Cook sausage, breaking into pieces, until no longer pink, about 5 minutes. Add garlic and cook until fragrant, about 30 seconds.

2. Stir in tomatoes, water, and pasta. Cover and cook, stirring occasionally, until pasta begins to soften, about 7 minutes. Reduce heat to medium-low and simmer, covered, until pasta is al dente, about 7 minutes. Stir in olives, capers, and basil. Sprinkle with cheese and bake until cheese begins to brown, 4 to 6 minutes. Serve.

TEST KITCHEN TIP: Sweet Italian sausage tastes great here, too.

CHICKEN, ARTICHOKE, AND SPINACH CALZONE Serves 4 to 6

WHY THIS RECIPE WORKS: Shredded rotisserie chicken provides a quick, hearty filling for these calzones.

- 1 rotisserie chicken, skin discarded, meat shredded into bite-size pieces (about 3 cups)
- 9 ounces frozen artichoke hearts, thawed, patted dry, and chopped
- 2 ounces (2 cups) baby spinach
- 6 ounces low-moisture mozzarella cheese, shredded (1½ cups)
- 4 ounces feta cheese, crumbled (1 cup)
- ¼ cup chopped fresh basil
- ½ teaspoon salt
- ¼ teaspoon pepper
- 1 (1-pound) ball ready-made pizza dough
- 2 tablespoons olive oil

1. Adjust oven rack to upper-middle position and heat oven to 450 degrees. Combine chicken, artichokes, spinach, mozzarella, feta, basil, salt, and pepper in bowl.

2. Divide dough in half. On lightly floured counter, roll dough into two 9-inch rounds. Working one at a time, place half of filling over half of dough, leaving 1-inch border around edges. Brush edges with water, fold dough over filling, and crimp to seal. Repeat with remaining dough and remaining filling.

3. Brush rimmed baking sheet with 1 tablespoon oil. Transfer calzones to prepared sheet and cut two 1-inch slits in top of each calzone. Brush calzones with remaining 1 tablespoon oil and bake until golden brown, about 20 minutes. Serve.

TEST KITCHEN TIP: The dough will be easier to roll if you let it sit at room temperature for 5 minutes before rolling out.

BEEF TENDERLOIN WITH PARMESAN RISOTTO

POTATO-CRUSTED HALIBUT WITH TARTAR SAUCE

SPICED CHICKEN WITH COUSCOUS

**PROSCIUTTO-WRAPPED PORK TENDERLOIN
WITH HERB PAN SAUCE**

POTATO-CRUSTED HALIBUT WITH TARTAR SAUCE Serves 4

WHY THIS RECIPE WORKS: Baking the fish with a crust of potato chips makes for a crisp, flavorful coating without deep frying.

- 1 cup mayonnaise
- 3 tablespoons finely chopped dill pickles, plus 1 teaspoon pickle juice
- 1 small shallot, minced
- 1 tablespoon capers, rinsed and chopped fine
  Salt and pepper
- 1 tablespoon lemon juice
- 2 teaspoons Dijon mustard
- ⅛ teaspoon cayenne pepper
- 4 (6-ounce) skinless halibut fillets, 1 inch thick
- 2 cups potato chips, crushed

1. Adjust oven rack to middle position and heat oven to 450 degrees. Combine ¾ cup mayonnaise, pickles, pickle juice, shallot, capers, ¼ teaspoon salt, and ¼ teaspoon pepper in bowl; set aside.

2. Combine remaining ¼ cup mayonnaise, lemon juice, mustard, and cayenne in second bowl. Pat fish dry with paper towels and season with pepper. Brush top and sides of fish with mayonnaise–lemon juice mixture and coat with potato chips, pressing to adhere.

3. Place fish on foil-lined rimmed baking sheet and bake until fish flakes apart when gently prodded with paring knife and registers 140 degrees, 12 to 15 minutes. Serve with tartar sauce.

TEST KITCHEN TIP: Any firm white fish like cod, haddock, or mahi-mahi works well here. The test kitchen's favorite potato chips are Lay's Kettle Cooked Original.

BEEF TENDERLOIN WITH PARMESAN RISOTTO Serves 4

WHY THIS RECIPE WORKS: Giving the rice a head start in the micro-wave ensures the risotto will be ready when the steaks finish resting.

- 4 cups low-sodium chicken broth
- 1 cup Arborio rice
- 6 tablespoons unsalted butter
- 1 tablespoon vegetable oil
- 4 (6- to 8-ounce) center-cut filets mignons, about 2 inches thick
  Salt and pepper
- 1 onion, chopped fine
- 2 garlic cloves, minced
- 2 ounces Parmesan cheese, grated (1 cup)
- 3 tablespoons minced fresh parsley

1. Microwave 3 cups broth, rice, and 2 tablespoons butter in covered large bowl until most of liquid is absorbed, 14 to 16 minutes.

2. Meanwhile, heat oil in 12-inch skillet over medium-high heat until just smoking. Pat steaks dry with paper towels and season with salt and pepper. Cook until browned and meat registers 120 to 125 degrees (for medium-rare), 3 to 5 minutes per side. Transfer to plate and tent loosely with foil.

3. Wipe out skillet with paper towels. Melt 2 tablespoons butter over medium heat. Cook onion until softened, about 5 minutes. Stir in garlic and cook until fragrant, about 30 seconds. Add parcooked rice and remaining 1 cup broth and simmer, stirring constantly, until rice is tender, 5 to 7 minutes. Off heat, stir in Parmesan, parsley, and remaining 2 tablespoons butter. Season with salt and pepper to taste. Serve with steaks.

TEST KITCHEN TIP: For a slightly more economical option, substitute boneless strip steaks of similar thickness cut in half crosswise.

PROSCIUTTO-WRAPPED PORK TENDERLOIN WITH HERB PAN SAUCE Serves 4 to 6

WHY THIS RECIPE WORKS: After browning the tenderloins, we finish cook-ing them in the oven and make a rich pan sauce from the fond in the skillet.

- 2 (12-ounce) pork tenderloins, trimmed
  Salt and pepper
- 6 ounces thinly sliced prosciutto
- 2 tablespoons vegetable oil
- 1 tablespoon all-purpose flour
- 2 garlic cloves, minced
- 2 teaspoons minced fresh thyme
- 1¼ cups low-sodium chicken broth
- ¼ cup lemon juice (2 lemons)
- 3 tablespoons minced fresh chives

1. Adjust oven rack to middle position and heat oven to 450 degrees. Pat tenderloins dry with paper towels and season with pepper. Wrap each tenderloin with prosciutto.

2. Heat 1 tablespoon oil in 12-inch skillet over medium-high heat until just smoking. Cook pork until browned on all sides, 5 to 7 minutes. Transfer meat to wire rack set in foil-lined rimmed baking sheet. Bake until meat registers 145 degrees, 15 to 18 minutes.

3. Meanwhile, heat remaining 1 tablespoon oil in now-empty skillet over medium heat until shimmering. Add flour, garlic, and thyme and cook, stir-ring constantly, until fragrant, about 1 minute. Stir in broth and lemon juice and cook, scraping up any browned bits, until slightly thickened, about 3 minutes. Off heat, add chives. Season with salt and pepper to taste. Slice pork and serve with sauce.

TEST KITCHEN TIP: You will need 4 to 6 slices of prosciutto per tenderloin.

SPICED CHICKEN WITH COUSCOUS Serves 4

WHY THIS RECIPE WORKS: Pumpkin pie spice—a combination of cinnamon, ginger, nutmeg, and allspice—combines with cumin to provide the warm spice profile found in many Moroccan dishes.

- 1 teaspoon ground cumin
- ¾ teaspoon pumpkin pie spice
  Salt and pepper
- 4 (12-ounce) bone-in split chicken breasts, trimmed and halved crosswise
- 1 tablespoon vegetable oil
- 1½ cups low-sodium chicken broth
- 1 (15-ounce) can chickpeas, rinsed
- 1 cup couscous
- ½ cup dried apricots, chopped into ¼-inch pieces
- ⅓ cup green olives stuffed with pimento, sliced, plus 1 tablespoon olive brine

1. Adjust oven rack to lowest position and heat oven to 450 degrees. Combine cumin, pumpkin pie spice, ½ teaspoon salt, and ¼ teaspoon pepper in bowl.

2. Pat chicken dry with paper towels and rub with spice mixture. Heat oil in 12-inch skillet over medium-high until just smoking. Cook chicken, skin side down, until browned, about 5 minutes. Arrange chicken, skin side up, in 13 by 9-inch baking dish and roast until meat registers 160 degrees, about 20 minutes.

3. Meanwhile, bring broth to boil in now-empty skillet. Stir in chickpeas, couscous, apricots, olives, and olive brine, cover, and remove from heat. Let stand for 5 minutes. Season with salt and pepper to taste. Serve with chicken.

Smoky Indoor Ribs

How do you duplicate the tender texture and smoky richness of slow-smoked barbecued ribs in your oven? BY KELLY PRICE

"SMOKE IS NO JOKE" is the barbecue mantra in my native North Carolina. What this means is, you can't have real barbecue without smoke. I was in full agreement until I moved to Boston, where barbecuing through the long winter is impractical. But living without the smoky, tangy, slightly spicy barbecue ribs I was raised on was not an option.

So I gathered a representative sampling of recipes for indoor "smoked" ribs and got cooking. The recipes used three approaches to try to introduce smoke flavor: placing wood chips on the oven floor, rubbing the raw ribs with smoked paprika, or broiling a liquid smoke–enhanced barbecue sauce onto cooked ribs. Fail, fail, and fail. The chips never smoked, the rubs didn't add much, and the smoky sauce didn't get inside the meat. If I wanted deeply smoky, tender ribs with a sticky, saucy crust, I'd have to start from scratch.

I knew to start with St. Louis–cut spareribs, which are meatier than baby backs but more manageable than regular spareribs (the latter has extra meat, bone, and bulk on one end). Next, I focused on getting smoke flavor into the meat. Traditional barbecue relies on long exposure to wood smoke (generated by soaked wood chips in backyard recipes). Could I get wood chips to work in the oven? Even at the highest temperature, even on ripping-hot baking sheets and pizza stones, the chips never smoked. Time to give up on the chips.

I'd already discovered that brushing a smoky sauce onto cooked ribs added only superficial smokiness. But what if I braised the ribs in a smoky liquid? I tested every smoky ingredient I could think of: chipotle powder, smoked paprika, liquid smoke, espresso powder, and Lapsang Souchong tea, all mixed with water. After the ribs had braised for about 1½ hours—enough time to start tenderizing and hopefully drink up some braising liquid—I baked them "dry" for another 1½ hours to get a crusty exterior that approximated real barbecue "bark." Except for a faint whiff of smoke in the liquid smoke batch, tasters detected no smoke. I upped the liquid smoke from 1 teaspoon to 2 tablespoons, and

now I was on to something. I added espresso powder; it hadn't done much on its own, but the two worked nicely together to deepen the smoke flavor.

To create a sticky coating, I slathered the test kitchen's basic barbecue sauce on the ribs twice while they were baking. That was good, and it got even better when I added some of the liquid smoke and espresso powder. Replacing the paprika with smoked paprika contributed yet more smoky depth. These ribs were pretty good, but I knew the true test was with the test kitchen's Southern contingent. "Tastes like home," said one tester. "Smoke is no joke," said another. Little did they know.

SMOKY INDOOR RIBS Serves 4 to 6

Use liquid smoke that contains no salt or additional flavorings.

RIBS

- 2 tablespoons instant espresso powder
- 2 tablespoons liquid smoke
- 1 tablespoon salt
- 2 (2½- to 3-pound) racks pork spareribs, preferably St. Louis cut, trimmed and membrane removed

BARBECUE SAUCE

- 1 tablespoon vegetable oil
- 1 onion, chopped fine
  Salt and pepper
- 1 tablespoon smoked paprika
- 1½ cups low-sodium chicken broth
- ¾ cup cider vinegar
- ¾ cup dark corn syrup
- ¾ cup ketchup
- ½ cup molasses
- 2 tablespoons brown mustard
- 1 tablespoon hot sauce
- 1 tablespoon instant espresso powder
- ½ teaspoon liquid smoke

1. FOR THE RIBS: Adjust oven rack to middle position and heat oven to 300 degrees. Bring 3 cups water, espresso powder, liquid smoke, and salt to boil in small saucepan. Pour mixture into large roasting pan. Place ribs, meat side down, in liquid. Cover pan tightly with aluminum foil and bake for 1½ hours.

2. FOR THE BARBECUE SAUCE: Meanwhile, heat oil in large saucepan over medium heat until shimmering. Add onion and ¼ teaspoon salt and cook until softened, about 5 minutes. Stir in paprika and cook until fragrant, about 30 seconds. Add broth, vinegar,

corn syrup, ketchup, molasses, mustard, hot sauce, and espresso powder and simmer, stirring occasionally, until thickened and reduced to 2 cups, 50 to 60 minutes. Stir in liquid smoke and season with salt and pepper to taste. Let cool for 20 minutes. (Sauce can be refrigerated for up to 1 week.)

3. Reserve ½ cup sauce for serving. Remove ribs from roasting pan and transfer, meat side up, to wire rack set in foil-lined rimmed baking sheet; discard braising liquid. Brush both sides of ribs with sauce. Bake until tender and fork inserted into meat meets no resistance, about 1½ hours, brushing meat side with sauce after 30 and 60 minutes of cooking. Tent ribs loosely with foil and rest for 30 minutes. Slice meat between bones and serve with reserved sauce.

Most recipes for indoor ribs use liquid smoke in the sauce. We follow suit but intensify the smoky effect by braising the ribs in a smoky liquid first.

▶ Never removed the membrane from a rack of pork ribs? For our method, go to CooksCountry.com/extra.

TEST KITCHEN TECHNIQUE
Bringing the Smoker Inside

We braise the ribs in a mixture of water, espresso powder, and liquid smoke. After 1½ hours, the ribs are ready to be slowly roasted with sauce for a caramelized "bark."

Meatloaf with Mushroom Gravy

For this back-to-basics meatloaf, we magnified the mushroom flavor and streamlined the kitchen work. BY REBECCAH MARSTERS

In my book, the world would be a better place without honey-chipotle, truffle, and pesto-swirled meatloaf. Perhaps meatloaf recipes have gotten out of control because plain meatloaf—in its pure form just ground meat, seasonings, binder, and maybe a glaze or gravy—is so simple that it's actually hard to get right. This point was driven home when I gathered eight recipes for meatloaf with gravy. One had so much oregano and Italian sausage that it resembled a giant meatball, and another was so full of vegetables that meatloaf seemed a misnomer. An herb- and bread-heavy loaf was akin to "Thanksgiving stuffing." Other recipes had gravies that were greasy, thin, or bland. I decided to scrap all of these and start with a clean slate.

Putting gravy on the back burner for the moment, I turned my attention to the loaf. Meatloaf mix, a combination of ground beef, pork, and veal, is the traditional choice, but I settled on pork and beef alone (mild, delicate veal seemed out of place in the rustic dish that I pictured). I included sautéed onion and garlic and went with basic seasonings: Worcestershire sauce, salt, and pepper. A simple mixture of cracker crumbs, milk, and eggs made for a neutral-tasting binder. (I subsequently learned that it's easier to add the binder to the pork and introduce the beef afterward. Our science editor explained that because the pork has more water than ground beef, it blends more easily.)

We use sautéed button mushrooms, dried porcini mushrooms (and their soaking liquid), and Worcestershire sauce to beef up the flavor of this meatloaf.

Over years of making meatloaf in the test kitchen, we've found that meat packed into a loaf pan stews in its own juices and fat, and only gets really crusty on the top. We prefer to bake meatloaf "free-form" on a rimmed baking sheet so the fat can drain and the entire loaf can get appealingly crusty and craggy (all the better for soaking up gravy). For a first stab, this loaf wasn't bad. But had I taken my quest for simplicity too far? Regardless of the fact that I'd be serving it with gravy, this meatloaf needed more oomph.

Since I'd be building a gravy based on mushrooms, I decided to try adding some to the meat mix. I chopped up button mushrooms and tossed them into the sauté pan with the onion and garlic. The flavor was definitely improved, but the cooked mushroom pieces were slimy in the loaf. To keep their flavor minus the unpleasant texture, I gave the mushrooms a few quick pulses in a food processor before sautéing them. Mission accomplished.

After the meatloaf had baked,

I poured the drippings from the baking sheet into a skillet to start the gravy. I browned more sliced button mushrooms in the drippings, whisked in flour and beef broth, and simmered. The beef broth muted the mushroom flavor, so I switched to milder chicken broth. Still, tasters wanted more depth, so, building on the mushroom theme, I tried adding dried porcini mushrooms to the gravy. I soaked the dried porcini in hot water to rehydrate them and then drained and chopped them before sautéing them with the other vegetables. With a dash of Worcestershire sauce and a bit of thyme, the gravy finally achieved depth and richness.

As a batch of gravy was thickening, it dawned on me that I was using the same skillet in which I had sautéed the onion and mushrooms for the meatloaf earlier—was I missing an opportunity to streamline the process? For my next loaf, I sautéed the vegetables as usual, but instead of fetching a rimmed baking pan on which to bake the meatloaf, I wiped out the skillet and shaped the meatloaf right in it. After baking, all I had to do was move the meatloaf to a cutting board (tented with foil to retain heat) and put the skillet back on the stove (carefully—the handle was hot) to make the gravy; the drippings were already right where I wanted them.

I was almost done, but I kept eyeing the leftover porcini soaking liquid on the counter, which experience has taught me packs a ton of rich, earthy flavor. Surely I could find a home for it. After a bit of trial and error, I learned that I could not only add ½ cup of the porcini liquid to the gravy but also boost the flavor of the meatloaf by using the liquid instead of milk. This hearty, robust meatloaf and rich mushroom gravy may not be fine-dining fare (thankfully), but all the same, it makes for some pretty fine dining.

Looking for something to eat with your meatloaf? Visit CooksCountry.com and search for "mashed potatoes."

MEATLOAF WITH MUSHROOM GRAVY
Serves 6 to 8

If you're short the 2 tablespoons of meatloaf drippings needed to make the gravy, supplement them with melted butter or vegetable oil. Swanson Certified Organic Free Range Chicken Broth is our taste-test winner.

- 1 cup water
- ¼ ounce dried porcini mushrooms, rinsed
- 16 saltines
- 10 ounces white mushrooms, trimmed
- 1 tablespoon vegetable oil
- 1 onion, chopped fine
  Salt and pepper
- 4 garlic cloves, minced
- 1 pound ground pork
- 2 large eggs
- 1 tablespoon plus ¾ teaspoon Worcestershire sauce
- 1 pound 85 percent lean ground beef
- ¾ teaspoon minced fresh thyme
- ¼ cup all-purpose flour
- 2½ cups low-sodium chicken broth

1. Adjust oven rack to middle position and heat oven to 375 degrees.

Microwave water and porcini in covered bowl until steaming, about 1 minute. Let sit until softened, about 5 minutes. Drain porcini through fine-mesh strainer lined with coffee filter, reserve liquid, and mince and reserve porcini.

2. Process saltines in food processor until finely ground, about 30 seconds; transfer to large bowl and reserve. Pulse 5 ounces of white mushrooms in processor until finely ground, 8 to 10 pulses.

3. Heat oil in 12-inch nonstick skillet over medium-high heat until shimmering. Add onion and cook until browned, 6 to 8 minutes. Stir in processed mushrooms and ¼ teaspoon salt and cook until liquid evaporates and mushrooms begin to brown, about 5 minutes. Add garlic and cook until fragrant, about 30 seconds. Transfer to bowl with saltines and let cool to room temperature, about 15 minutes. Wipe out skillet with paper towels.

4. Add pork, ¼ cup reserved porcini liquid, eggs, 1 tablespoon Worcestershire, 1 teaspoon salt, and ¾ teaspoon pepper to cooled mushroom-saltine mixture and knead gently until nearly combined. Add beef and knead until well combined. Transfer meat mixture to now-empty skillet and shape into 10 by 6-inch loaf. Bake until meatloaf registers 160 degrees, 45 to 55 minutes. Transfer meatloaf to carving board and tent loosely with aluminum foil.

5. Slice remaining 5 ounces white mushrooms. Discard any solids in skillet and pour off all but 2 tablespoons fat. Heat fat over medium-high heat until shimmering. Add sliced mushrooms and reserved porcini and cook, stirring occasionally, until deep golden brown, 6 to 8 minutes. Stir in thyme and ¼ teaspoon salt and cook until fragrant, about 30 seconds. Add flour and cook, stirring frequently, until golden, about 2 minutes. Slowly whisk in broth, ½ cup reserved porcini liquid, and remaining ¾ teaspoon Worcestershire, scraping up any browned bits, and bring to boil. Reduce heat to medium and simmer, whisking occasionally, until thickened, 10 to 15 minutes. Season with salt and pepper to taste. Slice meatloaf and serve with gravy.

TEST KITCHEN SOLUTION One Skillet, Start to Finish

ON THE STOVE
We brown the onion and ground mushrooms to give the meatloaf robust flavor.

INTO THE OVEN
We shape and bake the meatloaf in the same skillet.

BACK TO THE STOVE
While the cooked meatloaf rests, we use the drippings in the skillet to make the gravy.

TESTING GARLIC PEELERS

When you need to peel garlic, you can whack the clove with the side of a knife blade (which works beautifully, but you get a crushed clove) or you can use a garlic peeler. You roll these devices—simple silicone or rubber tubes, or sheets that you shape into a tube—with the garlic inside, a process that gently tugs the papery skin off the cloves and leaves them intact. Thus, garlic peelers are perfect for recipes calling for whole or sliced cloves. We tried three models priced from $6.50 to $8.79, peeling both single and multiple cloves, and evaluated them on their peeling performance, ease of use, and cleanup. While all were easy to wash in the dishwasher or by hand, the real differences lay in how comfortable they were—or were not—to press down on and roll, and how quickly and effectively they removed the peels. Our winner, the Zak! Designs E-Z Rol Garlic Peeler, lived up to its name. It was the thickest and most well cushioned, making rolling easy and painless. Its grippy silicone surface thoroughly and speedily removed the skins from cloves of all sizes without bruising them. It's our new favorite way to peel garlic. —LISA McMANUS

KEY **Good** ★★★ **Fair** ★★ **Poor** ★

HIGHLY RECOMMENDED	CRITERIA		TESTERS' NOTES
ZAK! DESIGNS E-Z ROL GARLIC PEELER Model: 069 $8.79 at www.cheftools.com Material: Silicone	Peeling Ease of Use Cleanup	★★★ ★★★ ★★★	The original, and still the best, garlic peeler on the market, the Zak! has a thick silicone sleeve that cushions your hands, so it's comfortable to roll over lumpy garlic cloves. It took just about five seconds to strip a clove, thoroughly removing peels from cloves of all sizes and shapes without bruising the garlic. It held and peeled up to five medium cloves at a time. The simple, open-ended tube cleaned up easily and dried completely, whether washed by hand or in the dishwasher (top rack recommended).

RECOMMENDED WITH RESERVATIONS			
NORPRO GARLIC PEELER Model: 1059DB $6.50 at www.amazon.com Material: Rubber 	Peeling Ease of Use Cleanup	★★ ★ ★★★	A flat 5-inch square of textured rubber that resembles a jar opener, this model does peel garlic, but it tends to unroll while you work. The thin rubber hurt our hands as we pressed on lumpy cloves, and the textured surface became spotted with juice, revealing that we'd bruised the garlic. When we peeled five cloves at once, we had to re-roll some multiple times. Finally, we had to pull off stray peels by hand—which wasn't necessary with our winner.

NOT RECOMMENDED			
OXO GARLIC PEELER Model: 1062036 $6.99 at www.oxo.com Material: Silicone tube in vented plastic box 	Peeling Ease of Use Cleanup	★ ★ ★★★	This thin, clear silicone tube bulges outward in the center, a design that is supposed to keep cloves contained. All it really did was make it hard to locate the best spot to press, and the thin material made our hands hurt as we rolled. Garlic became slightly bruised, and we had to repeatedly put cloves back in to finish peeling them. It held five cloves but took rounds of rolling to peel them. Washing the tube was easy, but the vented plastic storage box seemed pointless.

Crispy Potato Tots

We loved tots as kids, but frozen tots got an F when we revisited them. After 100 pounds of potatoes, we finally got a recipe for tots that adults can't get enough of, either. BY SARAH GABRIEL

HAVING EATEN MY weight in Tater Tots® as a child during the elder Bush's administration, I felt particularly qualified to develop a recipe for a homemade version. When my colleagues saw me researching recipes, many asked, "What's wrong with the frozen ones?" Good question. I prepared a big batch for the tasting table and was surprised to hear complaints about the powdery coating and raw-tasting, fishy-smelling interiors. Had tots always been this terrible? Even with a bad taste in my mouth, my childhood memory of super-crunchy, well-seasoned, fluffy potato pillows was unshaken. I wanted a recipe that lived up to those memories.

Bloodied but not unbowed after the store-bought frozen-tot tasting debacle, I gathered five promising recipes for homemade tots. (Yes, they're out there.) The standard method calls for chopping potatoes either by hand or in a food processor and then combining them (either raw or partly cooked) with egg, flour, salt, and pepper before shaping and deep-frying. I quickly learned two things: First, raw potatoes produced tots with decidedly undercooked interiors, so I'd need to start with partially cooked spuds. Second, the amount of flour that these recipes required (about ¼ cup per pound of potatoes) produced hard, rubbery tots, so I'd use less.

I started with five potatoes, peeled and roughly chopped. I pulsed them in the food processor (the grating disk made stringy shreds), scraped them into a bowl, and microwaved them. After eight minutes, they were slightly cooked but still firm enough to hold their shape. Unfortunately, the spud pieces were brown in spots. Fortunately, stirring a little salt into the raw potatoes corrected the color (frozen tots use a sodium-based preservative for the same reason). Now that I had bright white, partially cooked potatoes, I stirred in a beaten egg and just 1½ tablespoons of flour.

The good: The tots were unbelievably crunchy on the outside ("almost viciously crunchy," said one pleased taster). Our science editor explained that when I microwaved the potatoes, their starch granules expanded and absorbed water. When I fried the tots, the water evaporated and left behind the dry, brittle skeleton of the swollen starch molecules—the crunch. The bad: The mixture was very wet and hard to work

For just the right fluffy interior and crisp crust, we precook the potato shreds in salted water in the microwave before forming and deep-frying the tots.

with. I had to scoop it into the hot oil, tot by tot. And these tots fried up dense and gluey inside.

To reduce the glueyness, I'd have to reduce the amount of starch—but I had already taken most of the flour out. One recipe from the first round called for processing the potatoes with water, and I'd noticed that when I drained the spuds, the water was thick with potato starch. For my next test, I processed the potatoes with a cup of water (salted to prevent browning), drained them and discarded the starchy water, and then microwaved and stirred in the flour and beaten egg, as before. With some of the potato starch removed, these tots were fluffy, not gluey. However, they were

still wet inside. That proved an easy fix: I simply ousted the egg.

Now, for the shaping. As most of the recipes I'd found instructed, I had been scooping each tot individually into the hot oil. But now, without the egg, the mixture was drier and difficult to scoop. Was this a positive development? One recipe from my initial tests called for rolling the potato mixture into logs in plastic wrap, freezing the logs, then slicing them into individual tots. The rolling was messy, but slicing the chilled mixture was definitely easier than scooping each tot. I tried pressing my potato mixture into a foil-lined 8 by 8-inch baking dish and then freezing it. After an hour, it was easy to remove

the foil and slice the mixture into tots.

To speed the cooling process, I spread the hot potato mixture on a large sheet of foil on the counter for 10 minutes before packing it into the pan and freezing it. Now the block was ready to slice neatly after just 30 minutes in the freezer. With six easy cuts in one direction and eight in the other, forming individual tots was as simple as slicing brownies. From there, all it took was a quick fry, and these tots were ready to roll. Watching tasters stuff their faces like 10-year-olds fresh from recess, I knew this recipe was an A+.

CRISPY POTATO TOTS
Makes 4 dozen

If your food processor has a capacity of less than 11 cups, you'll need to process the potatoes in two batches. If any large pieces of potato remain after processing, chop them coarsely by hand. To make handling the uncooked tots easier, use a wet knife blade and wet hands.

2¼	teaspoons salt
2½	pounds russet potatoes, peeled and cut into 1½-inch pieces
1½	tablespoons all-purpose flour
½	teaspoon pepper
4	cups peanut or vegetable oil

1. Whisk 1 cup water and salt together in bowl until salt dissolves. Pulse potatoes and salt water in food processor until coarsely ground, 10 to 12 pulses, stirring occasionally. Drain mixture in fine-mesh strainer, pressing potatoes with rubber spatula until dry (liquid should measure about 1½ cups); discard liquid. Transfer potatoes to bowl and microwave, uncovered, until dry and sticky, 8 to 10 minutes, stirring halfway through cooking.

2. Stir flour and pepper into potatoes. Spread potato mixture into thin layer over large sheet of aluminum foil and let cool for 10 minutes. Push potatoes to center of foil and place foil and potatoes in 8-inch square baking pan. Push foil into corners and up sides of pan, smoothing it flush to pan. Press potato mixture tightly and evenly into pan. Freeze, uncovered, until firm, about 30 minutes.

3. Meanwhile, adjust oven rack to middle position and heat oven to 200 degrees. Heat oil in Dutch oven over high heat until 375 degrees. Using foil overhang, lift potatoes from pan and cut into 1¼ by 1-inch pieces (6 cuts

Keys to Making Tots at Home

Yes, ours are more work than commercial frozen tots—but they taste so much better.

DRY After chopping, we drain the potatoes, which removes starch that would otherwise make the tots gluey and heavy.

FREEZE We parcook the potatoes, add flour, and press into a baking pan to freeze briefly. Now the tots are easy to cut.

CUT We lift the firmed-up mixture out of the pan and cut the tots—it's as easy as slicing brownies.

---

in 1 direction and 8 in other). Fry half of potato tots, until golden brown and crisp, 5 to 7 minutes, stirring occasionally once they begin to brown. Drain on wire rack set in rimmed baking sheet and place in oven. Bring oil back to 375 degrees and repeat with remaining potato tots. Serve.

MAKE AHEAD
Cool fried potato tots, transfer to zipper-lock bag, and freeze for up to 1 month. To serve, adjust oven rack to middle position and heat oven to 400 degrees. Place potato tots on rimmed baking sheet and bake until heated through, 12 to 15 minutes.

LOTSA TOTS
Double ingredients for Crispy Potato Tots. Process and drain potato mixture in 2 batches. Microwave entire potato mixture for 12 to 14 minutes, stirring halfway through cooking. Spread potato mixture over large sheet of foil to cool and press into 13 by 9-inch baking pan. After freezing, cut potato rectangle in half crosswise before cutting into potato tots per recipe. Fry in 4 batches.

BACON-RANCH POTATO TOTS
Stir 1 tablespoon cider vinegar into potatoes after microwaving. Add 4 slices finely chopped cooked bacon, 1 teaspoon onion powder, ½ teaspoon garlic powder, and ½ teaspoon dried dill to potatoes with flour in step 2.

PARMESAN-ROSEMARY POTATO TOTS
Stir 2 minced garlic cloves into drained potatoes before microwaving. Add 2 ounces grated Parmesan cheese and 2 tablespoons minced fresh rosemary to potatoes with flour in step 2.

SOUTHWESTERN POTATO TOTS
Add 2 ounces shredded smoked gouda, 3 tablespoons minced fresh cilantro, and 2 tablespoons minced jarred jalapeños to potatoes with flour in step 2.

TEST KITCHEN PRIMER
Deep Frying

• **THE IDEAL OIL TEMPERATURE**
Most foods are fried at 350 to 375 degrees. But the oil temperature drops when food is added, so you have to adjust the burner to keep the oil at the right temperature.

• **THE RIGHT TOOLS**
We like to fry in a Dutch oven because its relatively low sides allow good visibility and easy access. A metal slotted spoon or "spider" skimmer makes it easy to remove food from hot oil.

• **THE PROPER FINISH**
Drain food on a wire rack set in a rimmed baking sheet and season it hot out of the oil.

Rinse Away the Starch
For tots with light, fluffy interiors, we found we had to process the potatoes with salt water and then drain them. This process washed away excess potato starch that was making the tots dense and gummy. The salt helpfully prevented the chopped potatoes from turning brown, too.

DENSE AND GUMMY
No rinse.

LIGHT AND FLUFFY
Saltwater rinse.

Quick Mixed Vegetables

Mixed vegetable side dishes are all over the freezer section, but most left us feeling lukewarm.

BY CAROLYNN PURPURA

A VEGETABLE MEDLEY is a nice side dish, so why let the frozen vegetable companies claim it? Inspired by the many mixes with cream sauce that I found in the freezer section of my supermarket (have you tasted them? Recap: Good idea, bad execution), I headed into the test kitchen to make my own version. The parameters? Freshness, speed, and, of course, great taste.

I used the classic mix of broccoli, cauliflower, carrots, and red bell pepper. The colors were bright and pretty, and I knew from experience that the vegetables would cook at about the same rate—assuming I chopped them correctly. I chopped the peppers into fat strips, the cauliflower and broccoli into same-size florets, and the less delicate, longer-cooking broccoli stems and carrots into ¼-inch-thick slices.

Simply boiling the vegetables imparted no flavor, so I turned to a classic test kitchen method: I sautéed the vegetables in oil, added a little water to the pan, and then simmered the vegetables, covered, until they were nearly tender. After a few minutes, I removed the lid to evaporate any remaining water. The sautéing developed color and flavor. I switched the water for chicken broth to further boost the taste.

For the sauce, my mantra was "quick and easy." White sauce with cheese was out. Even boiling down heavy cream to coat the vegetables seemed onerous, plus it tasted one-dimensional. What if I could avoid cooking the sauce altogether? Mentally checking off no-cook ingredients that might give the sauce body and flavor, I was struck by the promise of cream cheese. I stirred a bit into the heavy cream and then tossed this dairy mix with the hot vegetables. The cream cheese melted, adding instant body and tang. To turn a mere coating into a real sauce, I stirred in lemon juice, red pepper flakes, and chives. In some 10 minutes, I'd put a mixed vegetable side dish on the table that beat the pants off the freezer version.

This recipe is far fresher and tastier than the frozen version.

MIXED VEGETABLES WITH INSTANT CREAM SAUCE Serves 4

- 2 tablespoons heavy cream
- 1 ounce cream cheese
- 2 tablespoons minced fresh chives
- 2 teaspoons lemon juice
- ⅛ teaspoon red pepper flakes
- 2 tablespoons olive oil
- ½ pound broccoli, florets cut into 1-inch pieces, stalks peeled and sliced ¼ inch thick
- ½ pound cauliflower florets, cut into 1-inch pieces
- ½ pound carrots, peeled and sliced ¼ inch thick
- 1 red bell pepper, stemmed, seeded, and cut into ½-inch-wide strips
- ¼ cup low-sodium chicken broth
  Salt and pepper

1. Combine cream, cream cheese, chives, lemon juice, and pepper flakes in bowl; set aside.

2. Heat oil in 12-inch nonstick skillet over medium-high heat until just smoking. Add broccoli, cauliflower, carrots, and bell pepper and cook, stirring occasionally, until vegetables are spotty brown, 4 to 6 minutes. Stir in broth, cover, and reduce heat to medium-low. Cook until vegetables are nearly tender, about 2 minutes. Remove lid and cook until liquid evaporates and vegetables are tender, about 1 minute. Stir in cream mixture. Season with salt and pepper to taste. Serve.

Green Bay Booyah

This hearty, stick-to-your-ribs soup is a diehard favorite in northeast Wisconsin. Now we know why.

BY ADAM RIED

Booyah just may be the richest, heartiest chicken and beef soup you've never heard of—unless you happen to be from Green Bay, Wisconsin, that is. Little known even in the rest of the state, booyah is both a soup and an event in Green Bay, made in huge batches in outdoor kettles for fairs, fundraisers, and family gatherings. One cold, slushy morning at the Suamico United Methodist Church, just north of Green Bay, people were lining up for bowls of stick-to-your-ribs booyah at 7:30 a.m., never mind the 10 a.m. start time or the discouraging weather. Clearly, the soup is a celebration all by itself.

Later that same day, I attended my second booyah bash, this time sampling the handiwork of Suamico firefighters. When I got home, I tested several recipes I'd found in Wisconsin cookbooks. I was sure that this hearty soup could please crowds far beyond Green Bay, but first I'd have to bring it indoors, hacking back the 60-gallon batches to fit into a Dutch oven on a home stove. I'd also need to come up with a full-flavored broth without the endless simmering called for by the booyah faithful. And I'd have to limit the ever-present fat (although Green Bay fans actually measure the success of booyah by the grease—a defense against bitter Wisconsin winters?). I'd also cook the vegetables to tenderness instead of mush and keep the chicken from overcooking.

Most recipes for booyah follow the same outline: Simmer whole chicken(s) in water to make broth. Turn that broth

Booyah is a rich chicken and beef soup loaded with vegetables. If you're looking for a hearty one-pot meal for a crowd, look no further.

into the soup base, simmering beef and shredded cabbage in it until they practically disintegrate. At some point, add the other vegetables. Finally, discard the skin and bones from the chicken, dice the meat, and return it to the pot.

With an eye toward building a flavorful broth quicker, I replaced the water with canned chicken broth. But I'd still need chicken meat for the booyah. Instead of waiting for a whole chicken to cook, I'd use parts. And to avoid stringy, overcooked white meat, I'd use dark meat thighs, which I knew would stand up better to simmering and contribute better flavor. (They did, on both counts.) As added insurance against overcooking, I learned to pull them out after 30 minutes, stirring in the boned, shredded meat at the end. Taking advantage of my considerably scaled-down batch, I made another break from booyah tradition: I browned the chicken before simmering it. This is standard test kitchen practice for building flavor in braises and stews,

but I can see why booyah chefs in Wisconsin don't do it: Browning enough chicken for several hundred would be highly impractical, even crazy. Since my booyah would feed just 10, I could take advantage of the extra flavor that the technique supplies.

But while the flavor was good, the broth lacked the full-bodied, silken quality that comes from the gelatin released from bones that simmer for a long time (the thighs simmered for just 30 minutes). I enlisted the beef for help. Usually, booyah contains boneless beef chuck. I tried two bone-in cuts: short ribs and shin slices. Both "beefed up" the broth as I'd hoped. I opted for the short ribs, since they're easier to find. I handled them as I had the chicken, browning them to build flavor, before simmering them in the broth. Unfortunately, the short ribs set me back on another score: The soup was greasier than ever. Eventually I forged a three-pronged approach to limit the grease. I trimmed (and discarded) the fat between the raw short rib meat and bones, adding the two separately to the broth. I discarded the fatty chicken skin (but only after browning, so I could capture its flavor). And I defatted the broth before adding the vegetables.

Booyah never met a vegetable it didn't like. In addition to the constants (onions, carrots, celery, tomatoes, cabbage, and potatoes), you find beans of every stripe (green, fresh, and dried), peas (frozen and split), corn (usually as a component of frozen mixed vegetables), turnips, and even rutabaga. Since I was making a comparatively small batch, I left the frozen mix in the freezer aisle and replaced it (mostly) with fresh carrot coins and chunks of mellow rutabaga. I kept the frozen peas, as finding fresh ones is iffy in the fall and winter. Mushy vegetables may be unavoidable in 60-gallon batches, but all I had to do to prevent this in my scaled-down soup was add the vegetables in stages; the quickest-cooking went in at the end. I made an exception for the cabbage, which I added early so it would be very soft by serving time, just as I'd seen (and tasted) in Suamico. A final hit of lemon juice brightened the soup.

I sat down with a bowlful to assess. Warming, filling, and flavorful, this booyah could hold its own anywhere in the country, Green Bay included.

GREEN BAY BOOYAH Serves 8 to 10

The bone side of a short rib is especially fatty and requires the most trimming. To defat the broth, lay a paper towel over its surface, quickly lift it up by a corner (the fat will adhere), and discard. Repeat with more paper towels, as needed.

- 2½ pounds beef short ribs (3 to 4 English-style ribs)
- 2½ pounds bone-in chicken thighs, trimmed
  Salt and pepper
- 1 tablespoon vegetable oil
- 2 onions, chopped fine
- 2 celery ribs, minced
- 8 cups low-sodium chicken broth
- 2 bay leaves
- 4 cups shredded green cabbage
- 1 (28-ounce) can diced tomatoes
- ½ pound rutabaga, peeled and cut into ½-inch pieces
- 1 pound russet potatoes, peeled and cut into ½-inch pieces
- 3 carrots, peeled and sliced ¼ inch thick
- 1 cup frozen peas
- 1 tablespoon lemon juice

1. Remove bones from short ribs; reserve. Trim fat from meat and bones. Pat beef and chicken dry with paper towels and season with salt and pepper. Heat oil in Dutch oven over medium-high heat until just smoking. Brown beef on all sides, about 10 minutes; transfer to plate. Cook chicken until browned all over, about 10 minutes; transfer to plate. When chicken is cool enough to handle, remove and discard skin.

2. Pour off all but 1½ teaspoons fat from pot. Add onions and celery and cook over medium heat until softened, about 5 minutes. Stir in broth and bay leaves, scraping up any browned bits. Add beef, beef bones, and chicken and bring to boil.

3. Reduce heat to low and simmer, covered, until chicken registers 175 degrees, about 30 minutes. Transfer chicken to bowl. When chicken is cool enough to handle, shred into bite-size pieces, discarding bones. Cover chicken and refrigerate. Continue to simmer stew until beef is tender, about 75 minutes longer. Transfer beef to plate. When cool enough to handle, shred into bite-size pieces, discarding fat. Discard beef bones and bay leaves. Defat broth.

4. Add shredded beef, cabbage, tomatoes, rutabaga, 1¼ teaspoons salt, and 1 teaspoon pepper and bring to boil. Reduce heat to medium-low and simmer until rutabaga is translucent around edges, about 15 minutes. Stir in potatoes and carrots and cook until all vegetables are tender, about 20 minutes. Add chicken and peas and simmer until heated through, 2 to 3 minutes. Off heat, stir in lemon juice. Season with salt and pepper to taste. Serve.

EASIER THAN YOU THINK

Buckeyes

For the best peanut butter flavor, go easy on the sugar.

BY MEGHAN ERWIN

WHAT'S A BUCKEYE? You'd know if you lived in Ohio, where it's the official state tree, so named because its nuts resemble a deer's eyes. And you'd know if you went to the Ohio State University, where Brutus Buckeye is the beloved sports mascot. Most important to us, buckeyes are also chocolate-dipped peanut-butter candies that resemble this nut.

They're made by rolling a mixture of peanut butter, confectioners' sugar, and butter into balls and dipping each ball into chopped, melted chocolate. To create a hardened, shiny chocolate shell over the buttery filling, many recipes call for paraffin wax to be melted with bar chocolate.

The recipes we tested were bland and too sweet. Nor did we care for the waxy chocolate. To simultaneously fix the cloying quality and intensify the flavor, we adjusted the proportions, cutting back on sugar and butter and nearly doubling the peanut butter. Now, though, the buckeyes were too soft to dip. To fix that, we mixed melted white chocolate chips into our base. Once they re-hardened, they added structure.

In place of the wax, we tried corn syrup, shortening, and cream to firm up the chocolate coating. None provided the right texture. Eventually,

Buckeyes, a classic Ohio candy, use a classic combination: chocolate and peanut butter.

we figured out that using semisweet chocolate chips (which contain emulsifiers that harden into a sturdy coating) instead of melted bar chocolate made for delectable buckeyes.

BUCKEYES Makes 4 dozen pieces

Don't use natural peanut butter here.

- 1½ ounces white chocolate chips
- 2¾ cups creamy peanut butter
- 4 tablespoons unsalted butter, softened
- 3 cups (12 ounces) confectioners' sugar
- 1 teaspoon vanilla extract
- ⅛ teaspoon salt
- 2 cups (12 ounces) semisweet chocolate chips

1. Line rimmed baking sheet with parchment paper. Microwave white chocolate chips in bowl on 50 percent power, stirring occasionally, until melted, about 1 minute. Let cool for 5 minutes. Using stand mixer fitted with paddle, beat peanut butter, melted white chocolate, butter, sugar, vanilla, and salt on medium-high speed until just combined, about 1 minute. Roll dough into 1¼-inch balls and place on prepared sheet. Freeze until firm, about 30 minutes.

2. Microwave semisweet chocolate chips in bowl on 50 percent power, stirring occasionally, until melted, 1½ to 2 minutes. Using toothpick, dip chilled balls into melted chocolate, leaving top quarter of balls uncovered. Return balls to prepared sheet and refrigerate until chocolate is set, about 1 hour. Serve. (Buckeyes can be refrigerated for up to 1 week or frozen for up to 1 month.)

America's Best Lost Recipes

$25,000 GRAND PRIZE

Responding to our call, 1,200 of you entered beloved family recipes in our third Lost Recipes Contest, part of our ongoing project to preserve America's culinary heritage. We eagerly read your stories about how these recipes fit into the lives of your families. We researched how they fit into American history. And we tasted our way through many delicious dishes, culling some 100 for our new book (see below). Then, after months of pleasurable eating and agonizing over what to include (or rather, what to exclude), several dozen test cooks and editors cast their votes. These pages feature our five favorites, adapted and updated where necessary to simplify shopping and cooking. Bring them into your own kitchens to start your own new traditions.

Lisa Keys comes from a long line of frugal cooks. Her family's grand-prize-winning chocolate cake features stale bread crumbs and leftover wine.

115 Lost Recipes Found — in a Single Book

The third book in our Lost Recipes series, *From Our Grand-mothers' Kitchens* ($29.95) gathers more than 100 heir-loom family recipes, which together tell a story about how America cooks. We supplement these old-fashioned recipes with practical test kitchen tips, your personal stories, and culinary research that grounds them in time and place. But the book isn't just a nostalgic glance backward: We've tested the recipes rigorously to ensure that they work for today's cook, that they move easily *From Our Grandmothers' Kitchens* to yours. Try comforting casseroles and canning, Slumgullion and Scripture Cake, recipes born in faraway places and on these shores. Collectively, they add up to delicious home cooking now.

WINNER GRATED BREAD AND CHOCOLATE CAKE
Lisa Keys, Middlebury, Conn.

Serves 10 to 12
We used store-bought bread crumbs for convenience. Look for almond flour in the natural foods section of your market. This cake can overbake quickly, so check often once it begins to color.

CAKE
- 2 cups almond flour
- 2 tablespoons all-purpose flour
- ½ cup plain dried bread crumbs
- 1 ounce semisweet chocolate, grated
- 1 teaspoon baking powder
- 9 large egg whites
- 1½ cups (6 ounces) confectioners' sugar
- ¼ cup dry red wine
- 2 tablespoons lemon juice

FROSTING
- 2 cups heavy cream, chilled
- ¼ cup (1¾ ounces) granulated sugar
- 2 tablespoons Dutch-processed cocoa
- ¼ cup amaretto or other almond-flavored liqueur
- ½ ounce semisweet chocolate, grated

1. FOR THE CAKE: Adjust oven rack to middle position and heat oven to 350 degrees. Grease two 9-inch round cake pans, line with parchment paper, grease parchment, then flour pans. Whisk almond flour, all-purpose flour, bread crumbs, chocolate, and baking powder together in bowl.

2. Using stand mixer fitted with whisk, whip egg whites on medium-low speed until foamy, about 1 minute. Increase speed to medium-high and whip whites to soft, billowy mounds, 1 to 2 minutes. Gradually add sugar and whip until glossy, stiff peaks form, 1 to 3 minutes longer.

3. Gently whisk wine and lemon juice into whipped egg whites by hand. Gently fold in one-third of flour mixture to combine until a few streaks of flour remain. Fold in remaining flour mixture, in 2 additions, until incorporated.

4. Divide batter evenly between prepared pans and smooth tops. Lightly tap pans on counter to release air bubbles. Bake until light golden brown and cakes feel firm and spring back when touched, about 20 minutes, rotating pans halfway through baking.

5. Let cakes cool in pans on wire rack for 10 minutes. Run paring knife around pan edge. Remove cakes from pans, discarding parchment, and let cool completely, about 2 hours.

6. FOR THE FROSTING: Using stand mixer fitted with whisk, whip cream, sugar, and cocoa on medium-low speed until foamy, about 1 minute. Increase speed to high and whip until stiff peaks form, 1 to 2 minutes longer.

7. Mark middle of sides of each cake round at several points with knife. Using marks as guide, score edge of each round with long serrated knife, slowly cutting inward to slice each into 2 even layers. Place 1 bottom round on platter. Brush with 1 tablespoon amaretto and spread ⅔ cup whipped cream over top. Repeat twice, ending with cake layer. Press lightly to adhere. Brush with remaining 1 tablespoon amaretto. Frost cake with remaining whipped cream and sprinkle top with chocolate. Serve.

Crumbs to Cake

Using grated bread in place of flour is a creative use for stale bread that's more common in the Old World than the New. Many traditional German and Austrian torte recipes are based on bread, most notably Brod (bread) Torte, which like Lisa's recipe, often calls for almonds and wine, as well.

These cardamom-scented cookies are deep-fried, not baked.

FINALIST **DANISH KLEINER**
Ruth Okey, Costa Mesa, Calif.

Makes about 5 dozen cookies
If you don't have a diamond cookie cutter, cut the dough into 4 by 2¾-inch diamonds with a pizza wheel or knife.

- 3¾ cups (18¾ ounces) all-purpose flour
- 1 teaspoon baking powder
- ½ teaspoon salt
- 8 tablespoons unsalted butter
- 1½ teaspoons ground cardamom
- 1 cup (7 ounces) granulated sugar
- 3 large eggs
- ¼ cup heavy cream
- 1 teaspoon vanilla extract
- 4 cups vegetable shortening or vegetable oil
  Confectioners' sugar (optional)

1. Whisk flour, baking powder, and salt together in bowl. Microwave butter and cardamom in second bowl, until melted and fragrant, about 1 minute.

2. Using stand mixer fitted with paddle, beat granulated sugar and eggs on medium speed until smooth, 1 to 2 minutes. Add melted butter mixture, cream, and vanilla and beat until combined, about 30 seconds, scraping down bowl as needed. Reduce speed to low and slowly add flour mixture until just combined.

3. Transfer dough to clean counter and divide into 4 equal pieces. Place each piece on sheet of plastic wrap and flatten into 4-inch square. Wrap tightly and refrigerate until firm, about 1 hour.

4. Line 2 rimmed baking sheets with parchment paper. Working with 1 dough square at a time (keep remaining dough refrigerated), roll into 12 by 10-inch rectangle, about ⅛ inch thick, on well-floured counter. Using 4 by 2¾-inch diamond cookie cutter, stamp out cookies. Cut 1½-inch-long slit, lengthwise, in center of each cookie, then carefully pull tip of cookie through slit. Place cookies on prepared sheets and refrigerate until ready to fry.

5. Heat shortening in Dutch oven over medium-high heat until 350 degrees. Fry 8 cookies until golden brown, about 30 seconds per side, adjusting burner as necessary to maintain oil temperature at 350 degrees.

6. Drain cookies on wire rack set in rimmed baking sheet. Repeat with remaining cookies. Dust with confectioners' sugar, if using. Serve.

Shaping Danish Kleiner
After you've rolled the dough into a rectangle, use a cookie cutter or knife to cut it into diamonds. Next:

1. Cut a slit in the center of each diamond-shaped cookie.

2. Pull one tip of the cookie through the slit to create a twist.

Cookie Geography
Kleiner (also spelled klejner) is the Danish version of a cookie that exists with slight variations all over Europe. The cookies are deep-fried in oil (or lard) and are shaped as diamonds or rectangles with one end pulled through a hole in the center. Scandinavians use special cookie cutters to make them, *kleiner* or *fattigman* cutters, the latter after the Norwegian variation. The cardamom places this recipe firmly in Scandinavia, a region that loves the spice.

FINALIST *MOM'S GONE WITH THE WIND HEAVENLY PIE*

Sandy Farler, Bellevue, Wash.

Serves 8

Don't skimp on the resting times in the oven or the refrigerator. If you do, the pie may be gooey, making it hard to slice. Meringue is tricky to make on humid days.

- 4 large eggs, separated, room temperature
- ¾ teaspoon salt
- ½ teaspoon cream of tartar
- 1½ cups (10½ ounces) sugar
- 1 tablespoon grated lemon zest plus 3 tablespoons juice
- 2 cups heavy cream, chilled

1. Adjust oven rack to middle position and heat oven to 300 degrees. Grease 9-inch deep-dish pie plate.

2. Using stand mixer fitted with whisk, whip egg whites, ½ teaspoon salt, and cream of tartar on medium-low speed until foamy, about 1 minute. Increase speed to medium-high and whip whites to soft billowy mounds, 1 to 3 minutes. Gradually add 1 cup sugar and whip until glossy, stiff peaks form, 3 to 6 minutes.

3. Spread meringue into prepared pie plate and smooth into even layer. Run finger around inside edge of pie plate to create small gap between edge of meringue and rim of plate. Bake meringue until golden brown and set, about 1 hour. Turn off oven and let meringue dry completely for 3 hours longer. Let meringue cool completely on wire rack, about 30 minutes. (Meringue will crack and deflate after baking to form crust.)

4. Meanwhile, whisk remaining ½ cup sugar, egg yolks, lemon zest, lemon juice, and remaining ¼ teaspoon salt together in medium saucepan until smooth. Cook over medium-low heat, stirring constantly, until mixture is thickened and registers 170 degrees, about 5 minutes. Strain curd through fine-mesh strainer into large bowl. Place plastic wrap directly on surface of curd. Refrigerate until completely cooled, about 1 hour.

5. Using stand mixer fitted with whisk, whip cream on medium-low speed until foamy, about 1 minute. Increase speed to high and whip until soft peaks form, 1 to 3 minutes.

6. Fold half of whipped cream into cooled lemon curd until no white streaks remain. Spread lemon mixture into cooled meringue shell and smooth into even layer. Spread remaining whipped cream over top and refrigerate until set, about 1 hour. Serve.

For the lemony Mom's *Gone with the Wind* Heavenly Pie, a meringue forms the crust, and the topping is whipped cream.

Ensuring Even Meringue

After spreading the meringue in the pie plate, run your finger around the inside edge. The gap between the dish and the meringue will help the meringue rise and fall more evenly.

HOLLYWOOD EXCLUSIVE: **The Story Behind the Pie**

"We lived in Southern California in the beautiful little town of Encino, a suburb of Los Angeles, in the 1950s. My mother was the leader of our Brownie troop, and one spring, our troop was holding a bake sale in our front yard. Mom baked a delicious lemon pie (that she had always called Heavenly Pie) and added it to the sales table. Almost immediately, an extremely handsome gentleman pulled up in his Mercedes-Benz convertible sports car and proceeded to browse. His eye fell upon my mom's tempting creation, and he asked to purchase her Heavenly Pie. Mom packed up the pie, a blush starting at her toes and heading to her cheeks. After he drove away, Mom could barely contain her joy—our customer was the legendary Clark Gable! From that day forward, we always referred to her pie as Mom's Gone with the Wind Heavenly Pie!" —SANDY FARLER

READ MORE stories behind the recipes in our new book, *From Our Grandmothers' Kitchens*.

FINALIST ITALIAN LOVE NESTS

Tracy Zampaglione, Orlando, Fla.

Makes 12 pasta nests
Spray the muffin cups with vegetable oil spray to keep the nests from sticking.

- 8 ounces angel hair pasta
  Salt
- 1 cup heavy cream
- 2½ ounces Parmesan cheese, grated (1¼ cups)
- 3 ounces thinly sliced prosciutto, chopped fine
- ¼ cup dry white wine
- 2 large eggs
- 2 teaspoons minced fresh sage
- 1 teaspoon white pepper
- ½ teaspoon ground nutmeg
- ⅛ teaspoon hot sauce
- 12 green olives stuffed with pimento

1. Adjust oven rack to middle position and heat oven to 350 degrees. Grease 12-cup muffin tin. Bring 4 quarts water to boil in Dutch oven. Add pasta and 1 tablespoon salt and cook, stirring often, until al dente. Drain pasta and return it to pot.

2. Whisk cream, ¾ cup Parmesan, prosciutto, wine, eggs, sage, pepper, ½ teaspoon salt, nutmeg, and hot sauce in bowl. Pour over pasta and toss.

3. Using tongs, portion pasta mixture into prepared muffin cups, twisting pasta to form uniform nests. Pour any remaining sauce evenly over pasta, sprinkle with remaining ½ cup Parmesan, and press 1 olive into each nest.

4. Bake until centers are set and tops are golden brown, 20 to 25 minutes, rotating tin halfway through baking. Let nests cool in pan on wire rack for 5 minutes. Run small knife around edges, unmold, and serve warm.

Fill muffin cups with pasta and creamy sauce.

FINALIST CHAPEL SQUARES

Jeanne Holt, Mendota Heights, Minn.

Makes 24 squares
You'll need an 18 by 13-inch rimmed nonstick baking sheet. Use almond paste, not marzipan (which is sweeter and smoother).

CRUST
- ½ cup whole milk
- 2 large eggs, separated, whites beaten lightly
- 2½ cups (12½ ounces) all-purpose flour
- 2 tablespoons granulated sugar
- ½ teaspoon salt
- 11 tablespoons vegetable shortening, cut into ½-inch pieces and chilled
- 5 tablespoons unsalted butter, cut into ¼-inch pieces and chilled

FILLING
- ¾ cup dried sour cherries
- 4 teaspoons water
- 1¾ pounds Haralson or Granny Smith apples, peeled, cored, and sliced thin (about 4 apples)
- 12 ounces Fireside or Golden Delicious apples, peeled, cored, and sliced thin (about 2 apples)
- ⅔ cup (4⅔ ounces) granulated sugar
- ½ teaspoon ground cinnamon
- ⅛ teaspoon salt
- 4 ounces almond paste, cut into ¼-inch pieces

GLAZE
- 1¼ cups (5 ounces) confectioners' sugar
- 3 tablespoons whole milk
- ¼ teaspoon almond extract

1. **FOR THE CRUST:** Whisk milk and egg yolks together. Pulse flour, sugar, and salt in food processor until combined, about 3 pulses. Add shortening and pulse until mixture resembles coarse cornmeal, about 10 pulses. Add butter and pulse until mixture resembles coarse crumbs, about 10 pulses. Transfer mixture to large bowl.

2. Pour milk mixture over flour mixture and combine, using rubber spatula to press dough firmly until it comes together. Transfer dough to clean counter and divide into 2 equal pieces. Place each piece of dough on sheet of plastic wrap and flatten into 4-inch square. Wrap tightly and refrigerate for 1 hour.

3. **FOR THE FILLING:** Adjust oven rack to lowest position and heat oven to 400 degrees. Microwave cherries and water in covered bowl until steaming, about 1 minute. Let sit until cherries have softened and cooled to room temperature, about 30 minutes. Combine softened cherry mixture, apples, sugar, cinnamon, and salt in large bowl; set aside.

4. Let dough soften at room temperature for 10 minutes. Roll 1 dough square between 2 large sheets of parchment paper into 19 by 14-inch rectangle. Remove top piece of parchment. Loosely roll dough around rolling pin, then unroll dough over 18 by 13-inch rimmed baking sheet. Gently fit dough into sheet and up the sides and sprinkle with almond paste. Drain apple mixture thoroughly, then spread over dough-lined sheet. Cover with plastic and refrigerate until needed.

5. Roll remaining 1 dough square between 2 large sheets of parchment into 19 by 14-inch rectangle. Remove top piece of parchment. Loosely roll dough around rolling pin, then unroll it over filling. Trim and fold edges of dough together. Crimp, using fork.

6. Cut 1-inch slits in top crust at 2-inch intervals, then brush with egg whites. Bake bars for 10 minutes, then reduce oven temperature to 350 degrees and continue to bake until juices are bubbling and crust is golden brown, 40 to 45 minutes, rotating sheet halfway through baking. Let bars cool in sheet on wire rack for 30 minutes.

7. **FOR THE GLAZE:** Whisk sugar, milk, and almond extract together in bowl until smooth. Drizzle glaze over bars and let cool until filling has set, about 2 hours. Cut into squares. Serve.

Chapel Squares pair almond paste with sour cherries and apples in a flaky pastry square.

Marzipan in the New World

Though marzipan and almond paste have been popular in Europe for centuries, they're completely absent from early American cookbooks. In 1943, though, Irma Rombauer plonked a recipe for marzipan into *Joy of Cooking*. (Her mother's family hailed from Lübeck, a German town known for marzipan.) Today, you can find almond paste and marzipan at the supermarket.

Equipment Review Travel Mugs

The best traveling companion should open and close easily, seal tightly, and keep the contents hot. With hundreds of mugs out there, far too many miss the mark. BY AMY GRAVES

ENJOYING YOUR OWN coffee or tea on the way to work beats spending $4 for a latte in a paper cup, but not if the vessel it's in offers no better heat retention and proves harder to sip from. After surveying the vast travel mug market, we narrowed our choices to seven, ruling out plastic and ceramic for lousy insulation, mega-mugs that hold 24 or more ounces (for the rare monster commute), and anything that requires complete lid removal (you're in transit, after all). Prices ranged from $15 to $39.

A travel mug is supposed to keep your coffee hot. Although experts disagree about the perfect drinking temperature, we find that coffee below 140 degrees is lukewarm, not hot. We filled the mugs with freshly brewed coffee at exactly 155 degrees. Then we threaded thermometer probes into the mugs so we could read their contents' temperatures over four hours without opening them. We knew from previous tests that ceramic travel mugs don't retain heat for longer than 30 minutes, plastic for about an hour. With only double-wall stainless steel mugs in this lineup, we were surprised that one, the Trudeau Board Room 16-Ounce Travel Mug, lost heat just as quickly as any plastic mug.

Most of our mugs kept coffee above 140 degrees for just over an hour. A few mugs retained heat remarkably well: After three hours, the Zojirushi 17-Ounce Clear Stainless Mug had "cooled" to only 152 degrees. The Thermos Element 5 Travel Mug stayed between 145 and 150 degrees for more than two hours. We let colleagues test-drive these two mugs for a few weeks; users reported that they had to wait a long time before the contents were cool enough to drink, and the Zojirushi user actually added cold water to her hot tea before she left home. The Thermos Sipp 16-Ounce Vacuum Insulated Tumbler maintained an optimal temperature the longest, staying above 140 degrees for two hours.

We demand that our travel mug be rugged, with a snug-fitting lid that won't leak or drip, so we turned full mugs over and shook them. The good news is that all were leak-proof, but only when they were filled properly (overfilling disrupted the seal). The OXO Liqui-Seal Travel Mug had no fill line; on the first try we overfilled it, and it leaked.

Mugs with complicated gaskets in their lids, such as the OXO and the Trudeau Board Room, presented another problem: The gaskets trapped liquid, so when we closed the lids and began sipping, coffee dribbled out. Mugs that were hard to close all the way, like the Thermos Element 5, had us rechecking them before we put them in our bag, fearing a leaky mess.

When we filled the mugs with coffee for a car ride, we cottoned quickly to those we could open single-handedly, since that let us keep both eyes on the road. Mugs with handles didn't fit in all car cup holders, and using them distracted us from driving. The Timolino Icon 16-Ounce Signature Vacuum Travel Mug, a sleek, slightly curved tumbler, uses a sturdy snap-open lid that proved simple to operate. Plus, the lid didn't partially obstruct our view—the chief flaw of the Zojirushi mug (though that's not a concern for commuters who don't drive).

When you're drinking a hot beverage from a lidded mug, you need the flow of liquid to be predictable and manageable—neither a torrent nor a trickle. The single half-inch opening on the Timolino mug was neither stingy nor overly generous. Mugs with 360-degree openings, such as the Thermos Element 5, let coffee rush out from too many exits.

We'd love to blast our mug clean in the dishwasher, but we'll take anything we can attack with hot, soapy water and a sponge. Narrow openings like the one on the Thermos Element 5 had us struggling to squeeze in a sponge. Mugs with wide bodies and uncomplicated lids that didn't trap odors, such as the Timolino, made cleanup a breeze. As a bonus, both the carafe and its lid are top-rack dishwasher-safe.

Many hot drinks later, we had a winner. The Timolino Icon 16-Ounce Signature Vacuum Travel Mug offered adequate heat retention; straightforward, comfortable handling; a lid that's easy to sip from and doesn't leak; and a design that cleans up nicely, with no hidden nooks and crannies.

	CRITERIA		TESTERS' NOTES
HIGHLY RECOMMENDED			
TIMOLINO Icon 16-Ounce Signature Vacuum Travel Mug **Model:** PCT-46K **Price:** $28.00 at www.koozio.com **Dishwasher:** Top rack only	Sipping & Handling ★★★ Leakproof ★★★ Heat Retention ★★		This sleek mug kept coffee drinkably hot for twice as long as it took for us to get to work (over an hour), but what really made this a top tumbler was its simple, leakproof lid design, which made it super easy to handle and a cinch to clean.
RECOMMENDED			
ZOJIRUSHI 17-Ounce Clear Stainless Mug **Model:** SM-DA50AX **Price:** $38.99 at www.amazon.com **Dishwasher:** No	Sipping & Handling ★★ Leakproof ★★★ Heat Retention ★★★		This slender, pretty carafe had the best heat retention of any mug in our lineup, and it opens easily with the press of a button. Too bad the open lid almost obstructed our view as we were driving (though train commuters won't mind). A colleague found her tea too hot to safely drink for the first half of her commute.
THERMOS Sipp 16-Ounce Vacuum Insulated Tumbler **Model:** NS105BK004 **Price:** $29.99 at www.shopthermos.com **Dishwasher:** Yes	Sipping & Handling ★ Leakproof ★★★ Heat Retention ★★★		A button in the center of the top opened this mug easily, but liquid poured out of opposite sides of the lid—we had to check alignment carefully. But it kept the contents hot, was impossible to overfill, and never leaked. The small hook inside the lid bottom designed to hold the string to a tea bag is a nice touch.
THERMOS Element 5 Travel Mug **Model:** E10500 **Price:** $34.99 at www.shopthermos.com **Dishwasher:** No	Sipping & Handling ★ Leakproof ★★★ Heat Retention ★★★		This rugged-looking mug retained heat superbly, staying well above 140 degrees for 2½ hours. But we needed two hands to twist open the lid unless the mug rested securely on a flat surface. The narrow neck made it hard to clean by hand, and the handle gets in the way of some car cup holders.
OXO LiquiSeal Travel Mug **Model:** 1055291 **Price:** $19.99 at www.bedbathandbeyond.com **Dishwasher:** No	Sipping & Handling ★★★ Leakproof ★★ Heat Retention ★★		With a soft rubber grip for comfortable handling and flawless, one-touch opening, our former test kitchen favorite was still a pleasure to take along. Coffee stayed above 140 for only an hour. It was easy to overfill this tumbler, which leaked if coffee got into the lid mechanism before we closed it.
BODUM Double Wall Travel Press with Bonus Lid **Model:** K11057-01 **Price:** $29.95 at www.zappos.com **Dishwasher:** Yes	Sipping & Handling ★★ Leakproof ★★★ Heat Retention ★★		A good mug but a flawed French press: Stray grinds seeped into the brew, and the lid prevented us from easily adding milk and sweetener. A non-French press lid (included) worked much better. Plus it retained heat reasonably well, sealed completely, and cleaned up in the dishwasher.
NOT RECOMMENDED			
TRUDEAU Board Room 16-Ounce Travel Mug **Model:** 087588 **Price:** $14.95 at www.cappojim.com **Dishwasher:** No	Sipping & Handling ★ Leakproof ★★ Heat Retention ★		Dressed to impress, this faux-leather encased mug didn't. It lost heat like a sieve, letting coffee cool below a drinkable temperature in less than an hour. Liquid that got trapped inside the lid when we sipped dribbled out when the mug was turned upside down to test its seal. And the handle got in the way of the car's cup holder.

Taste Test Tomato Soup

Canned tomato soup is often disappointing, loaded with salt and sugar to prop up processed, flavorless ingredients. Does any brand actually taste like tomato? BY HANNAH CROWLEY

FOR CONVENIENCE, a can of tomato soup is hard to beat: Open, heat, eat. Unfortunately, its contents rarely excite us. Canned or homemade, tomato soup should taste like bright, fresh tomatoes.

Yeah, right.

In our quest to find a product worth buying, we rounded up eight national brands of tomato soup (seven canned and one from a box), heated them according to the instructions on the label, and called our tasters to the lunch table. Twenty-one editors and test cooks spooned their way through 4 gallons of soup. It wasn't pretty. The soups earned comparisons to "hospital food" and "tomato-flavored dishwater." But in the end, we emerged with two brands that we could recommend, even if not highly.

You'd think it would be a safe bet that tomato soup would include, well, tomatoes. But only half of our soups did—the top-ranking half. The four bottom-ranking soups derive their only tomato flavor from tomato puree, a combination of water and tomato paste. Three of the top four soups also include tomato puree, but all four add fresh, unprocessed tomatoes. It was no surprise that tomato flavor was an important factor in our tasters' preferences. Our winner, Progresso Vegetable Classics Hearty Tomato, earned the highest ranking for tomato flavor, while our three least favorite soups ranked lowest in the same category.

Tomatoes are naturally sweet, so a certain level of sweetness in tomato soup is desirable; sure enough, some of the sugar on the nutrition label comes from the tomatoes. But several of our samples went overboard adding sweeteners. Our four lowest-ranking soups list sugar or high-fructose corn syrup (HFCS) within the first three ingredients. (By law, the order of the ingredient list must reflect the percentage of an ingredient within.) Tasters unflatteringly compared these sugary brands to SpaghettiOs and Fruit Roll-Ups.

Tasters were equally exacting about texture. "You could mortar a house with this stuff," one noted of a thick soup. As for Healthy Choice Tomato Basil, it was so thick that one taster dismissed it as "tomato soup chewing gum"; that particular brand uses more cornstarch than any other we tasted. No wonder it ranked near the bottom in our lineup. Soups with the opposite problem—those that were too thin—were panned as "red water." Our two favorites struck tasters as closest to homemade, with medium body and slightly chunky texture that was created by pieces of real tomato.

From soup to soup, seasoning varied widely. One soup tasted of celery, onion, and other "vegetal" components—anything but actual tomatoes. A low-sodium sample tasted washed out; its watery flavor and weak seasoning failed to deliver the sweet, tangy punch of ripe tomatoes. In fact, the two bottom-ranked soups contained the least sodium. While all the soups featured herbs and spices, the aggressively herbaceous seasoning of Muir Glen Organic Tomato Basil and Healthy Choice Tomato Basil pushed these two down in our ranking. Even for tomato-basil soups, these were over the top.

In the end, we still vote for homemade tomato soup. But we're willing to concede that in a pinch, our two recommended brands, Progresso Vegetable Classics Hearty Tomato and Imagine Organic Vine Ripened Tomato Soup, will do. Both had just enough seasoning to add depth without stealing the show. They were salted but not salty. We also liked their pleasantly sweet flavors—which tasted like ripe, sweet tomatoes—and their home-style textures. A grilled cheese sandwich seen in their company could hold its head high.

TEST KITCHEN TIP

Improve Canned Soup

After your soup is warm, lend it a helping hand. Off-heat, sprinkle on or stir into 1 can of soup any of the following: 2 to 3 tablespoons sour cream, 2 to 3 tablespoons shredded cheddar cheese, or 1 tablespoon minced fresh chives or basil.

RECOMMENDED

TASTERS' NOTES

PROGRESSO
Vegetable Classics Hearty Tomato
Price: $2.69 for 19 oz.
Sugars: 13 g per 1-cup serving
Sodium: 690 mg per 1-cup serving
Tomato: Tomato puree, tomatoes
Sweetener: Sugar, less than 2 % corn syrup solids

The "deep red" color and "tangy" flavor of this soup suggested actual tomatoes. Although it has the second highest amount of sodium among the brands we tasted, the flavors were balanced, and the "slightly herbaceous" seasoning "allowed the tomato to bloom."

IMAGINE
Organic Vine Ripened Tomato Soup
Price: $3.29 for 14.5 oz.
Sugars: 12 g per 1-cup serving
Sodium: 610 mg per 1-cup serving
Tomato: Tomato puree, tomatoes, tomato juice, tomato paste
Sweetener: Evaporated cane juice

This canned soup had the texture of homemade and nicely trod the line between sweetness and tang. "Tastes like real tomato, a balance between acidic and sweet flavors," one impressed taster noted. Although this soup contains no cheese, a few tasters thought they detected traces of Parmesan.

RECOMMENDED WITH RESERVATIONS

IMAGINE
Organic Creamy Tomato Soup
Price: $3.99 for 32 oz.
Sugars: 7 g per 1-cup serving
Sodium: 620 mg per 1-cup serving
Tomato: Tomatoes
Sweetener: Rice syrup

Unlike our top picks, this bright orange soup wasn't chunky. Instead, it was "comforting" and "thick." But many tasters objected to the strong vegetal flavors (primarily celery), which they felt "overpowered the tomato."

MUIR GLEN
Organic Tomato Basil Soup
Price: $2.99 for 14.6 oz.
Sugars: 11 g per 1-cup serving
Sodium: 740 mg per 1-cup serving
Tomato: Tomato puree, tomatoes
Sweetener: Raw sugar

Some tasters praised this "zesty" canned soup for its "good balance of spice and roast-y flavors" and "present tomato" taste. Others felt that the herbs sabotaged the tomato flavor. As one taster put it, "A little too herby—almost like a canned pizza sauce."

CAMPBELL'S
Condensed Tomato Soup
Price: $0.99 for 10¾ oz.
Sugars: 12 g per 1-cup serving
Sodium: 480 mg per 1-cup serving
Tomato: Tomato puree
Sweetener: HFCS

This soup incited no passion. "Not too thin, not too thick, just kind of dead center," one taster wrote. Other verdicts included "mild" and "bland but not off-putting." High-fructose corn syrup (which tastes sweeter than sugar) is the second ingredient listed; some tasters found this soup too sweet.

NOT RECOMMENDED

PROGRESSO Vegetable Classics Tomato Basil Soup
Price: $2 for 19 oz.
Sugars: 14 g per 1-cup serving
Sodium: 680 mg per 1-cup serving
Tomato: Tomato puree
Sweetener: Sugar, less than 2 % corn syrup solids

Although similar in some respects to our winning soup, this sample had no yeast extract (an ingredient that adds depth). Tasters found this variation "sickeningly sweet"; one likened it to SpaghettiOs. The third ingredient listed is sugar, and this soup had the most total sugars per serving of all the brands we sampled.

HEALTHY CHOICE
Tomato Basil Soup
Price: $2.69 for 15 oz.
Sugars: 12 g per 1-cup serving
Sodium: 470 mg per 1-cup serving
Tomato: Tomato puree
Sweetener: Sugar

A glut of herbs doomed this "heart healthy" soup. Tasters couldn't get past the "disgusting, powdery dried-herb dust." The "gelatinous" texture didn't help. As one taster wrote, the soup "seems thickened with duck sauce."

CAMPBELL'S Condensed Soup Healthy Request Tomato
Price: $1.49 for 10¾ oz.
Sugars: 10 g per 1-cup serving
Sodium: 410 mg per 1-cup serving
Tomato: Tomato puree
Sweetener: HFCS

This "healthier" version of regular Campbell's uses a lot more water than the original. Our tasters found the soup "watery, thin, and bland." As one taster summed up, "Looks like tomato dishwater and tastes like it, too."

Cooking Class How to Braise Short Ribs

Short ribs are relatively inexpensive because they contain lots of tough connective tissue. But when ribs are properly braised, the toughness literally melts out, leaving tender, moist, intensely beefy meat and rich sauce.

Short Ribs 101

Get to Know Your Ribs

As their name says, short ribs are, well, short ribs cut from any part along the cow's ribs: the lower belly, the shoulder (or chuck), or the forward midsection. Here are the three cuts of short ribs that you're most likely to encounter at the meat case.

TOP CHOICE
Boneless

Boneless short ribs are the easiest to work with and eat—if you know to compensate for the flavor and body lost by evicting the bone. Our recipe is boldly flavored and uses gelatin to give the sauce body and silkiness.

BEST BONE-IN CHOICE
English-Style

English-style short ribs are 2- to 4-inch lengths of bone with a wide piece of fatty meat attached. They are easy to find at the supermarket and usually cheaper than flanken, which is why we prefer them in the test kitchen.

NOT RECOMMENDED
Flanken-Style

Flanken-style short ribs are about ¾ inch thick, cut across the ribs and grain, and they include two or three segments of rib bone. We find them harder to eat than English-style short ribs, thus we don't recommend them.

BRAISED BEEF SHORT RIBS

Serves 6

Use ribs that are at least 4 inches long and 1 inch thick. If you can't find boneless ribs, substitute 7 pounds of bone-in beef short ribs that are also at least 4 inches long (with 1 inch of meat above the bone) and cut them off the bone. (See method at right.) Use a bold red wine, such as Cabernet Sauvignon.

- 3½ pounds boneless short ribs, trimmed
-    Salt and pepper
- 2 tablespoons vegetable oil
- 2 onions, halved and sliced thin
- 1 tablespoon tomato paste
- 6 garlic cloves, peeled
- 2 cups red wine
- 1 cup beef broth
- 4 large carrots, peeled and cut into 2-inch lengths
- 4 sprigs fresh thyme
- 1 bay leaf
- ½ teaspoon unflavored gelatin
- ¼ cup water

1. Adjust oven rack to lower-middle position and heat oven to 300 degrees. Pat ribs dry with paper towels and season with salt and pepper. Heat 1 tablespoon oil in Dutch oven over medium-high heat until just smoking. Brown half of beef on all sides, 10 to 12 minutes; transfer to plate. Repeat with remaining 1 tablespoon oil and remaining beef.

2. Reduce heat to medium, add onions, and cook, stirring occasionally, until softened and browned, 12 to 15 minutes. Stir in tomato paste and cook until paste begins to darken, 1 to 2 minutes. Add garlic and cook until fragrant, about 30 seconds. Stir in wine and bring to boil over medium-high heat. Simmer, scraping up any browned bits, until reduced by half, 8 to 10 minutes. Add broth, beef and any accumulated juices, carrots, thyme, and bay leaf and bring to simmer. Cover and bake until tender and fork inserted into meat meets no resistance, 2 to 2½ hours, turning meat twice during cooking.

3. Sprinkle gelatin over water and let sit until gelatin softens, about 5 minutes. Transfer beef and carrots to serving platter and tent loosely with aluminum foil. Strain contents of pot through fine-mesh strainer into bowl, pressing on solids to extract as much liquid as possible; discard solids. Pour liquid into fat separator and let settle for 5 minutes. Return defatted liquid to pot and cook over medium heat until reduced to 1 cup, 5 to 10 minutes. Off heat, stir in gelatin mixture. Season with salt and pepper to taste. Pour sauce over beef and carrots. Serve.

MAKE AHEAD

Ribs and sauce can be refrigerated separately for up to 3 days. To serve, heat sauce and ribs together over medium heat until ribs are heated through, about 10 minutes.

> ▶ The quality of store-bought beef broth varies widely. Search for our favorite brands at **CooksCountry.com.**

Make Your Own Boneless Ribs

If you can't find boneless ribs, make them yourself from bone-in English-style ribs. All it takes is a few minutes and a sharp chef's knife. Position the knife as close to the bone as possible, then carefully slice away the meat. Trim and discard the hard fat and silverskin from both sides of the meat.

SECRET INGREDIENT
Powdered Gelatin

By using boneless ribs, we can make short ribs without the usual fattiness (read: grease). But we pay a price. Boneless ribs lack bone marrow, which normally gives sauce extra flavor and body. We restore the texture by stirring in gelatin.

Twelve Steps to Braising Short Ribs

1. HEAT OVEN Adjust the oven rack to the lower-middle position and heat the oven to 300 degrees. **WHY?** We like to braise in a moderate oven, which provides more even heat than the stovetop can.

2. BROWN IN BATCHES Sear the ribs in two (or more) batches until they're well browned. **WHY?** Caramelizing the crust will mean a more flavorful braise. If you crowd the pot, the ribs will steam instead of browning.

3. SAUTÉ AROMATICS Brown the onions and then add the tomato paste. Finally, add the garlic cloves. **WHY?** Sautéing onions, tomato paste, and garlic in the rendered beef fat creates a rich base of flavor for the braising liquid.

4. ADD WINE, THEN BROTH Pour in the wine and reduce it by half, scraping up the browned bits (fond) in the pot. Then add the broth. **WHY?** Reducing cooks some of the alcohol out of the wine and concentrates its flavor.

5. COVER AND BRAISE Place the lid on the pot and braise the ribs for two hours or more, until they're fork-tender. **WHY?** The lid traps heat and steam and prevents evaporation, letting the ribs slowly simmer and tenderize.

6. TURN RIBS TWICE During cooking, turn the meat in the braising liquid twice. **WHY?** Turning ensures that the ribs will cook evenly in the simmering liquid.

7. PIERCE WITH FORK After two hours, test the ribs for tenderness by sticking a fork into the meat. **WHY?** To see if it's done. If the fork is difficult to remove, cook the meat longer.

8. REMOVE AND REST Using tongs, move the meat and carrots to a platter and let them rest. **WHY?** So the meat juices, squeezed outward during cooking, can redistribute, ensuring juicy ribs.

9. STRAIN SAUCE Strain the contents of the pot into a large bowl. **WHY?** To turn the vegetable-studded braising liquid into a smooth sauce. By this time, the onions are spent.

10. DEFAT SAUCE Pour the sauce into a fat separator. Let it settle for five minutes and then return the liquid to the pan, leaving the fat behind in the separator. **WHY?** So the strained sauce isn't greasy.

11. REDUCE SAUCE Reduce the strained, defatted sauce on the stovetop for five to 10 minutes. **WHY?** To thicken the sauce slightly and concentrate its flavor.

12. ADD GELATIN Dissolve the gelatin in a small bowl of cold water and then stir it into the pot. **WHY?** The gelatin makes the sauce silken and full-bodied (even though you used boneless ribs).

Braising Q&A

What Is Braising?
Braising is slow, covered cooking with liquid. You can braise vegetables relatively quickly, but for most people braising means meat—usually tough, cheap cuts that tenderize through long, gentle cooking. Pot roast, pork shoulder, shanks, brisket, and ribs all have enough connective tissue to be good options for braising. Leaner, more tender cuts (like most steaks) don't benefit from braising.

How Does Braising Work?
Connective tissue, which is made primarily of collagen, is what makes some meat (like short ribs) tough. When it is cooked beyond 140 degrees, it begins to break down into gelatin, the protein that makes for tender meat. Collagen breaks down most efficiently in a moist environment at temperatures around 200 degrees. We've found that the best way to encourage collagen to break down into gelatin is by putting the meat and liquid in a covered Dutch oven in a 300-degree oven and letting it cook for a long time.

What Pot Should I Braise In?
When braising meat in the test kitchen, we almost always reach for our trusty Dutch oven. The sturdy, roomy pot conducts heat well (helping the meat get a good sear), and it has plenty of space. It's also outfitted with a tight-fitting lid.

TEST KITCHEN FAVORITE
Le Creuset 7¼-Quart Round French Oven ($270)

TEST KITCHEN BEST BUY
Tramontina 6.5-Qt. Cast Iron Dutch Oven ($39)

Can Braised Meat Be Overcooked?
You can indeed overcook braised meat, driving out so much of the meat's moisture that it becomes dry. In that case, your pot roast will go beyond sliceable and on to shredded. You can salvage it for a sandwich, salad, or soup. But it won't make a presentable Sunday roast. Cook braises just until fork-tender, then stop.

Looking for a Recipe

Swiss Chocolate Sauce
Elmira A. Conlon, Altoona, Pa.

I am looking for a recipe from my childhood: the Swiss chocolate sauce from Gifford's, an old-fashioned ice-cream parlor that has been in the D.C. area since 1938. All of their sauces were wonderful, but I especially loved the Swiss sauce. I've never been able to find one like it. Perhaps your readers can help?

Date Bar Fruitcake
Debbie Hansen, Lebanon, N.H.

I am looking for a sentimental favorite from my childhood in the 1950s—a fruitcake recipe that was printed on the box of Dromedary Date Bar Mix. The product no longer exists. I would be delighted if you could reproduce that wonderful cake.

Amish Butter Pie
Karen Shelley, Warsaw, Ind.

A few years ago I ate at the Amish Family Center, in Nappanee, Indiana. One of the choices for dessert was called butter pie. It was different from a custard pie, although perhaps it is in the same family. Since then, I haven't been able to find a recipe that was quite right. Can you help?

Hamburger Pinwheels
Debra Pratt, Whitehall, N.Y.

A good many years ago, when I was in school, the school cafeteria used to serve hamburger pinwheels. They were made from biscuit dough with ground beef rolled up—pinwheel-style—inside the dough, and they were served with brown gravy. The pinwheels were comforting and delicious. I'd love to be able to make them at home.

Tomato Soup Cake
Laura Major, Paonia, Colo.

My mom used to make this recipe when I was a kid, and it was always a hit. It called for a can of tomato soup and had raisins, nuts, and a cream cheese frosting (the best part!). I attempted to make it once, but it was a disaster. I'd like to try it again—and get it right this time.

Peanut Butter Streusel Pie
Adele Alford, Middletown, R.I.

I would love to have a recipe for a pie that a diner here in Newport, Rhode Island, used to make. (The owner of the diner and his wife were Southerners.) They filled a standard pie crust with a custard/pudding, topped it with meringue, and finally sprinkled on a peanut butter streusel. I know it sounds odd, but it was the best!

Piccalilli Relish
Marcia Lang, Two Harbors, Minn.

My mother used to make a relish she called piccalilli. It was like a cabbage slaw that was packed into green peppers and put in a crock to pickle, somewhat like sauerkraut. I have searched and can find nothing that seems similar. Can you help? I'd love to eat this again.

Apple Cider Doughnuts
Jessica Trompeter, Chicago, Ill.

I absolutely love going to apple orchards in the fall and snagging a couple of warm doughnuts dusted in cinnamon sugar. I have tried to make apple cider doughnuts at home, but they lack that robust apple cider–cinnamon flavor. Can anyone share a recipe for a tried-and-true, real orchard-style cider doughnut?

Lemon Chiffon Pie
Ermine Owenby, Tallahassee, Fla.

My mother used to make Lemon Chiffon Pie back in the 1960s. Can you revive a recipe for this pie? My mother made this for Sunday suppers when the minister and his wife would be our guests.

German Apple Cake
Deanne Weber, Northfield, Minn.

My 103-year-old grandmother is now living in a nursing home, and when we cleaned her house, I looked in her recipes for her delicious apple cake. I couldn't find the recipe, and she is no longer able to relate it to us from memory. The cake was dark and sweet (like a spice cake or coffee cake) but I don't think it had molasses (which I do not like). It did have chunks of apple and raisins, and sometimes she put nuts in it. She baked it in a 9 by 13-inch pan and topped it off with a delicious creamy chocolate frosting. She is 100 percent German, if that helps in the search.

Così's Flatbread
Kristie Macbean, Astoria, N.Y.

I would like a recipe to make flatbread similar to what they make at the restaurant chain Così—it is absolutely delicious. Theirs is made in a large open flame hearth oven, so I would also need some tips on how to approximate that baking environment at home. Thanks.

Sesame Pie
Frances W. Little, Kannapolis, N.C.

In the late 1950s, my sister made a pie called sesame pie (or open sesame pie). The recipe came from a package of dates, or maybe from a magazine that published the winners of some sort of contest. (Neither my sister nor I remember.) The pie is memorable to me because I figured the dates meant that I wouldn't like it. I was very wrong—it was good! So good that I'm still looking for the recipe. Does anyone out there have it?

SIZZLING CHEESE PINWHEELS
Makes 2 dozen pinwheels
Leo Torrente, Yorktown, N.Y.

"This makes a couple dozen pinwheels, but they're so good, you better take care or you'll eat the entire batch yourself!" Leo warned us. Broilers vary dramatically, so watch the pinwheels carefully. Begin checking for doneness after a couple of minutes of broiling on the first side.

- **8** ounces cream cheese, softened
- **6** ounces sharp cheddar cheese, shredded (1½ cups)
- **2** ounces thinly sliced deli salami, chopped fine
- **3** scallions, minced
- **1** tablespoon hot sauce
- **2** teaspoons Dijon mustard
- **12** slices hearty white sandwich bread, crusts removed
- **12** ounces bacon, halved crosswise

1. Adjust oven rack 6 inches from broiler element and heat broiler. Set wire rack in rimmed baking sheet. Process cream cheese and cheddar in food processor until smooth, about 30 seconds. Transfer to bowl and stir in salami, scallions, hot sauce, and mustard.

2. Working with 1 slice bread at a time, roll bread as thin as possible with rolling pin. Evenly cover with 2 heaping tablespoons cheese mixture. Starting at short edge, roll bread into tight cylinder. Cut in half crosswise and wrap each half with 1 piece bacon, covering bread completely. Secure bacon with toothpick.

3. Transfer to prepared baking sheet and repeat with remaining bread, filling, and bacon. Broil until bacon is crisp, 10 to 12 minutes, flipping halfway through broiling. Let pinwheels cool for 10 minutes. Serve.

Maple-Walnut Cake

A great American ingredient, maple syrup, makes for a Great American Cake.
Its pairing with walnuts is classic—and with good reason.

To make this cake you will need:

- **2 cups (8 ounces) walnuts, toasted**
- **1 recipe yellow layer cake***
- **¾ cup maple syrup**
- **¾ cup (5¼ ounces) sugar**
- **4 large egg whites**
- **½ teaspoon maple extract**

FOR THE CAKE: Adjust oven rack to middle position and heat oven to 350 degrees. Grease three 8-inch round cake pans, line with parchment paper, then grease and flour pans. Process 1½ cups walnuts in food processor until finely chopped, about 1 minute. Prepare yellow layer cake batter according to directions, stirring in ground walnuts until just combined. Scrape equal amounts of batter into prepared pans and bake until toothpick inserted in center comes out clean, about 25 minutes. Cool cakes in pans on wire rack for 10 minutes. Remove cakes from pans, discarding parchment, and cool completely, about 2 hours.

FOR THE CANDIED NUTS: Line rimmed baking sheet with aluminum foil and set wire rack in sheet. Simmer ¼ cup syrup in small saucepan over low heat until reduced by half, 2 to 3 minutes. Stir remaining ½ cup walnuts into syrup, then pour onto wire rack. Let sit until coating is firm, about 10 minutes.

FOR THE FROSTING: Whisk sugar, remaining ½ cup syrup, egg whites, and extract together in bowl and place over medium saucepan with ½ inch of barely simmering water. Using hand mixer, whip mixture on medium-high speed until stiff peaks form, 6 to 8 minutes. Remove from heat and whip until mixture has cooled and is very thick and glossy, 8 to 10 minutes.

TO ASSEMBLE: Place 1 cake round on serving platter. Spread 1 cup frosting over cake, then top with second cake round. Spread another 1 cup frosting over cake, then top with third cake round. Spread remaining frosting evenly over top and sides of cake. Garnish with candied walnuts. Serve.

*Go to **CooksCountry.com/extra** for our Yellow Layer Cake recipe or use your own.

Recipe Index

Cook's Country

DECEMBER/JANUARY 2012

Moravian Chicken Pie

Crown Roast of Pork

Chocolate Pound Cake

Slow-Cooker Turkey Breast
You Get Great Gravy, Too

Cookie Contest Winners
New Holiday Favorites

Low-Fat Apple Crisp
Super-Crunch, Full Apple Flavor

Diner-Style Omelets
Fluffy and Foolproof

Hearty Spinach Lasagna
You Won't Miss the Meat

Tasting Breakfast Sausage
Could Frozen Beat Fresh?

Cheesy Potato Cakes
Crisp Outside, Creamy Inside

Harvey House Chocolate Puffs
American Classic Rediscovered

Cheese Fondue
No Fondue Pot Required

Testing Oven Mitts
Are New Materials Better?

www.CooksCountry.com
$4.95 U.S./$6.95 CANADA

Down around Winston-Salem, North Carolina, Moravian Chicken Pie is the centerpiece of weekly church fundraisers. Now that we've perfected our version of this sumptuous all-chicken double-crust pie, we're making it a centerpiece of our comfort food repertoire. PAGE 20

0 74470 05251 7   0 1>

Cook's Country

Dear Country Cook,

My sister Kate and I did a fair amount of cooking as we were growing up. She spent many days at the Yellow Farmhouse in our small town in Vermont helping Marie Briggs bake whole-wheat and Anadama breads, molasses cookies, and lemon meringue pie. I started off with cakes, recipes found in *Fannie Farmer* or *Joy of Cooking*, enjoying decidedly mixed results. Our parents were always kind enough to ask for seconds, even when the results were lopsided or underbaked or when the frosting dripped down the side of the cake like thin gruel.

As a kid, what I always loved about cooking was that I was taken seriously. I couldn't fix my father's Country Squire station wagon, be of much help when an addition was being built onto our small cabin (though I do remember hammering in 20 penny nails), or handle a chain saw. I could milk a cow, clean a gutter, and throw bales of hay, but most of all I could cook. I could throw together a batch of cookies or a cake, hand-churn ice cream in our White Mountain, whip up spaghetti sauce, or boil corn, and I could do it just as well, or so I thought, as either of my parents. Cooking was my ticket into the world of grown-ups.

These days, everyone wants kids to remain childish. In the country, youngsters sat in the pickup along with mom or dad, endured long hours of adult discussions about breeding pigs, or picked up a brush and slopped creosote onto rough-hewn fence posts. Childhood isn't just for childish things; it's also a time for finding out what you are capable of, in the kitchen as in life.

Christopher Kimball
Founder and Editor, Cook's Country

Cook's Country

Founder and Editor Christopher Kimball
Editorial Director Jack Bishop
Executive Editor, Magazines John Willoughby
Executive Editor Peggy Grodinsky
Managing Editor Scott Kathan
Senior Editors Lisa McManus, Cali Rich,
Bryan Roof, Diane Unger
Test Kitchen Director Erin McMurrer
Associate Editors Lynn Clark, Amy Graves
Test Cooks Sarah Gabriel,
Rebeccah Marsters, Kelly Price
Assistant Editors Hannah Crowley, Taizeth Sierra
Assistant Test Cooks Nick Iverson,
Carolynn Purpura MacKay
Copy Editors Nell Beram, Megan Chromik
Executive Assistant Christine Gordon
Assistant Editor Shannon Friedmann Hatch
Assistant Test Kitchen Director Gina Nistico
Senior Kitchen Assistants Meryl MacCormack,
Leah Rovner
Kitchen Assistants Maria Elena Delgado,
Andrew Straaberg Finfrock, Ena Gudiel
Executive Producer Melissa Baldino
Associate Producer Stephanie Stender

Contributing Editors
Erika Bruce, Eva Katz, Jeremy Sauer
Consulting Editors Anne Mendelson, Meg Ragland
Science Editor Guy Crosby, Ph.D.
Executive Food Editor, TV, Radio & Media
Bridget Lancaster

Online Managing Editor David Tytell
Online Editor Kate Mason
Online Assistant Editors
Eric Grzymkowski, Mari Levine
Video Operations Manager Peter Tannenbaum
Media Producer Alexandra Pournaras
Associate Editor/Camera Operator Nick Dakoulas
Assistant Editor/Camera Operator Jesse Prent

Design Director Amy Klee
Art Director, Magazines Julie Bozzo
Deputy Art Director Susan Levin
Designer Lindsey Timko
Staff Photographer Daniel J. van Ackere
Color Food Photography
Keller + Keller, Anthony Tieulli
Styling Mary Jane Sawyer, Kelly Upson

Art Director, Marketing/Web Christine Vo
Associate Art Directors, Marketing/Web
Erica Lee, Jody Lee
Designers, Marketing/Web
Elaina Natario, Mariah Tarvainen
Online Photo Editor Steve Klise

Vice President, Marketing David Mack
Circulation Director Doug Wicinski
Circulation & Fulfillment Manager Carrie Fethe
Partnership Marketing Manager Pamela Putprush
Marketing Assistant Lauren Perkins
Customer Service Manager Jacqueline Valerio
Customer Service Representatives
Jessica Amato, Morgan Ryan

Retail Sales & Marketing Manager Emily Logan
Client Service Manager, Sponsorship Bailey Snyder

Production Director Guy Rochford
Senior Project Manager Alice Carpenter
Production & Traffic Coordinator Kate Hux
Asset & Workflow Manager Andrew Mannone
Production & Imaging Specialists Judy Blomquist,
Heather Dube, Lauren Pettapiece

Technology Director Rocco Lombardo
Systems Administrator Marcus Walser
Software Architect Robert Martinez
Software Project Manager Michelle Rushin
Senior Business Analyst Wendy Tseng
Web Developers Chris Candelora,
Cameron MacKenzie

VP New Media Product Development Barry Kelly
Social Media Manager Steph Yiu

Chief Financial Officer Sharyn Chabot
Human Resources Manager Adele Shapiro
Publicity Deborah Broide
ON THE COVER:
Moravian Chicken Pie, Keller + Keller
ILLUSTRATION: Greg Stevenson

Cook's Country magazine (ISSN 1552-1990), number 42,
is published bimonthly by Boston Common Press Limited
Partnership, 17 Station Street, Brookline, MA 02445. Copyright
2011 Boston Common Press Limited Partnership. Periodicals
Postage paid at Boston, Mass., and additional mailing
offices. Publications Mail Agreement No. 40020778. Return
undeliverable Canadian addresses to P.O. Box 875, Station A,
Windsor, Ontario N9A 6P2. POSTMASTER: Send address changes
to Cook's Country, P.O. Box 8382, Red Oak, IA 51591-1382.
Customer Service: It's easy to subscribe, give a gift subscription,
change your address, and manage your subscription online.
Visit www.americastestkitchen.com/customerservice for all of
your customer service needs or write to us at Cook's Country,
P.O. Box 8382, Red Oak, IA 51591-1382. PRINTED IN THE USA

Contents

DECEMBER/JANUARY 2012

BABKA, 24   CROWN ROAST OF PORK, 12   CHERRY TARTS, 8

Features

In Every Issue

**Attend Cooking School
with America's Test Kitchen** (NEW!)
Learn how to think—and cook—like
a pro from the test kitchen experts
you know from our TV shows. Our new
online cooking school combines per-
sonalized instruction with leading-edge
technology to offer an unparalleled
learning experience. To learn more, visit
TestKitchenSchool.com.

America's TEST KITCHEN
America's Test Kitchen is a 2,500-square-foot kitchen located just outside of Boston. It is the home of *Cook's Country* and *Cook's Illustrated* magazines and is the workday
destination of more than 50 test cooks, editors, and cookware specialists. Our mission is to test recipes until we understand how and why they work and arrive at the best
version. We also test kitchen equipment and supermarket ingredients in search of brands that offer the best value and performance. You can watch us work by tuning in to
Cook's Country from America's Test Kitchen (CooksCountryTV.com) on public television.

Ask Cook's Country

BY SARAH GABRIEL

Why does green salad wilt if you dress it ahead of time? How can I prevent this?

Robert Gladden, Sukagawa, Japan

Several food science reference books attribute wilting to the oil, which dissolves the protective waxy cuticle on the lettuce leaves, allowing them to lose moisture and wilt. In the name of due diligence, we did a few experiments.

The main components of vinaigrette are acid (vinegar or citrus), oil, and salt; often sugar is included, too. We tossed several different kinds of lettuce in six different preparations: just oil, just vinegar, just salt, just sugar, a combination of oil and vinegar, and a combination of oil, vinegar, and salt. All of the lettuce that had been tossed with vinegar or salt, whether alone or in combination with oil, began to wilt in minutes and was inedible after an hour. To our surprise, the lettuce tossed in oil remained relatively pert and crunchy even after four hours. So oil doesn't dissolve the protective waxy coating on lettuce after all? We turned to our science editor for clarification.

Leafy vegetables wilt because they lose "turgor pressure," or the pressure supplied by the water within the cells to keep cells plump, he told us. As soon as water starts to leak out of the cells, the turgor pressure falls and they deflate and become limp. Oil can dissolve the waxy cuticle on lettuce and cause it to wilt, but that would take a very long time.

Vinegar, however, can cause relatively rapid wilting. Vinegar is made up of water and molecules of acetic acid, at approximately 5 percent by weight, plus a small concentration of hydrogen ions and acetate ions. A high concentration of dissolved ions outside the lettuce creates strong osmotic pressure, which draws the water out of the cells fairly quickly. The influence of osmotic pressure draws water from a dilute solution (inside the cells) to a concentrated solution (the vinegar) until the concentrations of dissolved molecules inside and outside the cells are equal. Salt creates even more dissolved ions and accelerates this process.

THE BOTTOM LINE: Vinegar makes lettuce wilt. To prevent sad, wilted salad greens, dress them right before serving.

SAD SALAD
Salad dressed with vinaigrette after one hour.

Can I add flavors to dried beans that are soaking in water?

Francisco Betancourt, Cambridge, Mass.

In the test kitchen, we often soften dried beans before cooking not simply by soaking them in water but by actually brining them, which seasons them and improves their texture. When beans soak in brine, sodium ions from the salt replace calcium and magnesium ions in the skin of the beans. Sodium ions weaken the pectin holding the cells together, allowing more water to penetrate the skins to produce softer, more tender beans. Our formula is to soak a pound of dried beans overnight in a solution of 3 tablespoons of salt dissolved in 4 quarts of water.

To find out if you can add other flavors via the brine, we soaked a pound of chickpeas in three brines: plain, brine with four pureed garlic cloves and an onion, and brine with ⅓ cup of pureed oregano. Many flavor compounds are only oil soluble, so we suspected that our water-based brines would not flavor the beans.

Before cooking the chickpeas, we rinsed them well. Tasters were nearly knocked over by the onion and garlic flavor in the second batch. All tasters detected herb flavor in the oregano-brined batch. We repeated these tests with other dried beans and other herbs with similar results.

THE BOTTOM LINE: Yes, you can add flavor to dried beans by introducing herbs, onions, or garlic to the brine that the beans soak in.

GARLIC AND ONION

FRESH OR DRIED HERBS

I've seen recipes for scrambled eggs that call for water or milk. Does this do anything for the eggs?

Amy Cronin DiCaprio, Amherst, Mass.

When eggs are scrambled, the mechanism that transforms the liquidy beaten eggs into a fluffy mound on the plate is protein coagulation—the process by which, when exposed to heat, proteins unfold and then tangle up with one another and set, forming a latticed gel. The more tender the scrambled eggs, the more loosely the proteins have coagulated. Adding water to scrambled eggs dilutes the proteins a little, thereby raising the temperature at which they coagulate and making it harder to overcook the scramble. Water also increases the amount of steam, which puffs up the eggs, producing fluffy scrambled eggs. As for milk, it contains water but also fat, which coats the protein molecules so that they can't bind with one another as tightly. The key to scrambled eggs that are both fluffy and tender is a balance of water and fat.

We scrambled eggs with water, milk, half-and-half, and heavy cream and found that half-and-half provided the best balance of fat and water when we used our favorite scrambled egg formula: two additional yolks for every eight eggs to boost richness. When we simply scrambled whole eggs without the benefit of the extra fat from the yolk, some tasters preferred the eggs made with heavy cream.

THE BOTTOM LINE: Scrambled eggs benefit from added liquid, preferably a liquid with fat; use 1 tablespoon of liquid for every two eggs. For fluffy and tender scrambled eggs for four, use eight eggs, two yolks, and ¼ cup of half-and-half.

I see all kinds of honey at the supermarket (clover, buckwheat, tupelo, etc.). Some are quite expensive. What's the difference?

Beth Youmell, Stowe, Vt.

The raw material that bees use to produce honey is nectar, a sweet liquid created by plants for the purpose of attracting pollinating birds and insects. Most honeys are made from the nectar of many different flowers, but there are some "monofloral" varieties made in controlled environments from the nectar of a single type of flower. The flavor and chemical makeup of honey depend on the nectar that it's made from. Are the different kinds interchangeable in the kitchen?

To find out, we tasted four varieties of honey—three monoflorals (tupelo, orange blossom, and buckwheat) as well as wildflower honey—three different ways: plain, in tea, and baked into honey cake. In the plain and tea tastings, we found tupelo honey to be subtly floral and piney. Orange blossom was thicker and slightly less sweet, with a perfumed aroma and a flavor that one taster likened to an orange Popsicle. Wildflower honey bowled us over with its flowery flavor and aroma, which one taster compared to "fancy soaps," and buckwheat honey was dark, "malty," "robust," "barnyard-y," and "molasses-y," according to various tasters. As for the honey cake tasting, all honeys were fine, save one. Buckwheat honey has an uncommonly high protein content; the protein reacts with the sugar, producing the dark pigments, toasty aromas, and signature bold flavor. The flavor of buckwheat honey is so strong that some tasters didn't care for it in the honey cake.

THE BOTTOM LINE: Try different varieties of honey to determine what you like. Strongly flavored varieties like buckwheat honey can be too assertive for many recipes—save these honeys for your tea.

Recently, I went to make a batch of cookies and found that I was out of brown sugar. Do you have a substitution?

Margaret Sorenson, St. Paul, Minn.

Most brown sugar is made by adding molasses (a byproduct of refining sugarcane into solid sugar) either to granulated white sugar or to the sugarcane syrup before it has crystallized. (A few gourmet brown sugar manufacturers have reverted to the old-fashioned method of halting the refining process early.) In the test kitchen, we've found that pulsing 1 cup of granulated sugar in the food processor with 1 tablespoon of molasses makes a fine substitute for light brown sugar. For dark brown sugar, use 2 tablespoons of molasses for the same 1 cup of granulated sugar.

THE BOTTOM LINE: Don't have any brown sugar in the cupboard? Make your own by mixing molasses into white granulated sugar. Or simply add the molasses along with the wet ingredients in your recipe.

To make 1 cup of light brown sugar:

1 cup granulated sugar + 1 tablespoon molasses

To make 1 cup of dark brown sugar:

1 cup granulated sugar + 2 tablespoon molasses

To ask us a cooking question:
Visit **CooksCountry.com/askcookscountry**. Or write to Ask Cook's Country, P.O. Box 470739, Brookline, MA 02447. Just try to stump us!

Kitchen Shortcuts

COMPILED BY CAROLYNN PURPURA MACKAY

DOUBLE DUTY
Wine Chiller
Colleen Niles, San Diego, Calif.

I don't own a wine bucket to keep wine cold, but I've discovered that instead, I can use the insert from my ice-cream maker (which lives in my freezer). The insert keeps white wine nice and cool for hours.

DOUBLE DUTY
Improvised Cake Cover
Anathea O'Brien, Milwaukee, Wis.

I don't have a cake cover (but I do have several decorative cake stands without covers). Instead of buying yet another specialized item to hog space in my cabinets, I use the bowl of my salad spinner to cover cakes and keep them fresh. The salad-spinner bowl is light, easy to clean, and since it's clear, I can tell at a glance how much cake I have left.

BETTER BAKING
Quicker Biscotti Crisping
Kristie Swanick, Cooperstown, N.Y.

After slicing biscotti logs that must be returned to the oven to dry, I place the cookies on a cooling rack on the cookie sheet instead of directly on the sheet. The air circulates and both sides dry, so I no longer need to flip the cookies partway through this second round of baking.

HANDY TIP
Easy Vinaigrette
Cooper Clark, Somerville, Mass.

I've found a great way to make my favorite vinaigrette. Instead of measuring everything out, I use a Sharpie to mark an old plastic dressing bottle with measuring lines for each ingredient. I add each ingredient to the dressing bottle according to the lines and then shake. Presto—I've got vinaigrette.

DOUBLE DUTY
A Nutty Idea
Phyllis Meeker, Manchester, N.H.

Sometimes I have a difficult time opening bottles that seem to get glued shut, especially those containing sticky things like maple syrup. I found that using my nutcracker around the screw cap gives me the leverage I need to open bottles easily.

BETTER BAKING
Flatter Parchment
Valerie Sullivan, Denver, Colo.

My parchment paper comes in a roll, like plastic wrap. This used to pose a problem when I baked cookies, as the edges would curl up and mar the tender cookies as they baked. Now as soon as I get a new roll of parchment I cut it to size and store the sheets between the baking sheets, which keeps the parchment flat. Now my cookies look as good as they taste.

NEAT TRICK
Splatter Saver
Carol Mayer, Sparta, Ill.

Melting butter in the microwave always used to mean having to clean up splatter. Covering the butter with a paper towel didn't help much. I've found that laying the waxy butter wrapper over the container that the butter is in keeps my microwave clean, and the melting butter stays where it should.

Submit a tip by e-mail at **CooksCountry.com/kitchenshortcuts** or send a letter to Kitchen Shortcuts, Cook's Country, P.O. Box 470739, Brookline, MA 02447. Include your name, address, and phone number. If we publish your tip, you will receive a free one-year subscription to *Cook's Country*. Letters may be edited for clarity or length.

Recipe Makeover Apple Crisp

Would cutting fat and calories give us the chance to put the apples front and center?

BY CAROLYNN PURPURA MACKAY

APPLE CRISP IS often too sweet, maybe even too rich. So when I got the assignment to trim calories and fat from this classic American dessert, I figured I could make crisp both lighter and better, putting the focus where it should be: on the apples. After calculating that a single serving of ordinary apple crisp has 540 calories and 23 grams of fat, I headed to the test kitchen intending to bring the numbers down and the apple flavor up.

Among the handful of low-fat recipes that I tested, I encountered some seriously out-of-place flavors (like molasses) and some practically flavorless crisps, as well as toppings that were anything *but* crisp. But I also came across some good ideas. I decided to begin with a classic recipe for crisp, which topped sliced, spiced, and sweetened apples with a crunchy mix of butter, sugar, flour, nuts, and oats. Then I figured I'd borrow from and rearrange the best aspects of the low-fat recipes to develop my own.

Many low-fat recipes remove the sugar from the filling. Hoping to do the same, I reached for six Golden Delicious apples, which are naturally sweet, and baked a crisp of plain sliced apples topped with the (for now) high-fat topping. This filling fell apart and didn't taste like much. For my next attempt, I stole a trick from a low-fat recipe that I'd tested: I poached the apples in apple juice concentrate and cinnamon before sprinkling on the topping and baking the crisp. This technique both jumpstarted the cooking of the apples and turbo-charged their flavor. Since the concentrate was still too caloric, I substituted lower-calorie apple juice. Both apples and juice were already sweet, so just 2 tablespoons of brown sugar sweetened the filling.

Homemade applesauce binds the apple slices in the filling and moistens the crunchy topping.

The flavor of the filling was under control, but its texture was more like apple sauce than crisp. If I cooked the apples less, though, I got slices floating in juice. After a week of experimentation, I devised a solution: I chopped three of the apples, boiled them in the juice, and mashed them into applesauce. I sliced the three remaining apples and folded them into the mash. Then I briefly cooked the two together.

Now I examined the topping. Reluctantly, I ejected the calorie-dense nuts. Next, I went after the butter (I was using 10 tablespoons). The low-fat recipes I had tried offered a variety of replacements: egg whites, juice, and jam, to name three. All had produced chewy (as opposed to crisp) toppings. OK, I'd just slowly decrease the butter. Removing the first 3 tablespoons actually made the crisp taste better—more apple-y. But further cuts left me with too little fat to coat the dry ingredients. Since the flour added no flavor, I reduced the amount that I was using. To make up for its lost cohesive qualities, I ground half of the (far more flavorful) oats into oat "flour" in the food processor. But the calories and fat were still too high, so I reconsidered the butter. As is typical with crisps, I had been cutting in cold butter to make coarse crumbs. I was happy to discover that if I melted it, it coated the ingredients better, allowing me to further cut back on butter. Finally, I stole 1 tablespoon of the apple mash that I'd (conveniently) already made for my apple filling and used it to replace yet more butter in the topping. These measures meant that the topping needed just 3 tablespoons of butter.

At this point, the fat and calorie numbers were so low that I hoped to restore the nuts. No can do, I concluded after a bit of number crunching. But I did look around for a less fatty alternative. While I was eating cereal one recent morning, the "nuts" on the Grape-Nuts package practically leapt off the box at me. (Not only does the famously misnamed cereal contain no nuts, but it contains no grapes, either.) Back in the test kitchen, I stirred ⅓ cup of the cereal into the crisp topping. When I tried a spoonful of this apple crisp, the crunch was loud enough to be heard out of state. The fact that I'd saved 240 calories and 17 grams of fat was nice, too.

TEST KITCHEN TECHNIQUE **Apple Every Way**

1. START WITH APPLE PIECES
Peel, cut, and stew one-inch chunks in apple juice.

2. MAKE APPLESAUCE
After stewing, mash the pieces into sauce for the filling and the topping.

3. ADD APPLE WEDGES
Peel, slice, and fold these into the mash to complete the filling.

SECRET INGREDIENT **Grape-Nuts**
Are we off our nut? Figuratively, no. Literally, yes. We love the flavor and crunch that nuts add to apple crisp but not the fat and calories. For guilt-free crunch, we used Grape-Nuts cereal in place of walnuts or pecans.

REDUCED-FAT APPLE CRISP

Serves 6

Instant or quick oats turn the topping sandy; use old-fashioned oats. Note that the apple pieces and apple wedges are cooked differently.

TOPPING

- ⅔ cup (2 ounces) old-fashioned rolled oats
- ⅓ cup Grape-Nuts cereal
- 5 tablespoons packed light brown sugar
- ¼ cup (1¼ ounces) all-purpose flour
- 3 tablespoons unsalted butter, melted and cooled
- ½ teaspoon ground cinnamon
- ⅛ teaspoon salt

FILLING

- 6 large Golden Delicious apples (8 ounces each), peeled, cored, and halved
- 1 cup apple juice
- 2 tablespoons packed light brown sugar
- ¾ teaspoon ground cinnamon
- 2 teaspoons lemon juice

1. FOR THE TOPPING: Process ⅓ cup oats in food processor until finely ground, about 20 seconds. Combine processed oats, remaining ⅓ cup oats, Grape-Nuts, sugar, flour, butter, cinnamon, and salt in medium bowl; set aside.

2. FOR THE FILLING: Adjust oven rack to upper-middle position and heat oven to 400 degrees. Cut 3 apples into 1-inch pieces and slice remaining 3 apples into ¼-inch-thick wedges. Bring apple pieces, apple juice, sugar, and cinnamon to simmer in 12-inch nonstick skillet over medium heat. Cover and cook, stirring occasionally, until apples are tender, about 15 minutes. Transfer mixture to bowl and mash apples using potato masher. Reserve 1 tablespoon mashed apple mixture. Return remaining mashed apple mixture to skillet with apple wedges and cook, covered, until wedges just begin to soften, 3 to 4 minutes. Off heat, stir in lemon juice.

3. Scrape apple filling into 8-inch square baking dish and press into even layer. Add reserved mashed apple to topping mixture, stirring until mixture appears crumbly. Sprinkle topping over filling and bake until juices are bubbling and topping is deep golden brown, about 25 minutes. Let cool on wire rack for 15 minutes. Serve.

How do you transform this most luxurious of roasts from a special-occasion feast into an outstanding (and easy) dinner for two? BY LYNN CLARK

JUICY, ULTRA-TENDER PRIME rib is the ultimate roast beef. Unfortunately, its steep price tag means that it's usually saved for large, festive dinners. But I think a dinner for two can be as special an occasion as any, so I set out to convert this lavish cut of beef into a luxurious but easy dinner for two.

I knew that even the smallest prime rib roast (the term refers to any roast that contains only the highly prized rib section of the cow) was far too big for just two people. But I also knew that this cut could be divided into bone-in rib steaks (usually called rib eyes) that are about 1½ inches thick and weigh around 1½ pounds each—perfect for two. You can sometimes find these thick-cut steaks in the meat case, but if not, you can request them at the super-market meat counter.

But how do you best cook a cut of meat that looks like a steak but demands to be treated like a roast? Clearly, I needed to combine the two cooking techniques. After a few false starts I hit it right: I seared the meat on the stovetop and then moved it to a low oven to cook through. The hybrid technique gave me just what I wanted: a roast with a crusty brown exterior and an interior that was juicy and rosy red from one edge to the other.

While the roast rested, I made the accompanying jus (using ketchup instead of the more typical tomato paste so that I didn't have to open a can for a single tablespoon of paste). Everything was ready, but when I plated it up, something was wrong. The cut is basically a steak, so when you remove the bone, cut it in half, and serve it, each person gets just that—half a steak. The plate lacked that big, rosy slice of meat that distinguishes prime rib from other "lesser" cuts. The solution? Creative carving. I experimented with butterflying the steak, but this was tricky and the results weren't stellar. Next I tried cutting the meat in half on the bias; that didn't look right either. I finally succeeded by slicing the roast on the bias into four pieces. The technique gave me beautiful pieces of meat that showed off

These slices may not be quite as thick as traditional slabs of prime rib. But they are just as rosy, tender, and delicious.

more of the rosy interior and presented like honest-to-goodness prime rib. I'd done it: I'd produced a delicious "prime rib" dinner that didn't require a special occasion or a gathering of the tribe.

PRIME RIB FOR TWO

Be sure to brown the edges of the steak to render the fat. You can do this easily by using tongs to hold the steak on its side in the hot pan.

- 1 (1½-pound) bone-in rib-eye steak, 1½ inches thick
  Salt and pepper
- 1 tablespoon vegetable oil
- 2 tablespoons minced shallot
- 1 teaspoon ketchup
- ¼ teaspoon dried thyme
- ½ cup beef broth
- ¼ cup red wine

1. Adjust oven rack to lowest position and heat oven to 200 degrees. Pat steak dry with paper towels and season with salt and pepper.

2. Heat oil in 12-inch skillet over medium-high heat until just smoking. Brown steak all over, 10 to 12 minutes. Transfer steak to wire rack set in rimmed baking sheet. Roast until meat registers 120 to 125 degrees (for medium-rare),

25 to 30 minutes. Transfer steak to cutting board, tent loosely with aluminum foil, and let rest for 5 to 10 minutes.

3. Meanwhile, pour off all but 2 teaspoons fat from now-empty skillet. Add shallot and cook over medium heat until softened, about 1 minute. Stir in ketchup and thyme and cook until fragrant, about 30 seconds. Add broth and wine and simmer, scraping up any browned bits, until reduced to ⅓ cup, about 10 minutes. Carve bone from steak and cut steak on bias into four ½-inch-thick slices. Serve with jus.

> **TEST KITCHEN TECHNIQUE**
> **Roast for Two?**
> To approximate "prime rib" presentation from a single rib steak, make four cuts on a 45-degree angle to "carve" the steak.
>
>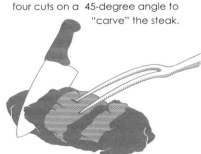

Slow Cooker Turkey Breast and Gravy

You don't need a whole bird to create a satisfying version of this holiday classic. But you do need to figure out how to make a rich, savory gravy in the slow cooker. BY REBECCAH MARSTERS

THERE'S A REASON I roast a turkey only at holiday time: It's a chore to haul such a big bird from store to refrigerator to oven to table—and then there's the carcass to deal with. Working with just the turkey breast was more feasible for a weeknight dinner (my family prefers white meat anyway), and given the size of a whole, bone-in breast, it seemed tailor-made for the slow cooker. I figured that if I could add gravy to the package, this meal just might fall into my weekly rotation.

Traditional gravy starts with a stock made from the browned neck and giblets—two elements that aren't included when you buy a turkey breast at the market. Also, though lean turkey breast does shed a lot of liquid during cooking—and I'd certainly use what I got—it's not the fatty, rich drippings that are produced when you cook a whole bird, and which make the gravy tastes so good. With these challenges in front of me, I was eager to get cracking.

> ▶ For our Slow-Cooker Holiday Ham recipe, go to CooksCountry.com/extra.

I kept my first test simple: I plunked the whole bone-in, skin-on breast into the slow cooker, scattered the usual chopped carrot, celery, onion, and garlic around it, and let everything cook on low for about five hours, until the meat reached 160 degrees. The good news was that on my very first try the meat was tender and juicy. Unfortunately, the carrot and celery hadn't contributed much flavor to the turkey

Save Your Skin
It's cumbersome to brown a whole turkey breast. Instead, we removed and browned the skin only, getting fat, fond, and flavor for our gravy. We added the rendered skin to the slow cooker for yet more flavor.

juices, and the skin of the bird was pale, limp, and flabby—a ghastly sight.

For the vegetables to give up their flavor, I'd have to brown them first. Since I was pulling out my skillet, I decided to try making the roux (the mixture of fat and flour that thickens the gravy) now, instead of after the meat was done. This way, my theory went, the gravy would essentially make itself as the turkey juices combined with the roux while the meat cooked. I sautéed the carrot, celery, onion, and garlic cloves in butter. Once the vegetables were browned, I added flour, using a typical roux ratio of about 1½ parts flour to 1 part fat. I stirred in white wine and chicken broth, added a few bay leaves and thyme sprigs, poured everything into the slow cooker, and set the turkey breast on top. Five hours later, when the meat was done, I strained out and discarded the vegetables, which, having added their essence to the "gravy," were spent. Why the quotation marks around "gravy"? Because while what was left in the cooker was flavorful, it was way too watery to qualify as gravy.

Obviously, for the gravy to have the proper consistency after absorbing all the turkey juices, my starting point would have to be a very thick liquid. To this end, I decreased the amount of added broth by a third and introduced extra flour to the roux. Now the gravy came out of the cooker thick enough to merit the name "gravy."

It was good as far as it went, but the gravy still tasted anemic. I hoped that browning the whole skin-on breast at the outset would solve this problem. The rendered turkey fat improved the gravy, but wrestling the 7-pound hunk of bird in the pan was no fun. As I eyed the turkey breast warily, I realized that during the browning, it was only the skin that was contributing fat and flavor anyhow. For my next test, I removed the skin, cut it into a few smaller pieces for ease, and threw it into the skillet. Much like bacon, the fat rendered and the skin became crisp. I could then use the drippings (along with some butter) to sauté the vegetables and build the roux. Instead of discarding the browned skin, I added it to the slow cooker so that it could lend depth to the drippings, and hence to the gravy. I proceeded as before, and by the time the turkey was

The gentle, moist heat of the slow cooker is ideal for producing juicy white meat.

cooked, I had a thick, rich, savory gravy to go with it. It may not have been the full Thanksgiving spread, but this was a flavorful turkey and gravy combo that I could handle any night of the year.

SLOW-COOKER TURKEY BREAST AND GRAVY
Serves 8 to 10
If you don't have quite 3 tablespoons of drippings after browning the turkey skin in step 1, supplement with additional butter.

- 1 (6- to 7-pound) bone-in turkey breast, trimmed
- 1 tablespoon unsalted butter
- 1 onion, chopped coarse
- 1 carrot, peeled and chopped coarse
- 1 celery rib, chopped coarse
- 6 garlic cloves, peeled and smashed
- 7 tablespoons all-purpose flour
- 2 cups low-sodium chicken broth
- ½ cup dry white wine
- 2 sprigs fresh thyme plus 1 teaspoon minced
- 2 bay leaves
    Salt and pepper

1. Pat turkey dry with paper towels. Remove skin from breast and cut into 4 equal pieces. Cook turkey skin in 12-inch skillet over medium heat until browned, 8 to 10 minutes. Transfer skin to slow cooker. Pour off all but 3 tablespoons fat from skillet. Add butter, onion, carrot, celery, and garlic and cook until vegetables are browned, 8 to 10 minutes. Whisk in flour and cook, whisking constantly, until golden, about 2 minutes. Slowly whisk in broth and wine and bring to boil. Transfer gravy, thyme sprigs, and bay leaves to slow cooker.

2. Season turkey with salt and pepper and place meat side up in slow cooker. Cover and cook on low until breast registers 160 degrees, 5 to 6 hours.

3. Transfer turkey to carving board, tent loosely with aluminum foil, and let rest for 15 to 20 minutes. Pour gravy through fine-mesh strainer into serving bowl; discard solids. Stir minced thyme into gravy and season with salt and pepper to taste. Carve turkey and serve with gravy.

Five Easy Recipes Braised Hearty Greens

Now that we've figured out how to cook them faster, we give you four variations to further tempt you to "go green." BY KELLY PRICE

SLOW-BRAISED GREENS ARE a beautiful thing: tender and mildly bitter, nutritious and deeply satisfying. I find them particularly appealing when someone else makes them, devoting their time—not mine—to waiting for the greens to simmer to softness. Luckily, the test kitchen figured out a simple recipe that gets braised greens on the table in under an hour.

The first obstacle was the sheer volume of greens: You need a full 2½ pounds to serve four to six people. Such a mass of greens easily overflows a skillet and even a Dutch oven. To solve the problem, we added half of the greens to the pot with a cup of water and covered them for one minute. By this point, the first batch of greens had wilted down so that the pot could handle the other half.

We took a hard look at how long greens really needed to cook, and we discovered that 40 minutes of simmering was perfect. (Some old Southern recipes suggest cooking greens for up to five hours.) We removed the lid during the last 10 minutes of cooking to help some of the liquid evaporate, leaving just a bit of juice, which is affectionately known as "pot liquor." To bump up the flavor, we started by sautéing onion and then added salt, brown sugar, and cayenne to the pot with the greens. Using chicken broth instead of water approximated the meatiness sometimes supplied by a ham hock. Vinegar and butter added at the end of cooking brought depth.

With a simple master recipe complete, I could focus on creating a few flavor variations so that home cooks (and those they were feeding) would never tire of these greens. Chorizo and jarred pimento peppers add a smoky, complex, and meaty dimension in one variation. (The peppers also bring a welcome pop of color.) For a simple, elegant version with an Italian accent, we top the greens with crisped pancetta and toasted pine nuts. One of my tasters' favorite variations features crunchy toasted almonds and sweet, slightly chewy golden raisins. In the final variation, small white beans add a creamy element, and the natural sweetness of shallot balances the greens' bitter bite.

Armed with a simple, efficient cooking technique and easy-to-make variations, I now had recipes for greens to suit any occasion.

Our greens take on a Spanish flavor with chorizo, pimento peppers, and sherry vinegar.

TEST KITCHEN PRIMER
Hearty Greens

Kale
If frilly kale (pictured) is too strong for your liking, try milder Tuscan kale.

Collards
These greens can have very thick stems—take care to stem them thoroughly.

Mustard Greens
The peppery bite of mustard greens mellows during cooking.

Turnip Greens
Younger, smaller turnip greens are sweeter than older, larger ones.

BRAISED HEARTY GREENS
Serves 4 to 6
Don't be alarmed by the giant mound of greens. They wilt significantly when cooked. Collards may need a few extra minutes of covered cooking in step 1.

- 4 tablespoons unsalted butter
- ½ cup thinly sliced red onion
- 2½ pounds hearty greens (kale, mustard, turnip, or collards), stemmed and leaves chopped
- 1 cup low-sodium chicken broth
- 1 tablespoon packed brown sugar
    Salt and pepper
- ⅛ teaspoon cayenne pepper
- 2 tablespoons cider vinegar

1. Melt 2 tablespoons butter in Dutch oven over medium heat. Cook onion until softened, about 5 minutes. Add half of greens, broth, sugar, ½ teaspoon salt, and cayenne. Cover and cook until greens are beginning to wilt, about 1 minute. Stir in remaining greens and cook, covered and stirring occasionally, over medium-low heat until completely tender, about 30 minutes.

2. Remove lid and cook over medium-high heat, stirring occasionally, until liquid is nearly evaporated, about 10 minutes. Stir in remaining 2 tablespoons butter and vinegar and cook until butter is melted, about 30 seconds. Season with salt and pepper to taste. Serve.

BRAISED HEARTY GREENS WITH CHORIZO AND PIMENTOS
Omit 2 tablespoons butter and cayenne in step 1. Cook 8 ounces chorizo sausage, halved lengthwise and sliced ¼ inch thick, in Dutch oven over medium heat until browned, 6 to 8 minutes. Using slotted spoon, transfer chorizo to paper towel–lined plate. Proceed with remainder of step 1. Replace cider vinegar with 2 tablespoons sherry vinegar. Add chorizo and ½ cup chopped jarred pimento peppers with butter and vinegar in step 2.

BRAISED HEARTY GREENS WITH PANCETTA AND PINE NUTS
Toast ⅓ cup pine nuts in Dutch oven over medium heat until golden, about 2 minutes; set aside. Omit 2 tablespoons butter in step 1, and cook 6 ounces chopped pancetta in Dutch oven until browned, 6 to 8 minutes. Using slotted spoon, transfer pancetta to paper towel–lined plate. Proceed with remainder of step 1. Replace cider vinegar with 2 tablespoons red wine vinegar. Top greens with pine nuts.

BRAISED HEARTY GREENS WITH RAISINS AND ALMONDS
Toast ⅓ cup sliced almonds in Dutch oven over medium heat until golden, about 5 minutes; set aside. Proceed with step 1. After removing lid in step 2, add ½ cup golden raisins. Replace cider vinegar with 2 tablespoons balsamic vinegar. Top cooked greens with almonds.

BRAISED HEARTY GREENS WITH WHITE BEANS AND SHALLOTS
Replace 2 tablespoons butter and onions in step 1 with 2 tablespoons vegetable oil and 6 thinly sliced shallots. Cook shallots over medium heat until browned, 6 to 8 minutes. Using slotted spoon, transfer shallots to paper towel–lined plate. Proceed with remainder of step 1. After removing lid in step 2, add 1 (15-ounce) can rinsed small white beans. Top cooked greens with shallots.

Christmas Cookies

We tasted more than 600 cookies. Through them, we traveled the world—Italy, France, Wales, Bosnia, Latvia . . . We tested our language skills (can you say Piparkoogid?). We lost track of how many grandmothers we met and how often we heard "I've been making this cookie for more than 50 years." Your recipes allowed us to attend long-ago weddings and Christmas dinners and to honor legendary family bakers. We took note of new trends in baking (chai, dulce de leche) and old ones (margarine, "soured heavy cream"). We considered cookies flavored with Arizona honey, and we marveled at dough made with mayonnaise and at filling that combined chickpeas, chocolate, and rum. One contest entrant speculated that we work at "the happiest kitchens on earth." At this time of year, immersed in your delicious recipes and delightful stories, it's hard to argue with her. Here are this year's seven winning recipes.

WINNER CHERRY TARTS Sara Cowley, Winamac, Ind.

"I got this recipe from a friend over 30 years ago. My mom is the expert cookie baker in the family, but one year I brought these cookies as my contribution to the family's Christmas cookie tray. Everyone loved them, and my mom asked for the recipe. For a little while they were known as Sara's Cherry Cookies, but then a couple of years in a row we both made them for the Christmas tray. I took the hint and let her make them from then on."

Makes about 18 large cookies

2½ cups (12½ ounces) all-purpose flour
¼ teaspoon baking soda
¼ teaspoon salt
12 tablespoons unsalted butter, softened
¾ cup (5¼ ounces) granulated sugar
¼ cup milk
1 large egg plus 1 large white
1 teaspoon almond extract
¾ cup cherry preserves
1 cup (4 ounces) confectioners' sugar
½ teaspoon vanilla extract

1. Adjust oven racks to upper-middle and lower-middle positions and heat oven to 350 degrees. Line 2 baking sheets with parchment paper. Combine flour, baking soda, and salt in bowl.

2. Using stand mixer fitted with paddle, beat butter and granulated sugar on medium-high speed until pale and fluffy, about 2 minutes. Add 2 tablespoons milk, whole egg, and almond extract and beat until incorporated. Reduce speed to low, add flour mixture in 3 additions, and mix until just combined, scraping down bowl as needed.

3. Lightly beat egg white in bowl. Working on lightly floured counter, divide dough in half and form each into 4-inch disk. Roll each disk into ¼-inch-thick circle. Using 2½-inch cookie cutter, cut out rounds, gathering and rerolling dough as necessary. Transfer half of rounds to prepared sheets, 1 inch apart. Place heaping teaspoon of preserves in center of each round. Top with remaining rounds and crimp with fork. Brush filled rounds with beaten egg white and cut ½-inch X into center of each.

4. Bake until edges are lightly browned, 12 to 14 minutes, switching and rotating sheets halfway through baking. Let cookies cool on sheets for 5 minutes and then transfer to wire rack to cool completely, about 1 hour. Whisk confectioners' sugar, remaining 2 tablespoons milk, and vanilla in bowl until smooth. Brush cookies with glaze and let sit for 30 minutes. Serve. (Tarts can be stored at room temperature for up to 2 days.)

$1,000 GRAND PRIZE

SANDIES BY THE SEA Linda Hanson, Madison, Wis.

"Friends and family know that the week before Christmas I am totally enveloped in cookie making, baking seven different kinds of cookies to give away. Since I found this recipe several years ago, my friends and my husband always ask, 'You are making those buttery, salty, caramel-y cookies, aren't you?'"

Makes about 4 dozen cookies

1	cup pecans, toasted
2	cups (10 ounces) all-purpose flour
¼	teaspoon table salt
16	tablespoons unsalted butter, softened
⅔	cup packed (4⅔ ounces) light brown sugar
1	large egg
1	teaspoon vanilla extract
25	soft caramel candies
¼	cup heavy cream
½	cup (3 ounces) bittersweet chocolate chips
	Coarse sea salt

1. Process pecans in food processor until finely ground, about 30 seconds. Combine flour, processed pecans, and table salt. Using stand mixer fitted with paddle, beat butter and sugar on medium-high speed until pale and fluffy, about 2 minutes. Add egg and vanilla and beat until incorporated. Reduce speed to low, add flour mixture, and mix until just combined, scraping down bowl as needed. Refrigerate until dough is firm, about 1 hour.

2. Adjust oven racks to upper-middle and lower-middle positions and heat oven to 350 degrees. Line 2 baking sheets with parchment paper. Roll heaping tablespoons of dough into balls and place 2 inches apart on prepared sheets. Using back of floured ½ teaspoon measuring spoon, make indentation in center of each ball.

3. Bake until edges are lightly browned, 12 to 14 minutes, switching and rotating sheets halfway through baking. Remove cookies from oven and gently reinforce existing indentation with teaspoon measure. Let cookies cool on sheets for 5 minutes and then transfer to wire rack to cool completely, about 40 minutes. Repeat with remaining dough.

4. Cook caramels and cream in small saucepan over low heat, stirring frequently, until smooth, 8 to 10 minutes. Meanwhile, microwave chocolate chips in bowl, stirring occasionally, until smooth, 1 to 2 minutes. Fill each cookie dimple with ½ teaspoon melted chocolate and spread up sides of dimple. Top with ½ teaspoon caramel mixture. Sprinkle cookies with sea salt and let sit until centers are firm, about 1 hour. Serve. (Cookies can be stored at room temperature for up to 3 days.)

PISTACHIO-FENNEL COOKIES

Pam McCollow, Pewaukee, Wis.

"This recipe is a bit different than traditional Christmas cookies, but the subtle taste of fennel is very pleasant and the pistachios add a festive color. It's a relatively new recipe, but it's going to become a yearly tradition."

Makes about 3 dozen cookies
Pulverize the fennel seeds in a spice grinder or mortar and pestle.

2	cups (10 ounces) all-purpose flour
1½	tablespoons fennel seeds, ground
1	teaspoon baking powder
½	teaspoon salt
16	tablespoons unsalted butter, softened
1½	cups (10½ ounces) sugar
1	large egg
1	tablespoon grated lemon zest
2	teaspoons almond extract
1	cup shelled pistachios, chopped

1. Adjust oven racks to upper-middle and lower-middle positions and heat oven to 350 degrees. Line 2 baking sheets with parchment paper. Combine flour, ground fennel, baking powder, and salt in medium bowl.

2. Using stand mixer fitted with paddle, beat butter and sugar on medium-high speed until pale and fluffy, about 2 minutes. Add egg, lemon zest, and almond extract and beat until incorporated. Reduce speed to low, add flour mixture in 3 additions, and mix until just combined, scraping down bowl as needed. Add ½ cup pistachios and mix until incorporated.

3. Roll heaping tablespoons of dough into balls and place 2 inches apart on prepared sheets. Press dough to ½-inch thickness using bottom of greased measuring cup. Top cookies with remaining ½ cup pistachios, pressing lightly to adhere. Bake until edges are lightly browned, about 10 minutes, switching and rotating sheets halfway through baking. Let cookies cool on sheets for 5 minutes and then transfer to wire rack to cool completely, about 40 minutes. Serve. (Cookies can be stored at room temperature for up to 3 days.)

FINALIST OLD WORLD BUTTER HORNS Shelley Kempner, Forest Hills, N.Y.

"When I was growing up … my parents' friend Nick, originally from Italy, always made these cookies for Christmas and brought them over still warm on a large cardboard tray (which I later figured out was a clothing box; he was a tailor). This kept them in a single layer—important, since they're quite fragile. These cookies never made it to the communal table. They disappeared one by one, eaten secretly with a large napkin underneath to catch the shards (too good to lose!)."

Makes 4 dozen cookies

4	cups (20 ounces) all-purpose flour
2¼	teaspoons instant or rapid-rise yeast
½	teaspoon salt
18	tablespoons (2¼ sticks) unsalted butter, chilled and cut into ½-inch pieces
½	cup sour cream
2	large eggs, separated, plus 2 large yolks
1¾	teaspoons vanilla extract
¾	cup walnuts, toasted and chopped fine
⅛	teaspoon ground cinnamon
⅛	teaspoon cream of tartar
⅔	cup (4⅔ ounces) sugar

1. Adjust oven rack to upper-middle and lower-middle positions and heat oven to 400 degrees. Line 2 baking sheets with parchment paper. Process flour, yeast, and salt in food processor until combined, about 30 seconds. Add butter and pulse until mixture resembles coarse meal, 10 to 12 pulses. Add sour cream, 4 egg yolks, and 1 teaspoon vanilla and pulse until dough forms, about 10 pulses. Divide dough into 8 equal pieces and form each into 4-inch disk. Wrap disks in plastic wrap.

2. Combine walnuts and cinnamon in bowl. Using stand mixer fitted with whisk, whip 2 egg whites and cream of tartar together on medium-low speed until foamy, about 1 minute. Increase speed to medium-high and whip whites to soft, billowy mounds, about 1 minute. Gradually add sugar and remaining ¾ teaspoon vanilla and whip until stiff, glossy peaks form, 2 to 3 minutes. Using rubber spatula, fold in nut mixture.

3. Working one at a time, roll each disk into 7-inch circle. Cut disk into 6 equal wedges. Place heaping teaspoon of egg white–nut mixture into center of each wedge and pinch points of dough together to seal. Place dough triangles on prepared sheets, 1 inch apart. Let shaped cookies stand for 15 minutes.

4. Bake until lightly browned, 12 to 14 minutes, switching and rotating sheets halfway through baking. Cool cookies on sheets for 5 minutes and then transfer to wire rack to cool completely. Repeat with remaining dough and filling. Serve. (Store cookies at room temperature for up to 2 days.)

FINALIST COCONUT-LIME DREAM BITES

Elizabeth Pokrivka, Seven Valleys, Pa.

"This recipe came from my great-great aunt Violet. It was originally made with lemon and is a family favorite. My mom and I like to experiment with flavors, so one Christmas we decided to try making them with lime."

Makes 15 bars

CRUST

1⅔	cups (6⅔ ounces) cake flour, sifted
¼	cup (1¾ ounces) granulated sugar
¼	teaspoon salt
11	tablespoons unsalted butter, cut into ½-inch pieces and chilled

FILLING

1	cup packed (7 ounces) light brown sugar
4	large eggs
1	teaspoon vanilla extract
½	teaspoon salt
¼	teaspoon baking powder
1	cup sweetened shredded coconut
1	cup walnuts, toasted and chopped

GLAZE

4	teaspoons grated lime zest plus ¼ cup juice (2 limes)
1	tablespoon granulated sugar
2	cups (8 ounces) confectioners' sugar, sifted

1. FOR THE CRUST: Adjust oven rack to middle position and heat oven to 350 degrees. Lay sheets of aluminum foil perpendicular to each other in 13 by 9-inch pan, with extra foil hanging over edges of pan. Push foil into corners and up sides of pan, smoothing foil flush to pan. Process flour, sugar, and salt in food processor until combined, about 30 seconds. Add butter and pulse until mixture resembles coarse meal, about 10 pulses. Transfer mixture to prepared pan and press into even layer. Bake until edges are lightly browned, about 15 minutes. Let crust cool in pan for 5 minutes.

2. FOR THE FILLING: Whisk sugar, eggs, vanilla, salt, and baking powder together. Stir in coconut and walnuts. Pour filling over warm crust and bake until filling is set, about 25 minutes. Cool bars in pan for 5 minutes.

3. FOR THE GLAZE: Combine lime zest and granulated sugar in bowl. Whisk confectioners' sugar and lime juice together in second bowl until smooth. Pour glaze over warm bars and spread into even layer. Sprinkle with lime sugar. Let bars cool completely in pan on wire rack, about 2 hours. Using foil overhang, lift bars from pan and cut into 15 pieces. Serve. (Store bars at room temperature for up to 2 days.)

FINALIST NOCHE BUENA CHOCOLATE SANDWICH COOKIES

Paula Bonchak, Bonham, Texas

"This is one of my best holiday cookie recipes. Everyone enjoys receiving them. They look special (and yummy) on my cookie trays and are always one of the first cookies to go."

Makes about 20 cookies

Use either Kahlua or Tia Maria for the coffee liqueur. Dulce de leche, a Latin American caramel, is sold in the baking aisle of most supermarkets.

- ⅓ cup blanched almonds
- 1½ cups (7½ ounces) all-purpose flour
- ¼ cup (¾ ounces) Dutch-processed cocoa
- ½ teaspoon salt
- ¼ teaspoon cayenne pepper
- 12 tablespoons unsalted butter, softened
- ⅔ cup (4⅔ ounces) granulated sugar
- 4 ounces bittersweet chocolate, melted and cooled
- 2 large egg yolks
- 2 tablespoons coffee liqueur
- 1 teaspoon vanilla extract
- ¼ cup dulce de leche

1. Adjust oven racks to upper-middle and lower-middle positions and heat oven to 350 degrees. Line 2 baking sheets with parchment paper. Process almonds in food processor until finely ground, about 30 seconds. Combine flour, cocoa, salt, and cayenne in bowl.

2. Using stand mixer fitted with paddle, beat butter and sugar on medium-high speed until pale and fluffy, about 2 minutes. Add melted chocolate, egg yolks, liqueur, and vanilla and beat until incorporated. Reduce speed to low, add flour mixture in 3 additions and mix until just combined, scraping down bowl as needed.

3. Working with 2 teaspoons dough at a time, roll dough into balls and place 1 inch apart on prepared sheets. Sprinkle ground almonds on top, pressing lightly to adhere. Bake until edges appear dry, 8 to 10 minutes, switching and rotating sheets halfway through baking. Let cookies cool on sheets for 5 minutes and then transfer to wire rack to cool completely, about 40 minutes.

4. Spread ½ teaspoon dulce de leche over bottom of half of cookies and then top with remaining cookies to form sandwiches. Serve. (Cookies can be stored at room temperature for up to 3 days.)

▶ Find past winning holiday cookie recipes by visiting CooksCountry.com/recipes.

FINALIST CARIBBEAN BISCOTTI **Diana Singer,** New York, N.Y.

"I was supposed to go on a Caribbean vacation but had to cancel it due to work. I wanted to make a cookie that would transport me to the islands, so I chose ingredients that reminded me of warm, beachfront locations."

Makes about 3 dozen cookies

For a decorative finish, brush the logs with a beaten egg white and sprinkle with turbinado sugar before baking.

- ½ cup light rum
- 1 cup dried papaya, chopped fine
- 1 cup dried pineapple, chopped fine
- 2 cups (10 ounces) all-purpose flour
- 1 cup (7 ounces) sugar
- 1½ teaspoons baking powder
- ¼ teaspoon salt
- ⅛ teaspoon ground allspice
- 2 large eggs, lightly beaten
- 2 tablespoons vegetable oil
- 1 teaspoon vanilla extract
- ½ cup macadamia nuts, toasted and chopped
- ½ cup sweetened shredded coconut

1. Adjust oven rack to middle position and heat oven to 350 degrees. Line 1 baking sheet with parchment paper. Combine rum, papaya, and pineapple in bowl. Microwave, covered, until rum begins to boil, about 1 minute. Let sit until dried fruit softens, about 5 minutes. Strain fruit, reserving 3 tablespoons rum. Combine flour, sugar, baking powder, salt, and allspice in large bowl. Whisk reserved rum, eggs, oil, and vanilla together in medium bowl. Stir rum-egg mixture into flour mixture until combined. Stir in reserved dried fruit, macadamia nuts, and coconut.

2. Form dough into two 12 by 2-inch logs 3 inches apart on prepared baking sheet. Bake until lightly browned, about 35 minutes. Let logs cool on sheet for 15 minutes. Transfer to cutting board and, using serrated knife, cut logs on bias into ¾-inch-thick slices. Place cookies cut side down on sheet and continue to bake until dry, about 10 minutes, flipping cookies after 5 minutes. Let cool on sheet for 1 hour. Serve. (Cookies can be stored at room temperature for 1 week.)

Crown Roast of Pork

A crown roast looks impressive, but its unique shape poses problems for the chef.
If we could get it to cook evenly, this roast would taste as regal as it appears. BY SARAH GABRIEL

For an impressive presentation around the holidays, butchers take two bone-in pork loin roasts, strip the meat off the bone ends (that's "frenching" in butcher-speak), and tie the roasts together in a crown shape. But the striking appearance hides a culinary challenge: The odd shape—think big spiky doughnut—makes it difficult to cook a crown roast evenly.

Most recipes treat a crown roast like any other big roast: Season, brush with oil or butter, set in a roasting pan, and cook in a moderate oven. But the ring of meat and bone insulates the pork on the inside, making that section take much longer to cook because the oven's heat can't efficiently travel into the hole. This leads to a dry, overcooked, overbrowned perimeter by the time the interior meat is done. Additionally, simply salting and peppering the exterior amounts to seasoning that's only superficial. As I stared at 40 pounds of nearly inedible pork and a pile of problems on the heels of my initial tests, my goal crystallized: an evenly cooked, richly seasoned, and well-browned roast.

To get the hot oven air to circulate through the hole in the center of the meat, I tried elevating the roast on a V-rack. Lifting the meat off the pan this way only marginally improved the doneness discrepancy and did nothing to even out the browning. As I was staring

▶ Never carved a crown roast? To learn how, go to CooksCountry.com/extra.

dejectedly at yet another unevenly cooked roast, a colleague asked me if I had tried roasting the crown upside down. It sounded a little crazy, but then sane-sounding techniques weren't getting me anywhere. I flipped a roast, rubbed it with salt and pepper, brushed on 4 tablespoons of melted butter, and put it in a 300-degree oven. Because the large mass

A bonus: Potatoes and shallots set underneath the roast make for an easy, super-flavorful side dish.

of meat on the bottom was now exposed to more heat, this roast emerged much more evenly cooked, although the browning still needed work.

It took me more than a week to work through a cooking technique that resulted in both evenly cooked and well-browned meat, but eventually I got there. To blast the thick, meaty bottom of the ring with heat and start the browning, I cooked the roast upside down for about an hour (until it registered 110 degrees) at 475 degrees. Then I turned down the

oven to 300 degrees and flipped the roast right side up to gently finish cooking for about 40 more minutes (until the roast hit 140 degrees).

Yes, the meat was perfectly cooked, but I hadn't solved the problem of superficial seasoning. A crown roast was too unwieldy to easily brine (one of the test kitchen's favorite techniques to deeply season meat), but I knew that salting the roast and letting it sit overnight should have the same effect. Sure enough, it did. For even more flavor, I

added thyme, rosemary, and garlic to the mix. Now the roast was seasoned throughout. Fortunately, further tests determined that six hours of salting was enough to get the job done. The added seasoning also made the savory pan drippings (of which I had about half a cup) even more flavorful.

Crown roasts are often presented with stuffing or a side dish filling the hole in the middle. Stuffing seemed a little heavy with so much meat, so I concentrated on roasting some potatoes and shallots along with the pork. Because I was cooking the crown roast on a rack and flipping it, cooking the vegetables inside the hole was obviously out (although I could certainly serve them there). But roasting them in the pan, under the rack, imbued them even more completely with the meaty drippings.

One taster suggested that I add apples, a classic pork accompaniment. Apple pieces that I cooked with the vegetables were too mushy to serve but added a pleasantly sweet-tangy dimension to the drippings. Instead of discarding them, I pureed the softened apples with the pan drippings. This mixture, bolstered with a little chicken broth, made for a fine sauce. Adding ½ cup of apple cider to the roasting pan midway through cooking reinforced the apple flavor, making the sauce even better.

Juicy and perfectly cooked, with simple roasted vegetables in the center and a sweet-and-tangy sauce on the side, this roast was just the crown I needed for the head of my Christmas table.

CROWN ROAST OF PORK
Serves 10 to 12
Buy a pork loin roast with rib bones that have been trimmed clean, or "frenched." Check with the butcher that the chine bone has been cut from the crown roast; leaving this bone attached hinders even cooking. You want to buy the roast tied, but we tie it an extra time for more support during flipping. Use potatoes that measure 1 to 2 inches in diameter.

Kosher salt and pepper
3 tablespoons minced fresh thyme
2 tablespoons minced fresh rosemary
5 garlic cloves, minced
1 (8- to 10-pound) bone-in pork loin roast (chine bone removed), tied into crown
2 pounds small red potatoes, scrubbed
10 ounces shallots, peeled and halved
2 Golden Delicious apples, peeled, cored, and halved
8 tablespoons unsalted butter, melted
½ cup apple cider
1 cup low-sodium chicken broth

1. Combine 3 tablespoons salt, 1 tablespoon pepper, thyme, rosemary, and garlic in bowl; reserve 2 teaspoons for vegetables. Pat pork dry with paper towels and rub with remaining herb salt. Wrap kitchen twine twice around widest part of roast and tie tightly. Refrigerate roast, covered, for 6 to 24 hours.

2. Adjust oven rack to lower-middle position and heat oven to 475 degrees. Place V-rack inside large roasting pan. Toss potatoes, shallots, apples, 4 tablespoons butter, and reserved herb salt in large bowl and transfer to pan. Arrange roast bone side down in V-rack and brush with remaining 4 tablespoons butter. Roast until meat is well browned and registers 110 degrees, about 1 hour.

3. Remove roast from oven and reduce oven temperature to 300 degrees. Using 2 bunches of paper towels, flip roast bone side up. Add apple cider to pan and return to oven, rotating direction of pan. Roast until meat registers 140 degrees, 30 to 50 minutes. Place meat on carving board, tent loosely with aluminum foil, and let rest for 15 to 20 minutes.

4. Transfer apple halves to blender and potatoes and shallots to bowl. Pour pan juices into fat separator, let liquid settle, and then pour into blender. Process apples and pan juices until smooth, about 1 minute. Strain sauce through fine-mesh strainer into medium saucepan. Add broth and bring to simmer. Season with salt and pepper to taste. Remove twine, slice meat between bones, and serve with vegetables and sauce.

KEY STEPS **Crown Roast of Pork**
When roasted directly on a roasting pan, the perimeter of a crown roast overcooks by the time the interior ring is done. Here's how we solved that problem and produced evenly cooked pork.

1. TIE ROAST
Using kitchen twine, make two loops around the widest part of the roast and tie securely to help the crown hold its shape when flipped.

2. SET BONE SIDE DOWN Place the pork bone side down on the V-rack and adjust the bones to steady the roast. Roast about 1 hour, until meat is 110 degrees.

3. FLIP BONE SIDE UP
Using paper towels to protect your hands, flip the hot roast bone side up and set it back on the V-rack to finish cooking in a gentle oven.

Tuscan White Bean and Pork Soup

Leftover crown roast gave our Tuscan white bean soup heft and substance—but it took too long to cook for a weeknight dinner.

BY SARAH GABRIEL

Swiss chard stems are tougher than the leaves, so it's important to cook them longer.

HERE IN THE test kitchen, we like Tuscan bean soup so much that we have several different versions to recommend. The basic recipe is a home run: Dried white beans are soaked and cooked slowly to creamy perfection, then blended with tomatoes and vegetables (carrots, onion, celery, and lots of garlic), and cooked with pancetta, bay leaf, kale, and fragrant rosemary. Stirring in chopped leftover meat from a crown roast made a great recipe even better, except for one drawback: the almost-three-hour cooking time.

For the sake of convenience, I decided to use bacon instead of pancetta; I usually have it around. The bacon combined with the leftover pork added so much flavor that no one noticed when I omitted the celery and bay leaves from the basic recipe. Canned beans were an obvious move and a huge timesaver. The kale was delicious but took a while to soften, so I switched to Swiss chard, which cooks much more quickly (especially when I sautéed the heartier stems with the onion and carrots and added the leaves later). With these shortcuts, I had this warming, delicious soup on the table in about 40 minutes.

TUSCAN WHITE BEAN AND PORK SOUP
Serves 8
You can substitute an equal amount of ham steak for the pork roast; remove the rind before chopping.

4 slices bacon, chopped fine
1 pound Swiss chard, stems chopped, leaves sliced ½ inch thick
3 carrots, peeled and cut into ½-inch pieces
1 onion, chopped
8 garlic cloves, minced
2 teaspoons minced fresh rosemary
6 cups low-sodium chicken broth
2 (15-ounce) cans cannellini beans, rinsed
1 (14.5-ounce) can diced tomatoes
4 cups chopped leftover pork roast
Salt and pepper

1. Cook bacon in Dutch oven over medium heat until crisp, 6 to 8 minutes. Using slotted spoon, transfer bacon to paper towel–lined plate. Pour off all but 1 tablespoon fat from pot.

2. Add Swiss chard stems, carrots, and onion to now-empty pot and cook until softened, 6 to 8 minutes. Stir in garlic and rosemary and cook until fragrant, about 30 seconds. Add Swiss chard leaves and cook until wilted, 3 to 4 minutes.

3. Stir in broth, beans, and tomatoes and bring to boil. Reduce heat to medium and simmer until carrots are tender, about 15 minutes. Add pork and cook until heated through, about 1 minute. Season with salt and pepper to taste. Serve.

Braised Brisket with Mushrooms

Dry meat and wan mushroom flavor can ruin what should be a tender, flavorful winter classic. We set out to fix those flaws. BY SARAH GABRIEL

I'VE ALWAYS LOVED the idea of rich, meaty braised beef brisket paired with earthy mushrooms. But the versions I've had were never satisfying. The brisket was dry and shred-y, and the mushroom flavor got lost. It was time to figure out this homey dish.

The test kitchen has a lot of experience with brisket. I started out with a trick we've discovered—piercing holes in the brisket's fat cap so that the rendering fat will drip down and moisten the leaner interior meat—and then proceeded with our standard braising method. I seasoned and browned the meat, set it aside, and then cooked a pound of sliced mushrooms in the skillet before adding onions and brown sugar (for caramelization), garlic, thyme, and a little flour to thicken the sauce. Then I whisked in 1 cup each of chicken broth and red wine and let the sauce simmer a bit to thicken. I cooked meat and sauce in a tightly covered baking dish in a 300-degree oven.

Brisket is always dry if you eat it right away. We have a technique for cooling the brisket in the pan juices to allow it to reabsorb them. After a few hours, the meat was indeed moist and sliceable. But did I have to wait that long? Cutting the brisket in half might help, I thought, since it would expose more liquid-reabsorbing surface area. And perhaps turning it over during the soaking would even out absorption. Happily, those two tricks let me reduce the post-cooking soak to one hour.

Now I got to work on the sauce. Tasters wanted more mushroom flavor and wondered where the pound of

sliced mushrooms had disappeared to. Quartering instead of slicing the mushrooms prevented the vanishing act but didn't boost flavor. Adding more fresh mushrooms made the dish unwieldy, so I turned to dried porcini. I microwaved ¼ ounce of dried porcini in a cup of water, strained the liquid and added it with the wine and broth, and stirred in the minced dried mushrooms. That did it: I had deep, full, balanced mushroom flavor. A little balsamic vinegar was the perfect foil to rich beef and mushrooms.

Despite the simple method, this dish had deep, complex flavors and super-tender meat. It was a brisket hit.

BRAISED BRISKET WITH MUSHROOMS Serves 8 to 10
Flat-cut brisket is easier to find and more uniform in texture than point cut.

    1   (4- to 5-pound) brisket roast,
        fat trimmed to ¼ inch
        Salt and pepper
    ¾   cup water
    ¼   ounce dried porcini mushrooms, rinsed
    1   tablespoon vegetable oil
    1   pound white mushrooms, trimmed
        and quartered
    2   onions, chopped
    1   tablespoon packed brown sugar
    3   tablespoons all-purpose flour
    3   garlic cloves, minced
    1   teaspoon minced fresh thyme
    1   cup low-sodium chicken broth
    1   cup dry red wine
    3   bay leaves
    1   teaspoon balsamic vinegar

1. Adjust oven rack to middle position and heat oven to 300 degrees. Pat brisket dry with paper towels. Place roast fat side up on cutting board and prick all over with fork. Cut brisket in half crosswise into 2 roasts. Season with salt and pepper. Microwave water and porcini in covered bowl until steaming, about 1 minute. Let sit until softened, about 5 minutes. Drain porcini through fine-mesh strainer lined with coffee filter, reserve liquid, and mince and reserve porcini.

2. Heat oil in 12-inch skillet over medium-high heat until just smoking. Brown 1 roast on both sides, 10 to 14 minutes; transfer fat side up to 13 by 9-inch baking dish. Repeat with remaining roast.

3. Pour off all but 1 tablespoon fat

For the most tender, juicy brisket, braise until fork-tender and then let it rest for an hour.

from skillet. Add mushrooms and ¼ teaspoon salt and cook over medium-high heat until liquid evaporates and mushrooms are golden brown, about 8 minutes. Add onions and sugar and cook, stirring occasionally, until browned, 8 to 10 minutes. Add flour, garlic, and thyme and cook until golden and fragrant, 1 to 2 minutes. Slowly whisk in broth, wine, ½ cup reserved porcini liquid, reserved porcini, and bay leaves, scraping up any browned bits, and bring to boil. Reduce heat to medium and simmer until thickened, about 8 minutes.

4. Pour sauce over roasts and cover dish tightly with aluminum foil. Bake until tender and fork inserted into meat meets no resistance, 4½ to 5 hours.

Let brisket cool at room temperature in dish, uncovered, for 1 hour, flipping halfway through cooling. Discard bay leaves. (Cooled brisket can be refrigerated in sauce for 2 days; reheat gently, covered, in 300-degree oven for 1 hour before proceeding with step 5.)

5. Transfer roasts to carving board. Strain sauce through fine-mesh strainer into fat separator; reserve mushrooms. Let liquid settle, then pour into bowl. Stir vinegar into sauce and microwave until warm, 30 to 60 seconds. Slice roasts against grain into ¼-inch-thick slices and return to dish with mushrooms. Pour 1½ cups sauce over meat. Serve with remaining sauce. (Refrigerate sliced brisket in sauce for up to 3 days; reheat meat in sauce.)

KEY STEP Halve the Brisket
We cut the raw roast in two to create more surface area, so that it can better reabsorb the pan juices after cooking. Translation: moist meat.

Crispy, Cheesy Potato Cups

When we tried to improve upon classic scalloped potatoes, we found ourselves in a sticky situation. BY SARAH GABRIEL

THE CREAMY INTERIOR of a cheesy potato casserole is delicious, but the edges and top, where the cheese gets brown and crisp, are irresistible. Would it be possible, I wondered, to improve on perfection by engineering a cheesy potato casserole with more crisp brown edges?

After testing (and rejecting) every type of baking pan in the test kitchen, I spotted a muffin tin and realized that if I divided the mixture among the muffin cups, each serving would get its own crisp brown shell.

Adapting a favorite test kitchen recipe for scalloped potatoes, I cut russet potatoes into ¼-inch pieces (they fit nicely into the muffin cups) and microwaved them with half-and-half until they were just tender. I stirred in lots of cheddar cheese tossed with cornstarch (to prevent separating) and spooned the mixture into a muffin tin treated with nonstick spray. After I'd sprinkled each with Parmesan cheese, I put the tin in a 425-degree oven.

The top of each potato "muffin" browned quickly. But when I inverted the pan to release them, they slumped into messy piles revealing oily, blond bottoms. Switching to the lowest oven rack produced well-browned bottoms, but now they were cemented to the pan. Well-browned bottoms also came at the expense of properly cooked tops: Mine were now leathery and overcooked. Laying a sheet of foil over the pan for the first 10 minutes of cooking evened out the browning, but when I inverted the pan to remove the cakes, the brown bits still clung while the creamy interior spilled out.

I figured that a drier mixture would hold together better so I used less half-and-half and added Parmesan cheese with the cheddar. This time, I tried greasing the muffin cups with butter instead of spray. No amount of prying would free these cakes. The next few weeks were a blur of greasing, coating, and prying (and praying). I tried melted butter, softened butter, chilled butter, and all manner of sprays but made scant headway—and I wasn't forging any friendships in the dishwashing room.

Buttering and flouring the tin, as I would for a cake, made a small improvement regarding sticking. Then a colleague suggested that I coat the tin with bulkier bread crumbs instead of flour.

This batch of potato cakes virtually leapt out of the pan. Further testing showed that tasters preferred lighter panko bread crumbs to ordinary ones. I ground them to meld them with the cheesy crust.

When it comes to crisp, creamy, and cheesy potato cakes, it turns out that you can have it all—it just takes some engineering.

CHEESY POTATO CUPS

Makes 12 potato cups
Don't use preshredded cheese here.
Do use a nonstick 12-cup muffin tin.

- ½ cup panko bread crumbs
- 1 tablespoon unsalted butter, softened
- 2 pounds russet potatoes, peeled
- 1¼ cups half-and-half
- 1¼ teaspoons salt
- ¾ teaspoon pepper
- 5½ ounces sharp cheddar cheese, shredded (1⅓ cups)
- 1¼ ounces Parmesan cheese, grated (⅔ cup)
- 2 teaspoons cornstarch

1. Adjust oven rack to lowest position and heat oven to 425 degrees. Pulse panko in food processor until finely ground, about 5 pulses. Evenly coat each muffin cup with softened butter and then with ground panko. Cut each potato in half lengthwise, then cut each half into 3 wedges. Cut each wedge crosswise into ¼-inch-thick slices. Combine potatoes, half-and-half, salt, and pepper in large bowl and microwave, covered, until just tender, 12 to 15 minutes, stirring once.

2. Meanwhile, toss cheddar, Parmesan, and cornstarch together in bowl; reserve ⅓ cup for topping. Add remaining cheese mixture to hot potato mixture, stirring until smooth. Divide potato-cheese mixture evenly among muffin cups and smooth. Sprinkle cups with reserved cheese.

3. Cover muffin tin with aluminum foil sprayed with vegetable oil spray and bake for 10 minutes. Discard foil and continue to bake until golden brown, 13 to 15 minutes. Run paring knife around perimeter of muffin cups. Let potato cups cool in muffin tin on wire rack for 5 minutes. Place rimmed baking sheet on top of muffin tin and invert potato cups, tapping on muffin tin to release cups. Invert cups onto wire rack and let cool for 5 minutes. Serve.

Coating the tin with softened butter and ground panko bread crumbs ensures a clean release.

Anatomy of a Potato Cup
The best thing about scalloped potatoes is the contrast between the creamy center and the crusty edges. We engineered a recipe in a muffin tin to get the most of both attributes.

THE POTATOES We cut the potatoes small and thin so they'd cook evenly, fit into the muffin cups, and make layers that resemble standard scalloped potatoes.

INSIDE For the ultimate creamy, cheesy interior, we used sharp cheddar, Parmesan, half-and-half, and cornstarch.

ON TOP We sprinkled each potato cake with extra cheese.

BOTTOM AND SIDES For the crispest, cheesiest crust, we coated the muffin cups with softened butter and ground panko bread crumbs.

Getting to Know Winter Fruit

In the 19th century, an orange in a Christmas stocking was a rare treat for American children. Nowadays, winter offers a wide variety of fruit. Here are 11 that are at their best from October through February.

Tangerine
KID GLOVES

Tangerines are named for the Moroccan city of Tangier and are part of the mandarin family, all members of which have loose, easily removable skin, hence the nickname "kid glove" oranges. They are the most common mandarin in the United States. We like chopped tangerines in salads or relishes (but watch out for the plentiful seeds) or juiced for a tangy, citrus-spiked stir-fry.

Grapefruit
BREAKFAST BUDDY

Today grapefruit—whether white, red, or pink—is a breakfast staple, but it was unknown in this country before the 18th century. That's when a cross between an orange and a pummelo (a thick-skinned, cantaloupe-or-bigger-size citrus) gave birth to the sweet-tart grapefruit. Try grapefruit in salsa, relishes, and salads.

Navel Orange
SUPERMARKET STAPLE

The navel orange is seedless, easy to peel, and notably sweet and juicy. Its name comes from the blossom end's resemblance to (what else?) a human navel. From flavoring cakes to rice pilafs to vinaigrettes, this orange has dozens of uses, and the zest and juice are as flavorful as the flesh. We use a rasp-style grater to zest it, freezing the zest for up to one month; the flavor declines minimally, and it's convenient to have at the ready.

Sour Orange
MARMALADE MATE

If you've tasted bracingly bitter Seville orange marmalade, you've eaten sour oranges. This orange is also used in much Latin American cooking, which is why in this country you see it in Latin food stores. Use the juice from sour oranges (along with oregano, garlic, and cumin) to make a tasty marinade for grilled chicken. If you can't find it, use a test kitchen trick to mimic its flavor: Combine lime and orange zests with ordinary orange juice.

Kumquat
THE WHOLE PACKAGE

This pygmy of the citrus family is about the size of an olive, and the entire fruit, from peel to flesh, is edible. It's actually the sweeter rind—not the tart, dry flesh—that houses most of the flavor. Kumquats are often candied or pickled; alternatively, we suggest slicing or halving and seeding them before adding them to desserts or baked goods.

Prickly Pear
DESERT DIVIDEND

Prickly pears, aka *tunas*, are full of crunchy little edible seeds and taste like melon. The fruit—the berry of the prickly pear cactus—is common in the Southwest. If you run across these pears at the market, the spines will probably have been removed (and that's a good thing). Use prickly pears to make jams or marmalade, or enjoy them the traditional Mexican way: raw—peeled and sliced—with a squeeze of lime.

Persimmon
SOFT SPOT

Sweet, creamy persimmons taste like a luscious cross between pumpkins, fresh dates, and plums. Supermarkets carry the acorn-shaped Hachiya (pictured here) and the round Fuyu persimmon, both from Asia. The Hachiya must be extremely soft and squishy before you eat it or its tannins will dry out your mouth; the Fuyu can be eaten sliced while firm-tender. North America has a native persimmon, too. While you won't find it at the grocery store, it accounts for the many old American recipes for persimmon pudding.

Blood Orange
FLESH AND BLOOD

From the outside, a blood orange looks like an ordinary orange. Expose its crimson flesh, however, and you'll appreciate the macabre name. Enjoy its striking color and wonderful sweet-tart flavor juiced or sectioned into salads. To segment, cut off the ends of the fruit so that it stands flat, cut away the peel and pith, and insert your paring knife between each segment and membrane—on both sides—until the segments fall free.

Pomegranate
CROWN JEWELS

The hundreds of small, sparkling crimson kernels inside a pomegranate are tart, slightly crunchy, and completely edible—seed and all. To release the kernels with less mess (the juice stains), halve the pomegranate and submerge it in a bowl of water. As you gently pull it apart, the seeds will sink, separating from the bitter pith and membrane that hold them. Use the seeds in green or fruit salads or to top a pudding or a custard pie.

Quince
PECTIN POWERHOUSE

The fragrant quince was once commonplace in American kitchens. No more—a pity. Although hard, dry, and astringent when raw, quince is delicious cooked. Peel and poach for tarts or compotes; roast to serve alongside meats; or add a few slices to your next apple pie. Thanks to loads of pectin (a natural thickener), quince is also ideal for jams, jellies, and preserves.

Cranberry
SAUCE STUDDER

Unshackle the cranberry! Sure, it's great in sauce for Thanksgiving, but this berry can go way beyond the bird. For starters, try pairing cranberry sauce with pork. In the test kitchen, we also like to add cranberries to apple pie or apple crisp. During the fall and winter, cranberries are sold fresh, but the frozen ones—available year-round—work equally well for cooking.

PORK CHOPS WITH RADICCHIO SLAW

GARLICKY POTATO SOUP WITH PARMESAN TOASTS

BISTRO SALAD

HERB-ROASTED CHICKEN WITH DIJON GREEN BEANS

GARLICKY POTATO SOUP WITH PARMESAN TOASTS Serves 4
WHY THIS RECIPE WORKS: The cheesy toasts make a fast, weeknight soup special.

- ¼ cup grated Parmesan cheese
- 3 tablespoons unsalted butter, softened
- Salt and pepper
- 1 (6-inch) piece baguette, cut into 8 slices on bias
- 3 scallions, white parts minced, green parts sliced thin
- 3 garlic cloves, minced
- 1 tablespoon all-purpose flour
- 3 cups low-sodium chicken broth
- ½ cup heavy cream
- 1½ pounds Yukon Gold potatoes, peeled and cut into ½-inch pieces

1. Adjust oven rack to middle position and heat oven to 475 degrees. Combine Parmesan, 2 tablespoons butter, and ½ teaspoon pepper in bowl. Spread Parmesan butter on 1 side of baguette slices. Place bread, buttered side up, on rimmed baking sheet and bake until golden brown, 6 to 8 minutes; set aside.

2. Meanwhile, melt remaining 1 tablespoon butter in Dutch oven over medium heat. Cook scallion whites until softened, about 2 minutes. Add garlic and flour and cook until fragrant, about 1 minute. Stir in broth, cream, and potatoes and bring to boil. Reduce heat to medium-low, cover, and cook until potatoes are tender, 10 to 12 minutes.

3. Working in batches, process soup in blender until smooth, 1 to 2 minutes. Return soup to pot. Season with salt and pepper to taste and sprinkle with scallion greens. Serve with Parmesan toasts.

PORK CHOPS WITH RADICCHIO SLAW Serves 4
WHY THIS RECIPE WORKS: Preparing the slaw before cooking the pork allows the radicchio to soften and the flavors to meld.

- 1 tablespoon balsamic vinegar
- Salt and pepper
- ¼ cup extra-virgin olive oil
- 1 small head radicchio (6 ounces), sliced thin
- 1 fennel bulb, stalks discarded, bulb halved, cored, and sliced thin
- 1 grapefruit, peeled and segmented
- ½ cup pitted kalamata olives, halved
- 2 tablespoons minced fresh parsley
- 2 scallions, sliced thin
- 4 (6- to 8-ounce) boneless pork chops, ¾ to 1 inch thick, trimmed

1. Combine vinegar, ½ teaspoon salt, and ¼ teaspoon pepper in bowl. Slowly whisk in 3 tablespoons oil until emulsified. Toss radicchio, fennel, grapefruit, olives, parsley, and scallions with vinaigrette in large bowl; set aside.

2. Pat pork chops dry with paper towels and season with salt and pepper. Heat remaining 1 tablespoon oil in 12-inch skillet over medium-high heat until just smoking. Cook chops until well browned and meat registers 145 degrees, 5 to 6 minutes per side. Transfer to platter, tent loosely with aluminum foil, and let rest for 5 minutes. Serve chops with slaw.

TEST KITCHEN NOTE: You can substitute half of a small head of red cabbage, thinly sliced, for the radicchio.

HERB-ROASTED CHICKEN WITH DIJON GREEN BEANS
Serves 4
WHY THIS RECIPE WORKS: A mustardy compound butter flavors both chicken and green beans.

- 5 tablespoons unsalted butter, softened
- 2 tablespoons Dijon mustard
- 2 tablespoons minced fresh thyme
- 3 garlic cloves, minced
- Salt and pepper
- 2 teaspoons honey
- 4 (12-ounce) bone-in split chicken breasts, trimmed and halved crosswise
- 2 pounds green beans, trimmed and cut into 2-inch lengths
- ¼ cup water

1. Adjust oven rack to lowest position and heat oven to 450 degrees. Combine butter, mustard, thyme, garlic, ½ teaspoon salt, and ½ teaspoon pepper in bowl. Transfer 2 tablespoons butter mixture to second bowl and stir in honey; reserve. Pat chicken dry with paper towels and rub with unsweetened butter mixture. Cook chicken, skin side down, in 12-inch nonstick skillet over medium-high heat until browned, about 5 minutes. Arrange chicken, skin side up, in 13 by 9-inch baking dish and roast until meat registers 160 degrees, about 20 minutes.

2. Meanwhile, melt reserved honey butter over medium-high heat in now-empty skillet. Add green beans and cook, stirring occasionally, until spotty brown, 8 to 10 minutes. Stir in water and ½ teaspoon salt, cover, and reduce heat to medium-low. Cook until beans are nearly tender, 3 to 5 minutes. Remove lid and cook until liquid evaporates and beans are tender, about 1 minute. Season with salt and pepper to taste. Serve with chicken.

BISTRO SALAD Serves 4
WHY THIS RECIPE WORKS: Thick-cut bacon and a fried egg add heft to these greens, turning a quick salad into supper.

- 1 tablespoon red wine vinegar
- 1½ teaspoons minced shallot
- ½ teaspoon mayonnaise
- ½ teaspoon Dijon mustard
- Salt and pepper
- 3 tablespoons extra-virgin olive oil
- 8 slices thick-cut bacon, cut into 1-inch pieces
- 4 large eggs
- 1 head frisée (6 ounces), cut into 1-inch pieces
- 1 romaine lettuce heart (6 ounces), cut into 1-inch pieces

1. Combine vinegar, shallot, mayonnaise, mustard, ⅛ teaspoon salt, and ⅛ teaspoon pepper in bowl. Slowly whisk in oil until thoroughly incorporated; set aside.

2. Cook bacon in 12-inch nonstick skillet over medium heat until crisp, about 8 minutes. Using slotted spoon, transfer bacon to paper towel–lined plate. Pour off all but 1 tablespoon fat from skillet. Heat fat over medium-low heat. Fry eggs, covered, until whites are just set, 2 to 3 minutes.

3. Meanwhile, toss frisée and romaine with dressing and divide among individual bowls. Top each salad with fried egg and bacon. Season with salt and pepper to taste. Serve.

TEST KITCHEN NOTE: You can substitute 8 cups of mixed greens for the frisée and romaine.

**SKILLET BURGERS WITH SAUTÉED ONIONS
AND HORSERADISH SAUCE**

GINGER-GLAZED PORK TENDERLOIN

TOASTY SKILLET SPAGHETTI WITH SHRIMP

FLANK STEAK WITH LOADED SMASHED POTATOES

GINGER-GLAZED PORK TENDERLOIN Serves 4 to 6

WHY THIS RECIPE WORKS: A cornstarch-thickened sauce makes quick work of glazing pork tenderloins.

- ¼ cup water
- ¼ cup dry sherry
- 3 tablespoons honey
- 2 tablespoons soy sauce
- 1½ tablespoons grated fresh ginger
- 2 teaspoons cornstarch
- 2 (12-ounce) pork tenderloins, trimmed
  Pepper
- 1 tablespoon vegetable oil
- 1 tablespoon sesame seeds, toasted

1. Whisk water, sherry, honey, soy sauce, ginger, and cornstarch in bowl. Pat pork dry with paper towels and season with pepper. Heat oil in 12-inch nonstick skillet over medium-high heat until just smoking. Cook tenderloins until well browned and meat registers 145 degrees, about 4 minutes per side (16 minutes total). Transfer pork to carving board, tent loosely with aluminum foil, and let rest for 5 minutes.

2. Whisk sauce to recombine and add to now-empty skillet. Simmer over medium heat until thickened, about 5 minutes. Add pork and any accumulated juices and cook, turning occasionally, until glazed, about 1 minute. Slice and sprinkle with sesame seeds. Serve with any extra sauce.

TEST KITCHEN NOTE: Serve over rice.

SKILLET BURGERS WITH SAUTÉED ONIONS AND HORSERADISH SAUCE Serves 4

WHY THIS RECIPE WORKS: Horseradish sauce and charred onions dress up these simple indoor burgers.

- ¼ cup sour cream
- 1½ tablespoons prepared horseradish
- 1 tablespoon minced fresh chives
- 2 teaspoons lemon juice
  Salt and pepper
- 1½ pounds 85 percent lean ground beef
- 3 garlic cloves, minced
- 1 tablespoon vegetable oil
- 1 onion, halved and sliced thin
- 4 hamburger buns

1. Combine sour cream, horseradish, chives, and lemon juice in bowl. Season with salt and pepper to taste; set aside. Gently knead beef, garlic, ½ teaspoon salt, and ¼ teaspoon pepper together in large bowl until well combined. Shape into four ¾-inch-thick patties and press shallow divot in center of each.

2. Heat oil in 12-inch nonstick skillet over medium-high heat until just smoking. Add patties and cook until well browned and meat registers 120 to 125 degrees (for medium-rare), 3 to 4 minutes per side. Transfer burgers to plate and tent loosely with aluminum foil.

3. Pour off all but 1 tablespoon fat from pan. Cook onion over medium-high heat until browned, 6 to 8 minutes. Place burgers on bun bottoms and top with onions and horseradish sauce. Serve.

TEST KITCHEN NOTE: We recommend Boar's Head Pure Horseradish.

FLANK STEAK WITH LOADED SMASHED POTATOES Serves 6

WHY THIS RECIPE WORKS: These smashed potatoes pack the flavorful punch of a loaded baked potato without the considerable baking time.

- 1 (1½- to 2-pound) flank steak, trimmed
  Salt and pepper
- 8 slices bacon, chopped fine
- 2 pounds small red potatoes, halved
- 2 tablespoons vegetable oil
- ¾ cup sour cream
- 4 ounces sharp cheddar cheese, shredded (1 cup)
- 2 scallions, sliced thin

1. Pat steak dry with paper towels and season with salt and pepper. Cook bacon in 12-inch nonstick skillet over medium heat until crisp, about 8 minutes. Using slotted spoon, transfer bacon to paper towel–lined plate. Pour off all but 1 tablespoon fat from pan. Cook steak over medium-high heat in now-empty skillet until well browned and meat registers 120 to 125 degrees (for medium-rare), 5 to 7 minutes per side. Transfer to cutting board, tent loosely with aluminum foil, and let rest for 5 minutes.

2. Meanwhile, microwave potatoes and oil in large covered bowl until tender, 10 to 12 minutes. Add sour cream and, using potato masher, mash until combined. Stir in cheddar, bacon, and scallions. Season with salt and pepper to taste. Slice steak thinly against grain and serve with potatoes.

TEST KITCHEN NOTE: Use potatoes that are between 1 and 2 inches in diameter.

TOASTY SKILLET SPAGHETTI WITH SHRIMP Serves 4

WHY THIS RECIPE WORKS: Cooking the pasta right in the pasta sauce infuses it with flavor and streamlines cleanup.

- 2 slices hearty white sandwich bread, torn into quarters
- 3 tablespoons extra-virgin olive oil
- 6 garlic cloves, minced
- ¼ teaspoon red pepper flakes
- 1½ pounds extra-large (21 to 25 per pound) shrimp, peeled, deveined, and tails removed
  Salt and pepper
- 1 (28-ounce) can crushed tomatoes
- 2 cups water
- 8 ounces spaghetti, broken in half
- ¼ cup chopped fresh basil

1. Pulse bread in food processor until coarsely ground, about 5 pulses. Heat 1 tablespoon oil in 12-inch nonstick skillet over medium heat. Cook bread crumbs until golden, about 5 minutes. Add half of garlic and ⅛ teaspoon pepper flakes and cook until fragrant, about 30 seconds; transfer to bowl. Wipe out skillet with paper towels.

2. Pat shrimp dry with paper towels and season with salt and pepper. Heat 1 tablespoon oil in now-empty skillet over medium-high heat until just smoking. Add half of shrimp and cook without moving it until spotty brown on first side, about 1 minute; transfer to bowl. Repeat with remaining 1 tablespoon oil and remaining shrimp. Add tomatoes, water, pasta, remaining garlic, and remaining ⅛ teaspoon pepper flakes to now-empty skillet and bring to boil. Cover and cook over medium heat until pasta begins to soften, about 7 minutes. Reduce heat to medium-low and simmer, covered, until pasta is nearly al dente, about 5 minutes. Add shrimp and cook over medium-low heat until shrimp is cooked through, 1 to 2 minutes. Stir in basil. Sprinkle with toasted bread crumbs. Serve.

Chocolate Pound Cake

Pound cake is wonderful. Chocolate cake is wonderful.
Why is the combination so often a disappointment? BY LYNN CLARK AND SHANNON FRIEDMANN HATCH

WE LOVE POUND cake and we love chocolate cake. So why don't we love chocolate pound cake? Because most versions fail to capture the best of either: the buttery, mild, dense, and velvety nature of pound cake or the deep, rich chocolate of chocolate cake. You would think it would be simple: Just add chocolate to a proven recipe for plain pound cake and voilà, chocolate pound cake.

Instead, the chocolate pound cakes that we tested missed the mark. Some were so timid that we barely pegged them as chocolate. Others went to the other extreme: Chocolate (and sometimes sugar) overload annihilated all traces of pound cake. Textures ranged from coarse to crumbly to fudgy; none evinced the tight, compact crumb that should characterize pound cake. We were determined to develop a recipe that walked the line between pound and chocolate cake.

We decided to start with a classic recipe for plain pound cake: Cream 1 cup of sugar with two sticks of butter. Add ½ teaspoon of vanilla extract and five eggs, beating after each egg to help the cake rise in the oven (most pound cakes have no chemical leaveners). To finish, stir in 1 cup of flour and bake.

To this basic cake we added cocoa, figuring that it was the simplest way to add chocolate flavor. After testing varying amounts, we settled on ¾ cup. However, by introducing this additional dry ingredient into our batter, we turned our formerly moist pound cake dry as well. We looked into adding milk or buttermilk but then came up with a better idea: We'd "bloom" the cocoa. The test kitchen uses this technique—stirring cocoa into hot water (in this case ⅓ cup of water)—because it frees the cocoa's flavor particles, amping up chocolate taste. In one stroke, we hoped to get a cake that was both more moist and more flavorful. And we did.

But the chocolate flavor remained a wee bit harsh and sharp. To fix that, we pitted the regular cocoa we'd been using against Dutch-processed cocoa; there was no question that the mellow, rounded flavor of the latter suited pound cake better. At this point, a fellow test cook asked why we were limiting ourselves to cocoa. Wouldn't chopped bar chocolate further soften and deepen the cake's flavor? Good question. Many pound cakes later, we'd determined that 2 ounces was the right amount and milk chocolate the right type. One final change assured both optimal chocolate flavor and moist texture: We added ¼ cup of brown sugar to the batter. Brown sugar is more moist than granulated sugar, and its complex, caramel nuance underlined the taste of the chocolate.

Despite all the work we'd done, tasters continued to insist that the cake tasted "flat." Fortunately, that complaint disappeared when we quadrupled the vanilla (it seems counterintuitive, but vanilla actually enhances chocolate flavor) and doubled the salt. Finally, our pound cake was moist, buttery, and mildly sweet, with a tight crumb and deep, rounded chocolate flavor. A hybrid of pound cake and chocolate cake, this version did both proud.

▶ Visit **CooksCountry. com** and search for "loaf pans" to see a video highlighting the winner of our equipment testing.

Just a quarter cup of light brown sugar helped deepen this cake's chocolate flavor.

CHOCOLATE POUND CAKE
Serves 8
Our favorite loaf pan (Williams-Sonoma Goldtouch Nonstick) is slightly smaller than a standard 9 by 5-inch pan. If you're using a standard pan, begin to check the cake for doneness after 55 minutes.

- 1 cup (5 ounces) all-purpose flour
- 1 teaspoon salt
- ⅓ cup boiling water
- ¾ cup (2¼ ounces) Dutch-processed cocoa
- 2 ounces milk chocolate, chopped fine
- 16 tablespoons unsalted butter, softened
- 1 cup (7 ounces) granulated sugar
- ¼ cup packed (1¾ ounces) light brown sugar
- 2 teaspoons vanilla extract
- 5 large eggs, room temperature

1. Adjust oven rack to lower-middle position and heat oven to 325 degrees. Grease and flour 8½ by 4½-inch loaf pan. Combine flour and salt in bowl. Pour water over cocoa and chocolate in second bowl and stir until chocolate is melted and no dry streaks of cocoa remain. Let mixture cool 5 minutes.

2. Using stand mixer fitted with paddle, beat butter, cocoa-chocolate mixture, granulated sugar, brown sugar, and vanilla on medium-high speed until fluffy, 2 to 3 minutes. Add eggs, one at a time, and beat until combined. Reduce speed to low and add flour mixture in 3 additions, scraping down bowl as needed, until just combined. Give batter final stir by hand (it may look curdled).

3. Scrape batter into prepared pan and gently tap pan on counter to release air bubbles. Bake until toothpick inserted in center comes out clean, 60 to 70 minutes. Cool cake in pan on wire rack for 10 minutes. Remove cake from pan and cool for 2 hours. Serve.

Foolproof Cheese Fondue

You don't need a fondue pot—or an invitation to a 1960s theme party—to make our easy, foolproof fondue. All you need are the right ingredients and a little know-how. BY DIANE UNGER

Fondue originated in Switzerland in the 18th century, when both cheese and wine were staples of the Swiss kitchen. The easy-to-make meal transformed these ordinary ingredients into a rich, satiny mixture just begging to be scooped up by crusty bread. Here in the States, fondue didn't take off until the 1960s when, thanks in large part to jet planes and transatlantic travel, Americans became enamored with international cooking. But as the '60s gave way to the '70s, fondue slowly fell out of favor. By 1980, most Americans had stowed their fondue pots in their attics, along with their leisure suits and eight-track players. But I was determined to head into the test kitchen and bring creamy, authentic Swiss-style fondue back to the table.

Apple slices and steamed broccoli florets are also delicious dipped in fondue.

Fondue isn't complicated. So how come it so frequently disappoints? Well, as is commonly the case in cooking, the devil is in the details. Often, the flavor balance is askew—too boozy or sour or bland. Sometimes, the cheese is stringy or gummy. And if the host doesn't have a proper fondue pot (called a *caquelon* in Swiss French), the cheese can quickly cool and begin to solidify. I wanted to create a foolproof, indestructible recipe that would be not only easy and delicious but also sturdy enough to withstand cooling and reheating without breaking. That way, people could enjoy fondue with or without the pot.

Typically, Swiss-style fondue is made by melting at least two varieties of cheese—usually Gruyère and Emmentaler—in a dry white wine. Garlic and other flavoring agents are added to complement the cheese blend and in many cases, kirsch (a clear cherry brandy) lends a tinge of tartness. Newer recipes use flour or cornstarch to keep the cheese from separating. There are lots of variables and, thus, lots of opportunities to go wrong, especially when you're operating without a fondue pot. I decided to start at the beginning, with the cheese and a saucepan.

Gruyère is the classic fondue cheese, so it was a definite. I was less committed to Emmentaler. Suspecting that American cooks might try replacing the latter with (convenient, inexpensive) deli-counter Swiss, I tried the swap myself. But when I melted deli Swiss in the saucepan with the Gruyère and the wine, the resulting fondue was stringy. Our science editor explained that the deli Swiss was probably aged less than the Emmentaler, meaning that its proteins were less tightly bonded together and stretched more easily,

turning my fondue rubbery and gummy. Next, I replaced the Emmentaler with cheeses like fontina, cheddar, and Monterey Jack, but my luck was no better; none tasted right. So, many fondues later, I was back where I started: Emmentaler and Gruyère it would be. A further series of tests determined the right ratio: 2 cups of each cheese, plus 1½ cups of wine. To my surprise, using room-temperature cheese proved key. That's because if cheese is overheated rapidly, it breaks down and separates into fat, water, and curdled protein. Starting with cheese at room temperature helped prevent that.

Old recipes for fondue use neither cornstarch nor flour. Don't look to me to second-guess the Swiss on fondue—I tried to get rid of both. But it turned out they're necessary for stability; without them, the cheese was prone to break. Next, I did a side-by-side test, preparing one batch of fondue with cornstarch, a second with flour, and a third with a mixture of the two. I found that the cornstarch, tossed with the grated cheese and then activated by the simmering wine, did a fine job of holding the cheese together and lent a silkier texture than the flour alone.

Now that I had the basics in place, I turned to refining the flavor. I added a pinch of nutmeg and, to bring the traditional garlic accent to my fondue, I minced a clove and added it to the boiling wine. Alas, the flavor was too intense. It was better to simply halve a clove and let it simmer briefly in the wine before removing and discarding it. As for the kirsch, my tasters found that it added little, so I gave it a pass. At this point, to assess my progress, I made up a batch of fondue, whisking the cheeses into the simmering wine until they

started to bubble and the fondue was creamy—less than three minutes total. (Some authentic Swiss recipes swear by a wooden spoon, but I found that the whisk better incorporated the cheese.) A careful pour into the serving pot and a few baguette cubes later and I had perfect, foolproof fondue.

But one problem remained—my initial mission was not merely to make a great stovetop fondue but to make a great stovetop fondue that could be made ahead of time, held, and reheated without any loss in quality. After experimenting with electric blankets, thermoses, tea cozies, and aluminum foil, I finally found something that worked: a pair of nested Pyrex bowls. The fondue goes into the smaller bowl and the larger bottom bowl is filled with hot water. Kept in this manner, the fondue stayed creamy for up to 15 minutes. To hold it longer, I moved the entire setup to the microwave and zapped it. I could repeat this process up to three times before the fondue started to become grainy.

My fondue may lack the romance of a flickering flame and a groovy, high-design fondue pot, but it's got something better—great flavor, ease of assembly, and staying power.

FOOLPROOF CHEESE FONDUE

Serves 4 as a main dish or 8 as an appetizer
Don't substitute deli Swiss cheese for the Emmentaler—it will make the fondue stringy. Do use a crisp, un-oaked wine, such as Sauvignon Blanc. Try dipping steamed broccoli and cauliflower florets, apple slices, and chunks of cured meats.

- 8   ounces Emmentaler cheese, shredded (2 cups), room temperature
- 8   ounces Gruyère cheese, shredded (2 cups), room temperature
- 2   tablespoons cornstarch
     Pinch ground nutmeg
- 1½ cups dry white wine
- 1   garlic clove, peeled and halved
- ¼   teaspoon pepper
- 1   (12-inch) baguette, cut into 1-inch pieces

1. Toss Emmentaler, Gruyère, cornstarch, and nutmeg together in bowl until well combined. Bring wine and garlic to boil in medium saucepan over high heat; discard garlic.

2. Reduce heat to medium-low and slowly whisk in cheese mixture 1 handful at a time. Continue to cook, whisking constantly, until mixture is smooth and begins to bubble, 2 to 4 minutes. Stir in pepper. Serve with bread.

The American Table
Chafing Dish Cookery

An early electric chafing dish.

We Americans like to consume things in the kitchen—and not just food. Tell us about a new toy, be it a crème brûlée torch, wok, or George Foreman Grill, and soon every home cook who prides herself on her kitchen and cooking boasts one. But kitchen crazes are nothing new. Consider the chafing dish. As far back as the 1890s, it appeared in the social pages of the *New York Times*: "The furor for chafing dish cookery is 'on,' and the most fashionable luncheons are those where nearly if not everything eaten is cooked on the table." Within a decade, an electric version had been developed, and during the first half of the 20th century, chafing dishes saw many a hostess safely through chicken à la king, lobster Newburg, Swedish meatballs—and fondue. In the 1950s, chafing dishes won praise (and a prominent spread) in the pages of *Life* magazine as handy for entertaining in "maidless households." That same article gloried in a subset of chafing dish cookery—flaming food—including must-have recipes for flaming kippers, flaming cabbage with meatballs, and flaming fruitcake. Are we ripe for a comeback?

TESTING FONDUE POTS

You don't need a fondue pot for our Cheese Fondue, but these specialty pots do make it easier to keep the fondue warm and at the right consistency. We gathered six pots (read the full testing at CooksCountry.com) priced from $30 to $170, including three electric and three traditional fuel-burning models, and prepared a batch of our Cheese Fondue in each. Our initial bias toward the flickering flames of traditional pots changed as soon as we began testing. Though the metal burners are adjustable, we could never get the fire low enough to prevent the sauce from scorching. Electric pots have dials to control the heat, but the heating elements attached beneath two of the pots created hot spots. The third worked better: Constructed like a double boiler with a stainless steel outer bowl to hold water and a ceramic insert for the fondue, it regulated heat well and kept the fondue creamy. Several pots feature a nonstick coating that was easy to scratch with metal dipping forks. The two electric pots with attached elements are dishwasher-safe (as long as the dial and cord are detached), but scorched-on cheese did not come off in the dishwasher, and hand washing was a pain. We preferred the double boiler–style pot, which can be removed from the heating element, making it easy to clean. In the end, this pot, the Trudeau Electric 11 Piece 3-in-1 Fondue set, was the only one we can recommend highly. Except for the romance of flame, it has it all. –TAIZETH SIERRA

HIGHLY RECOMMENDED

TRUDEAU Electric 11-Piece 3-in-1 Fondue Set
Model: 0823004
Price: $79.95
Source: www.cooking.com

CRITERIA
Performance ★★★
Design ★★★

TESTERS' NOTES
Easy to use and clean, this 3-in-1 fondue pot held our fondue at the right temperature for over an hour. Chocolate fondue also turned out well, and when we removed the insert and used just the stainless steel pot, we got good results for oil and broth fondues, too. Cheese and chocolate fondue must be prepared in a separate pan and transferred to the double boiler.

RECOMMENDED WITH RESERVATIONS

OSTER 3 Quart Fondue Pot
Model: FPSTFN7700
Price: $29.99
Source: www.target.com

Performance ★★
Design ★★

This model has the best temperature control, and we could prepare the cheese fondue directly in the pot. Unfortunately, the nonstick interior was easy to scratch, and the heating element created a hot spot.

CUISINART Electric Fondue Pot
Model: CFO-3SS
Price: $59.95
Source: www.cuisinart.com

Performance ★★
Design ★

Though the suggested temperature settings on this model's dial are off (the sauce quickly overheated and broke on the setting recommended for holding fondue), this pot functioned well once we compensated for that problem. Unfortunately, its nonstick coating was easily scratched.

EMILE HENRY Flame Top Cheese Fondue Set
Model: 619922
Price: $125
Source: www.emilehenryusa.com

Performance ★
Design ★★

Our favorite among the fuel-burning fondue pots, this model was the largest in that group, with a 2.6-quart capacity. Our only complaint (but a crucial one): Even when we turned the heat down to the lowest setting, the flame was still too high, scorching the fondue.

TEST KITCHEN TECHNIQUE
Reheating Fondue
Even our foolproof fondue eventually cools down and firms up. We tested dozens of ways to keep it warm and reheat it and found this method works best: Fill a microwaveable bowl one-third full of boiling water, then nest a slightly smaller microwaveable bowl inside it. Pour the fondue into the smaller bowl and serve. To reheat, microwave the double-bowl setup for 2 to 3 minutes, stirring halfway.

Moravian Chicken Pie

Instructions for making this fantastic, old-fashioned savory pie left a lot to the imagination.
We set out to get rid of the guesswork. BY KELLY PRICE

For more than 40 years, my grandmother and the ladies of Fairview Moravian Church, in Winston-Salem, North Carolina, have gathered the second Tuesday of every month, a flurry of chicken and chatter, to make The Pies. They simmer the chicken, whisk the gravy, fill the crust, and exchange updates on everything from gardening to grandchildren. To raise money for their churches, a lot of other local ladies are making the very same home-spun pies: tender chicken meat in a rich, golden-brown crust and a good dousing of gravy. But as with many old dishes, recipes are vague at best, merely instructing the cook to "boil the chicken until cooked" and "bake until ready." Was my grandmother's refusal to divulge her recipe part of her plot to keep me close to home?

The traditional sour cream crust turned out to be especially flaky, tender, and easy to roll out.

Almost a thousand miles from home, I was frustrated that I could enjoy Moravian chicken pie just a few times a year: when I was visiting. I needed a reliable recipe. I looked up some online, in the test kitchen cookbook library, and in my own Moravian cookbooks, finding, among others, one from the Old Salem Tavern, a 200-year-old tavern in the Moravian village of Old Salem that's renowned for its pie. In most cookbooks, the writers plainly assumed that the cook already had plenty of chicken pie expertise. If you couldn't fill in the missing information yourself, you could expect pies that were either dry or so soupy that they couldn't be sliced, as well as soggy, tricky-to-make crusts. Plus, these recipes required the cooks to spend many hours in the kitchen.

Most older Moravian chicken pie recipes start by simmering a whole chicken in water until tender, then shredding the meat and concentrating the broth into rich chicken stock. Doubtless it was a fine method back when flavorful yard-roaming hens were the norm, but made with supermarket chickens today, the filling was bland. To develop old-fashioned chicken flavor, I borrowed a test kitchen technique from our recipes for chicken soup: I browned bone-in, skin-on breasts and thighs to develop fond and flavor, discarded the skin, and simmered the chicken pieces in store-bought broth. Now I had both juicy chicken and a quick broth with amplified chicken flavor to use for my gravy.

To build the gravy, I made a roux by stirring flour and a little butter into some chicken fat that I had from browning the chicken. I whisked in the fortified broth and a glug of half-and-half; simmered the mixture for 10 minutes; and ended up with a thick, full-bodied gravy. As most recipes suggest, I intended to use some of the gravy to moisten the filling—exactly 1 cup produced a juicy yet sliceable pie—and the remainder to serve with the pie. But while my gravy was perfect for the filling, it was too thick to serve with the pie. To get pourable gravy, I thinned out a portion of the thick stuff with additional fortified broth.

The filling and double-use gravy settled, I turned to the crust. Among the recipes I'd tested, the Old Salem Tavern pie crust stood out. Typically, pie crust doughs are made from flour, butter, shortening, and water. The tavern's crust had no shortening, but it did include two less common ingredients: sour cream and egg. I had to tinker with the recipe to get it to work, but once I did, I had an especially flaky, tender pie crust that was unusually easy to roll out.

Our science editor explained that acidic sour cream inhibits gluten development. Gluten, the protein that's formed when water bonds with flour, is necessary to hold a crust together, but too much can toughen it. The egg was providing emulsifiers to help disperse the fat evenly throughout the dough, resulting (again) in less gluten development, hence more tenderness.

As with most pie dough recipes, my working recipe required a variable amount of water to make the dough coalesce, depending on the humidity in the air, the age of the flour, and other factors. Frustrating. To eliminate the guesswork, I tried using more sour cream, which has water in it. I discovered that if I used exactly ½ cup, I could skip the water entirely. My crust was flaky and tender. The dough was a dream to work with. Best of all, the recipe was precise and turned out perfect every single time.

Well, not quite perfect: The bottom crust was soggy. Fortunately, the test kitchen knows how to handle that. I baked the pie on the bottom rack in a 450-degree oven to let the bottom crust crisp. After 20 minutes, I turned down the oven to keep the pie from over-browning before cooking through.

I pulled a final chicken pie out of the oven. A labor of love and an antidote to homesickness, this golden pie didn't make my grandmother, the church ladies, or Fairview Moravian Church materialize. But on every other count, it delivered.

MORAVIAN CHICKEN PIE
Serves 8
If you get less than 2 tablespoons of fat from browning the chicken in step 4, supplement it with butter. The pie may seem loose when it comes out of the oven; it will set up as it cools.

CRUST
- ½ cup sour cream, chilled
- 1 large egg, lightly beaten
- 2½ cups (12½ ounces) all-purpose flour
- 1½ teaspoons salt
- 12 tablespoons unsalted butter, cut into ½-inch pieces and chilled

PIE
- 2 (10- to 12-ounce) bone-in split chicken breasts, trimmed and halved crosswise
- 3 (5- to 7-ounce) bone-in chicken thighs, trimmed Salt and pepper
- 1 tablespoon vegetable oil
- 3 cups low-sodium chicken broth
- 1 bay leaf
- 2 tablespoons unsalted butter
- ¼ cup all-purpose flour
- ¼ cup half-and-half
- 1 large egg, lightly beaten

1. FOR THE CRUST: Combine sour cream and egg in bowl. Process flour and salt in food processor until combined, about 3 seconds. Add butter and pulse until only pea-size pieces remain, about 10 pulses. Add half of sour cream mixture and pulse until combined, 5 pulses. Add remaining sour cream mixture and pulse until dough begins to form, about 10 pulses.

2. Transfer mixture to lightly floured counter and knead briefly until dough comes together. Divide dough in half and form each half into 4-inch disk. Wrap each disk in plastic wrap and refrigerate for at least 1 hour or up to 2 days. (Dough can be wrapped tightly in plastic and foil and frozen for up to 2 months. Thaw completely at room temperature before using.)

3. Remove 1 dough disk from refrigerator and let sit for 10 minutes. Working on lightly floured counter, roll into 12-inch round and transfer to 9-inch pie plate, leaving ½-inch over-hang all around. Repeat with second dough disk and transfer to parchment–lined rimmed baking sheet. Cover both doughs with plastic and refrigerate for 30 minutes.

4. FOR THE PIE: Pat chicken dry with paper towels and season with salt and pepper. Heat oil in large Dutch oven over medium-high heat until just smoking. Cook chicken until browned all over, about 10 minutes; transfer to plate. Pour fat (you should have 2 tablespoons) into small bowl; reserve. When chicken is cool enough to handle, remove and discard skin. Add broth, chicken, and bay leaf to now-empty pot and bring to boil. Reduce heat to low and simmer, covered, until breasts register 160 degrees and thighs register 175 degrees, 14 to 18 minutes. Transfer chicken to bowl. When chicken is cool enough to handle, shred into bite-size pieces, discarding bones. Pour broth through fine-mesh strainer into second bowl and reserve (you should have about 2¾ cups); discard bay leaf.

5. Adjust oven rack to lowest position and heat oven to 450 degrees. Heat butter and reserved fat in now-empty pot over medium heat until shimmering. Add flour and cook, whisking constantly, until golden, 1 to 2 minutes. Slowly whisk in 2 cups of reserved broth and half-and-half and bring to boil. Reduce heat to medium-low and simmer gravy until thickened and reduced to 1¾ cups, 6 to 8 minutes. Season with salt and pepper to taste. Combine 1 cup gravy with shredded chicken; reserve remaining gravy for serving.

6. Transfer chicken mixture to dough-lined pie plate and spread into even layer. Top with second dough round, leaving at least ½-inch overhang all around. Fold dough under itself so that edge of fold is flush with outer rim of pie plate. Flute edges using thumb and forefinger or press with tines of fork to seal. Cut four 1-inch slits in top. Brush pie with egg and bake until top is light golden brown, 18 to 20 minutes. Reduce oven temperature to 375 degrees and continue to bake until crust is deep golden brown, 10 to 15 minutes. Let pie cool on wire rack for at least 45 minutes.

7. When ready to serve, bring remaining ¾ cup reserved gravy and remaining ¾ cup reserved broth to boil in medium saucepan. Simmer over medium-low heat until slightly thickened, 5 to 7 minutes. Season with salt and pepper to taste. Serve pie with gravy.

TEST KITCHEN DISCOVERY
Really Easy Pie Crust
Most recipes for pie crust call for a variable amount of ice water to bind the dough, depending on the humidity, the flour, and the phases of the moon. OK, we made up that last part, but still, making crust is nerve-racking enough without having to guess how much water to add. Fall short and the dough won't ever come together. Overdo it and you'll get a tough crust. The magic of our recipe is that by including exactly one egg and precisely ½ cup of sour cream, we produce an especially tender crust and we eliminate the water and the guesswork.

TEST KITCHEN TECHNIQUE **Double Duty Gravy**
We use gravy to form the base for the filling in our Moravian Chicken Pie and also to serve with slices of the pie.

GRAVY FOR FILLING Combine 1 cup of thick gravy with the shredded chicken for a sliceable filling.

GRAVY FOR SERVING Thin the remaining thick gravy base with fortified chicken broth to make gravy for serving.

Spinach and Tomato Lasagna

So you think that lasagna with no meat and no béchamel is missing something?
Think again. BY REBECCAH MARSTERS

Some people think of spinach lasagna as less hearty than the "real" meat version of the dish. Not me. I have a soft spot for it: Tender noodles layered with chunky tomato sauce, earthy spinach, and gooey cheese make for a meal that's satisfying but still feels fresh. I wanted to do justice to spinach lasagna and prove to even the most dubious carnivore that it needn't play second fiddle.

I gathered various recipes to try, but after a marathon of layering and baking, my tasters had a question: Where's the spinach? A few flecks of the green stuff barely discernible between layers was not enough, plus the spinach we could find was often watery and slimy—attributes that certainly didn't earn any fans. My tasters also dismissed the lasagnas that used a white sauce (usually a dairy-based béchamel) for being too rich and obliterating the main ingredient. The tomato-based recipes, on the other hand, underlined the fresh flavors instead of covering them up. We did learn something useful from this first round, though: Surprisingly, frozen spinach was just as good as fresh judged on both flavor and texture, and it saved a considerable amount of kitchen time.

Now that I knew the problems I needed to fix, I put together my own recipe. The first change that I made? Triple the spinach. To eliminate the watery texture that plagued so many of my initial attempts, I thawed the frozen spinach (three whole boxes) and squeezed it dry in a clean kitchen towel. (When I saw how much liquid came out, it was clear why the lasagnas I'd tested were slimy.) I mixed the drained spinach with ricotta, a couple of eggs, and Parmesan cheese; made a quick sauce using canned crushed tomatoes; and layered both with no-boil noodles and plenty of mozzarella cheese. An hour and a half later, we dug in. Now here was a spinach

Frozen spinach tastes just as good as fresh in this lasagna—and it's cheaper and easier.

lasagna with the namesake ingredient front and center.

But by tripling the greens, I'd unintentionally damaged the texture: The lasagna was riddled with grassy, uneven chunks of spinach. Unwilling to sacrifice texture for flavor, I went to work on the thawed spinach. It was already "chopped," but I pulled out the food processor, pulsed the stuff until it was truly finely chopped, and proceeded as before. This time we all liked its texture as well as its flavor, but I felt that it

wasn't evenly distributed. So the next time I made the sauce, I stirred ½ cup of the spinach in with the tomatoes. There was plenty left for the ricotta mixture, and when this lasagna baked up, the spinach had more presence—in the best possible sense.

Next came the ricotta. This fresh cheese has long been a lasagna staple, and for good reason. At its best it's fluffy and rich, but it can easily turn grainy and dry if it's not given a little attention. I already had the food

processor out for the spinach, so I whirred the cheese. The creamier texture pleased my tasters, but now they found the filling dry. Had I been overzealous when squeezing out the spinach? We had all tasted the unappetizing results of too much water, but surely we could reach a middle ground. The next time I wrung out the greens I warily eyed the bowl of murky liquid. It didn't look appealing, but I knew it held lots of good favor. By adding a measured amount of the spinach water to the food processor with the ricotta, I hoped I could control the consistency of the filling, preventing either dry or soggy lasagna. In addition, the warm liquid would smooth out any lingering graininess. I processed ⅓ cup of spinach water with the ricotta and then added eggs and Parmesan. When I was satisfied with the creaminess, I stirred, layered, and baked as before. This filling was moist, rich, and smooth, with plenty of spinach flavor.

▶ For more lasagna recipes and our taste test of no-boil lasagna noodles, do a search for "lasagna" at CooksCountry.com.

To finish, I adjusted the seasoning, adding a generous amount of garlic (five cloves) and a pinch of red pepper flakes to the sauce, plus a healthy handful of basil to both the sauce and the filling. In the end, this lasagna was hearty yet fresh, with enough bold flavor to leave its meaty cousin green with envy.

SPINACH AND TOMATO LASAGNA
Serves 8 to 10

Our favorite lasagna noodles are Barilla No Boil. You can thaw the spinach overnight in the refrigerator instead of microwaving it. But do warm the spinach liquid to help smooth the ricotta.

- 30 ounces frozen chopped spinach
- 2 tablespoons olive oil
- 1 onion, chopped fine
- 5 garlic cloves, minced
- ⅛ teaspoon red pepper flakes
- 2 (28-ounce) cans crushed tomatoes
  Salt and pepper
- 6 tablespoons chopped fresh basil
- 24 ounces (3 cups) whole-milk or part-skim ricotta cheese
- 3 ounces Parmesan cheese, grated (1½ cups)
- 2 large eggs
- 12 no-boil lasagna noodles
- 12 ounces whole-milk mozzarella cheese, shredded (3 cups)

1. Adjust oven rack to middle position and heat oven to 375 degrees. Microwave spinach in covered large bowl until completely thawed, about 15 minutes, stirring halfway through. Squeeze spinach dry, reserving ⅓ cup liquid. Pulse spinach in food processor until ground, 8 to 10 pulses, scraping down bowl every few pulses. Wipe out large bowl with paper towels. Transfer spinach to now-empty bowl; set aside.

2. Heat oil in large saucepan over medium heat until shimmering. Add onion and cook until softened, about 5 minutes. Stir in garlic and pepper flakes and cook until fragrant, about 30 seconds. Add tomatoes, ½ cup processed spinach, 1 teaspoon salt, and ½ teaspoon pepper and cook until slightly thickened, about 10 minutes. Off heat, stir in 3 tablespoons basil; set aside.

3. Process ricotta and reserved spinach liquid in food processor until smooth, about 30 seconds. Add Parmesan, remaining 3 tablespoons basil, eggs, 1½ teaspoons salt, and ½ teaspoon pepper and process until combined. Stir ricotta mixture into remaining processed spinach.

4. Cover bottom of 13 by 9-inch baking dish with 1¼ cups sauce. Top with 3 noodles and spread one-third of ricotta mixture evenly over noodles. Sprinkle with ⅔ cup mozzarella and cover with 1¼ cups sauce. Repeat twice, beginning with noodles and ending with sauce. Top with remaining 3 noodles, remaining sauce, and remaining 1 cup mozzarella.

5. Cover pan tightly with aluminum foil sprayed with vegetable oil spray and bake until bubbling around edges, about 40 minutes. Discard foil and continue to bake until cheese is melted, about 10 minutes. Cool on wire rack for 30 minutes. Serve.

KEYS TO Spinach Flavor

To make lasagna that Popeye the Sailor Man could love—in other words, lasagna that actually tastes like spinach—it isn't enough to just toss some of the leafy stuff into the mix and call it a day.

USE MORE We tripled the amount of spinach called for in most recipes.

INCLUDE THE JUICE
After we squeezed the spinach dry (to avoid soggy lasagna), we added some of the spinach water to the ricotta cheese for a creamy, spinach-flavored filling.

BREAK IT DOWN
We further chopped the spinach in the food processor for a fine, even texture that distributed nicely in both the cheese filling and the sauce.

ON THE SIDE
Catalina Salad Dressing

This 1970s relic depends on vinegar, sugar, ketchup, and onion for its sweet-and-tangy flavor. Alas, most recipes are just plain sweet. BY REBECCAH MARSTERS

CULINARY HISTORIANS DEBATE whether it was named for the California island or the Catalan region of Spain. Whatever its history, Catalina dressing is a zesty cousin to French dressing with a striking red-orange hue. If this is news to you, then you probably never visited a steakhouse or salad bar in the 1970s or '80s. The dressing may have tasted good then, but today the painfully sweet bottled versions seem caught in a time warp. I set out to freshen up this modern classic.

I gathered and tested eight recipes, producing results that were only minimal improvements over the bottled version. Most were too sweet (with an entire cup of sugar to dress six portions of salad); one outlier was too sour. Some versions tasted like ketchup dumped on lettuce, and in more than a few, the raw onion was overbearing. As a group, these dressings lacked balance. I cherry-picked the successful elements (yes, there were some), giving the nod to ketchup (but not too much), celery seed, cider vinegar, and chili powder (which tasters preferred to the more common paprika).

I whisked these ingredients into neutral-tasting vegetable oil and tackled my first order of business: cutting down on sugar. I eventually landed on 3 tablespoons of sugar and ⅓ cup of ketchup to ½ cup of oil (for 1 cup of dressing). I also backed off on grated onion. When I got to just 2 tablespoons, it made more sense to use a shallot, so I did. To tame the shallot's bite, I microwaved it with some of the oil and used the flavored oil in the dressing. Tasters applauded the now mellow onion flavor.

But if the flavor was on target, the texture wasn't. To get rid of the stringy bits of grated shallot, I whirred the dressing in the blender. That got me to rethink my earlier technique. I dispensed with the grater and simply chopped the shallot before microwaving it.

With just a handful of pantry ingredients, I'd made a bright, balanced dressing that restored dignity to the Catalina name.

Use this recipe to dress greens, as a marinade for chicken, or as a dip.

CATALINA DRESSING
Makes 1 cup
Be sure to use celery seed, not celery salt, in this dressing.

- ½ cup vegetable oil
- 2 tablespoons chopped shallot
- ⅓ cup ketchup
- ¼ cup cider vinegar
- 3 tablespoons sugar
- 1 teaspoon salt
- ½ teaspoon chili powder
- ½ teaspoon celery seed

Combine ¼ cup oil and shallot in bowl and microwave until shallot is softened, about 2 minutes. Let cool slightly, about 5 minutes. Combine shallot mixture, ketchup, remaining ¼ cup oil, vinegar, sugar, salt, chili powder, and celery seed in blender and process until smooth, about 30 seconds. Cover and refrigerate to let flavors meld, about 30 minutes. Serve with greens. (Dressing can be refrigerated for up to 1 week.)

Bringing Babka Home

This rich bread is defined by its many twisting layers of gooey cinnamon-sugar filling. But the dough was so rich and tender that the fabulous filling made it collapse. BY ERIKA BRUCE

The roots of the traditional Jewish bread known as babka (a diminutive of "baba," the Polish word for grandmother) are planted firmly in Eastern Europe. Over there, it was a round yeast bread reserved for holidays. But after immigrants brought the bread to America—specifically the New York City area—it gradually morphed into a loaf-shaped coffee cake served year-round. Popular in both Jewish and other bakeries, babka also came to accommodate different fillings, such as chocolate or jam. But across time and geography, the defining characteristics of the classic version have remained constant: a moist, rich yeasted bread layered with sweet, gooey cinnamon-sugar filling. You could think of it as the ultimate cinnamon bread.

Unfortunately, if you don't live within striking distance of New York City, it's hard to get your hands on really great babka. Born a Gentile with no Jewish grandmother to bake me treats, I was tired of mail-ordering babka from New York bakeries, so I decided to devise a foolproof recipe to use in my own kitchen.

I started by baking four of the most promising-sounding versions from among the wildly varying recipes I'd found. The babkas I wound up with ran the gamut from lean and bready (like stingy cinnamon bread) to too rich and inundated with oozing filling (like too-indulgent cinnamon buns). But at least I had zeroed in on what I was looking for: a bread that was moist, rich, and tender

Babka started life in Eastern Europe as a rare treat for holidays. Today, you can find it in many a New York City bakery.

but also sturdy enough to support lots of layers of filling. The filling should be sweet and gooey but not so abundant that it oozed out of the bread. And most important of all, the filling should swirl in layer after layer throughout the bread.

I started by searching for the right dough. After those initial tests, I had selected brioche-style dough (a yeasted dough made with butter, eggs, sugar, and milk) as the best model. But once I introduced the standard filling (a generous amount of brown sugar, cinnamon, and melted butter), the bottom layers of dough got weighed down, and the loaf emerged from the oven with a huge gap at the bottom. I backed off on the butter by a couple of tablespoons, but if I removed more than that the dough seemed too lean to qualify as babka. To increase its richness without adding too much liquid, I substituted two egg yolks for the whole egg and injected just a splash more milk. This mimicked the tenderness of the lost butter without compromising the structure of the dough.

Next, I needed to plug the leak: The filling was pooling in the bottom of the pan, causing the dough to steam instead of bake and leaving me with huge pockets of filling interspersed with chunks of plain bread. The simple jelly roll–style shaping method that my recipe and most others employ didn't integrate the filling very well. After a long phone call to the very helpful folks at Green's, a Brooklyn bakery famous for its babka, I decided to try what they described as the traditional babka approach; though more labor-intensive than the jelly roll technique, it'd be worth it if it worked. The key concept was to roll out the dough super-thin—so thin that after rolling it formed a rectangle twice the size that it was before. Next, the rectangle gets rolled up, creating a much longer and skinnier jelly roll, which is then folded in half lengthwise, given a couple of twists, and deposited in the loaf pan.

This traditional shaping technique was a real challenge with a tender dough and slippery filling. I struggled with it mightily until I realized that I could make my work a lot easier by chilling the dough for at least an hour before handling it. With the chilled dough, the new technique was well worth the extra time and effort, since it almost quadrupled the number of layers in my babka, ensuring cinnamony goodness in every bite. A perfectionist, I went so far as to reserve a small amount of filling for the fold in the roll (where dough meets dough) to ensure cinnamon in the center of the babka.

Despite all the folds and undulations, the filling still sank some in the oven, leaving the top layers thin and wimpy and tasters fighting over the delicious gooey bottom. I'd need to thicken the filling to get it to stay put during baking. To do so, some recipes suggest introducing ground nuts or dried fruit like raisins or currants, but since I didn't want to alter the pure cinnamon-sugar filling, I chose additional flour as the best course of action. The extra starch bound the filling nicely but also left an unpleasantly pasty aftertaste. I could get away with ¼ cup of flour without my tasters noticing, but that alone wasn't enough to do the job of thickening.

A few chocolate babka recipes call for a layer of whipped egg whites in the filling (which is then sprinkled with chopped chocolate). My first attempt to borrow this technique for my cinnamon babka resulted in some sadly deflated egg whites once I'd plopped on the heavy, flour-thickened streusel filling. However, the filling did stay put, so I knew I was on the right track. The second time, I didn't bother whipping the egg white to peaks; instead, I just mixed it in with the other filling ingredients. Easy to spread, this filling stayed evenly distributed throughout the babka.

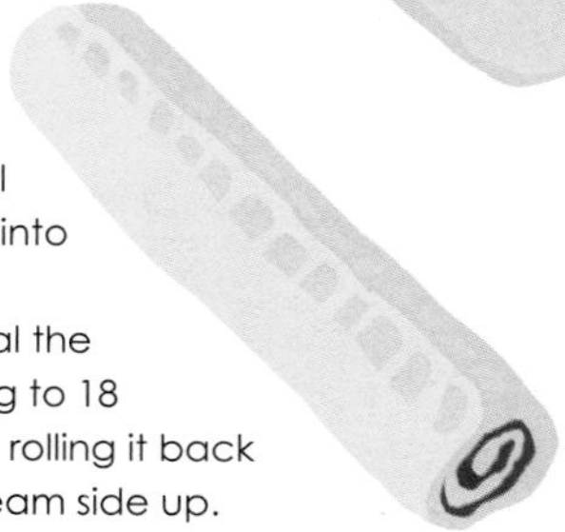

The loaf was beautiful. The aroma in the kitchen was heavenly, and the babka tasted so good, we practically inhaled it. My mail order days were behind me.

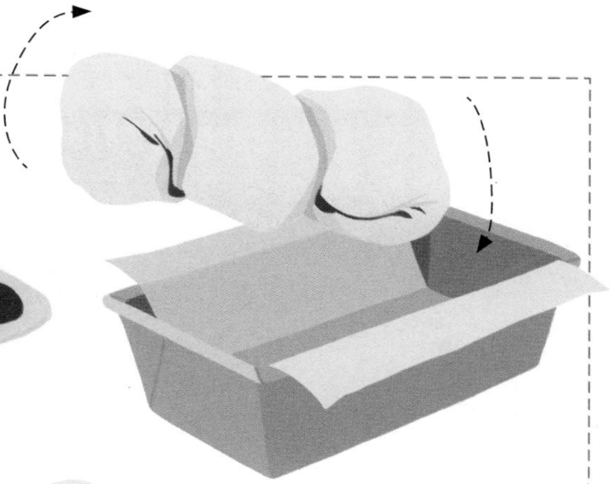

▶ Yes, the brand of cinnamon matters. Find which is our favorite by searching for "cinnamon" at CooksCountry.com.

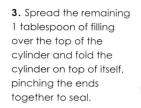
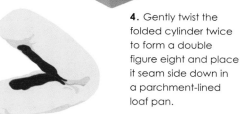
CINNAMON BABKA

Serves 8

Once you've added the butter in step 3, if the dough is still sticking to the sides of the bowl after five minutes of mixing, add 2 to 4 tablespoons of extra flour. The test kitchen's favorite loaf pan measures 8½ by 4½ inches; if you use a standard 9 by 5-inch loaf pan, start checking the babka for doneness after 40 minutes.

FILLING

- 1 **cup packed (7 ounces) light brown sugar**
- ¼ **cup (1¼ ounces) all-purpose flour**
- 2 **tablespoons unsalted butter, melted and cooled**
- 1 **large egg white**
- 2 **teaspoons ground cinnamon**
- ⅛ **teaspoon salt**

DOUGH

- ½ **cup whole milk, heated to 110 degrees**
- 2 **large egg yolks plus 1 large egg**
- 1 **teaspoon vanilla extract**
- 2 **cups (10 ounces) all-purpose flour**
- ¼ **cup (1¾ ounces) sugar**
- 1½ **teaspoons instant or rapid-rise yeast**
- ½ **teaspoon salt**
- 8 **tablespoons unsalted butter, cut into 8 pieces and softened**

1. FOR THE FILLING: Combine all ingredients in medium bowl. Set aside 1 tablespoon filling.

2. FOR THE DOUGH: Adjust oven rack to middle position and heat oven to 200 degrees. When oven reaches 200 degrees, turn it off. Grease large bowl. Whisk milk, egg yolks, and vanilla together in 1-cup liquid measuring cup.

3. Using stand mixer fitted with dough hook, mix flour, sugar, yeast, and salt on low speed until combined. Slowly add milk mixture and mix until dough comes together, about 3

minutes. Increase speed to medium-low and add butter, 1 piece at a time, until incorporated, about 1 minute. Continue to mix until dough is smooth and comes away from sides of bowl, 10 to 12 minutes. Transfer dough to prepared bowl, cover with plastic wrap, and place in turned-off oven until dough has risen slightly, about 1 hour. Place in refrigerator until dough is firm and has doubled in size, at least 1 hour.

4. Line 8½ by 4½-inch loaf pan with parchment paper, allowing excess to hang over edges. Punch down dough on lightly floured counter. Roll out dough to 20 by 14-inch rectangle. Spread all but 1 tablespoon reserved filling over dough, leaving ½-inch border around edges. Working from short side, roll dough into cylinder and pinch along seam to seal. Position cylinder seam side up and roll back and forth until stretched to 18-inch length. Spread reserved filling over top of cylinder. Fold cylinder on top of itself and pinch ends to seal. Gently twist double cylinder twice to form double figure eight. Place shaped dough seam side down in prepared pan, cover loosely with plastic, and let rise in turned-off oven until doubled in size, about 1 hour.

5. Lightly beat whole egg in bowl. Remove loaf from oven and discard plastic. Heat oven to 350 degrees. Brush loaf with beaten egg. Bake until deep golden brown and loaf registers 190 degrees, about 45 minutes. Let cool in pan on wire rack for 20 minutes. Remove loaf from pan and cool completely, about 2 hours. Serve.

TO MAKE AHEAD

Instead of letting dough rise in step 4, cover shaped loaf with plastic wrap and refrigerate for up to 24 hours. Let dough sit at room temperature for 1 hour before baking.

Harvey House Chocolate Puffs

With a chocolate shell and a whipped-cream and strawberry filling, how could these puffs from a famous old restaurant chain fail? Let me count the ways… BY DIANE UNGER

L ong before there were highway rest stops with fast-food courts, late-19th-century train travelers on the Atchison, Topeka & Santa Fe Railway in search of quick, tasty meals found them at Harvey House, a network of exactingly run restaurants in the stations. (Few trains in those days had dining cars.) In 1946, Judy Garland immortalized the chain's famously comely, efficient, and well-bred waitresses in MGM's "The Harvey Girls." And in recent years, several books about the chain have credited it with no less than civilizing the American West. So with all that attention, why have Harvey House Chocolate Puffs (with strawberry cream, no less) fallen into obscurity?

I first ran across these puffs in *The Harvey House Cookbook: Memories of Dining along the Santa Fe Railroad* (2006), and though the recipe was vague, the pastry sounded incredibly delicious. To a standard cream puff recipe, a Harvey House chef added an ounce of melted chocolate. The puffs were then baked in a "gem pan," the precursor to today's muffin tin, "until done" and subsequently filled with strawberry jam and whipped cream. I dashed down to the test kitchen and followed the recipe as best as I could, substituting a muffin tin for the gem pan and using my experience to help me figure out how long to stir and bake the puffs, what size to make them, what temperature to set the oven, and how to sweeten and flavor the cream.

Since the last few Harvey Houses dis-

We used a large zipper-lock bag to pipe these chocolate-flavored cream puffs.

appeared some 60 years ago, I couldn't compare my puffs to the real thing. But it wasn't necessary: The shortcomings stared me in the face. The puffs fell almost as soon as they came out of the oven. They were soggy and the chocolate flavor was almost imperceptible. Instead of fresh, bright berries, I tasted overly sweet jam. And when I dug my spoon into the puffs, the whipped cream squished out. But their promise was evident, too: strawberries and cream encased in crisp, almost custardy choco-

late pastry. All I had to do was get the recipe to work as smoothly as Harvey House restaurants used to: When a train pulled into the station, every last passenger was fed well and sent on his or her way in 30 minutes flat.

Cream puffs—or in this case, chocolate puffs—are made from a classic French mixture known as *choux* pastry; French pastry chefs use it for profiteroles (cream puffs) and chocolate éclairs. Recipes don't vary much, probably because the precise ratio of butter to eggs to liquid

(milk or water) is key to making the puffs puff—and stay puffed. Since the test kitchen has a foolproof recipe for choux pastry that has already solved the problems that I was experiencing, I turned to it for my next test.

Unfortunately, when I stirred in the melted chocolate, the normally delicate, airy puffs deflated faster than I could say Atchison, Topeka & Santa Fe. Choux paste, like popover batter, forms hollow centers, and the puffs rely on steam in order to rise. After they bake, the puffs will be soggy if the steam can't escape. I had cuts slits into each baked puff, as our recipe instructs, to let out the steam. Apparently, that hadn't helped. Figuring that the fat in the chocolate was to blame for upending the delicate choux ratios, I got rid of the milk (which also contains fat) to compensate and used an all-water dough. The puffs barely improved. Over the next week, I did one (futile) test after another, trying different types and amounts of bar chocolate. After creating dozens more puffs that failed to live up to their name, I phoned our science editor in frustration.

▶ Search for "food processors" on CooksCountry.com to read our testing story and see our favorite model.

He suggested that I switch to cocoa. The problem, he explained, was that once the steam escaped, my cream puff walls clearly weren't stiff and dry enough to offer structural support. (This despite my "drying" the puffs in a cooling, partly open oven.) Since bar chocolate is denser than cocoa, it was causing the puff walls to collapse. To make matters worse, our science guy added, the fat from the bar chocolate in the pastry was likely forming a barrier that prevented the steam from escaping and the walls from drying. So I experimented with cocoa and determined that 3 tablespoons produced tall puffs with good chocolate flavor. Before turning to the filling, I made one last change: I ditched the muffin pan in favor of piping the puffs directly onto a baking sheet. This allowed for better air circulation, which also helped prevent soggy puffs.

The original Harvey House Chocolate Puff called for simply plopping strawberry jam in the bottom of each puff and topping it with whipped cream. I folded the two together for better distribution but still found the strawberry flavor bland and too sugary. I opted for a quick homemade puree: I cooked frozen strawberries briefly on the stove to concentrate flavors and then mashed and cooled the berries. I folded my vibrant homemade puree into the whipped cream with a little sugar. To stabilize the cream, I tried and rejected gelatin—it was too much trouble. Whipping heavy cream with confectioners' sugar and 3 tablespoons of softened cream cheese proved a sturdy and simpler solution.

Technically, I was done, and maybe if I were a hungry 19th-century traveler worn out from a dirty and dangerous train trip, these puffs would taste perfect as they were. But since I was a comfortable and well-rested test cook, I had a more critical eye (and palate). What was missing? A final bit of chocolate reinforcement, I realized. I stirred together an easy chocolate glaze and drizzled it on the puffs. Bingo. The Harvey House

restaurants may be long gone, but I'd wager that my rejuvenated puffs will keep the name alive.

HARVEY HOUSE CHOCOLATE PUFFS
Serves 8

An accurate oven temperature is essential for puffs to puff. We recommend that you keep an oven thermometer in your oven (we like the Cooper-Atkins model). To prevent lumps in the whipped cream filling, be sure to sift the confectioners' sugar. The assembled puffs will hold in the refrigerator for up to 1 hour.

CHOCOLATE PUFFS
- 2 large eggs plus 1 large egg white
- 1 teaspoon vanilla extract
- ½ cup water
- 5 tablespoons unsalted butter, cut into ½-inch pieces
- 2 teaspoons granulated sugar
- ¼ teaspoon salt
- ½ cup (2½ ounces) all-purpose flour
- 3 tablespoons Dutch-processed cocoa

STRAWBERRY FILLING
- 8 ounces frozen strawberries, thawed
- 1 cup heavy cream, chilled
- 6 tablespoons (1½ ounces) confectioners' sugar, sifted
- 1 teaspoon vanilla extract
- 1½ ounces cream cheese, cut into 1-inch pieces and softened

CHOCOLATE GLAZE
- 1 cup (4 ounces) confectioners' sugar, sifted
- 3 tablespoons Dutch-processed cocoa
- 2 tablespoons water
- 1 teaspoon vanilla extract

1. FOR THE CHOCOLATE PUFFS: Adjust oven rack to upper-middle position and heat oven to 425 degrees. Line rimmed baking sheet with parchment paper. Whisk eggs, egg white, and vanilla together in bowl. Bring water, butter, sugar, and salt to boil in medium saucepan over medium-high heat. When butter is melted, remove pan from heat. Using rubber spatula, stir in flour until smooth. Return saucepan to low heat and cook, constantly stirring and smearing mixture against bottom of saucepan, until mixture is slightly shiny and registers 170 degrees on instant-read thermometer, 2 to 3 minutes.

2. Transfer flour mixture to food processor and process until slightly cool, about 30 seconds. Remove feed tube insert from food processor. With food processor running, slowly add egg mixture through feed tube until incorporated. Scrape down sides of bowl and process until smooth, thick paste forms, about 30 seconds. Sprinkle cocoa over paste and process until combined, about 15 seconds, scraping down bowl as needed.

3. Cut ½ inch from corner of large zipper-lock bag. Transfer cocoa paste to bag and pipe eight 2-inch-wide and 1¼-inch-high mounds 2 inches apart on prepared baking sheet. Dip small spoon in water and smooth exterior of mounds.

4. Bake puffs for 15 minutes (do not open oven door) and then reduce oven temperature to 350 degrees and continue to bake until firm, 20 minutes. Remove baking sheet from oven and turn off oven. Using tip of paring knife, carefully cut ½-inch slit into side of each puff. Return puffs to oven, prop door open with wooden spoon, and let puffs dry for 30 minutes. Transfer puffs to wire rack to cool completely, about 30 minutes. (Puffs can be stored at room temperature for up to 1 day or frozen in single layer in airtight container for up to 1 month.)

5. FOR THE STRAWBERRY FILLING: Meanwhile, cook strawberries in medium saucepan over medium-low heat, mashing occasionally with potato masher, until thickened and reduced to ½ cup, 10 to 12 minutes. Transfer to large bowl and refrigerate until cool, about 1 hour.

6. Using stand mixer fitted with whisk, whip cream, sugar, and vanilla on medium-low speed until foamy, about 1 minute. Increase speed to high and whip until soft peaks form, 1 to 3 minutes. Add cream cheese and whip until stiff peaks form, about 30 seconds. Gently fold chilled strawberries into whipped cream, return mixture to large bowl, and refrigerate until firm, about 1 hour. (Filling can be refrigerated for up to 1 day.)

7. FOR THE CHOCOLATE GLAZE: Set wire rack in rimmed baking sheet. Using serrated knife, cut puffs crosswise into 2 pieces, ½ inch from bottom. Top puff bottoms with strawberry whipped cream and replace tops; transfer to rack. Combine sugar and cocoa in bowl. Whisk in water and vanilla until smooth. Spoon 1 tablespoon glaze over each puff and let sit for 15 minutes until set. Serve.

TEST KITCHEN TECHNIQUE **Prevent Puff Droop**
Choux paste relies on steam in order to puff. But the steam that lifts the puffs can also make them soggy and flat. To help your puffs avoid that fate, follow these two steps.

1. CUT 'EM Cut a ½-inch slit into each puff to allow the steam to escape.

2. DRY 'EM Dry the puffs for 30 minutes in a partially open, turned-off oven.

Equipment Review Oven Mitts

Obviously, they should prevent burns, but the best mitts should also be comfortable, dextrous, and durable. BY TAIZETH SIERRA

KEY **Good** ★★★ **Fair** ★★ **Poor** ★

IN 2005, WE named the Kool-Tek 15-Inch Oven Mitt by KatchAll our favorite oven mitt. But we were always bothered by its high price ($44.95 each), and recently we began to wonder if newer (maybe cheaper) models might offer any advantages. We gathered eight mitts, including our former winner, priced from $14.95 to $44.95 each. We included the standard quilted cotton oven mitts but also many others made of fancier stuff, including leather, silicone, neoprene (a material used for wet suits), Nomex (a fireproof fabric worn by race-car drivers), and Kevlar (which is found in bullet-resistant body armor).

What were we looking for? Above all, a good oven mitt must be functional, offering protection from burns (obviously), but also letting the cook easily maneuver everything from a baking sheet to a heavy casserole dish to the handle of a hot skillet. We considered our level of control and comfort as we wore these mitts to perform our first task: moving hot sheet trays loaded with baking cookies. Many mitts were oversize, thick, and awkwardly shaped, making it hard to get a good grip and even leaving thumbprints in our cookies. Thinner, more form-fitting styles were easier to maneuver. In particular, Gloven Oven Gloves let us use all of our fingers. Moving a scorching hot oven rack posed the next challenge, and some models became downright painful the longer we had to hang on. Disappointingly, our early front-runner failed this test: The Gloven quickly became too hot around the fingers. And what good is dexterity if you can't take the heat?

So we turned up the temperature. Holding a full casserole dish that had just come out of a 450-degree oven, we walked around the test kitchen, timing the mitts' heat resistance. To measure how hot they got, we wired our middle finger and thumb with temperature probes. When the temperature reached an unbearable 110 degrees, we called it quits. Some mitts let us travel only a few feet, others several yards before we had to put down the casserole. Most mitts clocked in at a respectable 45 seconds. The worst models withstood the heat just a paltry 18 seconds. Our old favorite, made of Nomex and Kevlar, lasted 1½ minutes. The best performers? Silicone mitts that lasted well over two minutes—longer than most cooks would ever need to hold a hot dish.

HIGHLY RECOMMENDED			CRITERIA		TESTERS' NOTES
KOOL-TEK 15-inch Oven Mitt by KatchAll **Model:** KT0215 **Price:** $44.95 each **Source:** www.cooking.com			Dexterity Heat Protection Durability	★★½ ★★★ ★★★	After 18 rounds of testing, Kool-Tek still came out on top. Made with layers of Nomex and Kevlar for heat protection, these mitts won fans for heat resistance and all-around dependability. What's more, this mitt emerged from the laundry as good as new. It never let us down.
ORKAPLUS Silicone Oven Mitt with Cotton Lining **Model:** A82305 **Price:** $14.95 each **Source:** www.dillards.com	BEST BUY		Dexterity Heat Protection Durability	★★ ★★★ ★★★	Orka redesigned this mitt since our last testing. The old model had great heat resistance but was too stiff, plus it was unlined, so our hand got sweaty fast. This improved version features a removable cotton-terry lining that stays dry and comfortable and launders perfectly. This mitt is soft and extremely flexible.
RECOMMENDED					
CALPHALON 14-inch Oven Mitt **Model:** 52171 **Price:** $14.99 each **Source:** www.bedbathandbeyond.com			Dexterity Heat Protection Durability	★★ ★★ ★★½	The innovation for this otherwise standard cotton mitt was silicone striping over the hand portion. It performed solidly, though some testers found the mitt large and unwieldy. It shrank in the laundry, which actually improved the fit.
RECOMMENDED WITH RESERVATIONS					
OXO GOOD GRIPS Silicone Oven Mitt with Magnet **Model:** 1147503 **Price:** $14.99 each **Source:** www.bloomingdales.com			Dexterity Heat Protection Durability	★½ ★★★ ★½	The silicone grip had excellent heat and stain resistance. Unfortunately, it was also stiff and oversize, which compromised dexterity. This mitt emerged unscathed from the flames. However, it didn't fare as well against soap and water, fading after just one wash.
LE CREUSET Oven Mitt **Model:** TH4911 **Price:** $14.95 each **Source:** www.wayfair.com			Dexterity Heat Protection Durability	★★ ★★½ ★	This mitt was a tad oversize, which hindered dexterity, but it had decent heat resistance and performed well. But it failed on other counts: It shrank significantly in the wash; oil stains on the terry cloth grip remained after three cycles; and when it came in contact with flames, it caught fire within seconds.
NOT RECOMMENDED					
GLOVEN Oven Gloves **Model:** GRL01 **Price:** $39.99 pair ($19.99 each) **Source:** www.amazon.com			Dexterity Heat Protection Durability	★★★ ★½ ★	We immediately took a liking to the tight fit and total finger control possible while wearing these gloves. However, these gloves lacked insulation between the fingers, hence ranked at the bottom in heat resistance. The glove discolored when it came in contact with flames and it emerged from the washer flecked with lint.
BUILT Sizzler Oven Mitt **Model:** OMXL-FVE **Price:** $17.99 each **Source:** www.kitchenkapers.com			Dexterity Heat Protection Durability	★★ ★★ ★	These Neoprene mitts were thin and form-fitting. The manufacturer claims these mitts resist temperatures up to 500 degrees, but the grip started melting when we pulled a casserole out of a 450-degree oven, began smoking during our heat-resistance test, and caught fire when exposed to flames. We'd say the "sizzler" in the name is about right.
PADERNO WORLD CUISINE Three-Finger Oven Mitts **Model:** 48517-03 **Price:** $71.10 pair ($35.55 each) **Source:** www.buy.com			Dexterity Heat Protection Durability	★ ★★ ★	Below average when it came to heat resistance, these leather mitts began scorching when they came in contact with flames. Their biggest drawback was a complete lack of dexterity: The three-finger design was a hindrance.

Oven mitts must be washable. We stained each with a measured amount of ketchup, soy sauce, and vegetable oil and headed for the laundry room. (All mitts were machine-washable with the exception of the neoprene models.) The oil stain clung to some gloves, one faded, another emerged covered in lint, and a few shrank considerably. Only the Kool-Tek 15-Inch Oven Mitt and the OrkaPlus Silicone Oven Mitt emerged from the washer as good as new.

If your oven mitt accidentally comes in contact with a heating element, does it melt or scorch? With a fire extinguisher handy, we cranked the burner to high and stuck each glove in the flame for five seconds. Neoprene and terry cloth mitts caught fire (the neoprene smelled foul), leather gloves scorched, and Nomex models discolored. Again, silicone proved its mettle, emerging intact. The Kool-Tek glove, made of Nomex and Kevlar, was also unscathed.

Against its new crop of rivals, the Kool-Tek 15-Inch Oven Mitt once again came out on top. While it wasn't the most dexterous mitt we tested, its heat resistance and durability more than made up for a little stiffness. If $44.95 per mitt is too steep (and you will need two mitts for many tasks), we suggest the OrkaPlus Silicone Oven Mitt ($14.95 each), our Best Buy. It performed almost on par with our winner, with slightly less control in the thumb.

Taste Test Breakfast Sausage Patties

Shaping and frying breakfast sausage meat is more work than simply browning
a frozen, fully cooked patty. Is it worth the effort? BY HANNAH CROWLEY

THE MANTRA OF modern cooking is that fresh is always better than frozen. But frozen is usually faster. And most mornings, time is of the essence. Fact: Dumping a box of fully cooked, frozen breakfast sausage patties into a skillet is easier than shaping and cooking patties from raw tube-style rolls of sausage meat. Plus frozen cooked patties take half as long to cook. Then again, the extra work might be worthwhile if the end result tastes better. Several years ago, we pitted fresh breakfast sausage links against precooked and were surprised when the precooked products won. We set out to see if the same would hold true for patties.

Our ideal breakfast sausage patty is meaty, savory, and a little peppery, with a nice hint of salt, herbs, and sweetness. Some fat is to be expected—it's sausage, after all—but not too much, and it shouldn't be tough or gristly. And it goes without saying that good sausage shouldn't be rubbery. Armed with 11 national pork breakfast sausage products, we held pretastings to eliminate the worst and winnow our lineup to seven. Our final lineup included two products that were fully cooked patties, one that consisted of raw patties, and four tubes of raw "roll-style" breakfast sausage meat that we sliced into patties. Twenty-one America's Test Kitchen editors and test cooks sat down for a blind tasting.

Texture, it turned out, was the most important factor. Four of the seven products scored poorly for being "rubbery" and "spongy." Tasters described their texture as "processed" and "artificial" and wondered whether "weird" binders or fillers were used. According to Iowa State University meat-processing and -preservation expert Joe Sebranek, fillers are actually uncommon in breakfast sausage: Sausage is made from pork trimmings. Manufacturers analyze the fat content of the meat and combine trimmings of various fat levels to achieve the ratio that they desire—a process called blending. The way that each sausage is blended directly affects its texture. Too much lean protein and not enough fat makes for chewy sausage, Sebranek explained.

Conversely, our least favorite product seemed so fatty that one taster dubbed it a "grease bomb." A peek at the nutrition label verified that this sausage had the most fat (23 grams) per 2-ounce serving. Our winner isn't lean by any means, with 19 grams of fat in 2 ounces;

obviously, we like sausages that have some sizzle. But its fat ratio made for a tender bite without the grease puddle.

Traditional breakfast sausage seasonings are salt, black pepper, and sage; manufacturers then add their own blend of spices, which labeling laws do not require them to reveal. Tasters panned one "all natural" sample for being under-salted (the label confirmed that it had the least sodium per serving), while another product by the same manufacturer was "overwhelmingly" salty (it had the most sodium). Our winning sausage ranked second for saltiness. Our top four sausages all added a sweetener. Two products added no sweetener (one was faulted for its lack of seasoning). Sausages with evident black pepper flavor were also praised. Overall, tasters preferred a harmonious blend of salty, sweet, and spicy.

Tasters also liked the winner's "meaty" flavor. This could be from the pork itself, but it certainly got a helping hand from monosodium glutamate (MSG), the seventh ingredient on its nutrition label. (Glutamates increase people's perception of savory flavor.) One other product we tasted added MSG, but that sausage was tough and stringy so tasters barely noticed its enhanced flavor.

In the end, the two precooked patties ranked highest, followed by the raw, preformed patties. All four tubes of breakfast sausage sat at the bottom of our ranking. Precooked patties have an advantage: Cooked in ovens to a carefully calibrated level of browning and flavor development, they are immediately frozen to minimize flavor changes. Exposure to oxygen makes fatty foods like sausage taste stale and pick up off-flavors, so manufacturers add antioxidants and vacuum-seal the packages, forcing out all air, to prevent flavor loss. It's more difficult for makers of "all natural" sausages to maintain freshness because they can't add the same antioxidants—which often leads to flavor loss.

We crunched numbers, and finally picked a favorite: Jimmy Dean Fully Cooked Original Pork Sausage Patties (note that no sausages in our tasting achieved "highly recommended" status). This particular Jimmy Dean sausage was meaty with "tender yet substantial texture," tasters said. It was fatty but didn't go overboard, and it had an appealing blend of salt, sugar, and spices.

RECOMMENDED

TASTERS' NOTES

JIMMY DEAN
Fully Cooked Original
Pork Sausage Patties
Price: $3.49 for 8 patties
Style: Precooked patties
Fat per 2-oz serving: 19 g
Sodium per 2-oz serving: 502 mg

These fully cooked patties earned the top spot for being "meaty and well seasoned," with a "spicy, not too greasy taste." "Seasoning was perfect," according to one taster. Agreed another: "Coarser grain makes it more interesting and tender."

RECOMMENDED WITH RESERVATIONS

JONES DAIRY FARM
Golden Brown All Natural
Fully Cooked Sausage
Price: $2 for 6 patties
Style: Precooked patties
Fat per 2-oz serving: 20 g
Sodium per 2-oz serving: 373 mg

These fully cooked patties struck tasters as "smoky" and "sweet," with a "peppery spice," but they lost points on texture with some tasters. "Thick and spongy, rubbery ... like fast-food-restaurant style," wrote one. "Too bouncy!" agreed another.

JOHNSONVILLE
Original Recipe
Breakfast Sausage
Price: $3.99 for 8 patties
Style: Raw patties
Fat per 2-oz serving: 16 g
Sodium per 2-oz serving: 385 mg

Tasters found these raw, pre-formed breakfast patties "way too chewy" and "chunky." They were compared to "fake vegan sausage" and "tofu." On the upside, they earned points for a "nice level of saltiness" and a "smoky," "mesquite-like flavor."

JIMMY DEAN
All Natural Regular Pork Sausage
Price: $3.49 for 16-ounce roll
Style: Roll-style, raw
Fat per 2-oz serving: 15 g
Sodium per 2-oz serving: 420 mg

Tasters praised this sausage for a "well-seasoned" flavor that "tastes real, more like good sausage than fast food." However, its "grainy" and "coarse" texture proved its downfall.

FARMLAND
All Natural Original Pork Sausage
Price: $2.49 for 16-ounce roll
Style: Roll-style, raw
Fat per 2-oz serving: 16 g
Sodium per 2-oz serving: 310 mg

Tasters found this sausage bland despite its "good meaty" taste and "tender" texture. It had the least amount of salt per serving, and tasters noticed. "Tasted like a tiny hamburger, not sausage," said one.

NOT RECOMMENDED

BOB EVANS
Original Recipe Pork Sausage
Price: $4.29 for 16-ounce roll
Style: Roll-style, raw
Fat per 2-oz serving: 15 g
Sodium per 2-oz serving: 460 mg

While we liked this sample's "large black pepper grains" and "good herbal flavors," the texture was "rubbery," "chewy," and "dry, tough, and stringy," according to tasters. "Reminds me of beef jerky," one wrote.

FARMLAND Original
Pork Sausage Roll
Price: $1.99 for 16-ounce roll
Style: Roll-style, raw
Fat per 2-oz serving: 23 g
Sodium per 2-oz serving: 510 mg

This product had the most fat and salt per serving among our samples, so it is no wonder we found it "salty," "extremely fatty," and "a grease bomb."

Cooking Class How to Make Fluffy Omelets

Order an omelet at a diner and chances are good that something extraordinarily high and fluffy will come out of the kitchen. How do short order cooks do it? If you asked them, they might tell you to beat it.

FLUFFY DINER-STYLE CHEESE OMELET Serves 2

We recommend using a hand-held mixer for this recipe, as 3 tablespoons of cream is too small an amount to whip in a stand mixer. Alternatively, whip the cream by hand and continue the recipe with a stand mixer.

- 3 tablespoons heavy cream, chilled
- 5 large eggs, room temperature
  Salt
- 2 tablespoons unsalted butter
- 2 ounces sharp cheddar cheese, shredded (½ cup)
- 1 recipe omelet filling (optional)

1. Adjust oven rack to middle position and heat oven to 400 degrees. Using hand-held mixer set at medium-low speed, whip cream in medium bowl until foamy, about 30 seconds. Increase speed to high and whip until soft peaks form, 1 to 2 minutes; set aside. Beat eggs and ¼ teaspoon salt in large bowl on high speed until frothy and eggs have at least doubled, about 2 minutes. Gently fold whipped cream into eggs.

2. Melt butter in 10-inch nonstick ovensafe skillet over medium-low heat, swirling pan to coat bottom and sides. Add egg mixture and cook until edges are nearly set, 2 to 3 minutes. Sprinkle with ¼ cup cheddar and half of filling, if using, and transfer to oven. Bake until eggs are set and edges begin to brown, 6 to 8 minutes.

3. Remove skillet from oven and sprinkle with remaining ¼ cup cheddar. Cover with lid and let sit until cheddar begins to melt, about 1 minute. Tilt skillet and, using rubber spatula, push half of omelet onto cutting board. Tilt skillet so that omelet folds over itself to form half-moon. (If filling omelet, after cheese melts, slide omelet onto board. Sprinkle half with remaining filling. Fold closed.) Cut omelet in half. Serve.

Enjoy a plain cheese omelet or fill it with potatoes, scallions, and bacon, as is pictured here.

SAUSAGE AND PEPPER OMELET FILLING

- 4 ounces bulk pork sausage
- 1 small onion, chopped fine
- ½ red bell pepper, chopped fine
  Salt and pepper

Cook sausage in 10-inch nonstick skillet over medium-high heat, breaking up meat into small pieces, until browned, about 5 minutes. Using slotted spoon, transfer sausage to paper towel–lined plate. Pour off all but 1 tablespoon fat from skillet. Cook onion and bell pepper in skillet until softened, about 5 minutes. Stir in sausage and season with salt and pepper to taste.

LOADED BAKED POTATO OMELET FILLING

- 1 large Yukon Gold potato, peeled and cut into ½-inch pieces
- 4 slices bacon, chopped
- 2 scallions, sliced thin
  Salt and pepper

Microwave potatoes in covered large bowl until just tender, 2 to 5 minutes. Cook bacon in 10-inch nonstick skillet over medium heat until crisp, about 8 minutes. Using slotted spoon, transfer bacon to paper towel–lined plate. Pour off all but 1 tablespoon fat from skillet. Cook potatoes in skillet until golden brown, about 6 minutes. Combine potatoes, bacon, and scallions in bowl and season with salt and pepper to taste.

TEMPERATURE CONTROL

Warm This, Chill That

Our recipe for Fluffy Diner-Style Cheese Omelet calls for *chilled* heavy cream and *room temperature* eggs. Why?

The colder the heavy cream, the more easily it will whip. Luckily, this is no trouble for the cook. Simply leave the heavy cream in the refrigerator until just before you measure and whip it. (For the same reason, cooks often chill the bowl before whipping cream.)

As for the eggs, they'll beat more easily and take in air faster when they're at room temperature (we beat them until doubled in size). Does that mean you have to wake up early to set your eggs on the counter? No, simply fill a bowl with warm water from the tap, submerge the eggs carefully, and let them warm up for five minutes.

WARM THE EGGS
They'll beat more efficiently.

Moderate the Heat

Overcooking has turned many a good omelet bad, which is why most of us have had the disappointing experience of eating a rubbery omelet. We engineered our recipe to guarantee your omelet will be moist and tender:

We start it in a skillet on the stove over medium-low heat until the edges barely set—no more than three minutes. We move it to a hot oven, so the interior can cook through evenly in the circulating heat. After sprinkling on the last bit of cheese, we cover the skillet with a lid and let the omelet sit off heat briefly so the cheese can melt without the omelet overcooking. Together, these techniques safeguard against tough omelets.

SHOPPING
Size Matters

Our recipes almost always call for large eggs. If you're working with a different size, the corresponding average weights will help with substitutions. For example, a dozen extra-large eggs are about equivalent to 14 medium eggs.

EXTRA-LARGE	LARGE	MEDIUM
1.9 ounces	1.7 ounces	1.6 ounces

Twelve Steps to Perfect Fluffy Omelets

1. HEAT OVEN
Set the oven to 400 degrees. **WHY?** Ordinarily, omelets cook on the stove from start to end. But these thick omelets finish cooking in the oven's even heat.

2. BEAT CREAM
Using an electric mixer, beat the cream to soft peaks. **WHY?** Cream makes for richer omelets. Whipping it gives these omelets extra lift.

3. BEAT EGGS
Using the electric mixer, beat the eggs and the salt until doubled in volume. **WHY?** Beating the eggs for two minutes is how we get high, fluffy omelets.

4. FOLD TOGETHER
Gently fold the whipped cream into the whipped eggs. **WHY?** If you stir vigorously or overmix the eggs and cream, they can deflate.

5. MELT BUTTER
Melt the butter on the stovetop in an ovensafe 10-inch nonstick skillet. **WHY?** What, you make omelets with oil? Butter tastes better.

6. POUR IN EGGS
Add the egg mixture and cook for two to three minutes over medium-low heat until the edges set. **WHY?** The hot pan sets the bottom and edges of the omelet.

7. ADD CHEESE
Sprinkle half of the cheese (and half of the filling, if using) over the eggs. **WHY?** To give the cheese time to melt.

8. BAKE OMELET
Place the omelet in the oven and bake for six to eight minutes. **WHY?** The oven's ambient heat is the best way to set the top and interior of the omelet.

9. ADD REMAINING CHEESE
Remove the pan from the oven and sprinkle on the remaining cheese. **WHY?** If you added all the cheese at once, the interior would take too long to set.

10. COVER AND WAIT
Cover the pan with a lid and let it sit, off heat, for one minute. **WHY?** The cheese melts while the omelet very gently finishes cooking.

11. SLIDE OUT
Uncover, tilt the pan, and nudge half of the omelet onto the cutting board. **WHY?** A big omelet needs support to come out of the pan intact.

12. FOLD OVER
Tilt the skillet so the omelet folds into a half moon (if filling, slide out the whole omelet, top with remaining filling, and then fold). **WHY?** So the skillet does the work of flipping the omelet.

Egg-cellent Advice

Fluffy Rules
Is there anything wrong with an ordinary, flat omelet? Absolutely not. But our fluffy omelets are extraordinarily light and, well, fluffy. Give them a try.

FLAT IS FINE BUT...
Not nearly as nice as fluffy.

Don't Break It!
Omelets usually tear because they're overstuffed or they get manhandled in the pan. Our filling recipes don't overstuff the delicate egg base, and our sliding/folding technique protects against breakage.

HANDLE WITH CARE
Overfill your omelet or turn it out roughly and it'll look like this.

Fill the Omelet Twice
Wonder why we fill our omelet in two stages, using just half the filling before baking the omelet? If we added all of it at once to the delicate whipped eggs, they would deflate. After the omelet has set in the oven, we gently slide it from the skillet, distribute the remaining filling over half the baked omelet, and fold it closed.

Use a Hand Mixer
We usually prefer a stand mixer, but to whip such a scant amount of cream, a hand mixer is more effective. Our favorite is powerful, quiet, and agile with simple digital controls.

TEST KITCHEN FAVORITE
Cuisinart Power Advantage
7-Speed Hand Mixer

▶ Go to CooksCountry.com/how-to-cook for cooking lessons on everything from fried chicken to chocolate cake.

Looking for a Recipe

READER TO READER

Did you misplace a favorite recipe? Can you almost taste a chocolate cake from childhood but the bakery—and the recipe—are long gone? Ask a reader. While you're at it, answer a reader. Post queries and finds at **CooksCountry. com/magazine**; click on **Looking for a Recipe** (or write to Looking for a Recipe, Cook's Country, P.O. Box 470739, Brookline, MA 02447). We'll share all of your submissions online—hundreds are already posted—and print several on this page. Include your name and mailing address with each submission.

Orange-Cocoanut Cake
Ann Bartlett, Richardson, Texas

I am looking for the recipe for orange-cocoanut [sic] cake from an old Spry cookbook. When I was a kid, I earned most of my spending money by baking for our neighbors in Houston, Texas. Mrs. K ordered this cake about every other week. Mrs. G ordered oatmeal crispies (icebox cookies) and Mrs. R ordered five-minute devil's food cake quite often. I still have the recipes for the cookies and the chocolate cake but I have long since lost the orange-cocoanut one. The Spry cookbook came out in the 1930s. Spry was favored over any other shortening brand back then. I am 84 but I still do a lot of cooking. I'd love to find that recipe.

Walnut Bars
Cris Neuman, Houston, Texas

I am looking for a recipe for a type of blond brownie that I made for 20 years (but have misplaced for the past five years). The recipe came from the back of a Diamond walnuts bag. Made in an 8-inch square pan with less than a cup of flour and more than a cup of walnuts, the blondies were terrific and very moist. The Diamond website is no help. Can you clever folks find the recipe?

British Pork Pie
Virginia Markey, Woodstock, Ga.

I'm looking for a recipe for British pork pie similar to those sold at Thwaites Market in Methuen, Massachusetts. We have lived in Georgia for 18 years now and I've never been able to dupli-cate the pie's flavor. I've looked into having them shipped but the cost is way over my budget.

Dutch Fritessaus
Brian Opitz, Red Wing, Minn.

I would love to find a recipe that replicates fritessaus, the mayonnaise-like sauce served with french fries in the Nether-lands and Belgium. Mayonnaise is not a sufficient substitute. I have sometimes ordered fritessaus online but that is not convenient, especially when one wants some immediately! Now I'm going to be thinking of it all day.

Fresh Mint Sauce
Patti Hare, Los Angeles, Calif.

My grandmother used to make a mint sauce to serve with roast leg of lamb. She used fresh mint that grew in the yard; I had to fill a 4-cup bowl with it . . . but that's where I get lost. I remember that she used powdered sugar because it dissolved more easily but I don't remember how much. I think there was a little vinegar, too, to cut the sweetness. She would get it started on the burner early in the afternoon and then take it off and set it on the back of the stove, where the heat from the roasting lamb would help cook it more. By the time we were ready to eat, it was thick and lovely. My grandmother and mother have passed on, and my sister doesn't remember the recipe because she doesn't like lamb, so she didn't care about how to make it.

Vinegar Dumplings
Pat Szostek, Valparaiso, Ind.

I'm looking for a recipe that my mom used to make years ago. She called it vinegar dump-lings. It was basically a noodle dumpling with a sweet-and-sour sauce made from white vinegar and sugar. The sauce, which had no color, was a perfect balance of tart and sweet. I wrote the recipe down years ago but can't find it now. My mom passed away five years ago and I would love to make this recipe for my siblings. I hope you can help.

Sweet Potato Casserole
Gwen Hunt, Houston, Texas

As a young bride in the late 1970s, I was delighted when I received my first food processor as a Christmas gift. Around that time, I came across a fantastic recipe for a sweet potato casserole. The recipe called for mashing the cooked sweet potatoes in the processor and then adding milk, orange juice and rind, cinnamon, brown sugar, and egg. It quickly became a family favorite and one that is expected on every holiday table. Unfortunately, during a recent kitchen renova-tion the recipe was lost. Can you please help me find it? My family would be grateful. Thanks very much.

WHIPPED CREAM–CHERRY CHEESECAKE
Serves 12
Nancy Clark, East Falmouth, Mass.

"For special occasions, my mom would tie a ribbon around this cake and set it out on a tall cake stand. When it was time for dessert, she'd have the guest of honor untie the ribbon and cut the first slice." You can find cake-style ladyfingers in the bakery section of most supermarkets. A serrated knife slices this cake neatly.

- 36 cake-style ladyfingers (three 3-ounce packages), halved
- 16 ounces cream cheese, softened
- ¾ cup (5¼ ounces) sugar
- 2 teaspoons vanilla extract
- ¼ teaspoon almond extract
- 2 cups heavy cream, chilled
- 1 (21-ounce) can cherry pie filling

1. Line sides and bottom of 9-inch springform pan with 48 ladyfinger halves. Using stand mixer fitted with paddle, beat cream cheese, sugar, vanilla, and almond extract on medium-high speed until smooth; transfer to large bowl. Using dry, clean bowl and whisk attachment, whip cream on medium-low speed until foamy, about 1 minute. Increase speed to high and whip until soft peaks form, 1 to 3 minutes. Gently fold whipped cream into cream cheese mixture.

2. Pour half of whipped mixture into prepared springform pan, spreading into even layer, and cover with remaining 24 ladyfinger halves. Top with 1 cup pie filling. Scrape remaining whipped mixture over pie filling and spread into even layer. Cover with plastic wrap and refrigerate until set, at least 4 hours. Refrigerate remaining 1 cup pie filling.

3. Spread chilled pie filling over top of cake. Remove sides of pan. Serve.

U.S. POSTAL SERVICE STATEMENT OF OWNERSHIP, MANAGEMENT AND CIRCULATION

1. Publication Title: Cook's Country; 2. Publication No. 1552-1990; 3. Filing Date: 9/15/11; 4. Issue Frequency: Dec/Jan, Feb/Mar, Apr/May, Jun/Jul, Aug/ Sep, Oct/ Nov; 5. No. of Issues Published Annually: 6; 6. Annual Subscription Price: $29.70; 7. Complete Mailing Address of Known Office of Publication: 17 Station Street, Brookline, MA 02445; 8. Complete Mailing Address of Headquarters or General Business Office of Publisher: 17 Station Street, Brookline, MA 02445; 9. Full Names and Complete Mailing Address of Publisher, Editor and Managing Editor: Pub-lisher: Christopher Kimball, 17 Station Street, Brookline, MA 02445; Editor: Jack Bishop, 17 Station Street, Brookline, MA 02445; Managing Editor: Scott Kathan, 17 Station Street, Brookline, MA 02445; 10. Owner: Boston Common Press Limited Partnership, Christopher Kimball, 17 Station Street, Brookline, MA 02445; 11. Known Bondholders, Mortgagees, and Other Securities: None; 12. Tax Status: Has Not Changed During Preceding 12 Months; 13. Publication Title: Cook's Country; 14. Issue Date for Circulation Data Below: August/September 2011; 15a. Total Num-ber of Copies: 358,460 (Aug/Sep 2011: 356,253); b. Paid Circulation: (1) Mailed Outside-County Paid Subscriptions Stated on PS Form 3541: 266,376 (Aug/Sep 2011: 267,201); (2) Mailed In-County Paid Subscriptions Stated on PS Form 3541: 0 (Aug/Sep 2011: 0); (3) Paid Distribution Outside the Mails Including Sales Through Dealers and Carriers, Street Vendors, Counter Sales, and Other Paid Distribution Outside the USPS: 27,161 (Aug/Sep 2011: 23,828); (4) Paid Distribution by Other Classes of Mail through the USPS: 0 (Aug/Sep 2011: 0); c. Total Paid Distribution: 293,536 (Aug/Sep 2011: 291,029); d. Free or Nominal Rate Distribution: (1) Free or Nominal Rate Outside-County Copies Included on PS Form 3541: 2,452 (Aug/Sep 2011: 2,434); (2) Free or Nominal Rate In-County Copies Included on Form PS 3541: 0 (Aug/Sep 2011: 0); (3) Free or Nominal Rate Copies Mailed at Other Classes Through the USPS: 0 (Aug/Sep 2011: 0); (4) Free or Nominal Rate Distribution Out-side the Mail: 515 (Aug/Sep 2011: 515); e. Total Free or Nominal Rate Distribution: 2,967 (Aug/Sep 2011: 2,949); f. Total Distribution: 296,503 (Aug/Sep 2011: 293,978); g. Copies Not Distributed: 61,957 (Aug/Sep 2011: 62,275); h. Total: 358,460 (Aug/ Sep 2011: 356,253); i. Percent Paid: 99.0% (Aug/Sep 2011: 99.0%).

Holiday Rum Cake

Bring joy to the world with our moist, buttery Bundt cake,
scattered with streusel, soaked in sweetened rum, and finished with a rum glaze.

To make this cake you will need:

- 1 cup pecans, toasted and chopped fine
- ½ cup packed (3½ ounces) light brown sugar
- 6 tablespoons unsalted butter, softened
  Batter for Classic Rum Bundt Cake*
- ⅔ cup (4⅔ ounces) granulated sugar
- ½ cup dark rum
- 2 tablespoons water
- 1 cup (4 ounces) confectioners' sugar

▶ *Visit **CooksCountry.com/extra** for our **Classic Rum Bundt Cake** recipe.

FOR THE CAKE: Adjust oven rack to middle position and heat oven to 350 degrees. Grease and flour 12-cup nonstick Bundt pan. Reserve 2 tablespoons pecans. Use fork to combine remaining pecans, brown sugar, and 2 tablespoons butter in bowl to make streusel. Scrape two-thirds of Classic Rum Bundt Cake batter into prepared pan, sprinkle with even layer of pecan streusel, and top with remaining batter. Bake until toothpick inserted in center comes out clean, 50 to 60 minutes. Cool cake in pan on wire rack–lined rimmed baking sheet for 20 minutes.

FOR THE RUM SYRUP: Meanwhile, bring granulated sugar, rum, and water to boil in small saucepan and simmer over medium-low heat until sugar dissolves, about 2 minutes. Whisk in remaining butter until smooth. Cool rum syrup to room temperature, about 30 minutes. Remove cake from pan and prick all over with fork. Brush warm cake with ¾ cup rum syrup and cool completely, about 2 hours.

FOR THE GLAZE: Whisk confectioners' sugar into remaining rum syrup until smooth. Drizzle glaze evenly over top of cake and sprinkle with reserved pecans. Let sit until glaze is firm, about 30 minutes. Serve.

Recipe Index

 = Recipe Card

Visit us online at CooksCountry.com

Follow us on **Twitter**: twitter.com/TestKitchen
Find us on **Facebook**: facebook.com/CooksCountry